QUALITATIVE RESEARCH

QUALITATIVE RESEARCH

An Introduction to Methods and Designs

STEPHEN D. LAPAN
MARYLYNN T. QUARTAROLI
FRANCES JULIA RIEMER
EDITORS

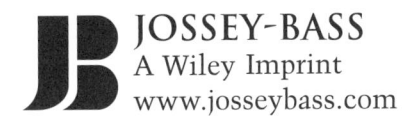

JOSSEY-BASS
A Wiley Imprint
www.josseybass.com

Copyright © 2012 by John Wiley & Sons, Inc. All rights reserved.

Published by Jossey-Bass

A Wiley Imprint

One Montgomery Street, Suite 1200, San Francisco, CA 94104-4594—www.josseybass.com

No part of this publication may be reproduced, stored in a retrieval system, or transmitted in any form or by any means, electronic, mechanical, photocopying, recording, scanning, or otherwise, except as permitted under Section 107 or 108 of the 1976 United States Copyright Act, without either the prior written permission of the publisher, or authorization through payment of the appropriate per-copy fee to the Copyright Clearance Center, Inc., 222 Rosewood Drive, Danvers, MA 01923, 978-750-8400, fax 978-646-8600, or on the Web at www.copyright.com. Requests to the publisher for permission should be addressed to the Permissions Department, John Wiley & Sons, Inc., 111 River Street, Hoboken, NJ 07030, 201-748-6011, fax 201-748-6008, or online at www.wiley.com/go/permissions.

Limit of Liability/Disclaimer of Warranty: While the publisher and author have used their best efforts in preparing this book, they make no representations or warranties with respect to the accuracy or completeness of the contents of this book and specifically disclaim any implied warranties of merchantability or fitness for a particular purpose. No warranty may be created or extended by sales representatives or written sales materials. The advice and strategies contained herein may not be suitable for your situation. You should consult with a professional where appropriate. Neither the publisher nor author shall be liable for any loss of profit or any other commercial damages, including but not limited to special, incidental, consequential, or other damages. Readers should be aware that Internet Web sites offered as citations and/or sources for further information may have changed or disappeared between the time this was written and when it is read.

Jossey-Bass books and products are available through most bookstores. To contact Jossey-Bass directly call our Customer Care Department within the U.S. at 800-956-7739, outside the U.S. at 317-572-3986, or fax 317-572-4002.

Wiley also publishes its books in a variety of electronic formats and by print-on-demand. Not all content that is available in standard print versions of this book may appear or be packaged in all book formats. If you have purchased a version of this book that did not include media that is referenced by or accompanies a standard print version, you may request this media by visiting http://booksupport.wiley.com. For more information about Wiley products, visit us at www.wiley.com.

Library of Congress Cataloging-in-Publication Data

Lapan, Stephen D.
  Qualitative research: an introduction to methods and designs / Stephen D. Lapan, MaryLynn T. Quartaroli, Frances Julia Riemer.—1st ed.
    p. cm.
  Includes bibliographical references and index.
  ISBN 978-0-470-54800-4 (pbk.); 978-1-118-11883-2 (ebk.); 978-1-1181-1884-9 (ebk.); 978-1-118-11885-6 (ebk.)
  1. Qualitative research. 2. Research–Methodology. 3. Education–Research–Methodology. 4. Social sciences–Research–Methodology. I. Quartaroli, Marylynn T., 1950- II. Riemer, Frances Julia, 1955- III. Title.
  H62.L293 2012
  001.4′2–dc23
                                                                                        2011030028

Printed in the United States of America

FIRST EDITION

PB Printing   10 9 8 7 6 5 4 3 2 1

Stephen D. Lapan
October 23, 1940–April 19, 2011

Our colleague Steve Lapan passed away unexpectedly just as this book went to press. This edited text was Steve's idea, and although we each brought our own experiences and expertise to its organization, the book would not exist without his initiative. Steve was our friend, our colleague, our mentor, our co-conspirator. Steve loomed large. He was funny and irreverent, curious and cynical. As a mentor, Steve was clear, strong, and indefatigable. When Steve was on your side, you knew you had an advocate who would fight with heart and soul for your cause. When he wasn't, you knew you needed to lay low and hope for the best.

I (Frances) first met Steve as a colleague not long after I came to Northern Arizona University (NAU). We were office neighbors and immediately recognized a shared interest in research in schools. We talked methodology and methods, students and administrators. Later we played poker once a month; we played for pennies and nickels—not much money, but plenty of entertainment. Steve brought his chips, I brought my cheat sheet, and with five colleagues (eventually including Steve's wife, Pat), we spent the occasional Friday night wagering and bluffing, and enjoying every minute.

I (MaryLynn) first interacted with Steve as I was entering my second year in NAU's Curriculum and Instruction Doctoral Program. Despite his somewhat gruff demeanor and intimidating physical presence, I found him to have both high expectations and a generous heart. It is because of his expertise and enthusiasm for research in its many forms that my career took the path it did. Without Steve's encouragement and support, I would never have pursued editing a methodology book, much less two!

There aren't too many people like Steve in one's life; we're grateful that he blessed ours. We dedicate this text to him.

CONTENTS

Tables, Figures, and Exhibits xi

Preface xiii

The Editors xix

The Contributors xxi

Part One A Qualitative Frame of Mind

1 **Introduction to Qualitative Research** 3
   Stephen D. Lapan, MaryLynn T. Quartaroli, and Frances Julia Riemer

2 **Ethics in Qualitative Research in Education and the Social Sciences** 19
   Donna M. Mertens

3 **Grounded Theory** 41
   Robert Thornberg
   Kathy Charmaz

4 **Methodology, Methods, and Tools in Qualitative Research** 69
   Jean J. Schensul

Part Two Drawing on the Disciplines

5 **Biography and Life Story Research** 107
   Cynthia E. Winston

6 **Mystery Solved: Detective Skills and the Historian's Craft** 137
   Laurie Moses Hines

7 **Ethnographic Research** 163
   Frances Julia Riemer

8 **Trekking Through Autoethnography** 189
   Tony E. Adams
   Carolyn Ellis

Part Three Integrating the Disciplines

9 **Narrative Inquiry: Stories Lived, Stories Told** 215
   Christine K. Lemley
   Roland W. Mitchell

10 **Case Study Research** 243
   Tricia S. Moore
   Stephen D. Lapan
   MaryLynn T. Quartaroli

11 **Arts-Based Research** 271
   Sharon Verner Chappell
   Tom Barone

12 **Practitioner Action Research** 291
   Stephen D. Lapan

13 **Program Evaluation** 321
   MaryLynn T. Quartaroli

Part Four Emancipatory Discourses

14 **Preliminary Considerations of an African American Culturally Responsive Evaluation System** 347
   Pamela Frazier-Anderson
   Stafford Hood
   Rodney K. Hopson

15 **What Makes Critical Ethnography "Critical"?** 373
Angelina E. Castagno

16 **Feminist Research** 391
Lucy E. Bailey

17 **Reclaiming Scholarship: Critical Indigenous Research Methodologies** 423
Bryan McKinley Jones Brayboy
Heather R. Gough
Beth Leonard
Roy F. Roehl II
Jessica A. Solyom

18 **Democratizing Qualitative Research** 451
Ernest R. House

References 473

Index 509

TABLES, FIGURES, AND EXHIBITS

Tables

Table 3.1	Initial Coding	47
Table 3.2	Focused Coding	49
Table 3.3	Examples of Glaser's Coding Families	52
Table 4.1	Sampling Plan for In-Depth Interviews in a Depression Study	75
Table 4.2	Main Classes of Data Collection at Individual and Community Levels	88
Table 4.3	Guide to Qualitative Research Tools	93
Table 6.1	High School Enrollment by Year, Ethnicity, and Parentage	154
Table 10.1	Two-Column Journaling Template	262
Table 12.1	Comparison of the Lewin (1948) and Kemmis and McTaggart (1982) Research Models	305
Table 12.2	Eight Practitioner Research Areas with Sample Questions	307
Table 12.3	Example of an Actual Stimulated Recall Interview	310
Table 12.4	Other Methods of Data Collection for Practitioner Research	312
Table 13.1	Guiding Principles for Evaluators	327
Table 13.2	Evaluation Questions for the Ke Aka Ho'ona Project	333
Table 13.3	Data Collection Methods for CIPP Evaluation of the Ke Aka Ho'ona Project	335

Figures

Figure 4.1	Formative Model of Research Areas	73
Figure 4.2	Initial Conceptual Model of HIV Exposure Factors Among Older Adults	87

Figure 5.1   Identity and Success Life Story Method   121
Figure 13.1 Simple Logic Model   331
Figure 14.1 Sankofa Bird Model of the ACESAS   361

Exhibits

Exhibit 1.1	Chapter Summaries 13
Exhibit 3.1	Early Memo Example 55
Exhibit 3.2	Example of a Memo Taken During Focused Coding 57
Exhibit 10.1	Moore (2009) Tutor Study—Case, Limits, and Purpose 248
Exhibit 10.2	Tutor Study Theoretical or Conceptual Framework 250
Exhibit 10.3	Tutor Study Questions 250
Exhibit 10.4	Tutor Study Example of Questions Linked to Data Sources and Types 252
Exhibit 10.5	Tutor Study Researcher Skill Development 254
Exhibit 10.6	Tutor Study Minimizing Bias 255
Exhibit 10.7	Tutor Study Pilot and Field Testing Interview Protocol 257
Exhibit 10.8	Tutor Study Excerpt of Tutor Interview Protocol 258
Exhibit 10.9	Tutor Study Data Recording 260
Exhibit 10.10	Tutor Study Coding 264
Exhibit 10.11	Tutor Study Contrary Findings 265
Exhibit 10.12	Tutor Study Member Checking 266
Exhibit 10.13	Tutor Study Example of a Descriptive Statement of Patterns and Findings 267
Exhibit 12.1	Scenario Examples of the Practitioner Research Stages 304
Exhibit 12.2	Guidelines and Suggestions for a Practitioner Research Study 314
Exhibit 13.1	Evaluation Criteria for the Ke Aka Ho‘ona Project 332
Exhibit 18.1	Considerations for Implementing Guiding Principles 469

PREFACE

THIS BEGINNING TEXTBOOK, *Qualitative Research: An Introduction to Methods and Designs*, is designed specifically for students taking their first, and possibly only, qualitative research course. Writing a text for students in education and the social sciences, we set out to serve three main purposes:

1. Provide a broad spectrum of research approaches, ranging from such recognizable investigative areas as historical and ethnographic research to emerging methodologies including autoethnography and arts-based research

2. Detail the basic purposes and processes of research approaches, explaining in each case how they are planned, conducted, and reported

3. Offer explanations and examples of how educational and social scientific research study results can be interpreted, evaluated, and applied across many professions

This book can also serve as an introductory source for students who plan to pursue advanced study and conduct their own qualitative research, but its primary aim is to offer readable, accessible content for the practitioner-consumer. As students graduate from college and begin their career, they become both professional practitioners of their discipline and potential consumers of research findings.

To the Instructor

This introductory research text is intended as a guide for your students who are most likely to be consumers, but not necessarily producers, of qualitative research. Although the book might serve as a primer for fledgling researchers, the overarching goal is to support your efforts in teaching students to become more intelligent readers and interpreters of this kind of research conducted by others.

The specific audiences are students in upper-level undergraduate and beginning graduate research courses who are not likely to pursue additional research course work on their own. Thus no prior experience or prerequisite course work would be required before using this text, although an introductory quantitative and qualitative survey course would be a useful foundation.

The book is structured to support your instructional endeavors in encouraging students to recognize important distinctions between research-based work and alternative sources of knowledge, to be able to understand the language and procedures normally encountered in different types of qualitative research studies, and to make practical sense of such studies in translating findings for use in everyday practice. Our purposes emphasized in this text include the following:

- Using, where possible, nontechnical language to explain research ideas
- Providing practical explanations of research approaches and the kinds of questions each answers
- Presenting clear-cut descriptions of most qualitative approaches used in education and the social sciences
- Making distinctions among a wide array of research approaches
- Offering explanations for necessary technical terms needed to understand how research is reported
- Examining forms and criteria for planning and conducting research
- Showing how each approach can be critically evaluated and interpreted from a practitioner's perspective
- Identifying actual research studies to allow students to practice critical analysis

The book is organized for a college course format in which one to two chapters may be assigned each week. And, because the chapters are of a stand-alone quality, you may use the sequence offered or may select a sequence that suits your unique instructional plans. Additional instructional features of the text are

- Chapters specifically relevant to qualitative research on ethics, the role of grounded theory, and data collection methods and tools
- A writing style that makes ideas accessible to students new to the field

- A diverse and balanced perspective of a broad spectrum of qualitative research methodologies ranging from discipline-based and interdisciplinary to emancipatory approaches

- An ending chapter on democratizing qualitative research designs

- Challenging questions distributed throughout each chapter to aid in instructional planning

- Key research ideas, concepts, and terms identified in each chapter

- An annotated set of relevant readings and an array of journals, organizations, and Web sites as sources for assignments and class discussions at the end of each chapter

- Expert authors for each chapter

To the Student

This text is based on the assumption that you have little or no background in how qualitative research is conducted in your field. Most who take a course of this kind will neither major in research nor become researchers one day. As students you will need to know how to read, understand, and interpret this kind of research so that you can judge its worth and practical value.

The material here is therefore presented using nontechnical language whenever that is possible. When technical terms are needed, they are offered along with practical explanations to increase your understanding. Further, you are provided with a broad coverage of qualitative research approaches (sometimes called methodologies) ranging from the recognized field of ethnography (the study of cultures and practices) to the emerging framework of indigenous research.

As a student your objectives for a course using this text should include learning about how qualitative studies are planned, carried out, and reported so that you, as a practitioner, might be able to read and interpret the results. Whether or not each research study's results should be used depends on your ability to determine if the studies are done well. To be an effective reader and evaluator of research in education and the social sciences, you should gain from this text the ability to

- Recognize and judge ethical issues in research

- Understand the inductive role of most qualitative approaches

- Comprehend the ideas and terms used to explain how each kind of research study is conducted
- Determine how each approach is organized and planned
- Recognize that practitioner questions may be answered differently depending on which research methodology is used
- Explain the similarities and differences found among qualitative research methodologies
- Understand how data are ordinarily collected and interpreted
- Develop ways of evaluating actual research studies to determine whether or not findings can be trusted
- Gain insight into how or when research might be translated into policy and practice

Some Study Suggestions

Many students find the language and procedures associated with research to be frightening or at least foreign to their everyday world. The following suggestions may assist you in tackling this relatively new and unusual area of study:

- Read the textbook before the course begins, making margin notes
- Commit new terminology and definitions to memory along with at least two examples for each
- Use chapter questions to monitor understanding
- Rewrite class notes and compare them to assigned readings
- Form a study group to test understanding "out loud"
- Talk with advanced students who have successfully completed the course for suggestions on content and study habits

Acknowledgments

Many have contributed to the publication of this textbook. The most prominent are the expert authors who patiently adjusted their individual writing style to match the rhythm and tone of the manuscript. We are grateful for their commitment to this complicated effort.

In addition, we very much appreciate the insightful critiques offered by these thoughtful reviewers: Valicia Boudry, Michel Coconis, Janet W. Colvin, Nancy Curtin, Jennifer K. Holtz, Dave Shen-Miller, Tara J. Schuwerk, and Julia Storberg-Walker. Most of their ideas and suggestions were incorporated into subsequent drafts of the text.

Certain people have a lasting impact on our lives and our work. Ernie House was Steve's instructor, mentor, colleague, friend, and critic to the world— "the best I know at reconstructing meaning through story."

For MaryLynn it was Steve Lapan, whose confidence in her has provided much-needed support through many challenges and (ad)ventures.

And Frances will always be grateful to Fred Erickson, who helped her find her voice, and taught her to look, ask, watch, and listen.

We are once again indebted to our editor, Andy Pasternack, who assisted in formulating the structure and content of the text. Also, we offer a special thanks to Seth Schwartz, who guided the development of this work from beginning to end. Finally, we are thankful for the thorough feedback by our fabulous copyeditor, Francie Jones, and to Kelsey McGee for shepherding the book through to its publication.

A Tour of This Text

This text, *Qualitative Research*, includes four chapters that prepare the reader in how this overall approach to research is planned, outlining philosophical assumptions that shape research studies (Chapter One), ethical dilemmas and guidelines for qualitative researchers (Chapter Two), the vital role of inductive grounded theorizing (Chapter Three), and the basic methods and tools used in these investigations (Chapter Four).

Chapters Five through Eight contain explanations of study approaches that are founded in recognized areas of study (discipline-based approaches). These include biography and life story research that examines individuals using biography and psychology as lenses for analyses (Chapter Five); historical research that employs the historian's craft to fill in gaps or reconsider histories already written (Chapter Six); ethnographic research that applies field studies in understanding a range of practices and beliefs from a cultural perspective (Chapter Seven); and autoethnography, an emerging research methodology used to offer dense descriptions of an individual's experience with a culture (Chapter Eight).

Chapters Nine through Thirteen address approaches that have blended disciplinary frameworks (interdisciplinary methodologies). These include narrative inquiry that seeks ways to understand and represent experiences through the stories that research participants live and report (Chapter Nine); case study research that isolates and reconstructs elements of a program or other phenomena (Chapter Ten); arts-based research that designs new research or critiques completed studies, in each case using principles and procedures from the arts (Chapter Eleven); practitioner action research, whereby groups or individuals study their own professional practice or examine important social issues (Chapter Twelve); and program evaluation that emphasizes the study of educational or social programs to determine their quality and effectiveness (Chapter Thirteen).

A decidedly more emancipatory perspective is emphasized in Chapters Fourteen through Eighteen. In Chapter Fourteen, the authors demonstrate that the undue influence of Eurocentric views reflected in research can be addressed in one way by using a culturally responsive system in evaluation studies involving African Americans; in Chapter Fifteen on critical ethnography, the primary goal is to highlight cultural aspects that represent oppression and identify avenues for equity; in Chapter Sixteen, feminist and other perspectives are used to demonstrate alternative explanations to the ordinary white male views found in traditional studies; and in Chapter Seventeen, the authors present ideas rooted in both indigenous knowledge systems and an anticolonial perspective and focus explicitly on the needs of the community. Finally, in Chapter Eighteen, qualitative researchers are challenged to incorporate strong conflicting values and interests of stakeholders by including stakeholder perspectives and interests, thereby democratizing their research.

Stephen D. Lapan
MaryLynn T. Quartaroli
Frances Julia Riemer

THE EDITORS

Stephen D. Lapan was professor emeritus at Northern Arizona University, where he directed the Curriculum and Instruction Doctoral Program. He taught courses in statistics, tests and measurements, program evaluation, action research, introduction to research, advanced research design, and paradigms for research. He received a PhD in educational psychology from the University of Connecticut. He conducted various types of research including several program evaluations. Among his publications are three books, *Survival in the Classroom* (with E. House), *Foundations for Research* (with K. deMarrais), and *Research Essentials: An Introduction to Designs and Practices* (with M. T. Quartaroli). Awards include the Arizona Association for Gifted and Talented Honor Board Life Achievement Award and Northern Arizona University College of Education Distinguished Service Award for Research. He served as editor for the *Excellence in Teaching Journal*, as consulting editor for the *Journal of Research in Childhood Education*, and as a review editor for the *International Journal of Teaching and Learning in Higher Education*.

MaryLynn T. Quartaroli has bachelor's degrees in theater, history, and geology, a master's degree in geology, and her doctorate in curriculum and instruction. Her areas of specialization include research methodologies, evaluation and assessment, science education, and Native American and adult education, as illustrated in her dissertation, *An Evaluation of the American Indian Air Quality Training Program*. She is the undergraduate research coordinator in the Office of the Vice President for Research at Northern Arizona University; she is also an external evaluator for programs funded by the U.S. Department of Education in projects as diverse as the Math and Science Partnerships and the Carol M. White Physical Education Program. She occasionally teaches research and curriculum classes for Northern Arizona University's Curriculum and Instruction Doctoral Program. With Stephen D. Lapan, she coedited and authored the data analysis chapters in *Research Essentials: An Introduction to Designs and Practices*.

THE EDITORS

Frances Julia Riemer received a PhD in educational anthropology from the University of Pennsylvania. She is currently an associate professor in the College of Education and the Women and Gender Studies Program at Northern Arizona University. She is an ethnographer who has conducted both long- and short-term ethnographic research in the United States, southern and eastern Africa, and Latin America. She has published a monograph, *Working at the Margins: Moving off Welfare in America*, and has had articles published in *Anthropology and Education Quarterly*, *Practicing Anthropology*, *Research Methods: Current Social Work Applications*, *Action in Teacher Education*, and *Educational Technology and Society*. She is currently working on *We Got the Light: Botswana and Stories of African Development*, based on ten years of ethnographic data collection in the southern African country of Botswana. She is the recipient of a Fulbright Scholar Award, a postdoctoral fellowship from the National Academy of Education/Spencer Foundation, a dissertation fellowship from the Spencer Foundation, and an Elva Knight research grant from the International Reading Association. She has developed and taught courses in educational sociology, ethnographic research methods, qualitative data analysis, and women's studies research.

THE CONTRIBUTORS

Tony E. Adams, PhD, is an assistant professor in the Department of Communication, Media and Theatre at Northeastern Illinois University. He teaches courses on relationships, gender, persuasion, identity, qualitative research, and communication theory. His work has appeared in such journals as *Qualitative Inquiry*, *Soundings*, *Cultural Studies <=> Critical Methodologies*, *Symbolic Interaction*, and the *Review of Communication*, and in such books as *The Handbook of Critical and Interpretive Methodologies*. He is currently working on a book about sexuality, same-sex desire, and coming out (tentatively titled *Narrating the Closet*).

Lucy E. Bailey is an assistant professor of social foundations and qualitative inquiry at Oklahoma State University. She is also core faculty in the Gender and Women's Studies Program. She holds graduate degrees in women's studies and cultural studies in education from The Ohio State University. Her interdisciplinary research interests include feminist, critical, and poststructuralist methodologies; American women's educational history; and diversity issues in higher education. With Nancy L. Rhoades, she published *Wanted—Correspondence: Women's Letters to a Union Soldier*.

Tom Barone's doctoral dissertation at Stanford University investigated the possibilities of literary nonfiction for researching and writing about educational matters. Since then he has explored, conceptually and through examples, a variety of narrative and arts-based approaches to contextualizing and theorizing about significant educational issues. He has written three books: *Aesthetics, Politics, and Educational Inquiry: Essays and Examples*; *Touching Eternity: The Enduring Outcomes of Teaching* (which received Outstanding Book Awards from Division B of the American Educational Research Association [AERA] and the AERA Narrative Research Special Interest Group); and *Arts Based Research*, coauthored with Elliot Eisner. As a professor of education in the Arizona State University Mary Lou Fulton Teachers College, Barone teaches courses in curriculum studies and qualitative research methods. He is the recipient of the AERA Division B Lifetime Achievement Award.

Bryan McKinley Jones Brayboy is an enrolled member of the Lumbee Tribe of North Carolina. He is Borderlands Associate Professor of Educational Leadership and Policy Studies in the School of Social Transformation at Arizona State University and visiting President's Professor of Indigenous Education at the University of Alaska Fairbanks. Most recently his research has been focused on exploring the role of indigenous knowledge systems in the academic experiences of indigenous students, staff, and faculty. He has published numerous articles and book chapters, and his recent research has appeared in such journals as *Anthropology & Education Quarterly*, *Harvard Educational Review*, *Journal of Black Studies*, *Review of Educational Research*, *Review of Research in Education*, and the *Urban Review*.

Angelina E. Castagno is an assistant professor of educational foundations in the Department of Educational Leadership at Northern Arizona University. She received her doctorate in educational policy studies from the University of Wisconsin-Madison. Her research focuses on issues of diversity, equity, and race in schools, with a particular emphasis on indigenous education and critical race theories. She has authored and coauthored articles in such journals as *Anthropology & Education Quarterly*, *Review of Educational Research*, and the *International Journal of Qualitative Studies in Education*.

Sharon Verner Chappell's doctoral dissertation at Arizona State University explored arts criticism methods of understanding young people's art works expressing social justice concerns in community-based settings. She is currently an assistant professor in elementary and bilingual education at California State University Fullerton, where she teaches topics in English language learning and cultural pluralism in education, as well as curriculum theory and arts education. Her research focuses on arts-based qualitative methods of analyzing issues of difference, language, culture, and power in childhood and youth studies.

Kathy Charmaz is professor of sociology and director of the Faculty Writing Program at Sonoma State University, a program she designed to help faculty complete their research and scholarly writing. She has written, coauthored, or coedited nine books including *Good Days, Bad Days: The Self in Chronic Illness and Time*, which won awards from the Society for the Study of Symbolic Interaction and the Pacific Sociological Association, and *Constructing Grounded Theory: A Practical Guide Through Qualitative Analysis*, which received a Critics' Choice Award from the American Educational Studies Association and has been translated into Chinese, Japanese, Polish, and Portuguese. Recently she has participated in two multiauthored book projects, *Developing Grounded Theory: The Second Generation*, and *Five Ways of Doing Qualitative Analysis: Phenomenological Psychology, Grounded Theory, Discourse Analysis, Narrative Research, and Intuitive Inquiry*. She currently serves as president of the Society for the Study of Symbolic Interaction.

Carolyn Ellis is professor of communication and sociology at the University of South Florida. She has published five books and four edited collections, the most recent of which are *The Ethnographic I: A Methodological Novel About Autoethnography*; *Revision: Autoethnographic Reflections on Life and Work*; and *Music Autoethnographies: Making Autoethnography Sing/Making Music Personal*. She has published numerous articles, chapters, and personal stories situated in interpretive representations of qualitative research. Her current research focuses on interactive interviews and collaborative witnessing with Holocaust survivors.

Pamela Frazier-Anderson, PhD, is the principal investigator for and founder of Frazier-Anderson Research and Evaluation, LLC in Norwalk, Connecticut, where she provides technical assistance in project and program development and collaborates with other evaluators on evaluation projects in the public and private sectors. Her research interests include educational issues affecting African American students from pre-K through grade 12 and in higher education, as well as program evaluation topics relevant to underserved populations. She currently serves as an adjunct faculty member in the Department of Psychology at Lincoln University within the department's distance learning program, in which she implements Web-based distance education courses in general psychology and program evaluation. She also serves as program cochair of the Multiethnic Issues in Evaluation Topical Interest Group of the American Evaluation Association, and as cochair of the Research on Evaluation Special Interest Group of the American Educational Research Association.

Heather R. Gough is currently working toward her doctorate in justice studies at Arizona State University. She earned her Juris Doctor degree from University of California, Berkeley, where she was honored with the Prosser Prize for Academic Excellence in Social Justice Practice, and subsequently earned her master's in social work from the University of Denver. Prior to her doctoral studies, she worked as an attorney, practicing in the fields of mental health, administrative, education, and dependency law. She has also worked as a social worker, providing therapeutic services to children and families involved in the foster care system.

Laurie Moses Hines earned her PhD in history of education and American studies from Indiana University-Bloomington. Before joining Kent State University, where she is currently an assistant professor, Hines worked for The College Board as lead developer and writer of an online public history project about The College Board's role in higher education. She was an assistant editor for the *History of Education Quarterly* and has published in that journal and *Education Next*, as well as in a number of edited texts. Her research focuses on the history of teachers, teacher education and higher education, and teacher professionalization. She currently is working on the historical dimensions of assessment of teacher dispositions for an edited volume on teacher assessment. Hines has presented research on historical topics and on teaching in higher education. She currently teaches courses in U.S. history, world history, and cultural foundations of education at Kent State University-Trumbull, where she was awarded a Kent State University teaching fellowship in 2003. She also is on the board of directors of Pi Lambda Theta, an educational honorary and professional association. She would like to thank the editors for their helpful comments.

Stafford Hood is the inaugural Sheila M. Miller Professor and head of the Department of Curriculum and Instruction and professor of educational psychology in the College of Education at the University of Illinois at Urbana-Champaign. His research and scholarly activities focus primarily on the role of culture in educational assessment and culturally responsive approaches in program evaluation. He serves, and has served, on numerous national advisory boards and committees including the American Indian Higher Education Consortium's National Science Foundation–funded Building an Indigenous Framework for STEM Evaluation project, as well as on Educational Testing Service's Visiting Panel for Research. He is president of the American Educational Research Association (AERA) SIG/Research Focus on Black Education and coeditor of the Feature Articles section of the AERA journal, *Educational Researcher*. He currently serves on the editorial boards of the *American Journal of Evaluation*, *New Directions for Evaluation*, and *Review of Educational Research*. He has also served as a program evaluation and testing consultant to the federal government, state departments of education, school districts, universities, foundations, and regional educational laboratories, and in New Zealand.

Rodney K. Hopson is the Hillman Distinguished Professor in the Department of Educational Foundations and Leadership in the School of Education, and faculty member in the Center for Interpretive and Qualitative Research at Duquesne University. His research interests lie in social politics and policies, foundations of education, sociolinguistics, ethnography, and evaluation. With funding support from the W. K. Kellogg Foundation, National Science Foundation (NSF), Robert Wood Johnson Foundation, Annie E. Casey Foundation, and other funding streams in the United States, he has secured support for graduate and postgraduate students of color in the natural and social sciences to contribute to the development of interests that focus on democratically oriented evaluation and research approaches and practices in traditionally underserved communities in the United States. With Rosalie Torres and Jill Casey, he is currently involved in an in-depth study of the logic model use of selected NSF-funded Math and Science Partnerships (MSPs). And, with Don Yarbrough, Lyn Shulha, and Flora Caruthers, he is involved in the study and application of program evaluation standards in preparation for the third edition of *Program Evaluation Standards for the Joint Committee on Standards for Educational Evaluation*.

Ernest R. House is a professor emeritus at the University of Colorado, Boulder, where he was professor of education, specializing in evaluation (1985–2001). Previously, he was professor of education at the University of Illinois at Urbana-Champaign (1969–1985). He has been a visiting scholar at University of California, Los Angeles, Harvard, New Mexico, and the Center for Advanced Study in the Behavioral Sciences at Stanford, as well as in England, Australia, Spain, Sweden, Austria, and Chile. His books include *Politics of Educational Innovation*; *Survival in the Classroom* (with S. Lapan); *Evaluating with Validity*; *Professional Evaluation*; *Values in Evaluation and Social Research* (with K. Howe); *Regression to the Mean*; and *Cherry Street Alley*, a childhood memoir. He received the Lasswell Prize in policy sciences and Lazarsfeld Award for Evaluation Theory.

Christine K. Lemley is an assistant professor in the Department of Teaching and Learning, Secondary Education at Northern Arizona University in Flagstaff. She earned a bachelor's degree in French, minor in English with certification to teach, from Lawrence University in Appleton, Wisconsin. She earned her master's degree in French from Middlebury College in Middlebury, Vermont. After completing two years of service as a Peace Corps volunteer, she pursued and earned her doctoral degree in curriculum and instruction from the University of Wisconsin-Madison. Her research interests focus on indigenous education and indigenous language revitalization efforts through narrative inquiry. Her most recent work focuses on social justice and equity issues, including historically marginalized populations. With Susan U. Marks and Gerald K. Wood, she coauthored the article "The Persistent Issue of Disproportionality in Special Education and Why It Hasn't Gone Away" in *Power Play: A Journal of Education Justice*.

THE CONTRIBUTORS

Beth Leonard (Deg Hit'an Athabascan) is originally from Shageluk, Alaska. Her father is James Dementi, who was raised in the traditional Athabascan subsistence lifestyle. Her mother is the late Reverend Jean Dementi, originally from California. Leonard earned her PhD from the University of Alaska Fairbanks (UAF) in 2007 in the Interdisciplinary Studies Program focusing on cross-cultural studies. She is currently an assistant professor in the UAF School of Education, instructing undergraduate and graduate courses on such topics as Alaska Native education, communication in cross-cultural classrooms, and documenting indigenous knowledge. Her research interests include indigenous pedagogies, indigenous teacher preparation, and Athabascan oral traditions and languages.

Donna M. Mertens is a professor in the Department of Educational Foundations and Research at Gallaudet University in Washington DC, where she received the Most Distinguished Faculty Award. She is a past president of the American Evaluation Association and has been honored with its awards for contributions to the association and to the development of theory in the field of program evaluation. She received her bachelor's degree in psychology at Thomas More College and her master's and doctoral degrees in educational psychology at the University of Kentucky. Her current interests focus on the linkage between research methods and social justice. She works with culturally diverse communities around the world to coconstruct approaches to research that address issues of human rights. She is the coeditor, with Pauline Ginsberg, of *The Sage Handbook of Social Research Ethics*, and is the author of *Research Methods in Education and Psychology: Integrating Diversity with Quantitative, Qualitative, and Mixed Methods*; *Transformative Research and Evaluation*; and the forthcoming *Program Evaluation: Theory to Practice*. She is the editor of the *Journal of Mixed Methods Research* and serves on the editorial board of *New Directions for Evaluation*.

Roland W. Mitchell is assistant professor of higher education and codirector of the Curriculum Theory Project at Louisiana State University. He received his PhD in educational research from the University of Alabama. He has published in numerous education journals including the *Journal of Negro Education*, the *International Journal of Education and the Arts*, the *Journal of Excellence in College Teaching*, and the *Review of Higher Education*. He provides consulting services to K–12 schools, not-for-profits, and universities on multicultural issues. He is currently at work on his first book, titled *Racing Higher Education: Representations and Refractions of Race in College Classrooms*.

Tricia S. Moore is a professor in the Department of Dental Hygiene at Northern Arizona University. She received a bachelor's in dental hygiene and master's and doctoral degrees in education from Northern Arizona University in Flagstaff. Her research interests include oral health, tobacco use, evidence-based practice, and professional development. Her most current work involves the use of students as tutors in a problem-based learning course as part of a dental hygiene curriculum. She serves on the editorial board for the *Journal of Dental Education*, the *Journal of Dental Hygiene*, and the *Journal of Contemporary Dental Practice*. She also serves on the Dental Hygiene Committee of the Arizona Board of Dentistry and as a curriculum consultant for the American Dental Association Commission on Dental Accreditation.

Roy F. Roehl II is an Alaska Native of Aleut descent. As an assistant professor he currently teaches mathematics methods, research methods, and calculus for the University of Alaska Fairbanks. He also spent fourteen years teaching mathematics and science at the high school level. He has been honored with a 2010 Mellon Foundation Fellowship, the 2004 Alaska Federation of Natives Eileen Panigeo MacLean Education President's Award, the 2001 Railbelt Conference Coach of the Year Award, and the 1998 Tandy Technology Outstanding Educator Award.

Jean J. Schensul, with her PhD from the University of Minnesota, is senior scientist at and founding director of the Institute for Community Research in Hartford, Connecticut. She is an interdisciplinary medical-educational anthropologist whose research cuts across the developmental spectrum, addressing contributions of ethnography to reveal disparities and structural inequities in early childhood development, adolescent and young adult substance use and sexual risk, reproductive health, and chronic diseases of older adulthood. She has received more than twenty National Institutes of Health research grants and is widely published in journals including the *Anthropology & Education Quarterly*, *AIDS and Behavior*, *American Behavioral Scientist*, and the *American Journal of Community Psychology*. She and Margaret LeCompte wrote and edited the widely celebrated seven-volume series, *The Ethnographers' Toolkit*. In 2010 she received the Bronislaw Malinowski Award for Lifetime Achievement in the application of anthropology to human problems. She has served as president of the Council on Anthropology and Education and is a member of the executive board of the American Anthropological Association.

Jessica A. Solyom is pursuing her doctorate in justice studies at Arizona State University. Her research interests focus on social justice and equity, American Indian activism, and immigration. She completed her master's degree in communication with emphases on interpersonal communication and critical cultural studies at the University of Utah. She currently serves as a managing editor for the *Journal of American Indian Education*. She has coauthored pieces in the *Nevada Law Journal* and the book *Research in Urban Educational Settings: Lessons Learned and Implications for Future Practice*.

Robert Thornberg is an associate professor in the Department of Behavioural Sciences and Learning at Linköping University in Sweden. He received his master's and doctoral degrees in education from Linköping University. His current research is on school bullying and peer harassment as social processes. His second line of research is on school rules, student participation, and moral practices in everyday school life. His main research methods are qualitative interview, focus group, grounded theory, and ethnographic methods. He is also a board member of the Nordic Educational Research Association (NERA) and a coordinator for the NERA Network for Empirical Research on Value Issues in Education as well.

Cynthia E. Winston is an associate professor in the Howard University Department of Psychology and principal investigator of the Identity and Success Research Laboratory. She is also the principal and founder of Winston Synergy, LLC, a narrative personality psychology consulting firm. She earned a BS from Howard University and a PhD in psychology and education from the University of Michigan. Her research interests focus on narrative identity, achievement motivation, and the psychology of success of adolescents and adults. She also has a special expertise in mixed-methods research design and analysis for inquiry related to engineering education and the cultural psychology of race as well as personality development within racialized societies. The National Science Foundation granted her an Early Career Award for her narrative psychology methodology development to study the lives of successful African American scientists and engineers.

QUALITATIVE RESEARCH

PART ONE

A QUALITATIVE FRAME OF MIND

CHAPTER 1

INTRODUCTION TO QUALITATIVE RESEARCH

Stephen D. Lapan
MaryLynn T. Quartaroli
Frances Julia Riemer

Key Ideas

- Empirical knowledge may be generated using scientific or social scientific approaches to study both physical and human phenomena.

- Qualitative research, as contrasted with quantitative studies, places more emphasis on the study of phenomena from the perspective of insiders.

- Quantitative researchers attempt to remain independent of the phenomena they study with the aim of generalizing findings, whereas qualitative researchers immerse themselves, viewing meaning as more context- and time-specific and, in most cases, not generalizable.

- Qualitative research from the critical theoretical view uses interpretive frameworks but also reveals ways that power is embedded in social contexts.

- Research *methods* refer to the kinds of tools used to collect data in studies, whereas *methodologies* are the more comprehensive designs and frameworks used in investigations.

- The qualitative methodologies presented in this text share important themes, including the view that reality is complicated and socially constructed and that qualitative research designs must be open to change during investigations.

Most of us seek knowledge and understanding as we attempt to make sense of the world around us. We use whatever means available to us as we negotiate the events in our lives. In some instances we might use *personal experience—*

knowing from earlier encounters that leaning against a cactus, for example, may not turn out well. Or we might rely on *tradition*, our well-developed habits—without thinking about it much, we decide to buy the same trustworthy automobile or go to the same coffee shop every morning. At other decision moments we may choose to depend on *reasoning*—we carefully examine the pros and cons before arriving at what we determine to be a logical conclusion about which car to purchase or coffeehouse to visit. And, finally, there are many circumstances in which we trust *authority*, the judgments of experts or respected others, to guide our final decision about such important areas as selecting a school or finding a good physician. So, as we consider the range of events and issues we must resolve, we are likely to apply any combination of personal experience, tradition, reasoning, and authority as our principal **sources of knowledge.**

Disciplined Inquiry

In **research-based knowledge,** conclusions are derived from carefully planned studies based on systematic observation using **disciplined inquiry** (involving an organized research plan or design that is considered acceptable by those with long experience in each relevant field of study). Characteristic of these inquiries are time-tested frameworks that are subject to critical review by peers in each area of investigation.

Some disciplines tend to focus on **quantitative research.** Chemists and other scientists conduct quantitative experimental research to study the physical world and its phenomena. Economists employ micro- and macroanalyses to study production, distribution, and consumption of goods and services. Some sociologists use demographics, organizational analysis, surveys, and correlational research to learn about social organization. Linguists employ discourse analysis to study language.

Other disciplines rely on qualitative inquiry. Anthropologists conduct ethnographic research to study culture. Historians employ their craft to interpret past events. Political scientists use policy and organizational analysis to understand the nature and distribution of power. Other researchers conduct arts-based inquiry to study phenomena aesthetically. Across all these disciplines, the reasons for knowing differ, and may include testing theory, learning something new, assessing needs, improving programs to inform practice, or evaluating. Whether quantitative or qualitative approaches are used, research findings should be and usually are subject to inspection and replication by those who conduct similar studies.

The gathering of **empirical information,** derived through direct observation, experience, or experiment, is usually referred to as either scientific or social scientific research. We commonly use the term *scientific* when applied to physical areas, such as chemistry or biology, and *social scientific* when used to study people and their interaction with environments in such research areas as anthropology and history. Scientific studies are more often those investigations carried out in highly controlled, laboratory-like settings in which potential causes are manipulated and observed to measure the effects. Social scientific inquiry, however, is generally conducted in real-life environments in which events are observed as they unfold without manipulation of normal patterns. Current research practices reflect a variety of strategies, procedures, and rules used in both scientific and social scientific studies that represent differing emphases in their designs. It is the case, though, that particularly in the physical domains, most approaches can be traced to what has been called the scientific method. This historic framework is characterized by the quantification of even qualitative events and the application of statistical analysis.

The **scientific method** begins with stating the problem and formulating a **hypothesis,** a reasoned and research-supported guess about what might cause a result or desired outcome. One might hypothesize, for example, that involving staff in decisions is likely to result in staff members' feeling more a part of the organization. Using the scientific method, such a hypothesis could then be pre- and posttested to arrive at conclusions either proving or disproving the hypothesized effect of staff involvement.

The development of the scientific method cannot be easily traced, but evidence of its application is found long Before the Current Era (BCE). Aristotle (384–322 BCE) is responsible for refining the process associated with the scientific method of establishing hypotheses, making observations, and determining answers through repeated experiments in order to test the relative truth of an original problem statement. Many other philosophers and mathematicians furthered Aristotle's work. A thoroughly modified and advanced current generation of quantitative designs is best represented in the early work of Campbell and Stanley (1963) and has evolved into conceptualizations found in Shadish, Cook, and Campbell (2002). This formulation of quantitative research is best characterized by **true experiments** found in the literature today, studies that include treatment and control groups, with participants randomly assigned to each hypothesized cause or intervention.

REFLECTION QUESTIONS

1. Explain in your own words the ideas behind the term *disciplined inquiry.*
2. How would you define the concept of empirical information or knowledge?

Historical Roots of Qualitative Research

The proliferation of qualitative studies in current research literature can be traced to at least one clear historical benchmark—the application to the human or social sciences of the German term *Verstehen,* loosely translated as "to understand" or "to interpret," by the German philosopher Wilhelm Dilthey (1989) in the mid-nineteenth century. Dilthey and other philosophers used the term to describe an individual's first-person perspective on his or her own experience, culture, history, and society. Subsequently, German sociologists Max Weber and Georg Simmel advocated *Verstehen* as a mode of sociological research in which an outside observer systematically gathers information on a particular phenomenon from the perspective of insiders, rather than interpreting it in terms of the researcher's outsider view. Advocates of this perspective argue that researchers are not really able to see the world as study participants experience it. These investigators are therefore obligated to gain insider views that may well differ from their own.

In the early twentieth century, German philosopher Edmund Husserl's (1913/1982) work on phenomenology advanced a research method to capture the processes through which humans come to know the world. In the early decades of that century, University of Chicago sociologists (called the Chicago School) listened to and recorded the views of those underrepresented in society, including immigrants, criminals, and the impoverished (Merriam, 2009). These and other social theorists laid the groundwork for qualitative researchers, who now use different methodologies and methods, seeking to uncover the meanings individuals bring to life experiences. The growth in the application of qualitative research approaches was pronounced by the 1970s, with the most significant expansion occurring in the last two decades of the twentieth century. Today there are dozens of journals, handbooks, research texts, and organizations devoted to qualitative designs and strategies (for examples, see Organizations and Web Sites at the end of this chapter).

The assumption in popular discourse and among novice researchers is that quantitative researchers count and qualitative researchers describe. And in truth, from the terms *qualitas* and *quantitas,* the term *qualitative* implies observing the *kinds* of things in the world, whereas the term *quantitative* suggests locating the *amount.* Quantitative researchers, on the one hand, do ask such questions as "How many of something are there in this place in the world?" Qualitative researchers, on the other hand, ask questions like "What are the kinds of things that are important for the conduct of social action in this local community of social practice?" Specifically, the quantitative investigator is likely to pose such a research question as this: "Is there a measurable increase in students' achievement after they experience the special science program?" The qualitative researcher, by contrast, might ask: "What are the participants' experiences with and reactions to the special science program?" In practical terms, though, quantitative researchers also describe, and qualitative researchers also count.

As a cautionary note, Strauss and Corbin (1998) remind us to carefully examine studies that may purport to be qualitative but do not actually follow the dictates of the paradigm:

> The term "qualitative research" is confusing because it can mean different things to different people. Some researchers gather data by means of interviews and observations, techniques normally associated with qualitative methods. However, they code the data in a manner that allows them to be statistically analyzed. They are, in effect, quantifying qualitative data. (p. 11)

Thus the terms *quantitative* and *qualitative* function as shorthand for differences far more complicated than the simple dichotomy of counting or not counting. They illuminate different assumptions about how we come to know the world. These differences are **epistemological,** asking questions about knowledge and how knowledge is acquired, and **ontological,** inquiring about the nature of reality and what it means to be or exist. These underlying assumptions reflect what Thomas Kuhn (1962) called different **paradigms,** or sets of practices that define a scientific discipline or approach to conducing research.

For the quantitative researcher, seeking understanding involves the concerted effort to remain independent of the phenomenon being studied, and when possible to establish cause-and-effect relationships that may be generalizable to other settings. This perspective has a long history beginning with the scientific method and early ideas of **positivism** (a precursor to current quantitative frameworks), but it has been thoroughly revised in a more advanced framework.

Current literature suggests that quantitative researchers have become ever more circumspect in regard to the trustworthiness of their research designs. These cautions are based on proposing generalization of findings only after recognizing the unique characteristics of both the nature of each study setting (**ecological validity**) and the explicit characteristics of each study sample (**population validity**). In addition, emerging issues identified as **conflict of interest validity** threats have been exposed related to insiders in pharmaceutical and other industries conducting their own research (House, 2011). Many standard research sources are available that provide more complete discussions of experimental and other quantitative or statistical research frameworks (see, for example, Gall, Gall, & Borg, 2003; Martin & Bridgmon, 2009; Shadish, Cook, & Campbell, 2002).

In contrast to those adhering to the more or less quantitative views outlined earlier, those who conduct **qualitative research** place much less emphasis on examining cause and effect and seldom find it necessary or even possible in most cases to draw conclusions that can be generalized beyond the research setting. For qualitative researchers, truth is context- as well as time-specific. As Merriam (2009) summarizes,

> Rather than determining cause and effect, predicting, or describing the distribution of some attribute among a population . . . [qualitative researchers] might be interested in uncovering the meaning of a phenomenon for those involved . . . [by] understanding how people interpret their experiences, how they construct their worlds, and what meaning they attribute to their experiences. (p. 5)

Whereas quantitative researchers seek to find what works best or which variables best explain a particular result, qualitative investigators strive to thoroughly explore day-to-day interactions, how things transpire, and the individual meanings of these events for the people involved. Certainly, this detail-oriented investigative approach can involve an intermix of both quantitative and qualitative observations (methods), but the underlying assumptions concerning the general views of research are distinctly different from those of quantitative researchers.

Qualitative researchers generally hold one of two research perspectives: **interpretivist** or **critical.** Interpretive researchers in this text (in the fields of biography and life story research, historical research, ethnographic research, autoethnography, narrative inquiry, case study research, arts-based research, practitioner action research, and program evaluation) assume that people create their own meanings in interaction with the world around them. For interpretive researchers, there is no single, unitary reality apart from our perceptions, and because each individual is unique and lives in a unique reality, individuals cannot be aggregated or averaged to explain phenomena. This notion of uniqueness applies to the researcher as well; in interpretive research, the effect of the researcher on the research itself is acknowledged. Interpretive investigators attempt to understand phenomena by accessing the meaning and value that study participants assign to them. These researchers ask open questions about how participants experience the world, and even allow questions to emerge and change as a situation becomes familiar.

Research grounded in critical theory draws on many of the same assumptions as the interpretive view, which acknowledges that reality is constructed through the meaning individuals give to a particular phenomenon. The important difference is that critical theorists focus on the ways power is embedded in the structure of society and how individuals become empowered to transform themselves, the social organization around them, and society as a whole. The critical researchers in this text (who focus on African American evaluation, critical ethnography, feminist research, indigenous research, and democratic research) are informed by principles of social justice, in terms of both working with and affecting outcomes in the community. Critical theorists ask about the sources of inequality and oppression in society, how language and communication patterns are used to oppress people, and how individuals achieve autonomy in the face of societal oppression.

As noted earlier, current educational and social scientific research literature continues to reflect both quantitative and qualitative views, represented by studies that employ many methodologies. Quantitative research may take a range of forms, including true experiments, quasi-experiments (with nonrandom sampling), correlational studies, and survey research. These all share the characteristics of linearity, precise quantitative measurement (often testing), and statistical analysis. Qualitative research, however, emphasizes texts over numbers. As Strauss and Corbin (1998) explain, "It can refer to research about persons' lives, lived experiences, behaviors, emotions, and feelings as well as about organizational functioning, social movements, cultural phenomena, and interactions between nations" (p. 11). These qualitative studies focus on giving voice to those who live experiences no one else could know about directly, asking research questions that encourage reflection and insight rather than assessing performance on tests or other quantitative measures emphasized in traditional quantitative research.

REFLECTION QUESTIONS

1. When Strauss and Corbin (1998) caution us about qualitative data's being transformed to quantitative, what do you think they mean?
2. What do you see as the main differences between interpretive and critical research approaches?

A Word About Method and Methodology

The goal of most research, especially applied studies, is to find the answer to some question or solution to some problem and translate that answer into findings or reports that may lead to practical decisions of one kind or another. As discussed above, findings from these kinds of studies might be presented in the form of words, numbers, or both. Numbers, often generated as scores on tests or ratings on surveys, are usually presented in tables and charts based on descriptive or inferential statistical procedures. When words are the primary reporting medium, it is ordinarily the result of analyzing what are known as *qualitative data* (not to be confused with the term *qualitative research*), obtained from such collection methods as long-answer questionnaires, interviews, or field notes.

These data collection, analysis, and reporting options are specified by research plans, often called research designs, which are usually characterized by an emphasis on either qualitative or quantitative data collection methods. Some plans may even emphasize both types of data, often referred to as **mixed-methods** designs. Researchers often refer to these data collection tools, such as interviews or tests, as **methods.** Research plans emphasize one kind of data over the other or, in the case of mixed methods, a mixture of both. Again, in this context the terms *qualitative* and *quantitative* refer to the kinds of data collected, not to the methodology or research approach being used (such as an experimental, survey, case study, or ethnographic approach) or to the more abstract idea of research paradigm.

Working within the qualitative and quantitative nomenclature, researchers must also select an overall research approach, sometimes called a **methodology** (also known as disciplined inquiry). Choosing a particular form of inquiry involves determining what is to be investigated (for example, the question, problem, or hypothesis) and which methodological design may best respond to the object and concerns of the proposed study. For example, a researcher may be faced with two kinds of concerns related to a school program. She may need to find out how the program works and what the overall short-term effect has been. Or she may need to determine if a program produces the kind of improved student achievement initially promised. The first question is one that may be best answered using an evaluation design (a methodology) in order to thoroughly describe the day-to-day program operation along with its overall immediate worth. The second might be better resolved through some kind of experimentation (another methodology) in which student results are assessed in terms of outcomes or gains. Thus, selection of which methodology to apply grows directly out of the problem faced.

In this text, for the purposes of convenience and clarity, we have requested that the authors make as fine a distinction as possible between the terms *method* (tools) and *methodology* (form of inquiry). In everyday research practice, however, we fully recognize that method and methodology have a tendency to interact to the point of becoming indistinguishable from one another. Although we portray method as a *way of doing* and methodology as a *way of thinking* about designing research, some argue that much of research is about method (Wolcott, 1990). One respected researcher notes that methodology is really a set of methods, practices, and procedures normatively followed by members from each discipline or field of study. As this investigator explains, "What researchers do in their reports of (empirical) research is list the methods used. They don't write a section properly labeled 'methodology'" (G. V Glass, personal communication, October 4, 2010). One must be cautious in creating such neat and clean categories as method and methodology, recognizing that, as with most human activity worth understanding, the act of conducting research is a complicated enterprise.

At a more abstract level, as suggested earlier in regard to paradigms, the terms *quantitative* and *qualitative* are also commonly used in yet other ways when discussing general views of research. As a shorthand form of communication, professional researchers often express the paradigmatic idea of traditional statistical research by using the term *quantitative*, whereas interpretive and critical investigators use the word *qualitative* to refer to any number of methodologies in their paradigms. It should come as no surprise that these multiple applications of these two terms create confusion, especially among those new to educational and social research.

REFLECTION QUESTIONS

1. Is it important to make a clear distinction between method and methodology? Why or why not?
2. In your estimation, why might it be difficult to separate method and methodology in research studies?

Overview of the Text

Our aim for this text is to offer an up-to-date guide to qualitative research design, data collection, analysis, and reporting written by articulate and accessible scholars. Learning about research methodologies from expert investigators themselves is particularly revealing, especially when their choices of paradigms are shaped by both discipline and personal beliefs. As Schwandt (1989) observes,

Our constructions of the world, our values, and our ideas about how to inquire into those constructions, are mutually self-reinforcing. We conduct inquiry via a particular paradigm because it embodies assumptions about the world that we believe and values that we hold, and because we hold those assumptions and values we conduct inquiry according to the precepts of that paradigm. (p. 399)

As you read the authors' step-by-step explanations of their research methodologies and the methods they employ for collecting and analyzing data, you will learn about both the research approaches and the decisions on which an actual study is based.

The reader will notice that most of the qualitative methodologies discussed in this text share common traits and themes. The chapter author-researchers seek a greater understanding of how the world works in all its complexity and variability of phenomena and human interactions. They account for the view that reality is socially constructed and that studies must therefore take place within these sociocultural contexts, not in carefully controlled conditions. Qualitative researchers incorporate the **etic perspective** (outsider-researcher) and the **emic perspective** (insider-participant) as lenses for synthesizing and interpreting study findings (see, for example, Chapter Four).

Conducting research in these real-life contexts raises ethical issues and concerns for participants (see Chapter Two); researchers have the responsibility to thoroughly examine the risks and benefits of conducting the research and their own **positionality,** given the unique relationship that develops between the participants and the researcher as a data collection instrument. The reader should take special note of how and to what extent these expert researchers are sensitive to their close, interactive investigative roles, and of the attention they give to the standards of emancipation and social justice.

Finally, an essential feature of all of the qualitative methodologies outlined in this text is the **inductive process,** which involves building meaning from specific, rich descriptions of people and settings. Whether the research is theory driven or involves theory building, each approach considers the process of deriving meaning from collected data as a core design ingredient (see Chapter Three for a particular case of this framework—**grounded theory**).

REFLECTION QUESTIONS

1. How are the inductive process and grounded theory related?
2. What do the terms *etic* and *emic* mean, and why are these important ideas in qualitative research?

Preview of the Chapters

The first part of this book provides readers with an overview of the nature of—and assumptions, methods, and tools common in—qualitative research studies. The remaining three parts of this text focus on fourteen distinct, rich, and varied qualitative methodologies. Part Two is a grouping characterized by its discipline-specific roots, reflecting approaches that come from the recognized areas of biography, history, anthropology, and a variation of ethnographic research, autoethnography, which employs two distinct disciplines. Part Three of the book contains chapters reflecting approaches that further blend recognized areas of research. In Part Four, the reader is provided with five chapters that address methodologies characterized by their emancipatory qualities. In each of these chapters, emphasis is given to critical theoretical issues of social justice.

This text's chapters represent forms of qualitative research ranging from well-known designs to newer, emerging formats. Each approach is presented to prepare the reader, as a consumer of qualitative studies, to critically evaluate both the authenticity and the usefulness of a given methodology. As a concise reference source, Exhibit 1.1 contains a short summary of Chapters Two through Eighteen.

EXHIBIT 1.1
CHAPTER SUMMARIES

- **Chapter Two: Ethics in Qualitative Research in Education and the Social Sciences**

    The chapter presents guidelines for protecting research study participants and conducting ethical research with the goal of enhancing social justice.

- **Chapter Three: Grounded Theory**

    Chapter Three provides a guiding framework for most qualitative research. This chapter emphasizes conducting research from the ground up (inductively) to construct meaning and middle-range theories.

- **Chapter Four: Methodology, Methods, and Tools in Qualitative Research**

    The chapter gives an explanation and review of methods and instruments commonly used to collect data in qualitative studies, including face-to-face observation and in-depth interviewing.

(Continued)

EXHIBIT 1.1
CHAPTER SUMMARIES (Continued)

- **Chapter Five: Biography and Life Story Research**

    The methodology discussed in this chapter employs a biographical framework from a psychological perspective for the purpose of developing a narrative or constructing theories about a person's life.

- **Chapter Six: Mystery Solved: Detective Skills and the Historian's Craft**

    Chapter Six outlines strategies used to understand the past, employing data collection, analysis, and interpretation to fill gaps in historical knowledge.

- **Chapter Seven: Ethnographic Research**

    Ethnographic research documents the beliefs and practices of a particular cultural group or phenomenon in its natural environment from the perspective of insiders.

- **Chapter Eight: Trekking Through Autoethnography**

    Chapter Eight illustrates how the use of dense descriptions of the researcher's own experiences in a culture allows for a better understanding of the culture and the individual.

- **Chapter Nine: Narrative Inquiry: Stories Lived, Stories Told**

    Narrative inquiry research seeks ways to understand and represent experiences through the stories that individuals live and tell.

- **Chapter Ten: Case Study Research**

    Case study research uses descriptions of programs, events, or other phenomena to construct a complete portrayal of a case for interpretation and possible action.

- **Chapter Eleven: Arts-Based Research**

    Chapter Eleven discusses the application of principles and procedures derived from visual, literary, and performance-based arts to conduct studies or analyze social phenomena in the manner of an artist or art critic.

- **Chapter Twelve: Practitioner Action Research**

    Chapter Twelve outlines research in which practicing professionals collect data for individual or group self-reflection and improved practice.

- **Chapter Thirteen: Program Evaluation**

    Program evaluation develops case study descriptions but also renders judgments of worth about studied phenomena, with an emphasis on social or educational programs.

- **Chapter Fourteen: Preliminary Considerations of an African American Culturally Responsive Evaluation System**

    The chapter offers a research approach and model for culturally responsive evaluation studies, particularly for use in majority African American settings.

- **Chapter Fifteen: What Makes Critical Ethnography "Critical"?**

    Critical ethnography uncovers and explicates power and oppression, with the goal of working toward greater equity and justice for marginalized groups.

- **Chapter Sixteen: Feminist Research**

    Feminist research consists of a family of research strategies that explore women's practices in order to better understand and address their lived experiences.

- **Chapter Seventeen: Reclaiming Scholarship: Critical Indigenous Research Methodologies**

    The chapter describes research methodologies grounded in anticolonialism, with an emphasis on relationships among the researcher, the topic, and indigenous communities

- **Chapter Eighteen: Democratizing Qualitative Research**

    Chapter Eighteen offers a deliberative democratic research framework structured for situations in which strong, conflicting values and interests are present, negotiated, and incorporated into the study's results

REFLECTION QUESTIONS

1. What characteristics might distinguish biographical and life story research from historical investigations in this text?
2. At this point, what is your understanding of, and reaction to, arts-based inquiry as an approach to research?
3. In your own words, how would you explain emancipatory research studies, and why might they offer important perspectives?

Summary

Although there are several sources of knowledge for understanding our surroundings, research-based information developed through disciplined inquiry is a more trusted source. A quantitative research approach, on the one hand, is often used to study both physical and social phenomena, with current forms of quantitative research having advanced beyond earlier frameworks. Qualitative research, on the other hand, examines social settings from insiders' perspectives and generates descriptions and analyses of contexts, rather than applying numbers, to derive meaning.

Qualitative and quantitative research are guided by distinctly different views about how knowledge is defined and discovered; qualitative researchers see meaning as socially constructed, whereas quantitative researchers consider truth as more enduring, although somewhat influenced by contexts. Qualitative research has two dimensions: the *interpretive* perspective, which focuses on uncovering participants' views, and a *critical* perspective, which builds on the interpretive perspective but also examines ways in which power is embedded in social settings.

For purposes of clarity and convenience, it is important for readers to distinguish between methods and methodologies as they negotiate the chapters offered in this text while understanding the subtle ways the concepts interact in practice.

The methodologies presented share common themes, including the view that reality is complicated and socially constructed. In addition, the qualitative research designs offered here employ inductive reasoning, are constructed to be flexible and dynamic, and are subject to change as research studies unfold.

Key Terms

conflict of interest validity, 7
critical, 8
disciplined inquiry, 4
ecological validity, 7
emic perspective, 12
empirical information, 4
epistemological, 7
etic perspective, 12
grounded theory, 12
hypothesis, 5
inductive process, 12
interpretivist, 8
methodology, 10
methods, 10
mixed-methods, 10
ontological, 7
paradigms, 7
population validity, 7
positionality, 12
positivism, 7
qualitative research, 8
quantitative research, 4
research-based knowledge, 4
scientific method, 5
sources of knowledge, 4
true experiments, 5

Further Readings and Resources

Suggested Readings

Creswell, J. W. (2007). *Qualitative inquiry and research design: Choosing among five approaches* (2nd ed.). Thousand Oaks, CA: Sage.

Although not as comprehensive as Denzin and Lincoln's book (2005) described below, this book is thorough and practical in its presentation of the five qualitative research areas of narrative research, phenomenology, grounded theory, ethnography, and case study research.

Denzin, N. K., & Lincoln, Y. S. (Eds.). (2005). *The Sage handbook of qualitative research* (3rd ed.). Thousand Oaks, CA: Sage.

This authoritative and highly respected handbook is the most comprehensive source for qualitative research on the market, including such cutting-edge and traditional methodologies as narrative research, critical ethnography, indigenous inquiry, and arts-based research.

Green, J. L., Camilli, G., & Elmore, P. B. (Eds.). (2006). *Handbook of complementary methods in education research* (3rd ed.). Mahwah, NJ: Lawrence Erlbaum.

This is a thorough source for both quantitative and qualitative approaches, including chapters on both general philosophies and critical methodologies. Applications are exclusively for education, as the title suggests.

Merriam. S. B. (2009). *Qualitative research: A guide to design and implementation*. San Francisco: Jossey-Bass.

Although it is limited by a primary focus on case study research, this very readable introduction to and overview of qualitative research contains useful sections on sampling, data collection, and reporting of qualitative investigations.

Strauss, A., & Corbin, J. (1998). *Basics of qualitative research: Techniques and procedures for developing grounded theory* (2nd ed.). Thousand Oaks, CA: Sage.

This is the best source for understanding the philosophy, designs, and procedures associated with theory construction, or what is now commonly known as grounded theory—the construction of meaning and explanations through an inductive process.

Organizations and Web Sites

American Educational Research Association (AERA)—Special Interest Group on Qualitative Research (SIG #82) (www.aera.net/Default.aspx?menu_jd=208&id=772)

This subgroup of AERA provides a space for discussions of the philosophical, ethical, and methodological issues surrounding qualitative research.

American Evaluation Association (AEA) (www.eval.org)

This is an international professional association with approximately five thousand members who are primarily interested in evaluation studies.

Association for Qualitative Research (AQR) (www.aqr.org.au/)
This Australia-based group of qualitative researchers supports innovations in qualitative research practices.

International Association of Qualitative Inquiry (IAQI) (www.iiqi.org/C4QI/httpdocs/iaqi/home.html)
This multidisciplinary institute at the University of Illinois at Urbana-Champaign facilitates the development of qualitative research methods across disciplines, and publishes a newsletter and other periodic publications including the *International Review of Qualitative Research* listed below.

International Journal of Qualitative Studies in Education (www.tandf.co.uk/journals/tf/09518398.html)
This peer-reviewed journal aims to enhance the practice and theory of qualitative research in education.

International Review of Qualitative Research (www.lcoastpress.com/journal.php?id=8)
A peer-reviewed journal from the University of Illinois at Urbana-Champaign, this publication encourages the use of critical, experimental, and traditional forms of qualitative inquiry in the interests of social justice.

Qualitative Inquiry (http://qix.sagepub.com/)
This Sage publication offers current studies and commentary concerning emerging issues in qualitative and mixed-design research.

Qualitative Report (www.nova.edu/ssss/QR/)
This bimonthly online journal focuses on qualitative research.

Qualitative Research Journal (www.rmitpublishing.com.au/qrj.html)
This international online journal is devoted to the theory and practice of qualitative research in the human sciences.

Qualitative Social Work (www.sagepub.com/journalsProdDesc.nav?prodId=Journal201566)
This Sage publication regularly includes these features: "Response and Commentary"—responses to previous articles in the journal or contributions that initiate discussion of current research and practice issues; "Practice and Teaching of Qualitative Social Work"—critical "how-to" accounts and reflections on the methodology and practice of qualitative social work; and "New Voices"—articles by oppressed voices that often have been silenced, and from authors who are working in contexts that are new to publishing on qualitative research and practice and are exploring new possibilities for the use of qualitative research and practice.

CHAPTER 2

ETHICS IN QUALITATIVE RESEARCH IN EDUCATION AND THE SOCIAL SCIENCES

Donna M. Mertens

Key Ideas

- Qualitative researchers' interactions with individuals and communities provide fertile ground for the emergence of ethical dilemmas.

- Ethical guidelines and principles bind all researchers to standards of ethical practice as exemplified in government regulations and professional associations' codes of ethics. Qualitative researchers contribute additional layers of ethical concerns emanating from the "researcher as instrument" concept that is part of qualitative inquiry.

- The axiological branch of philosophy is one that explores the nature of ethics and provides a way to examine ethical issues in qualitative research.

- The National Commission for the Protection of Human Subjects of Biomedical and Behavioral Research (1979) issued the *Belmont Report*, in which they identified three ethical principles to guide researchers: beneficence, respect, and justice. These principles are expanded on from the perspective of qualitative researchers who situate their work with a goal of furthering social justice.

- The norms for research in the *Belmont Report* include the concept of rigor, defined in terms of valid designs and researcher competency, as a basis for establishing the ethical quality of studies. Qualitative researchers have expanded the norms related to valid designs and researcher competency to include the principle of authenticity, which encompasses the principles of balance (or fairness), ontological authenticity, educative authenticity, catalytic authenticity, and tactical authenticity.

- Members of communities that have been pushed to the margins of society are taking a more active role in articulating what they consider to be ethical research practices in their communities. Codes of ethics for researchers in education and the social sciences are beginning to address issues of culture and power differences.

Ethical Dilemmas in Research

Suppose a researcher is conducting research in a school setting and observes that the principal engages in illegal behaviors toward students and teachers. Suppose a researcher is studying illegal behaviors, such as drug use, and finds that he and the participants in the research are threatened with arrest. Suppose a researcher has made a promise of confidentiality, but the participants want their names attached to their stories. Suppose research participants are willing to be interviewed by a researcher but not willing to sign a consent form for fear of retaliation by more powerful "others." Suppose a researcher publishes a description of an individual that is rich in detail—rich enough that her identity is immediately obvious to others who know her. Suppose that description of the individual is not very flattering, or that the individual does not recognize herself in the way the researcher portrays her. Suppose a researcher describes a community and its values in ways that members of the community do not themselves recognize. Suppose members of a community view the results of research as a means to perpetuate a deficit perspective of their culture and way of life, with findings that only depict problems in the community without recognizing strengths. What is the researcher's ethical responsibility in such situations as these?

Guidance for the Ethical Conduct of Research

All researchers can find guidance in the ethical conduct of research from such sources as their professional associations, government-sponsored reports, ethical review board stipulations, funding agencies, research sponsors, and scholarly literature. (You can find Web-based resources for these types of organizations and documents at the end of this chapter.) The establishment of ethical review boards is a significant development that emerged in response to harm associated with unethical research.

ETHICS IN QUALITATIVE RESEARCH IN EDUCATION AND THE SOCIAL SCIENCES

In the United States, researchers who are part of a university or college that receives federal funds are required to have their research proposals approved by an **institutional review board (IRB)** (even if their proposed research is not supported by federal funds). IRBs provide very specific guidance in terms of what evidence they need from a researcher in order to approve a research proposal, including an explanation of how the researcher documents the validity of the research design, justification of sampling strategies, and detailed procedures for obtaining informed consent. However, researchers have found limitations in using standard forms that IRBs require for submission of a proposal because these forms do not allow them to address the broader scope of complexity of the research situations, especially with qualitative research studies.

Qualitative educational and social researchers face particularly complex ethical issues because their research involves personal interaction with individuals and communities. The concept of **researcher as instrument** brings to the fore ethical issues related to relationships that generally receive less attention or are not addressed in quantitative research studies. In addition, educators and social scientists work in contexts in which issues of diversity are more visible now than ever before. Hence, researchers encounter additional ethical concerns when the dimensions of diversity relevant to a given study are typically associated with those having less power in the researcher-researched relationship on the basis of age, diminished capacity, historical legacies of oppression and discrimination, or social stigma, such as children, ethnic and racial minorities, people with disabilities, deaf people, religious minorities, LGBTQ (lesbian, gay, bisexual, transsexual, and queer/questioning) persons, indigenous peoples, criminals, drug users, and older adults.

The remainder of this chapter examines the principles and scientific norms for the ethical conduct of research, beginning with a historical look at their emergence and continuing with specific concerns that qualitative researchers have raised. The role of ethical review boards and professional associations' codes of ethics are integrated into the discussion.

Ethical Principles

Cognizance of the critical need to attend to ethical issues in research arose from atrocities perpetrated in the name of research, such as the medical experiments conducted by the Nazis during World War II and the Tuskegee experiment, which involved studying the course of syphilis in black men in studies conducted in the United States from 1933 to 1972 even after a treatment for the disease had been discovered. These examples represent extremes in the unethical conduct of research; however, researchers also need to be aware of less obvious, yet still harmful, effects of research. In the United States, the National Commission for the Protection of Human Subjects of Biomedical and Behavioral Research was established in 1978 to develop regulations to guide ethical conduct for researchers. The results of the National Commission's work are found in the 1979 *Belmont Report*, which outlines three basic principles to guide researchers:

Beneficence: Researchers should strive to maximize the good outcomes for science and humanity and minimize risk or harm to individuals in the research.

Respect: Researchers should treat the people in their study with respect and courtesy, with particular concern for children and people who have mental retardation or senility.

Justice: Researchers should ensure that the people who participate in the research are those who reap the benefits of the research. They should achieve this by the use of procedures that are reasonable, nonexploitative, carefully considered, and fairly administered.

Qualitative Researchers and Axiological Belief Systems

Axiology is the branch of philosophy that explores the nature of ethics. Christians (2005) and Lincoln (2009) provide critical insights into the axiological assumptions of qualitative researchers who situate themselves in the **constructivist paradigm**. Paradigms are frameworks of philosophical assumptions that guide researchers. For example, constructivists assume that reality is socially constructed, and they see the purpose of research as to authentically understand multiple constructions of what is considered to be real. With each edition of *The Sage Handbook of Qualitative Research* (Denzin & Lincoln, 2005), constructivists have increased their concerns about social justice and human rights. Mertens (2009; 2010; Mertens, Holmes, & Harris, 2009) conceptualized axiological assumptions, while commensurate with those that are evolving from constructivist worldviews, explicitly reflect ethical beliefs of researchers who situate themselves in the **transformative paradigm**. Within this framework, researchers believe that there are different opinions about reality, but that some of those versions of reality constitute barriers to the furtherance of social justice and human rights. This leads to the need to use culturally responsive methods of research that take into account the lived experiences of those who face discrimination and oppression. Culturally responsive research is characterized by awareness of power differentials both between the researchers and the participants and within communities. The transformative researcher focuses on establishing relationships with participants that allow for voices of all relevant constituencies to be heard, especially those associated with positions of least privilege. For example, a researcher in a project designed to improve reading instruction for deaf students would ask about the role of a visual language in bridging between American Sign Language and English in print form (Harris, 2011). These two worldviews, constructivist and transformative, are associated with the use of either qualitative methods or mixed methods (in other words, the combination of quantitative and qualitative methods in one study or a program of study).

Researchers who focus on collecting quantitative data sometimes claim that their research is objective because their personal opinions are not involved in the collection and analysis of the data and thus the results of the study. However, constructivists object to the reduction of human experience to a single number and raise questions about whose judgment was used to decide what data to collect, how to analyze those data, and how to interpret them. Constructivists openly acknowledge that researchers need to do a careful critical analysis of themselves and be sensitive to how their values and biases influence the research situation. Transformative researchers agree on the importance of self-awareness, but they also emphasize awareness of the differences in power relations in the research situation and how their research can be used to address issues of social justice. Additional ethical issues arise in constructivist and transformative research because of closer involvement with researched communities and increased emphasis on the use of research findings for social transformation.

Reframing Ethical Principles from a Transformative Perspective

As mentioned previously, constructivists have begun to wander into the transformative paradigm's terrain by increasing emphasis on issues of human rights and social justice. The transformative paradigm provides stimulation to rethink the standard ethical principles for research because it raises explicit questions about how researchers can contribute to addressing issues of discrimination and oppression as a means of furthering social justice and enhancing human rights. The standard ethical principles are reexamined here in light of a transformative perspective.

Beneficence

The principle of beneficence directs researchers to strive to maximize the good outcomes of their studies for science and humanity and minimize risk or harm to individuals in the research. The challenge comes in interpreting what is meant by maximizing good and minimizing risk or harm, and in researchers' abilities to discern whether they are doing good or harm. Even the choice of a research topic comes under scrutiny, as does choice of methods and strategies for dissemination and use of research findings. For example, members of a minority community might acknowledge that sexual abuse occurred at the hands of a member of that community, but they do not want to "air their dirty laundry." If a qualitative researcher hears these two perspectives, will she or he do more harm to the community to make this public or more good if it is revealed? What are the ethical implications of choosing to research such a sensitive topic? What are the ethical implications if sensitive topics are avoided?

Researchers who work for social transformation reframe the principle of beneficence to focus on understanding what is viewed as beneficial to members of the researched community. For example, Sullivan (2009) writes about issues that arise in research with people who have disabilities and raises the following questions in regard to avoidance of harm and promotion of benefits: "Is the research intrusive and potentially harmful to the researched? Is there any reciprocity between the researched and the researcher?" (p. 70). Similar issues are raised by members of indigenous groups, especially by Maori researchers in New Zealand (Cram, 2009) and American Indians in the United States and Canada (Battiste, 2000; LaFrance & Crazy Bull, 2009). Indigenous communities are asking for explicit statements from researchers as to what the researchers will gain (funding, publications, notoriety); what the community will gain (findings that can be used to lift them out of poverty or to address other social challenges, such as alcoholism and illiteracy); as well as the potential harm to individuals and the community (ruining their reputation or belittling their cultural practices). The harm to individuals needs to be considered in terms of the potential revelation of their identity through provision of details in conversations, writing, and presentations based on the research, especially in small or close-knit communities (Haverkamp, 2005).

REFLECTION QUESTIONS

1. To what extent are researchers ethically obligated to select topics that provide the "promise of ameliorating ills and/or providing benefits" (Ginsberg & Mertens, 2009, p. 595)? Justify your answer.
2. What are the methodological implications of the principle of beneficence? Does this principle dictate a certain approach to research? Why or why not?
3. What are researchers' ethical obligations in terms of disseminating their findings? Is a researcher's ethical obligation satisfied when the findings appear in a scholarly journal, or are there further implications of the beneficence principle for the dissemination and use of research? What might these be?
4. Under what conditions should researchers take action to ensure that their work will be used for the good of humanity?

Respect

The second ethical principle, respect, is defined in the *Belmont Report* (National Commission, 1979) in terms of treating people in the study with respect and courtesy, especially if the participants are not autonomous, such as children, people with mental retardation, or people suffering from senility. Kitchener and Kitchener (2009) interpret this definition of respect as including two directives for researchers: (1) to allow research participants to freely choose to participate in the research or to refuse or withdraw without penalty; and (2) to not make promises to the participants that you cannot fulfill (such as not promising that their child will be just like a hearing child if he or she gets a cochlear implant).

Qualitative researchers have raised many ethical questions about the meaning of respect and strategies for establishing trust in various cultural groups. Maori researchers provide insights into the meaning of respect in their discussions of how researchers enter their community, whether they are members of the community or not (Cram, 2009). Everyone is expected to adhere to the cultural norms of their community; that means they need to identify who they are, where they are from, the purpose of the research, who will own the data, who will benefit from the research, and how the information will be disseminated.

From a transformative perspective, learning about cultural norms and practices from the viewpoint of community members is part of demonstrating respect and establishing trust with a community. This learning includes several aspects related to power issues, including the formation of relationships versus partnerships, the establishment of teams of researchers with community representation, and the choice of language used in the research study. For example, some indigenous peoples distinguish between partnerships and relationships, viewing partnerships as short-term arrangements made for the conduct of research and relationships as developing over long periods of time through involvement with a community (Bishop, 1996; Cram, 2009; LaFrance & Crazy Bull, 2009; Moewaka Barnes, McCreanor, Edwards, & Borell, 2009). Research agendas may be developed over many years of both formal and informal engagement with the community. The following quotation illustrates the importance of community involvement from an ethical perspective.

> The more closely researchers are involved with the researched, the more likely it is that they can be responsive and adaptable. Close relationships with the local community can ensure that the appropriate people will be supportive and able to provide expertise, endorsement, and guidance for the research. (Ginsberg & Mertens, 2009, p. 596)

Researchers who are not members of the community in which they are working need to be aware of how their own values influence their approach to the study, as well as their perceptions of the processes that they observe. Such researchers can also keep a journal of how their thinking progresses throughout the study and engage in dialogue with a trusted member of the community to help with reflection on these matters. Researchers who are members of the targeted community are not exempt from concerns about allowing their biases to influence the research. All researchers need to engage in this self-reflection and reflection in relation to a community in order to preserve the integrity of their work.

Participatory action researchers have explored strategies that demonstrate how to involve participants as active members of research teams (see Chapter Twelve in this text; Fine et al., 2003; Kemmis & McTaggart, 2003; Kidd & Kral, 2005). Although building teams of researchers that are inclusive of members of the targeted community is not unproblematic, it does represent a strategy that lends itself to demonstrating respect, building trust, and developing relationships (Harris, Holmes, & Mertens, 2009). Respect in team building means that members of the community will serve as principal investigators or coresearchers, not only as research assistants or token representatives. Respect in team building also means acknowledging the expertise that team members bring to the inquiry process, not assuming that a university researcher is the expert who has come to teach the less sophisticated. All members of the team bring value to the team; learning should be a synergistic process, with each contributing from his or her base of knowledge and experience. As deaf researchers point out, they can and do learn sophisticated research methods, but hearing researchers cannot really learn what it means to be deaf (Harris et al.).

Another very important dimension of respectful research is the relationship between language and culture and the associated power issues. Several groups raise questions about the use of a dominant language in research that dismisses the language of the community. Should the language of discourse in the planning and implementation of the research be the language of the dominant culture or the language of the community? Should interpreters be provided for community members or for the dominant language users? Deaf researchers note that when the language of discourse is spoken English, they are at a disadvantage because of the need to go through interpreters and the lag time between what is said and what is signed (Harris et al., 2009). What if the tables were turned? What if researchers who want to conduct research in the deaf community (or any minority-language-using community) who do not know their language were obliged to get interpreters to express what they want to say?

ETHICS IN QUALITATIVE RESEARCH IN EDUCATION AND THE SOCIAL SCIENCES

REFLECTION QUESTIONS

1. In which language should the planning and implementation of research occur? Why?
2. What are the ethical implications when working in a community in which the language is one that is not in written form (such as the Hmong language or American Sign Language)?
3. Under what conditions is there an ethical obligation to provide multilingual, visual or auditory, sign-based, or Braille reports back to the community?
4. In what ways can a researcher determine whether or how participants will benefit from the research?

Justice

The third principle found in the *Belmont Report* (National Commission, 1979) is justice, defined as the process of ensuring that the people who participate in the research benefit from the research. Researchers should achieve this by using procedures that are reasonable, nonexploitative, carefully considered, and fairly administered. This principle overlaps somewhat with the concept of beneficence; however, it has been interpreted to mean that such groups as college sophomores and prisoners, for example, should not be overburdened with expectations of research participation simply because they are easily accessible, but at the same time groups should not be excluded from the opportunity to participate in research that has the potential to benefit them because they are viewed as hard to reach. Members of the dominant culture might view members of a linguistic minority, people with disabilities, or members of stigmatized groups as hard to reach because they do not have experience with those groups.

When the principle of justice is reframed using a transformative perspective, researchers are reminded of the diverse nature of groups, some characteristics of which can be used as a basis for excluding members of marginalized communities from participating in and benefiting from research. For example, historical studies of women that assumed that researchers could study middle-class white women and then speak on behalf of all women exclude the perspectives of poor women of color (Brabeck & Brabeck, 2009). Feminist thinking has evolved to recognize that women reflect wide variations in terms of age, sexual orientation, socioeconomic status, education, ethnicity, disability, deafness, health, and so on. Similarly, researchers in the disability community note the diversity within their membership on these characteristics, as well as in terms of the types and severity of disabilities and their accompanying need for supportive accommodations for authentic participation in research (Mertens, 2009; Sullivan, 2009). Researchers of gender issues ask if categories of gender need to be expanded to include lesbian, gay, bisexual, transsexual, and queer, while at the same time expressing concerns about the risks of "outing" individuals and putting them at risk of harm (Dodd, 2009; Mertens, Fraser, & Heimlich, 2008).

REFLECTION QUESTIONS

1. What is the researcher's ethical obligation in terms of including members of marginalized groups in his or her research?
2. What are the important dimensions of diversity that need to be included in research in particular communities?
3. How can researchers address dimensions of diversity that have historically been used to exclude populations from involvement in research so that those populations' experiences can be accurately captured?
4. What is the ethical cost of ignoring or inappropriately representing relevant dimensions of diversity in research?

Ethical Norms for Research

In addition to the three ethical principles in the *Belmont Report*, the National Commission (1979) also identified six norms to guide research: (1) use of a valid research design; (2) evidence of researcher competency; (3) identification of consequences of the research in terms of keeping participants' identification confidential; (4) maximizing benefits, minimizing risks; (5) appropriate sample selection and voluntary informed consent; and (6) informing participants of compensation for potential harm. Of course, ethical challenges arise as researchers struggle with the meaning of these norms. For example, how do researchers defend their research design as valid or provide evidence of their competency? Quantitative, qualitative, and mixed-methods researchers agree that they have an ethical responsibility to conduct rigorous research (Lincoln, 2009; Mark & Gamble, 2009; Mertens, 2010). After all, if the research lacks rigor, the results can be erroneous, and subsequent use of such results could cause great harm.

Validity, Rigor, and Ethics in Qualitative Research

In Guba and Lincoln's early writings (1989), the authors proposed the following principles to guide researchers in terms of linking the quality of their research with ethical practice:

- **Credibility** is the qualitative parallel to internal validity (the confidence that a researcher has that his or her intervention caused the change in the dependent variable). Credibility is established by
  - Sustained involvement in the research setting: Does the researcher stay in the research setting long enough to really understand what is going on?
  - Peer debriefing: Does the researcher meet with another person periodically throughout the study to reflect on any biases or omissions?
  - Member checks: Does the researcher share the preliminary results with members of the community to be sure they think the researcher's portrayal is accurate?
  - Monitoring self-perceptions: Does the researcher keep a journal or notes about his or her own beliefs, biases, perceptions, and changes in thinking?
  - Use of multiple data sources: Does the research include data from interviews, observations, and document reviews?
- **Transferability** parallels external validity, which means that the results of a study can be generalized to other samples from the same population. Establishing transferability is accomplished by the provision of sufficient details about the research participants and setting so that readers of the research can make a determination as to whether or how the findings from a study might transfer to their own context.
- **Dependability** parallels reliability, which means that there is consistency in the measurement of the targeted variables. Establishing dependability requires that the researcher perform a dependability audit, showing the points at which changes occurred in the research process and understandings related to that process.
- **Confirmability** parallels objectivity, which relates to the absence of personal bias. Confirmability is based on the provision of a chain of evidence such that the reader can see the source of the data and illustrative examples from the data that support the researcher's conclusions.
- **Authenticity** refers to providing a balanced and fair view of all the perspectives in the research study.

Lincoln (2009) expanded on the authenticity principle as being crucial for ethical qualitative research. She identified five fundamental dimensions of authenticity: fairness or balance, ontological authenticity, educative authenticity, catalytic authenticity, and tactical authenticity. She defines these terms as follows (pp. 154–155):

- **Fairness, or balance**, references the researcher's strenuous efforts both to locate all stakeholders in the inquiry and to persuade them to become full partners in nominating issues of interest that should be investigated.

- **Ontological authenticity** references the ability of the inquiry's (and inquirer's) activity, particularly data collection and interpretation, to elicit from respondents constructions that they were unaware that they held. . . . This particular form of authenticity refers specifically to that mental awakening—the recognition that feelings, attitudes, beliefs, values, or other mental dispositions never were expressed previously, even to oneself.

- **Educative authenticity** refers to the mandate among phenomenological, qualitative, and interpretivist inquirers to make others aware of the social constructions of all stakeholder groups.

- Research data, however, have no impact if individual and group stakeholders are indifferent to them or if interpretations are those that the community of stakeholders had already recognized for themselves. Findings not only must shed new light on a phenomenon of interest, they must also engender sufficient interest, consequence, and weightiness to prompt stakeholders to some positive action. This prompt to action is termed **catalytic authenticity**.

- The final task of authenticity criteria . . . is the training of research participants to speak on their own or on their children's behalf. This criterion is termed **tactical authenticity**, for its purpose is to train participants on how to "speak truth to power" and how to utilize recognized policies and procedures to make their wishes known to those in authority.

REFLECTION QUESTIONS

1. How do these principles that establish rigor in qualitative research and the dimensions of authenticity contribute to researchers' ability to make claims about the ethical nature of their work?
2. Is it possible to locate all stakeholders in a research context? What arguments could a researcher use to persuade people to participate in the research? What happens if individuals or groups choose not to participate?
3. What complexities might arise in trying to share all the findings of all the groups with every group? Are there conditions in which some results of research should be withheld from specific subgroups in the study?
4. To what extent should researchers be held accountable for the use made of their research findings, as suggested under the catalytic authenticity and tactical authenticity dimensions?

Researcher Competency

As alluded to in the previous section, **researcher competency** involves a great deal more than knowledge about methods from textbooks. Qualitative researchers need to be able to demonstrate people skills in culturally appropriate ways. In particular, researchers have increased their attention to the concept of **cultural competency**. "Cultural competency is a critical disposition that is related to the researcher's or evaluator's ability to accurately represent reality in culturally complex communities" (Mertens, 2009, p. 89). Symonette (2004, 2009) argues that cultural competency is not a static state, but is a dynamic journey that researchers undertake through self-reflection and interaction with the community. Concerns about a lack of cultural competency on the part of educational and social science researchers led to revisions of the codes of ethics for several professional associations, including but not limited to the American Educational Research Association (AERA), American Psychological Association (APA), American Evaluation Association (AEA), and American Sociological Association (ASA). For example, the American Evaluation Association (2004) revised its guiding principles to include an explicit principle that addresses the role of cultural competency in ethical program evaluations.

The work of the American Psychological Association (2003) provides one illustration of the importance of the concept of cultural competency in research and the ethical codes that guide researchers. APA's Joint Task Force of Division 17 (Counseling Psychology) and Division 45 (Psychological Study of Ethnic Minority Issues) published *Guidelines on Multicultural Education, Training, Research, Practice, and Organizational Change for Psychologists*. In addition, APA's Council of National Psychological Associations for the Advancement of Ethnic Minority Interests published *Guidelines for Research in Ethnic Minority Communities* (2000). This excerpt from that document illustrates the way that APA links cultural competency and ethics in research.

> As an agent of prosocial change, the culturally competent psychologist carries the responsibility of combating the damaging effects of racism, prejudice, bias, and oppression in all their forms, including all of the methods we use to understand the populations we serve. . . . A consistent theme . . . relates to the interpretation and dissemination of research findings that are meaningful and relevant to each of the four populations [Asian Americans/Pacific Islanders, African Americans, Hispanic Americans, and American Indians] and that reflect an inherent understanding of the racial, cultural, and sociopolitical context within which they exist. (p. 1)

Although APA grounds this discussion of cultural competency in issues related to race and ethnicity as they are experienced in the United States, other professional associations and marginalized groups have also published statements that articulate their view of cultural competency in their various communities. These include, for example, Maori communities (Cram, Ormond, & Carter, 2004); the African Botswana community (Chilisa, 2005); Canadian natives (Mi'kmaq College Institute, 2006); Australasians (Australasian Evaluation Society, 2006); indigenous communities (Osborne & McPhee, 2000); Navajo people (Brugge & Missaghian, 2003); and deaf people who represent the American Sign Language community (Harris et al., 2009).

Part of the movement toward understanding the relationship between cultural competency and ethical research is reflected in the establishment of institutional review boards that are specific to individual communities, such as those for specific Native American tribes (LaFrance & Crazy Bull, 2009) and Maori communities (Cram, 2009; Moewaka Barnes et al., 2009). Although obtaining approval from review boards is at times viewed as onerous, especially by outside researchers, the members of these communities see great value in the time and effort it takes for such researchers to do so. They view this as an opportunity for the researchers to advance in their cultural understandings before they undertake their studies. Dodd (2009) recommends that when formal ethical review boards are not available for marginalized communities, communities should form advisory boards that are representative of the diversity of their members and with whom institutional review boards can consult.

REFLECTION QUESTIONS

1. What does cultural competency mean to you?
2. In what contexts would you describe yourself as being culturally competent?
3. What could a researcher in a specific community do to improve his or her cultural competency?
4. What evidence do you see in published research of cultural competency (or lack thereof) on the part of the researcher?

Informed Consent

As stated in the *Belmont Report* (National Commission, 1979), **voluntary informed consent** means that the participants must agree to participate without threat or undue inducement (voluntary), must know what a reasonable person in the same situation would want to know before giving consent (informed), and must explicitly agree to participate (consent). This description contains several terms that are open to different interpretations.

One of the problematic concepts is what it means for consent to be voluntary without undue inducement. Ethicists are concerned that people may agree to participate in research because they feel compelled to do so in order to get money or whatever the researcher is offering to volunteers. If people are very poor and hungry, and they are offered a meal or a small amount of money, would that still allow them to truly volunteer? For example, if I offer a college student twenty dollars to participate in research, is that undue inducement? Most IRBs have decided that researchers can pay students at the going hourly rate for doing other types of work at the university.

REFLECTION QUESTIONS

1. If I offer twenty dollars to a homeless woman who is living in her car with her three children, is that undue inducement?
2. Is it ethical to give the twenty dollars to the college student but not to the homeless woman for fear of coercing her to participate in research she might not otherwise agree to do?

Most IRBs in the United States interpret the terms *informed* and *consent* to mean that the researcher needs to provide a written document that explains the research in an understandable way and that the potential participants then willingly sign. As qualitative researchers know, explaining the research in an understandable way can be quite challenging and demanding, requiring cultural competency.

Obtaining a signature on a form can also be fraught with difficulties depending on the context of the research. Several of the ethical dilemmas introduced this chapter are based on these complexities. For example, Ntseane (2009) conducted a study of African women entrepreneurs, which required that she explain the study to people at multiple levels in the Botswana culture, including the tribal council, the community elders, the business association, and finally the women entrepreneurs themselves. When she asked the women to sign the informed consent form, they grew angry with her. They had already given her their word that they were willing to participate; for her to then ask them for a signature was considered an insult. Wilson (2005) studied funding agencies' perceptions of deaf people in Jamaica, as well as how the deaf people felt they were being perceived by these agencies. One particular funding agency had a very paternalistic view of deaf people, and the deaf people resented this. However, the funds provided by that agency were the only resources that members of this deaf community had as a means to gain access to education. Hence, the deaf people in that part of Jamaica did not want to sign an informed consent form for fear that their names would be made known to the funders, with the consequence that they would lose the little bit of support that they had. These deaf people would knock on Wilson's door in the night so no one would see that she was talking with them. They agreed orally to be interviewed, but they did not want to sign a paper.

The work of the American Anthropological Association (AAA) has been particularly helpful in understanding this challenge. An AAA paper (2004) explains how institutional review boards can be supportive of ethical conduct of ethnographic research. This online document states,

> It is often not appropriate to obtain consent through a signed form—for example, where people are illiterate or where there is a legacy of human rights abuses creating an atmosphere of fear, or where the act of signing one's name converts a friendly discussion into a hostile circumstance. In these and in other cases, IRBs should consider granting ethnographers waivers to written informed consent, and other appropriate means of obtaining informed consent should be utilized. . . . The regulations permit the waiver of written consent, either if the consent document would be the only form linking the subject and the research and if the risk of harm would derive from the breach of confidentiality or if the research is of minimal risk and signing a consent document would be culturally inappropriate in that context.

In order for a researcher to navigate the IRB in such situations, it is helpful if the IRB has a person with expertise in qualitative research and cultural competency. Having such a member of the IRB would facilitate review of qualitative proposals with flexible research designs that are expected to evolve throughout the course of the study. If such a person is not on the board, it might be possible to suggest an outside reviewer who has these skills. If that is not possible, then it is incumbent upon the researcher to educate members of the IRB about these ethical considerations.

Qualitative research designs are often described as being emergent, meaning that the focus, questions, and engagement with members of the community may change as the study progresses. This creates a challenge for informed consent if this is approached as a one-time thing at the beginning of the research. When the conditions of the research change, the researcher needs to revisit the informed consent to be sure that the participants continue to be willing to be part of the study.

Informed consent in research that involves children comes with its own challenges. Legally, children (under the age of eighteen in the United States) cannot sign an informed consent agreement (Vargas & Montoya, 2009). Generally researchers are required to obtain consent from the children's parents. However, children can then provide **assent**, meaning that they understand and agree to participate in the research. Complexities arise when researchers work with groups of children or youth who may not want their parents to know something very personal about them, such as if they are lesbian or gay and their parents do not already know (Dodd, 2009). In such cases, a researcher can obtain a **certificate of confidentiality**, a legal document that protects identifying information from subpoena for legal proceedings. Certificates of confidentiality provide protection against "compelled disclosure of identifying information about subjects enrolled in sensitive biomedical, behavioral, clinical or other research. The protection is not limited to federally supported research" (U.S. Department of Health and Human Services, 2003). The National Institutes of Health's Web site notes that the certificates are granted when disclosure of study information "could have adverse consequences for subjects or damage their financial standing, employability, insurability, or reputation" (U.S. Department of Health and Human Services, 2011). For example, for LGBTQ youths who are not "out" to their parents or who live in an unsupportive or even violent home, requesting parental consent for a research study involving LGBTQ issues could pose a serious risk. According to Dodd (2009, p. 482),

> In such cases a researcher may request that an independent adult advocate, who has an existing relationship with the youth through a social service agency or school, be used to establish informed consent (Elze, 2003) or that the sponsoring agency be judged in loco parentis and therefore provide informed consent (Martin & Meezan, 2003). Disclosure of sexual orientation or gender identity may have a negative impact for the individuals involved as subjects risk job discrimination, strained or severed family relationships, and possibly even violence.

Szala-Meneok (2009) discusses informed consent issues as they relate to older adults whose mental capacity may be either diminished or waning over the course of the study. Suppose an elderly person signs a consent form for a long-term study when she is lucid. Is that consent form still valid if she does develop dementia? Szala-Meneok suggests that researchers have an ethical obligation to revisit the informed consent periodically over the study, especially if they note changes in the person's mental and physical health. In a case of dementia, another person (a family member, a significant other) could be asked to sign the consent form for the elderly person.

Confidentiality

Researchers are ethically obligated to promise **confidentiality** to participants in a study; this means the data will be reported in such a way that they cannot be associated with a particular individual. This is different from anonymity, which means that no one knows the identity of the respondent, not even the researcher. As a part of the confidentiality issue, participants should also be informed that researchers and evaluators are required by law to inform the appropriate authorities if they learn of any behaviors that might be injurious to the participants themselves or that cause reasonable suspicion that a child, elder, or dependent adult has been abused.

As noted in the previous section, there are particular circumstances in research in which revealing the identity of a participant could be quite harmful. Brabeck and Brabeck (2009) provide another example in their report of a study of Mexican American women who experienced intimate abuse. One ethical decision made in the course of the study had to do with whether participants who wished to do so might disclose their identity. One particular woman wanted her name used because she wanted the world to know the identity of her abuser. Ultimately, the researcher used her power to veto disclosure due to concern for participants' safety. Brabeck had established a relationship of trust with the participants over an extended period of time; she was able to explain the possible consequences of revealing identities in this research and thus sustain their ethical research relationship.

In a contrasting example, Ntseane (2009) was also confronted with an ethical issue concerning whether participants might disclose their identity. Women entrepreneurs in her own nation, Botswana, wished to have the names of their businesses published as part of her dissertation. Their argument was that Ntseane would be using the names of authors in her literature review section who had only written about the Botswana people. The participants insisted that she include their names in her dissertation because they were providing the most important part of the research—the data. Ntseane had based her rationale for the study on telling the story of these women from their own perspectives. She was therefore sympathetic to their request to have their names associated with their stories. She also felt conflicted in her obligation to participants in the face of her need to comply with her United States–based doctoral committee and the

ETHICS IN QUALITATIVE RESEARCH IN EDUCATION AND THE SOCIAL SCIENCES

university IRB requirements for confidentiality. This dilemma threatened trust at two levels: that between researcher and participant and that between researcher and institution. Ntseane decided that it was important to include the names of the women who provided her with the data; she renegotiated the need for confidentiality with her university.

REFLECTION QUESTIONS

1. Think of particular groups in the communities in which you plan to conduct research or work that stand out as important based on characteristics that are used to marginalize people, such as race and ethnicity or poverty. What might be culturally appropriate guidelines for conducting research concerning these groups?
2. What should researchers include in the guidelines to indicate respect and show sensitivity toward their culture? How would researchers implement culturally appropriate research guidelines within these populations?
3. How can researchers who are conducting studies in marginalized communities incorporate the voices of community members when facing ethical and methodological issues?

Summary

The ethical principles that guide researchers include respect, beneficence, and justice. When these principles are used to frame ethical decisions in qualitative research, additional questions arise in terms of interactions with community members that are more involved than they are with quantitative research. Involvement in communities requires careful consideration of cultural and language issues. The transformative paradigm is used to examine ethical issues related to the use of research findings, especially in terms of confronting discrimination and oppression. Qualitative researchers need to be conscious of the implications of ensuring that participants are fully informed and that they consent to voluntarily participate in the research. Because of the richness of the data, it is sometimes possible for readers of a given research study to identify individuals who participated, even if their names are not used in the study. Therefore, qualitative researchers need to be aware of implications for maintaining the confidentiality of the participants and conditions under which it might be appropriate to reveal their identity.

I close this chapter with this thought, which in a way provides a summation of the major concepts discussed herein:

Power differences between researchers and vulnerable populations, as well as within those populations themselves, present not only the usual, well-defined ethical puzzles that must be addressed in any social research, but also those that may have odd pieces, indistinct edges, and come attached to value-laden dilemmas that have better solutions and worse solutions, but no certified good solutions. (Mertens & Ginsberg, 2008, p. 491)

Key Terms

assent, 35
authenticity, 29
axiology, 22
beneficence, 22
catalytic authenticity, 30
certificate of confidentiality, 35
confidentiality, 36
confirmability, 29
constructivist paradigm, 22

credibility, 29
cultural competency, 31
dependability, 29
educative authenticity, 30
fairness (or balance), 30
institutional review board (IRB), 21
justice, 22
ontological authenticity, 30

researcher as instrument, 21
researcher competency, 31
respect, 22
tactical authenticity, 30
transferability, 29
transformative paradigm, 22
voluntary informed consent, 32

Further Readings and Resources

Suggested Readings

Brabeck, M. M. (Ed.). (2000). *Practicing feminist ethics in psychology*. Washington, DC: American Psychological Association.
Brabeck provides an interpretation of the American Psychological Association's ethics code from the perspective of feminist theory.

Fisher, C. B. (2003). *Decoding the ethics code: A practical guide for psychologists*. Thousand Oaks, CA: Sage.
Fisher explains the American Psychological Association's code of ethics in terms of how psychologists can do ethically responsible research.

Liamputtong, P. (2007). *Researching the vulnerable*. London: Sage.

Liamputtong explains ethical dilemmas and potential solutions in the context of working with vulnerable groups, such as criminal offenders and drug addicts.

Trimble, J. E. (Ed.). (2006). *The handbook of ethical research with ethnocultural populations and communities*. Thousand Oaks, CA: Sage.

This edited volume examines a variety of ethical considerations for researchers who work in diverse ethnocultural communities.

Organizations and Web Sites

American Educational Research Association, *Ethical Standards* (www.aera.net/About AERA/Default.aspx?menu_id=90&id=222)

This professional association of researchers publishes ethical standards for researchers in education.

American Evaluation Association, *Guiding Principles for Evaluators* (www.eval.org/Publications/GuidingPrinciples.asp)

This professional association publishes ethical guiding principles for people who conduct program evaluations in all fields.

American Psychological Association, *Ethical Principles of Psychologists and Code of Conduct* (www.apa.org/ethics/code2002.html)

This professional association publishes ethical principles to guide psychologists in their research.

Certificates of Confidentiality, *Certifications of Confidentiality* (www.grants.nih.gov/grants/policy/coc)

These legal documents protect identifying information from subpoena for legal proceedings, and are available from the National Institutes of Health.

CHAPTER 3

GROUNDED THEORY

Robert Thornberg
Kathy Charmaz

Key Ideas

- Grounded theory methods consist of strategies that shape data collection and analysis for the purpose of constructing theories of the studied phenomenon.

- These strategies are flexible guidelines that researchers can use to fit their research objectives and specific topic.

- Grounded theory methods are particularly helpful for studying individual, social, and organizational processes as well as research participants' actions and meanings.

- Grounded theory research is an iterative process in which data collection and analysis occur simultaneously, with each informing the other.

- The approach taken here emphasizes constructivist grounded theory, a contemporary version of Glaser and Strauss's original statement (1967), which views both data and analysis as social constructions and takes into account the conditions of their production.

Grounded theory is an inductive, iterative, interactive, and comparative method geared toward theory construction (Charmaz, 2006). A theory states relationships between abstract concepts and may aim for either explanation or understanding. The **inductive** logic of grounded theory means that researchers begin by studying individual cases or instances from which they eventually develop abstract concepts. Because this method is also **iterative**, grounded theorists move back and forth between data collection and conceptualization. This iterative strategy keeps grounded theorists asking successively more focused questions of their data and nascent analyses. In short, the method involves researchers in an interactive form of inquiry. Much of the interactive work relies on making systematic comparisons throughout the research process to construct concepts.

This method provides rigorous yet flexible guidelines that advance data analysis, which we describe in this chapter. Sociologists Barney Glaser and Anselm Strauss (1967) created grounded theory when they explicated the qualitative research strategies that they had used in their studies of how staff organized care of dying patients in hospitals. They intended (1) to provide explicit, systematic strategies for analyzing qualitative data; (2) to oppose views of qualitative methods as anecdotal, impressionistic, and unsystematic; (3) to contest the dominance of quantitative research; (4) to demonstrate the significance of qualitative research for theory construction; and (5) to challenge the arbitrary division of labor between theorists and researchers.

Since 1967 the method has moved across disciplines and professions. Grounded theory has been widely invoked to legitimize inductive qualitative studies, although its strategies have often been misunderstood and divisions between its originators have spawned two different versions of the method—Glaser's so-called classic grounded theory approach (1978, 1998) and Strauss's version (1987), later developed in collaboration with Juliet Corbin (Strauss & Corbin, 1990, 1998; see also Corbin & Strauss, 2008). A third version, constructivist grounded theory, first developed by Kathy Charmaz (2000) and continued soon after by Antony Bryant (2002), emphasizes the flexibility of the method; acknowledges the standpoints, positions, and situations both of the researcher and research process and of the participants; and moves the method further into interpretive inquiry (see also Bryant & Charmaz, 2007; Charmaz, 2003, 2006; for further reading about different versions of grounded theory, see Morse et al., 2009).

Doing Grounded Theory Research

Several manuals provide different guidelines for conducting grounded theory research (see, for example, Charmaz, 2000, 2006; Clarke, 2005; Glaser, 1978, 1998; Glaser & Strauss, 1967; Strauss & Corbin, 1990, 1998). Despite this variation, grounded theory researchers aim to conduct studies of individual and collective actions and of social and social psychological processes, such as experiencing identity transformations, changing organizational goals, and establishing public policies. Grounded theorists emphasize what people are doing and the meanings of their actions, such as their intentions; their own stated explanations; and their implicit, taken-for-granted assumptions (Charmaz, 2003, 2006). Nevertheless, even if we most often focus on actions and processes, we can also use grounded theory strategies to investigate other phenomena (for an example of generating a category system of school rules, see Thornberg, 2008a).

As constructivist grounded theorists, we view our methodological strategies as flexible guidelines to adopt as indicated through our involvement with data collection and analysis. Hence we see the constructivist approach to grounded theory methods as much less prescriptive and procedural than its earlier versions (Charmaz, 2006; Charmaz & Bryant, 2010). Furthermore, we do not narrow the method's focus to overt actions, visible processes, and explicit statements, because "the most important issues to study may be hidden, tacit, or elusive" (Charmaz, 2003, p. 91). Robert Thornberg's grounded theory study (2007) of inconsistencies in school rules demonstrates how a deeper analysis indicated that many of these everyday inconsistencies could be explained by studying how teachers applied implicit rules. Kathy Charmaz's study (1991) explicates how chronically ill people form and act on tacit meanings of time, and how these meanings foster changes in their self-concept.

Data Gathering in Grounded Theory

Grounded theory research uses data collection methods that best fit the research problem and enable the ongoing analysis of the data. This approach is therefore open to many methods of data collection. At the outset, a research problem may point to one method or a combination of methods for data gathering. If, for example, you want to study how and why disruptive behavior occurs in the classroom, you might begin to conduct classroom observations alone or in combination with informal conversations with the students and the teachers whom you observe. If you aim to explore experiences of management-staff conflicts in the workplace, you could conduct intensive interviews with people who have had such experiences. During the research process, your analysis of data evokes insights, hunches, "aha!" experiences, or questions and subsequent reflections, which might lead you to change your data collection method or add a new one. As long as you are conducting your study you have to think about how, where, and when to gather the data you need to address initial and emergent questions.

The first question you ask your data is, "What's happening here?" In line with this question, you might also ask the following: "What are the basic social processes? What are the basic social psychological processes? What are the participants' main concerns?" (Charmaz, 2006; Glaser, 1978). As you can see, you do not wait to construct the analysis until you have collected all the data for your study. Instead, you gather and analyze data simultaneously to raise and check your emerging questions and ideas (Charmaz, 2006; Glaser, 1978; Glaser & Strauss, 1967; Strauss & Corbin, 1998). Furthermore, according to **constructivist grounded theory**, you and your participants construct data through your interpretive acts. Data are constructions of reality, not reality itself. For example, an ethnographer's conversation with a research participant reflects how each understands the other and their shared situation. The recorded field notes then reconstruct the conversation and situation but are renderings of the shared experience, not the experience itself.

Coding Data

Coding begins directly as the first data start to emerge in the study. Data collection and coding go hand in hand throughout the research project. Charmaz (2006) defines coding as "naming segments of data with a label that simultaneously categorizes, summarizes, and accounts for each piece of data" (p. 43). Grounded theorists create their codes by defining what the data are about. Glaser (1978) argues, "Coding gets the analyst off the empirical level by fracturing the data, then conceptually grouping it into codes that then become the theory which explains what is happening in the data" (p. 55). By coding, grounded theorists scrutinize and interact with their data, stopping and asking analytic questions of the collected data. This process may take them into unforeseen areas and new research questions. According to constructivist grounded theory, coding consists of at least two phases: initial coding and focused coding (Charmaz, 2000, 2003, 2006, 2008). Nevertheless, doing grounded theory is not a linear process. Sensitive grounded theorists move flexibly back and forth between the different phases of coding.

Initial Coding

When we conduct **initial coding**, which is also known as **open coding**, we stay close to the data and remain open to exploring what we define as going on in these data. Through the comparison of different segments of data, we also gradually begin to interpret and analyze (1) the main concern or concerns of the participants—that is, what they are focused on or view as problematic; (2) the tacit assumptions of the participants; (3) explicit processes and actions; and (4) latent processes and patterns. Glaser (1978, p. 57) states that during initial or open coding, the researcher asks a set of questions of the data:

GROUNDED THEORY

- What is actually happening in the data?
- What are these data a study of?
- What category does this incident, statement, or segment of data indicate?

Charmaz (2006, pp. 47, 51) adds to these the following analytical questions, which may help during initial coding (see also Charmaz, 2003):

- What do the data suggest? Pronounce?
- From whose point of view?
- What do actions and statements in the data take for granted?
- What process(es) is at issue here? How can I define it?
- How does this process develop?
- Under which conditions does this process develop?
- How does the research participant(s) think, feel and act while involved in this process?
- When, why, and how does the process change?
- What are the consequences of the process?

We intend that a researcher use such questions as flexible ways of seeing, rather than applying them mechanically. Such questions help to search for and identify what is happening in the data and to look at the data critically and analytically. We conduct initial coding by reading and analyzing the data word by word, line by line, paragraph by paragraph, or incident by incident, and we may use more than one strategy. In her study of suffering, Charmaz (1999) engaged in both **line-by-line coding** of interviews with her research participants and **incident-by-incident coding** of interview stories about obtaining medical help during crises. By comparing incidents, she found unequal access to care within health organizations. Coding practices help us to see the familiar in a new light, avoid forcing data into preconceptions, and gain distance from our own as well as our participants' taken-for-granted assumptions (Charmaz, 2003; Glaser, 1978, 1998). During this careful reading we construct initial codes grounded in these data. Labeling codes with gerunds (noun forms of verbs), such as *dissociating, controlling,* and *coping,* helps us as grounded theorists to remain focused on action and process as well as to make connections between codes (Charmaz, 2006, 2008). In order to gain a good pace and to generate clear, understandable, and manageable initial codes, we keep the codes short, simple, precise, and active. We make sure that the codes fit the data instead of forcing the data to fit them. Each idea should earn its way into the analysis (Glaser, 1978).

In the example in Table 3.1, Thornberg, Halldin, Petersson, and Bolmsjö (2011) conduct line-by-line initial coding. The four excerpts are taken from an interview with a fifteen-year-old female student who has experienced being bullied in school. Note that the codes are kept closely to data and are focused on action and process.

Initial coding often gives grounded theorists more than one direction to consider. We could, for example, use the excerpts in Table 3.1 to tentatively describe and further investigate (1) experiencing loss as a victim of school bullying; (2) the interplay between self-perception of being different and bullying victimization; or (3) the victim career trajectory by the phases of being devaluated by peers, developing self-worthiness, and self coming-back. Nevertheless, it is too premature to make such decisions yet, based on the limited set of data and initial codes in Table 3.1. More initial coding and constant comparisons have to be made in order to grasp a focus that is relevant to, works with, and fits the substantive field of study. Remember that initial codes are provisional and constantly open for modifications and refinements in order to improve their fit with the data. The **constant comparative method** expedites constructing a strong fit between data and codes. Because codes initially come very fast, recognize that these codes need to be constantly compared with new data. By using the constant comparative method, we compare data with data, data with codes, and codes with codes to find similarities and differences (Glaser & Strauss, 1967). These comparisons in turn might result in some sorting of initial codes into new, more elaborate codes.

REFLECTION QUESTIONS

1. How would you define initial coding?
2. What ideas does the example of initial coding in Table 3.1 give you about how researchers code their own data?
3. How does initial coding challenge the researcher to think analytically?

Focused Coding

By conducting initial coding, the researcher will eventually "discover" the most significant or frequent initial codes. In **focused coding**, the researcher uses

Table 3.1 Initial Coding

Initial Coding	Interview Data
Being bullied for different reasons; Being punished for being too social; Breaking-down process; Becoming silent; Being bullied for group-imposed social shyness	Anna: I was bullied during elementary school by different people. Well, for different reasons. When I was very little, I was very social and stuff, but they didn't think it was okay that I was talkative, so I had to be broken. And then I became silent, and they started to bully me because of that instead, because I never dared to talk and stuff....
Being different; Name-calling;	Anna: It was because I was a bit different, and then, you know, they started calling me names. I don't remember exactly what. Interviewer: Different? How?
Experiencing social disapproval because of being too outgoing; Breaking-down of self; Reacting with self-silencing;	Anna: Well, that I was more outgoing than most of the others and stuff. And they thought that you shouldn't really be like that. But I was like that so they thought I had to be broken down or stuff like that. So I stopped talking. Interviewer: How long did it go on before....?
Extending time for bullying; Experiencing social fear; Becoming shy	Anna: That was basically the whole junior level of the elementary school. During the third grade, I really didn't dare to talk to people. I was very shy then....
	Interviewer: How do you think that this thing with you being bullied has affected you long term?
Suffering loss of good time; Becoming stronger (by surviving bullying); Self coming-back	Anna: It feels like I have lost pretty much time when I might have had so much more fun with instead. But I think it also has resulted in me becoming stronger, like I have gone through it and come back....
	Interviewer: The thing that you have become stronger, how do you feel today?
Experiencing self-trust; Protecting self from taking in belittling;	Anna: Well, I am confident in all situations, I think, and whatever people say to me, I don't let the criticism get to me anymore. I just shrug my shoulders and go on. Interviewer: But at the same time you report that you have lost a lot of....?
Fearing of standing up for oneself; In-taking belittling; Developing self-worthlessness; Suffering loss of good time; Questioning self's worthiness to live	Anna: Yeah, you know, all these years you didn't dare to stand up for yourself, and you kind of just take it in and somehow thought that you are worthless. There is so much time you have lost.... that you might have done more fun stuff. Instead you have walked about and felt that you don't deserve to live.

Source: The excerpt and the codes are examples from the initial coding that preceded the results in Thornberg et al., 2011.

these codes to sift through large amounts of data (Charmaz, 2000, 2003, 2006). Glaser (1978, 1998, 2005) argues that you have to find and select *one* **core category**, the most significant or frequent code that also is related to as many other codes as possible and more codes than are other candidates for the core category. According to Glaser (1978), the core category "accounts for most of the variation in the pattern of behavior" (p. 93). This core category becomes a guide to further data gathering and coding (instead of focused coding, Glaser talks about **selective coding**, meaning that subsequent data gathering and coding are delimited to the core category and those codes or categories that relate to the core category; see also Glaser, 1998; Holton, 2007). The constructivist position of grounded theory is more flexible by being open for more than one significant or frequent initial code in order to conduct this further work. Such openness also means that the researcher continues to determine the adequacy of those codes during the focused coding (Charmaz, 2006).

Focused coding is more directed, selective, and conceptual than initial coding. By doing focused coding, we can begin to synthesize and explain larger segments of data. Grounded theorists are open-minded (in order to avoid preconceptions and to let unexpected ideas or insights emerge), sensitive, and active in the coding process. They return to study their earlier coded data to select focused codes among the initial codes or construct focused codes based on comparisons between clusters of initial codes. They also begin to code more data, guided by these more elaborated codes, but are still sensitive and open to modifying their codes and to being surprised by the data.

In the study of students whose peers bullied them, Thornberg et al. (2011) constructed the focused code "deviance-defining and breaking-down of self by peers" from constant comparison of many initial codes like "being punished for being too social," "breaking-down process," "being bullied for group-imposed social shyness," "being different," "experiencing social disapproval because of being too outgoing," and "breaking-down of self" from the initial coding of the interview data in Table 3.1, as well as other initial codes generated by the earlier coding of other interview data, such as "being rejected because of not sharing the peers' interest in sport," "putting-down process," "being defined as deviant by peers," "being constructed as a loner by peers and then punished for being a loner," and "being socially rejected and dejected for not being cool enough."

Thornberg et al. (2011) constructed the focused code "self-inhibiting" through the constant comparison of initial codes like "becoming silent," "reacting with self-silencing," "becoming shy," "fearing of standing up for oneself," and "inhibiting the social presence of self." The focused code "developing self-worthlessness" was selected among the existing initial codes as it captures many other initial codes, like "questioning self's worthiness to live," "initiating mistrust and bad thoughts of self," "feelings of unworthiness," and "beginning to devaluate oneself." As can be seen in Table 3.2, in which parts of the interview data displayed in Table 3.1 have been recoded, the focused codes or categories were used to capture and synthesize the main themes in the interviewee's statements.

During focused coding, researchers explore codes and decide which best capture what they see happening in the data, and then raise these codes up to tentative conceptual **categories** for the grounded theory they are going to construct. The researchers give the categories conceptual definitions and assess the relationships between them. For example, the focused code "deviance-defining and breaking-down of self by peers" in Table 3.2 was later conceptualized as the category "stigma cycling," which refers to a cycling process between the following two subprocesses: peers (1) devaluing a student by defining and labeling him or her as different, odd, or deviant, and (2) breaking down

Table 3.2 Focused Coding

Focused Coding	Interview Data
Deviance-defining and breaking-down of self by peers;	Anna: It was that I was a bit different, and then, you know, they started to call me names. I don't remember exactly what. Interviewer: Different? How? Anna: Well, that I was more outgoing than most of the others and stuff. And they thought that you shouldn't really be like that. But I was like that so they thought I had to be broken down or stuff like that. So I stopped talking. Interviewer: How long did it go on before . . . .?
Self-inhibiting	Anna: That was basically the whole junior level of the elementary school. During the third grade, I really didn't dare to talk to people. I was very shy then. . . .
Self-inhibiting; Developing self-worthlessness; Suffering loss of time	Interviewer: But at the same time you report that you have lost a lot of . . . .? Anna: Yeah, you know, all these years you didn't dare to stand up for yourself, and you kind of just take it in and somehow thought that you are worthless. There is so much time you have lost . . . . that you have might done more fun stuff. Instead you have walked about and felt that you don't deserve to live.

Source: The excerpt and the codes are examples from the focused coding that preceded the results in Thornberg et al., 2011.

the student's self by repeatedly harassing and rejecting him or her. As long as the stigma cycling takes place, peers severely attack the victim's identity and self-value. This basic social process forces the victim to develop a negative-loaded deviant identity and a general expectation of being unwanted, rejected, and harassed by others—and to connect these two things. Nevertheless, further analysis also indicated a turning point among some of the victims, which broke the stigma cycling and initiated a coming-back trajectory. The names and definitions of the generated categories should be treated as approximate and provisional, and thus open for further development and revision during the entire analysis process.

In order to generate and refine categories, grounded theorists have to compare data, incidents, and codes, and then later compare their categories with other categories. According to Charmaz (2003, p. 101), making the following comparisons might be helpful during focused coding:

- Comparing different people (in regard to their beliefs, situations, actions, accounts, or experiences)
- Comparing data from the same individuals at different points in time
- Comparing specific data with the criteria for the category
- Comparing categories in the analysis with other categories

In addition, we suggest that the following comparisons are also useful during focused coding:

- Comparing and grouping codes, and comparing codes with emerging categories
- Comparing different incidents (for example, social situations, actions, social processes, or interaction patterns)
- Comparing data from the same or similar phenomenon, action, or process in different situations and contexts

In an ongoing study of school consultation and multi-professional collaboration between teachers and nonschool consultants concerning hard-to-teach students, Thornberg (2011) raised a focused code, "professional collision," to a category and tentatively defined it as collision between different professional perspectives, goals, and practices. By comparing this category with data and focused codes, he constructed other focused codes as categories, such as "remaining outsiders" and "resisting change of the school culture." By comparing these and other categories with each other, and with data and focused codes, Thornberg began to develop a grounded theory of consultation barriers between teachers and nonschool consultants.

According to this grounded theory, consultation barriers were constructed and maintained by social processes like professional collision; resisting change of the school culture, manifested in teachers' attitudes and actions; and nonschool consultants' remaining outsiders (professional marginalizing in the school context and failing to receive acceptance and legitimacy from teachers). The barriers served and protected each professional group's identity, self-serving social representations, and latent patterns. This complex social process of consultation barriers might be called, in Glaser's terminology (1978, 1998, 2005), the core category of the study. Thornberg linked the process of enacting professional and cultural barriers to most other categories and focused codes—including categories that indicated properties and dimensions of the process, such as professional collision, remaining outsiders, and resisting change of the school culture, as well as categories that indicated consequences of the process, such as consultation disengagement and consultation loss.

REFLECTION QUESTIONS

1. What is focused coding? When would researchers use it?
2. In which ways does Thornberg et al.'s focused coding (2011) of the data on bullying advance their analysis?
3. What challenges should researchers foresee when doing focused coding?

Theoretical Coding

In addition to conducting initial and focused coding, grounded theorists might also take advantage of what Glaser (1978, 1998, 2005) calls **theoretical coding**. Glaser (1978) introduces theoretical codes as tools for conceptualizing how categories and codes generated from data may relate to each other as hypotheses to be integrated into a theory. Theoretical codes "give integrative scope, broad pictures and a new perspective" (Glaser, 1978, p. 72). They "specify possible relationships between categories you have developed in your focused coding . . . [and] may help you tell an analytic story that has coherence" (Charmaz, 2006, p. 63). Holton (2007) defines theoretical coding as "the identification and use of appropriate theoretical codes to achieve an integrated theoretical framework for the overall grounded theory" (p. 283).

By studying many theories, grounded theorists may identify numerous integrating logics (that is, theoretical codes) embedded in these theories, and hence develop a repertoire or knowledge bank of theoretical codes (Glaser, 1998, 2005).

> One reads theories in any field and tries to figure out the theoretical models being used. . . . It is a challenge to penetrate the patterns of latent logic in other's [sic] writings. It makes the researcher sensitive to many codes and how they are used. He or she should take the time it takes to understand as many theoretical codes as possible by reading the research literature. This is a very important part of developing theoretical sensitivity. (Glaser, 1998, pp. 164–165)

Glaser (2005) argues that the more theoretical codes the grounded theorists learn, the more they have "the variability of seeing them emerge and fitting them to the theory" (p. 11). Glaser (1978) presented as a guide a list of theoretical codes organized in a typology of coding families, and made later additions to this list (Glaser, 1998, 2005). In Table 3.3 we have listed some of Glaser's coding families.

Glaser's list (1978, 1998, 2005) contains many more coding families. Nevertheless, Glaser's list is by no means exhaustive, and coding families reveal considerable overlapping. In addition, Charmaz (2006) points out that several coding families are absent from Glaser's list, and other coding families appear rather arbitrary and vague. Instead of being hypnotized by his list, researchers should investigate all kinds of theories they encounter in education and the social

Table 3.3 Examples of Glaser's Coding Families

Coding Families	Theoretical Codes
The "Six C's"	Causes, Contexts, Contingencies, Consequences, Covariances, and Conditions
Process	Phases, progressions, passages, transitions, careers, trajectories, cycling, and so on
Degree Family	Limit, range, grades, continuum, level, and so on
Dimension Family	Dimensions, sector, segment, part, aspect, section, and so on
Type Family	Type, kinds, styles, classes, genre, and so on
Identity-Self Family	Self-image, self-concept, self-worth, self-evaluation, identity, transformations of self, and so on
Cultural Family	Social norms, social values, social beliefs, and so on
Paired Opposite Family	Ingroup-outgroup, in-out, manifest-latent, explicit-implicit, overt-covert, informal-formal, and so on

Source: Adapted from Glaser, 1978, 1998.

sciences, as well as in other professional domains, in order to figure out for themselves their embedded theoretical codes. Subsequently they will view theoretical codes as analytic tools that, if relevant, they may draw on. If, for example, researchers discern a significant process in their data and emerging analysis, then they could draw on the concepts in Glaser's Process coding family (see Table 3.3) that fit the data (for example, phases, passages, careers, and so on).

However, the risk arises that grounded theorists might force theoretical codes into their analyses. Glaser (1978) strongly argues that theoretical codes have to earn their way into the grounded theory by constant comparison. They must work, have relevance, and fit with data, codes, and categories. Usually grounded theorists more or less consciously or unconsciously use a combination of theoretical codes in order to relate, organize, and integrate their categories into a grounded theory. By possessing a broad repertoire of theoretical codes, researchers can view their data and categories from as many different relevant theoretical perspectives as they can envision in order to explore and evaluate the usefulness of a lot of theoretical codes for relating, organizing, and integrating the categories and codes into a grounded theory.

In Thornberg's study (2010a) of how schoolchildren explain bullying, he combined different theoretical codes to develop a typology of children's social representations of causes of bullying: bullying as a reaction to deviance, bullying as social positioning, bullying as the work of a disturbed bully, bullying as a revengeful action, bullying as an amusing game, bullying as social contamination, and bullying as a thoughtless happening. By constructing a typology grounded in data and in codes and categories generated in the analysis, Thornberg actually established connections between categories in accordance with Glaser's Type Family (1978) included in Table 3.3, which fit very well with the data and the categories. He also used "social representation," which can be linked to the Cultural Family in terms of social beliefs, as a sensitizing concept. Blumer (1969) used the term **sensitizing concepts** to refer to general concepts that do not claim to be the truth but merely suggest a direction in which to look and to make possible interpretations. As Charmaz (2006) puts it, "These concepts give you initial ideas to pursue and sensitize you to ask particular kinds of questions about your topic" (p. 16). They give a loose frame to the empirical interest without forcing this frame on the data.

By comparing data, codes, categories, and memos (see the next section) with different theoretical codes, Thornberg (2010a) was able to see different possibilities of organizing and relating his categories in ways that reflected his data and the content of his categories. In addition, by doing a careful reading, grounded theorists might also detect many theoretical codes, such as normality-deviance, social norms, strategies, positioning, social control, power, and social influence, embedded in the children's social representations of bullying causes.

Even if theoretical coding has great potential to empower grounded theory research, Charmaz (2006) highlights some cautions that should be considered when conducting coding:

> These theoretical codes may lend an aura of objectivity to an analysis, but the codes themselves do not stand as some objective criteria about which scholars would agree or that they could uncritically apply. When your analysis indicates, use theoretical codes to help you clarify and sharpen your analysis but avoid imposing a forced framework on it with them. (p. 66)

Remember that the categories can be related to each other in many different ways depending on the grounded theorists' knowledge and meaning-makings of theoretical codes as well as on their preferences and perspectives as researchers. Grounded theories do not already exist out there in reality to be found but are always constructed by researchers through their interactions with and interpretations of the field and participants under study.

REFLECTION QUESTIONS

1. What are theoretical codes?
2. Why should researchers be cautious about using theoretical codes?
3. What challenges might using theoretical codes impose?

Memo Writing

While researchers are gathering, coding, or analyzing data, they will likely come up with ideas or thoughts about their codes or relationships between codes, or they might come up with questions they want to answer in their further investigation. In order to remember these thoughts and questions, researchers write them down. **Memos** are such analytic or conceptual notes. According to Glaser (1978), memos are "the theorizing write-up of ideas about codes and their relationships as they strike the analyst while coding" (p. 83). Memos can also be defined as "the narrated records of a theorist's analytical conversations with him/herself about the research data" (Lempert, 2007, p. 247). By **memo writing**, we take a step back and ask, "What is going on here?" and "How can I make sense of this?" For example, when Lempert was writing a memo from interview data in her study of domestic violence in South Africa, the concept of "shelter trap" occurred to her. Lempert then immediately defined this concept as a short-term solution that deflects "attention (and resources) away from the problem—structural inequalities" (p. 251).

We analyze ideas about the codes while conversing with ourselves and making comparisons. "Through memo writing, we elaborate processes, assumptions, and actions that are subsumed under our codes. Memo writing leads us to explore our codes; we expand on the process they identify or suggest" (Charmaz, 2000, p. 517). We write down ideas in process and progress. Memos help the researcher to "gain an analytical distance that enables movement away from description and into conceptualization" (Lempert, 2007, p. 249) and to build up and maintain "a storehouse of analytic ideas that can be sorted, ordered and reordered" (Strauss & Corbin, 1998, p. 220).

Grounded theorists engage in simultaneous data collection and analysis, and thus write memos from the beginning of the research process. Their early memos are often shorter, less conceptualized, and filled with analytical questions and hunches. Exhibit 3.1 illustrates an early memo.

EXHIBIT 3.1
EARLY MEMO EXAMPLE

Inconsistent Applying of School and Classroom Rules

My field notes and audio-recordings indicate that teachers often apply and uphold explicit school and classroom rules in a rather inconsistent manner. In all six classrooms observed in the study, the teachers have told the children the following rules: (1) don't talk during lessons/circle-times when teacher is talking, (2) don't talk during lessons/circle-times when another student who the teacher has given permission to speak is talking, (3) speak one at a time while the others are quiet, (4) raise your hand and wait for your turn if you want to speak, and (5) don't speak or answer without permission from the teacher. Nevertheless, I have for instance observed daily incidents when teachers apply these and other rules inconsistently. Sometimes, teachers correct or reprimand students when they break school and classroom rules. Sometimes teachers just ignore these rule transgressions. And sometimes they appear to positively reinforce the student behavior or act as if the student was doing the right thing.

(Continued)

> **EXHIBIT 3.1**
>
> **EARLY MEMO EXAMPLE (Continued)**
>
> - How are these rule inconsistencies constructed in everyday interactions?
> - Why do these rule inconsistencies occur?
> - How do teachers make meaning of these rule inconsistencies?
> - How do students make meaning of these rule inconsistencies?
> - What are the consequences?
> - Are there any hidden assumptions and/or latent patterns here?
>
> I should investigate this further and look for more examples of rule inconsistencies in order to grasp the variation by conducting more ethnographic observations. [Editors' note: See, for example, Chapters Four and Seven.] What happened in these situations and what appear to be the consequences? Do I see a latent pattern, when comparing incidents with incidents? I should also ask students who I observe participating in such events afterward about their experiences, concerns, and meaning-makings of the incidents. In addition, I should ask teachers themselves about these incidents.
>
> *Source:* This is one of the earlier memos in the analysis process that preceded the findings in Thornberg, 2007.

See, in Exhibit 3.1, how Thornberg takes an active, open, and critical stance by generating analytic questions about the social process of rule inconsistencies that he saw in many field notes and transcriptions from audio-recordings from classroom observations. All questions in the memo are expressions of the basic question in initial coding, "What is happening or actually going on here?" By asking these questions, Thornberg formulates hunches and strategies for further data gathering and coding. Later in a research process, memos become more elaborated and conceptual. Charmaz (2006, p. 82) argues that although memos vary, a researcher may do any of the following in a memo:

- Define each code or category by its analytic properties
- Spell out and detail processes subsumed by the codes or categories

- Make comparisons between data and data, data and codes, codes and codes, codes and categories, categories and categories

- Bring raw data into the memo

- Provide sufficient empirical evidence to support the definitions of the category and analytic claims about it

- Offer conjectures to check in the field setting(s)

- Identify gaps in the analysis

- Interrogate a code or category by asking questions of it

In Exhibit 3.2, Thornberg (2007) has come further in his research process on rule inconsistencies in school. He has now identified a basic social process—applying implicit rules—as well as its consequences for and relationships to other significant categories. Note that the memo begins with a title, "Applying Implicit Rules," which is the tentative name of the main category in the memo, and then provides a definition of this category. Furthermore, Thornberg relates the category to other categories and thus conceptualizes in the memo how this basic social process appears to affect students' meaning-makings and the possibility of their having a say about these rules. In the memo, "a latent pattern or a social process" refers to unarticulated and unconscious regularities in everyday social interaction.

EXHIBIT 3.2
EXAMPLE OF A MEMO TAKEN DURING FOCUSED CODING

Applying Implicit Rules

A deeper analysis of rule inconsistencies indicates a latent pattern or a social process that I would call "applying implicit rules." In everyday school life, teachers and students interact as if there were a set of unarticulated supplements or exceptions to the explicit rules. This unspoken set of rules appears to be unnoticed background features of everyday life. These implicit rules form patterned regularities of social interactions in classroom or other school contexts, produced by teachers' responses to students' behavior in the everyday stream of activities.

(Continued)

EXHIBIT 3.2
EXAMPLE OF A MEMO TAKEN DURING FOCUSED CODING (Continued)

Creating Confusion and Criticism Among Students

Informal conversations and focus group interviews with students indicate that many students appear to be unaware of these implicit rules and to perceive the teachers' behavior as inconsistent and confusing. John in grade 5 tells me, for example, "Well, but then you don't know what to do," and his classmate Robin said, "No, if you don't need to put your hand up or if you do have to put your hand up." Furthermore, several students claim that some rule inconsistencies result in unfairness.

Alice: It's unfair when she [the teacher] gives them the question, although they haven't put their hands up.
Robert: What do you mean? Why is it unfair?
Alice: That they still get the question. And those kids who have put their hands up, don't get it, although we have this rule.
(From a group interview with Alice and Johanna, fifth grade)

Children's difficulties in making sense of the inconsistencies can, at least in part, be explained by the latent pattern of implicit rules, which remain unarticulated in everyday teacher-student interactions.

Creating Rule Diffusion, Prediction Loss, and Negotiation Loss

Rule inconsistencies and unarticulated implicit rules create rule diffusion among students (that is, uncertainty and interpretation difficulties regarding which rules are in force and how they should be applied). This rule diffusion in turn leads students to a prediction loss (that is, they cannot always predict what would be appropriate behavior in particular situations, and how teachers would react to their behavior or fellow students' behavior). By remaining unarticulated and invisible for the students, the implicit rules also result in a negotiation loss for them (that is, they are not given any opportunity to join teachers in an open discussion and decision-making processes for developing and revising these rules). They cannot have a say in and openly negotiate rules of which they are unaware.

Source: This is one of the later memos in the analysis process that preceded the findings in Thornberg, 2007.

During focused coding, researchers raise focused codes into tentative conceptual categories in their memo writing. They begin to treat their focused codes as categories, which in turn inspire and push them to explore, develop, and analyze these codes more deeply. Early in her data collection concerning how people experienced chronic illness, for example, Charmaz (1991) created codes for disclosing illness and maintaining secrecy. She soon learned, however, that she needed to code for a greater range of responses, such as strategically announcing illness, avoiding disclosure, and imparting information. Grounded theorists evaluate their tentative categories and decide whether they are sufficiently robust to stand as categories. Furthermore, they compare categories, explore relationships between categories, and search for patterns and meanings in order to build up a grounded theory.

A memo should begin with a title, which is usually the tentative name of the main focused code or category. The grounded theorists then try to write down a working definition of the code or category and use the constant comparative method (that is, comparing the category with data, codes, subcategories, and other categories, and comparing the memo with other memos). When writing memos, researchers do not worry about the language and grammar because memos are for their own personal use (Glaser, 1978; Lempert, 2007). One tip is to use informal, unofficial language (Charmaz, 2006). The important thing is "to record ideas, *get them out*, and the analyst should do so in any kind of language—good, bad or indifferent" (Glaser, 1978, p. 85). Also, grounded theorists remember to treat memos as partial, preliminary, and provisional, and to compare, sort, and integrate memos (Charmaz, 2006). Through **memo sorting** researchers create and refine theoretical links by making more abstract and systematic comparisons between categories. They sort, compare, and integrate memos by the title of each category. They compare categories, look for relationships between categories, and consider how their sorting of memos and integrating of categories reflect the studied phenomenon. Memo sorting helps to reveal relationships between categories more clearly and helps researchers develop a grounded theory as well.

REFLECTION QUESTIONS

1. What purposes does memo writing fulfill in grounded theory analysis?
2. How do the examples of memo writing in Exhibits 3.1 and 3.2 help you to think about developing and analyzing the codes and the possible relationships between them?
3. How does memo writing challenge researchers to advance their analysis?

Theoretical Sampling and Saturation

Coding gives ideas for memo writing, which then leads to **theoretical sampling**. Glaser and Strauss (1967) define theoretical sampling as "the process of data collection for generating theory whereby the analyst jointly collects, codes, and analyzes his data and decides what data to collect next and where to find them" (p. 45). It is about "seeking and collecting pertinent data to elaborate and refine categories in your emerging theory" (Charmaz, 2006, p. 96). The iterative process of grounded theory moves to theoretical sampling when researchers have a theoretical category that they need to develop. Grounded theorists constantly analyze the data they have gathered, a process that evokes ideas, hunches, perspectives, and questions that will guide further data collection. Theoretical sampling is a highly interactive process in which the coding of data leads to further memo writing, which in turn sends the researcher back to the empirical field with hunches, new lenses, questions, and so on. The memo example in Exhibit 3.1 illustrates how theoretical sampling can take place quite early in the study.

Theoretical sampling prevents researchers from becoming overwhelmed and unfocused in data gathering and analysis. This form of sampling keeps grounded theorists focused on checking and refining their conceptual categories, and thus prompts them to gather specific data to illuminate the properties of these categories. When Charmaz (1991, pp. 228–256) developed her category of "situating the self in time," she returned to research participants from whom she had developed the category and followed up on hints and leads in their earlier interviews about how they saw themselves in relation to time.

Theoretical sampling should not be confused with an initial sampling strategy, such as convenience sampling, which is used to start a project (for example, choosing a specific school as a sample to begin doing the grounded theory study). Theoretical sampling directs the researcher as to where to go, where to collect data next. When Thornberg (2007) was trying to figure out how the day-to-day application of implicit rules in school affected the students (a direction of focus based on constant comparison and memo writing), he began to investigate their reactions and actions in such events by making ethnographic observations, as well as by conducting informal conversations with students to ask them more focused questions about how they perceive and make sense of these events. Theoretical sampling helps to "elaborate the meaning of your categories, discover variation within them, and define *gaps among categories*" (Charmaz, 2006, p. 108). The basic questions in theoretical sampling are where or to whom the researcher should go next in data collection, and for what theoretical purpose (Glaser & Strauss, 1967). Always remember that the aim of theoretical sampling is conceptual development in order to generate a grounded theory.

How do researchers know when to stop collecting data? In the grounded theory tradition, the answer is that you stop when the categories are saturated, a point that is called **theoretical saturation**. This point occurs "when gathering fresh data no longer sparks new theoretical insights, nor reveals new properties of your core theoretical categories" (Charmaz, 2006, p. 113). In order to evaluate whether the researchers have saturated their categories, they might ask questions like these:

- Are there any gaps in the categories?
- Are there any vague or underdeveloped definitions?
- Are we missing some data needed in order to more fully understand and conceptualize categories, relationships between categories, or our constructed grounded theory?

In addition, Charmaz (2006, pp. 113–114) suggests that researchers ask themselves the following questions in order to critically explore if the categories really are saturated or if the researchers need to continue with further theoretical sampling and analysis:

- Which comparisons do we make between data within and between categories?
- What sense do we make of these comparisons?
- Where do they lead us?
- How do our comparisons illuminate our categories?
- In what other directions, if any, do they take us?
- Which new conceptual relationships, if any, might we see?

Saturation is neither about seeing the same pattern over and over again nor about the absence of new happenings in data. Saturation refers to "conceptual density" and "theoretical completeness" (Glaser, 2001, p. 191). Grounded theorists keep sampling until their categories are saturated and their grounded theory is complete and without "holes" or hypothetical links that are not grounded in data. Nevertheless, judging saturation is always tricky and thus raises "concerns about foreclosing analytic possibilities and about constructing superficial analyses" (Charmaz, 2006, p. 115). Researchers who conduct small studies and adopt commonsense categories, for example, may saturate their categories quickly. Their categories become face-value endpoints *of* analysis rather than problematic foci *for* initiating further analysis and, likely, further data collection (see Charmaz, 2009). Therefore, researchers must be constantly open to what is going on in the field; use grounded theory guidelines wisely; and act on their data as active, reflective, and conscious analysts.

> **REFLECTION QUESTIONS**
>
> 1. Compare and contrast theoretical sampling with the sampling that grounded theorists do when they begin a project.
> 2. Why are the criteria for theoretical saturation problematic?
> 3. How does theoretical sampling challenge researchers to think about their emerging analysis?

Theoretical Sensitivity and Using the Literature

Theoretical sensitivity means that through data gathering and analysis researchers are able to "discover" relationships between their categories that lead them to construct a grounded theory that fits, works with, and is relevant to the field under study (Glaser, 1978). "To gain theoretical sensitivity, we look at studied life from multiple vantage points, make comparisons, follow leads, and build on ideas" (Charmaz, 2006, p. 135). One way of fostering theoretical sensitivity, according to Glaser (1978, 1998, 2005; Glaser & Strauss, 1967), is for researchers to delay reading theoretical literature and published research in the substantive area of their study until the analysis is nearly complete. The main reasons for this dictum are (1) to keep the researchers as free and open as possible to discovery, and (2) to avoid contamination (for example, forcing data into preexisting concepts that distort or do not fit these data or have no relevance to the substantive area). At the same time, Glaser (1978, 1998, 2005) argues that researchers should possess prior knowledge of and read literature in other substantive areas that are unrelated to the actual research project, for the purpose of enhancing their theoretical sensitivity by knowing many theoretical codes.

However, Glaser's dictum of not reading literature in the substantive area until the end of the analysis—that is, ignoring established theories and research findings—entails a loss of knowledge. "A dwarf standing on the shoulders of a giant may see further than the giant himself" (Burton, 1638/2007, p. 27; see also Stern, 2007, p. 123). The researchers have to recognize that what may appear to be a totally new idea to them in terms of an "innovative breakthrough" in their research may simply be a reflection of their own ignorance of the literature (Lempert, 2007). As constructivist grounded theorists, we argue that instead of risking reinventing the wheel, missing well-known aspects, coming up with trivial products, or repeating others' mistakes, researchers indeed *can* take advantage of the preexisting body of related literature in order to see further. We reject the very idea of an unbiased "tabula rasa" researcher who, without any prior theoretical knowledge and preconceptions, collects and analyzes value-neutral and theory-free data (in essence, empirical facts "as they really are," independent of the researcher) in order to discover and represent reality as it is in itself. No neutral position exists; no objective god's-eye view of the world is available. Glaser's emphasis on the researcher's neutrality and objectivity overlooks the embeddedness of the researcher within specific historical, ideological, sociocultural, and situational contexts.

In contrast to Glaser's position, Strauss and Corbin (1990, 1998; see also Corbin & Strauss, 2008) argue that the literature can be used more actively in grounded theory studies, as long as the researcher does not allow it to block creativity and get in the way of discovery. According to Strauss and Corbin, familiarity with relevant literature can enhance sensitivity to subtle nuances in data, provide a source of concepts for making comparisons to data, stimulate questions during the analysis process, and suggest areas for theoretical sampling. Our view assumes a similar logic. If grounded theorists reject naive empiricism as well as theoretical forcing, they need not dismiss extant theoretical and research literatures nor apply them mechanically to empirical cases. Instead, grounded theorists can use these literatures as possible sources of inspiration, ideas, "aha!" experiences, creative associations, critical reflections, and multiple lenses. "There is a difference between an open mind and empty head. . . . The issue is not whether to use existing knowledge, but how" (Dey, 1993, p. 63). We recommend that researchers remain open to the field under study and the data they are gathering, take a critical stance toward preexisting theories and research findings throughout the research process, and subject all ideas to rigorous scrutiny (for a further discussion, see Thornberg, in press).

REFLECTION QUESTIONS

1. When do you think grounded theorists should engage in a detailed literature review? Why?
2. In what ways can preexisting concepts and ideas from research literature enhance or diminish the researcher's theoretical sensitivity? Give your reasons.
3. How does conducting a grounded theory study challenge conventional conceptions about doing a literature review?

Summary

Grounded theory strategies enable researchers to build successive levels of abstraction that culminate in a theoretical analysis of their data. Through engaging in categorizing and conceptualizing data, grounded theorists have the tools to make explicit actions, meanings, and processes that otherwise would remain implicit. The method contains strategies that lead researchers to check and refine their emerging categories as well as establish relationships between categories. Grounded theory simultaneously gives researchers tools for making qualitative research manageable and for advancing their theoretical analyses.

As you may have discerned, grounded theory strategies offer rich possibilities for development in educational and social research because of their suitability for studying a wide range of research problems at varied levels of analysis. Although researchers typically have adopted the grounded theory approach to study individuals and interactional settings, it may be used to research organizations, cultures, and policies. Note that Thornberg's current work (2011) speaks to professional and organizational cultures that teachers and other professionals in schools face. Grounded theory is particularly useful for moving across classrooms and schools, as Thornberg's studies of school rules and implicit norms in everyday school life exemplify (see, for example, Thornberg, 2007, 2008a, 2008b, 2009, 2010b). Researchers can build on grounded theory strategies to broaden the specific contributions of grounded theory to qualitative educational research and more generally to qualitative inquiry across disciplines and professions.

Key Terms

categories, 49
coding, 44
constant comparative method, 46
constructivist grounded theory, 44
core category, 48
focused coding, 46

incident-by-incident coding, 45
inductive, 41
initial coding, 44
iterative, 41
line-by-line coding, 45
memos, 54
memo sorting, 59

memo writing, 54
open coding, 44
selective coding, 48
sensitizing concepts, 53
theoretical coding, 51
theoretical sampling, 60
theoretical saturation, 61
theoretical sensitivity, 62

Further Readings and Resources

Suggested Grounded Theory Studies

Bhopal, K. (2009). Identity, empathy and "otherness": Asian women, education and dowries in the UK. *Race Ethnicity and Education, 12,* 27–39.

The author shows that Asian women's entry into higher education affects how they view the practice of dowries in the United Kingdom, and argues that a black feminist perspective is useful in studying women who have been silenced.

Edwards, K. E., & Jones, S. R. (2009). "Putting my man face on": Grounded theory of college men's gender identity development. *Journal of College Student Development, 50,* 210–228.

This study finds that college men responded to perceived expectations of male gender identity by putting on a performance that felt like wearing a mask.

Jackson-Jacobs, C. (2004). Hard drugs in a soft context: Managing trouble and crack use on a college campus. *Sociological Quarterly, 45,* 835–856.

This study demonstrates that being able to keep drug use bounded and having residential mobility within a "safe" area without drug dealers alter the experience and meaning of frequent crack cocaine use.

MacDonald, H., & Swart, E. (2004). The culture of bullying at a primary school. *Education as Change, 8*(2), 33–55.

This ethnographic study locates bullying in the norms and values of an authoritarian culture in the school.

Qin, D., & Lykes, M. B. (2006). Reweaving a fragmented self: A grounded theory of self-understanding among Chinese women students in the United States of America. *International Journal of Qualitative Studies in Education, 19,* 177–200.

The authors analyze how Chinese women graduate students engaged in reweaving a fragmented self that they experienced first as students in their homeland and later as they became international women students in a new land.

Star, S. L. (1989). *Regions of the mind: Brain research and the quest for scientific certainty.* Stanford, CA: Stanford University Press.

Using the work of nineteenth-century brain researchers as a case example, this study examines how scientific theories become dominant and entrenched. The findings show that scientific theories change through solving problems in routine work, thus challenging notions of paradigm change through scientific revolution.

Thornberg, R. (2010). Schoolchildren's social representations of bullying causes. *Psychology in the Schools, 47,* 331–327.

This study investigates how schoolchildren explain the occurrences of bullying. The analysis results in a typology of social representations of the causes of bullying, and then links these social representations to the more general process of social categorization and also to the process of moral disengagement.

Wasserman, J. A., & Clair, J. M. (2010). *At home on the street: People, poverty and a hidden culture of homelessness.* Boulder, CO: Lynne Rienner.

This study focuses on men who choose to live on the street, where they find community and companionship and remain free from the constraints and dangers of the shelters.

Wolkomir, M. (2005). *Be not deceived: The sacred and sexual struggles of gay and ex-gay Christian men.* New Brunswick, NJ: Rutgers University Press.

This book explores the dilemma that Christian men who define themselves as gay or ex-gay experience in reconciling their sexual identity with conservative Christian beliefs.

Woodruff, A. L., & Schallert, D. L. (2007). Studying to play, playing to study: Nine college student-athletes' motivational sense of self. *Contemporary Educational Psychology, 33,* 34–57.

This study explores how student-athletes' conflicting motivations and self-perceptions influence their emotions, cognition, and behavior.

Other Suggested Readings

Bryant A., & Charmaz, K. (Eds.). (2007). *The Sage handbook of grounded theory.* Los Angeles: Sage.

This handbook includes contributions by leading proponents and practitioners of grounded theory that reflect the range of current thinking on the method.

Charmaz, K. (2006). *Constructing grounded theory: A practical guide through qualitative analysis.* London: Sage.

This book offers a contemporary statement of grounded theory that takes into account methodological developments occurring in the past four decades and presents accessible guidelines for using the method.

Clarke, A. E. (2005). *Situational analysis: Grounded theory after the postmodern turn.* Thousand Oaks, CA: Sage.

This book builds on Anselm Strauss's conceptions of social worlds and extends his version of grounded theory by including postmodern concerns and by acknowledging how the situation of inquiry affects the research process and product.

Corbin, J., & Strauss, A. (2008). *Basics of qualitative research: Techniques and procedures for developing grounded theory* (3rd ed.). Los Angeles: Sage.

This third edition of the textbook uses a less rule-bound approach to grounded theory than do its predecessors and demonstrates using the method with computer-assisted qualitative data analysis software.

Glaser, B. G. (1978). *Theoretical sensitivity.* Mill Valley, CA: Sociology Press.

This book provides the basic statement of Glaser's logic of grounded theory and the concept-indicator model of using the method. This approach develops new concepts from inductive analysis of empirical data and, in turn, specifies the empirical indicators of the concepts.

Glaser, B. G., & Strauss, A. L. (1967). *The discovery of grounded theory.* New York: Aldine.
This book is the original statement of the method. It challenged 1960s conventional views of theory construction, qualitative research, data collection and analysis, and methodological rigor.

Thornberg, R. (in press). Informed grounded theory. *Scandinavian Journal of Educational Research.*
In accordance with the constructivist position of grounded theory, this article presents good arguments for using literature as a source of analytical lenses and tools. In contrast to mechanical (and forcing) deductions, the article suggests and describes a set of data sensitizing principles of using literature.

CHAPTER 4

METHODOLOGY, METHODS, AND TOOLS IN QUALITATIVE RESEARCH

Jean J. Schensul

Key Ideas

- Qualitative research is an approach that enables researchers to explore in detail social and organizational characteristics and individual behaviors and their meanings. To obtain this information, qualitative researchers depend on primary, face-to-face data collection through observations and in-depth interviews.

- Qualitative research can be carried out through case studies, interviews with people who have relevant experiences, and observations in the places where study participants live, work, shop, and engage in leisure time activities.

- Qualitative research is always theoretically guided. The degree to which theory specifies or initiates and guides the process of data collection varies depending on which scientific paradigm the researcher prefers.

- The main qualitative paradigmatic choices are positivist (driven by theory); interpretivist (driven by the views of those in the study setting); and critical (shaped by the belief that individual behaviors are the result of systemic or structural inequities, such as discriminatory policies and practices that exclude some people from resources, policies, and power).

- Qualitative researchers can also choose participatory and collaborative approaches that involve stakeholders in research decisions and activities.

- Qualitative research designs must take into consideration the study population, the study sampling strategy and sample size, the study location, duration, and timing.

- Steps followed in qualitative research include posing study questions, selecting the guiding theoretical model, choosing data collection methods at the individual or cultural (community or organizational) level, data collection, analysis, and reporting the results to main audiences.

The focus of this chapter is on the methodology, methods, and research tools that qualitative researchers use. I define the conduct of qualitative research as using multiple qualitative (and sometimes quantitative) approaches to data collection that are designed to help the researcher learn about and obtain the perspectives, meanings, and understandings of people who live and work in specific social settings. I will differentiate between qualitative methodology and methods. **Methodology** refers to the blueprint or set of decisions and procedures that governs a study and renders it understandable to others and is subject to inquiry, critique, and replication or adaptation to other settings. I use **methods** to mean the data collection techniques that qualitative researchers use to gather data within the framework of the study that is defined by its methodology.

In the first part of this chapter I outline the kinds of decisions that qualitative researchers make about who and what to study, for what reasons, and with what tools. I also address the idea of formative research modeling, a way of summarizing the researcher's prior and then growing knowledge of the research question and the field situation. In the second part of the chapter I describe the most common tools that qualitative researchers use to collect their data. Readers are referred to other resources (for example, see Chapter Three) for details on data analysis, as this is not the focus of the chapter. Nevertheless, researchers should have from the outset a fairly clear sense of why they are collecting data using the methods or tools they have chosen, and of how they plan to organize, manage, analyze, and integrate the data they collect.

One of the unique features of qualitative research is the face-to-face nature of data collection. Some qualitative researchers choose to involve themselves in the field or the study setting and to participate in it. **Participation** entails presence in the location, including residence there; engagement in the activities of daily living of individuals and families; and attendance at special events, rituals, rites of passage, and other one-time or irregular events that illustrate important features of the study context related to the research topic. Other qualitative researchers may find it difficult or impossible to immerse themselves in a specific field setting and instead may choose to gather their data through various forms

METHODOLOGY, METHODS, AND TOOLS IN QUALITATIVE RESEARCH

of reporting obtained directly from respondents. But whether the research involves participating in daily life or conducting interviews, the basic forms of qualitative data collection involve the direct, face-to-face interaction of researchers with members of the study population. Researchers make choices about how and where this interaction takes place. In the end, however, researcher style, personal and interactional skills, and judgments are all critical in obtaining, analyzing, and interpreting data. For these reasons, qualitative researchers often take great pains to describe themselves and to locate their identities in time and space, and through class, ethnicity, race, and other signifiers. In this way, they enable others to assess what biases or other factors might affect the replication of similar research, making it difficult or even impossible.

REFLECTION QUESTIONS

1. Think about times you have asked another person some specific questions in the course of a conversation. What tools have you used to sharpen your questioning skills in order to learn something new from the other person?
2. What are some of the biases that you might bring to a study? What are some ideas with which you would be in serious disagreement? How would you handle a disagreement between yourself and an interviewee during an interview?
3. What are some of the most important characteristics of the qualitative research methodology and methods to consider when reading qualitative research reports?

Research Methodology

Research methodology refers to the strategies that researchers use to ensure that their work can be critiqued, repeated, and adapted. These strategies guide the choices researchers make with respect to sampling, data collection, and analysis. Thus there is and must be a close association and integration among research questions, research methodology, and methods of data collection. Research methodology is sometimes referred to as **research design**, or, as I said earlier, the blueprint or roadmap that guides a study. Here I use *research methodology* and *research design* interchangeably. Researchers, in developing their research methodology, must consider their assumptions; selection and perception biases; **positionality** (personal identity, status and influence relative to participants in the study, and the effect these might have on participants and data collection in general); and the rules they follow in research decision making (Traustadottir, 2001). An important consideration is the extent to which the researcher is from or is a long-term resident of the study community—that is, an insider, an outsider, or both (Brayboy & Deyhle, 2000; Fine, 1994b). Insider or outsider status and the way status is negotiated can exert some influence on the ways the researcher is perceived, what information can be collected, and how access to information may change over time as insider or outsider status is renegotiated.

All types of studies that are empirical require a design for research, regardless of which theories or approaches drive a given study. Methodology follows from the research questions and initial hypotheses. A discussion of methodology includes a consideration of the study setting or community and the **study population**—the people that are the focus of the study question and analysis. The researcher must also address sampling procedures and guidelines—what data are to be gathered and how, in relation to the study question, and how the data will be stored, managed, and analyzed. Dissemination of results may also be included in the study methodology. The case that follows provides an example of this methodological decision-making process.

CASE EXAMPLE

STUDY OF DEPRESSION IN OLDER LOW-INCOME ADULTS LIVING IN PUBLIC HOUSING DESIGNATED FOR PEOPLE OVER SIXTY-TWO

The Institute for Community Research and partners, including an area agency on aging and a network of public mental health clinics serving older adults, conducted a study of depression in a racially and ethnically diverse population of older adults living in senior housing in Connecticut (Diefenbach, Disch, Robison, Baez, & Coman, 2009; Disch, Schensul, Radda, & Robison, 2007; Robison et al., 2009; Schensul et al., 2006). The study addressed three main research questions:

1. What were the lay understandings of the meaning of depression, and what language was used to describe feelings of loss and sadness, and the associated lack of functionality?

2. What factors predicted clinical depression in the study population?

3. What barriers to mental health treatment did this population encounter?

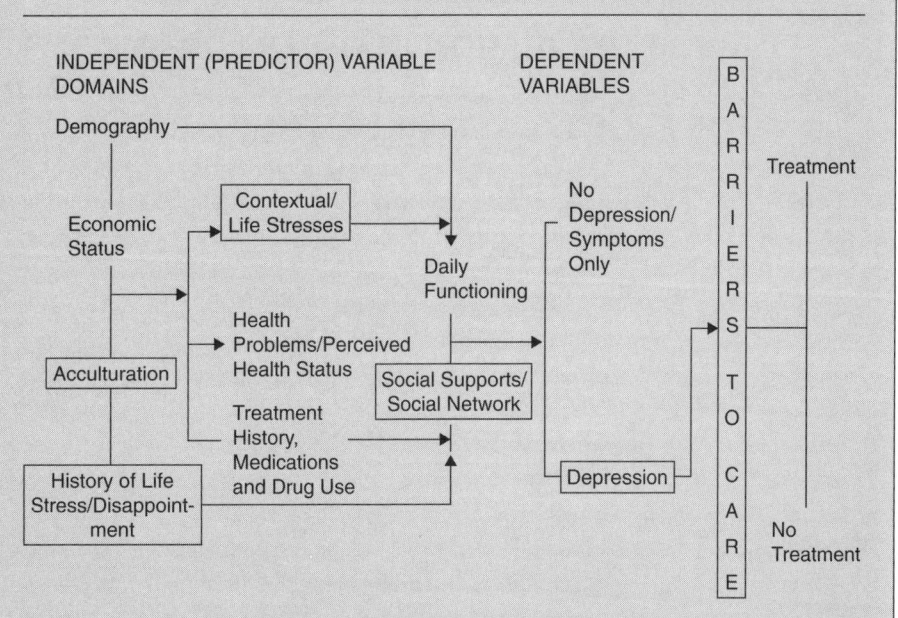

FIGURE 4.1 Formative Model of Research Areas

INDEPENDENT (PREDICTOR) VARIABLE DOMAINS

DEPENDENT VARIABLES

BARRIERS TO CARE

- Demography
- Economic Status
- Acculturation
- History of Life Stress/Disappointment
- Contextual/Life Stresses
- Health Problems/Perceived Health Status
- Treatment History, Medications and Drug Use
- Social Supports/Social Network
- Daily Functioning
- No Depression/Symptoms Only
- Depression
- Treatment
- No Treatment

The outcomes were both scientific (publications in peer-reviewed journals) and directed toward local use of the data to advocate for improvements in mental health services for older low-income adults.

Based on their own community and service provision experience, and on the literature on depression in older, racially and ethnically diverse, low-income adults, the interdisciplinary research team members first identified some of the factors they believed to be associated with clinical depression. In this way they generated and drew a formative model that highlighted their greater knowledge of contributors to depression and their gaps in understanding barriers to treatment (see Figure 4.1, in which boxed sections represent areas of ethnographic research).

Selecting the Study Population

There were over twenty-four large buildings in the community that were home to low-income, racially and ethnically diverse, older adults. The study team could not conduct interviews in all of these buildings and thus needed a rationale for selecting approximately half of the buildings. To make the choice, the team eliminated some buildings that had atypical characteristics (for example, the residents all were working; many of the residents were younger with disabilities; the

(Continued)

CASE EXAMPLE
STUDY OF DEPRESSION IN OLDER LOW-INCOME ADULTS LIVING IN PUBLIC HOUSING DESIGNATED FOR PEOPLE OVER SIXTY-TWO (Continued)

older adults lived in buildings that included many younger families; or the buildings were too small, with fewer than twenty-five residents). This left twelve buildings that were included in the final study building sample. The resident sample was a **census** (100 percent of the population) in each of the twelve buildings rather than another kind of sample, because the study included plans for network research to examine the relationships among each and every one of the residents in each of the buildings, and for this all residents had to be interviewed.

Identifying the Sample

The study included two components: qualitative data (to understand the language and meanings associated with depression) and quantitative data (composed of a survey plus a survey-integrate network component that asked about each respondent's relationship with others in the building). The study team had to make a decision as to how many qualitative interviews to conduct. They decided that they needed interviews with an equal number of African American/West Indian and Puerto Rican/Latino males and females, divided into three groups: (1) those who scored as depressed on an established diagnostic tool for identifying clinical depression, the Composite International Diagnostic Instrument (CIDI); (2) those who did not score as depressed but described symptoms of depression on the Center for Epidemiologic Studies Depression Scale (CES-D), an instrument that screens for depression using a symptom checklist; and (3) those who had no signs of clinical depression or symptoms (see Table 4.1). To obtain five people in each of nine cells, forty-five in-depth interviews were required.

Data Collection

The study was funded for three years, thus requiring staging of data collection. This included piloting instruments: implementing a survey that included questions about barriers to care for those who were already diagnosed as depressed, as well as for those who qualified as depressed in the study. Qualitative data collection followed survey data collection and was based on the diagnostic categories in Table 4.1. Forty-five in-depth interviews focused on the areas in the outlined boxes in Figure 4.1—acculturation, history of and current life stresses, social

Table 4.1 Sampling Plan for In-Depth Interviews in a Depression Study

	African American/West Indian	Puerto Rican/Latino	White Ethnic (Referring to members of European ethnic national groups, for example, Polish, Bosnian)
CIDI-Depressed	5	5	5
CES-D Depressed	5	5	5
Not Depressed	5	5	5

networks and supports, descriptions of depression, sadness and loss, and barriers to care.

Data Analysis

The study team included experts in the analysis of both qualitative and quantitative data. Team members divided into two working groups, one to make decisions about how to code and analyze qualitative interview data and one to decide on the best analytic strategies for the survey and network data.

Dissemination of Results

Decisions concerning dissemination involved the identification of interested audiences and the preparation of results reports appropriate for each audience. Results were reported to study partners, to the state department of mental health, and to legislators concerned about the mental health of older adults. They were also used to support a building-based intervention to alleviate depression among building residents that was conducted by a partnering hospital with a geriatric mental health service.

Making Methodological Decisions

Deciding which qualitative research tools to choose requires consideration of the research paradigms or approaches that guide or frame a study. It is also important to determine whether a study requires experiential understanding of the setting or community context within which the people who are the focus of the study live, or whether it requires researchers to learn from respondents their point of view on a topic. Even if direct experience in the study site is not part of the study design, understanding something about the cultural setting is critical in considering which tools of inquiry are likely to be most appropriate and when. For example, it is important to know enough about a setting to determine what procedures must be set into place in order to conduct a confidential in-depth interview on a sensitive subject, such as HIV risk behaviors. This can be a challenge in densely inhabited residential areas where there is little space and where neighbors may be curious, as in many low-income urban areas of India. Or, for example, deciding where, when, and how to interview patients in an emergency room setting calls for the acquisition of considerable information about the emergency room beforehand.

In addition to learning about the study context, researchers should consider the following: (1) which guiding research paradigm or paradigms they follow; (2) what their research questions and subquestions are in the initial stages of research; (3) what type of formative conceptual model they can develop with the information they have; (4) where, when, and with whom they will conduct the study; and (5) what their sampling plans are. They also should consider what methods and tools they will use to collect their data. These topics are considered in more depth in the following sections.

Guiding Paradigms

Qualitative research can be conducted within the framework of a number of different guiding paradigms. The term **paradigm** derives from the work of Thomas Kuhn (1970), who suggested that scientists are influenced by dominant ways of or frameworks for conducting science. In the social sciences we speak of several different influential views. The most commonly referenced are the positivist, interpretivist, critical, and participatory paradigms. **Positivists** believe that reality is external to the self, that it can be observed, and that the tools used in the conduct of research can produce information that is reproducible and potentially replicable if collected under similar circumstances. Positivists generally believe that researchers are observers and should minimize their interactions with and effects on the subject matter of the research while they are gathering data. Researchers who take a positivist position often prefer to test preexisting theories rather than to derive them inductively from the study situation.

Interpretivists take the position that social or cultural phenomena emerge from the ways in which actors in a setting construct meaning. The researcher comes to understand behaviors and the meanings attributed to them through immersion in the setting and interaction with the study participants. The earlier case example illustrating design decisions for the study of depression among older low-income adults of diverse ethnic and racial backgrounds included an interpretivist qualitative component examining the language and meanings associated with sadness, loss, stress, and life dissatisfaction in this population.

Mixed-paradigm research combines interpretivist and positivist approaches, highlighting the voices and views of the participants, in interaction with the results and interpretations of the researchers. Research on the use of the drug MDMA (Ecstasy) carried out in Hartford, Connecticut, with 120 young adult Ecstasy users provides a good example of this complementarity (Singer & Schensul, in press). The researchers explored the meanings and rituals these young adults attributed to the use of Ecstasy through in-depth interviews, and collected survey data on drug use, locations where drugs were used and bought, and other self-report data. More than half of the respondents maintained that, by balancing the risks of use with risk mediation, they were able to benefit from the use of Ecstasy and were in good control of their Ecstasy use. But their perspective did not include their other drug use. A separate analysis from the researchers' perspective showed variation in control based on the amount and frequency of Ecstasy use in conjunction with the use of other drugs. This analysis suggested that when Ecstasy users combined this drug with other drugs, their overall control of their use of substances, including Ecstasy, declined.

Critical researchers believe that social and political structures shape and hold power over the lives of individuals, creating various types of disparities. Critical researchers always locate the behaviors and meanings held by individuals and groups within larger systems of dominance and control. Although they may focus primarily on the structural determinants of disparities in their research, they always are concerned with how these factors differentially affect people living in communities by reinforcing and replicating benefits for those with more resources and reducing benefits for those with fewer. Critical researchers often base their work on secondary sources and historical reconstruction, using maps and graphs to illustrate structures of dominance; they also rely on in-depth interviews to reveal ways in which dominance and persistent inequities are transferred to the behaviors, opportunity structures, and meaning systems of vulnerable populations.

To illustrate, in a study of the role of temporary housing in the lives of injection drug users, researcher Julia Dickson-Gomez and her colleagues (Dickson-Gomez, Convey, Hilario, Corbett, & Weeks, 2007) were able to show that despite somewhat more progressive policies guiding permanent housing options for injectors, agency staffs that had the responsibility for helping drug users find permanent housing did not do so, in part because they did not believe that drug users could maintain a more permanent housing situation and benefit from social services. As a consequence, many drug-using men, for whom the chances of quitting drug use and getting a job were enhanced by permanent housing plus services, were deprived of this option. These men reported a variety of problems and challenges in finding housing other than temporary shelters. Their continued association with other drug users made it difficult or impossible for them to leave drug use behind and find a job.

The positivist position coincides with the critical paradigm insofar as each conducts observations through the lens of externally developed theoretical frameworks and each calls for the collection of data to demonstrate the veracity of hypotheses derived from the theory.

Researchers who take a **participatory or collaborative approach** join forces with stakeholders to conduct research toward some form of social action (see Chapter Eighteen as an example). Stakeholders may include community residents concerned with making positive changes in their community, state and local agencies, community organizations involved in the study problem or topic, and researchers. This approach acknowledges researcher expertise in scientific methodology, and at the same time engages stakeholders in contributing their knowledge and experience and decision making to research design, data collection, analysis, interpretation, and use of findings (Berg & Schensul, 2004; Minkler & Wallerstein, 2003). Participatory or collaborative research requires bringing positivist, interpretivist, and critical research approaches and tools to bear on issues and challenges presented by partners. The interaction of these frameworks or paradigms in actual field research results in improvements in theory, research methodology, and research tools, as well as interpretations and results that have local or partnership meaning. Partners can use these jointly forged results effectively to move toward desired social change. Social scientific research and social settings are complex, and a single research paradigm or approach may not be able to answer research questions or fulfill collaborator needs. Researchers should be aware that several research paradigms can be combined to guide a study, and many if not most research tools can be adapted for use within each of these paradigms.

REFLECTION QUESTIONS

1. Define the concept of paradigm for yourself.
2. Which of the paradigms described above is the most consistent with your own way of viewing the world? Which one is the least consistent? Why?

Defining the Research Questions

Qualitative researchers are most likely to raise research questions based on three factors: (1) what has personal meaning to them; (2) what they read and discover to be gaps in the literature; and (3) what they perceive during their first exposure to the field, or the study setting. Researchers usually frame their questions based on the research paradigm with which they feel most comfortable. For example, a qualitative researcher who favors a positivist perspective will build theory based on scientific literature, frame research questions from the literature, and structure data gathering to prove the theory. The researcher then gathers qualitative data to support the theory.

An interpretivist may identify research questions based on discussions with participants in the field about the meaning of an activity, ritual, artifact, or series of events. For example, researchers Stephen Schensul and colleagues (Kostick et al., 2010) found that the primary reproductive health complaint of women in Mumbai was *white discharge* (referred to in Hindi as *safed pani*). This complaint had no basis in infection or a medical problem. So the researchers undertook to learn from women what meanings they associated with the concept of *safed pani*, why they thought it was a health problem, and to what they attributed it in their lives. In-depth interviews with forty women revealed that they associated it with various sources of tension or conflict in their lives, including insufficient income, negative marital relationships, and abuse.

A critical researcher is more likely to raise questions about the factors that contribute to health disparities in minority communities, or how people experiencing disparities mobilize to address them. Young researchers in Hartford, for example, explored structural factors contributing to racism. They identified media, education, and economic disparities, and collected in-depth video-recorded interviews on those factors from other youth and adults (Mosher, in press).

Regardless of the researcher's choice of dominant perspective or paradigm, however, qualitative research questions tend to focus on explorations of behavior or social organization, of the many factors that might contribute to these, and of their meaning to the study population. Historical influence is also important in qualitative research, contributing to questions about how patterns of culture, social structure, beliefs, and behaviors came into existence; what historical factors might have contributed to current injustices in policy and practice; and whether things change over time.

Formulating a Conceptual Model

If research methodology or design constitutes a roadmap for the study as a whole, a **conceptual model** constitutes a theoretical roadmap. In many fields (psychology, sociology, economics), research begins with a theoretical model to be tested. Here the instruments are chosen in advance in relation to the components in the theoretical model. In qualitative research a conceptual model is a theoretical starting point, a pictorial map of the conceptual direction of the study. The conceptual model is a diagram that identifies the primary research **domains** that are likely to be addressed in the study based on initial assessment and the literature. A domain is a broad area of culture that a researcher considers to be important in the study.

For example, in a study of adolescent drug use, the starting point might be the hunches that youth involved in drug use learn through watching others and that the contexts in which they are exposed to drug use make a difference in what they use and why. Here the domains are *involvement in drug use, learning to use drugs,* and *family history of drug use.* Qualitative researchers would investigate and unpack each of these domains. For example, in-depth interviews might reveal information about current drug use, including the different drugs people use; how they use those drugs; how much they use; where they obtain the drugs; and the reasons why they use them, and with whom. The domain *learning to use drugs* would include any information about how a person started learning to use each of the drugs in his or her repertoire. This could include such subdomains as watching others use that drug, seeing close friends or parents use the drug, being taught by someone how to use the drug, anticipating effects of the drug, and first experiencing using the drug. *Family history of drug use* might include a history of drug use among family members and household members, involving what drugs were used, how they were used, and whether household patterns of drug use involved children—including the participant reporting the information. An initial working model would link these domains and their subcomponents. Thus different components of *family history of drug use* and *learning to use drugs* might be connected to a person's current drug use.

Models often are portrayed as diagrams. Domains are arranged as **predictor** and **outcome** domains (for example, learning by watching friends results in more drug use than trying drugs alone). Here *drug use* is the outcome domain; drug use may be "operationalized" or described in many ways. *Learning* is a predictor domain, which can include all the ways that people learn or become socialized into learning how to use drugs. These models are *not* quantitative tests of association. They are ways of illustrating patterns of interaction among domains and subdomains or qualitative variables. Domain associations can also be portrayed as **causal chains** or flow charts stated as hypotheses concerning how one domain may lead to another. For example, domain A (regulations combining regular and charter schools—an antecedent event) leads to domain B (overcrowding—a current condition) leads to domain

METHODOLOGY, METHODS, AND TOOLS IN QUALITATIVE RESEARCH

C (more student arguments in hallways—observed event). Matrices can also be used to show patterns of association among domains or subdomains across units of analysis. A **unit of analysis** is the social unit that is being compared with others to identify patterns of interaction among domains, subdomains, or qualitative variables. Units of analysis are usually persons, places, events, or things.

Domains can be deconstructed during or prior to fieldwork as ideas emerge and are clustered under domain headings. For example, in a current study of Ecstasy use in relation to sexual risk, researchers at the Institute for Community Research identified the use of Ecstasy for other purposes, including *coping with negative life situations*. This general theme initially emerged during in-depth interviews. Later we classified 118 in-depth interviews on Ecstasy use into two groups: use of Ecstasy for coping and use of Ecstasy for recreational or sex-related reasons. Approximately half of the interviews could be classified in the first group. Within this subgroup of cases, we identified five major subdomains, such as managing abusive situations, dealing with life stresses, and coping with the loss of a loved one. These subdomains are the independent variables predicting ecstasy use as well as the pattern of use (frequency and amount) (Moonzwe, Schensul, & Kostick, in press). In another example, researchers from the Institute for Community Research and the University of Connecticut Health Center, in collaboration with researchers from the Mauritius Family Planning Association and the University of Mauritius, produced an initial model in which peers, family, and media all were perceived to play a role in how young women and men related to one another. The model predicted that these relational domains were linked with sexual behaviors and consequences, such as HIV (Schensul, Oodit, Schensul, Ragobur, & Bhowon, 1994). Researchers modified this model in the field by asking respondents about their activities with their peers and their relationships with their family, as well as how they obtained information through the media and elsewhere about sexuality and HIV; what intimate behaviors they were involved in; and what the emotional, physical, and social consequences of these relationships were. The initial model was then expanded. Such models as these are developed in a rudimentary format, expanded in the field, and finalized during the analytic phase of a study.

Where, When, and With Whom the Study Will Be Conducted

All researchers must make decisions about study sites, the time period during which a study is to be conducted, and the boundaries of the study population. In this section I discuss some of the elements that researchers should consider in deciding where, when, and with whom their study is to be carried out.

Where: Study Location

Qualitative studies generally take place in one or more physical locations called study sites. A study site may be a sociopolitical community (a neighborhood, a municipality, a village, or even a city) or multiple communities (for example, a cluster of villages) included for comparative purposes. Or it may be an institution within a community (for example, one or more early childhood learning centers, health outposts, university campuses, clinics, or parks). Lately some researchers have been turning to the Internet to conduct qualitative research, using blogs, wikis, and social networking sites to collect data and share them with respondents. Social networks of individuals, organizations, or both may also constitute the focus of a qualitative study. Some qualitative research focused on topical interests, however, may not be place based, such as a study of couples who have chosen in-vitro fertilization or of individuals who have experienced sexual abuse as children. Here the location may be less significant than the identification of a scarce or hidden population.

When: Timing and Duration of the Study

All researchers have to make decisions about the timing and duration of their study. **Timing** refers to the time of year and time during the day, evening, or weekend when the research will take place. **Duration** refers to the length of time during which the study will take place. Many factors may determine both the timing and the duration of a study. Such external factors as available funds or the time period available to the researcher (for example, a sabbatical or half-sabbatical, or a six- or twelve-month period in the field required for dissertation work) are important considerations. Timing is important in research that focuses on the plans and activities leading up to a ritual occurring only once a year, combined with interviews about the actual conduct of the ritual. Interviews about conducting and participating in the ritual and observations of the ritual require that the researcher be in the field during the period of time that covers planning activities, the ritual, and its aftermath. Researchers doing qualitative work on asthma emergency room visits might want to time their study so that it coincides with peak periods (fall and spring in the Northeastern United States, for example) and regular times in order to see how experiences of asthma differ.

Taking into consideration recall time, or how long a person can remember the details of a specific event, is also important. Unless the event is highly unusual and dramatic, most people do not recall the details of an experience very accurately more than two or three days after it occurs. Research that calls for accurate recall of such an event as childbirth, a wedding, or a funeral; an eviction or the shift from one type of residential situation to another; or a recent visit to the

METHODOLOGY, METHODS, AND TOOLS IN QUALITATIVE RESEARCH

doctor for a health problem should take place within a week of the event. Life narrative interviews, however, do not require such timing because they call for recollection of a person's entire life history rather than a specific recent event (see Chapter Nine).

Finally, researchers need to take into consideration at what time during the day or week observations or interviews can best be conducted. Interviews with adolescents have to be timed for the after-school period between about 2:30 P.M. and 5:30 P.M. to avoid conflict with homework; but if adolescents are involved in after-school athletics, interviews may have to be conducted in the evening. Homeless people must be interviewed during the day because they are required to be registered in a shelter by later in the afternoon. Entrance and exit interviews with dance club clients can only be conducted in the evening and late at night as they are arriving at or leaving their club of choice. Families from northern India living in Mumbai usually go home for an extended period prior to the arrival of the rainy season in June; thus May through June is not a good time to plan to interview family members.

With Whom: Study Population

The term *study population* refers to the people who are the focus of the study. In a qualitative study there may be several study populations; for example, for a study on treatment programs for substance users, the two study populations may be service providers offering programs for drug users and the people who are using drugs. The study populations are always chosen in relation to the study topic, and the reasons why they are chosen—that is, their expected contribution to the study—must be given as part of the study design. As units of investigation and analysis, study populations may be chosen at different levels—census districts, town administrative bodies, local experts, family or household units, or individuals. In qualitative research the study population may or may not be equivalent to the study community, a place. Researchers conducting a study of barriers to female condom use might consider including those involved in reproductive health policymaking; potential or actual distributors, such as pharmacies and clinics; health care providers (for example, primary health care providers, nurses, health outreach workers, peer educators); and individual end users. Similarly, in a comparative study of the effects of social development curriculum on secondary school children's behavior, all middle schools would constitute the first-level study population. The research question would address differences in ways the curriculum is managed and delivered across schools. The second-level study population would be teachers who deliver the curriculum. Here the question might focus on how the curriculum is delivered and what facilitates or constrains delivery in each classroom. The third-level study population would be the students who engage with the curriculum; questions for these students might address their engagement with the curriculum, what they understand, what they might like to change, and how they feel about curriculum delivery. And the fourth-level study population might be parents, who could be asked about their knowledge of the curriculum content, how it is delivered, or their children's responses to it. A good study design might obtain some form of representative sample from each level or constituency to gain a holistic perspective on the study topic.

Sampling in Qualitative Research

Qualitative researchers sample for reasons that differ from those of quantitative or survey researchers, who usually prefer random or systematic sampling strategies that allow them to generalize or extend their results to the broader population from which a sample of respondents or events is selected. This is because qualitative research questions tend to focus on processes; on detailed contextual or historical descriptions; or on the meanings, interpretations, and explanations people assign to events, activities, and behaviors. Many qualitative questions are more concerned with **validity** (the degree to which the data and interpretation fit the situation) than with **generalizability** (the degree to which the study results can be generalized to the broader population from which the study sample is drawn).

Qualitative researchers use cases to illustrate the interactions among variables, recognizing that the same (or even different) variables may configure in different ways in other places or with other populations over time. They seek less for randomization and control than for understanding of the range of variation of behavioral phenomena or meanings in a population. Thus qualitative researchers turn to forms of purposive (also called purposeful), targeted, or systematic sampling, such as **criterion sampling** (identifying cases based on a set of criteria—for example, expertise in club drug use) or **theoretical sampling** (filling cells by characteristics of the study population defined in advance; cells may be filled according to such theoretical criteria as age, ethnicity, size, or level of empowerment). Another sampling option is **extreme or midpoint sampling** when the range of variation in a study population is known. Extreme sampling refers to choosing examples that represent the extreme ends or opposites of a continuum, whereas midpoint sampling involves choosing examples that are known to be typical of the study population. Or researchers may screen by study topic. In a study of drinking behavior in Mumbai, for example, researchers sought out married and unmarried men who had drunk a "little" (several times) or "a lot" (once a week or more) in the past thirty days, approximately twenty men in each of four cells. Finally, qualitative researchers use a variety of sampling strategies other than randomization to obtain representative samples from which generalizations can be made. For **targeted sampling**, researchers map all sites, or as many sites as possible, where people in the desired group gather; choose a sample of sites; and identify respondents from that site sample using preestablished protocols for choosing the number of respondents from each site. In **respondent-driven sampling**, respondents from randomly identified locations present recruitment cards to three others who volunteer for participation; these participants are asked to present cards to three others. This form of sampling is believed to result in an unbiased sample of the general population after approximately five such cycles (Heckathorn, 1997; Ramirez-Valles, Heckathorn, Salganik, & Heckathorn, 2004; Vázquez, Diaz, & Campbell, 2005) and is thus preferred to other forms of network sampling, provided that the respondents engage in behavior that is known to be networked. As with site selection, the researcher must justify each sampling approach. And it should be remembered that to choose a proper sample for validity or generalizability to the rest of the population or others like it requires knowledge of the study site, which is best obtained by spending as much time as possible learning about where people gather and in what numbers (sometimes referred to as **site mapping** or **ethnographic mapping**) (Tripathi, Sharma, Pelto, & Tripathi, 2010).

REFLECTION QUESTIONS

1. Find a qualitative study and define its sampling procedure. Do you think the procedure is adequate in this study?
2. Consider and outline situations in which you would consider using each of the approaches to sampling suggested above, and explain why.

Research Methods

Research methods are the tools qualitative researchers use to investigate their research topic and construct their argument and the decisions they make as to how to use those tools and with whom. As noted earlier, qualitative research methods share a common core of characteristics. They are generally used in face-to-face situations in which the researcher is relating to the respondent or the setting or both. The researcher is the primary (though not the only) tool for data collection, meaning that information is always filtered through the exchange between the individual, the research setting, and the respondents. This may introduce biases into the interview process. To try to reduce researcher bias and to enhance the voices and interpretations of respondents, while supporting researcher engagement, qualitative researchers attempt to minimize personal characteristics that could interfere with communication. Doing so requires researchers to reflect constantly on how they may be influencing the research setting and the research conversations by virtue of their identity, language capacity, knowledge of local culture, customs and etiquette, and perceived power or access to resources desired by the respondents. It also requires researchers' careful contemplation of their own possible biases or strongly held attitudes about local practices or people in the research setting that could wrongly influence interpretations or understandings of the field situation.

Two strategies researchers use to reflect on these issues are keeping a diary or personal log and creating an initial or formative conceptual model. The diary allows the researcher to record experiences in the field that are cause for reflection and consideration and that may require a change in approach or communication style. The conceptual model uses logical arguments drawn from the literature and personal experience in the study site to identify and link the main domains that are believed to be the most important for the study at initiation. Producing a conceptual model requires clear explication of both the reasons for choosing domains and the links among them. For example, the initial conceptual model for a study of HIV exposure among older adults consists of an outcome—exposure to HIV—and the factors believed to contribute to it, including the presence of injection drug users in their immediate networks, the presence of drug dealers in the neighborhood, and the involvement with drug-using commercial sex workers (see Figure 4.2) (Radda, Schensul, Disch, Levy, & Reyes, 2003; Schensul, Levy, & Disch, 2003). This model can then be expanded to include other factors as qualitative data on HIV exposure are collected and analyzed.

As another example, a researcher who proposes that inadequate school facilities, poor educational instruction, and a program of rental evictions result in poor school performance is biased in favor of structural or systemic explanations. The resulting model leaves out such factors as low parental education levels and peer norms favoring frequent cell phone texting. Thus a conceptual model will quickly reveal what domains researchers think are connected and should be explored in a study, where they have more or less information already, and what their biases and gaps in knowledge might be. In the early stages of a study, these can be corrected through **validity checks** carried out by asking local experts

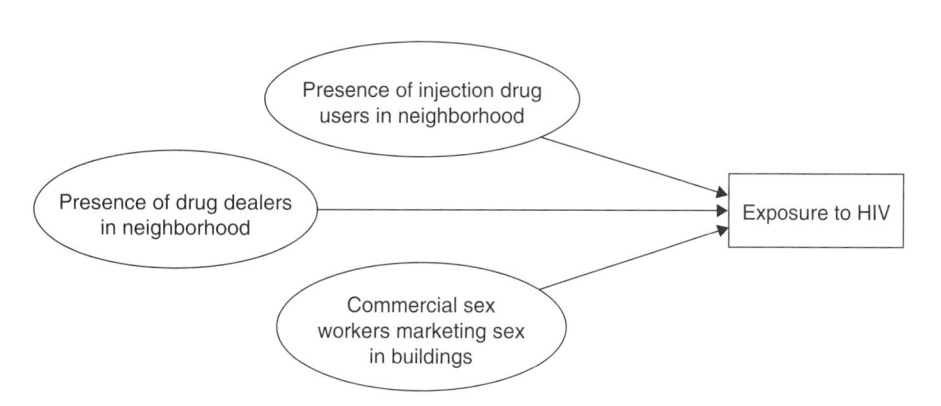

METHODOLOGY, METHODS, AND TOOLS IN QUALITATIVE RESEARCH

FIGURE 4.2 Initial Conceptual Model of HIV Exposure Factors Among Older Adults

```
   Presence of injection drug
     users in neighborhood
              \
               \
Presence of drug dealers ———————→ Exposure to HIV
   in neighborhood         /
                          /
   Commercial sex
 workers marketing sex
     in buildings
```

and other researchers who know the study setting whether the researcher's initial model and explanation for it make sense.

Although qualitative researchers collect many different types of data to answer their research questions, all types of qualitative research take an **emic perspective**, focusing on learning and understanding the perspectives of local residents and experts. The emic perspective is based on the belief that people's viewpoints, when set in the context of their lives, are understandable, whether or not the researcher agrees with them. The meanings that people attribute to their actions and behaviors, whether communicated directly or indirectly, are considered central to qualitative inquiry. Once the data are collected, the researcher can determine how and in what ways to represent the voices of the study participants. Always, however, qualitative researchers keep in mind that "sense-making through the eyes and lived experience of the people is at the heart of good qualitative research" (Schensul, 2008, p. 522).

It is useful to organize the collection of qualitative data into a four-cell matrix (see Table 4.2). The matrix juxtaposes two different primary ways of collecting face-to-face data, observation (what is seen and recorded by the researcher) and interviewing (what is told to and recorded by the researcher), against two different primary ways of organizing the data, the cultural level (including information about the community, organization, or collective cognition) and the individual level (including data obtained from individuals about individual beliefs and behaviors).

Table 4.2 Main Classes of Data Collection at Individual and Community Levels

	Observation	Interviewing
Cultural Level	Community maps, walkabouts, gatherings, celebrations and festivals, meetings, marches, markets	Open-ended in-depth interviews with key informants (community leaders and others knowledgeable about the topic of study)
Individual Level	People's daily activities, clinic visits, behavior in school, drinking behavior	Individual respondents' explanations for their participation in events, health or substance use narratives, reproductive health experiences, surveys

Researcher Position in Data Collection

Researchers may choose to be more or less engaged in the study site, or with the study participants, depending on the paradigms that drive their work and the requirements of the study. In addition, observations and interviews may be more or less exploratory or structured beforehand. The more the researcher prestructures or predefines either observations or interviews, the more focused and limited the nature of the collected data. Observations may be more or less **obtrusive** (intruding on the regular lives and behaviors of those who are the subject of study) depending on the degree to which the researcher structures the activities to be observed. For example, observation in a kindergarten classroom to document and describe predetermined types of interactions among teachers, aides, and students requires that the researcher become familiar with the study setting so as not to attract attention or interfere with the regular daily schedule. In this type of observational setting, the researcher can observe everyday behavior, document interactions, and define and code or classify them in the research site or later on. Conversely, experiments, in which respondents are asked to perform an activity and researchers code observations of the activity for the presence or absence of types of behavior—or for emotional responses that are derived from the study's theoretical framework—call for a high degree of structuring of both the behavioral setting and activities. A typical example might involve asking parents to use a standard set of developmentally appropriate toys in the same setting to demonstrate how they play with their toddlers.

In the same way, the more specific and structured the interview schedule, the less opportunity respondents have to express themselves as they would in a regular conversation. Semistructured, open-ended in-depth interviews in which

METHODOLOGY, METHODS, AND TOOLS IN QUALITATIVE RESEARCH

the interviewer is required to follow a sequence of questions limit the exploration allowed, as compared to more individualized and unstructured—or minimally structured—open-ended in-depth interviews. Further, the time limits imposed by requirements to ask all the questions in an interview schedule may reduce the possibilities for the researcher's engagement with the participant. At the same time, very open-ended interviews—which are conducted more like regular conversations—require the researcher to have considerable skill in focusing the questions so as to collect useful information relevant to the study and keep the respondent engaged.

Data Collection at the Cultural Level

At the cultural or collective level, qualitative researchers try to obtain information on community- or systems-level phenomena. These might include activities in which many or most people in the community participate, such as annual meetings, festivals, and religious celebrations that can illustrate community dynamics and tensions as well as cultural practices. Events that mark turning points in the history of a community or a group of residents also offer important information about the present. For example, stories obtained from residents of New York about the attack on the World Trade Center (WTC) buildings can provide a context for people's feelings about and behaviors in response to the placement of a Muslim cultural center near the WTC site. Further, in studies of drug use in Hartford, interviews about the destruction of public housing and the disbursement of public housing residents throughout the area provide a lot of information about the decentralization of social networks and the spread of specific drugs from the suburbs to the city and vice versa. In order to gather these types of data on community-level activities, beliefs, and interactions, the primary data collection tools are observations and interviewing. These are the building blocks of qualitative data collection.

Qualitative researchers may use other data collection methods to obtain information at the cultural level. These could include any or all of the following:

- **Cultural consensus modeling**, which provides information about the components or elements in cultural domains (such as leisure time activities, types of risk, illnesses, types of clothing, foods) and the different ways the way people organize and classify them; how people explain these mental or cognitive groupings; and the degree to which there is consensus or agreement about the ways the items in a domain are grouped
- **Network research**, which involves documenting through observation and measuring with surveys the ways organization members and organizations or

specific locations, such as bars, libraries, or senior centers, connect to each other, in what ways, and for what reasons

- **Archival research**, which involves using secondary data (primary data collected by others but available to the public for use) or library source data to help understand the history of a study site

- **Community mapping** in various forms, including drawing maps of the community or asking residents to draw such maps, and using existing to-scale maps or Google maps to locate activities and organizations spatially in relation to where people live and conduct their daily activities

- **Audiovisual documentation**, which involves filming or audio-recording activities that take place in the community for later coding and analysis

All of these methods round out the community-level data collection repertoire and provide the basis for a detailed description of a community or a study site.

Data Collection at the Individual Level

At the individual level, the focus is on the discovery of main themes and range of variation in the experiences, beliefs, norms, and practices of individuals. Again the primary means of data collection include interviews and observations, both open-ended and structured. These interviews are gathered from more than one person, because the goal is to identify differences and similarities across respondents in a sample. The following are the main ways of collecting data from individuals:

- **In-depth interviews** are conducted with unique individuals or a small number of people. There are several types of in-depth interviews. Life history narratives involve few interviews, which are usually very lengthy (up to fifteen or more hours of interview time); narrative interviews focus on specific and often sensitive topics, such as bereavement or HIV, and usually consist of three interviews of about one to two hours each, moving from less sensitive and more descriptive to more sensitive and more focused on personal meaning and feelings. One-time in-depth interviews usually address a specific topic and last about one to two hours (Seidman, 2006).

- **Semistructured interviews** are used to collect similar information from a larger sample of individuals, numbering at least twelve to fifteen and usually not more than ninety.

- **Qualitatively based surveys** are based primarily on prior qualitative research in the study population. These surveys are generated from the domains, subdomains, and individual items that emerge from in-depth and semistructured interviews. Usually they do not include standardized scales and other validated instruments, although there is no hard and fast rule about such inclusions. However, if preselected scales are used, it is always best to pilot them for meaning as well as to analyze the structure of these scales to make sure they are internally consistent. There is a strong possibility that any standardized measure will require adaptation when used with a new study population. The same principle applies to a standardized behavioral coding scheme, which will require adaptation to the study situation and setting.

- **Individual-level network data** (ego-centered data) describing the personal networks or relationships of individual respondents in a study can be collected, even in the context of in-depth interviews. Person-oriented network research can show what proportion of an individual's network members are involved in risk behavior (which is a more specific behavioral indicator of social influence than perceived influence). These data can also show what proportion of a personal network provides support for or extracts support from an individual (these are measures of positive and negative social support).

    A number of data collection methods or tools can be used at both the cultural (community or organizational) level and individual level for network research. For example, a researcher can collect network data to understand the structure of relationships among individuals in a **bounded system**, such as a classroom or buildings in which older adults live. In these cases it is possible to ask every member about every other member. In a **semibounded system**, such as a kinship network or peer network, the cutoff points demarcating network members may be unclear. It is then not possible to collect information from each and every member of the network about his or her relationships with all the others, so the network data are incomplete.

Most in-depth interviews or narratives can be coded, compiled, and even quantified to illustrate both the range of variation and cultural themes and patterns across individuals in a setting.

It is important to note that each of these approaches to data collection requires a design for site selection, observation, and recruitment. Discussions of recruitment strategies can be found in a variety of sources on qualitative methods (for example, see Bernard, 2000; Schensul, Schensul, & LeCompte, 1999).

Selecting Methods or Tools

Each researcher must decide which tools to use in order to answer study questions, how the tools should be implemented to the best effect, and who should implement them. The decisions researchers make about which tools to use will depend on the research questions, the training and skills of the research team, and the amount of time and money available to conduct research in the study setting. How much researchers actually know about the study setting also influences the tools they use for data collection. Those with prior experience in the setting, or who are already members of the study community, generally know more than novices or researchers new to the community and thus would resort less to exploratory approaches.

Further, the ability to engage in informed observation and interviewing and the sequencing of data collection activities is enhanced by being able to speak the local language. A student who is learning Swahili, Wolof, or Spanish in the field might like to begin with a few simple, structured interview questions that require limited mastery of the language (for example, asking vendors in a market where their products come from, asking teachers what languages their students speak, or asking people in a park where they live and how often they come there). Experienced researchers who speak the language used in the study site or researchers working in partnership with informed residents might not require these preliminary activities and can begin their qualitative research immediately by interviewing local experts on the study topic.

Table 4.3 summarizes the main types of qualitative research tools and provides some general suggestions as to when to use them in order to understand either the broader context of individual beliefs and behaviors (at the community level) or the individual perspective. Ideally these methods are complementary. It is convenient to introduce them sequentially, beginning with open-ended observations, interviews, and mapping, supplemented with various forms of cultural consensus modeling and photography. The community-level data provide the framework and information to move to semistructured observations and interviewing with specific samples of activities and individuals. In a true qualitative field study, participant observation (whereby the researcher observes and participates at the same time) and informal interviewing along with photographic documentation can occur throughout the life of the study, allowing the researcher to accumulate data on the community level. The data collected through these steps provide the basis for a qualitatively derived survey, the results of which can be explained with the qualitative data and by member checking, reviewing the results with members of the study community. The end result is an interpretive document or documentary that reflects both the views and voices

Table 4.3 Guide to Qualitative Research Tools

	Community Level	When to Choose	Individual Level	When to Choose
Observation				
Open-ended, nonparticipatory	Observing activities and interactions in public spaces	When collecting general information about demography, the history of setting activities, and rituals; when creating community- or setting-specific maps; when observing how parents and children interact in a park	Observing individual behavior	To identify possible dimensions of variation among individuals (for example, teachers instructing children in learning addition or reading when the dimensions are not known in advance)
Participatory	Engaging in and documenting regular routines of life in a household, community, school, or other setting	When it is considered important to learn the ways of behaving and thinking of a group of people by actually experiencing them	Participating in the daily routines or activities of individuals in the study community by following them	To understand through personal experience the differences in ways people do things
Structured	Noting systematic, observable similarities and differences using a checklist in public or quasi-public spaces or at events (for example, emergency rooms, bars, playgrounds)	For example, to study differences in the use of parks, malls, and clubs; to explore children's play patterns in school	Identifying and comparing activity patterns of individuals	To understand through quantification the different ways that people behave in a setting or over time (for example, parental behavior, teacher behavior throughout the day, clinicians' behavior toward different types of patients)

(Continued)

Table 4.3 (Continued)

	Community Level	When to Choose	Individual Level	When to Choose
In-Depth Interviews				
Open-ended	Asking interview questions and topics flowing from the interests of the interviewer and interviewee	To learn from community experts and gatekeepers who have knowledge relevant to the study topic	Asking interview questions and topics that flow from the interests of the interviewer and interviewee	To obtain pilot data using an informal or unfinished interview schedule to explore a particular topic, such as reproductive health choices or drug use
Semistructured	Covering a list of topics common to all respondents	To understand the range of perceptions of an issue by key people in a community	Identifying commonalities and differences across individual respondents on one or more topics	When using a common list of topics with corresponding open-ended questions, to identify intragroup differences in expressions of psychological stress, sexual dysfunction, child discipline practices, and so on
Structured	Obtaining systematic quantified or quantifiable data on study topics from a sample of community experts	For example, to conduct surveys with service providers about illnesses of clients, or surveys with pharmacists about purchases of over-the-counter substances	To obtain systematic quantified or quantifiable data on study topics from a sample of community residents	For example, to conduct surveys with respondents to identify variations in factors associated with illness management, HIV risk, and their correlates
Focused	Obtaining general information about a topic from a group of people who are interacting with each other	For example, to conduct focused group discussion of risks of HIV exposure in the community, important historical moments in the development of an institution, or key problems in service delivery	Focused group interviews are not held with individuals. Revealing personal information is not encouraged in focus group discussions.	N/A

Visual Documentation

Photography — Obtaining original or archival photographic images of a study setting and activities — For example, to understand spatial configurations of classrooms; to understand types of products sold in markets or produced by farmers — Obtaining visual evidence of differences in individual behaviors and representations related to performance or identity — For example, to illustrate variations in fashion by generation or how individual children interact with others through different play activities

Video documentation — Obtaining an audiovisual record of actual performances and practices, activities, and rituals over time — To record folk festivals, spoken word performances, political speeches and events, traffic flow, market activities, and so on — Obtaining narrative accounts of individuals' life stories, specific event narratives, and activities in which the events unfold over time — For example, to document narratives of escape from war zones, or the effects of climate change on individual lifestyles (such as shifts in the ways that households obtain water or firewood)

Mapping

Maps not to scale — Drawing physical layouts of important components of a study site — To situate items in relation to each other, and activities in space as observed or told — Drawing individual activity maps to show different ways respondents use space — For example, when documenting respondents' routes to and from work, and locations and sites on the route where they stop to drink alcohol

Maps to scale — Creating accurately scaled or GIS maps that locate data in relation to the earth's surface (and each other) — To locate sites where specific activities take place; for example, to locate sites with environmental toxins in relation to residential areas — Measuring accurately variations in individuals' use of physical space — For example, to obtain quantitative measures of the differences in daily activity spaces of urban residents to examine variations by age and ethnicity

(Continued)

Table 4.3 (Continued)

	Community Level	When to Choose	Individual Level	When to Choose
Social maps	Drawing locations people use for different purposes, and how they get there	To learn about how people use community resources; to situate historical events and populations; to hear how people talk with one another	Obtaining differences in respondents' perceptions and use of space	For example, to compare mothers', daughters', and sons' actual use of space in their neighborhood and their explanations for their use patterns, to identify generational and gender differences
Other Elicitation Techniques				
Listings and pilesorts	Obtaining information on how people identify and rank items in a domain and organize them cognitively into cultural groupings	For example, to monitor men's activities, sources of information on HIV, and sex behaviors	The listing of items in a domain provides the basis for exploring that domain with individuals in in-depth interviews.	N/A
Body maps	Obtaining information on where respondents situate items on the surface of the body	To obtain general data through key informants about where pain or emotions are located	Obtaining in-depth information from respondents on embodied experiences	When comparing individuals on dimensions included in the body mapping exercise
Items for classification	Obtaining cultural artifacts that represent important historical, ritual, or cultural meaning to a group	To explore collections of cooking utensils, weavings, beadwork, weapons, or clothing, and the stories behind them	Obtaining reports from individual respondents as to their ownership and use of such cultural items	To compare respondents on the degree of ownership of and familiarity with culturally identified items as a measure of identity or belonging

METHODOLOGY, METHODS, AND TOOLS IN QUALITATIVE RESEARCH

of the study community (the emic perspective) and the theoretically framed analysis of the researcher (the **etic perspective**).

> **REFLECTION QUESTIONS**
>
> 1. Can you identify any of the data collection methods described above that you would not feel comfortable implementing? Why? Which ones would you be most likely to choose, and why would you choose to apply them?
> 2. Can you think of any situations in which you could not apply one of these approaches?

Use of Cameras and Digital Recorders in Qualitative Research

Photo and video cameras and digital recorders are useful in recording live situations and in-depth interviews. All three aids to data collection are visible and to some degree intrusive. However, if the researcher has a good and trusting relationship with the respondents, obtains permission to film or record, and has undergone review by an institutional review board to ensure human subjects' protection and the absence of such threats as loss of confidentiality (see the next section for more on this review process), it is usually possible to use all three tools. Researchers should be sensitive to the possibility that certain people may not like to be photographed for a variety of reasons, including the belief that photographs capture the soul of the person, a desire for privacy, and gendered rules that preclude photographing women. Thus researchers should always ask permission before taking photographs of people in a research setting. Researchers should also be prepared to describe the storage, analysis, use, and destruction of audiovisual materials after the study is done. Finally, if the audiovisual materials will be used in any scientific productions (for example, a film, photographic exhibit, publication, installation, or Web site), the individuals involved should be asked to sign a release form and offered a clear explanation, in their own language, of how the materials will be used and what, if any, consequences there might be for the respondent and his or her community. (Chapter Two offers full details on these issues.)

Ethical Issues in Data Collection

All studies, including qualitative studies, require a review and approval by **institutional review boards** (**IRBs**). IRBs are university- or community-based ethics committees that meet regularly to provide an independent review of ethical considerations related to a study and the protection of "human subjects" or respondents, as well as the communities or other settings in which the research will be conducted. For example, qualitative researchers often pay respondents or give them small gifts for taking the time to participate in interviews or surveys. These payments are considered to be incentives. Researchers usually determine the value of incentives based on prevailing rates for similar studies in the area, and by taking into consideration what incentives could have a possible coercive effect on individual respondents in the study. Incentive amounts are intended to cover the cost of time required to participate in the study. They should be substantial enough to attract volunteers for a study, and small enough to avoid being considered coercive, especially when respondents have modest or low incomes, may need additional sources of financial support, or might not feel that they can refuse voluntarily. Insights and guidance in the ethics of qualitative research with diverse populations can be found on the Web site of the American Anthropological Association (www.aaanet.org/ar/irb/index.htm), and in publications by Trimble and Fisher (2006) and Hoonaard (2002, 2011), among others.

Although all interview schedules should be approved by an institutional review board, it is also important for IRB members to understand that in qualitative research interviewers do not always know in advance what all the relevant questions may be. Thus it is often the case that the community-level in-depth or focus group interview protocol or the individual-level in-depth interview schedule that is submitted to the IRB consists of only a few open-ended questions.

Data Analysis

Analytic decisions are generally made based on the research questions, the study model, and the types of data collected. Analysis of qualitative data progresses through classification of ideas, themes, topics, activities, types of people, and other categories relevant to the study. This process is referred to as coding. Coding involves the classification of elements in text data into categories that are related to the study topic and are useful in analysis. Corbin and Strauss (2008) discuss different types of coding categories, ranging from more concrete to more abstract and conceptual. These coding categories are created and refined as the researcher builds smaller units into larger domains. The researcher examines and describes variation within each code category, identifies links among code categories, tests these with further examples, and then explains and interprets them (see Chapter Three, Grounded Theory). As analytic codes emerge or initial codes are applied, a coding scheme is finalized that can be applied to the entire data set. All text-based observation and interview data can be coded, compared, and integrated into patterns by hand, or by using computer software, such as

Atlas-ti or NVivo (QSR International, 2010; Scientific Software, 2010). Furthermore, many of these programs allow for the incorporation of audiovisual, photographic, PDF, and JPG formats into files that can be coded.

Either with or without software, analysts make comments about interesting points or codes, and develop thematic, theoretical, methodological, or other types of memos than can be analyzed along with the data. Good qualitative researchers also write **analytic summaries** that provide the basis for overall project analysis and interpretation. An analytic summary is an interim write-up of the results of close examination of a specific coding category, for example, "partner relationship." To write a summary, the researcher would extract everything that has been coded or classified as about partner relationship. This could include different types of partners and different dimensions of relationships. An analytic report on this component of a study would sort out the different types of relationships and consider under each type the different dimensions of the relationship. The write-up would then summarize characteristics of relationships for each partner type and synthesize similarities and differences in relationships across all partner types. Chapter Three includes additional information about the process of data analysis.

Conceptual mapping, network research, drawings and photographs, geographic mapping, and other advanced qualitative methods or tools each require a different approach to analysis (LeCompte & Schensul, 2010; Miles & Huberman, 1994) and different software. Conceptual mapping often makes use of Anthropac, a program written by a sociologist for social scientists to facilitate free listing and grouping of items in a single domain (Analytic Technologies, 2010). Network analysis can be conducted with SPSS (for personal networks), and such programs as UCINET (for macro-network analysis) and Pajek or Krackplot (for macro-network display) are available. Many anthropologists use Microsoft ACCESS and GIS mapping software to create community maps or personal geographic spaces, which can then be compared and contrasted for differences across individuals, neighborhoods, or communities and villages.

To interpret their data, qualitative researchers **triangulate** different types of data, comparing and contrasting results to find and explain commonalities and differences. Triangulation refers to an examination of how different sources of data on the same topic may complement each other to deepen understanding of a study topic. For example, community-level interviews on perceptions of alcohol use among men in Mumbai can be complemented by consensus analysis that reveals the way men and women classify reasons men drink and the activities in which men are engaged (Berg et al., 2010; Schensul et al., 2010). The community-level interviews with local experts have shown the widespread belief that many men drink and that drinking leads to risky sexual activity. Consensus analysis showed that both men and women classified reasons for drinking into primary categories related to work conditions, stresses and conflict at home, influence of alcohol-consuming peers, parties and social life, and risky activities, such as going to ladies' bars to find women and seeing female sex workers. Consensus analysis broadens and complements the perspective provided by a much smaller number of local respondents.

> **REFLECTION QUESTIONS**
>
> 1. What are some codes that you could apply to a study that you might be planning or have selected?
> 2. How do these codes relate to the study model or research questions?
> 3. Can you think of some ways that you might organize your data for analysis?

Summary

Qualitative research is conducted on a face-to-face basis, and thus depends on the ability of the researcher to interact effectively with the study population in order to collect the required data. Maximum learning is achieved when researchers suspend their judgments and biases and use the tools of qualitative inquiry to learn from others and represent their perspectives. This is not to say that researchers must agree with everything their respondents tell them. It does mean that they have to listen carefully and sift through their own biases while doing so to be able to recall and record accurately what respondents say and do. The most effective ways of preparing for a qualitative study are thinking through in advance what the study is about and developing an initial conceptual model, learning something about the topic from people in the study site in order to determine how to ask the appropriate questions, and practicing by conducting pilot interviews and observations.

The qualitative data collection tool kit is substantial, and qualitative researchers have many choices to make in terms of study site, study sample, and the specific tools for data collection. Data can be collected on the cultural (community or organizational) level or the individual level. These decisions can only be made in the context of a specific study design or study plan of action. There are few right or wrong ways of making these choices, but there are standard guidelines for good interviewing, careful observation, and recording available in many qualitative texts (see Schensul & LeCompte, 1999). Audiovisual, network analysis, consensus analysis, and text management and analysis technology tools are widely available but are not required for many studies. New qualitative researchers should depend on their own data collection and analysis capacities without advanced technology, and should keep their studies simple by using small samples in order to practice their skills. Later, as they gain experience, it is easy to add more sophisticated components to a study.

Qualitative research results provide many insights into why people do what they do and what influences their thoughts, values, and behaviors. Qualitative research can also tell us why and how programs may be going well and can provide unexpected insights into programs and interventions. Qualitative research is especially useful in improving services; formulating locally or culturally specific interventions; examining the effects of policies on the lives of individuals, on families, and on neighborhoods; and understanding and explaining unknown or perceived variation in beliefs and behaviors in community, service, and educational settings. Thus, this approach has significant evaluative and intervention-oriented benefits for researchers, study participants, and the communities that constitute the focus of the research.

Key Terms

analytic summaries, 99
archival research, 90
audiovisual documentation, 90
bounded system, 91
causal chains, 80
census, 74
community mapping, 90
conceptual model, 79
criterion sampling, 84
critical researchers, 77
cultural consensus modeling, 89
domains, 80
duration, 82
emic perspective, 87
ethnographic mapping, 85

etic perspective, 97
extreme or midpoint sampling, 84
generalizability, 84
in-depth interviews, 90
individual-level network data, 91
institutional review boards (IRBs), 97
interpretivists, 76
methodology, 70
methods, 70
mixed-paradigm research, 77
network research, 89
obtrusive, 88
outcome, 80
paradigm, 76

participation, 70
participatory or collaborative approach, 78
positionality, 71
positivists, 76
predictor, 80
qualitatively based surveys, 91
research design, 71
respondent-driven sampling, 85
semibounded system, 91
semistructured interviews, 90
site mapping, 85
study population, 72
targeted sampling, 85

theoretical sampling, 84
timing, 82
triangulate, 99
unit of analysis, 81
validity, 84
validity checks, 86

Further Readings and Resources

Suggested Readings

Bernard, H. R. (2000). *Social research methods: Qualitative and quantitative approaches*. Thousand Oaks, CA: Sage.

This book, written by a well-known qualitative researcher and prolific methodological writer, summarizes key principles of qualitative and mixed-methods research design and data collection.

Denzin, N. K., & Lincoln, Y. S. (Eds.). (2005). *The Sage handbook of qualitative research* (3rd ed.). Thousand Oaks, CA: Sage.

This is one of the most comprehensive accounts of qualitative research, edited and with chapters by two well-known sociologists. Chapters written by numerous experienced researchers include explications of paradigms; specialized approaches from the perspectives of racial and ethnic groups; gender, sexual orientation, and other important demographic and political differences; as well as presentations on dissemination, research ethics, and other topics.

DeWalt, K., & DeWalt, B. R. (2002). *Doing participant observation*. Lanham, MA: AltaMira.

This unusual and very helpful publication by two experienced qualitative researchers highlights and solves central methodological and other problems in the collection, recording, organizing, and analysis of field notes based on participant observation ranging from positivist to participatory.

Pelto, P. J., & Pelto, G. H. (1978). *Anthropological research: The structure of inquiry* (2nd ed.). New York: Cambridge University Press.

This is one of the earliest explications of qualitative and mixed-methods research methodology and data collection methods, written by two anthropologists with extensive U.S. and cross-national qualitative research experience. The publication defines science for the social sciences, and outlines many different ways of collecting qualitative data in community and organizational contexts. It is used by social scientists from diverse disciplinary backgrounds, including educational researchers, and remains a widely read original piece of work.

Schensul J. J., & LeCompte, M. D. (1999). *The ethnographers' toolkit* (Vols. 1–7). Lanham, MD: Rowman & Littlefield.

This seven-volume set, currently in its second edition, covers all aspects of the qualitative research and ethnographic enterprise. The author-editors describe ethnography as mixed-methods research that generates cultural theories about the way communities and schools function and how individuals respond in terms of beliefs and practices. The set includes a general introduction (Book 1), a text on conceptualizing and designing qualitative research (Book 2), two books on basic and more specialized qualitative data collection methods (Books 3 and 4), and a book on approaches to analysis of qualitative data (Book 5). Book 6 is an examination of ethical considerations in qualitative research, including IRB reviews and partner relationships. Finally, Book 7 addresses the application of qualitative research results to solving social and other community problems. Book 1 of the second edition is now in print; Books 2 through 7 will be available by fall 2011.

Spradley, J. P. (1979). *The ethnographic interview*. New York: Holt, Rinehart and Winston; Spradley, J. P. (1980). *Participant observation*. New York: Holt, Rinehart and Winston. Both of these early books remain relevant accounts of the two critical data collection methods that qualitative researchers use: participant observation and in-depth interviewing. The author emphasizes the importance of the cultural domain in focusing the collection of interview and observation data, and uses the idea of domain analysis to describe and interpret cultural phenomena. This is necessary reading for those interested in cognitive or mental aspects of culture.

Organizations and Web Sites

Institute for Community Research (ICR) (http://incommunityresearch.org)
On this official Web site of the Institute for Community Research, you will find many examples of qualitative and mixed-methods studies and study results. You may also contact ICR researchers about their work or obtain their methods publications, including manuals for training youth to do their own qualitative research, through the Web site.

Online QDA: Learning Qualitative Data Analysis on the Web (http://onlineqda.hud.ac.uk/Intro_QDA/what_is_qda.php)
This Web site provides definitions for qualitative data analysis and is linked to an electronic mailing list and trainings in data analysis and software offered throughout Europe and the United States.

ResearchTalk (www.researchtalk.com/)
This institution, founded by qualitative sociologists, offers training throughout the year on analysis of qualitative data. ResearchTalk also provides specialized on-site training in the use of text management and analysis software.

PART TWO

DRAWING ON THE DISCIPLINES

CHAPTER 5

BIOGRAPHY AND LIFE STORY RESEARCH

Cynthia E. Winston

Key Ideas

- Many of the most influential theories in the field of psychology had their origins in biography and life story research.

- Biography and life story research can have the goal of theory development or of testing theory and general concepts about persons and lives.

- Historically biography and life story research has been a form of single case study research, although more contemporary research uses multiple cases as well as critical life episodes collected from a large number of participants.

- Steps followed in biography and life story research vary across researchers, but there are a few scholars who have developed data collection tools, analytic methods, and coding schemes that are guided by thematic content analysis and are widely available on the Internet.

- Biography and life story research focuses on internal validity in terms of narrative truth, as well as external validity in the form of the representativeness of the life episodes and topics within the whole life.

Biography and life story research blends elements of case study research (see Chapter Ten) and narrative methodology (see Chapter Nine) with the goal of producing rich descriptions and complex analyses of a single life or critical episodes within a person's life. As a form of case study research, biography and life story research treats the life as the case or bounded system. Biography and life story research is also a form of case study research in that the life is investigated in depth within the real-world context of meaning-making. At the same time, biography and life story research is a narrative methodology because the bounded system of a life is structured through experience in a storied form, and as such its study takes on the narrative form (Barresi & Jukes, 1997; Freeman, 2009). The core analytic goal of the biography and life story researcher is to interpret the meaning of the person's life experiences. The most influential theories in the field of psychology were developed using biography and life story research. This early grounding has led to biography and life story research's having a particular significance in the field of psychology. Narratives, autobiographical memories, self-defining memories, and personal memories are forms of biography and life story data. These types of data are collected by researchers using various interview methods. Biography and life story researchers also collect letters, personal documents, and other forms of archival data.

Historical and Theoretical Background

Biography and life story research is conducted in multiple disciplines in related forms, including history, psychology, and other social sciences. In history, biography research has evolved from what used to be the standard life and times approach. Historians placed the life within a historical period and context for the reader to learn about the historical period. In the last forty years, historians using biography have placed more emphasis on analysis of the life itself, rather than on the historical period.

Over time historians have become less interested in selecting the lives of "great men" for biography (see Carlyle, 1841) and have instead selected subjects of study who were not necessarily famous, but interesting. In the late 1900s it became much more common for the lives of women and individuals who were Black to be the subject of the biographies of historians because of a shift in historians' thinking about the importance of the lives of ordinary people. For example, Logan and Winston (1982) wrote a collective biography of the lives and achievements of over a hundred Black Americans, a group of people who had previously been ignored as subjects of biography and as contributors to American history. Biography within history during the nineteenth and early twentieth centuries was designed to be inspirational and entertaining. To a large extent it was not regarded as serious inquiry and scholarship.

In addition to biography and life story research's focus in the field of history, there is an interdisciplinary movement centered on the narrative study of lives called narrative inquiry (see Chapter Nine). Given the focus of Part Two of this book on qualitative research within the disciplines, as well as the long history of biography and life story research conducted within the field of psychology, the rest of the chapter will focus on the use of this research methodology within the field of psychology in particular.

Roots of Biography and Life Story Research in Psychology

Many of the most influential theories in psychology were developed using biography and life story research (McAdams, 2001; Singer, 2004). The origins of this research in the field of psychology have both formal and informal roots that began in the early 1900s. However, from the 1920s through the 1950s a branch of psychology called behaviorism, with its focus on observable behavior rather than on human thought and unconsciousness, dominated the field. This meant that there was a significant decline until the 1980s in researchers' use of biography and life story research.

Henry Murray, one of the key intellectual architects of personality psychology, most influenced the more formal development of biography and life story research. In the 1930s at the Harvard Psychological Clinic, Murray brought together an interdisciplinary group of renowned scholars and developed the personological tradition in personality psychology (Murray, 1938). **Personology** is the scientific study of the whole person in biographical and cultural context. This area of scientific study is distinguished from another area of research with the same name that is based on pseudoscience and involves using physiognomy and facial features to attempt to predict character traits and behavior (see Tickle, 2003). Murray introduced the concept of **person-centered psychology,** in which the researcher or analyst puts the person at the center of inquiry, believing that the investigator must become familiar with the person in many different contexts. Murray's goal in this research was to adopt what Gordan Allport (1937), the founder of personality psychology, coined an **idiographic approach** to personality study in which the researcher seeks to discover the specific and individual patterns in particular lives. This approach is in contrast to the **nomothetic approach** that was dominant during the 1930s in psychology and aimed to discover general principles or laws of behavior for all persons. For example, the five-factor model of personality developed by McCrae and Costa (1987) describes five dispositional traits that all humans possess to varying degrees and that are relatively stable across a person's life.

Theorists who were very famous in the field of psychology wrote psychobiographies, which in many ways more informally launched the study of lives through biography and life story methodology before Murray's formal introduction of personology. In 1910 Sigmund Freud wrote the psychobiography *Leonardo da Vinci and a Memory of his Childhood* (1910/1955); in 1958 Erik Erikson wrote *Young Man Luther*, and in 1969 he wrote *Gandhi's Truth*. Although not as famous and influential as Freud and Erikson in the field of psychology, Robert White (1938) developed the case of Earnst, which made an important contribution to biography and life story methodology, as it is considered the first intensive and methodologically sound study of a single case.

Psychobiography is a methodology designed for understanding personality and is focused on the analysis of a single life, most often of a person who is famous, exceptional, or unusual (see Schultz, 2007). Psychobiography researchers make a distinction between biography and psychobiography: in a biography the main goal is to tell the story of a life with a comprehensive focus, whereas in a psychobiography the goal is to focus on one facet of a person's life. For example, Elms and Heller (2007) conducted a psychobiography in which they asked the question of why Elvis Presley had difficulty performing the song "Are You Lonesome Tonight?" More contemporary psychobiography research has focused on dimensions of the lives of such famous people as George W. Bush, Adolph Hitler, Bill Clinton, Saddam Hussein, Abraham Lincoln, and Marilyn Monroe (Schultz, 2007).

After the beginning of World War II, due to the new emphasis on laboratory methods and psychometrics within the field of psychology, there was a turn away from biographical methods and the application of broad theories to the individual life (McAdams, 2009). Yet Murray was able to keep his personological approach alive during the war through his direction of a personality assessment program for the Office of Strategic Services (OSS), the agency that later became the CIA. The assessment plan used in the OSS focused on the whole person and used biographical narrative, as well as motivational, emotional stability, and intelligence assessments (Office of Strategic Services Assessment Staff, 1948).

Key Theoretical Underpinnings of Biography and Life Story Research

Within the field of psychology there are many ways in which researchers have studied lives. Scholars have called these such different names as biography research, life story research, and psychobiography research. All of these methodologies generally share the same underlying theoretical underpinnings that are important for understanding the research design and methodology used by biography and life story researchers, which are primarily grounded in personality and developmental psychology. Within these subareas of psychology it is well established that it is part of the nature of human beings to think in storied terms (McAdams, 2001), much in the same way human beings by nature are altruistic.

In other words, human beings think in terms of characters, plots, and settings as a way of making sense of human action and living.

From this perspective, the storied nature of human thought provides a way to think about **human individuality** and the human intention of making meaning of life experiences. Human individuality refers to the aspects of human personality that make a person unique or distinct from others. McAdams and Pals (2006), for example, have developed five principles for the science of the person. These principles describe human individuality in terms of evolution and human nature, dispositional signature, characteristic adaptations, life narratives and the challenge of modern identity, and the differential role of culture. In their emphasis of including studying life narratives as the aspect of human personality, they argue that persons develop life narratives that are internalized and evolving and that give individual lives their unique and culturally anchored meanings. Given this theoretical grounding, biography and life story researchers pursue answers to two overarching research questions:

1. How do we come to fully understand the life course of a person?
2. How do people make narrative sense of personal experience?

The storied nature of thought is often referred to as a narrative mode of thinking. Bruner (1986) suggests that human beings have evolved to interpret personal experiences in terms of stories. The **narrative mode of thought** focuses on stories and the vicissitudes of human intention organized in time (Bruner, 1986). Within this mode of thought, human needs, wants, and goals are explained in terms of human actors striving to do things over time (McAdams, 2009). In contrast, the **paradigmatic mode of thought** focuses on human experience in terms of tightly reasoned analyses, logical proof, and cause-and-effect relationships. In essence, the empirical discovery guided by reasoned hypotheses characteristic of the paradigmatic mode of thought is not the mode of thought persons use to make meaning of their life experiences. Instead, story, a key element of the narrative mode of thought, is the best available psychological structure that persons have for making sense of their lives in time (Bruner, 1990; McAdams, 2001; Sarbin, 1986). This narrative mode of thought helps shape behavior, establish identity, and integrate individuals into modern social life (Hermans, Kempen, & van Loon, 1992; Josselson & Lieblich, 1993; McAdams & Pals, 2006). The storied nature of human thought is so important that Sarbin argues that narrative is the "root metaphor" for the field of psychology.

Another very important element of the theoretical underpinnings of biography and life story research is the concept of time. Time within human lives is conceptually relevant to the idea of life span development. The **life course perspective** emphasizes that life stories are shaped by historical, economic, and cultural forces, as well as by social change and chance happenings. At the same time, people have **agency,** which is the capacity to make choices and to impose those choices on the world in the course of their development, actively constructing their lives in a complex and evolving social context (McAdams, 2009). Murray believed that human beings are time-binding organisms and that the history of the organism *is* the organism. In other words, the history of the individual is what really makes up who the individual is as a person. Thus, Murray believed, this mandated the use of biographical methodology (Murray, 1938). The concept of time within biography and life story research is also important in terms of the idea of **temporal order.** Sarbin (1986) describes temporal order as the idea that time is a key element of story, which always contains a beginning, middle, and end.

These key theoretical underpinnings of narrative, story, and time within biography and life story research are linked to more specific and formal theories about the nature of storied thought within the life course. **Storied thought** refers to the human capacity to think in terms of narratives that include people, settings, plots, or complicating actions, and the personal meaning of these narrative features. During the design phase of the research process these formal theories are critical in biography and life story researchers' decisions.

Contemporary Biography and Life Story Research Design

Within contemporary biography and life story research design, researchers have to develop a clear stance on their view of the world as it pertains to studying lives. In addition, they have to create a research design with well-articulated research questions, and they must identify the most appropriate theoretical framework for studying a life. The **design methodology** and the **data collection methods** are often closely aligned in biography and life story research in their incorporation of the same view of the world and nature of knowledge. What distinguishes them is that methodology is a way of designing a study of lives and thinking about the intricacies and compelling dynamics of lives, whereas the methods are the procedures and tools used to collect and analyze biography and life story data. Biography and life story research methods are often diverse in that the choice of the particular data collection strategies and tools is dependent on what data and insights emerge about a life throughout the research process. In other words, in addition to choosing the research methods identified as part of the design methodology at the outset, the researcher typically adopts further appropriate methods or techniques throughout the entire process as needed.

Nature of Knowledge, Worldview, and Research Approach

Within all forms of research, having a well-specified and meaningful research design framework is critically important. Aligning worldview, driving theory, research questions, strategies of inquiry, and research methods is a daunting conceptual task. As with all strong designs in social scientific research, biography and life story research design begins with researchers' identifying the assumptions and worldview they bring to the research enterprise. Within the context of research design, **worldview** can be defined as a general orientation toward the world and beliefs about the nature of knowledge. This includes the following epistemological questions: What is knowledge? How is knowledge acquired? What do people know? How do we know what we know? (see Lincoln & Guba, 2000). Although it is often taken for granted, when researchers choose a particular research design and specific methods of data collection, they are adopting a view about the nature of knowledge and sometimes go so far as to suggest which types of knowledge are most valuable for advancing the knowledge base on a particular topic within a specific field (see Creswell, 2009). The worldview researchers adopt shapes their selection of either a quantitative, qualitative, or mixed research methodology, which in turn guides the types of specific research strategies and methods of inquiry they use to study a life.

Although the designs used in biography and life story research are variable in terms of the types of data collected, most tend to use a qualitative research approach. The researcher's selection of a qualitative research framework is a research design decision to focus on the language and meaning of people's constructions of their attitudes, experiences, beliefs, and emotions as the central units of analysis. In selecting this focus, the researcher is making a decision to adopt a worldview that includes a philosophy of **constructivism** about the nature of knowledge and human experience. Constructivism emphasizes that individuals reflect on their own experiences to construct an understanding of the world in which they live (Mahoney, 2004). In other words, individuals create subjective meanings of their experiences and the world that are negotiated within the social, cultural, and historical context in which their lives are embedded.

Biography and life story researchers do occasionally develop a research design that includes using a quantitative approach. However, when researchers include the collection of quantitative data in their research, this is most often done using a **mixed-methods design.** There are a range of definitions of mixed-methods design, but what all definitions have in common is that such a design blends quantitative and qualitative research approaches through mixing that occurs at various stages in the research process. For example, a researcher can decide to blend the methods at the data collection stage, collecting both types of data simultaneously, or can combine the methods within the results or discussion stage of the research process (Johnson, Onwuegbuzie, & Turner, 2007).

For example, Nasby and Read (1997) conducted a case study of Dodge Morgan, who in 1986 completed a solo circumnavigation of the world in 150 days. Their goal was to study Morgan's life and the experience of his voyage, as well as other dimensions of his personality. These researchers used a battery of valid and reliable psychological scales to measure personality traits, needs, motives, emotional predispositions and states, interpersonal adjustment, and cognitive abilities before he went on his voyage. In addition, they collected data on mood during the voyage and analyzed his life experiences, which they collected from Morgan's memoir and correspondence.

After the biography and life story researchers make these initial design decisions about worldview and their corresponding approach, theory selection and the development of well-articulated research questions are important next steps in the process of research design.

REFLECTION QUESTIONS

1. What are the characteristics of a constructivist worldview that make it appropriate for studies that seek to answer the typical research questions pursued with biography and life story research?
2. Why would it be useful to use a constructivist worldview to understand the life of your favorite musician?

Selection of Theory and Research Questions

In terms of psychology, most of the research questions that are developed within contemporary biography and life story research evolve from the theoretical underpinnings of various **narrative theories of personality.** There are some exceptions in which researchers focus more on classic theories of achievement motivation, power motivation, and intimacy motivation to guide their conduct of biography and life story research (see Smith, 1992). For example, Winter (1987, 1996) has examined theories of power motivation, the recurrent preference for having an impact on people's behaviors, by examining the lives and inaugural addresses of American presidents.

As was previously discussed, there are several general theoretical underpinnings that are associated with studying a life related to narrative, story, and time. Narrative theories of personality are more specific in nature and are defined as theories about the storied nature of lives that describe and explain individuals' capacity to narrate and interpret the meaning of their life experiences (Singer, 2004). The most frequently used narrative theories of personality employed in biography and life story research are script theory (Tomkins, 1979); the life-story model of identity (McAdams, 1985); self-defining memories (Singer & Salovey, 1993); and dialogical self theory (Hermans, 1988).

The specific narrative theory of personality the researcher decides to use in a study will lead to specific types of research questions, as well as the use of a particular biography and life story research methodology. For example, a researcher using McAdams's **life-story model of identity** (1985) would ask the following type of research question: *Is there continuity and change in individuals' internalized and evolving narrative of self over time?* (McAdams et al., 2006). His model explains that individuals living in modern societies construct and internalize integrative life narratives beginning during adolescence and continuing throughout the life course. From this perspective, McAdams views identity itself as a life story that integrates disparate roles and brings together the reconstructed past, perceived present, and anticipated future in order to provide the person with a purposeful identity in modern life as a **psychosocial construction.** These integrative life narratives or life stories reflect an individual's narrative understanding of self in culture, an understanding coauthored by the person and by cultural influences providing the historical, religious, ethical, economic, and political contexts within which the person's life is situated (McAdams, Reynolds, Lewis, Patten, & Bowman 2001). Psychosocial construction is a process that individuals use to integrate personal psychological and social experiences in developing their autobiographical memories and internalized narratives of self.

A second example of the influence of the nature of the narrative theory of personality on the researcher's development of research questions can be drawn from **self-defining memories** (Singer & Salovey, 1993). A self-defining memory is an autobiographical memory that is linked to the individual's most self-relevant and important long-term goals. These self-defining memories are distinguished from other types of memories based on the five criteria of vividness, emotional intensity, repetition, linkage to similar memories, and these memories' relationship to a person's enduring concerns or unresolved conflicts (Singer, 2005). A researcher interested in studying self-defining memories would ask the following type of research question: *What is the relationship of the meaning and content of self-defining memories and self-restraint, distress, and defensiveness?* (Blagov & Singer, 2004).

In sum, there are several important considerations that researchers must address when designing a study of lives. They must account for their worldview, select an appropriate theory about lives, and decide what important research questions they need to answer in their study. All of these design decisions will guide the researchers in selecting the data collection instruments and approaches to analyze the biography and life story data.

REFLECTION QUESTIONS

1. Based on your understanding of the theoretical underpinnings of biography and life story research, what are some examples of research questions that you could pursue in a biography and life story study in your discipline?
2. What are the most important self-defining memories of your life, and what makes them self-defining?

Data Collection Instruments and Analytic Approaches

Within biography and life story research design, researchers use a range of strategies of inquiry to collect and analyze data. The strategies and research instruments researchers select for data collection depend on the narrative specificity that the researcher is interested in capturing with respect to a person's life. **Narrative specificity** refers to the time frame of the life experience. For example, some biography and life story researchers are interested in an **event-specific life experience** that occurs in a particular time and place. In contrast, a **lifetime period experience** spans a period of time longer than a single event in a person's life. A person's summer vacation or freshman year during college would be considered a lifetime period experience, whereas a person's sixteenth birthday party would be an event-specific life experience (see Conway & Pleydell-Pearce, 2000).

The goals related to the narrative specificity of the biography and life story research are often linked to differences in the researcher's selection of unstructured and semistructured interview instruments. An **unstructured interview,** sometimes also called an open-ended interview, is one in which the researcher only asks the participant a few questions. Unstructured interviews begin with what Spradley (1979) calls a "grand tour question" (p. 87). No further question is necessary until the participant has said all that is to be said about the topic that is the subject of the grand tour question (Benard, 1988). In an unstructured interview the researcher is able to let the participant lead the interview by providing the general framework for how the participant thinks about his life, the language used to describe the life experiences, and the contexts in which the life unfolds. In contrast, a **semistructured interview** in biography and life story research uses a very detailed interview guide that focuses on life chapters, critical life episodes, or specific self-defining memories. Unlike with an unstructured interview format, within the semistructured interview the participant is not expected to move too far beyond the scope of discussion that is defined by the interview guide.

Data Collection Tools

There are several examples of data collection tools for biography and life story research that have been developed recently. The **Life Story Interview** was developed by Dan McAdams (1995/2008) at the Foley Center for the Study of Lives at Northwestern University. The interview instrument is a selective and semistructured storytelling tool. It is divided into several sections that ask the participant to identify a few key scenes, characters, and ideas in her life. The researcher asks the participant to describe the most important things that have happened in her life and how she imagines her life developing in the future. The interview begins with the participant thinking about her life as a book or novel. Then the participant develops a chapter title and describes briefly what each chapter is about.

Next the researcher asks the participant to focus on key scenes that stand out in her life story. A key scene or **critical life episode** is a type of event-specific life experience because it describes an event or specific incident that took place at a particular time and place in the person's life that stands out for a particular reason. It could stand out, for example, because it was especially good or bad, particularly vivid, important, or memorable. The critical life episodes included in the Life Story Interview are as follows: high point, low point, turning point, positive childhood memory, negative childhood memory, vivid adult memory, wisdom memory, religious/spiritual/mythical memory, and anticipated future script. The future script includes the person's construction of the next life chapter, dreams, hopes, plans for the future, life projects, challenges, personal ideology, life themes, and reflections. For each of the critical life episodes the participant is asked to describe in detail what happened, when and where it happened, who was involved, what the participant was thinking and feeling in the event, why this particular scene is important or significant in the participant's life, and what the scene says about the participant as a person.

Robert Atkinson (1998) at the Life Story Center developed a life story research method that is also called the Life Story Interview. This method is not better than the Life Story Interview developed by McAdams; it is simply different in that it is an unstructured interview guided by only one question: *"Where would you like to start the story of your life?"* Atkinson's method of asking only one question is informed by his own conceptualization of a life story. He defines the life story as a fairly complete narrating of a person's entire experience of life as a whole. Moreover, Atkinson's method allows the person to construct both event-specific life experiences as well as general lifetime period experiences throughout the interview because no specific instructions are provided to only construct nuclear episodes, like they are in McAdams's Life Story Interview.

James Birren at California State University at Fullerton developed the guided autobiography method, largely influenced by his interest and pioneering work in adult development that established the field of gerontology (Birren & Deutchman, 1991). His **guided autobiography** is a semistructured method for life review that incorporates individual and group experiences with autobiographical writing. Birren uses a ten-week course to execute his guided autobiography method with adults. The course is structured using group work that a trained professional leads. The leader engages the group in a general discussion that includes posing questions as well as developing insights on individuals' writing of their life story. The trained professional also introduces concepts related to self-awareness and human development to the group. In each large group session, the researcher introduces one of nine themes and sensitizing questions to assist individuals in the recall of memories related to the theme. The themes include the following topics:

1. Major branching points in the life course
2. Family
3. The role of money in life
4. Major life work or career
5. Health and body
6. Sexual identity
7. Experiences with and ideas about death, spiritual life
8. Values
9. Goals and aspirations

In addition to the group session format, there is individual work in which each person writes two pages of personal history related to the theme or focus for the week. This individual assignment is followed by small group work in which each group participant reads the two pages, as well as gives supportive feedback and receives such feedback from group participants.

The guided autobiography instrument developed by McAdams (1997) both builds on his Life Story Interview and uses the same name as Birren's guided autobiography method. This semistructured instrument is designed to sample critical life episodes. The researcher asks the person to construct his own autobiography as the selective story of his life as he understands it in the past, present, and anticipated future. These critical life episodes are similar to those in McAdams's Life Story Interview and include the following topics:

1. Peak experience
2. Nadir (low) experience
3. Turning point experience
4. Earliest memory
5. Childhood experience
6. Adolescent experience
7. A morality experience
8. Important experiences of critical decisions
9. Future goals

However, unlike Birren's guided autobiography method, McAdams's guided autobiography instrument only engages a single person rather than a group. The instrument emphasizes the selective nature of this storytelling; many different events, characters, happenings, and themes of the person's life will be left out using this method. Like the Life Story Interview, the guided autobiography instrument asks the person to describe in detail what happened, when and where it happened, who was involved, what the person was thinking and feeling in the event, why this particular scene is important or significant in the person's life, and what the scene says about the participant as a person. These features of the method focusing on event-specific life experiences reflect the instrument's semistructured nature.

In yet another approach, the **Self-Defining Memory Task** was developed by Jefferson Singer and Kathie Moffitt (1991) at Connecticut College. As previously discussed in this chapter, self-defining memories capture emotional experiences. They are vivid, affectively charged, repetitive, and linked to other similar memories. They are also connected to an important theme of enduring concern in a person's life story. The Self-Defining Memory Task can be administered in either written or oral form. As part of this task the researcher collects at least five to ten memories from the participant. The task includes two stages. The participant is first asked to imagine an intimate moment with another person in which he divulges an important experience from his past that he feels provides particular insight into who he is as a person and what is most important to him. After constructing these self-defining memories, the participant rates each memory for the current emotional responses on twelve emotions and also indicates the intensity of the memories. These emotions include happiness, sadness, anger, fear, surprise, shame, disgust, guilt, interest, embarrassment, and contempt, and pride. The participant rates the intensity of the emotion associated with a memory in terms of its importance—whether or not the memory is self-defining or difficult to recall. The participant also rates the intensity by indicating the vividness of the memory in terms of the his having a visual image, sound, taste, touch, and smell associated with the particular memory. The memory emotion is important because positive emotional responses to memories have been linked in previous research to better psychological well-being, whereas negative emotional responses have been associated with distress (Blagov & Singer, 2004).

The **Identity and Success Life Story Method (ISLSM)** is a case study research method developed by Cynthia Winston at Howard University in the Identity and Success Research Lab (Winston, Philip, & Lloyd, 2007). The ISLSM is designed to guide an in-depth study of a person's life through the collection of multiple sources of evidence (see Figure 5.1). This method adopts a psychological, person-centered approach. The ISLSM incorporates several strategies of inquiry and research methods, including guided autobiography, survey, trait, and interview methods. More specifically, the ISLSM includes the following tools to acquire a rich understanding of a person's life: the Guided Race Autobiography, the Life Story Telling, the Developmental Success Matrix, the NEO Personality Inventory, the Identity and Success Survey, strategic interviews, and personal artifacts and documents. The ISLSM method was developed initially to study the identities, achievement motivation, psychology of success, and lives of African American scientists and engineers. It has also been used to create educationally and culturally relevant online learning environments that are psychologically accessible and beneficial for African American students and their non–African American peers in their schools, as well as for teachers and parents to learn more about lives and the psychological meaning of race experiences within racialized societies.

FIGURE 5.1 Identity and Success Life Story Method

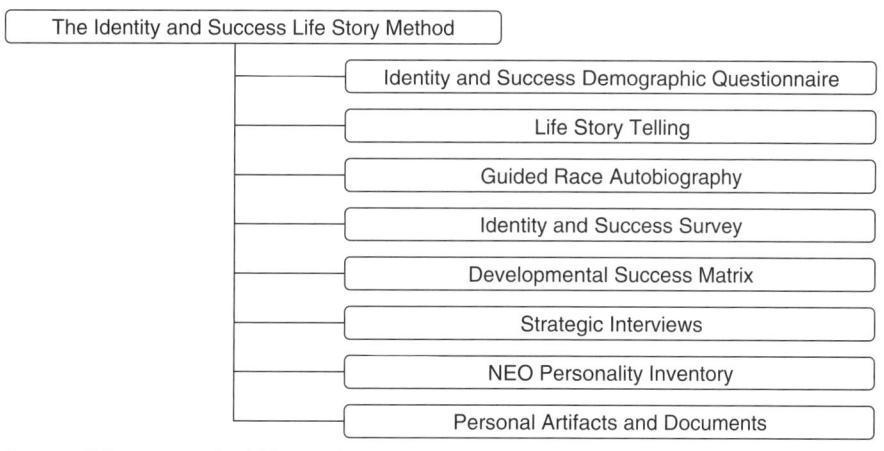

- The Identity and Success Life Story Method
  - Identity and Success Demographic Questionnaire
  - Life Story Telling
  - Guided Race Autobiography
  - Identity and Success Survey
  - Developmental Success Matrix
  - Strategic Interviews
  - NEO Personality Inventory
  - Personal Artifacts and Documents

Source: Winston et al., 2007, p. 34.

The **Guided Race Autobiography (GRA)** was developed by Burford and Winston (2005) to elicit autobiographical memories of race experiences across critical life episodes. It is one of the research instruments within the life story method that is novel and can be used independently from the ISLSM. The GRA, adapted from McAdams's guided autobiography instrument (1997), is a semistructured thematic tool. It is designed to elicit the construction of autobiographical narratives, based on six critical life episodes that reflect the meaning of race in each participant's life. These critical life episodes include the earliest memory of race, a childhood experience of race, an experience of race during adolescence, a peak experience of race, a nadir experience of race, and a turning point experience of race.

The Life Story Telling (LST) is an unstructured instrument that is designed to elicit a selective and free-flowing reconstruction of participants' life story. The LST is largely based on both McAdams's Life Story Interview (1995) and Atkinson's Life Story Interview (1998). As part of a selective life story reconstruction, participants do not tell the researcher about everything that has ever happened. Instead, the researcher encourages them to focus on what is important and significant about how they came to be. By design, this open-ended approach leads to a free association of thoughts, deep introspective sharing of experiences, and construction of multiple narratives. The LST is not guided by specific, ready-to-ask questions. The first and only question in the LST is "Where do you want to begin the story of your life?"

The Developmental Success Matrix (DSM) is a three-column matrix designed to stimulate participants to think about success across the life span. Using the DSM, participants include the names of as many people as they can remember who have contributed to their success in either positive or negative ways.

The NEO Personality Inventory is an assessment that is widely used within the field of psychology to measure personality traits that delineate personality structure. Guided by the five-factor model of personality (McCrae & Costa, 1999), the NEO measures the following five major dimensions of personality: (1) neuroticism, (2) extraversion, (3) openness, (4) agreeableness, and (5) conscientiousness. Each personality dimension is composed of several underlying and specific traits that further define the structure of personality.

The Identity and Success Survey includes compilations of validated and widely used measures within the field of psychology, as well as new open-ended survey questions about the psychology of race, racism, and success. The constructs that are measured include achievement motivation, ego identity, racial and ethnic monoracial and biracial identity, phenotypic variation, personal strivings, gender role stereotypes, and mental health symptomology.

Several strategic interviews are conducted as part of the Identity and Success Life Story Method. These strategic interviews are semistructured and designed to stimulate participants to talk in depth about specific life experiences and contexts of their development. For some participants there is considerable overlap between what is discussed in the Life Story Telling and the strategic interviews. However, participants are encouraged to continue discussing a topic, if it is relevant, even if it has been previously discussed. Topics within the strategic interviews include professional interests, educational experiences, interpersonal relationships, life interests, achievement motivation, influences on success, and the intersections of the meanings of race and gender within American society and culture. After the strategic interview, personal documents and artifacts are also collected from the participants. These documents and objects are selected by the participants and most often relate to what they discussed in their interviews as salient life experiences that shaped their identity and success. Some of the more rare documents that participants have included are certificates of their African ancestry along with their DNA sequences related to their ancestry. These participants are African Americans who have traced their African ancestry using a new service offered by African Ancestry (www.africanancestry.com) and who believe that the discovery of the specific African country and ethnic group with whom they share ancestry provides a life-transformative sense of their identity. The participants describe the inclusion of these documents as part of their life story as reflecting their identity and values. This is very similar to how people from other cultures preserve and share their family coat of arms or family crest as a key feature of the family story passed from one generation to the next.

Data Recording

Given the types of data that are collected using many of these life story research methods, a number of researchers use audio and video digital recording devices for data collection. The increasing availability and personal use of digital recording devices make this a particularly appealing medium for data collection for researchers, who in the past often used paper and pencil or cassette recording devices to collect the data.

There are some complexities, however, that biography and life story researchers face in using these types of devices. It is important for the researcher to consider which digital tools should be used for data collection and to think through all phases of the research process at the beginning of the project. For instance, once the data are collected, the size of the files, access to such backup devices as computers or external drives, and software availability for downloading will be important considerations for working with these data. These decisions can have a significant impact on the quality, timing, and feasibility of the data processing and data analysis stages in biography and life story research. Computers with older operating systems, for example, may not download video clips collected using newer video cameras. This can cause a problem for a researcher who has already collected data without testing the compatibility of the available hardware and software for the data analysis phase in the research process.

REFLECTION QUESTIONS

1. Compare and contrast the structure of McAdams's (1995/2008) and Atkinson's (1998) Life Story Interviews. What do you think the strengths and weaknesses are of each for conducting a research project on one of the oldest relatives in your family—a grandparent, aunt, or uncle?
2. How could a teacher use life story data collected from his students to increase the quality of the teaching and learning in his classroom? What types of life story questions would be important for the teacher to ask students? Would unstructured or semistructured life story instruments be most useful?

Data Processing

Processing of biography and life story data can be complicated. One of the characteristics of biography and life story data is that they are massive. Biography and life story researchers often create a protocol or set of procedures for data processing either during the research design phase of the project or once the data are collected. Hours of interviewing, for example, can create large audio and video files. The researcher's decision to use a video camera to collect data can be influenced by the availability of computing hardware and software. Having enough capacity to back up, process, and store the data can be a challenge for the novice researcher and even for the seasoned researcher who is accustomed to the simplicities of pencil-and-paper data collection methods. This is particularly a problem in research that includes multiple life story cases or large numbers of critical life episodes.

After data collection the researcher uploads, backs up, and stores the data in a secure location. This security entails protection of computer files of the downloaded video, audio, and transcribed data, as well as hard copy file security. One simple level of security for computer files of transcripts that biography and life story researchers use is to password-protect each file using the word processing program. If the life story research is being conducted in a team, it is important to make sure that the password is shared among all researchers who need access to the data. A consultation with a computer expert can be useful in trying to determine the size of potential audio and video files appropriate for the research design and to identify the need for additional hardware and software to complete the biography and life story project.

Another important element in the data processing of some forms of biography and life story research is masking and identification. In psychobiography research, the subject of the research is typically a person who is famous and identified by name in the publication. Therefore, creating identification transformations is not necessary. However, masking the identification of all of the actors the participant includes in the story may be necessary to meet the standards of ethics required by review boards for protection of human subjects, particularly with respect to the anonymity and confidentiality of the biography and life story data (see Chapter Two). **Masking** is a process that the researcher uses to transform the identities of persons and places represented in collected verbal data. Included in this masking process is the renaming of the storyteller and other persons mentioned by name using pseudonyms. A **pseudonym** is a fictitious name that the researcher assigns in the data processing phase to conceal the identity of the storyteller of the life story and, in some cases, other persons in the life story.

A very tedious element of data processing in biography and life story research is the transcription of audio and video life story materials into a word-processed document. **Transcription** is the verbatim translation of audio or video data into a written text document, usually completed with a word processing software application. The researcher can use multiple transcription methods, such as the widely used **Jeffersonian method** (Jefferson, 2004). This method is designed to guide the researcher to produce a transcript that is comprehensive, exhaustive, and verbatim, regardless of whether the speech contains fragments and incorrect grammar. It is important that the transcriber attempt to be as accurate as possible and transcribe how the words sound, even if they are not spoken within the conventions of Standard English. For this reason, one of the key features of the Jeffersonian transcription is a coding system of symbols that can be used in transcription to denote certain types of language features, including pauses, the use of "um," and other incomplete thoughts.

After the researcher has collected and processed the data, the next phase in the research process is data analysis. For many biography and life story researchers, informal analysis of the data begins when they first learn about the life during data collection. However, the data processing stage provides the researcher with the data in a form that is easier to work with to make systematic, reliable, and grounded interpretations.

Data Analytic Methods

Given the complexity of a life, the researcher has to approach the interpretation phase in the research process with an open mind, ready to learn new things about the person and the particularities of the life. Different theorists have very different perspectives on interpretation, and there are no explicit principles within the field to guide biography and life story researchers through the interpretation process. In general, **interpretation** is a process in which researchers engage that requires them to make sense of the data within the context of the historical, cultural, and relational context of the lived experience. Interpretation also includes the process of representing the data in another written form that describes and summarizes the core elements of how the researchers make sense of the data. Beyond this general conceptualization of the interpretation process are varying definitions, perspectives, and approaches used by researchers who work with data that are in the form of text (see Denzin, 2000). Given this variability and the challenge of the iterative process of interpretation, Denzin describes interpretation as an art. As a form of art, interpretation extends the role of the researcher as one of the data collection instruments to one of engaging in intensive critical thinking and grounded reasoning in an effort to make sense of the lived experience from the perspective of the person whose life is the subject of investigation.

General Analytic Mind-Set
In many ways biography and life story researchers adopt an analytic mind-set in which they engage throughout data analysis and the writing phases of the research process. That mind-set includes a constant striving to understand the meaning of experiences for the person living the life. Although it is difficult to construct a precise definition, **meaning** is a form of interpretation. The act of meaning-making requires the researcher to interpret the significance and sense of words, experiences, and symbols that emerge within the many episodes in the participant's life. When the participant negotiates and renegotiates meaning, she engages in a mental transaction in grappling with a pallet of representative symbols. This is precisely what the researcher is trying to uncover in the process of interpretation of the life story data. Meaning is personally and culturally shaped by the way people view themselves, others, and the world in which they live (Bruner, 1990).

> People construct and tell stories to make sense of their lives in time. These stories help people to find some degree of unity and purpose in life. But the stories also express variability, multiplicity, and flux. Any good interpretation, therefore, must strike a balance between coherence and complexity. Human lives are neither neat nor random. A life story will present certain unifying and integrating features of psychological individuality, providing a clear window into how some things fit together nicely, into a coherent pattern. But a life story will also present ideas that do not fit into any simple form. (McAdams, 2009, p. 473)

In biography and life story research, data analysis varies largely based on the units of analysis dictated by the data collection method or methods employed and by the specific research questions of the investigation. Most often the unit of analysis is a narrative. It can be a single life episode or life memory, as is the case when a researcher uses Singer and Moffitt's Self-Defining Memory Task (1991) or McAdams's guided autobiography instrument (1997). Bamberg (2004) calls this narrative unit of analysis a small story. It contains a beginning, middle, and end. In addition, it has the following narrative features: an abstract, an orientation that includes the setting and characters, a complicating action or plot that explains the reason for the telling of the story, an evaluation, a resolution, and a coda (Labov, 1972; Riessman, 1993). The other typical unit of analysis in biography and life story research is the whole life. Atkinson's Life Story Interview and psychobiographies are examples of methods that are typically subject to whole life data analysis. Although the researcher may select key episodes in the life story to analyze, what distinguishes the whole life data analysis is that the researcher is focused on trying to interpret the life as a whole.

The processes researches follow for making inferences from the verbal material in biography and life story research range in scope from sticking closely to the storyteller's words to departing significantly, as is often done in psychoanalytic approaches that look for latent or hidden content that is not necessarily obvious. There is a range of interpretive questions that a researcher can ask about a life that will also influence the scope of the inference. For example, a **discourse analytic question** within a biography and life story study would ask the following types of research questions:

- *What is the storyteller trying to accomplish by describing her life or a life episode of memory in a particular way?*

- *Is the person using language to position herself as a victim to the sexism pervasive in her experience?*

- *Is she trying to justify choices she made in her life?*

Another example of a biography and life story question using a **psychodynamic approach** is as follows:

- *What is the unconscious drive that underlies the storyteller's selecting this particular experience?*

An example of a biography and life story cultural psychology question about the meaning of race within the lives of people living in racialized societies is as follows:

- *What are the types of race experiences the person has in critical life episodes, and what do these experiences mean in the development of the person's internalized and evolving narrative of self?*

In sum, biography and life story researchers adopt a general orientation to the data and to answering specific types of questions when beginning to interpret those data. Researchers then join this general orientation with more specific approaches and analytic techniques to complete the process of data analysis.

Data Analytic Approaches

There are several types of approaches for interpretation of data that researchers have used in historical and contemporary biography and life story research. A data analytic approach is a more general orientation toward making sense of the data, which is in contrast to specific types of analytic methods that include specified procedures and coding frameworks for data interpretation (see Chapter Three). Historically in biography and life story research researchers have adopted various approaches to interpreting data, whereas more contemporary researchers focus on more specified methods and coding schemes for analysis.

The psychodynamic approach, grounded in Freud's psychoanalytic method (1940/1949), has had the most profound influence on methods of interpreting lives. Here the researcher searches for hidden meanings in the manifest content of everyday life. For example, Freud conducted a famous case study of a woman named Dora. Within this study, Dora described to Freud a dream she had about a jewel case. Freud's interpretation was that her dream was not really about the jewel case per se. Instead he believed that her dream had a hidden meaning and was about conflicts between Dora and her father during childhood and adolescence. Like Freud, Jung (1961) interpreted the dreams within an individual's life as having hidden meaning about that person's life. Rather than emphasizing hidden meaning related to sex and aggression like Freud did, Jung approached interpretation with an emphasis on universal themes, heroic conquests, the collective unconscious, and archetypes.

In contrast to researchers' espousal of the psychodynamic approaches to life interpretation, Stewart (1994) adopts a feminist approach to the interpretation of the lives of women. This approach is largely a response to the tendency for biographies and life stories to value and focus on White men whose various political, intellectual, artistic, and religious achievements have made them famous. Stewart advocates for researchers to use seven principles in interpreting life stories of women, each focusing specifically on the relations between identity, power, and societal roles. These principles direct researchers to do the following (McAdams, 2009; Stewart, 1994):

1. Look for what has been left out

2. Analyze their own roles and positions as they impact understanding the research process

3. Identify women's agency in the midst of social constraint

4. Use gender as an analytic tool

5. Be sensitive to the ways in which gender defines power relationships

6. Identify other significant elements of an individual's social position

7. Be suspicious of psychological perspectives that stem from experiences of the male elite

The approaches that have been described here are more specific than the general mind-set adopted by biography and life story researchers. And yet there is another level of analytic specificity in which biography and life story researchers engage when they interpret their data. **Thematic content analysis** is a form of interpretation that requires the researcher to engage in an iterative process of critical thinking, questioning, and categorizing. It can more simply be defined as a method of analysis for coding or scoring verbal materials to make inferences about characteristics and experiences of persons, social groups, or historical periods (Smith, 1992). The focus of the thematic content analysis should be guided by the specific research question or subquestions that guide the biography and life story study. The primary analytic goal in thematic content analysis is to make inferences from verbal material, analyzed in the form of text in written transcripts. In the context of thematic content analysis, an **inference** is a conclusion that the researcher develops from systematic thinking and reasoning about the meaning of the narrative data that are the subject of analysis.

Thematic content analysis is a method that has been widely used within the field of psychology, especially in the study of motivation and other dimensions of personality (see Smith, 1992). The thematic aspect connotes analysis of verbal material that is storied and has relatively comprehensive units of analysis or combinations of categories. A key component in thematic content analysis is **thought sampling,** which was developed by Murray (1943). Murray's idea was that the themes selected by individuals represent their characteristic sense of self and meaning within the cultural contexts of their lives. Given his interest, Murray primarily applied this idea of thought sampling to unconscious drives. But the basic idea has been extended to thematic content analysis more generally.

Some of the best and most widely used coding schemes for conducting thematic content analysis are detailed and include interpretive procedures for working with life story material from beginning to end. Smith (1992) edited a volume that includes over twenty thematic content analysis coding systems that are empirically derived, refined, and validated to assess the characteristics of persons and social groups. Stewart, Franz, and Layton (1988) developed a coding technique to analyze expressions of preoccupation with aspects of the adult self in personal documents and retrospective autobiographical writings of Vera Britten, a famous British writer, feminist, and pacifist who was born in the late

1800s. The focus of this original analysis was on the themes of identity, intimacy, and generativity, or the concern for and commitment to the well-being of future generations (McAdams & Logan, 2004). This analysis primarily draws on Erikson's theory of psychosocial development (1968). Further, Winter (1973) developed a coding scheme for analyzing power motivation in stories. Finally, McAdams has developed several coding systems to conduct thematic content analysis for themes of agency and communion, contamination sequences, and redemption sequences that are available on the Web site of the Foley Center for the Study of Lives at Northwestern University (see a complete list of relevant Web sites at the end of this chapter).

Winston and her graduate students (2007) in the Identity and Success Research Lab (ISRL) developed a thematic content analysis coding scheme to analyze the narrative experience and meaning of autobiographical memories of race (Burford, 2005). This thematic content analysis research method is designed to categorize the experiences constructed in oral and written autobiographical race narratives. Although this coding scheme was originally developed to analyze data collected by researchers using the Guided Race Autobiography, it can be used for analyzing any type of narrative and life story data. This method of analysis involves describing and interpreting the essence of the race experiences that individuals construct in narratives. Race is defined within this method as a psychological experience based on phenotypic variation in skin color, hair texture, facial features, as well as shared cultural-historical experiences associated with racial group membership within racialized societies (Winston & Winston, in press). The aim of this narrative analysis process is essentially to answer the following types of interpretive questions: *What are the experiences constructed in autobiographical memories of race about? In other words, what is the essence or nature of the experience that is constructed? How do the experiences relate to the universe of psychological and life experiences? Or, what is the universe of meaning of the experience, that is, the larger context in which the experience is embedded and made meaningful within the life?*

This coding scheme includes over thirty-five themes that were empirically derived from a collection of graduate student pilot studies conducted in ISRL (Burford, 2005; Mangum, 2006; Terry, 2008). Many of the themes capture ideas from existing theories about the psychological significance of race, including but not limited to the following: triple quandary theory (Boykin, 1986); Manichean psychology theory (Harrell, 1999); universal context of racism theory (Jones, 2003); whiteness theory (Lewis, 2004); and Nigresence theory (Cross, 1991). Cultural racism, racial pride, racial mistrust, interracial relationships, race shame, race attribution, multicultural validation, race progress, spirituality, and race stereotype exception are examples of some of the themes included in this thematic content analysis coding scheme. This coding scheme is available on the ISRL Web site.

Most of the thematic content analysis coding systems described here have been empirically derived, either inductively or deductively. Some biography and life story researchers use these schemes for deductive analysis, whereas others continue to inductively develop their own coding schemes or alter the existing ones as new themes emerge from their own inductive process. One challenge biography and life story researchers face in developing and using thematic content analysis coding schemes is determining the optimal way to achieve reliability and validity.

> **REFLECTION QUESTION**
>
> 1. Develop a data processing guide for a life story and biography research project, based on the following questions:
>   a. What is the research question that guides your study?
>   b. How many hours do you think it would take to construct your life story using one of the life story methods of data collection described in this chapter?
>   c. What kind of digital device do you prefer to use to collect data and why?
>   d. What kind of software is needed to download the data to your computer, and what are the minimum system requirements?

The Meaning of Reliability and Validity

Biography and life story research has been criticized for being too subjective as a form of research science. It has been characterized as too unwieldy and without a set of established and agreed-on methodological procedures. The defenders claim that biography and life story methods are of value because they are the best way to study the whole person, which was the fundamental goal of personality psychology during the 1930s at its founding. Sarbin (1986) also defends these methods by arguing that narrative is the root metaphor for the entire field of psychology.

There are some ways in which biography and life story researchers think about issues of the trustworthiness and usefulness of their research design, data collection methods, and analytic strategies of inquiry. Many of the ways these researchers think about reliability and validity are shaped by the arguments that scholars have made about the need to define reliability and validity differently in qualitative research (Anfara, Brown, & Mangione, 2002; Golafshani, 2003).

A key idea related to **external validity** has to do with **representativeness.** Within biography and life story research, representativeness can be thought of in terms of the appropriateness and completeness of the researcher's sampling design. A biography and life story researcher can engage in sampling among a group of individuals as well as sampling of topics and situations that the participant has conveyed to be important in making sense of her life (Brunswik, 1956; Dukes, 1965). In contrast, an experiment most often samples a single situation that is subject to the manipulation inherent in the experimental design. Thought sampling is another example of how external validity can be conceptualized within biography and life story research. This refers to sampling from within the set of life story data the thoughts that are representative of the general pattern of thinking of the individual about the meaning of his life. This form of thought sampling was described previously as part of the thematic content analysis process by which the researcher searches the life story data to understand and interpret the participant's characteristic sense of self and meaning within the cultural contexts of life.

Internal validity is often considered in terms of **narrative truth** (Schafer, 1981; Spence, 1982). This is the idea that a good interpretation of a life is linked to standards of a "good story," which includes its being internally coherent. In addition to coherence, McAdams (2009) also describes "openness, credibility, differentiation, reconciliation, and generative integration" (p. 423) as characteristics of a good story. Narrative truth extends the meaning of "truth" beyond the correspondence of objective facts of a life story event. In other words, the truth is not just what happened within the person's life in her story construction (scholars sometimes call this **historical truth**). The truth and internal consistency are also reflected in how the person felt about the experience when it was happening and how the person feels about it in the present (Rouse, 1978).

Another consideration of validity within biography and life story research is related to generalizability. By design, biography and life story research produces rich contextualized data. As such, these data provide opportunities for scholars not only to test existing theories but also to develop theories informed by meaning and human experience contextualized within a life. From this perspective the goal of the researcher is to use the life story data to make **theoretical generalizations,** which are generalized statements for which interpretive evidence can be found in the life story data.

The issues related to reliability and validity of life story data are complicated. Biography and life story researchers who disseminate their research in peer-reviewed journals that typically do not publish this type of research often are criticized by peer reviewers because of the ways in which validity and reliability are established within biography and life story research. This marks another of the many complexities inherent in the process of producing rich and thick descriptions of lives and their meaning. Nonetheless, biography and life story researchers have been successful in broadly disseminating their research in some peer-reviewed journals.

Dissemination of Findings

Biography and life story research is scientifically and practically useful for dissemination. Scholars employ several formats to write a biography and life story research report, making this research methodology beneficial for multiple types of audiences. These formats include journal articles, books written as biographies for both the general reader and the scholar, and book chapters in theory and methods handbooks. This range allows for the general reader to gain insight into the psychology of lives, and for a professional to gain theoretical knowledge as well as some technical insight into the practice of therapy, healing, and liberation. Disseminated biography and life story findings are also useful as case materials for professional development with teachers, as well as professionals in social work and psychology.

Well-developed biography and life story protocols guided by strong theoretical and methodological research design can also be disseminated in the form of coding systems and data protocols that serve as methodological guides for researchers to use in future biography and life story studies. The data collection instruments used in biography and life story research have practical applicability as another form of dissemination. For example, the Identity and Success Life Story Method has been used for life coaching with individuals, as well as in executive coaching and leadership development within corporations (see www.winstonsynergy.com).

Life stories have several useful functions for enhancing the lived experience. For example, life stories entertain, inform, and heal, and they also integrate and convey the overall purpose and meaning of a human life. In fact, most of clinical and counseling psychology practice is characterized by the professional's working with the client to engage in a process of storying and retelling the whole life or critical life episodes.

Summary

The majority of the most influential theories in the field of psychology had their origins in biography and life story research. Historically, biography and life story research has been a form of single case study research, although more contemporary research uses multiple cases as well as critical life episodes collected from a large number of participants. The goal of this research method can be theory development or testing theory and the development of general concepts about persons and lives. Steps followed in biography and life story research vary across researchers; a few scholars have developed data collection tools, analytic methods, and coding schemes that are guided by thematic content analysis and are widely available on the Internet.

As the field of psychology rethinks its core curriculum, undergraduate education, and the adoption of the goal to produce psychologically literate citizens among all liberal arts majors (see Halpern, 2009), the inclusion of biography and life story methods should be considered. As described in this chapter, biography and life story research provides a rich understanding of human agency, intentionality, human experiences, and lives. This is the heart of psychology as a human and social science and is particularly important given the centrality of understanding lives for all the professions in which these students are preparing to work. It will be the novice biography and life story scholars of today from across all disciplines who will ensure that these research designs are included and valued within researchers' methodological tool kit. As society becomes even more scientifically, technologically, and economically complex and diverse, this approach for understanding lives, culture, and meaning will become increasingly in demand (see Mack, Rankins, & Winston, in press). The question will be, Who will be ready to answer the call for more biography and life story research?

Key Terms

agency, 112
biography and life story research, 107
constructivism, 113
critical life episode, 117
data collection methods, 112
design methodology, 112
discourse analytic question, 127

event-specific life experience, 116
external validity, 132
guided autobiography, 118
Guided Race Autobiography (GRA), 121
historical truth, 132
human individuality, 111

Identity and Success Life Story Method (ISLSM), 120
idiographic approach, 109
inference, 129
internal validity, 132
interpretation, 125
Jeffersonian method, 125
life course perspective, 112
Life Story Interview, 117

life-story model of identity, 115
lifetime period experience, 116
masking, 124
meaning, 126
mixed-methods design, 113
narrative mode of thought, 111
narrative specificity, 116
narrative theories of personality, 114
narrative truth, 132
nomothetic approach, 109
paradigmatic mode of thought, 111
person-centered psychology, 109
personology, 109
pseudonym, 124
psychobiography, 110
psychodynamic approach, 127
psychosocial construction, 115
representativeness, 132
Self-Defining Memory Task, 119
self-defining memories, 115
semistructured interview, 117
storied thought, 112
temporal order, 112
thematic content analysis, 129
theoretical generalizations, 132
thought sampling, 129
transcription, 125
unstructured interview, 116
worldview, 113

Further Readings and Resources

Suggested Biography and Life Story Research Studies

Bamberg, M. (2004). Form and functions of "slut bashing" in male identity constructions in 15-year-olds. *Human Development, 47,* 331–353.

This journal article provides a good example of why and how researchers conduct discourse analysis of data about life story episodes.

Nasby, W., & Read, N. (1997). The life voyage of a solo circumnavigator: Integrating theoretical and methodological perspectives. *Journal of Personality, 65,* 785–1068.

This journal article provides a good example of a life story study that includes a mixed-methods approach to studying a single life. It also is one of the few case studies about a life that makes up an entire special issue of a journal.

Other Suggested Readings

McAdams, D. P. (2001). The psychology of life stories. *Review of General Psychology, 5,* 100–122.

This journal article is the most comprehensive source describing the theoretical orientation of life story research as grounded in other subareas of psychology.

Schultz, W. T. (2007). *Handbook of psychobiography*. New York: Oxford University Press.
This handbook provides a collection of psychobiographies, as well as some practical discussion about what psychobiographies are and why researchers are interested in conducting them.

Smith, C. P. (Ed.). (1992). *Motivation and personality: Handbook of thematic content analysis*. New York: Cambridge University Press.
This handbook provides the most comprehensive description available in a single volume of personality and motivation coding schemes and their theoretical background.

Organizations and Web Sites

Birren Center for Autobiography and Life Review (www.guidedautobiography.com)
The site describes and provides access to information about guided autobiography projects, products, events, and courses.

Center for Narrative Research (www.uel.ac.uk/cnr/forthcom.htm)
This site includes papers, seminars, workshops, and projects being conducted throughout the world on narrative. It also explains the mission of this center, which is located at the University of East London.

Foley Center for the Study of Lives (www.sesp.northwestern.edu/foley)
This Web site describes the work of an interdisciplinary research center led by Dan McAdams at Northwestern University to study psychological and social development in adulthood. The site includes access to multiple life story data collection instruments, including the Life Story Interview and guided autobiography, as well as numerous coding schemes for analyzing life story data.

Identity and Success Research Laboratory (http://web.mac.com/cwinston.isrl)
This site includes narrative and life story projects, courses, presentations, and data collection and analysis instruments.

Life Story Center at the University of Maine (http://webapp.usm.maine.edu/LifeStories)
This site includes a life story archive and resources, as well as mechanisms for individuals to create their own life story.

Psychobiography (www.psychobiography.com)
This site describes the historical and contemporary uses of psychobiography. It also provides an annual annotated bibliography of psychobiographies.

CHAPTER 6

MYSTERY SOLVED: DETECTIVE SKILLS AND THE HISTORIAN'S CRAFT

Laurie Moses Hines

Key Ideas

- The historian's craft is the method of collecting, analyzing, and interpreting information as a way to understand the past.

- Historians select specific questions or topics that may fill a gap in historical knowledge, reconsider how existing data are interpreted, or examine current policies.

- The foci of historical studies and the worldview of a historian provide guidance in determining which primary and secondary sources to consider when doing history.

- There are multiple categories of history and various philosophies of history that shape the story a historian creates.

Mysteries, detective stories, and whodunits remain well-liked forms of American entertainment, especially their current high-tech versions, such as the popular *C.S.I.* series of television dramas. In this new crop of investigative stories, science (either through criminal or medical forensics), intelligence (often gathered with the use of high-tech gadgetry), and pluck (that heady combination of luck and tenacity of central characters) solve the episode's mystery. Typically the characters of these dramas piece together the who's, what's, how's, and why's of crimes, and as the hour unfolds viewers come to see more clearly the puzzle as it is filled in with each piece of detail. These investigative shows hold our attention because we begin to guess or make assumptions about the who's, what's, how's, and why's of the crime, and we watch until the final moments because we want to see if our detective skills have correctly pieced together the puzzle. We become armchair detectives or, in today's modern lingo, forensic experts, without having to do the hard work of digging for information.

Embedded into each episode of these highly entertaining shows is the assumption that science and technology are accurate and practically fail-safe. Investigators become temporarily derailed because of human error in misinterpreting the science, handling the evidence, or becoming blinded by emotion. By the show's end, however, the characters have a breakthrough perception that allows them to see accurately the true story behind the mystery. They have figured out those who's, what's, how's, and why's. The story is clear; the mystery is solved; the case is closed.

History, as an academic discipline and a craft, shares a lot with these investigative dramas and with detective stories generally. Historians try to figure out the who's, what's, when's, where's, how's, and why's of earlier times. They use as much objective science as possible—usually by building on prior knowledge of the past, by adhering to certain standards in collecting and analyzing documents, and sometimes by using statistical models to help understand phenomena. Historians also mine intelligence by digging through old documents, following clues and trails to other historical materials, and attempting to be as thorough as possible in seeking out sources of information so that they can see the puzzle in all its entirety. And just like the characters in investigative dramas, historians also rely on pluck. For instance, there are many examples of historians happening on a document or a treasure trove of sources that leads to exciting, new historical knowledge. (Dusty closets and attics, and file cabinets destined for dumpsters, are only three examples from my own experience of places in which sources have been found and salvaged.) Just like those television detectives, historians also have hunches they follow—sometimes leading to dead ends and sometimes leading to insights. And, little by little, the past becomes clearer to historians, although it often takes months or even years of painstaking research rather than the hour-long episode to solve a puzzle.

Historians and detectives in investigative dramas part ways, however, on a key element, besides the dashing looks and charming smiles we see on television. Historians rarely close a case. Why? Because history is not about a story as much as it is about interpretation and analysis. And interpretation and analysis, at their heart, are subjective. They rely on historians making specific judgments about the who's, what's, how's, and why's. Although historians try as hard as possible to be as true as possible to the past—to capture the past as accurately as possible—the history historians write is always open to reinterpretation. Perhaps new data and sources are found. Perhaps relationships between historical actors are seen in a novel light. Perhaps a new way to interpret historical events and data is considered. All these things may change the interpretation and analysis of history—in essence, changing our view of the past. The case, then, is never completely closed.

This is what we will explore here: the approaches historians use to understand the who's, what's, how's, and why's of an earlier period. Whether you plan to engage in your own detective work on a historical research project or to simply read history, you should know that historians do write stories about the past by analyzing and interpreting historical data. These stories are shaped by the who's, what's, and how's that historians, like the agents in today's modern investigative dramas, pursue. Because we're dealing with the past, we'll toss in other considerations about when (the time period) and where (the place) before we come to conclusions about the most intriguing part of any investigative story—the why.

REFLECTION QUESTIONS

1. How are history and detective work similar?
2. How are they different?

The What: What We Are Trying to Understand

This seems like a straightforward question: What event or episode in history is under investigation? In reality, it is much more complex, especially because historical topics are not dropped on the historian's desk, like cases are dropped on those of crime detectives. Because history is an interpretation of the past rather than merely a chronicle of an event, considerations about what one studies are important and are sometimes the first step in any historical investigation. Historians investigate certain topics about the past for a number of different reasons.

Finding a Topic

Historians want to choose topics that are significant and by which they are intrigued. Significant topics may deal with relevant or perennial issues, such as child-rearing practices, religious beliefs, or government authority. They also may illuminate larger aspects of society and humanity, such as the ideas that motivated the antislavery movement or the ways in which U.S. citizens treated Irish or Chinese immigrants. Other topics may explore changes and continuities over time: Why did governments begin to take care of the poor or regulate business? Even comparisons trigger historical detective work, such as the varying experiences of working-class and middle-class women. Each of these topics is worth investigating because it tells us something about people's lives and society in the past.

Historians also choose topics to fill an existing gap in historical scholarship. Historians must be familiar with the body of historical knowledge to recognize an untold part of a story or to see how certain ideas or concepts may vary in different contexts. Novices to historical research may not recognize how a study fills in a gap simply because they have not gained command of the research. Becoming familiar with a body of scholarship requires time spent reading histories—including the endnotes or footnotes used by historians. In footnotes and endnotes historians indicate what sources they have used and what other histories they have read as part of their crafting an analysis and interpretation.

When filling in a gap in historical scholarship, historians often are so familiar with the existing research that they recognize when something has not been considered or when there is an untold part of the story. A good example of history that fills a gap in the research is the work of Linda Perkins (1987), who studies the history of African American women. Early in her career Perkins realized that histories about early schooling did not include the experiences of African Americans. Her scholarship fills this gap by including African Americans in the history of schooling, and by doing this Perkins also shows how concepts applied to white students change when historians consider African Americans.

Not all history fills in a gap. Historians may pursue topics that have been widely studied to provide a new interpretation of the data and therefore the story itself. Sometimes historians who engage in these types of studies use the same data others have used, or they consider additional information. The point, however, is that they are forwarding a new conclusion about prior research, usually as a way to challenge the existing interpretation. Such work often results in hot debates among historians about the past—again, the case is not closed, and different detectives pore over the information to come to different conclusions. Examples of these debates in the historical scholarship are the works of Michael B. Katz (1968) and Carl F. Kaestle and Maris A. Vinovskis (1980) on the creation of the public school system in Massachusetts in the nineteenth century. When reading histories in which there is vigorous disagreement on how to interpret the data, one can almost hear the historians refuting each other and offering their own interpretations. These differences in interpretation, then, can be another reason why historians pursue certain topics. As a reader of these histories, you act as a judge. You consider whether the new interpretation convincingly exposes weaknesses in prior research and if its own explanation is strong enough to displace prior research and usher in a reconsideration of existing scholarship.

Historians sometimes pursue certain topics because they have direct and immediate relevance to current social or government policy and practice. Such histories may investigate how policies and practices came to be or how the consequences of policies unfolded. In these cases historians believe that exploring a similar issue in the past will help to illuminate or critique current issues. History also may provide policymakers with a fresh understanding of how people addressed similar issues so that current policy will avoid the same mistakes that happened in the past.

If, indeed, the historian wants to make a connection between earlier and current times, then he or she should make this directly clear, rather than having the reader guess at the link. The historian should state the relationship between the history and the current policy; he or she also may provide suggestions for changing policy to accommodate the lessons the history teaches. Historians may do this in the introduction, in a conclusion, or even in a separate section of the study devoted to applying the research's lessons to current policy. Not all histories, however, are explicit about the connection between the past and current policy, so as a reader you may need to make these links yourself.

There are numerous examples of historical research that speaks directly to policy. Diane Ravitch and Maris Vinovskis's *Learning from the Past: What History Teaches Us About School Reform* (1995) and David Tyack and Larry Cuban's *Tinkering Toward Utopia: A Century of Public School Reform* (1995) both deal with past efforts at school reform. *The Rise and Fall of the New Deal Order* (Fraser & Gerstle, 1989) addresses government economic policy from Franklin D. Roosevelt through Ronald Reagan, and *Doughboys, the Great War, and the Remaking of America* (Keene, 2001) looks at how veterans shaped government social policies after World War II.

Historians choose their topics for a variety of reasons: because the topic is intriguing and tells us something about humanity and society; because it fills a gap in the research by considering untold stories or how current explanations may not fit different circumstances; because historians wish to advance a different interpretation; or because the topic may influence policy, either directly or indirectly.

Topic Categories

There are other ways to categorize topics historians explore, and that is by the type of history studied. There are many subdivisions within history, and each focuses on different topics. **Biography,** for instance, explores the life of one person in great detail, whereas **social history** explores the experiences of common people, usually as a group, such as the experiences of Italian immigrants, cowboys, or even teenagers. Common people are average, typical, everyday people who, individually, usually do not make news headlines or influence events. However, as a cultural group they are significant because they are the people of whom society is composed and they help to shape the atmosphere of a particular time. Biographies are typically written about headline-making people, whereas social history is history about the rest of us. **Cultural history** explores any range of cultural phenomena, from entertainment and sports to popular culture. Histories of jazz music, monster movies from the 1950s, and medieval patronage of the arts are all examples of cultural history. **Political or diplomatic history** focuses on politics and diplomacy, usually at a national or international level, and on such public figures as presidents, diplomats, or even military leaders, as well as the organizations in which they operate, like the army or a specific political lobbying group. **Intellectual history** encompasses ideas, their emergence, and their influence in society, such as feminism in the 1920s in the United States or the Enlightenment's ideals about man's rationalism that became popular in the eighteenth century. Often when historians explore different subdivisions within history they also use different sources, such as letters for a biography and government documents for a political history. We will discuss more about different sources later.

More specific topics for historical investigation are given their own category. Histories about geographic regions, such as U.S. history, world history, or Southern (U.S.) history, are considered **specialized topic areas,** which can include all the previous subdivisions of history within each special topic. For instance, one can explore a cultural history of the South, or women in the South. Likewise, women's history includes biographies (of famous women) and intellectual histories, such as one exploring the use and impact of the word *feminism*. Demographic groups also warrant their own topical subdivision, such as women's history, Latino/a history, or African American history. Labor history, military history, or the history of science and technology also are categorized separately. Historians usually work within a specific topic area because they specialize in one body of scholarship. In addition, even these subdivisions can be further divided; the history of education, for instance, includes the history of public education, the history of higher education, the history of the curriculum, and the history of teachers, among other things.

As we can see, when we consider what the historian studies there are many options. First, historians choose their topics—the "what" they study—based on any number of reasons. Topics also are categorized by the type of history under which they fall. As readers we must recognize that a study on the Civil Rights Movement, for instance, not only is about the U.S. Civil Rights Movement but also speaks to the larger African American experience and, even further, to the American experience more generally. By understanding how historians choose their topics or what category of history they are exploring, we see the larger significance of the research. Each historical study is not just a chronicle of an event or person; it is part of a larger mystery that historians are trying to understand. Therefore we try to understand one event or episode in history as a way to flesh out a larger topic—to add yet another piece to a big puzzle about the past.

REFLECTION QUESTIONS

1. What is a topic of interest to you that might lend itself to historical research?
2. Pose two or three different questions about this topic that require different historical approaches.

The When: The Historical Context of an Earlier Era

Like with our considerations about what historians study, the question of the "when" is similarly complex. It is not just a date. Historians study earlier eras or moments in time, and these earlier times are like completely different worlds from today. Each moment in time is unique because there are differing circumstances of a particular era. Historians refer to this as the **context.** Context gives meaning to past events; it helps us understand the importance of an event given the larger picture. Imagine, for instance, a picture of a flower. Without understanding what surrounds that flower, we cannot really understand its importance or even its meaning. Only when we step back and see what is around the flower does it make sense. Is it a flower in a field or in a bouquet? If a bouquet, is it being offered to a women by a man, or is it surrounded by flowers in a funeral arrangement? We cannot know the meaning of the flower unless we see the full picture around it. Likewise with history, we must see the full picture to understand the meaning of any one event. This is context.

Historians explore economic, cultural, social, intellectual, and political contexts. These contexts expose the norms, beliefs, values, and ideas of the time and allow the historian to assess an event or person on its own terms. Without understanding the economic context of the 1930s, for instance, there is little meaning to a family's migration from Kansas to California in 1936 during the height of drought conditions. Or, we cannot comprehend the American Civil War without knowing the political issue of states' rights, the economics of the slave labor system, or the social attitudes about slavery and Southern paternalism and honor. Understanding the context gives meaning to historical facts and information.

Historians must ground any historical topic in the larger context because the past is truly a different world from the one we inhabit, and only context gives meaning to any historical event. Historians try to take the perspective of people from earlier times rather than applying their own values and sensibilities to people from a previous era. The first person to do this was Herodotus, an ancient Greek who lived during the fifth century BCE. Herodotus is considered the father of history because he did not apply his own way of thinking on an earlier time and people. Historians use their **historical imagination** to understand earlier people, events, or concepts in their own right and on their own terms rather than using today's standards. Using today's standards or values to judge something in the past is called **presentism,** and historians consider this a violation of basic standards of historical research. Sometimes today's concepts, like the notion of psychology, for instance, were not even in existence in an earlier time—in this case, prior to the late nineteenth century when psychology and psychological concepts did not exist. Similarly, as abhorrent as we find slavery, we must try to understand the values and beliefs of antebellum Southerners that allowed them to find slave labor acceptable in their world. If we do not, we are not seeing these people on their own terms. Once we realize the importance of context—of understanding the broader economic, political, social, cultural, and intellectual aspects of an earlier period—we can focus on the time frame we wish to study.

Historical research varies according to the length of time under study. Some historians focus on a very short time span, say the integration of Boston's public schools in the early 1970s. Others explore a much longer time frame, such as the history of the laboring classes from the dawn of industrialization in the eighteenth century to today. What the former provides in extreme detail the latter usually treats in much broader terms that allow the historian to give an interpretation about continuities and sweeping changes over time.

Thus considering the "when" of historical research goes beyond a date. It is an attempt by historians to understand the full entirety of an earlier period. Context gives meaning to particular events and helps us see them as people then would have. If we try to master context and the ability to see the past on its own terms, then we are being pretty good historians. We also see that the length of time under study may determine the depth of interpretation. Either way, if historians are true to the context, then they are contributing a piece to a bigger puzzle of the past.

REFLECTION QUESTIONS

1. How does historical context give meaning to past events?
2. For a historical topic in which you are interested, what do you know about the economic, political, social, cultural, or intellectual context that would help you understand the topic better?

The Where: The Foci of Historical Studies

Historians can look at topics and events a number of different ways. The foci of where historians direct their attention will yield differing histories of even the same event. When considering where historians look, we focus on the scope of history and the view of history.

Scope of History

The scope of a historical investigation determines how wide a net the historian casts in finding sources and may reflect how influential the historian sees the topic or event. This, in turn, influences the interpretation made. Let us consider immigration policy during World War II to understand the foci of historical studies. We could look at the effect of U.S. immigration policies on Los Angeles. To do so, we would probably use some federal or national sources and local sources, like newspapers, diaries, and interviews of people in Los Angeles. This would be a local scope of study. We could broaden this to explore the effect of these policies on the entire American Southwest, using state and local sources in that region. This would be a regional study. Other regional studies would be studies of the Midwest, the South, or the West. Another alternative would have the historian examine national sources, using federal documents as well as many states' documents. National-level publications, like national newspapers, would help to chart the effect of immigration policy nationally. This would be a national study. We could make this an international study by focusing on the effects of immigration policy during World War II on Mexico. Thus the scope of study could be local, regional, national, or even international, but whatever it is, the sources must align with the scope of study. You cannot use only local sources and claim to be doing a national study.

When historians use a national scope, they are, by default, arguing that the topic had significance and influence at the national level. Likewise, local studies usually do not have national significance because the historian only explores the much smaller, local level, such as a city or community. However, sometimes a local person or event may have national impact. For instance, Jane Addams and her Chicago-based Hull House (a community reform organization aimed at assisting working-class immigrant women at the beginning of the twentieth century) were important beyond Chicago for the leadership and example they set in handling urban reform issues. Similarly, the 1925 Scopes Trial, which pitted evolution against creationism, was broadcast across the United States and was not just important in the state of Tennessee. Historians sometimes argue that local events exemplify a national issue. In this case the historian may rely most heavily on local materials but still pepper the research with relevant national sources to show how his or her localized topic stands as an example of a broader national trend or issue.

View of History

How a historian views a topic is related to the scope. The topic can be viewed from a top-down perspective or a bottom-up perspective—it just depends on where the historian looks. Let us again use our example of immigration policy during World War II to understand the view a historian takes. A **top-down view** of immigration would focus on the bigger picture about policy. A **bottom-up view** would focus on the people, their work, and their lives—in particular, the laborers themselves rather than famous people like labor leaders or presidents. Simply pursuing a local scope of study, however, would not always lead to a bottom-up perspective. One could examine the local aircraft industry in Los Angeles in terms of its growth and economic impact on the city without considering the lives of the aircraft factory workers.

The view historians take—either top down or bottom up—influences what is studied and the documents or sources used. A top-down view would focus on government policies, institutions, and influential people—the movers and shakers of the time and place. Government documents, letters, memos, materials from influential organizations and people, and widely read publications would be sources used. A bottom-up view considers common people and uses their documents: letters, diaries, oral interviews, as well as documents that get at the local culture, such as those produced by local organizations, clubs, churches, or other agencies that influenced the lives of the common people in a community.

Beyond helping to determine the sources used, the views historians take also provide a perspective on what historians think is important about the past and who they think effect change. Is it the little guy that makes change happen (the common person), or is it bigwigs (government and business leaders and their policies, for instance)? A historian's view (top down or bottom up) indicates to readers how he or she interprets history. Does the historian see institutions and influential people and policies as influencing the course of history, or does he or she see a give-and-take between people and policies? When reading historical research you should determine where the author's foci are to help you in understanding his or her interpretation.

REFLECTION QUESTIONS

1. Does the topic you chose earlier in the chapter have a local, state, regional, national, or international focus?
2. How does a top-down view of history differ from a bottom-up view, and what different places would you look for sources depending on which view you have?

The Who: Historical Actors

By now we should be recognizing that questions that once seemed simple (who, what, when, where) are far from that. Considerations about historical actors are equally complex. Historians must identify who or what are the historical actors that played a central role in shaping the time and topic under study. **Historical actors** more than likely are people, but sometimes they are things, such as organizations (including governments), demographic groups (such as laborers), or ideas (such as democracy).

As with the foci of historical studies, who a historian considers to be historical actors gives us a clue as to how the scholar sees the past. Are these individuals, or are the historical actors organizations or institutions, with a seeming life of their own beyond the persons who work within them? Sometimes the type of history indicates who can be historical actors. Social history and biography, for instance, usually see common people (individuals) as influential and important.

Intellectual history sees ideas as shapers of societal norms and values (see also Chapter Five, Biography and Life Story Research).

In considering whom they study, historians often categorize the historical actors according to various demographic or sociological traits. This helps to define them as members of specific groups and to understand their place in society. The three key markers are race and ethnicity, class, and gender. By looking at individuals as members of these groups, historians can see patterns of social relations in society. Usually, but not always, people with shared characteristics have similar legal and social standing in society. For instance, until very recently (the twentieth century), women were all but excluded from certain professions; thus the concept of gender helps historians understand the economic and social opportunities and limits on women as a group, rather than just limits on specific individual women in society. Furthermore, historians argue that race and ethnicity, class, and gender are key to understanding how the past unfolds, and that those characteristics provide central ways to interpret history.

Race and ethnicity, class, and gender are not the only categories we consider about individuals and their social groups. Historians also may consider religious affiliations and sexual orientation. Clearly people may not fit easily into such groupings and they may belong to more than one group. Historians try to flesh out how social groups may influence the lives of these people. Sometimes they do, sometimes they do not; but by considering social categories, historians try to better understand people in the past. Remember, too, that historians may not be considering just individuals but groups, examining, for instance, the experiences of gay and lesbian teachers, or even organizations that advocate for special groups. Thus individuals or groups may be historical actors.

The power that historical actors have to shape society or policy is sometimes referred to as **agency.** However, historians are very cautious about ascribing a motive or even assigning responsibility for change. Historians tend to describe events or changes and only attribute cause or motive on the part of historical actors if there is clear and compelling evidence. What constitutes clear and compelling evidence? Direct reference in materials to actions someone ordered or took, or to beliefs someone held that led to the outcome, would be compelling.

Overwhelming evidence (numerous documents that point to a certain historical actor) also would argue for cause or motive. Simple correlation (a rise in women's employment and a concurrent rise in divorce rates) would not indicate that one caused the other; it would be a basic correlation, but not causation. To clarify, a correlation simply indicates that when one thing happens (for instance, an increase in the daily average temperature in the Northeast from April through September), another thing happens (emergency room visits increase). Rising temperatures do not *cause* more accidents requiring emergency room visits. The rise in the number of bicycle or skateboard accidents—outdoor activities that increase in warm weather—*do* cause a rise in emergency room visits. Thus there is a correlation between warm weather and emergency room visits, but warm weather is not a cause; there is no causation. Historians are interested in correlation, but should never assume causation. Good historical research will consider all relevant sources of information, weigh the facts, and show any evidence of causation or motive, if indeed it is evident.

REFLECTION QUESTIONS

1. What is historical agency?
2. From your perspective, who affects change? Who are the historical actors?

The How: The Evidence Behind Historical Research

When trying to understand the past—whether it is individuals or groups, policies or people, or ideas or innovators—historians rely on evidence to determine what they know about the past. In understanding the evidence or sources behind historical research, we see the most similarity between the historian and the detective. Unlike other researchers, such as in the sciences or other social sciences in which scholars run experiments, administer surveys, or otherwise create data, historians dig for it. They are detectives on a search in a relatively great unknown. Historians typically find data or sources in old documents. Sometimes they use quantifiable data (census records, for instance) and run statistical analyses. More rarely they interview people who have experienced a past event, and thus create a written record of the past through oral interviews. The standard, however, is searching for and reading old documents.

Historians list all their sources in the endnotes or footnotes in writing up historical research. Unlike other types of social scientific research, historical scholarship does not have a specific section of the text devoted to a literature review. Rather, previous scholarship is embedded throughout the text and is used to build evidence and support for the interpretation as well as for a general understanding of the past. References to prior research are in the footnotes or endnotes, and historians are known to read the references as much as they read the actual text. This is one way they determine if the research is good—if it considers prior explanations and accepted knowledge about the past.

Any source used should be appropriate to the question under study (the what), to the foci of the research (the where), and to the time period (the when). Considering our earlier example of U.S. immigration policy during World War II, we would want to rely on federal documents, not local or state ones, if our focus is national or international. If that same study were to examine the effects of federal immigration and employment policy on Hispanics in Los Angeles, we would need to use local sources, such as documents from city government offices, businesses, organizations, or local newspapers, as well as any evidence, such as diaries, letters, or even interviews, from the people being studied. As a reader you should ask if the research uses the appropriate sources to build an interpretation, given the topic, the foci, and the time period.

In addition, historians try to use original sources. For instance, if you wanted to study the conversion of Native American Indians to Christianity in the eighteenth century, you would want to examine documents written by the missionaries and any available materials from the Indians themselves. Preferably you would do this by reading the original language, which may not be English. Relying on a translation of a document or an edited selection removes the historian one or two steps from the source. Translators may not have adhered to the original meaning, and editors determined what they believed was most important to include in the shortened or edited text. Rather, historians want to be able to make those determinations themselves and thus use the original source as much as possible.

When using documents, historians must analyze them in the proper context. They must consider the source's purpose when it was created: Was it to express feelings; persuade people; explain a phenomenon; provide legal, social, or moral guidance; or do something else? Historians also try to learn about the person or organization that produced the document, because that gives clues to the intended meaning and any biases in the source.

There are two sources of evidence on which historians base their analyses and interpretations: **primary sources** and **secondary sources.** Primary sources are documents or artifacts created during the time period under investigation. Secondary sources are interpretations of history—what historians produce. These may be articles, books, or other media. When using primary sources, historians must be careful in weighing the evidence. Sometimes primary sources provide conflicting accounts or experiences of the past. This is known as **counterevidence.** Knowing about the sources' authors or producers and their purposes assists the historian in weighing the evidence. Historians must also cross-check their documents with other sources and with existing knowledge and information to resolve any factual errors and expose any biases in creating an accurate interpretation of the past.

Primary Sources

Primary sources are data or documents created during the time period under investigation by people who actually witnessed or experienced an event. Primary sources can be documents (for example, newspaper articles, personal journals, reports, or memos) or artifacts (such as photographs, toys, clothing, or works of art). Often the interpretation that the historian makes depends on the types of primary sources used. Taking the immigration policy example, we can see that using federal government documents would yield one type of interpretation, whereas using local sources, especially from people affected by the policy, would yield another. When new primary sources become available, historians often argue that a new interpretation about a topic is necessary because the data may reveal a novel way to consider the subject or shed a new light on it. Because new data are uncovered from time to time, historical cases are rarely closed.

Public Records
Public records or documents typically have been published and therefore are accessible to anyone, especially now in the Internet age when you can simply "click" to get historical census data, for example. Unless classified, government documents and information are examples of public documents, but public documents are not just government-produced documents. They include any published or reproduced source that was made available to the public.

Examples of public documents include newspapers, magazines, books, published debates, and pamphlets. Local, state, or federal government documents, such as laws; reports; legislative records, such as the U.S. Congressional Record or even the minutes of a local city council or school board meeting; census data; birth, marriage, and death certificates; tax records; school enrollment figures; and deeds are public records. Sometimes private organizations, like labor unions, professional associations, or businesses, publish documents for general consumption. All these sources are available to a researcher with enough ingenuity to find them, either through a library or even through the Internet. Digitization projects currently aim to make older material accessible online. For instance, you can find online the text of published sermons from the seventeenth century and back issues of newspapers, to name only two examples.

Archival Documents
Other primary sources were not created to be widely distributed or available to the general public but instead were private or **archival documents,** such as letters, diaries, personal photographs, or even the documents of a private corporation or organization. These documents were created for personal or internal

use, and there may be only one copy in existence. (Some private documents have been published, as in the case of the letters and diaries of famous historical people. The correspondence between John and Abigail Adams is a prime example.) These private documents usually are accessible only through archives or specialized libraries that hold and preserve historical documents. The researcher must actually go to the archive, sometimes even requesting permission in advance to use a source. Depending on the sources' condition and age, strict rules apply for their usage, such as handling certain materials with special gloves or not making photocopies of materials.

Artifacts

Nonwritten items that historians analyze are **artifacts.** Any "thing" produced during an earlier time can be an artifact. This includes such items as toys, tools, clothing, furniture, and buildings, to name a few. Artifacts can even be images and recordings, like photographs, paintings and sculptures, music, movies, television productions, and advertisements. Historians can find additional information about artifacts produced for public enjoyment, such as artwork and entertainment media like movies or novels, and this helps them understand the impact or importance of the items. For instance, historians can scour critics' reviews, book reviews, and publication records that state the numbers of editions a book went through, the numbers of copies printed and sold, or the revenue earned by a movie or record to determine the influence that the artifact had on popular culture and society.

When reading a history that uses artifacts, check to see if the historian both interprets the artifacts (says what they mean) and gauges their influence on the broader culture. A historian can provide an illuminating description of an item, but if that item was culturally insignificant we learn little about the past. You can read in the text if the author has given a rationale for the importance of the artifacts being analyzed.

Oral Interviews

Within the last few decades historians have begun to use **oral interviews** with people who have direct knowledge of a historical topic or event. Oral interviews do create a new primary source, or at least elicit information that otherwise would not be part of the public record. Just like written documentation, oral interviews can sometimes conflict with other sources of information. With oral interviews this is doubly problematic as individuals may not remember things as they were. Their memories of a past event may be influenced by any of their experiences since that event or even by how the person collecting the oral history poses questions to them. In addition, there may be a great length of time between the original event and the time when the person is giving recollections, and this passage of time can affect the person's ability to remember the past as he or she experienced it.

Historians must account for any potentially faulty information through the confirmation of data by other witnesses or documented sources. Although oral interviews do show the experiences of people, researchers also must take caution not to overgeneralize an individual's experience to all people. You should ask of the historical scholarship you are reading what group of people those interviewed represent, and if and how their experiences reflect that of, or relate to, the larger society.

Quantitative Information

Quantitative data are numbers, facts, or figures that help historians show the significance of an issue under investigation, illustrate changes, make comparisons, and generally interpret the past. However, they provide their own set of interpretive issues because they are seen as "scientific" when in actuality they are simply another means to analyze information and are still subject to errors in the historian's method and interpretation. Some figures are problematic in themselves. Take, for instance, colonial literacy rates and the statistics associated with them. Does the researcher define literacy as applying to those people who can sign their name to legal documents or to people who read? E. Jennifer Monaghan (1989), in her study of colonial literacy in America, has shown that reading and writing were considered separate skills and taught independently. Thus just because some people, typically women, could not write, that did not mean they were illiterate. The historian using quantitative data must ensure that the statistics used actually measure the concept or category being studied. What, then, were the researcher's methods in determining this statistic? The number, as we see, may not actually say what it says it does. It may be more complex, and in evaluating historical research that uses quantitative data you must ask what, indeed, the statistics are illustrating. Are the numbers and even the categories of the things being tallied reliable? Do they actually measure what the historian claims they measure?

Historians sometimes compile statistical data from existing census records, survey statistics, or other quantifiable information. Historians will "create" quantitative data by counting, for instance, church membership records in a city and then organizing the numbers according to ethnic, residential, or other categories. How do they do this? They cross-check the information with books that provide common ethnic origins of surnames or with city documents recording residences. Statistical data may help to show the relationship between, say, income, ethnicity, and church membership. Historians can use sophisticated methods of

QUALITATIVE RESEARCH

Table 6.1 High School Enrollment by Year, Ethnicity, and Parentage

Father's Ethnic Group	1880	1900	1915	1925
Native white, native parent	27.4	36.2	52.5	57.8
Native white, foreign parent	15.9	15.2	45.3	—
Foreign-born white	3.5	11.5	29.4	46.1
Black	3.7	12.3	22.4	30.7

Source: Adapted from Perlmann, 1988, p. 186.

computer analysis to determine how significant the relationships are among these categories.

Historians also use statistical information to track or illustrate changes over time, or to make comparisons among groups or even across time. The numbers or figures often can be quite illustrative. To assist readers in seeing such comparisons or changes, historians will often place statistical information into charts, graphs, or other forms of visual representation. Table 6.1 is adapted from Joel Perlmann's *Ethnic Differences: Schooling and Social Structure Among the Irish, Italians, Jews and Blacks in an American City, 1880–1935* (1988). It shows the percentage of young people enrolled in high school by ethnicity and nativity (whether or not a person was born in the United States).

The table allows you not only to see the increase in school enrollment of the various ethnic groups across time but also to compare the percentages of students of the various ethnic groups enrolled in school at different times. For instance, the children of immigrants and black children had nearly equal high school enrollment rates in 1880 and in 1900; yet their rates of enrollment diverge beginning in 1915 and show clear differences by 1925, with black youths enrolling in high school at a lower rate. We could, as did Perlmann, ask what economic, cultural, and social circumstances accounted for these differences.

When reading historical research that incorporates quantitative data, therefore, it is important to ask if the measurements are consistent over time and reliable, and if the statistical information presented helps illustrate change or comparisons—or even if it provides instructive information that aids in describing or analyzing an earlier period of time.

Secondary Sources

Secondary sources are any interpretations of or histories about the past. Historians learn about earlier times not only through primary sources but also through what other historians have written. Secondary sources provide historians with existing knowledge about an earlier period. For instance, using our immigration policy example, you would need to read histories of Los Angeles and of immigrants during that time. Histories on wartime industry or other related topics also need exploration to understand current knowledge about immigrants, Los Angeles, and labor during the war. These secondary sources assist the historian in understanding the past and also in finding those unanswered questions or interpretative differences that may be the starting points for his or her research. Secondary sources also are good places to begin identifying primary sources.

Historians cannot simply use secondary sources of information. They must use primary sources because those are what speak directly from the past. If a historian uses only secondary information, or is overreliant on secondary sources, then the research is not considered primary source historical research. Analyzing secondary sources alone is usually characteristic of **historiography,** which is the study of the field of history and how historians see and write about the past. In any case, historians must strive to read the documents in their original form and analyze them according to their original meaning. This gets us closer to the "real" story of history—an understanding of the past on its own terms.

REFLECTION QUESTIONS

1. What are the differences between primary sources and secondary sources?
2. For the historical research questions that you posed in previous sections, what sources might provide appropriate data for your analysis and interpretation?

The Why: Historical Interpretation and Analysis

Rather than just telling a story, although sometimes historians do some very good storytelling, historical research is grounded in the analysis and interpretation of the past (see Chapter Nine, Narrative Inquiry, for another perspective on stories in research). Analysis and interpretation move historical research from being a chronicle of events to providing a larger understanding of why things were as they were in the past. History tells you about the past and why the past was as it was. That is the subjective part of historical research. Certainly, picking topics, determining the scope and foci of a study, and analyzing documents are all subjective because they rely on the historian's decisions and judgments. However, we most clearly see the subjectivity of historical research when we consider the interpretation advanced by a scholar. Here we can perhaps find additional similarities between historians and those detectives in our crime investigation dramas, because historians do bring a dose of pluck to this—both in following their hunches in finding topics and sources and in regard to the tenacity of their **worldview,** which does have an impact on how they interpret historical data. A worldview is the basic way in which a person sees relationships among people, institutions, and society. As much as historians try to see the past on its own terms and be objective, they can never be fully disengaged from their own worldview and personal and cultural biases and values. Ultimately these shape the history that is written.

Many things shape the worldview that a historian has and thus the interpretation he or she brings to historical research. The philosophy of history a researcher subscribes to, the trends in historical research, and the categories of analysis all contribute to the interpretation a researcher puts forth. These three things create the lens or worldview through which the historian looks at the data, whether or not the historian recognizes fully how much this does influence his or her work.

Philosophies of History

Previously I discussed causation and the caution historians take in ascribing motive or cause to a person or event. However, historians usually hold a foundational understanding (a **philosophy**) about the relationships between events and their causes and among the past, present, and future. The **cyclical philosophy** of history asserts that history repeats itself and that society is doomed to repeat history if it does not learn from the past. Seeing history and events as a struggle between good and evil, and believing that good will win in the end, encompass the **providential philosophy** of history. The **progressive philosophy** of history sees history as showing continuous progress or improvement in society because of humankind's efforts and abilities. Each of these **philosophies of history** supposes an objective researcher, and, yes, that is the ideal.

However, a recent philosophy questions this ability of researchers to disengage from their own values or worldview. For historians this would entail questioning their ability to leave behind the present when interpreting the past. This philosophy is called **postmodernism,** and it holds that the present taints and corrupts the historians' views of the past. Postmodern philosophers believe that historians, rather than uncovering the past in its truth, are creating the past.

Historiography

Historical research, just like television dramas, follows trends in interpreting the past. History, as an academic and professional discipline, is roughly one hundred years old. Many historians who study the development of the field of history, or historiography, see the first fifty years as promoting certain kinds of interpretations about the past. In general these years are characterized as producing **Whig histories,** accounts that typically celebrated progress. Whig histories generally downplayed social problems, such as inequalities or the negative impact of policies on society and people. Whig histories are criticized for focusing too narrowly on the development of institutions and prominent people, events, and ideas. Relying heavily on public documents for interpretation, Whig histories are criticized for taking those sources at face value rather than questioning their biases and purposes.

In the 1950s historians began to believe that the experiences of common people should be included in history and that sources from those people should be used. This led to new interpretations, often focusing on common people and how they experienced prominent events. The historians who followed this trajectory wanted to revise history to be more inclusive; thus they were termed revisionists, and their histories were considered **revisionist histories.** Revisionists examined new sources, asked new questions, and used new concepts, such as the sociological concept of social class, in analyzing and interpreting the past. Since the 1960s this type of historical scholarship has dominated the field, and Whiggish histories are seen as not taking a critical approach but instead defending unfair social or political practices and policies of the past.

Categories of Analysis

During the discussion of historical actors I explored how historians consider race and ethnicity, class, and gender to understand the people in the past and their experiences. These sociological **categories of analysis,** however, provide more than just a way to understand historical actors. They also provide a major means of analysis. By considering race and ethnicity, class, and gender as central in analysis and interpretation, historians try to see the past through the lens of one of these categories, with the assumption that the past will look different from, say, a race-based perspective.

When considering race and ethnicity, historians look at the influence of racial or ethnic groups. Historians who use a class-based analysis ask how social or economic differences shaped the past. Considerations of women's experiences, or conceptions of masculinity and femininity, are part of gender analysis. Not only do historians consider and describe the experiences of these groups of people but also their analysis or interpretation based on race and ethnicity, class, or gender assumes that these concepts structured events, social relations, policies, and ideas in the past. For instance, research on the North American slave labor system aims to describe the experience of slaves, but it further seeks to show that slave labor was central to the economic development of the British colonies and the United States (Smith, 1998), as well as to Southern cultural identity.

Other ideas have influenced historical analysis and interpretation. Literary theory and the other social sciences, such as sociology, have enriched historical scholarship. Historians have, for example, used Marxist theory and feminist theory in their analyses. The caution in applying these new theories to historical analysis, however, is that sometimes these new concepts may not have even been in existence in the past. Feminist theory, for instance, may help us understand gender relations in medieval Europe, but more than likely any man or woman transplanted from medieval Europe would not recognize those concepts in his or her world because the concept of feminism did not exist then.

REFLECTION QUESTIONS

1. What kind of story do you think history tells?
2. What is your worldview, and how does it affect how you interpret events in history?

Summary

Historians engage in detective work. They seek to understand the what's, when's, where's, who's, how's, and why's of the past. They attempt to be scientific by being objective and seeing the past on its own terms. They also follow rigorous procedures and standards for determining sources to be used and how to analyze them. They find data in all kinds of places, from documents in government offices to letters in archives, pictures in art galleries, and toys in museums. And they need pluck—especially their own tenacity in considering how to interpret and analyze the sources so that they can understand the past. But unlike with crime investigations, the case is never closed. Materials and documents surface to provide a new interpretation of an event. Other investigators bring different categories of analysis to the past or new ways of seeing it that change our understanding—sometimes simply by expanding our knowledge and other times by countering previously held views.

Historians, however, are not rogue detectives. They do follow standards of analysis and always judge their own interpretations in light of existing knowledge of the past. To help them, historians have organizations to serve as communities of scholars; journals to distribute new knowledge; and manuals to aid in teaching people how to engage in the historian's craft, or how to do history.

The best way to begin to think and act like a historian is to begin reading history books. Think of yourself as a detective reviewing another crime sleuth's report. Pay attention to how the scholar defines what is under investigation, who are the central historical actors, and how this study helps to expand our knowledge of the past. Also look at the sources used and even how the historian cites those materials in the footnotes. And, most significant, listen to hear the argument. Is the historian refuting previous scholarship? What is her view of history? How does he see the relationships among people and institutions in the work? Is this person writing a convincing argument by showing the evidence for his or her interpretation? Once you start reading history in this way, rather than as just an interesting story, you will begin to think and act like a historian.

Key Terms

agency, 148
archival documents, 151
artifacts, 152
biography, 142
bottom-up view, 146
categories of analysis, 157
context, 143
counterevidence, 150
cultural history, 142
cyclical philosophy, 156
historical actors, 147
historical imagination, 144
historiography, 155
intellectual history, 142
oral interviews, 152
philosophies of history, 156
philosophy, 156
political or diplomatic history, 142
postmodernism, 156
presentism, 144
primary sources, 150
progressive philosophy, 156
providential philosophy, 156
public records, 151
revisionist histories, 157
secondary sources, 150
social history, 142
specialized topic areas, 142
top-down view, 146
Whig histories, 157
worldview, 156

Further Readings and Resources

Suggested Historical Research Studies

Kerber, L. K. (1992). The paradox of women's citizenship in the early republic: The case of *Martin v. Massachusetts*, 1805. *American Historical Review, 97*, 349–378.
This article is an example of a legal history of women.

Lewis, J. (1998). *Walking with the wind: A memoir of the movement.* New York: Simon & Schuster.
This book explores issues of race and society from an autobiographical perspective of one of the acting, leading members of the American Civil Rights Movement.

Rogers, D. T. (1980). Socializing middle-class children: Institutions, fables, and work values in nineteenth-century America. *Journal of Social History, 13*, 354–367.
This article is an example of historical research on social class and culture.

Other Suggested Readings

Benjamin, J. R. (2007). *A student's guide to history.* Boston: Bedford/St. Martin's.
This book provides practical directions on how to analyze sources and research and write a historical paper. Also provided by Benjamin is a lengthy list of resources on historical topics, including organizations, bibliographies arranged by topic, reference guides, online resources, and digital resources, to name a few.

Clark, V. A. (2009). *A guide to your history course: What every student needs to know.* Upper Saddle River, NJ: Pearson-Prentice Hall.
Half of this text explains the historian's craft and how to write a research paper in history. The other half provides tips on how to succeed in a history course, from studying to participating in class and writing essays.

Rampolla, M. L. (2004). *A pocket guide to writing in history* (4th ed.). Boston: Bedford/St. Martin's.
This is a concise guide to what historians do and a great starter for those new in history.

Schrum, K., Gevinson, A., & Rosenweig, R. (2009). *U. S. history matters: A student guide to U.S. history online.* Boston: Bedford/St. Martin's.
This text provides an exceptionally thorough listing of online resources for historians and history students, including such secondary sources as interpretive essays and such primary sources as images, documents, and other digital media.

Organizations and Web Sites

American Historical Association (AHA) (www.historians.org); Organization of American Historians (www.oah.org)

MYSTERY SOLVED: DETECTIVE SKILLS AND THE HISTORIAN'S CRAFT

These are the two premier organizations for historians who actively produce historical scholarship. The AHA Web site has a link to all the scholarly societies with which it is affiliated.

Humanities and Social Sciences Online (www.h-net.org)
Also known as H-Net, this is an online, interdisciplinary organization dedicated to the scholarly exchange of ideas. Because historians engage in continuous debate over the past, and because there are numerous subdivisions within the field of history, online discussion forums for various topics exist and are accessible to anyone. Go to this Web site to access the multitude of options.

World History Association (www.thewha.org)
This is the major organization for world history. Its Web site has teaching aids as well as access to scholarship.

CHAPTER 7

ETHNOGRAPHIC RESEARCH

Frances Julia Riemer

Key Ideas

- Ethnography is the systematic study of a particular cultural group or phenomenon.

- Ethnography is naturalistic; ethnographers focus on real people and their everyday activities in their natural environment.

- Ethnographers engage in extended fieldwork to document beliefs and practices from people's own point of view.

- Written ethnographies have changed over time from texts exhibiting a disembodied, all-knowing perspective to experimental texts that are unconventional, polyphonic, and heteroglossic.

- Transparency in research methods and analysis improves the credibility and validity of ethnographic reports, as does the inclusion of researcher reflexivity and thick descriptions.

I have been intrigued by culture since I traveled to "the old country" with my grandmother at the age of ten. I was the oldest grandchild, my grandmother was widowed, and we were good traveling companions. We stayed in the village in southeast Austria where my aunts, uncles, and cousins lived. This was in the 1960s. I followed my older cousin as she took the cows out to the pasture every day. Her world, without indoor plumbing or electricity, was a far cry from my own in the industrial northeast United States. I learned then that people in other places lived lives that looked different from my own. I learned then that the differences, and also the similarities, were irresistibly fascinating. But I did not become an ethnographer until much later, after I found myself coordinating community-based development in the east African country of Somalia in the 1980s. Before moving to Somalia I had never had neighbors, colleagues, and friends who were no more than one generation removed from a nomadic existence. Although I understood the concept of culture, I remained confused in my interactions with my Somali friends and colleagues, and did not even know what questions to ask to address my confusion.

I studied to become an ethnographer in order to learn how to ask those questions. In the process I also came to understand that culture and cultural difference were not concepts applicable only to the old country or to pastoral economies on the other side of the globe. In fact, I conducted my first ethnography in the U.S. city in which I was living. In an attempt to understand how men and women negotiate the move from welfare to the workplace, I spent two years watching former welfare recipients assemble science kits in an area non-profit business, care for elderly residents in a long-term care facility, fill prescriptions in an inner-city hospital pharmacy, and build spiral staircases at a woodshop in the suburbs (Riemer, 2001). In conducting that research I saw the powerful role that economic status, when combined with race or ethnicity, played in expanding or narrowing an individual's employment options.

My current ethnographic research is back in Africa, this time in the southern African country of Botswana, where I am examining literacy practices (Riemer, 2008). These two projects illustrate a basic tenet of ethnographic research—an ethnographer must be able not only to make the strange familiar but also to make the familiar strange. In other words, as an ethnographer my task in Botswana is to make what I find there, the strange, understandable to people living outside Botswana. My challenge in investigating welfare-to-work transitions, however, was to make the ordinary—in that case, everyday workplace practices—strange to those of us who go to work in similar situations every day. Making the strange familiar and the familiar strange is a way of highlighting the intriguing nature of culture. We take our own culture for granted to such a degree that most times we do not even recognize that what we do is cultural. And at the same time, we find others' culture so strange that we have trouble making sense of their practices. In order to truly understand a cultural group or phenomenon, ethnographers must make cultural practices both accessible to those outside the group and identifiable as cultural to those inside the group.

In this chapter I lay out these and other basic tenets of ethnographic research in order to provide an overview both for the novice researcher who wants to know more about ethnographic research and for the reader of research who hopes to gain a better understanding of the ethnographies on the bookshelf and at the bookstore. I discuss how ethnographers ask questions and employ particular forms of data collection and analysis in order to learn and write about culture. I also consider the issues of validity and reliability, critiques of ethnography, and issues of representation and authority.

What Is Ethnographic Research?

Ethnography, from the Greek *ethnos* ("foreign people") and *graphein* ("to write"), is the systematic study of a particular cultural group or phenomenon. Ethnography is the primary research methodology for anthropologists; it seeks to answer anthropological questions concerning the ways of life of living human beings. Ethnographic research is also conducted by social scientists in other fields, including cultural studies, education, linguistics, communication studies, health care, and criminology. Historically ethnography has been defined in ways that focus on both the *what* and the *how*. In 1909, according to A. R. Radcliffe-Brown's later summation (1952), a group of British anthropologists defined ethnography as "the term of descriptive accounts of non-literate peoples" (p. 276). But Radcliff-Brown added two corollaries. He wrote that these "systematic field studies are carried out by trained anthropologists using scientific methods of observation," and that "the field worker did not confine himself to simple description but sought to include in his account some sort of theoretical analysis" (pp. 276–277).

American anthropologist Clifford Geertz (1973) famously differentiated ethnographic research from other kinds of research not by its methods, but by its "elaborate venture into thick description" (p. 6). By **thick description** Geertz refers to an action, practice, or event and the meaning and symbolic importance given to it by members of a particular society. Geertz's classic example is the difference between a wink, a blink, and a twitch. All three look similar, but their meanings are vastly different and are only understood within a broader cultural context. The concept of thick description suggests that ethnography goes a step further than simply describing. In fact, ethnographers talk about what they do as **cultural interpretation.** "Cultural interpretation involves the ability to describe what the researcher has heard and seen within the framework of the social group's view of reality" (Fetterman, 1989, p. 28). Interpretation of culture in its thick description requires both an insider's, or **emic,** perspective and an outsider's, or **etic,** perspective. The U.S. anthropologist Ward Goodenough (1970) advised ethnographers not simply to document facts about "a society, its organization, law, customs, and shared beliefs" but also to capture "what an individual must know to behave acceptably as a member of a particular group" (pp. 110–111).

This value on insider perspective shifts the relationship between researcher and research participant for ethnographers. Unlike respondents, who "respond to survey questions," or subjects, who are the "subject of some experiment," participants in ethnographic research are **informants** who "tell you *what they think you need to know* about their culture" (Bernard, 2005, p. 196). Informants are really teachers; they are experts about their lives and their practices. And if an ethnographer is fortunate, respectful, and successful, an informant will share that expert knowledge. As Richardson (1975, p. 521) wrote,

> Without the informant, the ethnographer cannot carry out his task. The ethnographer can go only so far with figures, newspapers, and histories, and even with observations. To complete his work, he has to turn to the informant; without the informant, he cannot be an ethnographer.

However, despite the best intentions of the ethnographer, informants are not always cooperative in providing open access to information.

Many ethnographers have written about the challenge of working with informants, who may provide different information in a private setting than they would in a public venue, who tailor information to create a certain impression, or who are simply uncooperative. Satish Saberwal (1969) recounted trying eighteen different times to obtain information from an informant in Kenya before finding any success. Norma Diamond (1970) wrote about the difficulties of working with Taiwanese women her own age who had no place to put Diamond's status as a single woman. Employing multiple informants and multiple research methods, relying on local assistants to make introductions and model appropriate social behavior, and allowing time to breed familiarity have all been cited as strategies to make the ethnographer's presence "more familiar and less threatening" (Sarsby, 1984, p. 118).

Ethnographers collect data in hospitals and family dining rooms, in geriatric centers and on the shop floor, in jungles and in recreational parks—wherever the activity in which they are interested takes place. In order to craft descriptions of cultural events and cultural practices, an ethnographer studies real people doing what they do to meet the everyday demands with which they are confronted. That is to say, ethnography is **naturalistic;** ethnographers focus on real people and their everyday activities in their natural environment, whatever that may be. Classic ethnographic research conducted in the early and mid-twentieth century was focused on a single society in a single place, and resulted in monographs on the practices of particular groups of people. Raymond Firth (1936) spent a year in Tikopia, in the western Pacific, and his account of that visit, *We the Tikopia,* has become one of the great classics of ethnography. Similarly, E. E. Evans-Pritchard (1940) studied the Neur people of east Africa and produced *The Nuer: A Description of the Modes of Livelihood and Political Institutions of a Nilotic People,* another classic of British social anthropology.

More recently ethnographers have found that the activities that are of interest take place over a range of sites, rather than at a single locale. Those ethnographies, termed **multi-sited ethnographies** (Marcus, 1998), cut across area studies to focus on process and connections through space and time, and often across borders and boundaries. An example of multi-sited ethnography is Nancy Scheper-Hughes's work on the black market for the trade of human organs. In her research Scheper-Hughes (2001, p. 2) follows

> the movement of bodies, body parts, transplant doctors, their patients, brokers, and kidney sellers, and the practices of organs and tissues harvesting in several countries—from Brazil, Argentina, and Cuba in Latin America to Israel and Turkey in the Middle East, to India, South Africa, and the United States

. . . and through various legal and illegal networks of capitalism.

It is important to remember that ethnographers do not study these sites—villages, classrooms, or global networks—themselves. They study *in* them. As Geertz (1973) wrote, "The locus of the study is not the object of study" (p. 22). The object of ethnography is not the place, but particular cultural phenomena that happen to be located in one or several places.

REFLECTION QUESTIONS

1. What are two important characteristics typical of ethnographic research?
2. How is an emic perspective different from an etic perspective?

How Does an Ethnographer Start?

The first generation of ethnographers of the late nineteenth and early twentieth centuries engaged in what has come to be known as **salvage ethnography** (Gruber 1970), an attempt to document the rituals, practices, myths, and languages of traditional cultures facing extinction from dislocation or modernization. However, over the past fifty years this emphasis on what Harry Wolcott (1999) has called place-based "ethnographic broadside" (p. 25), that is, the desire to document everything about a particular society, has shifted to a **problem focus** in which a particular problem or topic of interest guides the entire research endeavor. Such problems are guided and propelled by a specific set of research questions. As Margaret Mead (1928) explained about her own ethnographic research in Samoa, "I have tried to answer the question which sent me to Samoa: Are the disturbances which vex our adolescents due to the nature of adolescence itself or to the civilization? Under different conditions does adolescence present a different picture?" (pp. 14–17). More recently Rebecca Bliege Bird's questions about gender differences in fishing strategies guided her research among the Meriam (Torres Strait Islanders). Bird (2007) asked, "Are the differences in fishing preferences between the sexes predicted by resource variance or child-care trade-offs?" (p. 443).

Along with logistical opportunities and constraints, these questions shaped the decisions Mead and Bird, like other ethnographers, made about the location of their fieldwork, the focus of their study, and their data collection methods. Because ethnographic research involves extended fieldwork, ethnographers must identify and gain access to a field setting that will provide data sufficient to answer their research questions. Mead traveled to Samoa to collect data that would answer her questions; Bird traveled equally far, to the Meriam Islands on the northern Great Barrier Reef, for information on gender, familial responsibilities, and the division of labor. But as David Fetterman (1989) asserts, "The ideal site for investigation of the research problem is not always accessible" (p. 42). The ideal is always balanced by the possible, and concerns about travel funds, available time, and gaining access are always at the fore. Resources to support fieldwork are an issue; travel to foreign locales is costly, and next to impossible, unless outside funding can be secured.

Access, whether to a Pacific village or to a community center in the researcher's own neighborhood, also involves the consent and support of **gatekeepers,** that is, individuals who control access to something or some place. Ethnographers who hope to study learning and teaching in formal settings, for example, are dependent on the cooperation of school boards, school principals, and classroom teachers. In her research on social class and parental intervention in elementary school settings, Annette Lareau (2000) studied in two schools. Although she was granted access to both, her reception by school personnel differed drastically: she was welcomed by one school and regarded with some distrust at the other. Lareau traced the difference in reception to her points of contact at each school. She arrived at the first after two years as a graduate assistant on another project at the school. The school-based administrators knew her and welcomed her presence. They were interested in her research question, and the presence of previous researchers had made the school personnel "a bit *blasé* about the entire matter" (p. 203). She accessed the second school through the district office, and consequently had a far more formal relationship with the school principal and classroom teachers. In other situations, gatekeepers are not school principals, but central government officials and headmen. In my own research in Botswana I worked through several layers of gatekeepers: officials in Botswana's national government, department chairs and faculty at the University of Botswana, village chiefs, church leaders, and literacy teachers, to name just a few.

In addition to gaining access from gatekeepers, ethnographers, like other researchers, must obtain approval from **institutional review boards (IRBs)** in order to conduct research. Every university, as well as hospitals and government agencies, has an IRB that oversees all research conducted by faculty, staff, and students that involves humans as the subjects of a study (see also Chapter Two). The role of the IRB is to protect participants in proposed research projects.

However, ethnographic research differs from many other kinds of research in both length and depth of relationship with informants. Ethnographers have a distinctive obligation to the people they are studying. Anthropologists abide by a code of ethics developed and advanced by the American Anthropological Association (AAA) (www.aaanet.org/committees/ethics/ethcode.htm). It's important to note that ethnographers from other disciplines abide by the discipline's code of conduct; sociologists follow the Code of Ethics of the American Sociological Association (ASA) (www.asanet.org/about/ethics.cfm), whereas psychologists follow the Ethical Principals of Psychologists and Code of Conduct of the American Psychological Association (www.apa.org/ethics/code/index.aspx). Approval from an IRB requires submission of an application and the assurance that individuals who participate in a study will have given their **informed consent.** According to the AAA, informed consent includes "communication of information, comprehension of information, and voluntary participation" (American Anthropological Association, 2004, p. 1). However, although informed consent usually involves a signed form, in certain circumstances, such as when people are unable to sign or distrustful of signing their name to official-looking documents, ethnographers can request that oral informed consent be considered sufficient. In addition, the ethnographer must also guarantee the confidentiality of all research participants and that they will be neither harmed nor exploited by their participation.

REFLECTION QUESTIONS

1. What is the relationship between ethnographic research questions and the selection of a site or sites for study?
2. How do ethnographers gain access to fieldwork sites?

What Do Ethnographers Do?

How do ethnographers gather these multiple perspectives of insiders and outsiders? Ethnographers engage in **fieldwork,** that is, they collect data in natural settings to document beliefs and practices from people's own point of view. Ethnographic research is different from other forms of research in that fieldwork, so essential to ethnography, is conducted **in situ,** or in the setting or settings themselves. Basic to the fieldwork approach is the tenet that individuals' beliefs and actions cannot be detached from their context. Fieldwork provides the opportunity to take into account what anthropologists call people's **practices,** or activities, within the context in which they are enacted. James Clifford (1997) argues that this emphasis on fieldwork within anthropology "can be understood within a larger history of travel" (p. 64) that includes explorers, missionaries, colonial officers, colonialists, traders, and natural scientists. Yet before Bronislaw Malinowski, a Polish anthropologist, conducted fieldwork in the Trobriand Islands in 1914, scholars were armchair anthropologists who remained at home to process the ethnographic information sent to them by the travelers listed earlier. The discipline attributes the focus on fieldwork to Malinowski, who "has a strong claim to being the founder of the profession of social anthropology in Britain, for he established its distinctive apprenticeship—intensive fieldwork in an exotic community" (Kuper, 1973, p. 13).

Working in the Field

Because ethnographic research is conducted in an actual context in which practices of interest are taking place, ethnographers spend a good deal of time in the field. The rule is that time in the field should consist of at least one **full cycle of activities.** Because a full cycle encompasses the period from start to finish, an educational ethnographer would, on the one hand, typically spend a semester, if not an entire school year, in a classroom or other school setting. An ethnography of an agricultural society, on the other hand, would extend over at least one planting season. The rationale for the full cycle is that ethnographers want to see the beginning, the middle, and the end of a set of events.

The long-term, intensive nature of fieldwork is unique and rewarding; it can also be uncomfortable, frustrating, and full of anxiety. As William Shaffir and Robert Stebbins (1991) wrote, "Field researchers have in common the tendency to immerse themselves for the sake of science in situations that all but a tiny minority of humankind goes to great lengths to avoid" (p. 1). Finding a place among a group of people to whom you are a stranger, for example, and asking them questions that might seem too personal can certainly feel awkward.

Ethnographers also encounter difficulties that are unique to the settings in which they study. For Scott Grills (1998) the dilemma was how to remain nonpartisan in a highly politicized local cell of the Communist Party of Canada. For family researchers Karen Daly and Anna Dienhart (1998) the challenge was how to enter a "social psychological space . . . characterized by family loyalties, secrets, values, and practices" (p. 103) in order to study familial interactions. In my own fieldwork in companies that employed former welfare recipients, I was continually aware that for my informants who were low-level workers in a nursing home, my "enigmatic function, evident eavesdropping, and probing questions" made me suspect (Riemer, 2001, p. 14).

Shaffir and Stebbins (1991) identify four stages of fieldwork: "(a) entering the field setting; (b) learning how to play one's role while there, whether it be that of researcher or someone else; (c) maintaining and surviving the several kinds of relations that emerge; and (d) leaving the setting" (p. 7). Each stage requires unique social skills for ethnographers. In the growing literature on fieldwork experiences, ethnographers seem to agree that this social dimension of data collection "is usually inconvenient, to say the least, sometimes physically uncomfortable, frequently embarrassing, and, to a degree, always tense" (Shaffir, Stebbins, & Turowetz, 1980, p. 3).

Data Collection Methods

But ethnographers do not go into the field empty-handed. They bring data collection methods to help them organize their work and gain an understanding from an insider's, or emic, perspective (see also Chapter Four for more on data collection methods and tools). These data collection methods involve both direct and not-so-direct involvement in a research setting. **Participant observation** is the ethnographer's direct or active participation in local activities. Stephen Schensul, Jean Schensul, and Margaret LeCompte (1999) wrote that "participation means near-total immersion when ethnographers live in unfamiliar communities where they have little or no knowledge of local culture and study life in those communities through their own participation as full-time residents and members" (p. 92).

Participant observation has been an integral component of ethnographic research ever since the anthropologist Bronislaw Malinowski (1922) found himself unexpectedly stranded by the commencement of World War I while collecting data in the Trobriand Islands. During his prolonged tenure on the islands Malinowski assumed the life of a villager, gossiping, watching, asking questions, and taking part in ceremonies, festivals, and rituals. Contemporary ethnographers continue to rely on participant observation to understand the way insiders see and experience their world. In order to research the lives of college students, for example, Cathy Small (Nathan, 2006) lived in college dorms and took university classes for an academic year. In researching the aspirations of young people in a low-income neighborhood, Jay MacLeod (1987) developed and worked in a community youth project. In these and other cases, participant observation "requires close, long-term contact with the people under study" (Fetterman, 1989, p. 47). Given the ethnographer's unique role as participant-observer, the ethnographer has been called the primary research instrument in ethnographic research (Hammersley & Atkinson, 1983).

However, not all contexts provide opportunities for participant observation. An ethnographer who does not have a medical background, for example, cannot participate as a health care worker in a medical setting. In this case, the ethnographer finds herself in the role of what Wolcott (1999) referred to as **non-participant participant observer.** Wolcott ponders that the doubled "participant participant" straddles a politically contentious line by mediating the notion of observer. He wrote,

> Under present circumstances, . . . to identify oneself as observer perpetuates the idea that *we* are studying *them*, and that is no longer the way we prefer to portray either ourselves or our work. Thus I take the label of the "non-participant participant observer" as a self-ascribed label for researchers who make no effort to hide what they are doing or to deny their presence, but neither are they able fully to avail themselves of the potential afforded by *participant* observation to take a more active or interactive role. (p. 48)

In fact, ethnographers work within a continuum in which "participant observer" is at one end, and "non-participant participant observer" is at the other. In my own research on welfare-to-work transitions, I was a participant observer working alongside new employees as they packed science kits for area schools and piled boxes on skids (Riemer, 2001). In a nursing home, I helped the nursing assistants by wheeling elderly residents to and from lunch, making their beds, and listening to their stories. But I could not legally fill prescriptions at a pharmacy, nor did I have the woodworking skills to assist in building stairs in a custom woodshop. In those sites I was a non-participant participant observer, trying to watch unobtrusively while pharmacy technicians filled prescriptions and woodworkers shaped wood into custom-built spiral staircases.

Interviews

Ethnographers routinely couple observation with interviews. In his research with dealers of crack cocaine in New York City, Philippe Bourgois (1995) observed dealers and addicts on the streets and in crack houses; tape-recorded their conversations and stories; and interviewed "spouses, lovers, siblings, mothers, grandmothers, and—when possible—the fathers and stepfathers of the crack dealers"

(p. 13) as well as local politicians. Similarly, in their study of medical school as professional socialization, Howard Becker, Blanche Geer, Everett Hughes, and Anselm Strauss (1961) both attended school with the medical students they studied and conducted exploratory interviews with students and faculty. **Ethnographic interviews** are unique, however, in that they are more like guided conversations than structured interviews. Schensul, Schensul, and LeCompte (1999) describe ethnographic interviews as **in-depth** and **open-ended:** "By in-depth we mean exploring a topic in detail to deepen the interviewer's knowledge of the topic. Open-ended refers to the fact that the interviewer is open to any and all relevant responses" (p. 121). At times these interviews take the form of exchanges about particular events or topics; at other times they more closely resemble life histories (see Chapters Five and Nine for more information). Spradley (1979) describes ethnographic interviews as developing rapport and eliciting information. As I tell my students, "The best ethnographic interview is more like a conversation than a traditional interview" (Riemer, 2009, p. 208).

Ethnographic interviews can also take the form of **focus groups,** or interviews with multiple informants, in instances where a group context will elicit information that one-on-one interviews will not. Although focus groups are often associated with market-oriented settings, when used by ethnographers their structure, in terms of size, composition, and hetero- or homogeneity, is based on the focus and objective of the study. In academic contexts, focus groups often occur with five to ten people. However, they can also be smaller in number. In their research on female adolescence, for example, Michelle Fine and Pat Macpherson (1992) invited four teenage girls to dinners of pizza and soda to talk about "being young women in the 1990s" (p. 175). Fine and Macpherson describe this ongoing focus group as a space that allowed the girls to express gendered resistance both individually and together. Somewhat similarly, in their research on women's beliefs about abortion Andrea Press and Elizabeth Cole (1999) asked women to invite like-minded friends to their homes to watch and discuss a television show about abortion. The researchers listened as the women debated among themselves about justifiable abortions. Both of these cases illustrate the unique nature of ethnographic focus groups. Unlike more typical, market-oriented focus groups, ethnographic focus groups are unrestricted and animated. They meet in a comfortable, natural-feeling setting and are smaller, most often with two to five individuals who are like-minded friends rather than strangers.

Surveys
An ethnographer's toolbox holds a host of other data collection methods, their uses all directly related to the information the researcher needs to answer the

research questions. Because of their closed-ended nature, **ethnographic surveys,** or "structured ethnographic data collection methods" (Schensul, Schensul, & LeCompte, 1999, p. 166), are used when an ethnographer wants to collect information from a representative sample in a community. These surveys or questionnaires tend to be conducted toward the end of fieldwork, and are used to gather data that have been suggested by observation and interviewing. Schensul, Schensul, and LeCompte (1999) provide detailed instructions for developing ethnographic surveys:

> The difference between structured ethnographic data collection and standard surveys centers on the fact that ethnographers base their quantitative research measures on locally based formative ethnographic research. By contrast, non-ethnographic quantitative research often is generated *a priori* on the basis of the researcher's experience alone or on another researcher's theoretical perspective using instruments established for other purposes and other populations. (p. 167)

After observing literacy groups and conducting interviews with adult learners in Botswana, for example, I conducted house-to-house surveys on literacy practices in all three of my sites in order to learn more about who reads what, and how both practice and access differ across villages and towns.

Projective Techniques

Ethnographers also employ **projective techniques** to obtain a better understanding of the ways individuals make meaning of and organize their world. Conducted in the field alongside observation and interviews, projective techniques might include asking individuals to respond to images, identify objects, describe dreams, or rate or rank items. As part of their research on the culture of romance on a college campus, Dorothy Holland and Margaret Eisenhart (1992) asked male and female informants to sort gender-marked terms into piles. By gaining insight on how females categorized men and men categorized women, Holland and Eisenhart hoped to discover "shared implicit knowledge . . . about cross gender relationships" (p. 234). I employed a different kind of projective technique in my current research in Botswana. In an attempt to understand the experiences of rapid modernization, commodification, and change, I asked my informants to reflect on ethnographic photographs of local peoples and places taken during the early twentieth century. I listened to the stories that the photographs elicited: childhood memories of family and changes in clothing, work, and housing experienced over more than fifty years.

Key Informants

While conducting fieldwork ethnographers regularly find that some people are better informants than others. These individuals are called **key informants.** Key informants might be community members who have extensive knowledge of the community or play an important role in the setting—and who are willing to share information with the ethnographer. In his ethnography *Street Corner Society*, William F. Whyte (1943) introduced one of the most famous key informants in ethnographic research, Doc, who became Whyte's guide, adviser, and mentor. As Whyte explained, Doc quickly evolved from informant to collaborator.

> At first he was simply a key informant—and also my sponsor. As we spent more time together, I ceased to treat him as a passive informant. I discussed with him quite frankly what I was trying to do, what problems were puzzling me, and so on. Much of our time was spent in this discussion of ideas and observations, so that Doc became, in a very real sense, a collaborator in the research. (p. 28)

In my own work, I was fortunate to meet Mma Francinah, who is my guide and sponsor in her village in eastern Botswana. A community activist and self-proclaimed "somebody" in the village, Mma introduced me around, vouched for me, and even got me to judge a beauty pageant at the local school. She enjoyed taking me under her wing, and I was honored to be there.

These close relationships between ethnographer and key informant or informants present unique challenges. Overreliance on a single key informant, for example, may provide limited or skewed data. The intimacy that develops as an ethnographer gains acceptance, develops friendships, and, at times, becomes a member of a community makes the maintenance of objectivity difficult. Although ethnography itself has been a "delicate balance of subjectivity and objectivity" (Clifford, 1986, p. 13), Ilene Kaplan's caution (1991) remains relevant: "Breaking away from the role of objective researcher not only calls into question the legitimacy of the research itself, but also creates unrealistic expectations among those being studied regarding what the researcher can and cannot do in the future" (p. 236).

Written Records and Artifacts

Finally, ethnographers also collect and analyze written records and artifacts and, when relevant, conduct archival research. In researching literacy practices in Botswana, for example, I collected the adult primers used in literacy classes, postliteracy chapter books, reports from the country's Department of Adult Literacy, and evaluations conducted on literacy in Botswana. I also gathered reports on demographics, economic statistics, education levels, and per capita income. Further, I recorded what was sold in markets and street stalls, and attended church services and funerals. Later, in an effort to better understand relationships among literacy, identity, everyday practices, and "historically situated" meaning (Barton & Hamilton, 2000, p. 13), I supplemented ethnographically collected information with historical data found in the archives of the Council for World Mission/London Missionary Society (CWM/LMS).

> **REFLECTION QUESTIONS**
>
> 1. What do ethnographers do in the field?
> 2. How does an informant differ from a research subject or an interviewee?

What Do Ethnographers Do with Their Data?

Given both the depth and breadth of ethnographic research, ethnographers collect a good deal of data. Their job then becomes one of finding patterns in that body of collected information. As Wolcott (1999) wrote, "Pattern seeking is not limited to ethnographers—it is basic to good diagnostic procedure—but it is a behavior characteristic among them, something they do almost out of habit" (p. 257). Because ethnography is **iterative** in that it continually circles back on itself, pattern seeking begins with fieldwork itself. Right from the start, developing research questions, recording field notes, and writing analytic memos about the research process spur the iterative process. As questions emerge, existing questions are modified and new questions formulated. This practice, in which data shape decisions about fieldwork, is the start of ethnographic data analysis. (See also Chapter Three for additional information on handling data.)

At the same time as this ongoing, in-the-field analysis occurs, the ethnographer engages in what Margaret LeCompte and Jean Schensul (1999, p. 37) call "tidying up," or organizing data for storage and retrieval. Most fundamentally that organization should include making copies of and ordering field notes; creating a management system, perhaps in an Excel spreadsheet; indexing all documents and artifacts; and finding a place for their safekeeping. The end result is a catalog of and secure storage system for all data collected. Tidying up is essential. Because ethnographic research builds on itself, ethnographers are always mucking about in their data. A workable system that affords easily retrievable data is imperative to both data collection and analysis. Some ethnographers develop a management system early in their data collection; others organize after returning from the field. Either way, LeCompte and Schensul (1999) assert that tidying up is a "necessary and preliminary kind of analysis, one that he [the ethnographer] needed to do before he could even begin to approach a more indepth examination of his voluminous data" (p. 37).

The more in-depth analysis—the finding of patterns—happens in a **deductive** manner, or from the top down, and in an **inductive** manner, from the bottom up. Deductive research tends to be theory testing. For example, an ethnographer may test an existing theory or hypothesis by collecting data in two sites in order to compare how theoretically defined practices differ across contexts. William Julius Wilson and Anmol Chaddha (2009) provide the following illustration:

> Consider, for example, a researcher attempting to test William Julius Wilson's theory of the social transformation of the inner city, which includes a number of key hypotheses on the effects of living in highly concentrated poverty areas (Wilson, 1987). One of these hypotheses states that individuals living in extreme poverty areas are much less likely to be tied into the job information network than those living in marginal poverty areas. This hypothesis could be tested by a participant observer who selects one neighborhood that represents an extreme poverty area and another that represents a marginal poverty area and observes patterns of work-related interactions in each neighborhood over an extended period. (p. 550)

Another way that ethnographers analyze deductively is in the use of existing codes or the development of a set of categories from relevant literature to guide their analysis. For instance, anthropologists may draw on a subset of the eighty-eight major culture classifications in the Human Relations Area Files (HRAF) to code their own data (Murdock, 1971). The HRAF describes dimensions of cultural, social, economic, and political life across nearly four hundred cultural groups, and includes generic codes on communication (gestures and signs); structures (dwellings and outbuildings); and labor (wages and salaries, and labor relations). In his research on injection drug users in Miami, Bryan Page (LeCompte & Schensul, 1999) employed the HRAF classification of Health, Illness, Medicine, and Death to code his ethnographic interviews and observations.

But most ethnographic research does not start with a preexisting coding system. Ethnographers tend to work inductively—that is, they generate codes from their data. Martyn Hammersley and Paul Atkinson (1983) wrote, "The process of analysis involves, simultaneously, the development of a set of analytic categories that capture relevant aspects of these data, and the assignment of particular items of data to those categories" (pp. 208–209). Among ethnographers these codes and analytic categories have at times been treated as though they emerge from "a kind of mystical process" (LeCompte & Schensul, 1999, p. 68). Over the last twenty years, however, several texts have been published that focus specifically on how ethnographers analyze data. In addition, workshops and training sessions that provide hands-on opportunities to review ethnographic data and begin the process of analysis are offered regularly at professional conferences.

For ethnographers, several steps are involved in analyzing data inductively:

1. A careful reading of the entire body of data
2. The development of codes that describe chunks of data
3. The combination and reclassification of codes into categories
4. The systematic structuring of categories into **typologies,** or classifications based on characteristics, and **taxonomies,** the ordered hierarchies of particular classifications

Two concepts, constant comparison and analytic induction, are important to this process. In the **constant comparative method,** analysis begins early in the study, is ongoing, and is nearly completed by the end of data collection.

A highly simplified version of constant comparison looks something like the following:

The ethnographer begins to identify and create categories that emerge as data are collected.

As she continues to collect data, the new information that is collected is compared to these emerging categories.

Categories are then shifted, modified, and expanded to accommodate the new data.

Themes begin to emerge across categories, which are tested as new data are collected.

Barney Glaser and Anselm Strauss's study (1965) of death and dying in a hospital provides a first account of the process of constant comparison. Glaser and Strauss described an analytic process that produced a set of identifiers that both marked and conveyed the social worth attached to the stages of life from serious illness to death. Their process continued until **theoretical saturation,** or the point at which additional analysis no longer contributes to anything new about a concept. Glaser and Strauss (1967) wrote that this is the point when

> no additional data are being found whereby the sociologist can develop properties of the category. As he sees similar instances over and over

again, the researcher becomes empirically confident that a category is saturated. . . . [W]hen one category is saturated, nothing remains but to go on to new groups for data on other categories, and attempt to saturate these categories also. (p. 61)

More can be found on the constant comparative method in Chapter Three, Grounded Theory.

In contrast, **analytic induction** is a systematic and exhaustive examination of a limited number of cases to provide generalizations about—and to "search for negative or disconfirming cases" (LeCompte and Schensul 1999, p. 77) of—a particular phenomenon. Analytic induction uses some procedures similar to those of **grounded theory;** however, grounded theory researchers want the concepts to emerge, whereas those who do analytic induction are interested specifically in producing and confirming the causes of a problem (drug addiction, for example). To quote Florian Znaniecki (1934, p. 237), who first named and described the approach, the aim of analytic induction is to induce "laws from a deep analysis of experimentally isolated instances." Although both methods of analysis are inductive, researchers employing analytic induction develop a possible explanation from what they know of the field, and then evaluate, amend, and reevaluate their hypothesis based on the identified data. Donald Cressey (1953, p. 16), who employed analytic induction in his research on the social psychology of embezzlement, lists the stages of analytic induction as

- Define the phenomenon
- Hypothesize an explanation
- Study one case to see if it fits the facts
- Modify the hypothesis or the definition in light of this fit
- Review further cases

Rather than defining terms in advance of the research, ethnographers who employ analytic induction consider their hunches, developed prior to or during data collection, as hypotheses to be tested, and they modify themes and relationships among themes as they proceed through the research process.

In addition to analyzing by hand, researchers also employ software to analyze ethnographically collected data. Several software programs are on the market, and they all replicate to some degree the process of tidying up, coding, and categorizing described earlier. Software does facilitate the process; it allows the easy search of large databases, and affords, for example, the possibility of locating every instance of a particular emic term in a set of field notes. Choices about software tend to be made based on compatibility, price, and ease of use.

> **REFLECTION QUESTIONS**
>
> 1. When does analysis occur in ethnographic research?
> 2. What is the difference between inductive and deductive analysis?

What Does Ethnographic Writing Look Like?

The first generation of ethnographers wrote in a literary style termed **ethnographic realism.** Derived from natural science writing, ethnographic realism is "a mode of writing that seeks to *represent* the reality of a whole world or form of life" (Marcus & Cushman, 1982, p. 29). According to George Marcus and Dick Cushman, ethnographic realism is marked by (1) an all-encompassing description of another culture; (2) an all-seeing yet distant narrator; (3) composite rather than specific individuals; (4) references to fieldwork only to establish the actual presence of the ethnographer; (5) a focus on everyday practices; (6) a rigid assertion that the emic perspective is represented; (7) sweeping statements preferred over accounts of specific details; (8) the use of jargon; and (9) abstract concepts that disregard the context of native language. The style here is firsthand, present tense, perpetually existing; the ethnographer's past fieldwork is portrayed in the eternal present. As James Clifford (1983) wrote, "The goal of ethnographic realism is to give the reader a sense of 'you are there, because I was there'" (p. 118).

George Marcus and Michael Fisher (1986) write that these classic monographs tended to be organized around five possible frames: "life history, life-cycle, ritual, aesthetic genres, and the dramatic incident of conflict" (p. 57). These themes are described through narratives and **vignettes**—short, impressionistic scenes that focus on one moment or give a particular insight into a character, idea, or setting. Many contain a classic **trope,** or common theme, such as a first encounter or arrival during fieldwork. An oft-cited example is from Malinowski's *Argonauts of the Western Pacific* (1922). Malinowski wrote, "Imagine yourself, suddenly set down surrounded by all your gear, alone on a tropical beach close to a native village, while the launch or dinghy which has brought you sails away, out of sight" (p. 4). This and other arrival scenes, part adventurer's travel log and part colonial exoticism, were intended to set the stage for the reader and establish the researcher as the lone fieldworker surrounded by strangers.

Over the past fifty years, however, postcolonial writers (Bhabha, 1993; Said, 1979; Spivak, 1987) have developed a critique of ethnographic realism, accusing the strong authorial narratives of the first generation of ethnographers of ethnocentrism and questioning the authority of their monographs. They raise questions of **representation**, that is, questions about the ethnographer's ability and power to accurately portray something or someone else. In the 1980s several texts, including George Marcus and Michael Fisher's *Anthropology as Critique: An Experimental Moment in the Human Sciences* in 1986; James Clifford and George Marcus's *Writing Culture: The Poetics and Politics of Ethnography* in 1986; and James Clifford's *The Predicament of Culture: Twentieth-Century Ethnography, Literature, and Art* in 1988, shone new light on ethnographic writing. These authors declared a crisis in ethnography, maintaining that Western researchers could no longer portray non-Western peoples with uncontested authority, and asserting that cultural representation is always partial, contested, and political. The authors identified and encouraged experimental texts that are unconventional—that are **polyphonic,** or many voiced, and **heteroglossic,** or having contrasting styles of communication and points of view. Many examples of this experimental use of ethnography are available (Crapanzano, 1985; Fischer & Abedi, 2002; Mahmood, 2005; Masco, 2006; Maurer, 2005; Petryn, 2002; Stewart, 1996; Taussig, 1991, 2005; Tsing, 2004). To quote George Marcus (2007, p. 1127), these "messy" texts are "self-conscious experiments in bringing out the experiential, interpretive, dialogical, and polyphonic process at work in any ethnography."

These experimental ethnographers tend toward two strategies. They write with **reflexivity,** or introspection; their accounts examine their own sociohistorical locations, in which they are also actors in the story in order to lessen the distance between ethnographer and informant and to negate the suggestion of an all-seeing yet distant narrator. Or they include varied perspectives of ethnographic informants in an attempt to show rather than tell the reader. To address the critiques of ethnographic realism, alternative forms of writing have also appeared, including ethnographic drama (Allen & Garner, 1996; Richardson & Lockridge, 1991; Tillman, 2008); ethnographic poetry (Kusserow, 2002; Lowenstein, 2005); and autoethnography (see Chapter Eight for a detailed explanation of this form of writing).

REFLECTION QUESTIONS

1. What is ethnographic realism?
2. How does experimental ethnography differ from ethnographic realism? Why is this important?

How Do We Know an Ethnography Is Good?

Questions of **validity,** that is, how we know that research findings are trustworthy, are constants in conversations about research methodology. Like all researchers, ethnographers must convince readers and reviewers that their work is credible; that events in the field are described accurately, and in scientific terms; and that the research findings are valid. Ethnographers define validity in particular ways. According to Roger Sanjek (1990), ethnographic validity is determined "according to three canons: theoretical candor, the ethnographer's path, and fieldnote evidence" (p. 395). In other words, validity-rich ethnography is transparent.

The ethnographer shows how her choices about fieldwork—from the initial broad net to the more selective and systematic data collection that follows—were guided by emerging theory. She also clearly describes her research path, specifying the actual network of informants and contacts with whom she engages. Ideally, information about the ethnographer's path includes the ethnography's size and range; demographic data about the informants (gender, occupation, age); and the path from one informant to the next. Ethnographic validity is strengthened by knowing who and how many people participated in the research, and the range of perspectives they brought to the inquiry. Finally, it is incumbent on an ethnographer to show the relationship between the ethnographic report and the field notes, that is, actual excerpts of the data, on which it is based. However, as Sanjek (1990) notes, "My own admiration of fieldnote-rich ethnographies is obvious, but the canon of fieldnote evidence requires only that the relationship between fieldnotes and ethnography be explicit. Ethnographic validity is served by, but does not require, extensive fieldnote documentation" (p. 403). For ethnographic writers the challenge is to include selected or filtered field notes that make the results credible and the ethnographer's arguments plausible.

Triangulation, the process of using data from different sources (for example, historical documents, interviews, informal conversations, observations) to support a conclusion, is important to establishing validity. As Fetterman (1989) wrote, triangulation "is at the heart of ethnographic validity, testing one source of information against another to strip away alternative explanations and attempt to prove an hypothesis" (p. 94). Triangulation corroborates the researcher's findings across sources or techniques, seeks convergence of information on a common finding or concept, and is useful in proving hypotheses or constructing models.

External reliability, a term typically coupled with *validity* in discussions on the rigor of research, refers to the extent to which a study and its results can be replicated by another researcher. Yet, as Margaret LeCompte and Judith Goetz (1982) point out, the ethnographic process is "personalistic; no ethnographer works just like another" (p. 36). That said, issues of reliability can be challenging for ethnographers. LeCompte and Goetz maintain that ethnographers enhance the external reliability of their data when they describe their own status position in fieldwork relations, identify and justify their choices of informants, recognize how social situations and conditions shape informants' disclosure, explicitly identify the assumptions that underlie analytic constructs and premises, and clearly present methods of data collection and analysis. Transparency in regard to process is again key here.

Internal reliability refers to the degree to which another researcher would agree with the ethnographer's data analysis and conclusions. Ethnographers do several things to reduce threats to internal reliability. They use **low-inference descriptors,** or terms that are as concrete and specific as possible, including verbatim quotes and narratives, in their field notes. When possible they do **member checks** by having their informants review their own interview transcripts for accuracy. They confirm the accuracy of field notes with local informants, and they verify their results through the review of their peers. And when ethnographers use devices that record and preserve their data, they have a data trail that can be reviewed by other researchers (LeCompte & Goetz, 1982).

REFLECTION QUESTIONS

1. What strategies do ethnographers employ to enhance their research credibility? What strategies do you consider most critical to accepting an ethnographer's findings and interpretations?
2. How do ethnographers' understandings of validity and reliability compare with your previous understanding of these concepts?

What's the State of Ethnography Today?

Ethnography as research methodology has undergone many changes since the first generation of anthropologists took to the field in safari hats just after the turn of the last century. The end of colonization in Africa and Asia in the 1960s and 1970s was accompanied by a strong postcolonial critique of anthropology as a discipline and ethnography as methodology. Anthropologists were criticized for their dependence on colonial governments for funds, patronage, and at times protection, and on missionaries who provided "grammars, transportation, introductions, and in certain cases . . . a deeper translation of language and customs than can be acquired in a one- or two-year visit" (Clifford, 1997, p. 65). Equally important, according to postcolonial scholars, is that the ethnographies that were produced reinforced the image of the colonialist subject (Asad, 1995; Clifford, 1997; Salemink, 2000).

These critiques led to vigorous debates within and across disciplines concerning ethnographic methodology, researcher positionality, and representation. Postcolonial anthropologists (Kondo, 1990; Limón, 1994; Rosaldo, 1989; Taussig, 1997) have challenged and blurred anthropological distance while examining the organization of power by colonial governments, the modern state, and market systems. Feminist ethnographers (Abu-Lughod, 2000; Behar, 1993; Mahmood, 2005; Strathern, 2005) have critiqued dualisms of subject-object, researcher-researched, nature-culture, public-private, and self-other, and advocated examinations of authority, reproduction, emotion, and agency. Critical ethnographers (see also Chapter Fifteen) have expanded the role of ethnographer to include advocate, have widened the ethnographic focus to include both structure and agency, and have focused the ethnographic aim to embrace social justice and transformation.

The result is that rather than "a normative practice of outsiders visiting/studying insiders" (Clifford, 1997, p. 81), ethnography has become a practice of attending to "shifting identities in relationship with the people and issues an anthropologist seeks to represent" (Narayan, 1993, p. 682). That change is visible in course work, conferences, and publications. Classes on ethnography regularly address ethics, fieldwork identities, and researcher reflexivity, and conferences on ethnographic research center around themes like those of the 2010 Contemporary Ethnography Across the Disciplines (CEAD) conference hosted by the University of Waikato in Hamilton, New Zealand: emerging methods, practice and advocacy, and social justice and transformation. Increased reflexivity, or researchers' examination of their own sociohistorical locations, have typically become part of ethnographic narratives (Hammersley and Atkinson, 1983). The goal is to replace the disembodied, all-seeing anthropologists with ethnographers who are politically committed and geographically and historically situated.

Summary

Ethnographic research enables us to better understand the role of culture in both everyday and special practices and events. The goal of ethnographic research is to describe ways of life from an insider's, or emic, perspective, in a manner that is comprehensible from an etic, or outsider's, point of view. Through prolonged fieldwork involving participant observation, interviews, and other research methods, ethnographers describe and interpret cultural patterns, identify social reproduction and cultural continuities, and examine resistance and cultural change. Both theory testing and theory generating, ethnographers seek out patterns that help us understand and address problems on the micro level of the classroom and on the macro level of global exchange networks. Coming of age alongside dramatic changes in post–World War II global power structures, ethnographers have been the focus of a postcolonial critique concerning their role in reproducing first world–third world and north-south power structures. The result has been an emergence of experimental writing, increasingly reflexive accounts of fieldwork, and ethnographies informed by critical and postmodern theories.

Key Terms

analytic induction, 179
constant comparative method, 178
cultural interpretation, 165
deductive, 177
emic, 165
ethnographic interviews, 173
ethnographic realism, 180
ethnographic surveys, 174
ethnography, 165
etic, 165
external reliability, 182
fieldwork, 169
focus groups, 173
full cycle of activities, 170
gatekeepers, 168
grounded theory, 179
heteroglossic, 181

in-depth, 173
inductive, 177
informants, 165
informed consent, 169
in situ, 170
institutional review boards (IRBs), 169
internal reliability, 183
iterative, 176
key informants, 175
low-inference descriptors, 183
member checks, 183
multi-sited ethnographies, 166
naturalistic, 166
non-participant participant observer, 172
open-ended, 173

participant observation, 171
polyphonic, 181
practices, 170
problem focus, 167
projective techniques, 174
reflexivity, 181
representation, 181
salvage ethnography, 167
taxonomies, 178
theoretical saturation, 178
thick description, 165
triangulation, 182
trope, 180
typologies, 178
validity, 182
vignettes, 180

Further Readings and Resources

Suggested Ethnographic Studies

Abu-Lughod, L. (2000). *Veiled sentiments: Honor and poetry in a Bedouin society*. Berkeley: University of California Press.
This is an ethnographic study of gender relations, veiling, and the Bedouin code of honor based on two years of fieldwork in a Bedouin community in northern Egypt.

Bourgois, P. I. (1995). *In search of respect: Selling crack in El Barrio*. New York: Cambridge University Press.
This ethnography of crack cocaine use in New York's Spanish Harlem epitomizes the challenge of ethnographic observation in high-risk settings.

Crapanzano, V. (1985). *Tuhami: Portrait of a Moroccan*. Chicago: University of Chicago Press.
The study of an illiterate Moroccan tile maker is written as an experimental ethnography.

Evans-Pritchard, E. E. (1940). *The Nuer: A description of the modes of livelihood and political institutions of a Nilotic people*. Oxford, England: Clarendon Press.
Evans-Pritchard delineates the Neur lineage system in this classic ethnographic account of the social organization of pastoralists in Sudan.

Holland, D. C., & Eisenhart, M. A. (1992). *Educated in romance: Women, achievement, and college culture*. Chicago: University of Chicago Press.
This educational ethnography on gender relations and romantic and academic success is based on ten years of fieldwork with college women.

Lareau, A. (2000). *Home advantage: Social class and parental intervention in elementary education*. Lanham, MD: Rowman & Littlefield.
In this educational ethnography the author examines socioeconomic status and parental involvement in two elementary schools.

MacLeod, J. (1987). *Ain't no makin' it: Leveled aspirations in a low-income neighborhood*. Boulder, CO: Westview.
In this urban ethnography MacLeod theorizes on social reproduction, inequality, and the social mobility of young men in a public housing project.

Malinowski, B. (1922). *Argonauts of the western Pacific*. Long Grove, IL: Waveland.
Malinowski's ethnography on kula (shell necklace and armband) exchange among the Trobriand Islanders set the stage for modern ethnographic fieldwork.

Mead, M. (1928). *Coming of age in Samoa; a psychological study of primitive youth for Western civilization*. New York: William Morrow.
Mead's ethnographic fieldwork among Samoan youth, highly publicized upon publication, has been contested by succeeding anthropologists.

Riemer, F. (2001). *Working at the margins: Moving off welfare in America*. Albany: State University of New York Press.

The author's ethnographic research finds the transition from welfare to work to be a mechanism for social reproduction in urban America.

Whyte, W. F. (1943). *Street corner society*. Chicago: University of Chicago Press.

Whyte's urban ethnography of the intricate street worlds of "Cornerville," an Italian American slum in Boston's North End, is considered a classic in sociological research.

Other Suggested Readings

Clifford, J., & Marcus, G. (1986). *Writing culture: The poetics and politics of ethnography*. Berkeley: University of California Press.

The authors examine ethnographic realism and offer new ways of writing ethnography to reflect the postmodern world system.

Fetterman, D. M. (1989). *Ethnography: Step by step*. Newbury Park, CA: Sage.

This is a guide to conducting ethnographic research.

Geertz, C. (1973). *The interpretation of cultures*. New York: Basic Books.

This book contains classic essays on culture, its role in social life, and how it ought to be studied.

Marcus, G. E. (1998). *Ethnography through thick and thin*. Princeton, NJ: Princeton University Press.

This is an examination of the current state of ethnographic research and writing.

Wolcott, H. F. (1999). *Ethnography: A way of seeing*. Walnut Creek, CA: AltaMira.

This is an examination of the distinct nature of ethnography and what it means to conduct research in the ethnographic tradition.

Organizations and Web Sites

American Anthropological Association (AAA) (www.aaanet.org/)
Founded in 1902, the AAA is the world's largest organization of individuals interested in anthropology.

Annual Ethnography in Education Research Forum, University of Pennsylvania, Philadelphia (www.gse.upenn.edu/cue/forum)
This is the largest annual meeting of qualitative researchers in education.

Anthropology & Education Quarterly (www.wiley.com/bw/journal.asp?ref=0161–7761)
This peer-reviewed journal publishes ethnographic research on schooling in social and cultural contexts and on human learning both inside and outside of schools.

Ethnography (http://eth.sagepub.com/)
This is an international, interdisciplinary journal for the ethnographic study of social and cultural change.

Society for Applied Anthropology (SfAA) (www.sfaa.net/)
This professional society promotes the investigation of human behavior and practical applications to contemporary issues.

University of Surrey's Computer Assisted Qualitative Data AnalysiS (CAQDAS) Networking Project (www.surrey.ac.uk/sociology/research/researchcentres/caqdas/) The site provides practical support, training, and information on software programs designed to assist with qualitative data analysis. The site follows debates concerning methodological and epistemological issues arising from the use of software packages, and the project supports research into methodological applications of CAQDAS.

CHAPTER 8

TREKKING THROUGH AUTOETHNOGRAPHY

Tony E. Adams
Carolyn Ellis

Key Ideas

- Autoethnographers work to provide dense descriptions of a person's experience with a culture in order to better understand this culture and an individual's experience in it.

- Autoethnography developed in response to oppressive, colonialist, and inhumane research practices, and from recognition that human differences matter.

- Autoethnography is both process and product, a way of doing and representing research.

- Autoethnographers combine aspects of autobiography and ethnography: similar to autobiographers, they value personal experience and evocative writing; similar to ethnographers, they work to provide dense descriptions of cultural experience.

- Autoethnography can take a myriad of forms, all of which depend on an autoethnographer's goals for a project.

- Benefits of autoethnography include (1) its therapeutic possibilities, that is, its ability to help authors, research participants, and audience members transform their lives; and (2) its valuing of relational ethics—the interpersonal ties and responsibilities researchers have to those they study.

We begin this chapter by providing an example of what autoethnography is and does. We then discern characteristics of autoethnography and conclude by asking questions about our opening, introductory experiences. We weave conversation, personal reflection, and analysis throughout, and, in so doing, show how autoethnographic writing, research, and representation can look and feel.

Walking a Fine Line: Tony's Introduction

I (Tony) put on my pack and approach the start of a fourteen-mile overnight hike. I am with my friends Carolyn and Art, and two of their friends whom I have never met, Cindy and Susan.

Typically I am fine interacting with strangers for a short time. But with the length of time we'll spend together, two days and a night, I feel sure the unfamiliar others will ask about my life, particularly my relationships, research interests, and teaching. And I feel anxious: as a gay man who studies and teaches about gay identity, I put pressure on myself about deciding when and how to inform others of my identity and my work.

I fear negative responses to my identity, particularly from people who find gayness inappropriate or immoral. Persons who identify as or are perceived to be gay are often targets of physical violence (Pascoe, 2007), and in places like the United States, same-sex relationships are not recognized as a legitimate kind of coupling in many significant contexts (such as hospitals, governments, and families). Such institutions as the military (Brouwer, 2004); the education system (Gust & Warren, 2008); and some religious sects (Cobb, 2006) require a person to vigilantly regulate or stay silent about same-sex desire, and intimate same-sex affairs are often absent from or disregarded in mundane conversation (Foster, 2008).

Personal experiences of negative attitudes toward being gay also flood my memory: an aunt who, after I said, "I am gay," no longer allows me to visit; an ex-lover who may have killed himself after coming out to his father; and a student who reported me to the president of the university for being out in the classroom—the student and the president didn't think "gay" had any part in a college curriculum. I also recall the man interviewing me for a job who told me during the interview that he was gay but no one else at his university knew (he feared such information would tarnish his case for tenure); the female student who, the week after I came out to the class, wrote in a paper that she liked women but refused to talk about it with anyone (as of this writing, three years later, she still has told only one other person); and the high school acquaintance, who, after inferring from my Myspace Web page that I date men, e-mailed me for advice on getting out of reparative therapy, therapy required and funded by his parents to "correct" his same-sex desire.

These examples and experiences provide the context for the anxiety I feel as I approach a long, overnight hike with two strangers. I want to enjoy the experience but cannot *not* concern myself with whether, when, and how to disclose whom I like to love and what I like to study. I can keep my gay self and work secret, but I know it may be difficult should mundane questions about my relationships or my research enter the conversation—such questions as "Are you married?" "Do you have a girlfriend?" and "What do you teach about and study?"

But secrecy has its problems too. If I come out later into the hike, the strangers may consider me manipulative (Downs, 2005; Phellas, 2005) and possibly shameful of my identity and relational interests (Yoshino, 2006). The (potentially dangerous) reactions I experience on coming out may thus happen not because another finds gayness inappropriate or immoral but rather because I kept my identity and work interests hidden too long or because the others were upset that I wrongly assumed that they would be less than okay with my gayness. With self-disclosure being "embedded in the history of past disclosures" (Bochner, 1984, p. 610), an omission of personal information might mark me as having told a lie (Brown-Smith, 1998).

I could come out with my identity and interests immediately upon meeting unfamiliar others, but this might make for discomfort as well. From my perspective, I might say, "Hi, I'm Tony and I'm gay," a tactless greeting. Though it may make me feel better to tell others of my gayness, the fear that my statement might make others uncomfortable makes me uncomfortable. And so I decide against coming out immediately, and instead wait and hope for a more comfortable time to disclose (Adams, 2011).

"What do you do for a living?" Susan asks, a common one-liner that is about as safe as talking about the weather—usually.

"I teach college," I respond. I do not say, "I am also a researcher and writer," as these statements might invite her to ask what I research and write *about*. Given that my topic is gay identity, discussing my research and writing can serve as coming out. Even though I know numerous heterosexual-identified scholars who write about gay identity, I recognize that one who researches and writes about homosexuality may be marked and, consequently, evaluated as gay, at least until proving heterosexuality.

I recall advice from an interviewer for an academic job I did not get: "Say you research and write about 'sexuality,' not 'gay identity,'" she said. "I know you write about gay identity, and I am okay with it. But I also know that you made other faculty uncomfortable—they found the topic of gay identity inappropriate and immoral."

I remember dissonance rolling through my body: I felt sad for making other people uncomfortable, disingenuous for thinking about masking my work as more general ("sexuality") than specific ("gay identity"), angry that others still consider gay identity inappropriate and immoral, and regretful for hearing that had I changed a few words I might have been offered the job. I continue to feel unsure about the threshold of coming out—the threshold of needing and wanting to be open and honest with others while still being able to be open and honest with myself (Bochner, 1984).

Now I am in a similar situation, worried about how strangers may be offended by or uncomfortable with my gay identity or with hearing about work that may mark me as gay. But saying I study sexuality feels like a lie, and I hear the voices of friends, family, and pro-gay commentators who refer to being out as healthy, a sign of maturity, and politically responsible (Yoshino, 2006); choosing to *not* tell is rarely considered a good, viable option (Adams, 2011).

I compromise with myself: not wanting to start off on the "wrong foot," I feel fine saying "I teach college" at the start of the trip, but only as long as I force myself to come out later.

"What do you do for a living?" I ask Susan.

"I'm a dental assistant," she responds. "I primarily help dental surgeons with surgery."

"Sounds interesting," I remark.

"Oh, it is. I have some great stories."

"Do tell!" Carolyn says. "Entertain us—we have at least six more miles to hike today, and six more tomorrow."

"There was this time a male patient underwent anesthesia," Susan begins. "His girlfriend was in the room, and apparently the patient had done some time in prison."

I start to feel uncomfortable . . . again.

"The anesthesia started making the patient disoriented just as the male surgeon entered the room," she continues. "And, in front of his girlfriend, the patient begins talking about his attraction for men and is flirting with the oral surgeon."

I have a few ideas about where this story may go. Susan may describe the surgeon's response to the patient's flirting, the girlfriend's response to her boyfriend's flirting, or her own reaction. But regardless of the story's direction, I sense Susan may evaluate same-sex desire, either implicitly with the tone of her voice or explicitly with direct commentary.

I know I must act, but do I step in and say "I am attracted to men" to protect her from saying something offensive? Do I let her say something offensive, and *then* tell her that I am gay? Do I let her say something offensive, and hope that I can keep my same-sex desire hidden for the remainder of the hike?

"Apparently the patient had a few boyfriends in prison," Susan continues.

Nervously, I decide to protect Susan and myself by steering the conversation in another direction. "Did the girlfriend know of his attraction to men?"

"I don't think so," she responds. "But in prison he . . ."

"I bet his flirting made the girlfriend uncomfortable," I interrupt.

"I guess it may have," she says, sounding somewhat confused.

The tone of her voice indicates that the story has ended, the subject changed. I sense that I do not have to worry about being offended by an antigay remark or having to come out . . . yet (Adams, 2011).

Hiking into "Two Men's" Land: Carolyn's Introduction

"Hi," I (Carolyn) say to Cindy, as she gets out of the small rental car. It is 8:30 A.M., and we are committed to getting on the trail by nine. Cindy returns the greeting and then gets down to the work of adjusting her walking poles and backpack. Her friend Susan is performing the same task. Tony, a friend and former student, my partner, Art, and I lace up our shoes and help each other with our backpacks. I notice ours are considerably lighter than those of Cindy and Susan. Though I wonder what we forgot, I am glad not to have to carry such a heavy load.

Anxious to get on the trail, I take the lead. After an hour or so, I drop back behind Tony and between Susan and Cindy, who has been an acquaintance for many years.

"Hey, Cindy, we could introduce Tony to Judy. Wouldn't that be good?" Susan says. I cringe as I realize that Cindy and Susan do not know that Tony is gay. I feel anxious and wonder how to handle this. I have spent a lot of time with Tony, but it has always been around people who know he is gay. I'm used to Tony's being out, even flamboyant at times, celebrating his gayness. That's the Tony I know. I realize I don't know how to handle this situation. How would Tony want me to handle it? I don't want to out him if that isn't what he wants. Yet I don't want to hide that he is gay, which makes it seem I am in some way less than okay with that. I'm sorry Tony and I didn't talk about how to handle this situation before the trip. Now there is no opportunity to do so. I am surprised that Susan assumes Tony is straight. And then I am not. Why shouldn't she? Tony could pass for straight. I also am concerned for Susan. I don't know her well enough to know her politics, though I believe I have heard that she is a voting Republican. I feel nervous that she may say something untoward and embarrass herself and us. So what do I do? Her remark was not directed at me or at Tony. I am not sure Tony even heard her. I decide not to say anything and to wait until the time seems appropriate.

"Tony isn't married, is he?" Susan asks me quietly, a while later, perhaps noticing my silence in response to her earlier remark. Apparently she is still thinking about matchmaking.

"No, he isn't," I say hesitantly, "but . . ."

"I should've brought my sister on the hike," she interrupts. "The two of them would . . ."

"But he just moved in with someone in Chicago," I continue.

"Oh," she says, seeming disappointed though happy for Tony. Okay, I think, at least I've made the first step. I told the truth, but I didn't tell her Tony was gay. I could have said "with a man," but I didn't. Though he is partnered with a man, he is not literally married: being married is not an option for him where he lives. However, Susan didn't ask if he was gay or straight, rather if he was married. Did she notice I didn't say "with a woman?" I continue hoping to get some private time with Tony to talk about this. It feels strange not to be open about Tony's being gay. Certainly this lack of openness has little to do with me, but I worry that later others might assume that I felt Tony's gayness should be hidden. Or they might be upset that I didn't inform them earlier. I'm starting to feel viscerally some of the dilemmas that Tony has talked about in terms of revealing his gay identity.

Susan asks Tony what he teaches, and I notice that Tony gives a general answer. "I teach college." I feel he is underplaying himself. He does a whole lot more than that, but Tony doesn't elaborate, and I realize that he doesn't want to say what he teaches. I take this as a cue that he is not ready to come out or to talk about sexuality.

"What do you do?" Tony asks her back. This seems a safe question. I listen as Susan describes her work as an assistant to an oral surgeon. When she talks about people under anesthesia, I ask for stories. "Well, there was this one man . . ." she begins. Quickly I realize she is telling a story about a man who was attracted to men. Where will this go? Oh, please don't say anything that you'll later regret, I think, or that will hurt Tony. Besides, I like her, and I don't want her to have negative feelings about the man's attraction to men, which I fear would interfere with the way I see her. I am relieved when Tony changes the direction of the story, and I follow along.

But I keep thinking about Tony's identity. What will happen next? Outing him may not be the thing to do, but my silence feels wrong too. I want Susan and the others to know Tony is gay because they can't really get to know him as long as they assume he is straight. Perhaps his sexuality should make no difference, but it does. I realize that being gay permeates a lot of one's identity. The silence surrounding Tony's sexuality means that Tony has to go along with the pretense that he is something other than what he is. I think about how comfortable Tony is with being gay most of the time. I contemplate what I can do to make people on the trail aware of Tony's being gay without making too much of an issue out of it or making anyone uncomfortable.

"Would Jerry like this hike?" I ask Tony, in a strategic yet innocent voice loud enough for others to hear. I think that the meaning of this statement is obvious for those who are open to gay sexuality, yet can be avoided by anyone who doesn't want to know. It is also a statement that throws an opening to Tony to indicate how he wants to play the scene.

"I don't think so," Tony says, seemingly comfortable with my question. "He wouldn't have Internet access in many places, and the lack of access would be difficult given that he teaches an online class." Tony could have just said no and let it go at that.

"Who's Jerry?" Susan asks, taking the bait.

I hesitate a moment and then say, "Tony's partner."

"Oh," Susan says and nods thoughtfully.

"Well, I guess that takes care of partnering him with Judy then," Cindy says and chuckles. I felt sure that Cindy, who is open-minded and liberal, would have no trouble with Tony's being gay. But now it's Susan whose reaction I try to gauge. Her body language remains open, and I am hopeful that though this information has surprised her, it has not distressed her, except in terms of her matchmaking. We walk silently for a while.

Later, I get a chance to talk privately to Susan when she and I stop to urinate in the woods. "I'm sorry I didn't tell you earlier that Tony is gay," I say, and then feel almost disloyal to Tony. Why should this even demand a conversation? Why should I want to make sure Susan feels okay about this when it's really Tony's feelings that concern me more? Yet I don't want Susan to feel I intentionally deceived her by waiting too long to tell her.

"I am fine with his being gay," she says. "I know lots of gay people. That doesn't bother me at all." I listen and watch her closely. She speaks rapidly and is a little nervous, but I believe her. And if she's just saying that for me, then so be it; maybe if she says it enough it will be true.

REFLECTION QUESTIONS

1. Can you relate to Tony's or Carolyn's experience? Have you been in a situation in which you felt you had to hide your identity or in which you had multiple audiences who knew you from different contexts? Describe what happened and how you coped with the situation.

Teaching By Fire: Together, Talking About Autoethnography

After eight miles, we finally reach the summit of Mt. LaConte. Wet from the downpour that occurred halfway up the trail, we enter the lodge to dry off around the fire. Cindy offers us some Baileys Irish Cream that she has carried up the mountain in a plastic flask. We take her offering eagerly, and now understand why her pack was so much larger than ours!

"I don't really understand what you all do," says Cindy, looking at Art, Tony, and me. "I know you all work in the Communication Department at USF (University of South Florida), but you seem to write stories."

"We all do **autoethnography,**" Carolyn replies, as she pours Baileys into her steaming coffee. "Autoethnography is the study of self in culture. We're particularly interested in how people tell stories about their lives." Art and Tony make eye contact and smile, both seeming to know that an intellectual discussion about autoethnography is about to happen.

"But what is your method for doing research?" Cindy asks. "Do you study how people speak? Do you conduct interviews about social issues? Do you have a laboratory?"

"Autoethnography is a method for doing and writing research. It is a method that uses personal experience to understand cultural experience (Ellis, 2004; Holman Jones, 2005); it is a way of doing research that allows a researcher to use personal experience to describe and analyze the everyday 'actual empirical life' of culture" (Blumer, 1969, p. 31).

"Autoethnography doesn't sound like traditional research," Cindy says, "especially because it uses and values personal experience."

"The method isn't traditional," Carolyn replies. "Autoethnography developed in response to three issues with traditional research. First, there was the **crisis of confidence**—concerns about what research was; how research should be done; and ways a researcher can, and should, represent others. Second, there were scholars challenging the bias against the use and valuing of personal experience in research. Third, there was an increasing awareness of and respect for human difference and **identity politics**—that is, an awareness that the kinds of people we claim to be, or are perceived to be, matter (Ellis & Bochner, 2000).

"Gradually," Art says, joining the conversation, "scholars across a wide spectrum of disciplines began to consider what social sciences would become if they were closer to literature than to physics, if they privileged stories rather than theories, and if they were self-consciously value-centered rather than pretending to be value free (Bochner, 1994). Many of these scholars turned to autoethnography because they wanted to concentrate on ways of producing meaningful, accessible, and evocative research grounded in personal experience, research that would sensitize readers to experiences shrouded in silence and to forms of representation that deepen our capacity to empathize with people who are different" (Ellis & Bochner, 2000).

"I've never heard of the crisis of confidence," Susan responds, "but I understand the importance of leaving out personal experience in research—so that the research won't be biased. How does a person's identity influence the research process or what this person knows?"

"Well, let me first describe the crisis of confidence," Art replies. "This will provide a better understanding of the need for and use of personal experience as well as the increased importance of identities."

"In the 1980s," he says, "many scholars became troubled by social science's limitations (Ellis & Bochner, 2000). In particular, they realized that the 'facts' and 'truths' scientists 'found' were inextricably tied to the vocabularies and paradigms the scientists used to represent them (Rorty, 1982). They began to understand the impossibility of and lack of desire for **master, universal narratives**—that is, stories that apply to and are relevant for all people in all places at all times (Lyotard, 1984). Scholars began to recognize new relationships between authors, audiences, and texts (Radway, 1984). And they began viewing stories as complex, formative, meaningful phenomena that taught morals and ethics, introduced unique ways of thinking and feeling, and helped people make sense of themselves and others" (Bochner, 2001, 2002).

"There was also a growing need to resist colonialist, inhumane research practices," Tony adds, "specifically the researcher's practice of entering a culture; exploiting cultural members; and then recklessly leaving to write about the culture for personal, monetary, and professional gain, all the while disregarding the researcher's relationships to the culture and with cultural members" (Ellis, 2007).

"And even though some researchers still assume that research can be done from a neutral, impersonal, and objective stance" (Atkinson, 1997; Delamont, 2009), Art says, "most recognize that such an assumption is not tenable (Bochner, 2002; Rorty, 1982). For instance, a researcher decides who, when, where, and how to research, what questions to ask, and what topics to avoid. These decisions are tied to institutional requirements (such as institutional review boards), resources (such as funding), and personal circumstance (such as a researcher's studying cancer because of personal experience with cancer). A researcher may also change names for protection (Fine, 1993), compress years of research into a single text, and construct a study in a predetermined way (such as using an introduction, literature review, methods section, findings section, and conclusion). Autoethnography emerges as a method to acknowledge and accommodate a researcher's influence on research; the method doesn't advocate hiding from this influence or assume that it doesn't exist."

"In addition," Tony says, "scholars interested in identity and standpoint theory began recognizing that different people possess different ways of speaking, writing, valuing, and believing. These differences can stem from race (Boylorn, 2006; Marvasti, 2006); gender (Crawley, 2002; Pelias, 2007); sexuality (Foster, 2008); age (Paulson & Willig, 2008); ability (Couser, 1997); and class (Dykins Callahan, 2008). For the most part, those who advocate for traditional ways of doing and writing research advocate for a white, masculine, heterosexual, middle- and upper-class, able-bodied perspective. Following this logic, a traditional researcher not only disregards other ways of knowing but also implies that these other ways are unsatisfactory and invalid. Conversely, autoethnography works to recognize how the kinds of people we claim or are perceived to be influence interpretations of what we study, how we study it, and what we say about what we study" (Adams, 2005).

Doing Autoethnography: Continuing the Conversation

"I think we're telling Cindy and Susan more than they want or need to know here," Carolyn remarks, worrying that the academic tone of the conversation is off-putting. "What else would you like to know?" she asks.

"What you've said is helpful, though a bit complex," says Cindy; Susan nods. "I'd like to know more about how to use or do or write autoethnography."

"Let's go back to the basics," Carolyn replies. "Autoethnography combines characteristics of autobiography and ethnography. Are you familiar with autobiographies, particularly how autobiographies are written?"

"A person writes the story of a life, yes?" says Susan, hesitantly.

"That's the basic premise, but there are methods for doing this. For instance, when writing an **autobiography,** a person retroactively and selectively writes about past experiences. Usually the person does not live through these experiences solely to make them part of a published document; rather, these experiences are assembled using hindsight" (Denzin, 1989a).

"Autobiographers also tend to write about **epiphanies,**" Art interjects, "moments perceived to have significantly influenced the trajectory of a life, events after which life never seems quite the same" (Couser, 1997; Denzin, 1989a).

"So if I write about my epiphanies, am I doing autoethnography?" Susan asks.

"Not yet," says Carolyn. "This is where the **ethnography** aspect of autoethnography comes in. An ethnographer studies a culture's practices, common values and beliefs, and shared experiences in order to help **insiders**—cultural members—and **outsiders**—cultural strangers—better understand the culture (Maso, 2001). Ethnographers do this by becoming **participant observers** in and of the culture by taking notes of their part in and others' engagement with cultural practices (Geertz, 1973; Goodall, 2001). An ethnographer may also interview cultural members (Berry, 2005); examine ways of speaking and relating (Ellis, 1986); investigate uses of space and place (Makagon, 2004); and analyze artifacts, such as clothing and architecture (Borchard, 1998), and such texts as books, movies, and photographs" (Goodall, 2006; see also Chapter Seven, Ethnographic Research).

"Does this make sense?" Carolyn asks.

"I understand autobiography and ethnography separately," says Cindy. "I think I could write an autobiography. I think I could do ethnography. But I'm not sure how to combine them."

Carolyn glances at Tony and nods. "When a person does autoethnography," he says, "the person retrospectively and selectively writes about meaningful experiences—those epiphanies—that are made possible by being part of a culture and from possessing a particular cultural identity. But in addition to telling about these epiphanies, autoethnographers are often required by social scientific conventions to analyze these epiphanies by comparing them to existing research, interviewing others with similar epiphanies, and using their academic training to interrogate the meaning of an experience. The autoethnographer does this with the hope of making characteristics of a culture familiar for insiders and outsiders."

"How do you begin to write and do autoethnography?" Cindy asks Carolyn.

"I begin by describing meaningful personal experiences, my epiphanies."

"Such as . . . ?" asks Susan.

"Such as epiphanies about death and dying (Ellis, 1993, 1995b); abortion (Bochner & Ellis, 1995); racial tension and prejudice (Ellis, 1995c, 2002, 2009b); the use of emotions in research (Ellis, 1991); and the relational obligations researchers have to those they study" (Ellis, 1995a, 2007), Carolyn explains.

"Other autoethnographers have studied epiphanies related to eating disorders (Tillmann, 2009); troubled relationships (Adams, 2006; Kiesinger, 2002); race and ethnicity (Boylorn, 2008; Marvasti, 2006); and gender" (Crawley, 2002; Pelias, 2007), Art adds.

"Then what?" Cindy asks.

"Then I consider ways others describe their experience with similar epiphanies," Carolyn says. "I do this by reading research on a topic, interviewing people who may share my experience, and examining related artifacts like books, television shows, and movies."

Writing Autoethnography

"Okay, I understand how I might start to do autoethnography," says Susan, "but how do you go about writing it?"

"Good question," says Carolyn. "Autoethnography is not only a way of conducting research but also a way of representing research; it's both a process and a product. And, like the process, the product is a synthesis of autobiography and ethnography."

"So there are rules for writing?" asks Cindy.

"Yes," says Tony. "Consider what it might take to write an autobiography. In most cases, a person must possess a fine command of the print medium, and create an artful and evocative text that engages readers" (Adams, 2008).

"This often means using conventions of storytelling, such as character, scene, and plot development" (Ellis & Ellingson, 2000), says Carolyn. "The text should also illustrate new perspectives on personal experience—on those epiphanies—by finding and filling a gap in the existing, related story lines" (Couser, 1997; Goodall, 2001).

"Autobiographers can make texts artful and evocative by using other techniques as well," Tony says. "For instance, they can use the techniques of **showing** and **telling.**"

"Showing brings 'readers into the scene' (Ellis, 2004, p. 142)—into thoughts, emotions, and actions—in order to 'experience an experience'" (Ellis, 1993, p. 711), interjects Carolyn. "Most often done through the use of conversation, showing allows writers to make events engaging and emotionally rich. Telling is a writing strategy that works with showing; it provides readers with some distance from the events described so that they can think about the events more abstractly. Adding some telling to a story that shows is an efficient way to convey the context needed for the reader to appreciate what is going on, and a way to communicate information that does not necessitate the immediacy of dialogue and sensuous engagement" (see Adams, 2006).

"Autobiographers can also make texts artful and evocative by altering authorial points of view," says Tony. "Sometimes autobiographers may use first person to tell a story, typically when they personally observed or lived through an interaction and participated in an intimate and immediate 'eyewitness account' (Caulley, 2008, p. 442). Sometimes autobiographers may use second person to bring readers into a scene to actively witness an experience with the author, to be a part of rather than distanced from an event (Pelias, 2000). Sometimes autobiographers may use third person to establish the context for an interaction, to report findings, and to present what others do or say" (Caulley, 2008).

"Sounds like a call for creative writing. What rules does ethnography bring to the writing of autoethnography?" asks Cindy.

"Ethnographers work to produce a '**thick description**' of a culture" (Geertz, 1973, p. 10; Goodall, 2001), says Tony. "The purpose of this rich and detailed description is to help facilitate understanding of a culture, and it is created by discerning patterns of cultural experience—repeated feelings, stories, and happenings—as evidenced by field notes, interviews, and artifacts."

"By combining tenets of writing autobiography with tenets of writing ethnography, rules for and ideas about writing autoethnography emerge," says Carolyn. "When a person writes an autoethnography, the person seeks to produce an artful and evocative thick description of personal and interpersonal experience. The person accomplishes this by first discerning patterns of experience evidenced by field notes, interviews, and artifacts, and then describing these patterns using facets of storytelling, showing and telling, and alterations of authorial voice. The autoethnographer not only tries to make personal experience meaningful and cultural experience engaging but also, by producing accessible texts, works to reach the wider and more diverse audiences that traditional research usually disregards; such a move can make personal and social change possible for more people" (Ellis, 1995b; Goodall, 2006; hooks, 1994).

"Autoethnography treats writing as just as important as findings," says Art, looking up from a wildflower book he has been reading. "The method tries to motivate audiences to read and engage research, not produce research that sits on a shelf to be glanced at by only a few people."

"People are looking at us a little weird," Carolyn says, glancing around. "They're reading nature books, playing checkers, and talking about the hike up the mountain, and we're having this serious conversation." Everyone laughs. "Besides, we're out of Baileys and it's probably time to wash up for dinner." With that, they all go to their respective cabins, fill their wash basins with hot water from the centrally located outside pump, and wash as best they can.

REFLECTION QUESTIONS

1. Thus far, how has this chapter differed from other chapters you've read? How does autoethnography differ from other methods with which you're familiar?
2. What is a topic you might want to research using autoethnography?

Autoethnographic Forms

After dinner everyone ventures to Sunset Point to take in the sunset. Sitting on top of the rocks that jut out over the horizon, they feel on top of the world. After a few moments of silence and being in the moment, the discussion starts again. "Susan and I were talking," says Cindy. "And we're wondering, are all autoethnographies **personal narratives**?"

"No," Carolyn says. "But these narratives—stories by and about authors who view themselves as the phenomenon under study and write evocative narratives specifically focused on their academic, research, and personal lives (Goodall, 2006; Tillmann, 2009)—often are the most controversial forms of autoethnography for traditional social scientists, especially if they are not accompanied by traditional analysis or connections to scholarly literature."

"What is the purpose of personal narratives?" asks Susan.

"Personal narratives are used to understand a self or some aspect of a life as situated in a cultural context," Tony says.

"They work to invite readers to enter the author's world and use what they learn to reflect on, understand, and cope with their own lives" (Ellis, 2004), Carolyn adds.

"What other forms are there?" asks Susan.

"You all are gluttons for punishment," Art says. "Watch or you'll miss the sunset."

"We can watch the sunset and talk, too," says Carolyn. "There are a number of other forms that differ in how much emphasis is placed on the study of others, the researcher's self and interaction with others, traditional analysis, and the interview context, as well as on power in the researcher-subject relationship."

"For example," says Tony, "**indigenous/native ethnographies** develop from colonized or economically subordinated people, and are used to address and disrupt power in research, particularly a (outside) researcher's right and authority to study others. Once at the service of the (white, masculine, heterosexual, middle- and upper-class, Christian, able-bodied) ethnographer, indigenous/native ethnographers now work to construct their own personal and cultural stories; (forced) subjugation is no longer excusable" (see Denzin, Lincoln, & Smith, 2008; see also Chapter Seventeen in this text).

"I've heard of researchers once exploiting others for the purpose of research, such as the participants in the Tuskegee syphilis study and the Milgram experiments," Cindy says, "but I can't believe this exploitation still happens."

"Thankfully, exploitation is not as widely practiced," replies Tony, "though it still happens in different, more relational ways."

"What about the other forms of autoethnography?" Susan interrupts. "What is their focus?"

"**Narrative ethnographies** are texts presented in the form of stories that incorporate the ethnographer's experiences into the descriptions and analysis of others. In these the emphasis is on the ethnographic study of others, which is accomplished partly by attending to encounters between the narrator and members of the groups being studied" (Tedlock, 1991), says Carolyn.

"**Reflexive, dyadic interviews** focus on the interactively produced meanings and emotional dynamics of an interview," Carolyn continues. "Though the focus is on the participant's story, the words, thoughts, and feelings of the researcher also are considered—for example, the personal motivation for doing a project, the interviewer's knowledge of the topic, and ways in which the interviewer may have been changed by the process of interviewing" (Ellis, 2004).

"Similarly, **reflexive ethnographies** include something about the researcher's interest and experience in the topic being explored. These ethnographies exist on a research continuum ranging from the ethnographer's biography, to ethnographers' study of their lives alongside the lives of cultural members, to ethnographic memoirs (Ellis, 2004) or 'confessional tales' (Van Maanen, 1988) in which the ethnographer's backstage research endeavors become the focus."

"You haven't mentioned interactive interviews," says Art, joining the conversation.

"**Interactive interviews** provide an 'in-depth and intimate understanding of people's experiences with emotionally charged and sensitive topics' (Ellis, Kiesinger, & Tillmann-Healy, 1997, p. 121), says Carolyn. "They are collaborative endeavors between researchers and participants, whereby both discuss, together, issues that come up in conversation about particular topics (for example, eating disorders). Interactive interviews usually consist of multiple interview sessions, and, unlike traditional one-on-one interviews with strangers, are situated within the context of emerging and well-established relationships among participants and interviewers. The emphasis is on what can be learned from the interaction within the interview setting as well as from the stories that each person brings to the encounter."

"Similar to interactive interviews," Tony adds, "**community autoethnographies** use the personal experience of researchers-in-collaboration to illustrate how a community manifests particular cultural issues, such as whiteness (Toyosaki, Pensoneau-Conway, Wendt, & Leathers, 2009). Community autoethnographies thus not only facilitate 'community-building' research practices but also make opportunities for 'cultural and social intervention' possible" (p. 59).

"Art, because you were the coauthor with me on co-constructed narratives, why don't you say something about that approach?" Carolyn asks.

Art cautiously raises himself to a sitting position as he peers over the edge of the cliff. "**Co-constructed narratives** show how people collaboratively cope with the ambiguities, uncertainties, and contradictions of being friends, family, or intimate partners. Co-constructed narratives view relationships as jointly authored, incomplete, and historically situated affairs. Each person first writes a personal experience, often told about or around an epiphany, and then shares and reacts to the story the other(s) wrote" (Bochner & Ellis, 1995).

"Okay, I can't take in any more now," says Cindy, and everyone takes this as a cue to engage in the scene in front of us. "Anyone want some more Baileys?" she asks; we are amazed when she pulls out another flask from her down jacket, complete with five plastic cups.

Benefits of Autoethnography

The next morning we wake as the sun rises to one of the best days for hiking: sunny, cool, and dry. We head to breakfast, and we begin to stuff ourselves with pancakes and warm maple syrup, coffee, and Tang, followed by scrambled eggs, biscuits and gravy, grits, potatoes, and sausage. "I kept thinking last night about all you have told us," Cindy says. "And then I wondered about the benefits of autoethnography."

"There are many benefits, but let me focus on two," says Carolyn, digging into her second helping of hot pancakes. "First, there are many therapeutic possibilities of autoethnography for authors, participants, and audiences. Second, autoethnographers do not want to exploit others just for the purpose of research; consequently, one benefit of autoethnography is the method's focus on and valuing of the **relational ethics** in research—the interpersonal ties and responsibilities to those we study" (Ellis, 2007).

Therapeutic Possibilities

"Writing from personal experience can be therapeutic," Tony says. "Writing is, as hooks (1994) suggests, a way to name our pain and, in so doing, make this pain go away. Writing personal stories can be therapeutic for authors as we write to make sense of ourselves and our experiences (Kiesinger, 2002); purge our burdens (Atkinson, 2007); and question **canonical stories**—conventional, authoritative, and 'projective' story lines that 'plot' how 'ideal social selves' should live (Tololyan, 1987, p. 218; Bochner, 2001, 2002). In writing, autoethnographers seek to understand and improve relationships (Adams, 2006); reduce prejudice (Ellis, 1995c, 2002, 2009b); encourage personal responsibility and agency (Pelias, 2000, 2007); raise consciousness and promote cultural change (Ellis, 2002; Goodall, 2006); and give people a voice that, before writing, they may not have felt they had" (Boylorn, 2006).

"So writing can be therapeutic for an author, the researcher," Susan says.

"Yes, but it can also be therapeutic for participants and readers," Carolyn responds. "Personal stories can make **witnessing** possible—giving participants and readers the ability to observe and, consequently, better testify on behalf of an event, problem, or experience (Bochner & Ellis, 2006; see also Greenspan, 1998; Rogers, 2004). By way of researching and writing, an autoethnographer is able to identify cultural problems often cloaked in secrecy—for example, government conspiracy (Goodall, 2006); harmful gender norms (Crawley, 2002; Pelias, 2007); or how persons with same-sex desire navigate the disclosure of this desire. Autoethnographers not only work to alleviate and validate the meaning of their pain but also allow participants and readers, through witnessing, to feel validated and perhaps better able to cope with or change particular circumstances."

"Sounds like meaningful work," Cindy says. "I know that when I read, I often get joy from experiences similar to mine, or texts that motivate me to think and live differently."

Relational Ethics

"I think I'd like to do an autoethnography. But I'm wondering what happens when we include others in our stories. What do we owe them?" asks Susan.

"Excellent question," says Carolyn. "Autoethnographers recognize that research and researchers do not exist in isolation. We live connected to social networks that include friends and relatives, partners and children, coworkers, and students, and we work in universities and research facilities. As a result, when we conduct and write research, we implicate others. For instance, if a woman studies and develops antismoking campaigns within a university, tobacco companies may refrain from financially contributing to the university because of her research; even though she is doing the research herself, she may speak on behalf of others—in this case, on behalf of the university. Likewise, in traditional ethnographies the communities and participants being written about can usually be identified" (see Vidich & Bensman, 1958).

"In using personal experience, autoethnographers implicate not only themselves with their work but also close, intimate others" (Adams, 2006; Ellis, 2007), says Tony. "For instance, if a son tells a story that mentions his mother, it is difficult to mask his mother without altering the meaning and purpose of the story. Similar to people identifiable in a community study, such as the minister or town mayor, the author's mother is easily recognizable."

"Or if an autoethnographer writes a story about a particular neighbor's racist acts, the neighbor is implicated by the words even though the autoethnographer may never mention the name of the neighbor" (Ellis, 2009b), adds Carolyn. "She may try to mask the location of the community, but it does not take much work to find out where she lives and, therefore, may not take much work to identify the neighbor about whom she speaks.

"Autoethnographers often maintain and value interpersonal ties with their participants, thus making relational ethics more complicated," Tony says. "Participants often begin as friends or become friends through the research process. We do not normally regard them as impersonal 'subjects' only to be mined for data. As such, ethical issues affiliated with friendship become an important part of the research process and product" (Tillmann, 2009; Tillmann-Healy, 2003).

"Autoethnographers thus consider 'relational ethics' as a crucial component of research," Carolyn adds, "that should be foregrounded throughout the research and writing process" (Ellis, 2007).

"And how do you deal with these?" asks Cindy.

"On many occasions this obligates autoethnographers to show their work to others implicated in or by their texts, acknowledging how these others feel about what is being written about them and allowing them to talk back to how they have been represented," says Carolyn.

"Similar to traditional ethnographers, autoethnographers also may have to protect the privacy and safety of others by altering such identifying characteristics as circumstance or topics discussed, or characteristics like race, gender, name, place, or appearance," adds Tony. "For example, if we wrote about our hike, we might change your names or occupations."

"What would be interesting about the hike?" ask Susan and Cindy together. "There wasn't an epiphany here."

"Let's talk about that later," says Tony, not wanting to discuss negotiations of his gay identity. "For now, let me just say that autoethnographers must stay aware of how these protective devices can influence the integrity of their research as well as how their work is interpreted and understood. Most of the time they also have to be able to continue to live in the world of relationships in which their research is embedded after the research is completed."

Critical Responses to Autoethnography

"How do people evaluate autoethnographies?" asks Cindy.

"That's a great but tricky question," says Tony. "Often autoethnographies are erroneously evaluated by traditional research standards of reliability, validity, and generalizability. These standards function differently for autoethnographers."

"For instance," Carolyn interrupts, "establishing **reliability** means assessing an autoethnographer's credibility. This means asking such questions as Could the author have had the experiences described given available evidence? Does the author believe that this is actually what happened to her or him? and Has the author taken 'literary license' to the point that the story is better viewed as fiction rather than as a truthful, historically accurate account?" (Bochner, 2002).

Establishing **validity** for autoethnographers means assessing an autoethnography's verisimilitude—that is, trying to assess whether readers find the text lifelike, believable, and possible, and whether the story, the representation, is coherent and could be true" (Plummer, 2001), Tony says. "Validity is also related to whether an autoethnography helps readers communicate with others different from themselves or if the text offers a way to improve the lives of participants and readers, and the author's own life" (Ellis, 2004).

"And evaluating autoethnography in terms of **generalizability** means discerning how well a local, particular, personal text is able to illuminate global, general, cultural processes" (Ellis & Bochner, 2000; Ellis & Ellingson, 2000), Carolyn adds. "This means assessing how well an autoethnography applies to and is relevant for readers, how well a story speaks to them about their experience or about the lives of others they know. Generalizability is evidenced by responses like 'I know how you feel,' or 'My experience seems similar to yours.' Readers provide validation by comparing their lives to ours, by thinking about how our lives are similar and different as well as reasons for these similarities and differences" (Ellis, 2004).

"Although these are some ways to evaluate autoethnographies, are there people who discount autoethnography as an approach?" asks Susan.

"Yes," Carolyn says. "Many of the reasons why autoethnography is valued are reasons for which it is critiqued."

"To some, autoethnography is a threat to scientific orthodoxy," Tony adds.

"And when change is attempted," Carolyn continues, "it is often resisted by those who want to keep such orthodoxy in place, those who want to protect their own interests and power."

"What do these people say?" Cindy probes. "What are their concerns and critiques?"

"Some critics want to hold autoethnography accountable to criteria normally applied to traditional ethnographies or to autobiographical standards of writing," says Tony.

"Autoethnography is criticized for either being too artful and not scientific, or too scientific and not sufficiently artful," Carolyn adds.

"For instance," Tony says, "as part ethnography, autoethnography is dismissed according to social scientific standards as being insufficiently rigorous, theoretical, and analytical, and too aesthetic, emotional, and therapeutic (Ellis, 2009a). Autoethnographers are criticized for doing too little fieldwork and for not spending enough time with others (Delamont, 2009; Fine, 2003), and, in using personal experience, use supposedly biased data (Atkinson, 1997). They are also accused of being navel-gazing, self-absorbed narcissists who don't fulfill scholarly obligations of hypothesizing, analyzing, and theorizing" (Madison, 2006).

"And as part autobiography," Carolyn says, "autoethnography is dismissed according to autobiographical writing standards as being insufficiently aesthetic and literary and not artful enough. Autoethnographers are viewed as catering to the sociological, scientific imagination and trying to achieve legitimacy as scientists. Critics say that autoethnographers disregard the literary, artistic imagination and the need to be talented artists (Gingrich-Philbrook, 2005). Moro (2006), for example, says it takes a 'darn good' writer to write autoethnography."

"These criticisms don't seem fair," Cindy responds. "It's like people are resistant to change, and a double standard exists for autoethnography."

"They're not fair criticisms," Carolyn says, "especially because they erroneously and naively position art and science at odds with each other, a positioning that autoethnography seeks to disrupt. Autoethnographers believe research can be rigorous, theoretical, and analytical *and* emotional, therapeutic, and inclusive of personal and social phenomena."

"Autoethnographers also value the need to write and represent research in evocative, aesthetic ways" (Ellis, 1995b, 2004), Tony adds. "One can write in aesthetically compelling ways without citing fiction or being educated as a literary or performance scholar. The questions autoethnographers find most important are Who reads our work? How are they affected by it? and How does it keep a conversation going?"

"Why can't people let each other do their own work in the best ways they find possible?" Cindy asks.

"I don't want to speak for Carolyn," Tony says, "but I wonder the same thing."

"Me, too," Carolyn adds. "In a world of methodological difference, I find it futile to debate whether autoethnography is valid research" (Bochner, 2000; Ellis, 2009a).

"Unless we agree on a goal, we cannot agree on the terms by which we can judge how to achieve it," says Tony. "Simply put, autoethnographers take a different point of view toward the subject matter of social science. In Rorty's words (1982), these different views are 'not issue(s) to be resolved,' but 'difference(s) to be lived with'" (p. 197).

> **REFLECTION QUESTIONS**
>
> 1. Return to Tony's and Carolyn's opening experiences. How are they autoethnography?
> 2. How could we evaluate the opening experiences using autoethnographic perspectives on reliability, validity, and generalizability?

Talking the Talk and Walking the Walk

"I think we're ready for the walk down," says Carolyn. We all stretch and gather our much lighter packs.

"Thanks for the lesson on autoethnography," Susan says, adjusting her hiking stick. "But now we don't have much to talk about on the hike down."

"We can talk about my coming out yesterday," Tony says, as he takes the lead. Susan and Cindy exchange glances. "It was difficult," he continues. "I didn't know how you and Cindy would react. I felt torn about what to say and do. I wanted to be open and honest, but also wanted to maintain safety and protection."

"I felt bad that I assumed you were married," remarks Susan.

"How were you to know?" asks Tony.

"I could see you struggling," adds Carolyn. "I wanted to say something early on about your sexuality and take pressure off you. But I didn't say anything then because I didn't know if you wanted the others to know."

"It worried me for you to see me so uncomfortable," Tony says to Carolyn. "Research often suggests that being out is healthy, and I think that you think of me as a person who is out, often, most everywhere. By seeing me struggle with gayness, I worried that you might find me unhealthy and ashamed of myself, my partner, and my work."

"I was more concerned with how you saw me," Carolyn says. "It felt like a double bind. If I said something about your identity, then it might be perceived by you as inappropriate for me to have done so. If I didn't, then I feared you would think that I didn't want my friends to know."

"I also worried about how the others might perceive you for having a gay friend," says Tony. "I didn't want you to be considered by them to be inappropriate or immoral . . ."

"That wouldn't happen," says Cindy and Susan together. "We never had those thoughts."

"Do we have to talk about something just to talk?" Art interrupts. "You all are too serious, especially for this early in the morning."

Ignoring Art, Carolyn says, "So, Susan and Cindy, can you see how we could make an autoethnography project out of this discussion of Tony's gayness and how we negotiated it relationally? Here you have Tony, the gay, cultural actor, and us, who hold different cultural positions. Using autoethnography, we can now all talk about how we perceived the situation and why we said and did what we did. Then we'd have a relational portrayal of identity negotiation."

"Hey, I'm getting into this autoethnography stuff," says Susan. "Okay, let me tell you how I perceived what happened . . . "

"I want to go first," interrupts Cindy.

Tony, Art, and Carolyn laugh as the talking and walking continue.

REFLECTION QUESTIONS

1. How would you feel or respond if you were one of the hikers in our account? How would you tell your autoethnographic story?
2. How might Cindy and Susan now analyze their respective positions in the initial conversation? What might you learn from their analyses?
3. Think of some aspect of your life that is usually thought of as personal, such as sexual identity, and discuss how it might be negotiated relationally.

Summary

Throughout this chapter we tried to accomplish two things. First, we used our opening experiences to show how autoethnography might look and feel—that is, to demonstrate autoethnographic "products." Second, we discerned characteristics of autoethnography as a research method to describe the process we used to assemble these products. In so doing we worked to show what autoethnographic research and representation is and does.

Key Terms

autobiography, 198
autoethnography, 196
canonical stories, 204
co-constructed narratives, 204
community autoethnographies, 203
crisis of confidence, 196
epiphanies, 198
ethnography, 199
generalizability, 207
identity politics, 196
indigenous/native ethnographies, 202
insiders, 199

interactive interviews, 203
master, universal narratives, 197
narrative ethnographies, 203
outsiders, 199
participant observers, 199
personal narratives, 202
reflexive ethnographies, 203
reflexive, dyadic interviews, 203
relational ethics, 204
reliability, 207
showing, 200
telling, 200
thick description, 201
validity, 207
witnessing, 205

Further Readings and Resources

Suggested Autoethnography Studies

Adams, T. E. (2011). *Narrating the closet: An autoethnography of same-sex attraction*. Walnut Creek, CA: Left Coast Press.

This is a comprehensive autoethnography on the everyday negotiations of same-sex attraction, negotiations that are similar to those portrayed at the start of this chapter.

Ellis, C. (2004). *The ethnographic I: A methodological novel about autoethnography*. Walnut Creek, CA: AltaMira.

Ellis weaves both methodological advice and her own personal stories into a narrative about a fictional graduate course she instructs.

Holman Jones, S. (2007). *Torch singing: Performing resistance and desire from Billie Holiday to Edith Piaf*. Walnut Creek, CA: AltaMira.

Providing a description and critique of the torch singing genre, Holman Jones has created a text that slips in and out of prose, dialogue, and poetry.

Tillmann-Healy, L. (2001). *Between gay and straight: Understanding friendship across sexual orientation*. Walnut Creek, CA: AltaMira.

Tillmann-Healy explores the complexities of carrying on gay-straight friendships in this narrative ethnography of a gay community.

Other Suggested Readings

Ellis, C. (2007). Telling secrets, revealing lives: Relational ethics in research with intimate others. *Qualitative Inquiry, 13*, 3–29.

This is a thorough examination of the ethical issues that stem from doing autoethnographic research.

Ellis, C., & Bochner, A. P. (2000). Autoethnography, personal narrative, reflexivity: Researcher as subject. In N. K. Denzin & Y. S. Lincoln (Eds.), *Handbook of qualitative research* (2nd ed., pp. 733–768). Thousand Oaks, CA: Sage.

This classic, widely used essay on autoethnography can provide addition insight into the method and its applications.

Goodall, H. L. (2001). *Writing the new ethnography*. Walnut Creek, CA: AltaMira.
This book provides a foundational understanding of the writing processes associated with innovative forms of ethnographic and autoethnographic writing.

Organizations and Web Sites

Autoethnography Yahoo Group (http://groups.yahoo.com/group/autoethnography/)
Over three hundred scholars participate in this group by subscription.

International Congress of Qualitative Inquiry (www.icqi.org/)
This group's annual meeting takes place every May at the University of Illinois at Urbana-Champaign and offers many sessions on autoethnography.

National Communication Association, Ethnography Division (www.natcom.org/)
The annual meeting of this association takes place every November and offers numerous sessions on autoethnography.

PART THREE

INTEGRATING THE DISCIPLINES

CHAPTER 9

NARRATIVE INQUIRY: STORIES LIVED, STORIES TOLD

Christine K. Lemley
Roland W. Mitchell

Key Ideas

- Narrative inquiry is a qualitative research methodology that critically analyzes social and cultural contexts of human experience.

- Narrative inquiry, or "storytelling," is the first and oldest form of inquiry.

- Narrative inquiry is cross-disciplinary and is used by such fields as philosophy, education, science, religion, economics, law, and medicine.

- A critical event approach to narrative inquiry focuses on what the research participant identifies as important in the story.

- Narrative inquiry challenges positivist notions that only one truth exists.

- Narrative inquiry researchers continually question "What I know" and "How I know it."

Narrative inquiry is a qualitative research methodology that seeks ways to understand and represent experiences through the stories that individuals live and tell. A burgeoning interest in narrative inquiry underscores how stories can explain experiences as well as serve as a catalyst for personal and social change in the lives of the participants telling the stories and in the lives of their audience.

Narrative Inquiry: Introduction

According to Michael Connelly and Jean Clandinin (1990),

> Narrative inquiry, the study of experience as story, is first and foremost a way for thinking about experience. Narrative inquiry as a methodology entails a view of the phenomenon. To use narrative inquiry methodology is to adopt a particular view of experience as phenomenon under study. (quoted in Clandinin & Rosiek, 2007, p. 38)

The comments of narrative researchers Clandinin and Connelly illustrate both the **epistemic** (ways of knowing) nature and the **ontological** (ways of being) possibilities associated with the stories that we tell about our world. Throughout history the ability of these stories to shape meaning has been immeasurable. Numerous scholars, linguists, philosophers, and cultural workers in general have attested to the ways that communicating a shared understanding through stories is a social process and an essential building block for establishing a community (Bakhtin, 1981; Barthes, 1968/1977; Derrida, 1967/1980; de Saussure, 1916/1983). Further, the stories we tell and identify with are constantly in flux, malleable, negotiated, and highly contested. From competing tales of ancient biblical events in Greek, Aramaic, or Hebrew to more contemporary stories concerning the end of the Cold War and present East-meets-West global relations, the significance associated with the power relations structured into the stories we tell about ourselves and our world cannot be overstated (Delpit & Dowdy, 2002; Freire, 1973). Consequently, as Clandinin and Connelly (1990) argue, if you really want to understand a community, look closely at the stories that the community tells about itself.

We begin by positioning ourselves through (1) contexts that have shaped what we know about a given topic, (2) our views as individuals within communities, and (3) our views as researchers within institutions. As Catherine Riessman (1993) states, "The construction of any work always bears the mark of the person who created it" (p. v).

Christine Lemley's Position

I, Christine Lemley, am a white woman who grew up in the Midwestern region of the United States. I am committed to using power and privilege to address issues of social justice, equity, race, and diversity. I use narrative inquiry to privilege voices, at times voices of historically marginalized populations in the United States (for example, indigenous communities). For this chapter I will present a narrative inquiry study that I facilitated with an indigenous community in Wisconsin, the Menominee Nation. Although narrative researchers often maintain the confidentiality of their informants and use pseudonyms, in 2005 the Menominee Language and Culture Commission, the tribal legislative body that regulates language research on the reservation, requested that I use "Menominee," rather than a pseudonym that obscures the tribe's identity when referring to the Menominee Nation. In order to honor this request, I use "Menominee" in all written and oral presentations concerning this research.

My work with the Menominee explored how members of the Menominee Nation used indigenous knowledge and language practices to initiate change in their community (see also Chapter Seventeen, Reclaiming Scholarship: Critical Indigenous Research Methodologies). The participants shared knowledge they possessed, which enabled me to better understand how people strive for social and cultural change for themselves and others. For example, when a Menominee elder explained how education was something that no one could take away from her, I understood better how the Menominee lost language, culture, and land because of decisions made by the federal government. Through education, however, they transformed assimilative practices of learning English and going to school to advocate for themselves and others and survived the repeated hardships. I asked the participants (Menominee elders, teachers, and students) how they continue to resist assimilative practices, such as learning only English, today. A student explained,

> Well, Menominee language is sort of like picking flowers. You see these ugly old ones, they like make you stop speaking Menominee language and just speak English, it's like that. But the beautiful ones lets you speak your, what kind of language you want to try and speak, like Menominee.

I shared this student's sentiment with Menominee elders, who explained that this comment served as evidence that the Menominee language programs were positively influencing the students to embrace learning Menominee language. This research project demonstrated how narrative reflection enabled the participants, community members, and me to gain a deeper understanding of their experiences in the language programs. I have continued with narrative inquiry research projects that involve gathering stories from people in schools and communities to understand their lived experiences in more complex ways.

Roland Mitchell's Position

I, Roland Mitchell, am an African American man who grew up in the southeastern region of the United States. Stories about race and space have pervaded all parts of my being. As cultural theorist Stuart Hall suggests, the **historicity** or situatedness associated with these stories causes much of my research to explore the influence of power on stories that are told, those that are silenced, and the range of stories that remain somewhere in between. Exemplary examples of this approach to conducting narrative inquiry can be found in the work of such noted researchers as Janet Miller (2005), Tom Barone (2001), Jerry Rosiek and Becky Atkinson (2007), and Petra Munro-Hendry (2007).

In the research that I introduce in this study, I explore the ways in which race, gender, and subject matter inform classroom practice when an African American female teaches mathematics at a predominantly white university. In addition to drawing out some salient points about the relationships among race, gender, disciplinarity, and voice—especially as they pertain to those of us who are narrative inquirers studying those relationships—this line of research develops a more nuanced approach to hearing and then reporting the stories of those who, like the participant in the study, teach across cultural and racial boundaries (Delpit & Dowdy, 2002; Giroux, 2004; Ladson-Billings, 2005).

Stories Lived, Stories Told

Stories of black scholars in primarily white institutions and indigenous nation members participating in language revitalization efforts privilege and validate voices that are historically oppressed in an effort to institute social and cultural change. Narrative inquiry, therefore, empowers social, political, cultural, and economic identities.

Although our examples of the potential of narrative inquiry have to this point focused on historically marginalized communities, it is not our aim to suggest that narrative inquiry is essentially emancipatory or only useful when applied to marginalized communities. This is clearly not the case. Using narrative inquiry to mine the narratives of members of dominant groups is equally important. For example, from depictions of the United States as policing the globe to accounts of the former Soviet Bloc nations' attempts at establishing post–Cold War identities, stories arising from these events illustrate the rich potential of narrative inquiry to explore the stories of internationally powerful communities.

Narrative researchers look for ways to understand and represent experiences through the stories that research participants live and tell (Clandinin & Connelly, 2000; Creswell, 2005). The stories told provide guidance to better understand new knowledge or enhance existing knowledge about a topic. As researchers we set goals to represent individual stories as accurately and completely as possible. Narrative researchers center the research participant's story and use scholarly literature for background information (Creswell, 2005). Scholarly literature is important; yet the stories dictate which literature to seek rather than the literature's guiding the questions asked or topic of focus. Narrative researchers gather multiple forms of information (interviews, observations, letters, journals, newspaper articles, photos, movies) to most completely represent the research participants' stories in their own words (Creswell, 2005). Narrative researchers analyze the research participants' stories and present findings by "restorying" them through a framework (Creswell, 2005, p. 486; Mishler, 2004) that most accurately conveys the research participants' meaning. Using direct quotes is one way that we complete this act. We provide interpretations as well as invite the reader to make her or his own interpretation from the data presented.

Narrative inquiry at its core has always had the possibility to focus on positions of power and privilege, for it places the individual storyteller at the center of providing data that are valued. Leonard Webster and Patricia Mertova (2007) discuss literature concerning **critical events**, events that are described by the interviewee and have profound effects on this individual, continues to nurture this possibility. We anticipate other creative evolutions of narrative inquiry, and we invite researchers to consider options for turning a more critical eye on the narrative inquiry process. In using the word *critical*, different from the *critical* in "critical event approach" discussed in the next section, we mean to invite the reader to consider how narrative inquiry can be used to hear historically silenced voices in order to privilege this knowledge base and interrupt the status quo. Throughout our work we remain cognizant of issues of class, race and ethnicity, language, disability, gender, and sexual orientation. We continuously strive for ways to preserve the integrity of research participants' narratives, and to have their lived stories become stories told in the most complete way possible.

Narrative Inquiry: Critical Event Approach

We use narrative inquiry to understand human existence through personal stories. Hearing multiple people narrate living similar experiences, stories that talk *to* and *against* one another, sometimes highlights contradictory understandings of any given topic and always underscores the varied complexities of lived experiences. We use **raw narratives,** the interviewees' words reflected as accurately as when they interacted in the interviews, so that readers can draw their own conclusions before seeing others' (and our own) interpretations. As opposed to providing a basis for generalizing or affording a standard account of an experience, raw narratives highlight distinctive features and details that may be overlooked or undervalued as the researcher attempts to represent the experiences of others.

In addition to the previous narrative inquiry components, we underscore critical events, which produce stories and emotions that are unplanned, unanticipated, and uncontrolled (Webster & Mertova, 2007). Critical events could be spoken or unspoken parts of the interview. We believe critical events both literally and figuratively emphasize the essential parts of the story and frame what we should write and how we should write it. These critical events guide us to "think with the story" (Ellis & Bochner, 2000, p. 747) and to consider our connection to the speaker and the story, so that we can determine what we can learn from either the speaker or the story itself. The representation of the story, as shown in the following example, is then a specific set of questions leading to a meaningful silence that ultimately illustrate a critical event.

Mitchell's chapter in *Voice in Qualitative Inquiry: Challenging Conventional, Interpretive, and Critical Conceptions in Qualitative Research* (2008) considers the assertion that the more familiar researchers are with the communities (academic, political, familial, and so forth) to which their participants belong, the better positioned researchers are to understand the stories that their participants tell. In one particularly telling instance, an African American female mathematics professor stated that issues associated with race and gender had absolutely nothing to do with her subject matter, hence issues associated with race and gender would not be discussed in her class. However, when asked if her own racial and gendered identity influenced her professional advancement or the ways that her students related to her, she commented, "Absolutely, and if you turn that tape recorder off then we can talk" (p. 77).

Lacking familiarity with conversations about African American professors' experiences of teaching in majority European American schools, and given the scarcity of women who have historically participated in the science, technology, engineering, and mathematics areas, a researcher could be confused about the participant's unwillingness to be recorded when discussing the ways that her being African American and female influence her teaching experiences. However, recognizing her reasons for not discussing issues associated with race and gender in this context represents a critical event through which Mitchell was given insight into the nature of his participant's tenuous relationship to both the institution at which she is employed and the subject matter that she is teaching. Narrative reflection provides a valuable perspective from which to recognize this critical moment that brings together the collective experience of a historically marginalized community (black female academics in this case) in a specific academic discipline (mathematics) and in a specific university classroom (at a majority white institution) through the stories of an individual. To overlook this silence that we are referring to as a critical event risks overlooking the professor's perception of both her discipline and the institution at which she taught. In this regard it is not simply the story that is told that illuminates her experience but also the meaning that it holds for her and the researcher that make her silence the linchpin for conceptualizing this critical moment.

> **REFLECTION QUESTIONS**
>
> 1. What about the critical event example from this section stood out most to you? How? Why?
> 2. Why would a critical event approach be appropriate in your field?

Narrative Inquiry: Qualitative Research Methodology

Qualitative research generally uses **narratives,** verbal acts that include someone telling another person that an event occurred (Smith, 1981), for descriptive purposes to categorize and form **taxonomies** (classifications of themes based on similarities) to understand differences and similarities among and between stories. Narrative inquiry

> refers to any study that uses or analyzes narrative materials. The data can be collected as a story (a life story provided in an interview or a literary work) or in a different manner (field notes of an anthropologist who writes up his or her observations as a narrative or in personal letters). It can be the object of the research or a means for the study of another question. It may be used for comparison among groups, to learn about a social phenomenon or historical period, or to explore a personality. (Lieblich, Tuval-Mashiach, & Zilber, 1998, p. 2)

Distinguishing narrative inquiry from other forms of discourse, Catherine Riessman and Jane Speedy (2007) propose that narrative inquiry offers a focus on **sequence** (organization of events) and **consequence** (how and why events occurred). As they explain, "Events are selected, organized, connected and evaluated as meaningful for a particular audience. Analysis in narrative studies interrogates language—*how* and *why* events are storied, not simply the content to which language refers" (p. 430). So narrative inquiry focuses on the process of the story, how and why the story came to be, as well as what the story might become for the individual.

A distinction between qualitative research in general and narrative inquiry is that narrative inquiry includes the participants actively throughout the research process. The richness of detail in the participants' quotes conveys identity more powerfully than any interpretation. Placing the participant as the primary teller allows the reader to interpret the participant's story instead of a researcher's interpretation. The participant's voice is central to the telling.

The term *narrative inquiry* was first used by Connelly and Clandinin (1990) as a methodology to describe teachers' personal stories. Through their work Clandinin and Connelly (1995) have emphasized teachers' individual experiences and inquiries as legitimate sources of insight that can and should guide teacher practices. Further, they explain that telling stories of educational experiences allows teachers to determine and articulate what they know. Narrative inquiry, then, has teachers analyze and criticize the stories they hear and share as they work. Teachers use formal and informal stories to construct and make sense of knowledge in their everyday interactions and life (Webster & Mertova, 2007).

Robert Coles (1989) encourages the narrative researcher to (1) include participants in the storytelling process and (2) incorporate essential aspects of a story that help engage the audience. For example, according to Coles, the audience must consist of good listeners. Coles further guides researchers to consider the "manner of presentation; the development of plot, character; the addition of new dramatic sequences; the emphasis accorded to one figure or another; and the degree of enthusiasm, of emphasis, of coherence, the narrator gives to his or her account" (p. 23).

Narrative researchers play a dual role in establishing this type of relationship between themselves and the audience as they serve as their participants' narrators. The research participant's voice and story are her or his truth. The researcher's goal, then, is to present the truth according to the research participants.

Researchers from varying disciplines propose different ways to engage in narrative inquiry, yet the focus on the storied lived experiences of individuals and groups remains constant. Clandinin and Connelly (2000) view narrative inquiry as the study of **transactional** experience, the relationships between the people, places, and ideas involved in the research process. The transaction that they emphasize is between the narrator (interviewee), the listener (interviewer, potential listener or reader of the story), and the actual environment, or, as they would say, the landscape in which the events recounted in the story occur. Hence, these three phenomena (narrator, listener, environment) do not exist individually, but rather intersect where meaning is created and knowledge is produced. Narrative inquiry therefore positions researchers to examine the world of their participants as something both shaped by—and in some limited ways capable of shaping—historical interpretations. Through the use of narrative inquiry we, both researchers of teacher knowledge in traditional and non-traditional educational settings, seek to understand the stories of our participants. The researcher becomes involved by asking questions to better understand the story and its nuances. Narrative researchers frame the story as they determine what to tell and how to tell it in order to produce a full account in written form.

Narratives may guide people to better understand commitments for themselves, for their community, or for society at large. In *Recovering Language, Reclaiming Voice: Menominee Language Revitalization Programs,* Lemley (2006) interviewed a group of Menominee elders committed to revitalizing their indigenous language in communities on the reservation. Lemley asked the elders what being Menominee meant to them. One elder described how respect was an important aspect of her identity that she had learned throughout her upbringing. Her mother taught her self-respect that resulted in self-pride. She shared these notions when she recalled a conference she had attended at which the facilitator had asked her to respond to the question, "Who am I?"

> "Who am I?" was the question. I had to sit and think and answer this question, "Who am I? What's important to me as an individual?" And the first thing that came to my mind was 'I'm Menominee Indian.' That's who I am, that's what was important to me. So, I think it was the identification of self and the pride I had in myself as Menominee. And that's how I was taught . . . to be proud that you were Menominee even though your neighboring town looked down on you and discriminated against you and they were prejudiced because of who I am. And so I was taught by my mother . . . to be proud to be an Indian and not to walk in with your head down. Hold your head up, to be that kind of a person. And that was the first thing that came to mind . . . with the question "Who am I?" I'm Menominee Indian . . . the pride of being who I am. And to me it's a special, I'm a special person. I have my own culture. I have my own language. We have our own land. (Menominee elder, personal interview, quoted in Lemley, 2006, p. 115)

This passage underscores this elder's struggle and strong connection to her Menominee identity from her younger years. Her generation experienced violent political acts including forced assimilation through on-reservation and off-reservation boarding schools. Robbed of their indigenous identity, this generation was expected to adopt the dominant white culture's ways of speaking and acting. This elder's connection to this moment, when she identified who she was, highlighted the importance of not just the language but also the culture, the land, and the community ties. This particular story guided Lemley to identify how people had been influenced to continue speaking and learning Menominee, even when society punished the speakers. Noteworthy, too, are the pronouns *I* and *my* and then *we* and *our*, signaling that this elder had her own culture and her own language, yet the tribe had a collective investment in the land. These words and the pronouns guided Lemley to explore Menominee culture, language, and land as these relate to research participants' individual as well as collective meanings.

We primarily situate our own research in Clandinin and Connelly's conception of teacher knowledge (2000). However, the unique aspect that we hope to add to this rich literature is an exploration of the transactional relationship in our individually experienced yet collectively interpreted narratives. To date, most theories of teacher practical knowledge have emphasized teachers' individual experiences and inquiry as legitimate sources of insight that can guide teacher practices. This literature, however, has not emphasized the collective experiences that can—and should—inform teaching practice. Among the contemporary theories of teacher practical knowledge, Clandinin and Connelly's conception (1995) of **personal practical knowledge,** tacit knowledge about teaching that an individual acquires from the actual act of teaching, comes closest to a thorough development of this idea. They comment,

> We are clearer, at least in our own minds, about the relationship between teachers' personal knowledge and their practice because that relationship is part and parcel of our studies of teacher knowledge. What we mean by teachers' knowledge is that body of convictions and meaning, conscious or unconscious, that have arisen from experience (intimate, social, and traditional) and that are expressed in a person's practices. (p. 7)

Here Clandinin and Connelly highlight social and traditional experiences as sources of teacher knowledge. However, even in their work the emphasis remains on the individual's experience as a source of knowledge as opposed to collective historical experience as a source of knowledge. Our own research recognizes the utility of this collective approach to create and interpret narratives in marginalized communities in which strong communal ties have been an essential tool for survival throughout history.

Whereas our research focuses predominantly on K–12 teachers, in their chapter "Examples of Stories in Narrative Inquiry" Webster and Mertova (2007) provide examples of scholars and practitioners using narrative inquiry from such varied disciplines as legal education, medical education, neurology, adult education, primary education, theology, social history, and tertiary education. The stories, often based on reflections written by participants from diverse fields, reveal insights to improve existing conditions that quantitative measures, like satisfaction surveys, cannot. Narratives in these instances reflect the practical knowledge of lawyers, educators, physicians, and theologians who are describing, documenting, and subsequently conducting inquiry into the insights that govern their day-to-day practice. In their reflections the participants provide a case-study-like account of some of the most important moments of their practice for current colleagues and future practitioners, which often remain undocumented (see also Chapter Twelve, Practitioner Action Research, for a discussion of practical knowledge).

REFLECTION QUESTIONS

1. Why would narrative inquiry be beneficial to a research project in your own field of study?
2. Why might it be beneficial to participate as an interviewee in a narrative inquiry study?

Narrative Inquiry: Genres

Many genres of narrative inquiry exist. Biography, autobiography, life story research, and oral history are currently relevant forms of narrative research. In a **biography,** the researcher writes and records experiences about another person's life. **Autobiography** presents a narrative research form that includes a person or people recording their own experiences and writing about these experiences and themselves. In a **life story research** study, the researcher describes an individual's entire life. For an **oral history,** the researcher gathers information from an individual or groups of people about an experience and the causes and effects on the individual or individuals, the community, and society at large. We will describe examples of all four genres to show how we have engaged in these different forms of narrative inquiry.

To contextualize the processes involved in every research project, we want to explain that throughout our narrative inquiry studies we simultaneously observe the surrounding environment, note actions and speech, and participate in a dialogue. The outcome of the process is **reflexive knowledge,** insights into our participants' world that shed light on what we know about any given topic (Hertz,

1997). As researchers seeking to engage our participants and their stories in a reflexive manner, we continually question what we know, how we know it, and our relationship to this knowledge so we can collect multiple forms of data (observations, interviews, documents) in order to answer each question as thoroughly as possible. Our research projects take shape over time, capturing the iterative rethinking and revisions of topics and of ourselves (Lincoln, 1997; Reinharz, 1997). Further, reflexivity calls the researcher to raise questions of a cultural, historical, and political nature about what influences the assumptions and expectations inherent in his or her research (Miller, 1998), and to make explicit the constructed nature of the research produced by the researcher and the participants. The following research examples exemplify the aforementioned narrative inquiry genres: biography, autobiography, life story research, and oral history.

Biography

The narrative research in which I, Roland Mitchell, am currently involved concerns biographical inquiry into the stories that educators of color construct and subsequently rely on to navigate predominantly white and black U.S. higher education settings. The understandings that are being gleaned from the study suggest that although nearly half a century of legislation and hard-won victories against segregationist-era policies has resulted in greater inclusion of people of color, the lingering and ubiquitous influences of white supremacy still pervade the campuses, the practices, and specifically the stories that are told about U.S. postsecondary education. It is therefore not simply individuals along different continuums of this hard-fought battle who enter classrooms but entire communities with competing stories of struggle, resistance, success, and failure.

A significant part of a narrative inquiry is describing the landscape in which the narrative occurs. Collecting narratives for this study from faculty members of color through such mediums as individual interviews, focus groups, and class observations afforded a complex view of this landscape. Information gathered within and among these spaces demonstrates that even in cases in which only a single member of a family or community enters these once exclusively white environments, the insight that individual has gained from the stories about an entire community's resistance profoundly influences the ways in which he or she makes meaning and subsequently relates to his or her students. Further, the research suggests that educators of color who had the greatest success at providing service to students of color in predominantly white settings were able to draw on these stories of navigating historically segregated spaces as powerful pedagogical tools.

Autobiography

As a scholar of color, I found the stories my research participants narrated as both professionals and students in predominantly black and white universities to be similar to my own story. Consequently, one of the greatest strengths of an autobiographical approach to narrative is that it builds on insights and understandings with which the author has firsthand knowledge. Hence, as a student, administrator, and professor of color in these contexts, I had specific insights about the relationships between race, racism, and education. Recognition of the influence of autobiographically informed insights is a central part of coming to terms with these stories because immediate experience can be a double-edged sword. On the one hand, in some cases it provides the intricate details that are an indispensable part of communicating the complexities of an individual's experiences. On the other hand, being so close to a specific event or set of experiences (especially when considering the complexities associated with race and racism in the United States) risks causing me to potentially adopt bias that may influence the ways that he engages the stories of his participants.

My autobiographical accounts of the experiences that I had concerning race in varied educational contexts significantly informed my perspective as a researcher. For example, when considering the campus cultures of predominantly black and white universities, my understandings were informed by how I have personally observed issues associated with race and racism play out in different ways in multiple settings. For example, differences surfaced between predominantly white and predominantly black schools concerning the importance of titles (such as Doctor or Professor). This valuing of titles reflects a conservative culture in which predominantly black universities have historically functioned. The value attributed to more formal titles and a generally more conservative culture at black schools correspond to an intentional aim of presenting a more professional public image. In the postsegregation era these universities' relevance and overall value are often in question. In comparison, in predominantly white universities, in which institutional values appear to be more in line with the dominant culture, the adoption of a conservative public image is not necessarily a given.

The status or legitimacy afforded to predominantly white universities has little if anything to do with racial or racist perceptions about the competence of the educators or the educability of the student population. Their image is more closely related to their endowments, their retention rates, and the prestige of their alumni. In contrast, at historically black colleges there tends to be a more conservative institutional culture in which educators are typically referred to by their professional title, the dress by both students and staff members tends to be more formal, and "in loco parentis" approaches to student affairs translate to single-sex dorms and student curfews. Understanding these tensions on a personal level provided indispensable insight for conducting inquiry into the stories my participants told about their experiences in their classrooms and ultimately their relationships to their students and the material that they were teaching. Autobiographical approaches to narrative enable me to develop narratives that move beyond sweeping generalizations that describe predominantly black schools as rigid legalistic institutions or that portray predominantly white schools as places where academic credentials are unimportant.

Life Story Research

As previously described, research that I, Christine Lemley, completed for my doctoral dissertation (2006) included work with an indigenous people of North America. I gathered information to document their life stories of living and speaking their indigenous language. Through my studies I addressed the following question: How does language transmission between elders, teachers, and students influence the identity of the speakers and the sustainability of the language programs? I wanted to learn from people participating in the programs specifically about their identity and generally about what their thoughts were in regard to the language programs' sustainability. I learned the history of the tribe, noted how tribal members practiced their language in multiple sacred and public spaces, and engaged in dialogue with elders, teachers, and students to better understand their commitment to the language learning process.

Through the data analysis I came to understand how my initial focus on the language programs' sustainability needed to include the programs themselves as well as community events in which the participants engaged. Solely looking at the language programs would not accurately describe the Menominee Nation's commitment to language revitalization because language learning involved much more than translation and language program practice. So I altered my focus to explore my participants' lived stories of engaging in language learning as well as their actions and interactions including using sweat lodges, harvesting rice, collecting maple syrup, and attending storytelling sessions. I learned how the influence of involvement in the language programs on individual participants' identities revealed how people participating in the language programs expressed pride in their indigenous identity. The elders, teachers, and students explained how important speaking the language and practicing the culture were to them, their families, and their community. By focusing on the language programs' sustainability and listening to my participants' lived stories of learning and speaking their indigenous language, I found that Menominee language is learned both through acquisition of language knowledge and skills as well as through interactions with culture and living on the land.

I observed my research participants in multiple language learning settings and interviewed them about what learning the language meant to them personally as individuals and collectively as members in a community. I considered my position as an outsider in this community and the individual roles of elder, teacher, and student within the indigenous community, as well as the agency community members perceived within different spaces and places. Studying the participants' life story narratives led me to research Termination (1954–1973), a time when the federal government severed its previously established trust with some indigenous nations and eradicated their sovereign status, both of which had been defined in the Constitution and by federal law. These indigenous members no longer had an indigenous affiliation and became American citizens through forced assimilation and exploitation. Termination was a historical event to which the research participants repeatedly referred as threatening their indigenous identity, language, culture, and land. The life story research concerning forced attempts of assimilation revealed their obvious effect on contemporary challenges to learning and speaking the language. Talking to and against one another, the participants' narratives demonstrated the ease and tension the participants experienced in living, learning, and teaching the language.

Oral History

After I completed my dissertation work with the Menominee, I decided to explore positioning myself with "insider" status and study my own community in southwestern Wisconsin, where many people have moved from city dwellings to country living. I recalled hearing stories at family gatherings of my parents and family friends deciding to leave city life to take up rural living in the early 1970s. I invited my parents and their friends to share their stories of this move and narrate the challenges and rewards they experienced. This initial idea has continued, and I am currently involved with an oral history project focusing on lived experiences of people who moved to the Kickapoo Valley in southwestern Wisconsin from 1965 to 1985 as part of the back-to-the-land movement. I am focusing on two interview questions for this study: "What does 'back to the land' mean to you?" and "How did you participate (or not) in this movement?"

To understand the impact of the back-to-the-land movement on the ecological, economic, and social well-being of the Kickapoo Valley, I am completing extensive interviews about why the research participants moved and stayed (or left) and collecting artifacts (photos, journals, objects, newspaper articles, movies) that represent their lives. I am also investigating historical events that the participants mention were critical to their lives during the time they moved to and lived in the area. I completed an initial interpretation of the interviews and artifacts and now want to research the town's relocation of a flood plain, a historic event that many participants referenced as demonstrative of tensions and cooperation experienced as outsiders working with locals in the community. In addition to exploring the historic relocation, I have also decided to interview outsiders who moved to the area as well as locals who grew up in the area in order to collect multiple perspectives of this particular history and show the causes and effects of this movement on individuals, the community, and society at large. (For additional perspectives, see Chapter Five on biography and life story research, and Chapter Six on historical research.)

> **REFLECTION QUESTIONS**
>
> 1. Why might a researcher choose to tell a story through biography, autobiography, life story research, or oral history?
> 2. Do some parts of the studies described earlier seem particularly challenging or rewarding to complete? Explain your reasoning.

Narrative Inquiry: Responses to Critique

Narrative inquiry methodology challenges traditional research methodologies and "appears to reaffirm the plurality of stories that different cultures and subcultures may tell about themselves" (Hinchman & Hinchman, 1997, p. xiv). For narrative inquiry, no one truth exists, and storytelling often becomes an act of resistance against a dominant paradigm of rationality as the research participant can justify his or her actions or reactions throughout a narrative account. When conducted in a reflexive manner, narrative inquiry provides the possibility of reaching across the divide between researchers and the researched, giving marginalized communities the ability to take part in telling their own stories. In these cases narrative research serves as a conduit across static boundaries and objective notions of researchers gaining unmitigated access to the lives and experiences of their participants. And in so doing, this inquiry affords the reader the potential to see the relationship between the researcher and the researched and consequently the points that are tacitly accented or understated in the act of storytelling.

Plainly stated, narrative research highlights the fact that as long as there have been people, there have been stories by and about people. However, looking beyond the story itself, narrative inquiry focuses on who tells the story and how it is told. As with any other research methodology, narrative inquiry has its critics. We discuss three areas of criticism in the next section: (1) narrative inquiry and questions concerning reliability, objectivity, generalizability, and validity; (2) storytelling as therapeutic rather than analytic; and (3) the authenticity of the representation of narratives by narrative inquirers.

Reliability, Objectivity, Generalizability, and Validity

Such research elements as reliability, objectivity, generalizability, and validity are typically used as part of quantitative research measurement techniques that challenge qualitative research methodologies, including narrative inquiry (Mishler, 1990; Pinnegar & Dayne, 2007). In quantitative research, **reliability** indicates consistency and stability; **objectivity** represents separation between researcher and research participant; **generalizability** demonstrates predictability and control; and **validity** is equated with certainty (Webster & Mertova, 2007). These quantitative research elements are used as part of attempts to categorize research data and view them from an objective stance, generalizing in order to be efficient. These values and assumptions conflict with the philosophical underpinnings of narrative inquiry, which acknowledges human experience to be dynamic and constantly in a state of flux.

Reliability

Reliability in narrative research most often refers to dependability and trustworthiness of the data (Polkinghorne, 1988). And when considering trustworthiness, a narrative researcher is concerned that the story or narrative is recognizable to the participant storyteller and illustrative of the storyteller's experience. Narrative inquiry focuses on individual stories and experiences that expect and value differences between individuals (Webster & Mertova, 2007). The power of narrative inquiry lies in its ability to mine the unique insights and tacit understandings that inherently reside within and form the basis for the stories that we tell.

Objectivity

Narrative research dismisses the notion that research is a neutral activity. Similar to researchers from varied strands of qualitative research, narrative researchers suggest that the very desire to search for an objective stance within a person's lived experience is subjective in and of itself. Further, in the case of narrative research, the parts of a story that a participant chooses to highlight and the aspects of that story that a researcher most vividly reports are subjective as well. Alan Rumsey (2000) writes, "The landscape is read by *walking over it*" (p. 172), suggesting that narrative inquiry highlights the ways that each environment or landscape is different. Rumsey gives an example: someone could point to a rock formation and say, "There, that's the story." Speech relays the message but cannot serve an independent role to tell the whole story. Thus it is not simply the words, the rock, or the person, but instead the actual transaction between all three that is communicated through a narrative that provides rich and meaningful information.

Generalizability

In regard to generalizability, narrative inquirers look for the unique and significant meanings within a particular event. Narrative inquiry studies therefore tend to have a limited number of participants (small sample size) when compared to quantitative studies. This focus on the local and particular, as opposed to an expansive and general unit of analysis, contributes to narrative research's capacity for deep exploration and explanation of a phenomenon (see also Chapter Three, Grounded Theory). Consequently, whereas quantitative methods help researchers understand the what, where, and when of a phenomenon, qualitative approaches, and narrative research in particular, provide insight into how and why a phenomenon occurs (Creswell, 2005).

Validity

In a review of Catherine Riessman's book (2008) on narrative methods, Duque (2009) summarizes Riessman's view that the validity of narrative inquiry lies in a narrative's "ability to inform future studies and contribute to social change by empowering participants" (para. 25). Clearly this is an ambitious aim and is in direct conflict with quantitative approaches to research that aspire to objectivity. Duque concludes, however, that "these issues should serve as impetus for scholarly debates and 'added diversity' (Riessman, 2008 p. 200) in the field" (para. 25). We have found that a central part of informing future studies and subsequently empowering our participants in the way that Riessman describes as valid has been our ability to recognize critical events (Webster & Mertova, 2007) in our participants' stories. Critical events are important events recounted by the research participant and, as such, deserve focus from the researcher. Local knowledge informs the story and the researcher about cultural and personal interactions. What constitutes a critical event for narrative researchers is directly related to the relationship between the researcher and the participant. The researcher must be knowledgeable enough about the experiences of the individuals and community that he or she is researching to recognize what is critical and what is peripheral to the stories that participants are relaying. This recognition constitutes a meaningful type of validity.

Validity in narrative research emphasizes the inquirer's and even the participant's desire to understand. Jean McNiff (2007) explores issues of validity through an idea of goodness, focusing specifically on what counts as authentic practice and ethical research accounts. He writes, "I ask whether my work and my account may be judged as good, as I question whether my responsibility is to do good in the world or tell a good story" (p. 309). This conception of good is not simply a question for the researcher. It must be conceptualized against the backdrop of what participants consider to be a good representation, understanding, use, and so forth of their experiences. Further, the research must be conducted in a manner that recognizes that regardless of how detailed an account is, the distance between the research participants and the researcher can never be completely bridged because there is no unmediated access to the research participants' thoughts and actions. To facilitate the researcher's further inquiry into these issues, McNiff offers the following questions for the researcher-inquirer to understand and explain what he or she is doing (p. 310):

- What is my concern?
- Why am I concerned?
- What kind of experience can I describe to show the reasons for my concerns?
- What can I do about it? What will I do about it?

McNiff further explains, "For me, whether my story should be accepted is not a case of whether it abides by the conventions of the orthodox canon but whether the validity I am claiming for it can be justified" (p. 310). Hence what the narrative researcher obtains and subsequently how he or she presents or represents this information challenge status quo approaches to research that place the historically disenfranchised further on the margins by weighting the measures of accuracy and validity on the side of the researcher. Building on McNiff's earlier comments, we argue that narrative inquiry instead holds the potential for participants to play a greater role in justifying the validity of the narratives that researchers construct.

In contrast, in more orthodox approaches to research there is a clearly defined bifurcation between the researcher (rational subject) who produces knowledge and the researched (object under study) from whom the information is mined to create knowledge. Thinking of validity from a narrative perspective invites multiple epistemologies (ways of knowing), ontologies (ways of being), and axiologies (ways of valuing and judging) from research participants. As a result, narrative inquiry offers researchers the space to write stories with the expressed intent of capturing and engaging the experiences of their participants in a more complete and democratic manner than objectivist approaches to research allow. Therefore, the label and influence associated with being the subject or object—or the knower or known—are problematized; as opposed to there being a researcher and a participant, in a narrative inquiry there are costorytellers negotiating the spoken and unspoken landscape, events, understandings, and insights of which a given story consists.

Storytelling as Therapeutic

Carolyn Ellis and Art Bochner (2000) write, "If you are a storyteller rather than a story analyst then your goal becomes therapeutic rather than analytic" (p. 745). As educational researchers we do not feel particularly affected by this critique, yet we understand how this could affect researchers in educational psychology, especially in counseling and therapy professions. Regardless of the field in which we situate our inquiry, however, we acknowledge the power of stories to influence people's thinking and subsequently the ways they make sense out of phenomena. For instance, in the wake of the devastating earthquake that hit Haiti in January of 2010, American televangelist Pat Robertson is infamously remembered for his comments that the natural disaster that the small island nation faced was the product of a pact that Haiti made with the devil to gain its independence from French imperialists in the early nineteenth century. Despite the absurdity and outright racist connotations inherent in this explanation of Haiti's recent calamities, the decision to conceptualize the events through the narrative that Robertson presents clearly has different implications for an analyst of the tragic events—Does it accurately describe the event?—than for a therapist—Does it provide possibilities for psychic relief for the Haitian population? For narrative research, this distinction (accuracy versus psychic relief) provides the opportunity to contextualize and historicize the explanatory power or validity of Robertson's story against that of the counter-stories of the Haitian population. This distinction also highlights the contested nature of stories in general, causing us to give serious consideration to the perspectives of the story teller, those whom the story is told to, and those about whom the story is told.

Authentic Representation and Reproduction of Narratives

Another criticism of narrative inquiry is that narrative inquirers represent narratives as if they were authentic when the distortion of data may occur in any study. The events of stories may be too traumatic to recall, or the narrator may fear reprisal or simply have forgotten the events. This possible distortion of stories occurs for autobiographical narratives as well. Atkinson and Delamont (2006), for example, commented that

> autobiographical accounts are no more "authentic" than other modes of representation: a narrative or a personal experience is not a clear route into "the truth," either about the reported events, or of the teller's private experience. It is one of the key lessons of narrative analysis that "experience" is constructed through the various forms of narrative. (p. 166)

We agree with this critique, noting that cultural conventions shape human experience. As researchers we particularly consider here our research with marginalized populations. We wonder how the research participants were influenced by our cultural background and life experiences. We question whether the research participants were able to tell more or less of their stories—or preferred not to tell certain parts—because of our roles as insiders or outsiders of their respective communities.

So we return to our Haitian example in which Robertson posits a supernatural explanation for the disaster that is rooted in contrasting worldviews between evangelical Christian beliefs and indigenous Haitian religious beliefs. To really understand these ideas a researcher must be familiar with the competing cultural conventions and the historical moments within which they are situated. These conventions are rooted in meta-narratives that powerfully shape our perceptions of everything from finding the best ways to aid the Haitian population to actually providing a rationale—in Robertson's case—for why Haiti is experiencing its current hardships. There is little doubt, however, that if Haitians were able to tell their stories themselves, such issues as the cruelty they experienced under French colonial rule and the continuation of systematic economic isolation by current U.S. policies would provide a different narrative of who had been cavorting with the devil.

REFLECTION QUESTIONS

1. Which of the narrative inquiry critiques discussed earlier would you consider most important? Why?
2. How could you see a researcher overcoming the critique or critiques you listed in question 1?

Narrative Inquiry: How to Begin

In "The Future of Narrative" (2007), theorist Petra Munro-Hendry suggests that all research is narrative, and moreover that a strong case can be made that narrative research is the first and oldest form of inquiry. In addition, Clandinin and Rosiek (2007) believe that what feels new is the emergence of narrative research in the field of social scientific research. As a result of the growing interest in narrative inquiry over the last twenty years in both theory and practice, it has been employed as a tool for analysis across disciplines. Two specific reasons for this interest include (1) a critique of the inherent strengths and weaknesses of conventional positivist research methods, and (2) a focus on the individual and the individual's construction of knowledge (Webster & Mertova, 2007).

Conventional **positivist** research methods, which state that only one truth exists concerning any given notion, restrict accounting for the complexities of human actions and subsequently risk undermining the richness of human experiences by grouping them into discrete, objective measures. Although conventional positivist research, often portrayed through statistics, may provide much meaningful information, we assert that human actions are most complexly accounted for through narratives. However, we are not suggesting that narrative research necessarily explains life, recounts original experience, or provides unmediated access into an individual's world in a more authentic manner than traditional positivist research. Instead, our perspective on narrative research suggests that recounting any experience is a tenuous "contested territory" (Britzman, 2000, p. 30). As theorist Pierre Bourdieu (1990) argues, human life is incoherent and consists of elements standing alongside each other or following each other, without necessarily being related. Hence, narrative inquiry represents the work of researchers to provide a correspondence between life and a written description of it.

As researchers we construct or "story" lives by reducing them to a series of events, categories, or themes; we then put them back together again to make up a whole that is called narrative (Munro-Hendry, 2007). Clandinin and Connelly (2000, p. 48) provide the following procedures for conducting a narrative study:

1. Determine if narrative research is suitable,
2. Identify problems or questions to guide the study,
3. Gather stories,
4. Collaborate actively,
5. Consider literature,

6. Analyze and interpret data,

7. Consider context of stories, and

8. Re-story.

These steps, although not exclusive to narrative inquiry as a qualitative research methodology, are unique because of their focus on the research participants rather than on the research itself.

The emerging critical vein within narrative research has been attributed to its ability to provide a less exploitive method of inquiry than philosophical traditions evolving from positivist approaches to conducting research. Specifically, when examining historically marginalized communities (for example, women; people of color; the lesbian, gay, bisexual, transgender, queer [LGBTQ] community), narrative researchers offer the potential for a more egalitarian research relationship that honors **intersubjective** modes of knowledge production—that is, understandings that are negotiated and have varying meanings for different groups (Munro, 1993). Or, more plainly stated, research relationships are founded on the premise that knowledge is produced and subsequently communicated through the shared experiences and stories of individuals and communities. Furthermore, narrative inquiry portends the ability to add stories that traditionally had been excluded from mainstream educational research discourses (Munro-Hendry, 2007).

Some particularly powerful examples of the utility of narrative research can be found in the work of educators Rosiek (Dibble & Rosiek, 2002) and Miller (1992). Rosiek broadly describes the focus of his research to be an analysis of the ideas and practices that teachers use on a day-to-day basis to provide service to their students. He relates narrative inquiry to these aims because it provides the ability to impart stories about the nuanced aspects of teaching that cannot easily be measured, quantified, or communicated through traditional positivist approaches. For example, in an article Rosiek and his coresearcher Nancy Dibble, who is also the actual teacher in the article, conduct inquiry into Dibble's pedagogical practice in her biology class (Dibble & Rosiek). In the article Dibble comes to see her European American racial identity as influencing her attempts to counsel Mexican American students to pursue further science education. Their decision to frame the article in the voices of the researcher (Rosiek) in order to represent the complex insights that informed the teacher in the study's practice, and of the teacher (Dibble) in the form of the actual stories she told, reflects the authors' desire to move beyond a reductionist conclusion. Instead they use narrative to get at the teacher's reflections on the structure of the science curriculum, on her personal history, and on uncomfortable feelings that contain kernels of insight and eventually grow into reflexive insights about science, teaching, and her race.

Miller (1992) is interested in narrative research that primarily takes the form of autobiography; however, there is not necessarily a difference between narrative research and autobiography (see also Chapter Eight, Trekking Through Autoethnography). This is because a narrative can comprise information about persons and events that existed beyond the writer's personal experience. In "Exploring Power and Authority Issues in a Collaborative Research Project," Miller described her work conceptualizing curriculum as "cultural, historical, political, and biographical intersections that influence and frame interactions and interpretations among teachers, students, and texts" (p. 165). Miller's work demonstrates the complexity and potential rigor associated with the use of narrative research. Instead of resting on claims that narrative research inherently provides a more equitable and illustrative view of the experiences of teachers, Miller challenges simplistic depictions of teachers and the stories that they tell about their teaching. In "Autobiography and the Necessary Incompleteness of Teachers' Stories," Miller (1998) highlights the importance of studying stories by and about teachers by referencing Shari Benstock's critique of the sense that teachers are often told to just "tell your story." Benstock (1991, p. 10) states,

> Something is missing in this invitation. One difficulty arises when autobiographies, or narratives, or stories about education are told or written as unitary, and transparent, and are used as evidence of progress or success in school reform for example, so that the fabric of the narrative appears seamless, spun of whole cloth. The effect is magical—the self appears organic, the present appears as the sum total of the past, the past appears as an accurate predictor of the future.

Rosiek's and Miller's use of narrative inquiry not only demonstrates the potential for narrative research to describe and analyze "what is" but also raises questions and alternatives for "what might be" as both relate to the stories that are being conveyed (Miller, 1992, p. 169; Dibble & Rosiek, 2002). These possibilities are important in that they provide an approach to inquiry that accounts for the complexity of human experience while also recognizing that even in our most careful attempts at inquiry we still have significant epistemic and ontological limitations. However, these limitations are not intended to stop us as researchers from telling stories or learning from the stories that we tell but instead highlight the significant ways that we shape and are shaped by the world.

> **REFLECTION QUESTIONS**
>
> 1. What are defining characteristics of narrative inquiry?
> 2. How do you believe individual interests shape and are shaped by the world?

Summary

In this chapter we sought first to position ourselves and our work within the field of narrative inquiry. We then situated narrative research within the diverse family of interpretive approaches to research broadly termed as qualitative research. We described the applicability of narrative approaches to research, specifically outlining the critical and emancipatory possibilities that narrative affords. Through our discussions of critical events that occur within a narrative, we highlighted the importance of individual and collective narratives in giving traditionally marginalized communities the ability to tell their stories. Throughout this chapter we have underscored the creative potential of narrative approaches and the profound understandings that narrative approaches to research provide, while closely scrutinizing the stories that we and our participants tell about ourselves, each other, and the world.

We provided personal examples of our real-world experiences as narrative inquirers working with historically marginalized groups. Collecting these stories led us to delineate the differences between specific modes of narrative research (biography, autobiography, life history research, and oral history). And by recognizing these differences we emphasized our thinking about researcher reflexivity, or, more plainly stated, the relationship between the researcher (listener) and the researched (storyteller)—or in some cases where the line is blurred between the two. We also discussed the challenges and limitations of conducting narrative research by outlining narrative inquiry's relationship to conventional quantitative research concepts, for example, generalizability, validity, reliability, and objectivity. In this chapter we aimed to describe narrative research, seeking to highlight the possibilities that narrative inquiry offers researchers through the power of stories.

Key Terms

autobiography, 225
biography, 225
consequence, 221
critical events, 219
epistemic, 216
generalizability, 231

historicity, 218
intersubjective, 237
life story research, 225
narrative inquiry, 215
narratives, 221
objectivity, 231

ontological, 216
oral history, 225
personal practical knowledge, 224
positivist, 236
raw narratives, 219

reflexive knowledge, 225
reliability, 231
sequence, 221
taxonomies, 221
transactional, 222
validity, 231

Further Readings and Resources

Suggested Narrative Research Studies

Dibble, N., & Rosiek, J. (2002). White out: A case study introducing a new citational format for teacher practical knowledge research. *International Journal of Education & the Arts*, *3*(5). www.ijea.org/v3n5/index.html.

In this article a university researcher (Jerry Rosiek) and K–12 teacher (Nancy Dibble) explore the ways that narratives of historically marginalized communities can establish either obstacles or opportunities for educators teaching in racially and culturally diverse settings. In addition to including a practical application of narrative inquiry in the work of classroom teachers, this article also provides an instance of researchers and teachers' working together to situate stories in pedagogically powerful ways. In short, this article was not meant to sit on the shelves; instead it provides a case study for teachers seeking to address issues of racial and cultural diversity in the classroom.

O'Neil, M. (2006). Theorising narratives of exile and belonging: The importance of biography and ethno-mimesis in "understanding" asylum. *Qualitative Sociology Review*, *2*(1), 22–38.

This article reports a narrative inquiry into the experiences of Bosnian refugees in the East Midlands and Afghan refugees in London. The study is primarily situated in the field of sociology, and it reflects an application of participatory action research intended to inform public policy and praxis concerning the needs and treatment of asylum seekers and political exiles. The authors set out to develop a case for theory building based on lived experience. Using biographical materials and narrative inquiry was an essential part of their conceptual and methodological framework.

Other Suggested Readings

Clandinin, D. J. (2007). *Handbook of narrative inquiry: Mapping a methodology*. Thousand Oaks, CA: Sage.

This important text sets out to map the progression of narrative research over the course of the last few decades. It acknowledges the current popularity of narrative in the social sciences and attempts the difficult work of considering narrative inquiry as a methodology when conducting research.

Hurwitz, B., Greenhalgh, T., & Skultans, V. (2004). *Narrative research in health and illness.* Hoboken, NJ: Wiley.

This expansive text presents a comprehensive illustration of narrative inquiry's potential to inform the work of health care professionals. Patients' stories are examined to highlight social, cultural, ethical, psychological, organizational, and linguistic issues that are typically overlooked in the primarily positivist field of health care. The fields of health care and the social sciences are blended through the use of narrative to help health care providers become more effective in their everyday work with patients.

Miller, J. (2005). *Sounds of silence breaking: Women, autobiography, curriculum.* New York: Peter Lang.

Through the use of autobiographical narratives, Janet Miller, one of the most influential thinkers in the field of curriculum theory, provides an insightful portrait of the work of a narrative researcher. Included in the text are her reflections on over two decades of participation in the "reconceptualization of curriculum" movement; a consideration of her close engagement with classroom teachers; and, most important for our purposes, a thoughtful discussion of the constantly changing dimensions of narrative and interpretive practices.

Munro-Hendry, P. (2007). The future of narrative. *Qualitative Inquiry, 13,* 487–497.

In this article Petra Munro-Hendry directly addresses many of the primary challenges to narrative inquiry's acceptance as a more mainstream approach for conducting research. Questions concerning the validity, reliability, objectivity, and generalizability associated with narrative approaches to research are thoroughly addressed. However, Munro then moves to more complex questions concerning researcher reflexivity and the relationship between the tellers, recorders, and subsequent hearers of narratives. Further, by discussing the relationship between individuals and the stories that they tell, Munro forwards the possibility for narrative reflection to serve as a more socially just way of voicing the interests of historically marginalized communities.

Organizations and Web Sites

American Educational Research Association (AERA)—Special Interest Group on Narrative Research (SIG #145) (http://sites.google.com/site/aeranarrativeresearchsig/)

AERA is a national education association and affords opportunities to hear as well as dialogue with researchers and educators. The special interest group devoted to narrative inquiry holds conference sessions in which researchers present on topics that use narrative inquiry as a methodology.

International Congress for Qualitative Inquiry (ICQI), University of Illinois at Urbana-Champaign (www.icqi.org/)

ICQI meets annually on the University of Illinois at Urbana-Champaign campus. Interactive workshops begin the conference, and junior as well as veteran researchers and educators are invited to present, dialogue, and network. ICQI is much smaller than AERA and offers graduate students a supportive environment to present as well as talk about qualitative research methodologies, such as narrative inquiry.

CHAPTER 10

CASE STUDY RESEARCH

Tricia S. Moore
Stephen D. Lapan
MaryLynn T. Quartaroli

Key Ideas

- Case study research is used to describe complex phenomena and how people interact with them.

- Case studies often generate thick, rich descriptions of educational and social programs.

- Whereas survey research involves gathering wide-ranging surface-level data, by contrast case studies examine single instances in greater depth.

- Research questions help bound and focus the case study in ways that are meaningful to stakeholders and other audiences.

- A case study's design includes identifying the case, setting boundaries, developing research questions, employing methods of data collection that increase the validity of findings, and analyzing and synthesizing these data in reporting results.

- In addition to disclosing personal biases about the case, researchers often use triangulation and member checking to increase the validity of findings.

Case study research is an investigative approach used to thoroughly describe complex phenomena, such as recent events, important issues, or programs, in ways to unearth new and deeper understanding of these phenomena. Specifically, this methodology focuses on the concept of **case,** the particular example or instance from a class or group of events, issues, or programs, and how people interact with components of this phenomenon. For example, a case study of the 2010 U.S. Gulf Coast oil spill disaster (event) would represent an instance (a case) of offshore oil drilling accidents. A case study of an immigration law in Arizona (issue) would be an example of the issue of immigration policies instituted by governments. And the investigation of an effort to prevent drug use at a local high school is an example of a program case study.

Researchers focus case studies on defined portions of the phenomenon of interest, inquiry that is ordinarily limited to the investigation of contemporary events, issues, or programs rather than historical ones. In addition, the overarching purpose of this approach is to comprehensively "catch the complexity" (Stake, 1995, p. xi) of the activities, decisions, and human interactions. Case study results offer those directly affected by the case (**stakeholders**) and others interested in the event or program (**audiences**) extended awareness by providing rich detail about highlighted aspects of the case.

To provide a frame of reference for case study research, Scriven (1991) defines it as the polar opposite of survey research. Survey studies seek to gather broad surface-level data about a topic, such as state, regional, or national incidences of food poisoning. Conversely, case studies set out to examine the particular, portraying local topics or single instances, such as the case of food poisoning incidences and treatments at one health care facility. Lapan and Armfield (2009) explain the special nature of case study efforts as "a microscopic approach where intensive examination of the 'particular' is emphasized; this is what some call 'peeling the onion' to carefully view each layer of identified case-related program activity" (p. 166).

The term *case study* is not a new one and has been applied to many endeavors that are easily confused with case study research. Merriam (2009) crisply notes, "Case study research is not the same as casework, case method, case history, or case record" (p. 45). These uses of the term should be understood as distinct from the concept of case study research outlined here. As Merriam further explains,

> *Casework* is a term used in social service fields and usually refers to determining appropriate strategies for dealing with developmental or adjustment problems. *Case method* is an instructional technique whereby the major ingredients of a case study are presented to students for illustrative purposes and problem-solving experiences. *Case studies* as teaching devices have become very popular in law, medicine, and business. . . . *Case history*—the tracing of a person, group, or institution's past—is sometimes part of a case study. In medicine and social work, case histories (also called *case records*) are used in much the same sense as casework—to facilitate service to the client. (p. 45)

REFLECTION QUESTIONS

1. At this point, how would you define case study research?
2. How do case histories differ from case study research?
3. In your discipline, what might be an appropriate topic for case study research?

There are many uses in various fields for case study research, for example in the development of thick descriptions of educational and social programs. These studies are driven by research questions that determine the selection of program segments to investigate. Case studies can be focused in even more specialized ways or combined with other recognized methodologies, such as when ethnographers use thorough descriptions to study beliefs and practices to produce cultural interpretations (see Chapter Seven), when biography and life story researchers study how people interact with a significant event (see Chapter Five), or when researchers evaluate social and educational programs (see Chapters Thirteen and Fourteen).

Characteristics of a Case Study

Although case study research may be applied to many settings for many reasons, in this chapter we will focus on its use in illuminating educational and social programs. Program case study designs begin by identifying the specific program to be investigated followed by the selection of specific aspects that will be thoroughly studied. Unless very small and uncomplicated, most programs cannot be studied in their entirety. The selected program elements are then clarified using research questions that will guide the actual case study. Answering these questions through several forms of data collection becomes the principal task of the case study researcher.

Bounding the Case

Case study research involves the exploration of something with clear limits or boundaries. The case study researcher carefully defines and clearly specifies what elements of the case will be studied, that is, which portion of the program or other phenomena is to be the focus of the investigation. This **bounding** of the case includes identifying the aspects to be studied using research questions, the time frame to be included, and the exact physical locations that are part of the research. Such bounding communicates those parts of the case that will be included and those that will be excluded from the study. Identifying the study's location, the program within the facility to be observed, and the time frame within which the study will be conducted, for example, may bound a case study of a county mental health facility. In this study, the researcher could select the emergency care program within the mental health facility and decide to conduct the case study for at least three months to obtain a good sample of the facility's operation.

Focusing, limiting, or bounding case study efforts allows the researcher to use valuable investigative time for in-depth observations that produce rich and detailed case descriptions. These study limits are necessary given the usual time and resource constraints of any research effort.

Purposes of Case Studies

Lapan and Armfield (2009) note that many different purposes for case study research have been identified in the literature, including its ability to explain, explore, describe, and compare educational or social programs (Yin, 2003) and "to discover and communicate innovative ideas and programs" (Simons, 1977, in Lapan & Armfield, 2009, p. 167). Stake (1995, 2006) has provided one of the most efficient ways of explaining the purposes of case study research, recognizing it to be either intrinsic or instrumental.

Intrinsic case studies, on the one hand, focus on the case being studied, answering questions about that entity only to communicate the illuminated operations to its participants and other stakeholders. **Instrumental case studies,** on the other hand, use case results to support a theory or construct a new way of explaining some phenomenon.

In researching one or more reading classes for first graders, for example, an intrinsic case study researcher would observe several selected program elements during at least part of the school year and then summarize these findings to offer participants (teachers, parents, administrators) a deeper understanding about the program's operation. This intrinsic purpose would be served by focusing exclusively on the program itself.

Instrumental case studies, by contrast, explore instances or cases to build new theories or compare findings to current ones to either corroborate them or question their validity. In the first-grade reading example, the instrumental case study researcher would ordinarily collect data from dozens of classrooms, developing rich descriptions of teaching and learning patterns. By using large amounts of concrete data from real-life contexts, the theory-building or theory-testing case study researcher may be able to generate new or supporting explanations (theories) of how first graders learn to read.

Case Study Types

Case studies can be designed to include either one or several cases of the same phenomenon and can be conducted at any number of sites. **Single case studies** are those conducted using just one incidence or example of the case at a single site (one health care facility, one reading classroom). **Multiple case studies** can be conducted at one site where many examples of the case are examined, such as several first-grade reading classes in one school, or at multiple sites, such as first-grade reading classes in different schools or school districts. Multiple case studies and **multiple site case studies** are usually designed for purposes of comparison and sometimes referred to as **comparative case studies.** Whether at one or multiple sites, multiple cases are considered to be examples of the same type of case sharing common characteristics. Thus one might conduct a multiple comparative case study of state-level immigration policies in Arizona, Texas, New Mexico, and California, or of multiple high school drug prevention programs at five or six different high schools.

Most case studies, regardless of the design, can be completed in six weeks to three months depending on the number of researchers and the complexity of the case. However, some case study research can be designed for longer periods, perhaps for six months to more than a year, and are often called **longitudinal case studies.**

REFLECTION QUESTIONS

1. If you decided to conduct case study research of a university department of psychology, how might this be a single case study? How might it be a multiple case study?
2. Why might you decide to use a multiple case study rather than a single case design? When would you decide to use a single case study approach?

Planning Case Study Research

The elements and sequence of case study preparation are presented here so that the reader can determine the important characteristics of case study planning.

It should be noted, however, that these plans are likely to unfold in many different ways depending on the case to be investigated and the study questions to be answered. The case study examples provided here and elsewhere in this chapter are excerpted from a case investigation of a dental hygiene student tutor program conducted by the first author (Moore, 2009).

Conceptualizing the Study

The first step is conceptualizing the study, which includes clarifying the purpose, defining and limiting the case, identifying the questions, and considering potential audiences for the report (see, for example, Exhibit 10.1). This step helps the researcher verify that case study research is appropriate for what the researcher wants to know, or the purpose of the study. To accomplish this step the researcher asks such questions as these: What do I want to know about the case? Why do I want to know this? How will I limit or bound the case? Who else wants to know about or cares about this? This initial step influences everything else the researcher will do.

Bounding or Limiting the Case

As described previously, the case study researcher must define, limit, or determine the boundaries for the case. The case is often bounded by time (for

---

EXHIBIT 10.1

MOORE (2009) TUTOR STUDY–CASE, LIMITS, AND PURPOSE

Case: The case was limited to senior undergraduate dental hygiene students serving as tutors for beginning undergraduate dental hygiene students, or sophomores, in a course in the baccalaureate in dental hygiene (BDH) curriculum during one spring semester.

Limits: The case was limited to the tutor role and experience and did not focus on the students being tutored, except as they contributed to the tutor role.

Purpose: This is a single, intrinsic case study to better understand the nature of the student tutor role and experience and to illuminate the use of students as tutors.

example, examining the initial six months of a college nursing program) or by place (for example, examining an at-risk youth program as implemented in one community).

Writing Study Questions

Study questions provide the structure to capture the essence of the case in its context. The researcher asks, What do I want to know about the case? Asking good questions is one of the most important things the case study researcher does because the questions focus the inquiry and determine the plan. The researcher considers the questions during each aspect of the study. Decisions about the types of data gathered and the strategies used during interpretation and analysis depend upon the study questions. The researcher also considers the stakeholders in the study when crafting questions. The researcher asks, Who cares or wants to know about this? What do they want to know? Who will read the case study report?

Before defining the study questions, the researcher may choose to identify what is already known and what needs to be known about the case and its context. **Theoretical or conceptual frameworks** pertinent to the case can guide development of the study questions and may be discovered through a review of pertinent literature. A theoretical or conceptual framework explains or suggests a relationship between concepts or ideas. Sinclair (2007) likens a theoretical framework to a map or travel plan. Before undertaking a journey to an unknown place it is helpful to learn from the previous experience of others who have been on similar trips, to hear their suggestions about what to bring and what to expect. Likewise, before initiating a study, the researcher reads accounts of similar case studies by other researchers and discovers possible links and predictions of how those researchers' concepts or ideas may influence the case he wishes to study (see Exhibit 10.2).

Stake (1995) claims that a good study question will "direct the looking and the thinking enough and not too much" (p. 15). Case study research questions often begin with *how* or *why* (Yin, 2003). For example, *How* are patients screened for the mental health facility? *Why* are these criteria used? The researcher begins to formulate questions about the situation or problem to be studied, keeping in mind that a study question is bigger than simply what one source might reveal about the case. Questions should therefore be focused on the content of a program, not on data sources. One should ask such questions as How are participants selected? rather than What do the participants think of the selection process? Note how Moore (2009) wrote the questions for her tutor study in Exhibit 10.3.

EXHIBIT 10.2
TUTOR STUDY THEORETICAL OR CONCEPTUAL FRAMEWORK

A review of research on tutoring revealed a potential relationship between the learning potential of the student and the difference in age and expertise between the tutor and student. Expert, or more knowledgeable, peer tutors may have a different influence on collaborative learning than equal peer tutors (Rogoff, 1990). This led to questions about the tutor's use of knowledge and the nature of interactions between the tutors and the students.

EXHIBIT 10.3
TUTOR STUDY QUESTIONS

1. How does the student come to participate as a tutor?
   a. What influences students to become tutors?
   b. How are student tutors selected?

2. How does the tutor prepare for the tutor role?
   a. What is the nature of the training provided by the program?
   b. What preparation takes place for tutor tasks?

3. What does the tutor do during tutorials?
   a. What behaviors does the tutor exhibit during tutorials?
   b. In what ways does the tutor interact with students?
   c. In what ways does the tutor use his or her knowledge?
   d. In what ways does the tutor facilitate?

4. What does the tutor learn from the tutoring experience?

REFLECTION QUESTIONS

1. How are research questions used in case study research?
2. When considering study questions, what do you think Stake (1995) means by "direct the looking and the thinking enough and not too much" (p. 15)?
3. In your discipline, what might be appropriate questions for a case study?

Research Plan: How to Find Answers

Once the case is defined and questions are determined, the researcher can begin to plan the details of the study by asking, How can each question be best answered? Who has the needed information? What observations are needed? and Are there documents to review? The case study researcher looks at each study question to determine what data are needed and how best to acquire them. The plan will include

- The data that are to be collected
- From whom the data will be collected
- How, where, and when the data will be collected
- Who should collect the data

What Data Will Be Collected?

The researcher determines the types of data needed to best answer the research questions. Although there are no set rules about which types of data to use in case study research, the case study purpose is often to describe, illuminate, or provide insight, which will most likely require a substantial amount of qualitative data. Case study researchers can observe persons and things, such as participants, activities, interactions, and conversations. Case studies may also examine individuals' thoughts, feelings, and experiences, which are not easily observed and may be best revealed through interviewing key informants. For example, in the tutor case study, tutor interviews helped reveal what the student tutor role meant to the tutors. These are complicated ideas that are best communicated in complete thoughts and words to obtain their full meaning.

Case studies may also examine behaviors, which are easier to observe and can be described and portrayed through more quantitative means, such as a tally of events. Quantitative data might also include results from such instruments as tests and attitude measures. It is the researcher's task to strike a balance between quantitative and qualitative data in obtaining the best answers to research questions and communicating the case to stakeholders and other audiences (see Exhibit 10.4, which elaborates on question 2 from Exhibit 10.3).

The case study researcher creates a plan that incorporates a variety of data gathering methods to answer the questions. **Triangulation,** or finding agreement among evidence collected from multiple sources and using various methods, increases the validity and trustworthiness of findings. When the researcher obtains similar findings through two different methods, such as interviewing and observation, that information is considered more trustworthy or credible (for

> **EXHIBIT 10.4**
>
> **TUTOR STUDY EXAMPLE OF QUESTIONS LINKED TO DATA SOURCES AND TYPES**
>
> Question 2: How does the tutor prepare for the tutor role?
>
> a. What is the nature of the training provided by the program?
> b. What preparation takes place for tutor tasks?
>
> Possible methods and sources of data:
>   *Interview:* Tutors and administrators
>   *Observation:* Tutor training sessions and meetings
>   *Document review:* Training materials; tutor journals; or artifacts, such as textbooks, syllabi, or resource manuals

example, if interviews indicate that patients spend a considerable amount of time in the waiting room, and visits to the facility reveal standing room only). However, if the researcher observes something different from what an interview reveals, more investigation is needed to understand the discrepancy (for example, if interviews indicate that patients spend a considerable amount of time in the waiting room, but visits to the facility reveal an empty waiting room). Likewise, if two different sources agree about something (for example, if patients and doctors agree that the health care system is meeting the needs of the community), that information is more credible than when two sources disagree (for example, if doctors feel the health care system is meeting the needs of the community but patients do not).

REFLECTION QUESTIONS

1. How do you think triangulation works? Give two or three additional examples.
2. How would you define "credible information" in case study research?

From Whom Will Data Be Collected?

An **informant** is a data source, or someone who knows about the case and can help the researcher learn about the case. Stake (1995) defines an informant as "someone who knows a lot about [the case] and is willing to chat" (p. 67). The case study researcher creates a plan that incorporates collection of data from multiple sources and various perspectives to answer the questions. For example, a case study of a police academy training program would most likely include seeking data from the trainees and trainers, and could use interviews, questionnaires, and direct observation. In the dental hygiene tutor case study, this use of multiple methods and sources included interviewing and observing the tutors and those tutored.

Case study researchers often identify participants using **purposeful sampling** as opposed to random sampling. With **random sampling,** each item or person has an equal chance of being selected for study. For example, participants may be selected by drawing names from a hat. Purposeful sampling lends more strength in case study research because data sources, participants, or cases are selected by how much can be learned from them. This approach is described as seeking "information-rich" sources (Patton, 1987, p. 58) rather than producing representative samples. Additional considerations about sampling are outlined elsewhere in this text (see, for example, Chapter Four).

The case study researcher considers how many or how much to sample in order to answer the questions. Sometimes an estimate is made prior to the study, and then actual numbers are determined based on the data that are obtained. For example, the researcher may continue to search for data until **saturation** is reached, that is, the evidence becomes redundant, with no new information coming in (Lincoln & Guba, 1985).

How, Where, and When Will Data Be Collected?

The case study researcher concentrates on the case, collecting data from various sources using various methods for days, weeks, or perhaps even longer. The researcher must decide whether a longitudinal or cross-sectional approach will best reveal the complexities of the case. As previously discussed, longitudinal case studies are an exception in regard to time frame in that they may last for months or even longer depending on the purpose of the study. For example, if studying a health care system, the researcher must decide if he should spend an extended amount of time following the same patients over time from their acceptance to release (longitudinal), or if he should study different people at various stages, including some patients who are being accepted, some who are being treated, and others who are being released from care (cross-sectional).

Once the researcher has determined the kinds of data required and the data collection strategy, a timeline can be constructed. Depending on who and what are being studied, it may be necessary to make contacts and ensure access to the study site, a process similar to that required for ethnographic research (see Chapter Seven). The case study researcher also makes plans to protect participants, secures their consent to participate in study activities, and obtains necessary approvals (for example, from an institutional review board as discussed in Chapter Two).

> **REFLECTION QUESTION**
>
> 1. For the case study questions that you previously created, what sources and types of data would be likely to provide useful information?

Who Should Collect the Data?

The case study researcher needs a variety of skills in addition to information about the issues related to the case. A review of the literature helps familiarize the researcher with the case, the context, related issues, and theoretical or conceptual frameworks that can inform the study. Prior to conducting the study, a researcher who is new to case study research may need to acquire knowledge and gain skill in the methods commonly used in qualitative research, including interviewing, listening, observing, describing, and interpreting. An example from the tutor study may be useful (see Exhibit 10.5).

According to Seidman (1998), "There is an inherent paradox at the heart of the issue of what topics researchers choose to study" (p. 26), because researchers' interest in a topic is often related to how closely they are involved with it. Qualitative designs often call for the "persons most responsible for interpretations to be in the field, making observations, exercising subjective judgment, analyzing and synthesizing, all the while realizing their own consciousness" (Stake, 1995, p. 41). It is important for the researcher to carefully examine and

---

EXHIBIT 10.5

TUTOR STUDY RESEARCHER SKILL DEVELOPMENT

To prepare for case study research, the researcher took graduate courses in ethnographic research methods and qualitative data analysis. She read books (see the suggested reading list at the end of this chapter) and developed interviewing and listening skills by conducting and evaluating practice interviews. She solicited instruction and feedback on question construction from a mentor. She practiced interviewing and learned to rephrase, use probing questions, and wait a sufficient amount of time using silence to encourage the necessary information.

reveal her **researcher position.** If the researcher has a close relationship or a past history with the case being studied, this information should be made transparent. **Researcher biases** or predispositions can be made explicit in a bracketed interview prior to the study. In a **bracketed interview,** the researcher reveals what she believes the study may reveal, what she thinks the answers to the study questions might be, and other potential biases or beliefs that can influence the researcher's interpretation of study findings. The researcher and case study audiences must examine more carefully any results that match the researcher's preconceived expectations.

In addition to revealing and documenting predispositions and biases, depending on her position the researcher also considers who is best to collect the data. It may be necessary to involve multiple investigators. When different observers find similarities, there is strength; where they differ, there is a need for further investigation. Exhibit 10.6 describes how Moore (2009) minimized bias in her case study.

Research Protocols and Instruments

Design and choice of protocols and instruments will have a great impact on the overall quality of the study. For example, the researcher wants to select or design

---

EXHIBIT 10.6
TUTOR STUDY MINIMIZING BIAS

Because the researcher was a faculty member in the dental hygiene program, she knew that her insider position would influence the study. To help control for bias she stated what she thought the study would reveal and documented her prestudy biases and dispositions in a bracketed interview. For example, she believed that tutor facilitation style might change (improve) over time, from more directive (telling students what to do) to less directive (asking questions and letting students make decisions). During data analysis she was able to test the strength of actual findings by comparing these to her anticipated findings.

The researcher was so closely involved that she solicited external help. For example, a colleague with no special interest in the program interviewed some of the tutors. This use of an external interviewer helped ensure results were not simply due to the researcher's bias or to tutors' perceptions of her position as one of power.

an instrument that is **valid,** or measures what it intends to measure. Standardized instruments, such as questionnaires or observation protocols, may be identified from a review of the literature or special sources that report research tools (see Chapter Four). If an appropriate instrument cannot be identified (which often happens), the researcher may need to create an original instrument, or modify an existing one, to meet the study needs.

Surveys and Interviews

Interview and survey instruments are often used in case study work. Good interview and survey questions should be neutral rather than leading or implying answers. For example, "How have students reacted?" is much better than "What do students dislike?" Also, each question should ask only one thing rather than multiple things. For example, "Tell me about your training" is better than "Tell me how you were selected and trained." Open-ended questions will result in more detailed and useful data than questions that can be answered with a *yes* or *no*. For example, "What things are you trying to achieve with your students?" will lead to entirely different types of data than "Do you feel your main goal is to teach content?" (a good example of a leading question as well). Some styles of questions generate even richer data. These include (1) hypothetical questions, such as "Suppose that I am a student who is resisting the role, what would you say to me?"; (2) devil's advocate questions, such as, "Some would say that students shouldn't be tutors; how would you respond to that?"; and (3) questions that ask for interpretation or speculation, such as, "How would you say that tutoring was different than you expected?" or "If you were the director, what changes would you make in the program?"

In addition to using valid instruments for data collection, the researcher also specifies how the instruments will be used. Interviews can be highly structured, with specified wording and order, or conducted more like informal conversations, with room for flexibility or exploration. In either case the researcher's goal is to use the best approach to achieve the purpose of the case study. The order of the questions asked as well as the specific wording can also have an impact on the results.

Once data collection instruments are selected or designed, the researcher tests them. This helps ensure success in obtaining the desired information and allows problems to be worked out prior to the study. A **pilot test** may be as simple as sharing the instrument with a colleague to ensure that questions are worded appropriately and are understood and interpreted as intended. A **field test** involves using the instrument on participants similar to the actual participants who will be studied. Exhibit 10.7 explains this process in the context of the tutor study.

EXHIBIT 10.7
TUTOR STUDY PILOT AND FIELD TESTING INTERVIEW PROTOCOL

The tutor interview protocol was piloted and field-tested with six faculty members or students who had served as tutors in prior semesters. These individuals could best identify with the content and structure of the questions. Wording was modified or probing questions were added where the interviewer or the participants struggled. For example, "How would you describe your best student?" was changed to "How would you describe an ideal (A+) student?"

As a result of the field testing, the order of questions was rearranged and some questions were grouped together to help the natural flow. For example, "What is a typical day of tutoring like?" replaced "What do you do before the tutorial?" and "What do you do after the tutorial?" The introduction, explaining the study, was revised to include more comfortable and natural language based on the actual wording used in the field tests.

In spite of pilot and field testing one question was regularly misinterpreted. When asked, "Can you think of a particular situation where a student responded to the feedback they received?" a typical response was "He or she said thank you" rather than an explanation of behavioral change made as a result of suggestions from the student's peers. However, thorough pilot and field testing efforts will reduce such problems to a minimum.

Moore (2009) developed an **interview protocol,** or guide, for her tutor case study, which included instructions as well as the questions. The interview guide was designed to allow for exploration of participants' experiences. Exhibit 10.8 is an excerpt from the revised tutor interview protocol, after pilot and field testing.

Observations

An **observation plan** helps the researcher consider what exactly to observe, when, and for how long. In case study research the researcher observes and describes details, including specific observations about the **context**—the surrounding environment and physical, political, and social setting.

Depending on the purpose of the study, the observation can require various amounts of structure. Perhaps the study will require that the observer complete a specific protocol or instrument that has been validated for use. An educational example of an observational tool is Flanders Interaction Analysis (Flanders,

EXHIBIT 10.8
TUTOR STUDY EXCERPT OF TUTOR INTERVIEW PROTOCOL

First of all, thank you so much for participating in this interview. Do you know why you are being interviewed today?

***Pause, wait for response.**

We are hoping to learn more about the tutor, or facilitator, in the course. Your participation will help us better understand what tutoring involves and what it means to people like you and other tutors. Do I have your permission to audiotape this interview?

***Begin audiotape.**

I will be taking notes as we talk. I am interested in learning as much as I can about your experience tutoring. The information will be used for a doctoral dissertation. It is also possible that an article may be published at some point or that some of the findings may be presented at a professional meeting. Of course, if the study is published or presented, your name will not be used. Your identification will be protected through the use of a pseudonym, or code name.

***Check to be sure the tape is working.**

Do you have any questions before we begin?

Please let me know if I ask you something that you feel uncomfortable talking about, and we will go on to something else. Also, you can ask for an explanation at any time.

I would like to start with some questions about **your role as a tutor.**

Can you please tell me about tutoring? [Brackets have additional prompts or probing questions to solicit more explicit information.]

  [How does it work exactly?]
  [How is it going?]
  [Can you tell me a little more about it?]

How would you describe your role as a tutor?

  [What things do you do?]
  [What else do you do?]

What things are you trying to achieve?

  [Can you give me an example of what you mean?]
  [What strategies do you use to achieve that?]

> **In your opinion, what is the most important thing you do as a tutor?**
>
> *[Can you explain exactly how that works?]*
> *[Can you give me an example of what you mean?]*
>
> **What is a typical day of tutoring like?**
>
> *[What do you do before the tutorial session?]*
> *[What do you do during the tutorial session?]*
> *[What do you do after the tutorial session?]*
>
> **What do you spend the most effort on?**
>
> *[What do you spend the most time on?]*
> *[Can you think of a particular (instance, student, situation . . .) that . . . ?]*
> *[Can you give me an example of what you mean?]*
> *[Are there any areas that required more time than others?]*
>
> **How do you decide when to talk?**
>
> *[How do you decide what to say or ask?]*
>
> **Tell me a story** about something that stands out in your tutoring experience.
>
> Next I will ask you some questions about **your tutorial group and the students you tutor** . . .

1973). This protocol asks the observer to count and code teacher-student interactions using different numerical codes depending on whether a teacher uses direct influence (such as lecturing or giving directions) or indirect influence (such as asking questions, praising, or encouraging), and depending on the nature of student talk (such as responding, initiating, or silence; see also www.nova.edu/hpdtesting/ctl/fia.html for more information).

Some case studies call for less structured observations. For example, an experienced observer may begin with a blank page, draw maps and diagrams, and record whatever she feels is noteworthy. This offers details of the unique surroundings that could not be known until the observation begins.

The researcher must differentiate between what is observed, or what is happening in objective terms as others might see it, and what is interpretation. It is important for the researcher to note impressions and questions that arise in addition to describing more concrete observations, and to understand the difference. For example, "He began talking louder than everyone else and pointed his finger as he said, 'You will be hearing from me'" is descriptive; "He acted like he was angry and threatened someone" is interpretive.

Data Recording

Prior to the study, the case study researcher also chooses a method for recording information from interviews and observations. For example, will the interview be audiotaped, or will the interviewer take notes during or after the interview? Perhaps she will do both. Will observations be videotaped, or will the observer take notes or make tallies in real time? These decisions are made based on the nature of the observation. For example, if there are many things to observe at once, videotape, which can be reviewed multiple times, may best facilitate this but also requires additional time (see Exhibit 10.9). Studies suggest that people become accustomed to the camera quickly when there is no operator behind it and when people are intensely involved in what they are doing (Jordan & Henderson, 1995). If the observation is more targeted, it may make more sense to **observe in real time** (live observation). As with many studies that use direct observation in which the researcher is present, the researcher may actually serve as a participant observer and interact with participants, but it is more common for the observer to be as unobtrusive as possible to reduce her influence on the natural situation being observed. (See Chapter Four on methods and Chapter Seven on ethnography for more about participant observation.)

EXHIBIT 10.9
TUTOR STUDY DATA RECORDING

In the tutor case study videotape was used for observations of tutorials and tutor training sessions. Static videotaping equipment was situated on a tripod prior to tutorial sessions. Interviews were audiotaped.

Planning for case study research involves conceptualizing the study, identifying participants, establishing data collection methods, scheduling events, deciding who will be involved in collecting data, and attaining necessary approvals. Once planning is complete and appropriate approvals have been granted, the researcher begins data collection.

> **REFLECTION QUESTIONS**
>
> 1. You are considering a case study of a local unemployment office. Before narrowing the study questions to between two and six, try listing as many questions as you can about the case. Set a goal of at least fifty. Consider topics and issues related to the case. Consider the case from various perspectives. Once you have listed as many questions as possible about the case, narrow the list to a few questions that will help structure the data gathering.
> 2. Locate a survey instrument or questionnaire. Perhaps you have received one in the mail or can locate one online. Look at each question. See if you can identify any questions that might be improved. Are there leading questions? Are there questions that ask more than one thing? How would you improve the questions?
> 3. Practice your observation skills. Go to an area with a group of colleagues. Make a diagram of the area and observe all activities for a period of five minutes. Share and compare your observations with your colleagues.

Implementing Case Study Research

Once the researcher determines what to study, how and when to collect the data, and who will collect the data, and once all necessary approvals have been obtained, the plan is implemented. As Yin (2003) points out, there are no "routine formulas" (p. 57) for conducing case studies. With case study research, however, the researcher may learn something early in the study that can inform and improve the approach taken in the remainder of the study. It is important for the case study researcher to have a plan but also to remain open to discovery of the unanticipated or unexpected. For example, although the researcher is focusing on job placement in an unemployment office case study, he may also find that clients are offered more economical ways to purchase needed groceries. This is an instance of the case study researcher's being flexible in looking for certain answers but remaining open to other findings. The researcher is never sure how the case will unfold, what he will find, or what it will mean.

Data Collection

The attitude of a case study researcher during data collection remains one of an inquirer who is truly curious about the nature of the case, always searching for understanding and answers. The researcher keeps the purpose and study questions in mind and focuses on the case during data collection. The researcher understands that she is not the expert on the case, that the participants are the ones who have the information needed. Understanding elements of the case from participants' perspectives is vital as the researcher remains naive, open, nonthreatening, and nonbiased. The researcher watches closely and thinks deeply, endeavoring to understand the context and the issues, searching for meaning in behaviors and other observations.

The researcher strives to ensure the validity of information collected. When information is revealed, for example through interviews, the researcher attempts to corroborate what is said through observations or document review. When one source shares information, the investigator searches for confirmation from other perspectives. When multiple sources agree, the evidence is considered more trustworthy or valid.

Like other qualitative approaches, case study research often generates a large amount of data. This high volume of data requires careful management and regular writing of field notes or keeping a journal with important information, such as the date, location, and people present at each observation or interview. The researcher seeks to maintain a "chain of evidence" (Yin, 2004, p. 85) so that any findings can be traced back to the collected data in their original, raw form.

During data collection the researcher is primarily describing, but may also make notes about potential hunches concerning the meaning behind what is observed or said. The researcher also makes notes about what she is thinking during data collection and early analysis, in the form of dated memos that eventually become part of and inform the analysis and interpretation. The two-column approach is a method of journaling commonly used in case study research (see Table 10.1). Descriptions and objective data are recorded in one column, and notes of potential meanings or interpretations of the findings are recorded in the second column.

Table 10.1 Two-Column Journaling Template

Description	Interpretation
What is happening in objective terms, as others might see it	Possible meaning or meanings; other questions that arise
Tutor Study Example: The tutor was looking down rather than looking at the students.	*Tutor Study Example:* This could mean the tutor is not interested or not listening to the students. It might also be a strategy the tutor is using to discourage students from depending on her for approval and direction. Do any other tutors do this?

Data Analysis

In case study research, as in other methodologies included in this text, data collection and analysis ideally occur simultaneously in a dynamic and interactive process. Data collection is an important part of the process, but it is useless unless the researcher can make sense of the data; this is the goal of data analysis. For example, in a case study of a community program for teenage mothers, the researcher would be collecting data from participants and those who manage the program, and would want to carefully analyze these early data for clues about what subsequent issues to pursue and which data sources to select. Learning from initial data that certain individuals are asked to leave the program should cause the case study investigator to thoroughly follow up on this issue.

The initial level of analysis often involves **coding,** or classifying, qualitative data from observations, interviews, and other sources. Analysis literally means pulling things apart to examine them in their smallest components. The researcher deconstructs information and then puts things back together again in a more meaningful way. By dissecting the various parts, the researcher assigns meaning to them.

The researcher constantly compares the data, incidents, interactions, or remarks for properties, such as similarities and differences, that can help identify categories. The researcher assigns codes to the various categories. Merriam (1998) provides an example of coding and categories using food items at the grocery store. She suggests comparing each food item to other food items, thereby generating categories related to their characteristics. In this way food items could be classified into categories and subcategories. For example, an orange might be classified in the fruit category and also in such subcategories as citrus and domestic. Codes help the researcher sort and organize the data, just as file folders can help with organizing a stack of papers. When the researcher sees similarities between various components, these components will be assigned the same category or code. Codes a researcher generates should relate to the study purpose and be conceptually congruent (see Exhibit 10.10). Coding is just one level of analysis; Chapter Three provides a much more thorough discussion of the process of qualitative data analysis.

Often data collection and analysis reveal information that could not have been anticipated prior to the study and that can change the direction of the study. During the early stages of analyzing data the case study researcher makes notes about changes or additions concerning new data to collect that are not in the original study plan. The researcher notes initial insights or hunches, and then collects the data needed to confirm or disconfirm them. This evolving nature is one of the strengths of case study research design.

> ## EXHIBIT 10.10
> ## TUTOR STUDY CODING
>
> In addition to coding or classifying the nature of tutor interventions as either statements, questions (with subcategories of deep or surface), acknowledgments, or clarifications and confirmations, the researcher also classified tutor interventions according to whether their emphasis was on process, content, or social issues.
>
> Tutor facilitation style when requesting or encouraging students to act was also classified as directive, suggestive, or empowering.
>
> - A *directive facilitation style* was one whereby the tutor decided which direction students were to take or directly told the group or student what to do (for example, "Look up this," or "Don't focus on that") or controlled the process without giving options or choices (for example, "Why don't we just do this," or "We'll start with you").
>
> - A *suggestive facilitation style* was one whereby the tutor suggested a single direction to take but used softer language (for example, "Maybe you could do this") or left the decision somewhat open (for example, "We could do it this way," or "Does somebody want to do that?").
>
> - An *empowering facilitation style* was one whereby the tutor encouraged students to make their own decisions (for example, "How do you want to do it?" or "Do you know what to do next?") or offered more than one option from which to choose (for example, "You can do this first or do that first").

During data analysis the case study researcher also makes a concerted effort to remain open to findings that are contrary to preconceived notions identified prior to the study, and he attempts to disconfirm his own interpretations (see Exhibit 10.11). If no contrary evidence can be found, the researcher's interpretations are more strongly supported.

Data analysis leads the researcher to the findings that will be reported, most often including descriptions of the context and identification of meaningful themes or patterns, and sometimes including the application of models and theories to the data and the case, as discussed in the next section.

> **EXHIBIT 10.11**
> **TUTOR STUDY CONTRARY FINDINGS**
>
> Tutor facilitation style appeared to support the researcher's prestudy belief that tutor behavior would improve over time; however, week 9 showed tutors becoming more, rather than less, directive. Wondering if time pressures placed on tutors during week 9 had obscured a real trend, the researcher analyzed transcripts of observations from week 8. Her initial assumption, that tutor facilitation style might become less directive over time, was disconfirmed when the number of directive interventions per hour for week 8 also increased.

Validity

Tactics to improve the validity and trustworthiness of case study findings may include triangulation (the collection of data using a variety of methods [for example, interviewing, observing, and reviewing documents] and multiple sources [for example, tutors, tutees, and administrators]) and using piloted and field-tested (or standardized) protocols for interviews and observations. Conducting appropriate data analyses; examining researcher preparation and bias (for example, determining the extent to which the researcher's preconceived beliefs may have influenced the study findings); **member checking** (for example, reviewing draft findings by key informants to see if they affirm the validity of the report and recognize their contribution); and, if necessary, undertaking an external review and interpretation are also important measures to improve the validity and trustworthiness of case study findings. In the tutor study, member checking was used to ensure validity (see Exhibit 10.12).

> **REFLECTION QUESTIONS**
>
> 1. How might you explain the processes of data collection and analysis in case study research to a friend who has not read this chapter?
> 2. What are the most important characteristics that a case study must have for you to trust its findings? Why?

EXHIBIT 10.12
TUTOR STUDY MEMBER CHECKING

After initial data analysis, but prior to final analysis and report writing, tutors responded to preliminary patterns that had emerged at a focused group interview. Following a presentation, tutors were invited to react to and interact with the findings. The tutors contrasted the researcher's findings with their perceptions of the tutor role and experience. They also identified discrepancies between the preliminary analysis and their perceptions, which enabled the researcher to return to the data, applying new insights to a final analysis.

Case Study Reports

After data are collected and analyzed, the researcher keeps the purpose and the audience in mind in writing up the case study report. A case study researcher attempts to make a complex case and its context easier to understand. There is also no set format for a case study report; however, there are essential components to include. The report most often incorporates key elements to communicate the findings to interested stakeholders and audiences. In no particular order, these elements usually are (1) an introduction to the problem being investigated, (2) a theoretical or conceptual framework based on a review of the literature, (3) a definition or the limits of the case, (4) the purpose of the case study, (5) a description of the context of the case, (6) a description of the sample selected, (7) the methods used for data collection and analysis, (8) the efforts used to ensure validity of findings, (9) what the findings are, and (10) what the findings mean. Of course, it is important for the case study report to answer the study questions.

The content of case study reports can vary. The report is **descriptive** if it includes description only, such as providing a detailed account of what is happening in a particular program. A case study is **interpretive** if the report adds explanation in addition to description, for example, explaining why the program is implemented in a particular way.

The tutor case study report, for example, included description and excerpts of actual dialog spoken during tutorial sessions that portrayed some of the important aspects of the tutor experience. The report also included the analysis and categorization of tutor behaviors, revealed patterns in tutor behaviors (see Exhibit

EXHIBIT 10.13
TUTOR STUDY EXAMPLE OF A DESCRIPTIVE STATEMENT OF PATTERNS AND FINDINGS

One tutor's directive, content-focused, lenient style supported dependence on the tutor and maintenance of the status quo. She also saw the purpose of instruction as primarily to learn content. Other tutors, with more empowering, process-focused, persistent styles, had different ideas about the purpose of problem-based learning. They saw the purpose as individual growth and development of skills needed for the future, such as self-directed learning.

10.13), applied theory to the findings, answered the study questions, and compared study findings to other findings in the literature.

The goal of a case study report is to use description to provide the reader with a "vicarious experience," (Stake, 1995, p. 63) or a sense of being there in person, and to enable understanding of the experience from the informants' perspectives. The case study report is often fashioned to allow readers to make their own interpretation of what the study findings mean and how to use findings. When the report includes enough detail, or **thick description** (Lincoln & Guba, 1985), a reader can determine the extent to which the findings might generalize from the particular case to their situation. This is often referred to as **naturalistic generalization** (Stake, 1995, p. 85).

A good case study report helps the reader understand how the researcher came to the conclusions or assertions found in the study findings. The researcher's position is revealed, along with any biases that may have been introduced as a result. The report describes how data were collected and how categories were derived in enough detail that the reader can trace the path between the data collected and the findings reported. The report should contain no speculation without pointing out that this is what the researcher is doing. The report reveals the strengths and weaknesses of the study methods and the validity of findings. Tactics used to ensure that the research is trustworthy, credible, and confirmable are also described in the case study report.

Alternative representations of the case can also be made to improve the effectiveness of communicating the findings. These can include, but are not limited to, plays, poems, short stories, movies or videos, and live presentations with discussions. Readers of case studies should look for examples of these various formats.

REFLECTION QUESTIONS

1. From what you have read, why would some case study reports be more believable than others?
2. What are some benefits and uses for case study reports?

Summary

Case study methodology is an important set of strategies in social scientific research. It is an approach commonly used to better understand a complex phenomenon within its context. There are various ways of classifying case studies: single case studies, multiple case studies, multiple site case studies, and comparative case studies. They are intended to produce thick descriptions for the purpose of thoroughly explaining the case itself (intrinsic) or to build or test theories (instrumental).

This chapter addresses important aspects of planning, conducting, and reporting case study research including study conceptualization (for example, establishing the purpose, boundaries, study questions, and potential audiences for the report); planning (for example, determining how to answer the study questions in the best possible way, choosing the types of evidence to gather, deciding on methods of data collection, considering researcher position, employing techniques to ensure validity and trustworthiness, and preparing on the part of the researcher to gain skills); implementation (data collection and analysis); and reporting (describing versus interpreting, deciding what to include). Case study research offers participants and other interested groups thorough illuminations of their program efforts without the researcher's making judgments or placing value on the material. This creates opportunities for the stakeholders to decide how the results should be interpreted as well as what changes or improvements might follow.

Key Terms

alternative representations, 267
audiences, 244
bounding, 245
bracketed interview, 255
case, 243
case study research, 243
coding, 263
comparative case studies, 247
context, 257
descriptive, 266

field test, 256
informant, 252
instrumental case studies, 246
interpretive, 266
interview protocol, 257
intrinsic case studies, 246
longitudinal case studies, 247
member checking, 265
multiple case studies, 247
multiple site case studies, 247
naturalistic generalization, 267
observation plan, 257
observe in real time, 260
pilot test, 256
purposeful sampling, 253
random sampling, 253
researcher biases, 255
researcher position, 255
saturation, 253
single case studies, 247
stakeholders, 244
theoretical or conceptual frameworks, 249
thick description, 267
triangulation, 251
valid, 256

Further Readings and Resources

Suggested Case Study

Jenkins, K. (2008). Practically professionals? Grassroots women as local experts—a Peruvian case study. *Political Geography*, *27*, 139–159.

This is a good example of a case that was developed from a feminist perspective.

Other Suggested Readings

Merriam, S. B. (1998). *Qualitative research and case study applications in education: Revised and expanded from case study research in education* (2nd ed.). San Francisco: Jossey-Bass.

This book presents the components of case study research as they apply specifically to the field of education; it includes many illustrative examples.

Miles, M. B., & Huberman, A. M. (1994). *Qualitative data analysis: An expanded sourcebook* (2nd ed.). Thousand Oaks, CA: Sage.

This book provides a vast assortment of strategies and tools for data analysis.

Rubin, H. J., & Rubin, I. (2005). *Qualitative interviewing: The art of hearing data* (2nd ed.). Thousand Oaks, CA: Sage.

This serves as a good companion for the Seidman (1998) text, presenting various uses of interviews and different perspectives and examples from a husband and wife team.

Schensul, S. L., Schensul, J. J., & LeCompte, M. D. (1999). *Essential ethnographic methods: Observations, interviews, and questionnaires*. Walnut Creek, CA: AltaMira.

This includes guiding principles for and practical help with interviewing and observation techniques.

Seidman, I. (1998). *Interviewing as qualitative research: A guide for researchers in education and the social sciences* (2nd ed.). New York: Teachers College Press.

Seidman's book describes a process for in-depth interviewing that involves multiple interviews with the same participant. This text is helpful in understanding all aspects of using interviewing in research and includes many helpful techniques.

Stake, R. E. (1995). *The art of case study research.* Thousand Oaks, CA: Sage.

This book describes case study as an art, with few restrictions and guidelines. This approach is most appreciated by the experienced qualitative researcher and may appear vague for the novice. Stake uses an example of a case study throughout the text to illuminate each step in the case study research process so the reader can see how each step was applied to an actual case.

Wolcott, H. F. (1990). *Writing up qualitative research.* Thousand Oaks, CA: Sage.

This book provides helpful insight for when it is time to write the case study report (or any other kind of qualitative research report).

Yin, R. K. (2003). *Case study research: Design and methods* (3rd ed.). Thousand Oaks, CA: Sage.

This book provides a more prescriptive description of the process of designing and implementing a case study. It may be most helpful for the novice researcher to use this in conjunction with Stake's book (1995).

Yin, R. K. (2004). *The case study anthology.* Thousand Oaks, CA: Sage.

This book includes examples of case studies from a variety of disciplines.

Organizations and Web Sites

American Educational Research Association—Special Interest Group on Qualitative Research (SIG #82) (www.aera.net/Default.aspx?menu_jd=208&id=772)

This group offers discussions of the philosophy, purposes, and methodological issues surrounding the use of qualitative research in social and educational settings.

Center for Instructional Research and Curriculum Evaluation (www.ed.uiuc.edu/circe/Publications/CIRCE_Publications.html)

Several publications and papers can be found at this useful Web site from those who originated modern evaluation and advanced the status of case study research.

CHAPTER 11

ARTS-BASED RESEARCH

Sharon Verner Chappell
Tom Barone

Key Ideas

- Arts-based research is an approach to social research that employs premises, principles, and procedures that derive primarily from the arts (visual, literary, and performance based) rather than the social sciences.

- Arts-based researchers may either craft a research text that itself contains aesthetic or literary qualities or analyze the works of others (for example, students) in the manner of art critics.

- The primary purpose for engaging in arts-based research is to enable an audience to question commonplace educational or social phenomena, to perceive these from a different perspective, and to reflect deeply.

- Audience members make naturalistic generalizations by relating facets of the research text to analogous social phenomena with which they are already familiar.

- Many arts-based researchers engage in a multiphased qualitative problem-solving process in doing their research.

- Judgments about quality in arts-based research reflect the potential of the research study for achieving its heuristic aims through the plausibility and aesthetic power of the text.

Arts-based research is an approach that employs artistic design elements to study and reveal facets of social phenomena. These design elements may be associated with any form of art, including various literary, plastic, performance, musical, and digital arts, and allow the reader to expressively appreciate, perceive, and enjoy the research as a work of art. However, a few design elements may overlap with those found in the social sciences (such as ethnography, sociology, case study research, phenomenological research, and narrative research)—hence the term *arts-based* (rather than *artistic*) research. These design elements are employed in order to enable members of professional or lay communities to experience anew aspects of social and cultural phenomena. In doing so, arts-based researchers aim to raise fundamental questions about social issues, social practices, and qualities within cultural artifacts that have become taken for granted as obviously correct, useful, good, true, or beautiful.

For example, Coulter (2003) uses the genre of literary nonfiction to address the systemic processes that affect high school English language learners and works to communicate experiences from their perspectives and their stories. She uses the form of a novel to allow the reader to travel with these students and encounter the issues identified by the researcher through the design elements of theme, characterization, figurative language, and plot structure.

Background of Arts-Based Research

Arts-based research is both like and unlike many other forms of social research. First, it is distinguished from more scientific approaches to social research in a number of ways. Social research has been traditionally associated with the social sciences rather than the arts. Indeed, many of the premises, principles, and procedures associated with quantitative, and later qualitative, social research have been adopted and adapted from the physical sciences. Throughout most of the history of Western culture, the methodological "gold standard" for social research has been considered to be the experiment. The experiment, in the physical sciences as well as in social research, was long regarded as the form of research most likely to provide the highest degree of trustworthiness in research findings. Even in quantitative or qualitative research that did not offer the kind of rigor associated with the experiment, a premium was placed on high degrees of validity, reliability, and generalizability (see Chapters One and Four). The ultimate aim was to produce findings that accurately explained social phenomena, reliably predicted the outcomes of events within similar circumstances, and thereby (sometimes) afforded control over future events. For that to happen, social researchers found it necessary to engage in what John Dewey (1960) called a quest for certainty.

This epistemological predisposition toward certainty accorded with the fundamental aims of the European Enlightenment of the eighteenth century, a period of scientism during which two diametrically opposed, and hierarchically arranged, academic cultures were recognized. As identified by C. P. Snow (1959/1993), these two cultures were the scientific and the literary. In general, members of the scientific academic culture regarded the arts with much mistrust. Indeed, the arts and literature were often seen as merely ephemeral and ornamental; as sources of admiration and entertainment; or, even worse, as dangerous distractions from reality. They represented the embodiment of an ephemeral sort of aesthetics, one steeped in bias and subjectivity, inward feelings, emotions, and passions, at the expense of a rigorous devotion to objective truth discovered through a combination of scientific research and cold, hard logic.

However, arts-based research may also *share* certain features with other forms of research. Some latter-day aestheticians, philosophers, and proponents of arts-based research have refused what they see as a false dichotomy between the arts and sciences, noting that good artists employ rigorous technique, and that the work of science is in many ways artistic (Eisner, 1991). The philosopher Richard Rorty (1989) contended that, indeed, all forms of art are continuous with literature. If there is a continuum of scientific-artistic research, with no easily defined border between the two cultures, then the middle of that continuum may be occupied by qualitative research recognized as part of what has been called **genre blurring** (Denzin & Lincoln, 1998). A term coined by anthropologist-storyteller Clifford Geertz (1973), genre blurring implied an amalgamation of design elements, some associated with the social sciences, others with the arts and humanities. Especially in the 1970s and 1980s, among some social scientists there was new attention paid to the poetics of social research texts, to multimedia and various nonverbal forms of disclosure of findings, and to the performance (or "staging") of research results. It is perhaps ironic that the movement from the more scientific toward the artistic end of the continuum occurred primarily as a result of innovations by researchers trained in various fields of the social sciences.

It was against this backdrop that the term *arts-based research* was originated by Elliot Eisner of Stanford University and popularized in the 1990s by Eisner and Tom Barone of Arizona State University (formerly Eisner's doctoral student). Eisner and Barone were formally trained, not (primarily) in the social sciences, but in the arts and humanities. Attention to the approach grew, especially as a result of several professional institutes sponsored by the American Educational Research Association (AERA). These institutes were codirected by Eisner and Barone; over the years, these also included several prominent researcher colleagues as fellow instructors.

The purpose of the workshops was to introduce qualitative researchers and other academics from North America and elsewhere into a unique approach to social and educational research, one that bore little resemblance to traditional forms of quantitative or qualitative research in the social sciences. Since that time arts-based research has flourished in many fields, including the humanities, education, public health, and social work. Articles, books, and conference presentations that describe arts-based research, address issues surrounding it, and provide examples of it have proliferated. Nevertheless, among those who remain unfamiliar with the research approach, its nature and purpose are often misunderstood.

REFLECTION QUESTIONS

1. When you think of research, do you see researchers as being on a quest for certainty or as seeking to raise questions (or both)? Can researchers achieve both at the same time?
2. In your view, are the sciences and the arts diametrically opposed in terms of their purpose, form, and function? What is the importance of thinking about genre blurring in terms of the research process?

Purposes of Arts-Based Research Studies

Various proponents and advocates describe the primary purpose of engaging in arts-based forms of social and educational research in slightly different ways. In general, arts-based research texts reveal previously unattended-to aspects of social and cultural phenomena, or allow readers and viewers to vicariously experience those phenomena from an otherwise unavailable vantage point. This "reexperiencing" of facets of the social world may serve to problematize the value of commonsensical, orthodox ways of viewing the world in the minds of research audiences, producing doubt, disequilibrium, or skepticism toward dominant meanings habitually associated with social and cultural phenomena. Research with a **heuristic purpose** asks readers to examine phenomena in their own lives related to the worlds constructed in the research text. Research with an **interrogatory purpose** asks readers to reexamine commonly held assumptions about the phenomena. In other words, arts-based research texts aim toward a **critical persuasion** of readers and viewers to interrogate entrenched social norms, beliefs, and values.

For example, Cahnmann (2006) uses poetry both as an action research pedagogy (see Chapter Twelve) with bilingual elementary school students and teachers, and as a design for the research documentation. Throughout the research text she includes her own poetry as well as that of her research participants as a means of expressively portraying the importance of the art form to the language, culture, and identity of bilingual people. The reader reexperiences Cahnmann's own struggles with varieties of bilingualism in the poem "I Am That Good" when she does not receive what she thinks she has ordered in a restaurant: "So imagine my surprise when my / scrambled eggs arrived with French fries. 9am and soggy on the side / of my plate like a bad American joke" (p. 344). Her word choice, language play, and poetic voice are all expressive qualities that allow the reader to reexperience the phenomenon and question commonplace assumptions about language use and the relationship between language and culture.

The primary purpose of arts-based research is quite different from that of what has been called normal or **paradigmatic science**, insofar as it rejects a static, unified, and totalized notion of truth in favor of multiple versions of "truths" that are fluid, fragmentary, and even conflicting. But that is not to say that artists throughout history have not created works intended to convey some pure sort of truth, whether an inner, subjective reality or a heavy-handed expression of moral rightness. In other words, some works of propaganda or kitsch, posing as art, may indeed employ artful design elements to promote a single point of view, leading to constrained conversations rather than new ones. Some researchers may produce works in which a didactic, authoritative monologue privileges a singular point of view over all others. This is *not* the general purpose of arts-based research.

Instead, good arts-based researchers avoid knowledge claims of all sorts, and do not aim to advance singular orthodoxies or ideologies. Instead, arts-based researchers usually revel in the kind of ambiguity that is often associated with the arts. This does not mean that arts-based research is relativistic, value free, or apolitical. In a good work of arts-based research the artist's point of view is inevitably (if often implicitly) present. But the text is structured in a manner that is, to some extent, open to interpretation—that is, as Barthes (1968/1977) would say, writerly, inviting the reader into a conversation with the text and perhaps with other members of an audience. A piece of arts-based research may be said, therefore, to have achieved its purpose if consumers of the work are lured into rethinking (rewriting) their perspectives concerning that which has been thematically addressed in the research text. For example, in an address titled "The Shattered Mirror: Curriculum, Art and Critical Politics," Blumenfeld-Jones (2006) alternated the use of poetry and improvised dance sequences to explore the ways an aesthetic practice can link a person to the world around her through an ethical stance. Rather than promoting a certain point of view on right and wrong, this work allowed the audience to reexperience and converse with tensions produced in and through the aesthetic performance.

This shift in perspectives may sometimes be fundamental, producing an epiphany in the lives of those who engage with it. The result may be what Iser (1974) labeled **value negation**, persuading the reader (or viewer) to doubt previously held outlooks, attitudes, meanings, and values. At its most profound, arts-based research can lead to changes in practice by practitioners or a willingness on the part of readers to engage in new theoretical frameworks, or it may cause policymakers to reconsider the effects of their decisions on the lives of a citizenry.

For example, a/r/tography began out of the University of British Columbia but has influenced many researchers and educators internationally. It is a method that combines the perspective of artist, researcher, and teacher to explore classroom-based inquiry driven by aesthetic questions and social purposes of art making. In 2004 David Darts published an a/r/tography study, *Visual Culture Jam: Art, Pedagogy and Creative Resistance*. The study uses digital and still photography that asks how visual culture and art can affect students' social engagement, not only in the art-making process with the students but also in the design of the research document as a piece of visual culture itself. In 2008 Stephanie Springgay published another a/r/tography study, *Body Knowledge and Curriculum: Pedagogies of Touch in Youth and Visual Culture*, asking how art and visual culture can build awareness of the body as a site of encounter and as a process of exchange with high school students.

Since arts-based research's inception, other strands of this approach have also emerged. These include arts-informed research, performance ethnography or ethnodrama, narrative research, ethnopoetics, community-based participant action research in the arts, and research rendered in music- and dance-based forms or products. See the suggested readings and the list of organizations and Web sites at the end of the chapter for sources of information on some of these approaches.

REFLECTION QUESTIONS

1. Why is it important for research to allow audiences to "reexperience" a social phenomenon?
2. Why is it important for research to problematize commonplace assumptions? How is this related to critical persuasion?
3. Why might some researchers or fields have trouble with the promotion of ambiguity as a purpose of research? Why might other researchers argue for its importance?

Planning and Conducting Arts-Based Research Studies

The term *arts-based research* signifies not so much a category of research as an approach in which a high degree of aesthetic design elements are employed effectively in order to fulfill the heuristic and interrogatory research purposes discussed earlier. The processes engaged in during the planning and conducting of these studies embody some common features. This is especially true for arts-based research in which the final work resembles a work of art, one that could be conventionally labeled as nonfiction or fiction. According to Barone (1992), several phases may be identified in the processes of planning and conducting these studies. They parallel the five phases identified in a process of art making that Ecker (1966) discusses as **qualitative problem solving**. To illustrate the anatomy of arts-based research we will refer to the making of the study by Barone (1983).

Titled "Things of Use and Things of Beauty," this early piece of arts-based research took the form of a literary essay that also served as an evaluation report of a high school arts program commissioned by the Rockefeller Brothers Fund. In it the reader can identify many of the design elements discussed earlier, such as choice of theme, characterization, figurative language, and plot structure. But the aim of the report was not, primarily, to serve the intrinsic purpose (Stake, 2005; see also Chapter Ten) of documenting or providing a final portrait of the program under study. Rather, the report raised questions about the relationship between the arts and utilitarian crafts and about the reasons for including arts in a school curriculum. The text included a portrait of the school program and an arts teacher designed to prompt conversations about the tension between a utilitarian (practical) versus a self-liberatory (self-expressive) rationale for arts education. (Note: The fact that this study involved an arts program is not what makes this an arts-based piece of research; it is, rather, the presence of artistic design elements that does so). This theme was not as present, however, in the author's initial research reflections that engaged the big picture.

Phase One: Random Qualities

In Ecker's first phase of qualitative problem solving (1966), the artist-researcher encounters the big picture of the phenomenon, which may seem abstract, hazy, and even random. In this phase the researcher may have decided on (or been assigned) a setting, site, or set of phenomena to be studied, but has no clear focus on what issues or themes are significant. If fieldwork is involved, then phase one may occur prior to or after becoming immersed in the research site. If the former, then this phase involves the researcher's conducting "preproduction" activities, just as many novelists, playwrights, actors, and nonfiction storytellers research their characters and the contexts of their lives. The artist-researcher might read archival and historical documents; talk with the actual people whose lives are being represented or with others who are similar to those people; observe people as they go about living their lives; study the physical surroundings and settings of the time and period being portrayed; and so on.

In this phase, however, the researcher is in the process of becoming familiar with the specifics of the phenomena to be studied, but has no clear means for discriminating between what is worthy of attention and what is not. Some arts-based researchers have a tendency during phase one to record everything, whereas others prefer to record nothing. For Barone, the first encounter with the arts program was the reception of a huge portfolio that the director of the program supplied to him by way of the Rockefeller Brothers Fund. Barone read it carefully but had no idea at that point as to what would ultimately serve as data within his study and what would not. He encountered the kind of anxiety that many beginning social researchers encounter in their search for a topic of social significance that deserves their attention.

Phase Two: Tentative Relationships Between Qualities

In phase two of the process, the researcher, having become immersed in the phenomena under study, sees certain patterns, or qualities, but only as structured fragments (Ecker, 1966). There is still no ultimate theme or central set of insights around which a portrait or story can be woven. Barone (1983), upon visiting the program itself for one week on location in North Carolina, noticed a clash between the official utilitarian (or crafts) orientation of the arts program and the more expressive, aesthetic undertakings of the program. This dichotomy in purpose became obvious as a result of data gathering from administrators of the program, in student focus groups, in observations of the arts classrooms, in studying the arts and crafts of the Appalachian people of the area, even in the personality of the director-designer-teacher in the program, Don Forrister. But these observations remained fragmentary, with Barone still unable to imagine how they might serve as a theme around which to construct a literary essay.

Phase Three: An Emerging Theme

On the evening of the third intense day of the site visit, a crystallizing moment occurred—one in which the pieces of a puzzle seemed to fall into place. After reading, reflecting, rereading, ignoring, staring, pondering, and daydreaming about the mass of phenomena he encountered, Barone arrived at a controlling insight: a tension between the roles of the arts and crafts in the lives of the teacher and students. Barone came to the realization that the story of the arts program was one that could be best understood in the sociohistorical context of the relationship between the arts and crafts produced by the Appalachian people, of whom both Forrister and his students were members. This seeming tension between the crafts ("things of use") and the arts ("things of beauty") was indeed resolved in observing and portraying the ways in which these people existed in their daily lives, in the activities in Forrister's arts class, and in the hopes and dreams of his students who refused to label themselves as *either* artists *or* craftspeople, the students who saw themselves as in fact living lives in which creativity and work coexisted—that is, lives of productive artistry.

Phase Four: A Developing Theme

In phase four the researcher uses **qualitative control** to compose the research text, and employs the theme as a guide for selection of those data to be included in the report and those to exclude. This control is based on the construction of a coherent "whole" with aesthetic power, rather than on data that are episodic, that is, vignettes lacking such coherence from an artistic point of view. For Barone, this process occurred both in the final days at the research site and after the visit. It enabled the researcher, while still in North Carolina, to seek out and include telling details that served as thematic questions through additional observations, interviews, and collection of archival data. Moreover, during the last two evenings of the visit, Barone began a draft of the literary essay. He completed the essay several weeks later, after writing several drafts.

Phase Five: Work That Is Judged Complete

In the last phase of the problem-solving process, as Ecker (1966) states, "the work is finally judged complete—the total achieved—the pervasive has adequately been the control" (p. 67). This judgment must be based on a sense not that the work appears as the final word about the thematic issues attended to but that the work will serve a **metaphorical purpose**, reminding readers that the central characters and events in the study could be viewed both as real and as virtual, as analogues of characters and events that exist outside of the text with which readers are already familiar. That is, the researcher aims toward generating discussions about the thematic content.

Example Studies

Following are two example studies that illustrate issues with which arts-based researchers contend. The first is an arts-based construction, and the second is a piece of aesthetic social criticism.

Study 1: *Boundary Bay: A Novel* (Dunlop, 1999)

The dissertation that is discussed in the following paragraphs represents an example of literary arts–based research that explores issues of educational self-development inspired by interviews with secondary school educators, doctoral students, and university instructors. Such issues include the nature of teachers' lives, literary and artistic production, and the ways that social institutions affect women teachers' intellectual and creative lives. As a novel, Dunlop's research shows rather than tells about these issues in storied form, placing the epistemology of the ways lives are storied at the center of inquiry. The choice of the word *boundary* in the title suggests Dunlop's emphasis on calling attention to and blurring genre boundaries, such as by highlighting the ways disciplines, types of texts, and the lives of the researcher, subjects, and audiences are interrelated rather than separate and distinct.

Forms and Functions of the Study

Dunlop suggests that her novel is itself an act of inquiry, by which readers can extend their experiences through the perspectives of the characters, thus becoming more critical of the issues themselves. She positions her writing in relation to the genre of the educational development or self-formation novel (in German, the *Bildungsroman*), which explores the formative development of an individual within the context of sociocultural expectations and institutions. This genre, she suggests, has a pedagogical intent of raising questions in the reader about the origins of one's identity and purposes of personal growth in one's apprenticeship and in overall life meaning.

Social and Aesthetic Questions in the Study

The main character of Dunlop's novel is Evelyn, a new tenure-track professor in the English education department. She is recently divorced, a mentor to a new graduate student named Grace, and a teacher of literature. In one passage, Evelyn lectures about the literature of education and self-development to her graduate class, her public voice in lecture contrasting starkly with her interior voice:

ARTS-BASED RESEARCH

When the young man in the front row asks a question, Evelyn responds by rote, trying to be succinct, knowledgeable, erudite, falling into the role of lecturer, her academic language spilling from her. *Künstlerroman . . . the novel of the artist . . . traditionally the stories of men who journey away from society only to find through their educating adventures and their learning along the way how to adapt and fit into society.*

It occurs to Evelyn that the classic form of the novel does not seem to lend itself to the stories of women. Or the stories of others who simply never fit. . . .

Evelyn drifts away from the graduate seminar, thinking about reading novels about women. Her mind wanders, losing the grip of theory.

Evelyn reading through nights of despair and thirst, child crying on her shoulder, heating milk to feed Mara, book in hand, nights by the intensity of lamplight in the darkening quiet of her windowless office. Reading these women, their paginated presences. Can she save them, offer them alternatives? Read them again, give them second chances, other possible lives, different fictions. She thinks, do I reject these stories as they are written? Try to rewrite them as I read them? (p. 39)

In this passage, Dunlop uses the aesthetic tools of fiction (such as the shift in character perspective or voice) to explore issues of gender in the discipline of fiction writing and in the social sphere of the academy. Dunlop juxtaposes her character's vocal tone, word choice, and sentence structure when speaking publicly to a group of students and introspectively to the audience of only herself. This tension raises questions about how fiction's assumption of a male reader's experiences might affect various readers. It also raises questions about gendered discourse in the academy.

Implications for Arts-Based Research

Dunlop's novel positions itself as an epistemological departure from the traditional purposes of educational research through its pursuit of meaning over certainty, and its storied, aesthetic structure over **paradigmatic text** (it shows rather than tells). Further, it problematizes the ways that genres of research documentation affect the knowledge that audiences construct about issues of schooling. In particular, the research suggests the importance of increased interdisciplinary relationships in teacher education and more analysis of the gendered experiences of teachers and teacher educators through storied forms. This example also asks that serious attention be paid to the power of the novel (or other fictional genres) as a research genre that uniquely addresses issues of self-development through the form and function of the fiction itself. Dunlop's research methodology also raises questions about educational research from an aesthetic perspective. What does it mean, for example, to select stories to tell based on what moves you as a fiction writer?

REFLECTION QUESTIONS

1. How does turning qualitative research into a novel affect how the reader experiences the phenomenon through the reading process?
2. What methodological questions must researchers be prepared to discuss when choosing fiction as the primary genre for their research documents?
3. What might be a topic in your field of study that would lend itself to arts-based research?

Study 2: *Evidence of Utopianizing Toward Social Justice in Young People's Community-Based Art Works* (Chappell, 2009)

The dissertation discussed here represents an example of arts/educational criticism, a form of arts-based research that explores the aesthetic qualities and social content of young people's art works. Chappell selected art works from community-based organizations across the United States in which young people between thirteen and twenty-three years of age participated from 2001 to 2008. The study asked: What are young people's concerns for the world as expressed in and through their art works? What are their visions for better worlds, as they relate to their expressed concerns? What aesthetic tools and languages do young people use in their process of expressing concerns and visions? Drawing from E. P. Thompson's idea (1977) that art works educate desire, Chappell analyzed the ways that these art works might teach audiences alternative ways of thinking about and changing the world because of the ways that the art works prompt caring and action.

Form and Functions of the Study

In educational criticism, Eisner (2002) suggests that the critic chooses "the difficult task of rendering [some] essential ineffable qualities constituting works of art into a language that will help others perceive the works more deeply" (p. 213). Eisner responds to traditional conceptions of the critic as monologic, a person who functions to deliver singular, truthful, and accurate interpretations of aesthetic experiences in order to reeducate the public about works of art through the critic's personal viewpoint and language. Chappell joins Eisner and others (see, for example, Oliva, 2000) in asking the critic to build a **transactive space** through research so that multiple audiences can participate in the readings, reexperiencing the art works anew for themselves and contributing other readings to the conversation.

Eisner suggests that the critic "requires an ability not only to perceive the subtle particulars of educational life but also to recognize the ways those particulars form a part of a structure within the classroom" (Eisner, 2002, p. 217), or, in the case of this research, within works of art. He outlines four aspects of educational criticism: descriptive, interpretive, evaluative, and thematic. In this research Chappell addresses these aspects of educational criticism, weaving description of the art works with her interpretation of their meaning. The study constructs vicarious experiences of the art works for the reader, works to understand the meanings of art works and their social and aesthetic significance, and evaluates the art works for their facility to construct desire for social change.

Social and Aesthetic Questions in the Study

The study found that many young people's art works emphasized concerns with inclusion and exclusion, particularly marginalizations that affect their personal group memberships, access to resources, and equitable treatment. Their active political positions, beliefs, and experiences speak back to the public's imaginary, conceptualizing urban youth as hopeful of change and willing to participate in bringing it about. Aesthetic characteristics in the art works raise such social questions through the tools of the art forms themselves.

For example, hip hop artists from Youth Movement Records, an organization in Oakland, California, use emotion to compel audiences to reconsider the experiences of urban youth in the title song from their album *Change the Nation*. Youth artist Chuck Webster (2006) uses tone and word choice to compel a desire for restoration of social ills: "This the land of milk & honey / the land of spliffs and money / they aint wanting to change, clap pistols while tears runnin / yeah my house got busted at, better days id love that." The song engages an affective, relational aesthetic to carry the listener through the personal and political. Both desperate pain and desire are located in the forward momentum of the song and the intensity of Webster's views: "it would be worldwide the peace that I would provide/ who better than I—I seen hell with these eyes."

He uses metaphor to imagine better worlds, constructing images steeped in emotion. He places the capital of this new world on "top of Mount Zion," a reference to the area of Old Jerusalem in Israel. Mount Zion is a synecdoche, or a single aspect of a whole that comes to represent that whole. It becomes a symbol for the kind of world that Webster hopes for, a vision that stands in stark contrast to the "hell" he has seen with these eyes. But this place of hope and change seems almost out of reach, as it does not resemble the current nation, one that he wants to kiss goodbye. The kiss smack sound that he includes at the end of the verse echoes, even invokes sadness or dismay. Yet it is an unexpected personal touch, adding humor to the prospect of change. The kiss also passes the song over to the chorus, a call-and-response of multiple singers echoing each other's line: "If I could change the nation . . . If we could change the nation." Aesthetically and ethically, this polyvocal call-and-response builds a sense of collective desire that social change needs multiple voices and collaborative effort. It raises such questions as Who will change the nation? Who cares about its change? What role or roles do these young people want to take on themselves? How should we as various audience members be involved?

Implications for Arts-Based Research

This study is a form of arts-based research that engages in analytical discussion of art works while paying particular attention to the art forms themselves. As a piece of criticism, it raises questions about the role of the critic in social research, such as, What happens when discussion requires a movement away from the medium of the art work (such as from musical to written form)? and What is lost in that translation? This loss includes the limitation of using one language to describe the product of another language (such as using text to describe music, when the reader cannot hear the rhythms, mood, tempo, and so on of the song). This study also asks audiences to reexperience their values and beliefs about young people in different communities through taking on new perspectives offered aesthetically by viewing the art works in the context of critical research.

REFLECTION QUESTIONS

1. How is arts criticism a form of arts-based research?
2. How would you describe a transactive space?
3. How does this study explore the role of aesthetics in arts-based research?

Learning from Arts-Based Studies

Unlike most other forms of social research, arts-based studies do not make knowledge claims. Individual projects of arts-based research are not designed to add to a cumulative knowledge base. There is therefore no intent to have readers or viewers generalize in a traditional sense found in science-based studies. Instead, the generalization process is closer to what is called **naturalistic generalization** from case studies (see Chapter Ten), or **psychological generalization**, as the reader or viewer responds personally to the research text. This occurs as members of a research audience are allowed to vicariously inhabit a virtual world, enabled to reexperience parts of that world from a fresh perspective. When this virtual experience is sufficiently powerful it may call into question the comfortable, familiar, habitual meanings and values that adhere to social issues, events, and other phenomena, resulting, again, in value negation (Iser, 1974).

It is important to note that, according to reader-response theory, each reader or viewer will respond to the research text in a somewhat different manner. Discussion and conversation among members of a critical research community are ongoing as we work to understand the applications of meanings found within the text. For example, many researchers are now using performance to portray their observations of members of an ethnographic community under study. In a one-person theatrical production titled "Second Chair: An Autoethnodrama," Saldaña (2008) explored his own experiences with status in schooling, such as feelings of isolation and marginalization, as well as his overlapping identities, experienced during his time in the high school band. Audiences might respond differently to methodological, ethical, and practical issues related to Saldaña's work: how an artist-researcher collects data and turns it into a script to be performed, how the performance is representing self and others, and how this story relates to school group memberships and policies today.

Trusting Arts-Based Studies

Works of arts-based research are *not* to be trusted in two ways. First, a work of art may not be **phenomenologically truthful** in that it does not reflect exact, accurate experiences that can provide insight with certainty for the reader about a phenomenon. If readers expect texts of arts-based research to be literally true, they miss the point of arts-based research discussed earlier. Instead, the reader may expect a believable version of events, a plausibility, a kind of verisimilitude, but not a final "truth" in regard to "how things truly are" from a privileged perspective. Every work of arts-based research is a potential prevarication (Grumet, 1988). In this way the work serves as a framework for experiences that the reader is reminded of, and asked to connect with, through the work's expressive qualities.

Second, even if a piece of arts-based research is a well-crafted work of art, an issue of trustworthiness remains (Barone, 1995). A work of arts-based research may not succeed in fulfilling its heuristic purpose. In that regard it may remain superficial or fail to sufficiently interrogate prevailing worldviews. For that reason every reader or viewer must adopt a postmodern sense of skepticism toward a work. This means that trust must be earned by a work of arts-based research in every engagement between the text and the skeptical viewer.

Nevertheless, if a work succeeds in the ultimate purposes of arts-based research (raising questions, providing opportunities to reexperience phenomena, and questioning assumptions about those phenomena), then the result may be an emancipatory moment for readers or viewers. This moment is a heightened awareness through which the reader begins to actively construct new meanings and perceptions about a social phenomenon, calling previous ways of perceiving the world into question (Barone, 1995).

REFLECTION QUESTIONS

1. Why is a reader's response important to consider when evaluating what can be learned from arts-based research studies?
2. What is the role of trustworthiness in the realm of arts-based research?

Summary

Arts-based research is an exciting methodology and way of constructing knowledge about social phenomena. Accomplished works of arts-based research commonly possess several characteristics. These include but are not limited to the following, as further elaborated on in the work of Barone and Eisner (2006, 2011). The work of arts-based research must possess a potential for **illumination**. This is a capacity to reveal what has not been previously noticed in a set of social phenomena. Otherwise the work is redundant insofar as it rehashes the merely familiar, or the prevailing wisdom, concerning social issues, events, or topics. The work should have a potential for **generativity**. This is the capacity of the work to promote a disequilibrium in the reader or viewer, a kind of puzzlement that raises questions more than providing answers. Often this is the result of a purposefully crafted ambiguity in the text. The work should be **incisive**, focusing tightly on a social issue, theme, or topic. The work should be **socially significant**. That is, it should address social issues that are not trivial, but rather are important in and to a culture or society. The work should understand and engage **aesthetic qualities** (arts-based tools of language, their elements and principles) derived from the arts discipline or disciplines with which it converses.

Key Terms

aesthetic qualities, 286
arts-based research, 271
critical persuasion, 274
generativity, 286
genre blurring, 273
heuristic purpose, 274
illumination, 286
incisive, 286

interrogatory purpose, 274
metaphorical purpose, 279
naturalistic generalization, 285
paradigmatic science, 275
paradigmatic text, 281
phenomenologically truthful, 285

psychological generalization, 285
qualitative control, 279
qualitative problem solving, 277
socially significant, 286
transactive space, 283
value negation, 276

Further Readings and Resources

Suggested Arts-Based Research Studies

Barone, T. (2001). *Touching eternity: The enduring outcomes of teaching*. New York: Teachers College Press.

This book is a study of narrative construction and narrative analysis, through which Barone tells the stories of students affected by their high school art teacher and analyzes these stories for questions of "effectiveness" in teaching.

Belliveau, G. (2006). Engaging in drama: Using arts-based research to explore a social justice project in teacher education. *International Journal of Education & the Arts*, 7(5). www.ijea.org/v7n5/index.html.

This article uses drama in both the research methods and the form of research write-up to explore antibullying efforts by preservice teachers in a teaching practicum.

Chappell, S. (2009). A rough handshake or an illness: Teaching and learning on the border as felt through art-making. *Journal of Curriculum and Pedagogy, 1*, 10–21.

This article expresses the use of collage, bookmaking, and poetry in an exploration of linguistic and cultural borders in teaching for artists and educators.

Prendergast, M., Lymburner, J., Grauer, K., Irwin, R. L., Leggo, C., & Gouzouasis, P. (2008). Pedagogy of trace: Poetic representations of teaching resilience/resistance in arts education. *Vitae Scholasticae: The Journal of Educational Biography, 25*, 58–76.

This article explores how stories of teaching can overlap in the retellings in order to trace the effects or impacts of teachers on students derived through teachers' studying their own practice.

Other Suggested Readings

Barone, T. (2000). *Aesthetics, politics, and educational inquiry: Essays and examples*. New York: Peter Lang.

This book explores educational research using the tools of literature and narrative. Included is the essay "Ways of Being at Risk: The Case of Billy Charles Barnett," a sample study of narrative construction.

Barone, T. (2007). A return to the gold standard? Questioning the future of narrative construction as educational research. *Qualitative Inquiry, 13*(2), 1–17.

This article explores seven primary issues related to narrative forms of arts-based research.

Barone, T., & Eisner, E. (2011). *Arts based research*. Thousand Oaks, CA: Sage.

This introductory text from the academics who coined the term *arts-based research* addresses important issues and examples of arts-based social research.

Cahnmann, M., & Siegesmund, R. (Eds.). (2007). *Arts-based research in education: Foundations for practice*. New York: Routledge.

This foundational text explores purposes, tensions, and examples in arts-based research.

Eisner, E. (1997). The promise and perils of alternative forms of data representation. *Educational Researcher, 26*(6), 4–10.

The article addresses the potential strengths and weaknesses of arts-based research documentation, with attention paid to the ways that the arts construct knowledge.

Knowles, J. G., & Cole, A. L. (2007). *Handbook of the arts in qualitative research: Perspectives, methodologies, examples and issues*. Thousand Oaks, CA: Sage.

This book demonstrates how research in the social sciences has been informed by the arts, including diverse scholarly perspectives on the roles of the arts in research as well as examples of methodologies and genres used.

Marín, C. (2007). A methodology rooted in praxis: Theatre of the oppressed (TO) techniques employed as arts-based educational research methods. *Youth Theatre Journal, 21*, 81–93.

This article describes a community-based theatrical devising process known as theatre of the oppressed that the author used with her participants to construct and perform a theatrical script about their lives. Some devised portions of the creative writing are included in the article.

Sinner, A., Leggo, C., Irwin, R. L., Gouzouasis, P., & Grauer, K. (2006). Arts-based educational research dissertations: Reviewing the practices of new scholars. *Canadian Journal of Education, 29*, 1223–1270.

This article describes one decade of dissertations that use arts-based research in visual, literary, and performative modes. The authors of this article identify four shared principles in the dissertations: a commitment to aesthetic practices, inquiry, a search for meaning, and interpretation for understanding.

Springgay, S., Irwin, R., Leggo, C., & Gouzouasis, P. (Eds.). (2008). *Being with a/r/tography*. Rotterdam, The Netherlands: Sense.

This book explores the arts-based research method a/r/tography through three themes: self-study and autobiography, communities of a/r/tographic practice, and ethics and activism.

Organizations and Web Sites

American Educational Research Association (AERA)—Special Interest Group on Arts-Based Educational Research (SIG #9) (http://aber-sig.org/)

This Web site disseminates information about arts-based research to members of the Arts-Based Educational Research SIG. The site has information on conferences, awards, and resources. Members join this SIG through the AERA Web site (http://aera.net/).

A/r/tography (http://m1.cust.educ.ubc.ca:16080/Artography/)

This Web site provides an overview of the a/r/tography methodology, key researchers, art works, publications, news, and links.

Center for Arts-Informed Research (www.utoronto.ca/CAIR/airchome3.html)

This Web site describes the center, which is based out of the Ontario Institute for Studies in Education through the University of Ontario. This site is a resource for publications, events, and links in arts-based research.

Educational Insights (http://educationalinsights.ca/)

This online journal publishing arts-based research studies is hosted by the University of British Columbia's Centre for Cross-Faculty Inquiry in Education.

International Journal of Education & the Arts (www.ijea.org/index.html)

This online, open-access journal focuses on educational significances of the arts and the arts in education.

International Visual Methodologies for Social Change (www.ivmproject.ca/)

This Web site focuses on research that explores uses of visual methodologies to express participant observations and reflections on social experience.

Journal of Curriculum and Pedagogy (www.curriculumandpedagogy.org/Journal.html)

This journal focuses on interdisciplinary studies of the relationship between curriculum and pedagogy, including arts-based efforts.

Liminalities: A Journal of Performance Studies (http://liminalities.net/archives.htm)

This journal publishes scholarship focused on performance as a social, political aesthetic methodology and mode of critique.

CHAPTER 12

PRACTITIONER ACTION RESEARCH

Stephen D. Lapan

Key Ideas

- Practitioner action research, introduced by Lewin (1946, 1948), is an approach used by practicing professionals for individual reflection and shared study related to important social issues.

- Although practitioner action research is often conducted as critical social action, interpretive practical reasoning is an equally common application for professionals.

- Practitioner research as practical reasoning is characterized by professional self-reflection, tight time frames, and a work-related focus that is intended to improve practice.

- One useful format for implementing practitioner research, adapted from Kemmis and McTaggart (1982), offers a sequence of focusing, planning, acting, observing, reflecting, and revising, ordinarily followed by refocusing to initiate a new practitioner study.

- Stimulated recall is an underused but significant strategy practitioners can use to reflect on work-related decision making, especially those in highly interactive professions, such as counseling, community organizing, and teaching.

- Practitioner researchers should begin with small studies using tight study cycles and should involve colleagues in the research to create a culture of inquiry.

- Study validity can be checked by recognizing the practitioner researcher's biases, determining how natural and relevant the findings appear, and exhausting any potential alternative interpretations of the results.

- The practitioner researcher's professional knowledge is the most important validity test when findings are judged in comparison with that knowledge.

Although the main emphasis in this text is to explain qualitative research approaches to readers who are likely to be consumers of research studies, this chapter is an important exception in that nearly all professionals can readily apply the research designs described here. **Practitioner action research** (often called **action research** or **participatory action research**) is an investigative approach that emphasizes careful and systematic study by professionals interested in individual or shared self-reflection. Those who might use this form of research include architects, lawyers, social workers, educators, nurses, physicians, and most other professionals who want to more formally examine everyday issues of professional practice. As practitioner studies unfold, they are usually organized so that an individual or a small group of professionals can investigate these topics through the process of selecting issues, planning, collecting data, analyzing results, and reflecting on these findings by translating them into revised practice. A potential application could involve a team of physicians using a traditional experimental framework comparing different treatments of patients with similar conditions. In a more nontraditional qualitative application, a community activist group might study how to change state health policies, or a school principal could use practitioner action research to study ways to reduce school dropouts.

Practitioner action researchers using a traditional approach might ask research questions similar to these:

1. Does laboratory science significantly improve student learning when compared to textbook instruction?

2. Is this family of drugs more effective than another type for reducing cholesterol in patients over sixty-five years old?

3. Do lawyers who pass the bar exam in their first attempt make significantly higher salaries than those who fail the first try?

Practitioner action researchers who come from a nontraditional orientation think differently about how to approach research and what questions to ask. These are three examples of such questions:

1. What do we need to know to resolve the unemployment problems in our community?

2. How can we increase parent involvement in our after-school programs?

3. How can I more effectively explain treatment options to my patients?

Traditional researchers approach practitioner action research by using positivist ideas about conducting these studies, depending on experiments and similar plans to design and implement their studies. But, as the preceding questions imply, nontraditional investigators focus more on trying ideas to see if they work.

Nontraditional practitioner action research studies are seldom designed in a longer-term framework as most research tends to be. Instead they are likely to be scheduled and structured as small, manageable plans whereby data are collected in a time frame of less than an hour, although they can extend for up to a week or two depending on the nature and breadth of the research questions. The shorter study schedule is employed so that a practitioner can plan and carry out each investigation and immediately apply findings for reflection and adjustment in subsequent practice. Traditional applications may follow this pattern or adhere to the more typical long-term format.

REFLECTION QUESTIONS

1. What major differences do you see between traditional and nontraditional approaches to practitioner action research?
2. As you consider your future career, which approach would you rather use to study your own professional practice and why?

Historical Perspective

After World War II there were strong and well-deserved feelings against notions of totalitarianism of any kind, and there was profound interest in creating democratic social environments in many parts of the world. In this context the social psychologist Kurt Lewin (1946, 1948) considered ways to improve programs intended to assist the most troubled or deprived populations in the United States (Beattie, 1989). Although influenced by the work of others, Lewin is most often credited for creating the idea of practitioner action research, or what he called action research, to be used collectively by community workers as a strategy for solving problems. As Kemmis and McTaggart (1988) explain, "It was tried in contexts as diverse as integrated housing, equalization of opportunity for employment, the cause and cure of prejudice in children, the socialization of street gangs, and the better training of youth leaders" (p. 6).

Practitioner action research as conceived by Lewin provided legitimacy to this enterprise of collectively solving problems as a form of *real research*, offering an acceptable alternative to the orthodoxy of formal experiments and the like. However, this new area of professional self-study lost favor during the 1950s, in part because it usually consisted of such traditional applications as teaching elementary statistics to nonresearcher professionals and expecting them to produce studies (House & Lapan, 1988).

Renewed interest in practitioner studies was slow in coming. In the United States, for example, only a few organized training programs were reported (see, for example, Rogge, 1967), although it gained a firmer footing in Britain as a substantial part of the school curriculum reform movement in the 1960s (Elliott, 1988). An examination of the world's largest educational research association's annual conference program (that of the American Educational Research Association [AERA]) reveals a keen interest in research-based improved practice by 1973, but AERA listed no papers or presentations specifically related to practitioner research. Eighteen listings for the topic can be found in 1993, however, and in 2010 sixty sessions or papers were listed.

The revival of practitioner action research in the latter part of the twentieth century has many potential explanations, but Donald Schön's studies (1983) of successful professional practitioners represent a key contribution. Schön determined that the most effective professionals engaged in what he called **move-testing**, trying out small changes to obtain desired effects, then trying again with an altered move in the form of a new experiment. This kind of reflective practice, Schön explained, is an informal version of practitioner action research that has a direct influence on the overall quality of a professional's work. Those who regularly employ practitioner reflection, Schön discovered, were also found to be decidedly better at their profession (cited in House & Lapan, 1988).

Research and Professional Practice

The ordinary view of research and professional improvement comes from the world of traditional study designs in which experiments or other positivist forms of investigation conducted by experts are used to arrive at solutions. This perspective operates on the premise that principles or techniques that work in one place can be packaged or made into guidelines and applied elsewhere. It is an enduring aim of such experimental and correlation studies to influence the everyday practice of professionals from physicians in their treatment of patients to those who counsel and teach. The application of this idea of traditional research, sometimes called **technical or instrumental transfer** (which involves using findings from one setting in other venues), has worked reasonably well in such physically based professions as medicine, although even in medicine individual differences in susceptibility to various drugs, for example, often make medical research findings less than trustworthy. A prescription may effectively reduce one patient's blood pressure but could cause an adverse reaction in another.

As a general pattern, there has been what Berliner (2009) calls a "great disconnect" (p. 295) when it comes to any real influence of traditional research on most professional practice, particularly on the daily professional behavior of most practitioners. Many professionals report a lack of access to these research findings, but most describe them as neither relevant nor closely linked to what they need to know for solving real-life work-related issues.

Many contend that positivist research has not effectively influenced practitioners to improve the quality of their efforts. Atkin (1991), for example, explains that traditional research as a source for supporting change and improvement is problematic. Research conducted at universities, he explains,

> has its own purposes and values . . . but its guiding purpose is not necessarily to alter what people do. When university-based science does have practical impact, that influence is frequently incidental . . . in physical or biological science—and forced in the social and behavioral sciences. (p. 2)

Berliner (2009), who was trained in traditional research approaches, summarizes the issue in this way:

> I eventually learned that research data do not provide the surety that I believed such data possessed. I learned that practice is amazingly more complex than I first understood it to be, filled with variables not easily captured . . . [and] all of which are interacting with each other simultaneously. (p. 298)

Atkin, Berliner, and many others now advise that one more effective way of influencing professional practice is practitioner action research conducted by professionals in their own work environment. Such an approach has a longer history in education, but holds real promise in other fields as well. Applications of practitioner action research have ranged from the use of traditional positivist designs to the use of plans driven by a qualitative orientation—but in either case implemented by professionals themselves.

There are detractors as well, of course. Some professionals report that conducting these investigations is time-consuming and makes it even more difficult to keep up with the demands of their normal workload. And even those who consider practitioner action research a reasonable approach are not convinced that practitioners will use it. As Scriven reported in 1991, it is "an excellent idea, but one with a very poor track record" (p. 48).

REFLECTION QUESTIONS

1. What are some advantages and disadvantages of outside experts' conducting research on practice?
2. As a practitioner in your future career, what influence might most research have on your work?

Traditions That Shape Practitioner Research

Although there are still recommended uses of positivist experimental and correlational applications in some research contexts (see, for example, Johnson, 2008), practitioner action research finds its origins in what is known as **interpretive or critical traditions**. These traditions or worldviews stem from a distinct set of assumptions about where truth can be found and how research questions are formulated to discover meaning. Interpretive or critical researchers study real-life settings, focusing primarily on rich qualitative observations that recount multiple experiences and perspectives obtained from those who live in the studied settings. Unlike traditional researchers, interpretive or critical investigators expect findings that are primarily qualitative, complex, and dynamically dependent on time, location, and participant.

There are important distinctions even within the interpretive or critical perspectives. The critical side is identified by Kemmis (2009) as **critical social action** whereby individuals work collectively toward shared research topics using a practitioner research approach to resolve vital social concerns, such as local poverty or discrimination. Mills (2003) further explains critical social action as representing a "shared interest in liberating individuals from the dictates of tradition, habit, and bureaucracy" (p. 6).

By contrast, the interpretive approach to practitioner research directs professionals to research everyday practical issues associated with their own work-related efforts by designing studies for self-reflection and improvement. Kemmis (1993) calls this interpretive perspective **practical reasoning**, tracing it to Aristotle as a form of investigation that lone individuals or small study groups of like professionals employ to inspect and improve practice in the workplace. In the latter case, a practitioner action research group might design studies of interest to all members, or members might research their own individual topics with group assistance.

REFLECTION QUESTION

1. In your own words, what are the essential differences between critical social action and practical reasoning as approaches to practitioner action research?

Practitioner Research as Practical Reasoning

It can be argued that the technical or instrumental form of practitioner action research has an important advantage of being field based and thus more likely to represent current practices, unlike research conducted under artificial laboratory conditions. And without question the critical social action approach has its strength in galvanizing social or educational change, especially where those with the least power work toward gaining greater deserved equity. The theme of this chapter, however, is that of practitioner action research in the framework of Aristotle's practical reasoning that can be pursued by lone individuals or a community of professionals. This conception has the advantage of focusing on authentic, concrete, and relevant professional issues related to everyday practice. Local professionals are able to recognize and study those elements of practice that match the real-life pace and temporal flow of their professional setting. An additional characteristic of practitioner action research is that of professional autonomy, the control of the research by practitioners themselves without management or direction from outsiders. Practical reasoning and critical social action share this ingredient.

Practitioner action research as practical reasoning is designed by first identifying an issue, concern, or area of interest—it does not have to be a problem or serious event, but a topic that has the potential to influence the quality of professional work. A counselor may ask his patients to offer anonymous written comments about the effectiveness of a new role-playing technique, or a classroom teacher could study a video of a recent lesson to observe the clarity of her directions.

What follows are two very concrete examples of professionals engaging in practitioner action research as a form of practical reasoning, hereafter referred to as **practitioner research**. In these two scenarios, emphasis is given to **practitioner self-reflection**, an important characteristic of practitioner research. The primary focus is on one's own professional practice, not on audiences or others in the workplace.

Practitioner Research in Action: Two Scenarios

Prior to addressing the overall characteristics and usual designs associated with practitioner research, it is instructive to explore this idea through the use of fictionalized concrete examples. The two stories here are of two kinds, the first representing an individual teacher applying practitioner research to his own practice without the involvement of colleagues. The second is an example of a lawyer adopting it to her own practice, but engaging other lawyers in the process. In each of these examples a format adapted from Kemmis and McTaggart (1982) will be used to organize the phases of the investigative process. These phases or stages are *focusing, planning, acting, observing, reflecting*, and *revising* (cited in Jones et al., 1999, p. 12) and will be defined in each scenario.

Mr. Crane, Sixth-Grade Teacher

Our teacher, Mr. Crane, has determined that his students are reluctant to become verbally involved in classroom discussions (**focusing**). It is Mr. Crane's position based on both study and experience that increased verbal involvement by students is directly linked to student interest, motivation, and positive attitude, and ultimately to improved learning or at least to creating a better environment for learning.

Planning in this setting refers to Mr. Crane's thoughts about how to try something different that may have the potential to encourage greater student verbal involvement. Perhaps he could use more silence to give students increased opportunities to speak, or he might request that students respond to each other's ideas more often—a complicated idea in itself. He could also try to ask questions that are more open ended so that multiple responses are possible, making class members feel less need to produce one best answer. Mr. Crane must now decide during this planning phase what to try, perhaps selecting two ideas to keep the size of the "experiment" manageable. Limiting the variables in any tryout gives the practitioner researcher the ability to keep track of which strategies may cause the desired outcomes.

Mr. Crane decides to try the selected use of silence and, with some careful preplanning, the use of open-ended questions. He now teaches the lesson applying these new ideas (**acting**) and makes an audiotape of the lesson for later observation and reflection. When time first allows, Mr. Crane listens to the taped class, writing down what happens during the lesson when he attempts the use of silence at different intervals. The practitioner researcher, Mr. Crane, also writes down all the questions he asks during the lesson—as most teachers know, these are always different than those one plans to ask. He then examines these questions to gauge the extent of their open-endedness and if the better questions produced the student verbal involvement anticipated (**observing**).

By examining his observations, Mr. Crane is now reflecting on the relative effectiveness of his attempts to increase verbal involvement, deciding that these new questioning strategies did produce the wanted results, although he sees ways of refining these questions to make them even more effective (**revising**). However, Mr. Crane discovers that the use of silence was awkward, disturbing his normal teaching pattern and interrupting the pace of the class. Silence, he decides, looked like a much better idea on paper than in practice, and he will probably not experiment with it again, at least for purposes of increasing student talk.

This reflecting and revising by Mr. Crane leads to **refocusing** (focusing), that is, using the findings from the first set of observations, reflections, and revisions to make changes for the next research cycle. In turn, this revised planning moves Mr. Crane from the final stage of the Kemmis and McTaggart (1982) model to the beginning phase once again, thus designated as refocusing or focusing all over again, producing a new set of plans, acts, observations, reflections, and revisions. These full cycles, as suggested earlier, are quite close together, in this instance representing a lesson or activity of less than an hour that is subsequently observed and whose results are used for a new practitioner research plan.

Ms. Drake, Courtroom Lawyer

As an experienced defense attorney, Ms. Drake has learned that there is no such thing as too much information concerning the events surrounding each potential case. She also knows that most lawyers try to address this need for information during early interviews with clients and others associated with the case so they can determine if there is an actual case and, if so, how they will construct that case. Missing information or getting the ideas or facts wrong can be very costly later on.

Ms. Drake has decided that this is an important area to study using practitioner research following the Kemmis and McTaggart (1982) model. Some members of Ms. Drake's law firm have agreed to work with her on this issue and are interested in studying their own practice as well. To proceed, Ms. Drake has developed her own practitioner's theory that some of the information she gains from clients is probably clouded by her own biases and assumptions she brings to the early interviews. Ms. Drake guesses that she may well draw premature conclusions during these first meetings, thinking she understands what the case is before the client has fully disclosed the story *(focusing)*. This happens to many professionals whose experience makes them potentially wiser but too anticipatory in their judgments.

To investigate this phenomenon, Ms. Drake and her colleagues discuss what kind of data she might collect to learn about this issue. There is the potential of using audiotape, a questionnaire, and even a colleague observing the early interview sessions. Although they know they have not exhausted the possibilities, all agree that it is important to learn if the client has had the opportunity to recount relevant events as well as to determine what techniques Ms. Drake could use to draw out the client's story *(planning)*. Ms. Drake has the idea of using the technique of clarification by rephrasing what the client says at appropriate times both to clarify what has been said and to encourage the client to continue. This also can be achieved by asking clients to rephrase or restate what they have said. She had seen this used effectively in training seminars, but was not altogether comfortable with its use. She recalled an example in which a client said: "Well, my feeling was that explaining to the police that I saw the accident happen was the best thing to do even though they thought I caused it." The lawyer's clarification statement was: "So, you wanted to be certain the police got your side of the story. Is that it?" This seemed straightforward enough in Ms. Drake's mind. In the seminar at least, the technique did encourage the client to provide more details.

Ms. Drake's research practitioner group decides against the live observer idea as too distracting for the client, but concurs that an audio-recording would be part of normal events. Ms. Drake's colleagues also suggest the addition of a short questionnaire for completion by the client as a verification of what is observed on the tape recording. The questionnaire would ask the client if there was any information about the case not covered in the interview and would seek an overall reaction.

Ms. Drake meets with her first client who will be part of this practitioner research study *(acting)*, explaining that she is taping to be able to catch all of the information covered. Ms. Drake does her best to selectively rephrase the client's statements without sounding like a parrot (a great fear she had at the training seminar and going into this client interview session). Ms. Drake also makes certain the client completes the questionnaire before leaving the office, but has it administered by one of her practitioner research team members.

When she can find the time, Ms. Drake listens to the tape, *observing* her restatement strategy in action. She finds that in some instances the technique is having the desired effect, with the client pursuing thoughts further and producing more examples as a direct result of Ms. Drake's rephrasing. At other times, though, the lawyer's restatements sound almost absurd to her—she is the parrot she feared she would be. Ms. Drake will wait for her colleagues to observe the taped interview to see what they think. For further data, the questionnaire results show that the client thought his story was fully expressed, but was distracted on occasion by the lawyer's "just repeating what I said sometimes. That just didn't sound right."

Ms. Drake and her practitioner researcher colleagues discuss the findings (*reflecting*). Each member offers Ms. Drake suggestions about refining her clarifying statements to avoid the "parrot phenomenon." They also remark on when she might have used the technique and other times when she might have been better off not doing so.

While her colleagues are offering more examples of clarifying without repeating along with suggestions for the judicious use of the strategy, Ms. Drake is already thinking about how she might attempt this again with another client she will see in a few days (*revising* and *refocusing*). She is more enthusiastic about the process than she expected, but did not anticipate how complicated this seemingly simple restatement idea would become in practice. At the same time, the overall significance of examining this part of her professional practice has taken on heightened importance. Meanwhile, the other group members begin discussing their own projects—one decides to also study the clarification strategy in early interviews, whereas others have quite different areas of interest.

Scenario Analysis

In both of the examples the practitioner researchers followed the adapted Kemmis and McTaggart (1982) steps, and in both cases produced a pattern that Kemmis and McTaggart describe as a **spiral or spiraled cycle**—rather than just repeated cycles—whereby each subsequent practitioner research event conveys growth, change, and potential improvement in subsequent practice. The term *cycle* communicates a kind of redundancy or starting over in the same way that seasons of the year repeat themselves. It is a reasonable prospect, however, that a practitioner may engage in the study of a given topic during only one cycle, either resolving the issue or deciding that a different one is a more productive focus. The spiral or improvement idea would still result if professional growth and perhaps new insights were attained.

It should be an acceptable option that a lone individual could effectively conduct practitioner research, as Mr. Crane was able to do. However, the added advantages of a collegial effort evident in Ms. Drake's scenario included group support and multiple contributions from the team members. Conducting practitioner research in group settings usually offers discoveries that individuals reflecting by themselves will not see.

REFLECTION QUESTIONS

1. How might you approach your future career practice as a researcher in ways used by Mr. Crane or Ms. Drake?
2. What are other aspects of this practice you could study?

Characteristics of Practitioner Research

Any application of this kind of investigation is considered an unusual idea in the world of formal study in which most practitioners experience research as something outsiders do, not as something self-initiated. A shift in outlook is produced when research is experienced as local, relevant, and under a practitioner's own control. Further, as Atkin (1991) suggests:

> A feature that distinguishes this type of investigation sharply from conventional research is that the researcher . . . becomes a different professional as the research process unfolds, and as a result of it. His or her practices are modified continually because of the inquiry. (p. 9)

In addition, for a professional engaged in interpretive practitioner research, a primary aim is to design studies that assist in changing and improving everyday professional practice, not necessarily to look for direct results in audiences.

At this point it is worth recounting the characteristics of practitioner research addressed in the chapter:

- *Self-reflection*—an emphasis on self-study focusing on one's own professional work either alone or with peer assistance

- *Tight time frames*—study plans that may include observations of less than hour to no more than a week or two, making it possible to have immediate influence on everyday practice

- *Relevant research findings*—study results drawn from one's own practice and used to immediately revise professional action

- *Spiraled cycles*—an overall structure that moves from focusing and planning to using findings to revise and improve practice, enabling growth

- *Practitioner researcher autonomy*—a professional's ongoing experience of power over the selection of issues, the development of plans, and the use of results

Using Ms. Drake's scenario to highlight these characteristics, she began her practitioner research by focusing on her professional work, using peer assistance to reflect on her effectiveness in initial client interviews. Gathering data from the audiotape and questionnaire, Ms. Drake and team members reflected and made plans for revised practice within a very short time frame. Ms. Drake applied these ideas by making plans for new professional action and employed the spiraled cycle of changed practice for further study. It may be premature to determine if professional improvement has occurred, but Ms. Drake's plan included continued practitioner research to assess her effectiveness in subsequent early client interviews. Finally, the entire research enterprise was under the guidance and control of the practitioner researcher, Ms. Drake, with assistance from her team. This is a significant departure from most experiences practitioners have with research ordinarily directed by managers, academics, or other outsiders.

Another vital element of group practitioner research involves the opportunity to work in an environment steeped in professional discourse that fosters a sustained learning community. This environment, if made a part of the regularized activities of the workplace, increases interest and curiosity in the examination and improvement of practice.

Practitioner Research Designs

Practitioners will find it useful to follow some kind of guidelines for designing practical studies of their own work, and one such model (Kemmis & McTaggart, 1982) has been adapted and applied in our cases of Mr. Crane and Ms. Drake. To review, these stages are *focusing, planning, acting, observing, reflecting*, and *revising* (followed by *refocusing*). Using our two practitioner researchers as examples following this model, we see Mr. Crane and Ms. Drake conducting their research in each stage in Exhibit 12.1.

EXHIBIT 12.1
SCENARIO EXAMPLES OF THE PRACTITIONER RESEARCH STAGES

Focusing

- Mr. Crane finds his students reluctant to talk in class.
- Ms. Drake suspects she is obtaining only partial client reports in initial interviews.

Planning

- Mr. Crane thinks about using silence and more open-ended questions.
- Ms. Drake decides on applying a clarification strategy.

Acting

- Mr. Crane teaches using silence and open-ended questions, taping the experiment.
- Ms. Drake interviews a client using the clarifying statement technique, taping the experiment and implementing a questionnaire.

Observing

- Mr. Crane listens to the tape for examples of silence and questions.
- Ms. Drake listens to the tape and reads the completed questionnaire to gauge the effect of the clarifying statement experiment.

Reflecting

- Mr. Crane decides questions work but silence does not.
- Ms. Drake finds her restatements sometimes useful, sometimes parroting.

Revising

- Mr. Crane revises his questions and cancels the silence idea.
- Ms. Drake develops better clarifying statements and eliminates parroting examples.

Refocusing

- Mr. Crane has a new plan for increasing student verbal involvement.
- Ms. Drake has a new plan for encouraging client reporting.

Table 12.1 Comparison of the Lewin (1948) and Kemmis and McTaggart (1982) Research Models

Design Stage	Lewin	Kemmis and McTaggart
Selecting a topic or issue	Fact-finding Conceptualization	Focusing
Making a research plan	Action planning	Planning
Engaging in practice	Implementation*	Acting
Collecting data		Observing
Interpreting observed action	Evaluation	Reflecting
Determining needed changes	Problem analysis	Revising
Developing a new practitioner research plan	Fact-finding Conceptualization	Refocusing (Focusing)

Source: Adapted from Jones et al., 1999.
*Lewin's implementation phase encompasses K&M's acting and observing categories.

Kemmis and McTaggart (K&M) developed their design steps for practitioner research based on the work of Lewin (1948), who, as explained, originated the practitioner action research idea decades earlier. In Lewin's format, he outlines his stages as *fact-finding, conceptualization, action planning, implementation, evaluation,* and *problem analysis.* The elements of this structure are comparable to the K&M framework, as shown in Table 12.1.

There are two rather subtle but important differences between the Lewin and K&M designs that deserve attention. First, Lewin does not directly address the role of observation, incorporating it as part of his *implementation* category. And, although K&M consider *refocusing* an essential activity to emphasize the spiraled cycle pattern noted earlier, Lewin's model implies beginning once again with *fact-finding* and *conceptualization.* To be fair, though, Lewin made clear in his writing that a spiraled cycle of growth was a crucial aim of his recommended practitioner research sequence.

Most who write about practitioner research follow design sequences quite similar to those offered by Lewin and K&M, although some (Johnson, 1995, for example) have departed from this pattern by designating the initial stage as *problem identification.* This conception of beginning by locating difficulties may lead to a **deficit orientation,** implying that practitioner research should be conducted only when professionals experience trouble or serious problems in their work. However, as Schön (1983) has explained, professionals who frequently and effectively engage in move-testing (a form of practitioner research) are also those found to be superior performers in their practice. Practitioner research should not be just for teachers who have severe discipline problems or lawyers who too often improperly represent their clients.

> **REFLECTION QUESTION**
>
> 1. Why might a deficit orientation be a downfall in practitioner research?

Engaging in Practitioner Research

Our teacher, Mr. Crane, and our lawyer, Ms. Drake, seemed to decide rather easily and quickly how to get started in their research efforts, readily determining a focus and plan of action. But they were fictitious, of course, and most professionals approach this task with a good deal more reticence. Most have little or no experience in research of this kind and cannot fall back on past experience or on observing others going through the process. Perhaps the best advice at this stage is to just try something to get into the pattern and build experience through practice, even if the focus and the plan do not seem vital to one's work.

Choosing Study Questions

As mentioned previously, an important element in initiating practitioner research is the selection of a focus and formulation of a plan. This is achieved by deciding on an area of interest and a potential question or two that can guide the study. Those new to practitioner research are surprised how quickly the process moves along once a focus and questions are chosen. To get started, professionals may be able to find an area of interest from those suggested in Table 12.2. Two sample questions have been provided for each area as initial ideas for planning, but these would need to be revised to suit each professional's work characteristics.

Reviewing this list of focus areas and sample questions might offer a hospital administrator, for example, the opportunity to select the *time* focus area in order to pursue a practitioner research plan to make better use of patients' wait time in the emergency room. In another case, a librarian may choose the *talk* focus area to analyze what information he most often offers patrons during a given workday. And a museum guide could decide to study her *communication* effectiveness by getting feedback on the clarity of her spoken and written material. Although professionals may require at least some training or guidance before initiating practitioner research, and even though they may well need some advice along the way, most will find that the experience itself will provide nearly all of the direction needed.

Table 12.2 Eight Practitioner Research Areas with Sample Questions

Focus Area	Sample Questions
Time	1. How is time allotted for most important activities? 2. Are there ways for audiences* to be engaged during wait periods?
Talk	1. What content is represented by most professional talk? 2. Are there ways that audiences could be encouraged to talk more often?
Communication	1. How clear are spoken explanations or directions? 2. What written material do audiences have the most difficulty understanding?
Openness	1. To what extent are audience members encouraged to present their ideas? 2. How could audience member questions be increased?
Expertise	1. What limitations of skills or knowledge are demonstrated by the professional or professionals? 2. What areas of knowledge could be sought by audience members?
Expectations	1. How effectively are expectations of the audience members explained? 2. Is essential information, such as schedules and deadlines, effectively communicated to audience members?
Objectivity	1. How are the professional's or professionals' views used in appropriate or inappropriate ways? 2. To what extent are audience member perspectives encouraged and clarified?
Environment	1. What are the best and worst aspects of the workplace's physical environment? 2. How could availability of work space, seating, lighting, storage, or other physical elements be improved for audience members or professionals?

*The term *audience* is used as a convenient label for those served by professionals, such as patrons, patients, clients, students, or customers.

REFLECTION QUESTIONS

1. List at least one example in your future practice for identifying a focus and possible plan.
2. If you selected the *expectations* focus area in Table 12.2, how would you revise it and create your own question or questions to study?

Data Collection

A key element in the practitioner research cycle is that of selecting which data to use in answering study questions. Although specific details for collecting data are presented in Chapter Four, some ideas specifically useful for practitioner researchers should assist those who are relatively new to data collection. Data collection is, first of all, a deliberative process that requires some practical problem solving. There are very few settled rules about what instruments to use or what kinds of observations to employ. One important guideline is that open-ended tools better serve the purpose of capturing the complexity of the work environment, but more closed-ended instruments are very efficient ways of collecting corroborating information. Therefore, an open-ended questionnaire question might ask: "What are all the ways the intake experience could be improved?" But a questionnaire that asks audiences to rate experiences on a one-to-five scale is easier for audiences to complete and for researchers to summarize. One can use the first to collect in-depth data occasionally and the latter more frequently, allowing both to be useful sources of information.

Initially, as a rule of thumb, the practitioner researcher asks two basic questions as data collection methods and tools are determined:

1. Which data sources are probably the most useful in order to best answer the study questions? (Will colleagues, clients, support staff, or even outsiders have the best information?)

2. Which instruments or procedures can be used with the least intrusion? (Are observations best, or will questionnaires be better? Perhaps interviews are better yet.)

One seldom-used approach that offers insight into practitioner work is called stimulated recall. The idea is this: during **stimulated recall (S-R)** the interviewer makes notes about the practitioner's decisions during work, then stimulates the practitioner's recall about each decision and asks why it was made. This technique is particularly appropriate for such professionals as teachers, counselors, and community organizers who work in hectic interactive environments with audiences. It allows professionals to carefully review their work-related decision making but does not interrupt the work process. Also, it can offer a way to discover decision areas of focus for additional practitioner research. Shavelson and Stern (1981) explained this idea as an approach that demands thorough and deep reflections on the part of the practitioner by studying audio- or videotapes of practice, followed by a question-and-answer session in which practitioners reflect on why decisions were made. The interviewer is ordinarily a colleague who, along with the interviewee, has read about and discussed how the stimulated recall technique is applied.

Suppose that a social worker wanted to find out more about how she makes decisions during sessions with clients. The social worker would request a colleague to assist, make an audiotape of a session with a client, and then follow the guidelines below to gather insight into her professional decision making.

1. The colleague assistant (CA) carefully listens to the tape, writing down anything that even remotely sounds like a decision the social worker (SW) made, either in a planned way or "on the run." Tape recorder counter numbers are used to catalog where in the session the decision occurred if review is needed.

2. The SW listens to the tape to refresh her memory about the client session.

3. The CA and the SW review the purpose of S-R before beginning the process:

    a. The CA and the SW are primarily interested in decisions made that seem important, and in why each decision may have been made if the SW knows or can puzzle it out.

    b. Some decisions could be typical and even planned for, whereas others may be made spontaneously during the client session.

    c. To begin the S-R process and for each succeeding section of the taped client session, the SW first attempts to identify and give reasons for each decision she hears, keeping in mind that nothing should be considered too unimportant to address.

    d. The CA then follows up in each segment by reminding the SW of decisions she did not address (hence, S-R), asking for reasons behind them.

    e. The SW is reminded that it is altogether reasonable that she does not know why any number of decisions were made, but it is useful to know about these and whether they are important enough to reflect on for future sessions.

4. The SW and CA now listen to a beginning segment of the taped client session, keeping it to a minute or two unless there are very few decisions made. (This S-R session should be tape-recorded so that the SW can review the discussion for future practitioner planning and action.)

5. The SW now comments on decisions and possible reasons, and then the CA asks for clarification or stimulates the recall of the SW by pointing out decisions.

6. The process is repeated as time and energy allow, but most who experience S-R are surprised by how little is covered due to the volume of decisions that occur in most practitioner work. Teachers have found that reflecting on fifteen to twenty minutes of the taped teaching session requires up to ninety minutes of S-R (Lapan, 1986).

7. The SW is now on her own to decide what changes to make as a result of the S-R experience using the rich data she has gained, and she can review the taped S-R interview as needed.

Table 12.3, which shows a small excerpt from an actual S-R interview with a well-respected teacher reflecting on her decisions, can offer a clearer idea about how S-R works.

Table 12.3 Example of an Actual Stimulated Recall Interview

Interviewer:	*Can you talk to me a bit about what was going on so far?*
Teacher:	*It's interesting when I think back, when I asked the first question there were several hands up, but not a lot. The first person I called on is pretty immature and isn't very insightful—at least hasn't been on this novel. I figured he'd start at a pretty low level, but he'd get a chance to talk first . . . then he'd be calmed down. (Teacher noted earlier that this student was nervous about the taping as well.)*
Interviewer:	*You started the lesson by asking for their general opinion comparing the book to the movie rather than their specific opinions?*
Teacher:	*That was because they kept wanting, in informal discussion, to get off on one little thing. They'd want to talk about how the dog was hurt or what the house looked like. I wanted to keep away from that.*
Interviewer:	*Why?*
Teacher:	*Because everybody would talk about how the house was different. And that's all they would talk about is just the house. I wanted a broader viewpoint . . . what was important to look for here were the differences between the movie and the book . . .*
Interviewer:	*Lots of decisions teachers make are during preparation while others are made on the run. Which kind of decision was this?*
Teacher:	*That was prepared. I made the decision as soon as I heard them talking informally about the movie. I wanted them to focus on the bigger picture . . . get them to see a broader idea.*

Source: Lapan, 1986, p. 5.

In Table 12.3 the teacher is able to reflect on two decisions made during less than two minutes of her instruction (who to call on and what question to ask first). In this example at least, she had reasons for making these choices, but finds the first one revealing—it sounds as if she had not really reflected on it before. The teacher and the interviewer would continue this S-R process, leaving the teacher afterward to reflect and reconsider her decision making in subsequent lessons, determining to continue using some strategies while changing others. In the first twenty minutes of this lesson there were more than a hundred decisions this teacher discovered and reviewed.

This kind of self-reflection offers rich topics for the study of practice, but it is even more useful for identifying new avenues for self-study. Professionals who have engaged in the S-R process report that it is a thorough experience in reflection, but one that is both time-consuming and energy draining. They also have said that S-R's value is not readily evident, that practitioners need to go through the process to recognize its contribution. Insights gained are well worth the effort, but S-R is not a procedure that can be repeated very often. It is no surprise that it is an underused although profoundly revealing tool.

REFLECTION QUESTIONS

1. What, in your judgment, would be the best uses for S-R as a technique in practitioner research?
2. Under what circumstances might you find it useful, and when would you not use it?
3. How can S-R serve both as a strategy for practitioner self-study and as a way to discover new focus areas?

Table 12.4 provides a quick review of other methods of data collection for the practitioner researcher. Again, rereading Chapter Four of this text will provide much more detail about the selection and use of various data collection procedures and tools. There is, however, one caution that practitioner researchers should heed. As most investigators ought to know, there is an idea that has developed over the years from the field of ethnography known as the **law of the instrument**. This refers to the tendency for researchers to continually reuse a measure or protocol they really like. The motivation may be that it required considerable effort to develop initially and worked well when applied in the initial study. Indeed, it may have suited the first investigation quite well, but does it really make sense in every study? Even though requiring extra effort, it is usually best to reconsider for each study what kind of instruments and

QUALITATIVE RESEARCH

Table 12.4 Other Methods of Data Collection for Practitioner Research

Method	Advantages	Disadvantages
Audio/video	• This method is always best for reproducing actual events for later study. • It can be used repeatedly to answer different research questions.	• This method is a potential distraction for researchers and audiences. • It is time-consuming to locate data relevant to research questions.
Questionnaires	• The open-ended variety is particularly useful in revealing feedback from a broader audience base.	• Questionnaires can be labor-intensive to summarize and review.
Live observations	• Live observations are useful in collecting fresh data if observers know what to look for.	• Observer presence can disrupt the normal flow of events. • If data are missed, these cannot be recaptured.
Interviews	• Interviews can be the most powerful tool in gaining insights in that audiences recount experiences and reactions in ways they are not likely to record on questionnaires or other tools.	• Interviews are very time-consuming and require more expertise from interviewers than most appreciate.
Journals	• Journals are a realistic way to keep track of reactions to events during practice before time erodes memories.	• The recorded information may not be relevant to research questions.
Logs	• Logs can be used to collect supplemental information about attendance, participation, and time frames.	• Logs usually lack depth or context.

procedures make the most sense when linked to the study's set of research questions.

Structure for Practitioner Research

Most of the qualitative research approaches included in this text are described for those who may never design and conduct their own research. This chapter, however, as an exception to that theme, encourages professionals to engage in a kind of research that is both relevant and effective in regard to reflective practice and the promise of improvement. As noted earlier, the best-performing professionals are those who examine their work through careful and deliberate reflection and reformulate how to proceed even more successfully as a result (Schön, 1983). Kemmis (2009) describes this reformation and self-reflection as a "reversal of consciousness" (p. 465) that leads to a deepened self-awareness and self-presence in one's daily work that encourages ongoing inspection and reflection.

There are, of course, many aspects or areas that can be chosen for examination in applying practitioner research. In initiating a study, one important principle to follow is *to focus on one's own behavior and performance in the workplace*. All too often those who begin this kind of research readily shine the investigative light on others, perhaps observing clients in group therapy or examining student learning after particularly important lessons. Although clients, students, patients, and other audiences are vital data sources for practitioner research studies, it is the lawyer, nurse, social worker, counselor, teacher, or physician who most influences these audiences and who should be the primary study focus.

The practitioner researcher should begin by selecting an issue or topic of interest, one that is important enough to spend valuable time and energy investigating. But, as emphasized earlier in the chapter, an important second principle is to *start with something*. It is far too tempting, given the feeling of risk associated with self-study, to contemplate rather than act. One's selection of a focus may not be the most important element of practice, but it gets the research under way. Experiencing the process at the early stages is more important than the actual focus itself. This experience increases a professional's grasp of how this kind of research operates and will sharpen the researcher's ability to improve in choosing focus areas as the cycles unfold. It is also reasonable that the practitioner researcher may change the focus or at least adjust its definition before or during the planning or other phases of the research. As an overview of this methodology, some general guidelines and suggestions in Exhibit 12.2 will be useful reference points during all phases of the study.

REFLECTION QUESTIONS

1. What do you think the term *culture of inquiry* means as it relates to practitioner research?
2. Why might practitioner researchers want to use qualitative data in their studies?
3. Why would practitioner researchers want to use quantitative data?

EXHIBIT 12.2
GUIDELINES AND SUGGESTIONS FOR A PRACTITIONER RESEARCH STUDY

Starting the Research
- Begin small by examining one or two aspects at a time to maintain control over the move-testing, keeping track of how the new idea or ideas work or have influenced results.

Planning and Organizing
- Use tight cycles whereby each focus, plan, action, observation, and finding sequence can influence the next cycle (spiraled cycle) as immediately as possible (this will vary by profession, with some cycles repeating from day to day and others repeating weekly or monthly).

Focusing and Refocusing
- Make decisions during or after each cycle about the wisdom of pursuing the same issue or moving on to a different focus area.

Conducting Participatory Inquiry
- Involve colleagues, if at all possible, to increase the quality of ideas and create the potential for communities of reflection, learning, and improvement.
- Involve audiences (assistants, clients, patients, patrons, students) by sharing the purposes of conducting practitioner research; encourage their contribution to planning as a way of modeling a culture of inquiry.
- Involve audiences as important sources of data and useful sounding boards for sharing results (another way of creating a culture of inquiry and a useful check on the authenticity of results).
- Encourage colleagues to assist in entire cycles and to select their own focus areas for investigation.

Protecting Autonomy
- Maintain control over the practitioner research efforts even when conducting institutionally themed investigations (managers or outside academics may be tempted to offer assistance or possibly take some control of the effort).

> **Pursuing Complexity**
>
> - Explore areas of interest that are ever more complex but that continue to be relevant to each practitioner's everyday world.
>
> - If ever in doubt, emphasize qualitative over quantitative data, because more complete explanations are ordinarily required to understand the complexities of practice and are almost always more useful in seeking deeper meaning for reflection on and revision of practice.

Trusting Practitioner Research Results

It has been effectively communicated over the years that all research is really a kind of argument for truth and meaning. The practitioner researcher wants to know if study findings are a good representation of what is happening concerning his practice. This idea is often referred to in terms of **study validity**, a concept associated with all three traditions of research introduced earlier: technical or instrumental, interpretive or critical, and practical. In the case of practical or practitioner research, many ideas about what makes studies valid are similar to those of most interpretive or critical approaches. The following is a set of questions the practitioner researcher should answer to make a convincing argument that the results found are relatively trustworthy.

- Are the researcher's biases and other preformed expectations transparently known and therefore recognized for their potential influence on any findings?

- How natural and real do the findings appear in representing how things usually transpire in the work setting?

- Are the findings complete enough to be fully representative of the practice under study?

- Are the findings really meaningful to the professional in a way that makes them useful for change and improvement?

As practitioners move through this research process and gain more confidence and experience, more involved and complex practitioner research designs are possible. When professionals are ready to conduct these studies, additional study validity issues may be addressed as well. These are two additional validity questions for these advanced investigations:

- Were results confirmed by audiences by asking members if the findings made sense in their experience (called **member checking**)?
- Did using more than one source for data and more than one method of collecting the data (called **triangulation**) confirm results?

A final test of any set of research findings should be the extent to which it is consistent with the professional's knowledge of her practice and the profession. Although profoundly underappreciated as producers of research, professionals know considerably more than outside researchers about good practice and what should be done given the overwhelming number of varied situations in which they must make decisions in the moment. Schön (1983) contends, for example, that professionals are "able to describe deviations from the norm in their area of expertise . . . without describing the norm itself. . . . [T]hey can spontaneously perform tasks which they are unaware of having learned or be able to express" (quoted in House & Lapan, 1988, p. 75). This is a kind of tacit knowing that effective professionals already have but are often unable to explain. Yet they can apply this knowledge to their own practice by solving problems in their everyday world. Further, practitioners should take full advantage of this tacit knowledge or "knowing-in-action" when judging the quality of their own practitioner research findings. While testing their results against the list of validity checks presented earlier, in the final analysis professionals in the process of self-reflection should ask the following question: Does this fit with what I know about my work?

REFLECTION QUESTION

1. What is your definition of "knowledge of the profession"?

Summary

Practitioner action research, an idea introduced by Lewin in the 1940s, was first used by community groups to address such important social problems as racism and poverty. In addition to its use in social action, practitioner action research has since been applied using traditional technical and practical reasoning approaches as a way for practitioners to conduct their own research without outside supervision or control.

One model adapted from Lewin's earlier work (1948) that practitioners can follow includes focusing, planning, acting, observing, reflecting, revising, and then refocusing (Kemmis & McTaggart, 1982). This research approach is characterized by practitioner self-reflection, short turnaround schedules, a focus on real-life work-related topics, and practitioner autonomy. Practitioner researchers collect data from everyday practice for reflection, pursuing subsequent studies by trying out new strategies based on the previous research. In addition, they can test the validity of their findings against their own explicated biases, determining how realistic and useful the results are and judging the findings in terms of how well these correspond to their own professional knowledge as practitioners.

Key Terms

acting, 299
action research, 292
critical social action, 296
deficit orientation, 305
focusing, 298
interpretive or critical traditions, 296
law of the instrument, 311
member checking, 316
move-testing, 294
observing, 299

participatory action research, 292
planning, 298
practical reasoning, 297
practitioner action research, 292
practitioner research, 298
practitioner self-reflection, 298
reflecting, 304
refocusing, 299

revising, 299
spiral or spiraled cycle, 301
stimulated recall (S-R), 308
study validity, 315
technical or instrumental transfer, 295
traditional researchers, 293
triangulation, 316

Further Readings and Resources

Suggested Practitioner Action Research Studies

Luck, L., & Webb, L. (2009). School counselor action research: A case example. *Professional School Counseling.* http://findarticles.com/p/articles/mi_m0KOC/is_6_12/ai_n35574390/.

This is a good example of a traditional positivist application of practitioner action research that emphasizes quantitative data and is conducted over a three-year period.

Reed. J. (2006). Using action research in nursing practice with older people: Democratizing knowledge. *Journal of Clinical Nursing, 8,* 1064–1067. www.ncbi.nlm.nih.gov/pubmed/15840074.
This is a revealing application of practitioner action research in health care, with attention paid to the challenges of conducting studies in health care settings.

Other Suggested Readings

Berliner, D. C. (2009). Research, policy, and practice: The great disconnect. In S. D. Lapan & M. T. Quartaroli (Eds.), *Research essentials: An introduction to designs and practices* (pp. 295–313). San Francisco: Jossey-Bass.
This book chapter provides an excellent rationale for the use of practitioner research over traditional forms of study.

Coghlan, D., & Brannick, T. (2009). *Doing action research in your own organization* (3rd ed.). Thousand Oaks, CA: Sage.
This resource is often used by those conducting practitioner research in the health care, community, and education fields.

Kemmis, S., & McTaggart, R. (Eds.). (1988). *The action research planner* (3rd ed.). Geelong, Victoria, Australia: Deakin University Press.
This book is considered one of the best sources for applying practitioner research to professional practice. It includes rationales and specific guidelines for professionals to follow.

Kemmis, S., & McTaggart, R. (2006). Participative action research: Communicative action and the public sphere. In N. K. Denzin & Y. L. Lincoln (Eds.), *Handbook of qualitative research* (3rd ed., pp. 559–603). Thousand Oaks, CA: Sage.
Authored by the recognized experts in the field, this chapter is arguably one of the most thorough treatments of practitioner research and addresses issues of politics, ethics, and professional involvement.

Parkin, P. L. (2009). *Managing change in healthcare: Using action research.* Thousand Oaks, CA: Sage.
This book is a refreshing application of practitioner research designs and strategies for individuals and teams of professionals related to the patient-service interface.

Organizations and Web Sites

American Educational Research Association—Action Research Special Interest Group (SIG #2) (www.aera.net/Default.aspx?menu_id=368&id=4718)

According to the group's stated purpose, this SIG "builds community among those who are engaged in action research and those who teach others to do action research. This is accomplished through dialog about professional development strategies, educational practices and theory, and methods of action research."

Action Research Electronic Reader (www.scu.edu.au/schools/gcm/ar/arr/arow/default.html)
This source offers study reports of practitioner research across many fields, including health care and business; it also supplies information about conducting studies.

Action Research Network (http://actionresearch.altec.org/)
The Action Research Network provides very good, no-cost access, especially for teachers and professors engaging their students in practitioner research assignments.

Center for Action Research in Professional Practice (CARPP) (www.bath.ac.uk/carpp)
This Web site offers guidance in conducting practitioner research studies and includes links to other sites.

Collaborative Action Research Network (CARN) (www.did.stu.mmu.ac.uk/carnnew/)
Founded in 1976 in order to continue the development work of the Ford Teaching Project in U.K. primary and secondary schools, CARN has grown to become an international network. It draws its members from educational, health care, social care, commercial, and public services settings.

Voices from the Field (www.alliance.brown.edu/pubs/voices/3qrt1999/actref.shtml)
This Web site offers stories from practitioners' own research and includes links to other sites.

CHAPTER 13

PROGRAM EVALUATION

MaryLynn T. Quartaroli

Key Ideas

- Evaluations, like case studies, systematically scrutinize programs, products, personnel, materials, or policies, with the additional intention to determine their value, merit, or worth.

- Evaluators select the appropriate approach for specific evaluations from a multitude of methodological options, based on the underlying perspectives, assumptions, and needs of a program's stakeholders and audience.

- An extensive set of professional performance standards and principles guides the planning, implementation, and reporting of evaluation findings.

- Evaluators use a program description or a logic model to determine the possible criteria on which to focus an evaluation.

- Often in collaboration with program stakeholders, evaluators select standards by which to measure the quality or merit of the criteria under scrutiny.

- Trusting evaluation reports depends on the quality of the evaluation processes, the competence of the evaluators, and the use of such strategies as member checking and triangulation.

Have you ever read a movie or music review? Looked for information comparing products (for example, computers, cameras, or cars) or services (for example, computer repairs, mechanics, or extended warranties) on the Internet on sites like PCWorld or Yelp? Received a grade or comments on your academic, athletic, or artistic performance? Given advice to a friend about college or career choices? If so, you have been involved in an evaluation, either as an interested member of the **audience** (reading reviews or comparison information) or as a **stakeholder** (receiving a grade or giving advice) who has a vested interest in the results. But there is a fundamental difference between a personal opinion and an evaluation: an opinion is a belief or judgment that is ordinarily unsubstantiated by evidence or proof, whereas evaluations depend on systematic and disciplined procedures for data collection, analysis, and reporting conclusions.

What Is Evaluation?

Evaluation can be broadly defined as a systematic examination of programs, personnel, products, materials, or policies to determine their merit, worth, or value (Lapan, 2004; Scriven, 1991). Legislative bodies, foundations, and other funding agencies are increasingly demanding information on how their funds are used and what results can be attributed to those expenditures. Specifically, in this chapter I will be emphasizing evaluations of programs; a **program** is a planned set of expectations, procedures, and activities to produce specific outcomes or results. Examples of programs include drug treatment interventions, natural disaster relief efforts, adult literacy outreach, or get-out-the-vote campaigns.

In the current economic and political climate, programs are expected to operate effectively and efficiently. "Although accountability will continue to be an important purpose for program evaluation, the major goal should be to improve program performance, thereby giving customers and funders better value for money" (Wholey, Hatry, & Newcomer, 1994, p. 2). Stake (1967) goes further, including both program description and judgment of worth within the domain of evaluation. Stufflebeam (2001) concurs, defining evaluation as "a study designed and conducted to assist some audience to assess an object's merit and worth" (p. 11). Others have expanded the understanding of evaluation as having the "ultimate goal of evaluation as social betterment . . . by assisting democratic institutions to better select, oversee, improve, and make sense of social programs and policies" (Mark, Henry, & Julnes, 2000, p. 3). It should be apparent that studies done under the label of evaluation may have many different goals and present a wide variety of information to their audience.

Lapan (2004) describes many contexts and foci for evaluations, including public and private sectors; limited and broad scopes; and examinations of programs, personnel, products, materials, or policies. **Program evaluation** "emphasizes how educational and social programs are implemented, how they operate, and what effects they have" (p. 238). As Stake (1995, p. 95) notes, "All evaluation studies are case studies" that specifically examine programs to determine their merit and shortcomings. Each evaluation is thus "context specific, ongoing and formative, flexible and evolutionary, and personally and institutionally relevant" (House, 1996, p. 12).

> **REFLECTION QUESTIONS**
>
> 1. What are some programs in your discipline that could be evaluated?
> 2. What would be the purposes or goals for evaluating these programs?

Evaluation Approaches

Even a brief look at the research literature about evaluation reveals numerous options for planning and implementing a program evaluation. For the most part this diversity is the result of the context in which the evaluation takes place, the requirements of the program managers or funders, the knowledge and skill of the evaluators, and the stakeholders' preference from among evaluation perspectives discussed in the next section.

Evaluation Perspectives

Broadly, program evaluations can be viewed as framed by **utilitarian** and **intuitionist/pluralist** perspectives (House, 1980). A utilitarian approach makes judgments based on the notion of the greatest good for the greatest number of people. In contrast, an intuitionist/pluralist perspective seeks the widest representation of values from diverse populations.

Specific assumptions of the utilitarian perspective are that (1) the audience for the evaluation is a predetermined decision maker, either the managerial elite or mass consumers; (2) the evaluations rely on predetermined standards as a means of evaluating social utility of the greatest good for the greatest number; and (3) data and performance criteria relate to the total system rather than to individuals, program staff, or program recipients (Hamilton, 1977). Most utilitarian approaches rely heavily on specific mandated designs, the identification of objectives and standards, and the definition of variables in observable terms, placing an emphasis on primarily quantitative data (Gredler, 1996, p. 41).

In contrast, assumptions of the intuitionist/pluralist perspective differ as follows: (1) the audiences for the evaluation are all the individuals associated with the innovation or program, not just the managers or decision makers; (2) the role of evaluation is to reflect diverse perceptions of program worth, not to apply a uniform standard of value; and (3) the experiences of individuals associated with the program are important to understanding how a program works and what its impacts are, instead of summarizing or generalizing the data and performance criteria to the program as a whole (Gredler, 1996). "Likewise, the subjective utility of something is based on personal judgment and personal desires. Each person is the best judge of events for himself" (House, 1993, p. 56). Qualitative data play a much larger role in these evaluations.

Historical Foundations

A pioneer in the development of evaluation as a professional field, Robert Stake (1967) identified these program elements in his "countenance model" in order to capture the complexity of educational or other social programs:

1. **Program antecedents** (resources): the plans, personnel, supplies, and funds that are available to design and implement a program

2. **Program transactions** (implementation): how a program operates and functions, including its routine and nonroutine activities

3. **Program outcomes** (impacts or effects): the short- and long-term actual effects of the program's transactions, whether these are expected or unexpected

According to Stake (1967), these three elements form the organizational basis for a matrix of evaluation process which include both program description and judgment of quality. To describe a program, evaluators gather data to determine the amount of congruency between a program's *intended* and *observed* antecedents, transactions, and outcomes, while making note of any discrepancies. Evaluators also identify standards of excellence for use in making judgments about a program's elements (also see the Selecting Standards section of this chapter). To implement an evaluation examining all of these aspects of a program can be an expensive and time-consuming undertaking; a program's managers, funders, or sometimes both groups may choose to request an evaluation that places a priority on one or more of these elements as needed for their purpose.

For example, an evaluation of a teen pregnancy prevention program might assess the plans, personnel, and funds available to design and implement the program (its antecedents) to determine if the community has sufficient resources available. Another evaluation might focus on whether that program is being implemented as planned (its transactions): Are the activities (such as public information events and free condom distributions) being planned and carried out in the most effective and logical locations? Alternatively, evaluators could focus on whether or not teens are using the program's activities as intended and on the rates of teen pregnancies over time (its outcomes).

Over the past thirty-five years, Daniel Stufflebeam and his colleagues at the Western Michigan University Evaluation Center have developed another framework for guiding evaluations of programs, projects, personnel, products, institutions, and systems, particularly those aimed at effecting long-term, sustainable improvements—the **CIPP Evaluation Model** (Stufflebeam, 2003). The name is an acronym for the fundamental components of the model, to address the following questions:

- **C**ontext: What needs to be done? What assets are there? What needs or problems can be addressed by the program? What are the political dynamics in this setting?

- **I**nput: How should it be done? What are the competing strategies, work plans, and budgets of the selected program approach?

- **P**rocess: Is it being done? How well is the program implementing its strategies and work plans?

- **P**roduct: Did it succeed? Did the program have an impact on its targeted recipients? What are the quality and significance of the program's outcomes? To what extent are the program's contributions successfully continued over time? How successfully can the program be adapted and applied elsewhere?

More information about the CIPP Model is available from the Evaluation Center Web site listed among the resources at the end of the chapter.

This model has been used effectively for a wide range of program evaluations in such areas as education, transition to work, training and personnel development, welfare reform, nonprofit organization services, community development, community-based youth programs, and community foundations. One of these evaluations, of the Consuelo Foundation's Ke Aka Hoʻona self-help housing and community development program, will serve as the representative study in this chapter.

Many other evaluation framework options are evident in a search of the research literature, such as goal-free evaluations, cost-benefit analyses, empowerment evaluations, needs assessments, and so forth. These do not represent rigid methodologies, but rather idealized approaches (House, 1980). Because the various evaluations are developed to address different needs, and because each evaluation is unique, the evaluator must identify what approach is useful in a specific situation. As Worthen, Sanders, and Fitzpatrick (1997, p. 68) note,

> The purist view that looks noble in print yields to practical pressures demanding that the evaluator use appropriate methods based on an epistemology that is right *for that evaluation,* or even multiple methods based on alternative epistemologies within the same evaluation.

Thus strict adherence to only one approach is unlikely. Evaluators tend to be eclectic in using these models, choosing and combining concepts from the various approaches to fit the particular situation. Recognizing that there are important differences in the contexts and activities of individual social services and educational programs, evaluators must tailor their approach to meet the needs of the stakeholders (Fitzpatrick, Sanders, & Worthen, 2003).

REFLECTION QUESTIONS

1. Considering the programs that you previously identified for evaluation, what perspective (utilitarian or intuitionist/pluralist) would be most appropriate to use? Why?
2. When should each component of the program be evaluated? Why?

Guiding Principles for Evaluators

Whichever approach fits a particular program, designing and implementing a high-quality evaluation is critically important to trusting the findings and making appropriate decisions. In 2004 the American Evaluation Association (AEA), the premier international organization of professional evaluators, developed a set of five guiding principles to promote ethical practice in the evaluation of programs, products, personnel, materials, and policies. As described in Table 13.1, these principles, with their corresponding standards, serve as a checklist for ensuring high-quality evaluation research.

As is evident from these principles, evaluators must embody a great number of technical skills, dispositions, and ethical values to work collaboratively with their clients to design and execute an evaluation that is valid, just, and useful.

Table 13.1 Guiding Principles for Evaluators

Principle	Standards
Systematic inquiry: Evaluators conduct systematic, data-based inquiries.	Ensure that clients adhere to the highest technical standards appropriate to the methods they use.
	Explore with clients the shortcomings and strengths of evaluation questions and approaches.
	Communicate the approaches, methods, and limitations of the evaluation accurately and in sufficient detail to allow others to understand, interpret, and critique their work.
Competence: Evaluators provide competent performance to stakeholders.	Ensure that the evaluation team collectively possesses the education, abilities, skills, and experience appropriate to the evaluation.
	Ensure that the evaluation team collectively demonstrates cultural competence and uses appropriate evaluation strategies and skills to work with culturally different groups.
	Practice within the limits of their competence, decline to conduct evaluations that fall substantially outside those limits, and make clear any limitations on the evaluation that might result if declining is not feasible.
	Seek to maintain and improve their competencies in order to provide the highest level of performance in their evaluations.
Integrity and honesty: Evaluators display honesty and integrity in their own behavior, and they attempt to ensure the honesty and integrity of the entire evaluation process.	Negotiate honestly with clients and relevant stakeholders concerning the costs, tasks, limitations of methodology, scope of results, and uses of data.
	Disclose any roles or relationships that might pose a real or apparent conflict of interest prior to accepting an assignment.
	Record and report all changes to the original negotiated project plans, and the reasons for them, including any possible impacts that could result.
	Be explicit about their own, their clients', and other stakeholders' interests and values related to the evaluation.
	Represent accurately their procedures, data, and findings, and attempt to prevent or correct misuse of their work by others.
	Work to resolve any concerns related to procedures or activities likely to produce misleading evaluative information, decline to conduct the evaluation if concerns cannot be resolved, and consult colleagues or relevant stakeholders about other ways to proceed if declining is not feasible.
	Disclose all sources of financial support for an evaluation, and the source of the request for the evaluation.

(Continued)

Table 13.1 (*Continued*)

Principle	Standards
Respect for people: Evaluators respect the security, dignity, and self-worth of respondents, program participants, clients, and other stakeholders.	Seek a comprehensive understanding of the contextual elements of the evaluation. Abide by current professional ethics, standards, and regulations concerning confidentiality, informed consent, and potential risks or harms to participants. Seek to maximize the benefits and reduce any unnecessary harm that might occur from an evaluation and carefully judge when the benefits from the evaluation or procedure should be foregone because of potential risks. Conduct the evaluation and communicate its results in a way that respects stakeholders' dignity and self-worth. Foster social equity in evaluation, when feasible, so that those who give to the evaluation may benefit in return. Understand, respect, and take into account differences among stakeholders, such as culture, religion, disability, age, sexual orientation, and ethnicity.
Responsibilities for general and public welfare: Evaluations articulate and take into account the diversity of general and public interests and values.	Include relevant perspectives and interests of the full range of stakeholders. Consider not only immediate operations and outcomes of the evaluation but also the broad assumptions, implications, and potential side effects. Allow stakeholders access to, and actively disseminate, evaluative information, and present evaluation results in understandable forms that respect people and honor promises of confidentiality. Maintain a balance between client and other stakeholder needs and interests. Take into account the public interest and good, going beyond analysis of particular stakeholder interests to consider the welfare of society as a whole.

Source: Adapted from AEA, 2004.

REFLECTION QUESTIONS

1. Select one standard from each of the five principles. What scale or evidence could you use to determine how well an evaluator has met each standard?
2. Under what conditions might evaluators find living up to these principles and standards problematic? How should they negotiate or resolve these conflicts?

Evaluation Design

As mentioned previously, there is no single approach to designing and conducting evaluations. Each is tailored to a specific program's particular context, mandates, and potential uses. "Evaluations should be based on the content, purpose, and outcomes of the program, rather than being driven by data collection methodologies" (Lapan, 2004, p. 239). As such, evaluation research uses multiple sources and methods of data collection and analysis. These may generate both quantitative and qualitative data. In any case, evaluators should design and carry out studies that meet the AEA (2004) principles and standards (see Table 13.1) for ensuring high-quality evaluations.

As compared to case study research, which focuses either on thorough descriptions of programs or on building and validating theories from multiple case studies (see Chapter Ten), the hallmark of an evaluation is the determination of criteria for judging the quality of a program, with standards of performance clearly explained. In his article with theater critic Charles Isherwood, Alastair Macaulay, the chief dance critic for the *New York Times,* explains,

> We're critics: our first task is not to determine what big-theater audiences will like but what we think is good and why. We're critics because we have criteria and we use them: different criteria on some occasions, but serious criteria to us. Sometimes we're both going to object strongly to shows that we can see are very popular indeed; sometimes we're both going to enthuse passionately about productions that leave most people cold. (Isherwood & Macaulay, 2010, p. C1)

This evaluation process is different from informal reviews and critiques in that the criteria and standards are predetermined, unlike an ad hoc critique: "I just like this show, and I don't like this other one."

Selecting Criteria to Study

Central to the selection of criteria for an evaluation are two questions: What is the purpose of the evaluation? and Who needs to know the information provided? A source to identify possible criteria for a program evaluation is often the program's logic model or detailed description.

Whether formalized into a written document or implied by program goals, objectives, activities, and outcomes, a **logic model** provides a graphic representation for understanding how a program works (see Chapter Fourteen for one example). This includes the theory and assumptions that underlie the program. A logic model is "a systematic and visual way to present and share your understanding of the relationships among the resources you have to operate your program, the activities you plan, and the changes or results you hope to achieve" (W. K. Kellogg Foundation, 2004, p. 1). More and more funding agencies, including private foundations and government offices, require a logic model as part of a grant proposal.

According to the W. K. Kellogg Foundation (2004), at its most basic level a logic model includes five components:

1. *Resources and inputs*—human, financial, organizational, and community

2. *Activities*—processes, tools, events, technology, actions, and interventions

3. *Outputs*—products of the activities, including types, levels, and targets of services delivered by the program

4. *Outcomes*—changes in program participants' behavior, knowledge, skills, status, and level of functions, both short-term (within 1 to 3 years) and long-term (within 7 to 10 years)

5. *Impact*—fundamental intended or unintended change in organizations, communities, or systems as a result of program activities over the long term

This is most commonly represented as a simple linear sequence (see Figure 13.1), although it is also possible to create much more complex logic models that include theories of change.

An evaluator uses a logic model to assist stakeholders in determining the criteria that are critical to evaluate a program's design, implementation, and results. Examples of criteria from an unemployment support services program logic model might include financial assets and program staff (resources), daily program operating procedures (activities), information events or training sessions delivered (outputs), participants' employment status and job performance (outcomes), and unemployment rate trends in the community (impact).

If no written logic model exists, evaluators, with the stakeholders, first write a detailed program description that provides essentially the same information. By examining program documents and talking to the program stakeholders, evaluators identify a program's antecedents, intended transactions, and expected outcomes and impact. Often these interactions with the program stakeholders can also result in the creation of a program logic model.

Stufflebeam and his associates at the Evaluation Center of Western Michigan University conducted an evaluation of the Consuelo Foundation's Ke Aka

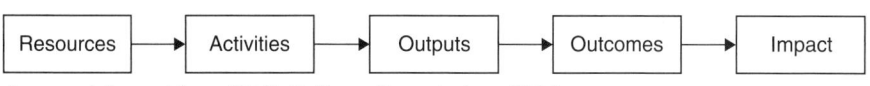

FIGURE 13.1 Simple Logic Model

Resources → Activities → Outputs → Outcomes → Impact

Source: Adapted from W. K. Kellogg Foundation, 2004.

Hoʻona project between 1994 and 2001. This initiative was a self-help housing project in which low-income families worked together, under the supervision of a licensed contractor, to construct their own homes in the Honolulu (Hawaiʻi) County community of Waiʻanae. Their evaluation included a report on the program's antecedents, a second report on its implementation, and a third report on the project's results (Stufflebeam, Gullickson, & Wingate, 2002). These were the three goals for the project (p. 22):

1. Build a community of low-income working families with children who commit to live in and help sustain a nurturing neighborhood free from violence and substance abuse and devoted to helping others.

2. Increase Waiʻanae's supply of affordable housing

3. Develop a sound approach to values-based, self-help housing and community development

In this section of the chapter I will use the third report to provide examples of designing and implementing an evaluation study. All of the evaluation reports for this program are available from the Evaluation Center Web site, listed at the end of the chapter. Exhibit 13.1 identifies the criteria selected for the evaluation of the Ke Aka Hoʻona project.

Forming Study Questions

Once the criteria for the evaluation project are identified, the development of specific study questions follows. These may be predetermined, such as when a program's source of funding requires answers to specific questions. These most likely will emphasize accountability: the effectiveness (in terms of costs, benefits, and services) and the impacts of the program (for example, improved student achievement scores, reduction in the rate of recidivism for paroled prisoners, increased voter turnout for primary elections). The purpose of these types of research questions is **summative**, used for making judgments after the

> **EXHIBIT 13.1**
>
> **EVALUATION CRITERIA FOR THE KE AKA HO'ONA PROJECT**
>
> The use of the CIPP Evaluation Model provided a comprehensive assessment of the Ke Aka Ho'ona project for the Consuelo Foundation's board of directors and other stakeholders. The model includes assessing the
>
> 1. *Context,* the nature, extent, and criticality of beneficiaries' needs and assets and pertinent environmental forces (adherence to Foundation values and relevance to beneficiaries)
>
> 2. *Input,* including the responsiveness and strength of project plans and resources (state-of-the-art character, feasibility)
>
> 3. *Process,* involving the appropriateness and adequacy of project operations (responsiveness, efficiency, quality)
>
> 4. *Product,* meaning the extent, desirability, and significance of intended and unintended outcomes (viability, adaptability, significance)
>
> *Source:* Stufflebeam et al., 2002, p. 65.

program is complete for the benefit of an external audience or decision maker (Scriven, 1991).

Other program stakeholders, including managers, staff, and sometimes recipients, may choose to ask questions that determine information for improving the program, often called **formative** evaluations. Patton (1997, p. 68) provides these examples of formative questions:

- What are the program's strengths and weaknesses?
- To what extent are participants progressing toward the desired outcomes?
- What is happening that wasn't expected?
- How are clients and staff interacting?
- What are staff and participant perceptions about the program?
- Where can efficiencies be realized?

Table 13.2 Evaluation Questions for the Ke Aka Hoʻona Project

Context		To what extent was the project targeted to important community and beneficiary needs?
Input		To what extent were the project's structure and procedural resource plans consistent with Foundation values, state of the art, feasible, and sufficiently powerful to address the targeted needs?
Process		To what extent were the project's operations consistent with plans, responsibly conducted, and effective in addressed beneficiaries' needs?
Product	Impact	What beneficiaries were *reached,* and to what extent were they the targeted beneficiaries?
	Effectiveness	To what extent did the project *meet* the needs of the involved beneficiaries?
	Sustainability	To what extent was the project institutionalized in order to sustain its successful implementation?
	Transportability	To what extent could or has the project been successfully adapted and applied elsewhere?

Source: Stufflebeam et al., 2002, p. 66.

For a long-term program such as the Ke Aka Hoʻona project, over time both formative and summative evaluations provided feedback during the program to help the Consuelo Foundation leaders and staff strengthen project plans and operations. The final summative report appraises what was done and accomplished. The Evaluation Center used the CIPP Evaluation Model to carry out this long-term study. The main questions that guided the study are shown in Table 13.2.

Selecting Standards

Once the specific criteria for the evaluation are identified, clearly identifying its purpose and audiences, and the questions are developed, evaluators determine appropriate standards by which to measure program quality, value, or success. These may be predetermined by the program's funding agency or developed in collaboration with one or more of the program's stakeholders. The following are the standards for the CIPP evaluation of the Ke Aka Hoʻona project (Stufflebeam et al., 2002, p. 66):

- Positive answers to the evaluation questions would rate high on merit, worth, and significance.

- Negative findings to any of the evaluation questions indicate areas of deficiency, diminishing judgments of program soundness and quality, and possibly discrediting the project entirely.

- Failure to meet the assessed needs of the targeted beneficiaries indicates overall failure of the project.

Data Collection

Evaluations can and should generate both quantitative and qualitative data by incorporating multiple types of **instruments** (data collection tools) and multiple sources of information. Just as in case studies (see Chapter Ten) and the other research methodologies in this text, the questions determine which instruments (such as tests, questionnaires, observations, or interviews) should be carefully selected, adapted, or developed to generate useful and valid data (see Chapter Four).

Similarly, the study questions also imply the best sources of data (such as documents, program staff, or recipients of services). Unlike quantitative methodologies, evaluations do not usually incorporate **random sampling** (also called probability sampling) to select a small group of study participants, because evaluators are not trying to generalize results as representative of a specific population. Rather, evaluators are more concerned with maximizing the representativeness of information. They therefore seek out people who can best answer each kind of question; this is known as **purposeful (or purposive) sampling**. This process is similar to collecting data in ethnography (see Chapter Seven) and case study research (see Chapter Ten), for which **key informants** who have the most information are actively sought. It is also most desirable to seek out alternative views and incorporate these into the results of the evaluation.

For the Ke Aka Hoʻona project, multiple methods were used to gather data; each part of the CIPP Evaluation Model incorporated at least three different data collection methods, as is evident in Table 13.3.

Data Analysis

Evaluators use the same data analysis strategies as other researchers. Because of the multiple types of data collected, evaluators must develop skills in coding and synthesizing qualitative data (see Chapter Three) and in descriptive and inferential statistics for quantitative data. I refer you to statistical texts or other quantitative research resources (such as Lapan & Quartaroli, 2009, or the

Table 13.3 Data Collection Methods for CIPP Evaluation of the Ke Aka Ho'ona Project

	Context	Input	Process	Impact	Effectiveness	Sustainability	Transportability
Environmental Analysis	✓						
Program Profile		✓	✓				
Traveling Observer			✓	✓	✓	✓	
Case Studies			✓	✓	✓	✓	
Stakeholder Interviews	✓		✓	✓	✓	✓	✓
Goal-Free Evaluation			✓	✓	✓		
Task Reports and Feedback	✓	✓	✓	✓	✓	✓	✓
Synthesis and Final Report	✓	✓	✓	✓	✓	✓	✓

Source: Stufflebeam et al., 2002, p. 67.

Research Methods Knowledge Base online at www.socialresearchmethods.net/kb/) for further information.

According to Patton (1997), there are four distinct processes involved in making sense of evaluation findings. The first task is to organize the data into a format that makes evident any basic patterns or relationships. For example, evaluators can create concept maps, tables, frequency diagrams, and flow charts to illustrate and summarize the data. Once this is accomplished, the evaluators must make interpretations of the data: "What do the results mean? What's the significance of the findings? . . . What are possible explanations of these results?" (p. 307). Next, the key component of evaluation is addressed: What is the merit, value, or worth of the program? In what ways are the results positive, and in what ways are the results negative? How do the results compare to the standards selected for the evaluation? A final step is likely to be included, although it is not mandatory: What action or actions should be taken in regard to the program? Often these are presented as a list of recommendations.

REFLECTION QUESTIONS

1. For the programs that you identified for evaluation, what might be important formative evaluation questions to answer? Summative questions?
2. Considering the formative and summative questions you have written, what data collection methods and sources would most likely provide the most useful and diverse data?

Reporting Study Results

Many if not most evaluation reports are submitted to the program management or funding agency without being published in the research literature. An evaluation report often includes an **executive summary**, or the summary of findings in brief. It may also articulate "recommendations for changes or . . . program elements that should be supported or receive greater emphasis" (Lapan & Haden, 2009, p. 193). The report should also provide specific details about the program, including a thorough description of the context for the evaluation and the evaluation design (data collection methods, sources, analyses, and syntheses of findings). Alternative views about the program's quality are also incorporated into the final evaluation report as part of what is often called a **minority report**.

The dissemination of findings to different stakeholders and audiences may require different formats and vocabulary. Most often the results are presented in writing, but other visual formats (such as multimedia videos or slide shows) may be appropriate, depending on each audience's expectations, levels of understanding, and language competencies.

Throughout the Ke Aka Hoʻona project (see Table 13.3) the evaluation team held feedback workshops with project leaders and staff, as well as with other stakeholders invited by the Consuelo Foundation, to go over draft reports. The workshop participants discussed the findings, identified areas of ambiguity and inaccuracy, and updated evaluation plans. A similar process occurred with the draft composite report before it was finalized in 2002.

Believing Evaluation Findings

A key concept in conducting and using evaluations is that of validity. In scientific research, **validity** is a benchmark of the rigor and truthfulness of findings. According to Shadish (1995, p. 421),

> Validity is a property of knowledge, not methods. No matter whether the knowledge comes from an ethnography or an experiment, we may still ask the same kind of questions about the ways in which that knowledge is valid. . . . A hammer does not guarantee successful nailing, successful nailing does not require a hammer, and the validity of the claim [to have nailed two boards together] is in principle separate from which tool was used. The same is true of methods in the social behavioral sciences.

House (1980) extends a very broad meaning to validity in evaluation as "worthiness of being recognized" (p. 249); he further suggests that program evaluations for external audiences must meet the criteria of being "true, credible, and right" (p. 250). Scriven (1991) defines valid evaluations as "ones that take into account all relevant factors, given the whole context of the evaluation (particularly including the client's needs), and weight them appropriately in the synthesis process" (pp. 372–373).

The Program Evaluation and Methodology Division of the United States General Accounting Office (GAO), arguably the most influential evaluation policymaking body at the national level, endorsed the use of multiple methods of data collection and analysis to improve the quality of evaluations. The GAO manual *Designing Evaluations* (Wisler, 1991) describes "strong evaluations" as those that employ methods of analysis that are appropriate to the question, support the answer with evidence, document the assumptions, procedures, and modes of analysis, and rule out the competing evidence. . . . Neither infatuation with complexity nor statistical incantation makes an evaluation stronger. . . . That is, the strength of an evaluation has to be judged within the context of the question, the time and cost constraints, the design, the technical adequacy of the data collection and analysis, and the presentation of the findings. A strong study is technically adequate and useful—in short, it is high in quality. (pp. 15–16)

Recent preferences by government and other funding agencies for conducting randomized control group experiments as evaluations have challenged the prevailing wisdom of the GAO guidelines and most practicing evaluators. Indeed, some evaluations do involve experimental procedures; the validity and reliability of these studies would then best be judged according to the standards for the methodologies selected for use. This topic is beyond the scope of this text; I would refer you to other texts (such as Lapan & Quartaroli, 2009) or Web resources (such as the Research Methods Knowledge Base online at www.socialresearchmethods.net/kb/) for further information.

Rather than appealing to the standards of reliability, precision, and internal and external validity typical of experimental research, the truthfulness of an interpretation of qualitative data is based on the standards consistent with the perspectives and criteria of the methodologies discussed in the other chapters in this text. In addition to noting the aforementioned traditional standards, Patton (2002) also lists standards for judging the quality and **credibility** of qualitative inquiry. He suggests that credibility

> depends on three distinct but related elements: (1) rigorous methods for doing fieldwork that yield high-quality data that are systematically analyzed . . . ; (2) the credibility of the researcher, which is dependent on training, experience, track record, status . . . ; and (3) philosophical belief in the value of qualitative inquiry, that is, a fundamental appreciation of naturalistic inquiry, qualitative methods, inductive analysis, purposeful sampling, and holistic thinking. (pp. 552–553)

Methods to improve the rigor and credibility of evaluation studies include a conscious analysis of predispositions and biases; **triangulation** (open inclusion of multiple sources and types of data); and a systematic search for alternative themes, divergent patterns, rival explanations, and negative cases (Patton, 2002). "By combining multiple observers, theories, methods, and data sources, [researchers] can hope to overcome the intrinsic bias that comes from single-methods, single-observer, and single-theory studies" (Denzin, 1989b, p. 307). Review by experts, program stakeholders, study participants, and audiences may also extend this process of improving the credibility of evaluations.

Because the researcher is the instrument for data collection and analysis in many qualitative approaches, some accounting of personal experience, training, and perspective should be included in the report (Patton, 2002). House (1980) concurs that an important component of establishing the validity of an evaluation is the trustworthiness of the evaluator. A related issue is how the presence of the researcher or the fact that an evaluation is taking place may distort the findings. "Evaluators and researchers should strive to neither overestimate nor underestimate their effects but to take seriously their responsibility to describe and study what those effects are" (Patton, 2002, p. 568). Finally, because there are no simple formulas or clear-cut rules about how to do a credible, high-quality analysis, it is important for the evaluator to maintain high standards for intellectual rigor, professional integrity, and methodological competence to establish a "track record" of quality work (Patton, 2002, p. 570).

Bias in research refers to "systematic errors or a disposition to errors . . . [that are] due to a tendency to prejudge issues because of beliefs or emotions that are wrong or irrelevant" (Scriven, 1991, p. 67). The role of an evaluator is to remain impartial and to reflect the biases of the various stakeholders (House, 1980). Many scholars suggest that it is impossible to remove researcher bias from the research process under any methodological paradigm (Guba & Lincoln, 1989; House & Howe, 1999; Patton, 2002; Silverman, 2001). However, attempts to control for bias should be addressed in the study design.

The use of **external evaluations** is one way to minimize bias. Ideally these evaluations are carried out by researchers working under contract who are not affiliated directly with the program, the staff, or the funding agency. The evaluators often come from universities, consulting firms, or research organizations; they are presumed to be independent, objective, credible, and less likely to be manipulated by program administrators or pressured to present only positive findings. But there is still potential for such influence because they are under contract to the program. In addition, these contracts can be quite costly in terms of time and money. There are also limitations to outside evaluators' depth of knowledge about the program being evaluated, as they are dependent on stakeholders to fully disclose the necessary information to answer the evaluation questions.

Internal evaluations are those done by project staff members, who may be specifically designated to conduct evaluations external to the design and delivery of a program (Scriven, 1991). Many would consider an insider too biased to produce a high-quality evaluation. Internal evaluators do have a number of advantages, including knowing the program better, which helps them avoid mistakes due to ignorance; knowing the people better, which allows them to talk to these people more easily; most likely having a better understanding of the subject matter and comparable projects; having a continuous relationship with the program to facilitate implementation of the results; and costing less (Scriven).

The use of an outside, external reviewer as a "**triangulating analyst**" (Patton, 2002, p. 560) can serve as a check on internal evaluation bias. All data collected are duplicated and provided for interpretation and evaluation to this independent reviewer, who synthesizes the information. The internal evaluator then compares the results of this analyst's results, to triangulate these with her own initial interpretations. Any discrepancies are then investigated and resolved, possibly through more data collection and analysis, prior to the preparation of the final report (Lapan, 2004). This process acts to minimize interpretive bias in the analysis of the program data.

The use of **member checking** also assists in validating the results and overcoming evaluator bias. The evaluator shares preliminary evaluation findings with as many stakeholders as possible to obtain their comments and feedback; they are asked to say if these findings accurately reflect their understanding of and experiences with the program. As Lapan (2004, p. 243) explains,

> In program evaluation it is appropriate to share findings during the study, especially when participants have finished providing observations about the program. . . . By sharing preliminary findings, the evaluator is able to gauge how early results fit with the understanding of participants and sponsors . . . [and] allows others to question the findings or request clarification, thus challenging the evaluator to reveal evidence, change interpretations, or collect additional data.

REFLECTION QUESTIONS

1. For the programs that you identified for evaluation, who would be the best evaluator to plan and implement the evaluation in each case? Why?
2. What would you look for in an evaluation report to determine how trustworthy or credible the findings are?

Evaluation Use

In too many instances, all the hard work and insightful analyses done by evaluators end up in a report that is filed away, never to see the light of day again. To avoid this wasteful use of time and resources, evaluators should clarify up front the intended uses of an evaluation by its intended users. Working in collaboration with the stakeholders in the program to determine the most useful evaluation questions to be answered, followed by actively encouraging these stakeholders to participate throughout the evaluation process with design, data collection, analysis, and interpretation, as appropriate, will promote use of the evaluation findings.

In general terms, there are three primary uses or purposes for evaluation findings (Patton, 1997):

1. *Facilitating program improvements* by providing valuable information to the program providers about what is working well and what needs attention while the program is being implemented

2. *Making overall judgments* by providing data to support making an informed decision about whether or not the program should be continued

3. *Generating knowledge* by providing evidence of lessons learned in relation to best program practices, offering the opportunity for enlightenment or illumination concerning the way programs are working and how outcomes can be measured, or elaborating policy options

When the evaluators and the stakeholders agree at the outset about the primary purpose and uses for the evaluation—and write these expectations into the project contract—then the likelihood of the findings' being used is significantly increased.

Summary

In these challenging economic times, with even more emphasis placed on accountability and efficiency, program evaluation continues to grow as a profession. Some become evaluators by accident (as their jobs require more data collection and analysis); others intentionally study to develop the knowledge, skills, and dispositions necessary to produce high-quality evaluations for program stakeholders, funders, and the general public to use to make informed decisions.

Similar to case studies, evaluations systematically scrutinize programs, products, personnel, materials, or policies; however, evaluations must also include judgments of value, merit, or worth. There is no single methodology or approach used for evaluations; evaluators instead choose from many options to design a study that will answer the specific questions suggested by the purpose and intended use of the findings. All aspects of a program, its resources, activities, outputs, outcomes, and impacts, can be evaluated. Guided by an extensive set of principles and performance standards, evaluators incorporate diverse perspectives, data collection tools, and methods of analysis to measure the quality or merit of the program criteria under scrutiny. The quality and trustworthiness of the evaluation results depend on the qualifications and competencies of the evaluators, the level of involvement of program stakeholders, and the use of appropriate strategies to manage issues of bias.

Key Terms

audience, 322
bias, 339
CIPP Evaluation Model, 325
credibility, 338
evaluation, 322
executive summary, 336
external evaluations, 339
formative, 332
instruments, 334
internal evaluations, 339
intuitionist/pluralist, 323
key informants, 334
logic model, 329
member checking, 340
minority report, 336
program, 322
program antecedents, 324
program evaluation, 322
program outcomes, 324
program transactions, 324
purposeful (or purposive) sampling, 334
random sampling, 334
stakeholder, 322
summative, 331
triangulating analyst, 340
triangulation, 338
utilitarian, 323
validity, 337

Further Readings and Resources

Suggested Evaluation Study

Stufflebeam, D. L., Gullickson, A., & Wingate, L. (2002). *The spirit of Consuelo: An evaluation of Ke Aka Ho'ona*. Kalamazoo: The Evaluation Center of Western Michigan University. http://rszarf.ips.uw.edu.pl/ewalps/teksty/consuelo_eval.pdf.

This is a classic, long-term evaluation of a nonprofit foundation's self-help housing and community development program. It is designed using the CIPP Evaluation Model and presents findings of all aspects of the program: antecedents, transactions, and outcomes.

Other Suggested Readings

Fitzpatrick, J. L., Sanders, J. R., & Worthen, B. R. (2003). *Program evaluation: Alternative approaches and practical guidelines* (3rd ed.). New York: Longman.
This is a comprehensive text, providing an overview of a wide variety of evaluation approaches and practical tips on designing and implementing a successful evaluation.

Patton, M. Q. (2008). *Utilization-focused evaluation* (4th ed.). Thousand Oaks, CA: Sage.
This book provides expert, detailed advice on conducting program evaluations, including a unique utilization-focused evaluation checklist.

Scriven, M. (2007). Key evaluation checklist. www.wmich.edu/evalctr/archive_checklists/kec_feb07.pdf.
Created by the eminent evaluator Michael Scriven, this checklist is intended for use in designing and evaluating programs, plans, and policies; writing evaluation reports on them; assessing their evaluability; and evaluating evaluations of them.

Stufflebeam, D. L. (2002). CIPP Evaluation Model checklist. www.wmich.edu/evalctr/archive_checklists/cippchecklist_mar07.pdf.
The checklist assists evaluators, clients, and other stakeholders to review and assess a program's history; to provide timely reports for program stakeholders to plan, implement, and disseminate effective services to beneficiaries; and to issue a summative report on the program's merit, including lessons learned.

Organizations and Web Sites

American Educational Research Association (AERA)—Division H: Research, Evaluation, and Assessment in Schools (http://aera.net/divisions/Default.aspx?menu_id=94&id=73)
This organization has more than twenty-five thousand educational researchers as members. AERA's Division H focuses on applied research in schools, program evaluation in school settings, assessment in schools, and accountability in schools.

American Evaluation Association (AEA) (http://eval.org/)
This national organization of over 5,500 professional evaluators from all disciplines, from all fifty U.S. states and sixty foreign countries, provides conferences, contacts, information, training, and other resources to support the work of evaluators.

Centers for Disease Control and Prevention Evaluation Working Group (www.cdc.gov/eval/index.htm)

This site provides a framework, steps, standards, and resources for program evaluation in public health.

The Evaluation Center of Western Michigan University (www.wmich.edu/evalctr/)
The center provides a wide variety of services and resources for evaluators that include publications, presentations, checklists, archived videos of the speakers at the "Evaluation Café," and an interdisciplinary PhD in evaluation.

Research Methods Knowledge Base (www.socialresearchmethods.net/kb/evaluation.php)
This is a comprehensive Web-based textbook covering the topics that are typically included in introductory social research methods courses. The section on evaluation research introduces several models as examples of this form of social research.

University of Wisconsin-Extension: Program Development and Evaluation Unit (www.uwex.edu/ces/pdande/index.html)
This Web site provides resources on planning evaluations and enhancing programs through the development of logic models, and offers many examples of tools and reports.

PART FOUR

EMANCIPATORY DISCOURSES

CHAPTER 14

PRELIMINARY CONSIDERATIONS OF AN AFRICAN AMERICAN CULTURALLY RESPONSIVE EVALUATION SYSTEM

Pamela Frazier-Anderson
Stafford Hood
Rodney K. Hopson

Key Ideas

- Culture and cultural context are viewed as essential components of a culturally responsive evaluation. A certain level of cultural competence is necessary to successfully conduct evaluations within majority African American settings.

- Notions of logic models rarely position culture and context as important elements in program theory, development, implementation, or evaluation.

- The African American Culturally Responsive Evaluation System for Academic Settings (ACESAS) is a logic model proposed to visually represent the key steps used when implementing culturally responsive evaluation in majority African American communities and with majority African American populations.

Note: The authors would like to acknowledge Kevin E. Favor for his critique of earlier drafts of this chapter.

- The steps of the ACESAS logic model are based on select approaches of culturally responsive evaluation and the practical application of those theories in recent literature.

- The steps of the ACESAS logic model include an examination of the cultural and sociopolitical assumptions underpinning the scope of the evaluation, a contextual analysis, establishment of the culturally responsive evaluation (CRE) team, an inventory of CRE team resources, the implementation of the CRE action steps, the creation of CRE products, and an indication of the influence and impact of the evaluation on the cultural group.

- Although the ACESAS logic model was created to address how evaluations are handled in majority African American settings, the steps presented in the ACESAS can be generalized to other settings and used by other evaluators across professional fields who evaluate services and programs with similar populations.

Evaluations are conducted to provide program operators with information about the success of their particular program with reaching its goals (see Chapter Thirteen). Program operators are increasingly held accountable by funders (government organizations, private foundations, corporate and nonprofit boards, as well as individuals) to provide cost-effective programs whose **outcomes** ultimately have a significant impact on the "bottom line" (which could be capital in the form of people or income). Evaluations may be qualitative, quantitative, or mixed-methods (using both qualitative and quantitative approaches) to gather information and analyze data about a given program.

Within the last decade **culturally responsive evaluation (CRE)** has emerged as a key methodological approach within the field of evaluation with the potential to address critically important concerns pertaining to how evaluations are conducted, as well as the interpretation and use of results for marginalized groups whose culture has historically been viewed as inconsequential within the context of an evaluation (Hopson, 2003, 2009). The purpose of this chapter is to introduce a visual framework called a **logic model** that represents the stages of an evaluation. This logic model expands on the theory and practice of CRE in the field of evaluation and enhances the ability of CRE to advance areas of social justice, which attends in part to the equitable distribution of opportunities and resources among marginalized cultural groups.

One advocate for social and political equity was Asa Hilliard (1933–2007). The acronym for the logic model (ACESAS) presented in this chapter is a homophone of the possessive noun *Asa's* in honor of his efforts to foster educational and social mobility for African American youth. We contend that our proposed logic model identifies critically important steps for conducting culturally responsive evaluations within African American communities. This logic model further delineates a level of uniformity as to what it means to be a culturally responsive evaluator and how one proceeds when conducting culturally responsive evaluations in majority African American communities or with majority African American participants. It is believed that this logic model will at least further the dialogue on CRE, particularly in regard to working with populations in which there are cultural power differentials at work.

Before introducing the African American Culturally Responsive Evaluation System and providing a detailed explanation of the logic model that we believe best reflects CRE, and prior to operationalizing the views of an increasing number of evaluators who maintain that culture is a central consideration in evaluation, we will begin with the following discussions:

1. We will differentiate *culture* from *race* and identify the implications of these terms within the context of the African American experience.

2. We will define culturally responsive evaluation and its relevance when conducting evaluations in African American communities.

3. We will summarize the purpose and use of logic models in evaluation studies and their use in planning evaluations in cultural minority communities.

Culture and Race

The need to acknowledge culture has been expressed by numerous scholars and social change advocates (such as Hilliard, 1991; Hopson & Kirkhart, 2011; Ladson-Billings, 1994) who recognize the wealth of information that is gained when data are analyzed and interpreted within a cultural context. However, culture is generally a difficult **construct** (a speculative framework for a concept or idea) to operationalize. Steven J. Heine (2008), a cultural psychologist, offered that the construct of culture is interpreted in light of one's profession and field of study. He proposes two definitions for this construct. In one definition **culture** is identified as "any idea, belief, technology, habit, or practice that is acquired from others" (p. 3). In the other definition culture is described as "a particular group of individuals . . . who are existing within some kind of shared context" (p. 3). Individuals within this shared context tend to engage in similar activities, prefer similar things, visit similar places, and have frequent social interactions.

Characteristics of African American Culture

Heine (2008) notes that culture is dynamic and fluid, and that cultural boundaries may shift as society changes due to an increase in cross-cultural interactions. For example, American slavery resulted in a unique cross-cultural interaction between Africans and American "whites" that morphed African American culture into a mixture of both African culture and the cultural beliefs and practices of their oppressors. Another example is the landmark case of *Brown v. Board of Education* in 1954, which was responsible for major changes across American society when it legally eliminated racial segregation and created social, economic, political, and educational opportunities for African Americans and others. At the same time, those interactions that had previously been illegal between African Americans and whites resulted in social exchanges that produced various levels of **acculturation,** or "the extent to which ethnic-cultural minorities participate in the cultural traditions, values, beliefs, and practices of their own culture versus those of the dominant 'White' society" (Landrine & Klonoff, 1996, p. 1). Therefore cultural characteristics for African Americans may exist along a continuum ranging from a Eurocentric value of **individualism** to the Afrocentric value of **collectivism.** Values associated with individualism are competitiveness, putting the self above others, domination of nature, and maintaining an internal locus of control. An African value system is characterized by cooperation, pursuing survival of the group, having harmonious relations with nature, and maintaining a functional external locus of control.

One assertion is that the more acculturated a person from a traditional African American background becomes, once he or she begins to interact with the majority culture the less he may identify with his own cultural background (Landrine & Klonoff, 1996). However, it may be practical to reflect on the idea that many African Americans are able to successfully make the transition from one cultural environment to another without forfeiting their original cultural identity and could be considered "bicultural" (Landrine & Klonoff, p. 1). Such a notion can probably find its grounding in W.E.B. Du Bois's earlier articulation of the "**double consciousness**"—in which African Americans desire to hold onto both identities—in his seminal work *The Souls of Black Folk* (1903/2005, p. 5). Du Bois states that the African American "simply wishes to make it possible for a man to be both a Negro and an American, without being cursed and spit on by his fellows, without having the doors of Opportunity closed roughly in his face" (p. 5).

African Americans have used their ability to **code-switch** in order to transition between both cultures and in some instances as a critical strategy for survival. Broadly defined, this term refers to a person's capacity to alternate between using two different languages (such as English and Swahili), or to alternate between two forms of the same language (as with the change in dialect when some African Americans alternate between "Black English" and "Standard English" in order to meet the social demands of a given environment) (Greene & Walker, 2004; Harrison & Trabasso, 1976). Code-switching may also occur with nonverbal actions because behaviors in one cultural setting may or may not be appropriate for successful interactions in another setting, but these nonverbal actions may provide critically important information for understanding the phenomena that are being observed. For example, Akbar (1975) notes that the African American child expresses himself or herself through considerable body language, adopts a systematic use of nuances of intonation and body language (such as eye movement and position), and is highly sensitive to others' nonverbal cues of communication.

Traditional African American cultural characteristics have been developed by those of African descent in part to survive in a system in which remnants from past generations remain evident through the presence of such organizations as the Ku Klux Klan, discriminatory housing and financial practices, a lack of access to health care, poorly funded educational programs, and a shortage of educational and employment opportunities. The African American experience served and continues to serve as a catalyst for the development and preservation of a specific cultural behavioral style.

Landrine and Klonoff (1996) assert that there remain cultural behaviors and practices embedded in the dominant U. S. white culture that, when analyzed, could be discernibly and characteristically linked to the culture of African Americans. More specifically there are characteristics reflected in core attitudes, values, beliefs, and practices of African American culture in which an individual's level of participation (or nonparticipation) is indicative of his or her level of cultural immersion within the African American cultural group. These categories of life practices include the following:

1. "Traditional Family Structures and Practices" (for example, focusing largely on extended family and extended family networks) (p. 72)

2. "Preference for Things African American" (for example, reading such magazines as *Ebony* or *Essence* and listening to rhythm and blues or hip-hop radio stations) (p. 72)

3. "Preparation and Consumption of Traditional Foods" (eating traditional Southern foods, such as collard greens or grits) (p. 72)

4. "Interracial Attitudes and Cultural Mistrust" (such as a the belief that "most White people are racists" or a mistrust of whites) (p.73)

5. "Traditional African American Health Beliefs and Practices" (such as a belief that "prayer can cure disease," a belief in voodoo, and the practice whereby church members can be so emotionally moved during worship that they collapse or faint) (p. 73)

6. "Traditional African American Religious Beliefs and Practices" (for example, membership in an African American church or the ability to get the Holy Ghost or "speak in tongues") (p. 73)

7. "Traditional African American Childhood Socialization" (for example, residing in and attending school and church in a predominantly African American neighborhood) (p. 74)

8. "Superstitions" (such as eating black-eyed peas and collard greens on New Year's Day to bring prosperity in the upcoming year) (p.74)

REFLECTION QUESTIONS

1. What are some of the attributes of culture?
2. How has culture been defined within the African American community?

Difference Between Race and Culture

It is often the case that both scholarly discourse and popular media outlets portray the construct of *culture* as interchangeable with the construct of **race.** Race has been defined as "a group or category or person connected by common origin" (Cashmore, 2003, p. 334). People belonging to certain "racial" groups are generally believed to share certain physical features and behavioral patterns.

It is true that within some geographical contexts, as group differences are explored the construct of race may appear to hold some validity; but upon closer examination, the idea of classifying individuals by race or suggesting that race and culture are synonymous can be fallible. When working with many groups, particularly those of blended nations, such as the United States, it quickly becomes obvious that the terms *race* and *culture* cannot consistently be juxtaposed. For example, if we look within the African American population there are individuals who would be racially categorized as white due to their physical attributes (such as skin color and hair texture) but who culturally identify as African American.

Some have argued that race, particularly as defined in the United States, is a socially contrived construct rather than a biological one. It has been argued that the ability to biologically categorize people by race would necessitate the presence of significant genetic differences that do not occur within the human population (Cashmore, 2003; Graves, 2001). Although research exists that disputes the concept of race as a valid classification system, the use of the term persists in popular culture as well as among researchers and practitioners as a means of grouping people. The problem with racial categorization is that it has been used as a means of subjugation, justifying the superiority of one group over another. Cultural practices and traits can be fluid and more difficult to identify, whereas racial characteristics (which most often address a person's physical features) are generally perceived as constant and less likely to change.

REFLECTION QUESTION

1. Are race and culture interchangeable constructs? Why or why not?

Implications of Racial Group Classification for African Americans

African Americans have generally been classified as a racial group with little consideration given to cultural differences in research and practice. Mainstream research has gradually acknowledged that African Americans are culturally distinct. However, those whose cultural beliefs and practices differ from the dominant culture are generally perceived to be culturally deficient in multiple regards. The lack of empirically reported evidence of African Americans' strengths, as well as of how programs and services can be refined to meet the specific needs of this community, must be comprehensively addressed. Although there are those who readily acknowledge cultural differences, these differences remain a cursory consideration across many disciplines, a behavior that has been transmitted into general practice.

Distinguishing a common cultural identity of people of African descent in the United States is complex due to the numerous methods and periods of entry for members of this group. Also, individuals who identify as African American vary in their physical features, sometimes making them indistinguishable from individuals with physical characteristics typically associated with other cultural groups. However, one cannot deny that an attribute uniting members of this group is that the historical presence of the African in the United States is intricately woven into an existence that has been strongly influenced by systemic discriminatory racial practices. Although individuals who first perpetuated these ideas and behaviors expired decades and even centuries ago, the base of these ideals remains a part of U.S. culture. For example, Winfield (2007) asserts that "definitions about race, ability and human worth, provided by race theorists from the nineteenth century, entered into the public vernacular and, subsequently, the **collective memory** of our nation" (p. 155). The French sociologist Maurice Halbwachs (1941/1992) has generally been credited with the first articulation of collective memory, arguing that what we know about past events is influenced by the perspectives and viewpoints of the social context of that time. Consequently, this collective memory influences how events are recalled and passed down to future generations.

It may be asserted that the institution of racism and the "racial" and economic caste systems established in the United States, as well as the collective memory of the dominant majority worldview (Winfield, 2007), have produced an insensitive mind-set with respect to diversity, particularly against those cultural groups perceived as not having much value. The failure to identify and acknowledge cultural subgroups within the U.S. population is an example of **cultural egoism** (the perception that one's culture is the only one of value) that has made its way into the social and political institutions of this country.

Researchers and practitioners working to facilitate programs in African American communities must have awareness about how a community's past and current experiences (as well as community members' individual experiences) have shaped its current perspective on the world (or **worldview**). They must also be aware of how others view African Americans and how this view can be influenced by a host of factors including both past and present attitudes about the group.

So the idea of racial superiority exists in the United States in part because it has been transmitted from generation to generation by the U.S. majority culture. Thus the idea that humans are better identified as belonging to a cultural group rather than a racial group directly challenges the notion of racial superiority in this country, where one's "whiteness" is a beneficial and profitable means of categorization (Lipsitz, 2006).

REFLECTION QUESTIONS

1. What are the implications of the constructs of race and culture when applied to a cultural group such as African Americans?
2. Why is it important to consider the historical implications of the treatment of African Americans when working with and evaluating members of the African American community?

Culturally Responsive Evaluation

Drawing from a cross-disciplinary synthesis of scholarship by researchers who have addressed the centrality of culture in their work, Hopson (2009) has provided a critically important and refined definition of CRE. He defines CRE as

> a theoretical, conceptual and inherently political position that includes the centrality of and attunes to culture in the theory and practice of evaluation. That is, CRE recognizes that demographic, sociopolitical and contextual dimensions, locations and perspectives, and characteristics of culture matter fundamentally in evaluation. (p. 433)

Thus, in an effort to place culture at the center of the evaluation, CRE advocates for a comprehensive assessment of culture, its implication or implications, and its effect on the complexities of life for specific cultural minority groups.

Origin of CRE

The National Science Foundation (NSF) published *The 2002 User-Friendly Handbook for Project Evaluation*. It was within this handbook under the section titled "Strategies That Address Culturally Responsive Evaluation" that the basic tenets of CRE were combined and succinctly presented by Henry T. Frierson, Stafford Hood, and Gerunda B. Hughes (2002). They were not the first to address the role of culture and **cultural context** (the cultural setting and situation) as an integral component in practice and research within evaluation or other fields of study (Hopson, 2003). However, these evaluators and educational researchers opened a major discourse within the evaluation community by summarizing and presenting a functional framework and rationale for CRE. They articulated a set of principles for CRE in the design, implementation, interpretation, and dissemination of evaluation results that would be echoed in the work of other evaluators whose evaluative research and practice were to be viewed as culturally responsive (Hood, 2009; Hopson & Kirkhart, 2011; Manswell-Butty, Daniel Reid, & LaPoint, 2004; Thomas, 2004).

Characteristics of the CRE Evaluator

The credibility of the evaluator in communities of color is essential to conducting a thorough and accurate assessment. An evaluator who lacks a shared lived experience with the targeted cultural group and its community will have difficulties implementing culturally responsive strategies. Consequently the evaluator's ability to accurately make judgments about the value and worth of programs or services serving racial minority groups, economically disadvantaged groups, or both may be suspect. These evaluators will most likely have an insufficient level of knowledge and understanding about the meaning of certain cultural traditions, language patterns and phrases, and subtle cultural nuances recognizable to those who have substantive experiences in the culture. In order for there to be systemic change that improves the effectiveness and accuracy of the evaluations of programs serving cultural minorities, the evaluation community must accelerate its efforts to address this critically important concern. The evaluation community must show more tangible signs that it recognizes (and values) that any continuing failure to meaningfully address culture, and its sociopolitical influence and impact, will certainly have detrimental repercussions on both evaluations and traditionally disenfranchised cultural groups intended to be served by the programs being evaluated.

As the need for more effective and accurate evaluations of programs in African American communities continues to grow, it is only reasonable that those entities making considerable financial investments in programs to serve these communities should have similar expectations. Major government and private funding sources have intensified their scrutiny concerning how to ensure that the evaluations of their funding initiatives in communities of color produce meaningful and accurate information for decision making. Such concern could increase the extent to which culturally responsive evaluators are sought to lead evaluation efforts in these communities. At the same time, it is quite likely that there will also be an increase in the number of evaluators seeking to do work in these communities who are masquerading as evaluators skilled in CRE strategies.

One of the primary tenants of CRE is to protect or prevent the exploitation of cultural minority and economically disadvantaged stakeholders, with the evaluator being the central conduit in this mission (Frierson et al., 2002). Highly trained evaluators whose culture and cultural experiences are congruent with those of the target population are in a unique position to gauge the impact of their proposed or implemented evaluation due to their insight as part of the cultural group that is to be evaluated. Frierson et al. assert that an evaluation is culturally responsive when it is "based on an examination of impacts through lenses in which the culture of the participants is considered an important factor, thus rejecting the notion that assessments must be objective and culture free, if they are to be unbiased" (p. 63). They go on to note,

To ignore the reality of the existence of the influence of culture and to be unresponsive to the needs of the target population is to put the program in danger of being ineffective and to put the evaluation in danger of being seriously flawed. (p. 63)

It is reasonable to assume that people who have a similar cultural background and similar cultural experiences are more likely to share a similar worldview. Worldviews are shaped in part by formal education and training; however, social learning through observation and experience both significantly contribute to one's cultural frame of reference and one's ability to interpret life from that perspective. In the event that an evaluator lacks (or has minimal) knowledge, experiences, and sensitivities relative to the cultural community and context in which the evaluation is being conducted, then from a CRE perspective it would be considered to be critically important that the evaluator establish an evaluation team to compensate for these shortcomings.

Implementing CRE in African American Community Settings

It is not difficult for an evaluator to find cultural community settings in the United States in which the implementation of CRE techniques and procedures would be appropriate. Unfortunately there are too many examples of cultural minority groups in regard to which the implications of culture have been historically disregarded, rejected, or misinterpreted by members of the evaluation community. Clearly the preceding statement could easily be asserted with a certain level of conviction within the African American community. There are encouraging signs that progress is being made within the evaluation community to more fully acknowledge and understand the relevance of culture, cultural context, and cultural nuance when conducting evaluations in African American communities. However, considerable work remains to address the persistent shortcomings of the standard procedures administered when the goal has been to evaluate programs and services whose participants are primarily African American.

Major professional associations, such as the American Evaluation Association (AEA) and the American Psychological Association (APA), have each established a set of principles designed to serve as guidelines for researchers and practitioners working with culturally diverse populations and in culturally diverse settings (Hopson, 2003). However, these principles in general remain somewhat implicit when delineating specific methodological approaches that are necessary as evaluators undertake assignments in cultural settings in which the culture of the target population differs from their own. For example, AEA's *Guiding Principles for*

Evaluators identifies competencies necessary for evaluators in five areas: systematic inquiry, competence, integrity and honesty, respect for people, and responsibilities for general and public welfare (American Evaluation Association, 2004). Although AEA provides brief examples of the requisites in these areas and lists some of the qualities necessary for evaluators working with diverse populations, the evaluator is generally left to determine his or her own level of competence and the methods used to meet those standards. Therefore additional measures are needed to ensure that the application of methods and the interpretation of results provide further support, protection, and adequate representation for those cultural groups targeted for research and evaluation.

Benefits of CRE

There are a number of benefits associated with the use of CRE in majority African American settings. First, it recognizes and brings to the forefront of the evaluation the culture of African Americans, a culture that has been devalued in the United States for hundreds of years. In his book *The Afrocentric Idea*, Molefi Kete Asante (1998) introduces the concept of **Afrocentricity,** which advocates for the study of Africans from their perspective rather than from a Eurocentric point of view. He suggests "taking the globe and turning it over so that we see all the possibilities of a world where Africa, for example, is subject and not object" of study (p. 1). Culturally responsive evaluation gives those of African descent, as Asante suggests, "a place to stand" (p. 13) that is based on the African (which includes the African American) perspective and is not compared or held to majority cultural group standards that may or may not be similar.

Another benefit is that CRE is a collaborative process involving multiple stakeholders during all phases of the evaluation. So one gains insight not only from program administrators, staff, and program participants but also from parents and community representatives relative to their needs, concerns, and any other information valuable to the evaluation. In part this assists with strengthening relationships between evaluators and stakeholders by reducing the apprehension of stakeholder groups who may question the cultural integrity of evaluators and the intent and purpose of the evaluation. Evaluators can establish a level of cultural trust by consistently behaving in a manner that exemplifies their respect for and knowledge of the particular community of color. When such cultural trust has been established the potential for the evaluation to positively influence how the results will be used by the stakeholder groups in the community of color increases.

An additional advantage of using CRE when conducting evaluations in majority African American settings is that standards are established to ensure that the evaluator has some level of cultural competence (which includes cultural knowledge and sensitivity) when working with specific cultural populations, particularly when the evaluator is from a different cultural background. As mentioned previously, one of the primary safeguards in CRE to guarantee some degree of cultural competence is that the evaluator must "share a lived experience" with the people that are part of the evaluation (Frierson et al., 2002, p. 70). This is particularly useful in assisting the evaluators with understanding issues of cultural context that may be operating within programs and services. This competency is better fulfilled and the research process more accurate when the evaluator has to some extent walked in the shoes of members of the target population.

This does not necessarily suggest that only African American evaluators are able to evaluate programs designed for African American populations, but it does mean that evaluators should have a substantial degree of knowledge and sensitivity in order to address needs; to create or adapt culture-fair tests and assessments; to provide a more comprehensive interpretation of results; and to examine the evaluation's impact on multiple levels, including the cultural and sociopolitical factors related to the target group (Frierson et al.).

Finally, CRE identifies "what works, for what groups and in what context" (Johnson, 2005, p. 229). Thus comprehensive contextual evaluations like those advocated by CRE lead to better identification of what programs or what components of programs are effective in improving outcomes for what groups of African Americans and under what circumstances. Therefore CRE is a tool of empowerment because it supports social justice themes: there is the potential to better define what aspects of programs and services lead to increased opportunities and benefits for African Americans as a whole as well as for subgroups within this population.

REFLECTION QUESTIONS

1. What is CRE?
2. Why is CRE a practical approach for evaluators working in the United States with cultural groups such as African Americans?

Logic Models

A logic model is a "graphic way to organize information and display thinking" (Wyatt Knowlton & Phillips, 2009, p. 4) that demonstrates the causal relationship between the program's "planned work" and the program's "intended results" (W. K. Kellogg Foundation, 2004, p. 2). Logic models were first introduced in the 1970s and have been used in the private, public, and nonprofit sectors. Evaluators may create logic models to visually demonstrate the planning, implementation, and intended outcomes of the evaluation. According to the W. K. Kellogg Foundation, logic models typically consist of the following steps: **resources or inputs** and **activities** (or the work you plan to do), and **outputs,** outcomes, and **impact** (the intended results of the evaluation). Logic models traditionally promote a linear way of thinking and typically use boxes and arrows to demonstrate the content and flow of evaluation activities.

Although logic models such as those developed by the United Way, the Centers for Disease Control and Prevention, and the W. K. Kellogg Foundation (2004) take one through the evaluative process (Taylor-Powell & Henert, 2008), logic models representing culturally responsive evaluations have only recently emerged in the literature. For example, in the American Indian Higher Education Consortium, Joan LaFrance and Richard Nichols suggest how the use of culturally relevant metaphors (common in indigenous ways of knowing) can be used in logic model development. They believe that a model incorporating symbols reflective of cultural knowledge and worldviews is a better indicator of logic models for indigenous populations than a traditional linear (and narrative-driven) logic model (American Indian Higher Education Consortium, 2009). The logic model described in this chapter builds on this way of thinking specifically for African American communities, for which it is necessary to create logic models that accurately depict CRE activities.

African American Culturally Responsive Evaluation System for Academic Settings

The **African American Culturally Responsive Evaluation System for Academic Settings (ACESAS)** is an adaptation of a logic model for use in African American communities. To date there has not been a systematic set of procedures to guide evaluators in their efforts to conduct culturally responsive evaluations with African American populations. We believe that the ACESAS is a first step in this process. The ACESAS is a logic model developed to visually conceptualize culturally responsive evaluations of educational programs for African American students from pre-K to grade 12, as well as in institutions of higher learning. The authors believe that the ACESAS can be a useful tool for effectively conducting culturally responsive program evaluations in most

THE ACESAS LOGIC MODEL

FIGURE 14.1 Sankofa Bird Model of the ACESAS

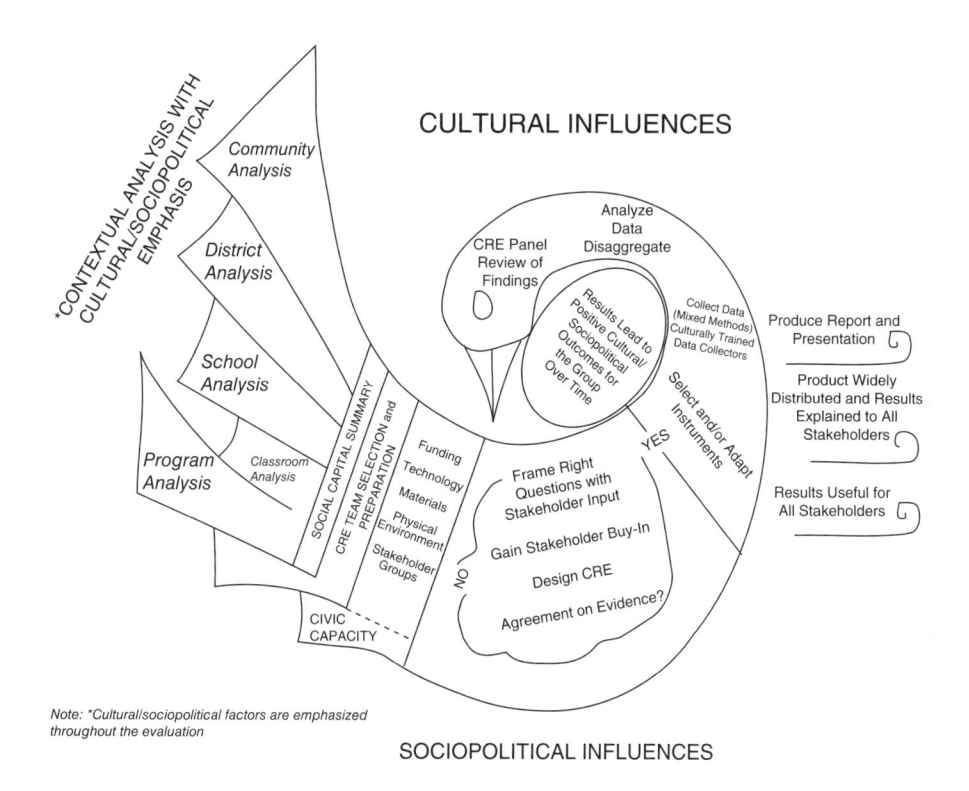

*Note: *Cultural/sociopolitical factors are emphasized throughout the evaluation*

noneducational settings as well, such as when evaluating health care prevention programs targeting African American men and prostate cancer, nonprofits focused on green initiatives in African American communities, and businesses' employee retention efforts for African American workers. However, the reference group for which the theoretical development of the ACESAS is tailored is African Americans in the context of educational settings.

The ACESAS was initially created in the form of a traditional logic model. However, it has evolved into an alternate visual depiction of CRE in order to (1) recognize that the African way of thinking is not necessarily linear and (2) provide a visual of symbolic significance for the community in which it will be used, as you can see in Figure 14.1.

We selected the image of the **sankofa bird** as the visual for our alternate model. The traditional image is of a bird with an egg in its beak whose body is facing forward but whose head and neck are extended backward. According to Elleni Tedla, author of *Sankofa: African Thought and Education*,

Sankofa is an Akan word which roughly translates as: "Return to the source and fetch." The source is our culture, heritage and identity. It is the power that is within us. Sankofa means that as we move forward into the future, we need to reach back into our past and take with us all that works and is positive. (1996, p. 1)

Thus the model of the ACESAS is an adaptation of the principle represented by the sankofa bird. This model seeks to visually represent the manner in which CRE fulfills the principles of sankofa in its evaluation practices: looking back (from a cultural and sociopolitical perspective) in order to move forward as a program, as a community, and as a cultural group.

Framework for the ACESAS

The conceptual foundation for the ACESAS logic model is reflective of insights and concerns expressed from a number of evaluation approaches, models, and theories:

- Stufflebeam's CIPP (Context, Input, Process, and Products) Evaluation Model (Stufflebeam & Shinkfield, 2007)
- House and Howe's views addressing deliberative democratic evaluation (House, 2001; House & Howe, 2000)
- Stake's responsive evaluation (1983)
- Chen's intervening mechanism evaluation (1990)
- Ladson-Billings's culturally relevant pedagogy (1994, 1995a, 1995b)

Stufflebeam's CIPP Evaluation Model (Stufflebeam & Shinkfield, 2007), House's (2001) and House and Howe's (2000) comments on deliberative democratic evaluation (see Chapter Eighteen), as well as Stake's comments on responsive evaluation (1983) call for equity in evaluation through the inclusion of stakeholder groups (such as program participants) who may not otherwise have a voice in the evaluation process. The ACESAS serves to facilitate this process by requiring input and active participation from all represented stakeholder groups at each stage of the evaluation, and, further, the logic model itself serves as a platform for discussion and deliberation among stakeholders and evaluation team members.

The ACESAS also expands on Chen's intervening mechanism evaluation (1990), whose purpose "is to uncover the causal processes underlying a program so that the reason(s) a program does or does not work can be understood" (p. 191). The ACESAS attempts to visually represent the idea that both culture and sociocultural factors are two of a number of key "moderators" that have the potential to influence programs and evaluations. Bledsoe (2005) defines a **moderator** as "a factor that can affect the strength of the program intervention and strategy" (p. 183).

When the ACESAS is used in educational settings, Ladson-Billings's culturally relevant pedagogy (1994, 1995a, 1995b) also helps drive some of the ACESAS methodology, particularly at the outset of the evaluation during the contextual assessment process (see the description of this process in next paragraph). Culturally relevant pedagogy uses strategies that place culture at the center of the instructional and learning process; CRE does the same for evaluation. It is believed that these strategies not only can contribute to improving the academic achievement of African American students but also can be a vehicle for cultural and individual empowerment (Ladson-Billings, 1998).

During the contextual assessment of an academic setting, one of the evaluator's major priorities is to assess the extent to which the current environment or environments at the school, district, and classroom levels are reflective of the cultural or ethnic backgrounds of the students and the positive attributes or positive qualities of the neighborhoods in which the students reside. Educational settings that successfully incorporate and use culturally relevant strategies are more likely to facilitate better outcomes and opportunities for their African American students. The evaluator's familiarity with culturally relevant strategies that contribute to the success of learning environments and with how these manifest themselves is critically important for assessing the group's social capital.

Purpose of the ACESAS

The ACESAS has been developed for the purpose of assisting program evaluators in their planning and designing of an evaluation that is **culturally competent** (the evaluator has considerable knowledge of and practical experience with the cultural group) and culturally responsive. Central to the ACESAS is the evaluator's ability to identify cultural and social justice themes critical to the evaluation and to effectively address them at each stage of the evaluation's development and implementation.

The ACESAS is intended to provide a visual guide for the evaluator through each step of an evaluation. Cultural and sociopolitical factors that are considered to be specifically relevant to the African American experience are central to the ACESAS logic model, unlike in most existing logic models, which view these factors as minimally important to the evaluation process or not important at all. The ACESAS requires the evaluator to consider the cultural influences and nuances when initially entering the setting throughout each stage in the evaluation of program inputs, outcomes, and dissemination of the evaluation results. Finally, the culturally responsive evaluator encourages stakeholders to look beyond the evaluation findings and consider how the information (whether positive or negative) can assist them with advancing their cultural or sociopolitical agenda. This applies not only to the local community of African American stakeholders but also to the broader African American community.

REFLECTION QUESTION

1. What is the ACESAS?

ACESAS Logic Model Components

Within the ACESAS model, cultural and sociopolitical realities of the African American experience serve to guide fundamental assumptions at each stage of the evaluation. Evaluators proceed through the following steps, which are further defined in the upcoming sections:

1. Examine the cultural and sociopolitical assumptions (or perceived influences) underpinning the scope of the evaluation
2. Conduct a contextual analysis
3. Establish the CRE team
4. Identify CRE team resources
5. Use CRE action steps to design and implement the evaluation plan
6. Create the evaluation products
7. Report evaluation results to all stakeholder groups.
8. Determine the program's influence and impact on the cultural group being served

Cultural and Sociopolitical Influences

In CRE, evaluators have substantive knowledge about the cultural beliefs and practices of the cultural group being served by the program as well as how these constructs could potentially play a role in the various stages and outcomes of the evaluation. Therefore it is reasonable that cultural influences and nuances should be prominent considerations across each phase of the evaluation. Family structure, health beliefs and practices, and religious beliefs and practices are culturally influential (Landrine & Klonoff, 1996) and are highly likely to be culturally specific. Therefore it is important for the evaluator to be knowledgeable of these influences as well as issues related to cultural attitudes, trust, and mistrust.

It is reasonable to argue that racism, discrimination, limited access to adequate health care, community violence, and inequitable education outcomes and opportunities are part of the sociocultural reality of the African American experience in the United States. Although it is true that the majority of African Americans live at or near the poverty level, they are still subject to issues of racism and discrimination across all income levels.

An in-depth understanding of relevant sociopolitical factors within African American communities is of major importance. This understanding contributes to the formulation of hypotheses about the extent to which these sociopolitical factors influence the external and internal behavioral dispositions, actions, and interactions of individuals and groups within these communities. An understanding of the types, nature, and influence of the sociopolitical factors embedded in communities of color contributes to a meaningful understanding of the evaluation results and findings therein.

Contextual Analysis

Prior to and upon initial entry into the evaluation setting, the principal evaluator conducts a **contextual analysis** of the community, the district, the school, the classroom, and the program. The purpose of this analysis is to obtain a thorough description of the environment in which the evaluation is to occur. The information collected at each level (community, district, school, classroom, or program) should include (1) a history of each level (for example, the origin of the community, district, or program); (2) an explanation of how the environment at each level has changed (or remained the same) culturally, economically, or in some other manner since the program's inception; and (3) the primary issues, strengths, and challenges at each level.

Information is gained through the use of interviews, observations, focus groups, and surveys, and through review of any relevant documentation and records. For example, in their evaluation of the Talent Development school-to-career program, Manswell-Butty et al. (2004) used a culturally responsive framework to conduct a process that is similar to what is suggested in the ACESAS. The evaluation team met with stakeholder groups during the planning phase of their evaluation. The purpose of these meetings was to "fully understand the sociocultural context of the environment in which the intervention and evaluation would take place" (p. 41). The team worked collaboratively by sharing school records and research findings, and staff, students, and administrators provided feedback on the strengths and challenges of the program, as well as on evaluation methods and proposed instruments (Ellison, 2004; Thomas, 2004).

An advantage of providing a contextual analysis is that it allows the evaluator to assess the cultural value and importance of the target population in all of these settings. The final product of the contextual analysis is therefore a description of the **social capital** of the group being served by the program. Noguera (2008) defines social capital as the "value of the cultural group in the broader society" (p. 24). Discussing social capital in relation to educational settings, he asserts that when the relationship between the community (including students and parents) and school personnel is limited and of low quality, then the school, which is an extension of the community, is "more likely to operate as negative social capital" (p. 24). For example, offering another perspective of the Talent Development program, Thomas (2004) indicated that many of the parents had negative views of school due to their own personal experiences. It is also possible that in some instances school officials may have negative views toward the clientele they serve (Noguera). Knowing the social capital of the group provides evaluators with insight into the cultural dynamics of the environment and creates a starting point for determining the methods they will use to engage stakeholder groups.

Completion of the contextual analysis also allows the evaluation team to perform a self-analysis (or self-reflection) to determine if team members have the level of competence necessary to conduct the evaluation. This analysis provides insight for the team to assess not only whether it has an adequate level of professional knowledge but also whether team members are familiar with the cultural group's strengths and challenges in a particular setting. This will help to facilitate the next stage in the process, which is to establish the culturally responsive evaluation team.

CRE Team
It is the responsibility of the principal investigator to ensure that members of the culturally responsive evaluation team include evaluators who (because of their shared lived experience with the target population) may be more effective in synthesizing information and interpreting the results of the contextual analysis from the cultural perspective of the group. The team also seeks to include key

representatives from all relevant stakeholder groups who would be involved throughout the evaluation. This helps in part to promote key stakeholder buy-in as well as to address issues of internal validity that may arise in regard to the evaluation design. It may also be necessary or more advantageous to empower individuals within stakeholder groups as evaluators. For example, Penn Towns and Serpell (2004) discussed using a project team with a "statistician, sociologist, educator, psychologist, and an anthropologist" (p. 52) for their study on exemplary urban schools. In 2007, with funding from the NSF, Stafford Hood and Melvin Hall developed the Relevance of Culture in Evaluation Institute (RCEI) Implementing and Empirically Investigating Culturally Responsive Evaluation in Underperforming Schools Project to train school-based teams (made up of teachers and principals) in basic evaluation and CRE through workshops to build evaluation capacity to conduct their own evaluations with support from consultants who were to provide technical assistance. To further ensure validity, evaluation teams and consultants were matched according to cultural background and level of knowledge about specific cultural groups (Hood, 2009).

CRE Team Resources

An inventory of the resources available to the team, as well as those needed in order to effectively complete a culturally responsive evaluation, is essential to the evaluation's success. Some of the resources to be considered include

1. Funding (the money required to pay for the evaluation)

2. Technology (the type of technological equipment needed to fulfill the contractual obligations for the evaluation, such as computers, printers, video- and audio-recording devices, and transcription machines and services)

3. Materials (the tools and equipment needed to complete the evaluation, including the software needed for survey tool development and data analysis)

4. Physical environment (the headquarters where evaluators are to be stationed during the course of the evaluation)

These are general items to consider for any evaluation, but even these resources may be influenced by both the cultural and the sociopolitical factors relevant to African American students and the school environment. For example, a sociopolitical factor, such as inequitable funding for educational programs in African American communities, may influence the type and scope of technology available in the school setting. Therefore, in classrooms requiring students to share computers (or in some classrooms with no computer access at all), the variety in the types of data evaluators will be able to collect (particularly qualitative data from such Web 2.0 resources as blogs or discussion groups or from online tests or surveys) would be negatively affected.

CRE also considers the civic capacity of stakeholders. **Civic capacity** is broadly defined as "various sectors of the community coming together in an effort to solve a major problem" (Stone, Henig, Jones, & Pierannunzi, 2001, p. 4). To make it more applicable within the context of evaluation, it is the building and maintaining of stakeholder groups across all populations that the program or project serves and their ability to assist in the design, implementation, and interpretation of the evaluation in both social and political contexts. Therefore the evaluators solicit participation and feedback from district and school personnel, parents, students, and additional community stakeholder groups (if relevant to the evaluation) at each stage of the evaluation. For example, an evaluation of a program in an urban community may include such individuals as staff members, students, program administrators, and parents (Manswell-Butty et al., 2004; Penn Towns & Serpell, 2004; Thomas, 2004). However, local community leaders (including social and political leaders) may also prove to be a valuable resource to the evaluation team, particularly in interpreting some of the findings and examining community dynamics, which may or may not have the potential to influence stages of the evaluation.

CRE Action Steps

At this stage the key procedures constituting the core of the evaluation are implemented. If a contextual analysis has been conducted, a CRE team identified, and resource capacity addressed, and if stakeholder groups representing the population the program or project serves are included in the process, then the **action steps,** or the actual procedures used to conduct a culturally responsive evaluation, are easier to facilitate and more likely to be considered valid. Similar to the stages of evaluation as discussed in Chapter Thirteen, the basic steps of this evaluation are derived from the work of Frierson et al. (2002) and summarized below as well as in the logic model.

1. Framing the right evaluation question or questions with stakeholder input

2. Designing the evaluation from a culturally sensitive perspective

3. Generating agreement with stakeholders on what is accepted as credible evidence

4. Selecting and adapting instruments

5. Collecting data using culturally trained data collectors who adhere to a mixed-methods approach in evaluation

6. Disaggregating the data

7. Assembling a CRE review panel to review and accept findings

The **culturally responsive evaluation review** panel is composed of a special group of individuals responsible for the review of the evaluation findings. This is an added safeguard in culturally responsive evaluation to ensure there is a mechanism in place to provide stakeholders, who are from the same cultural background as the program participants, with the ability to deliberate over the results of the evaluation prior to submission of the final report. Stakeholder groups help serve as a system of "checks and balances" in order to guarantee that as evaluators prepare to release the results, the manner in which the data have been and are being interpreted is culturally valid as it relates to the target population. These stakeholders work collaboratively with the evaluation team to ensure due diligence in maintaining this sort of validity. **Multicultural validity** refers to our ability to accurately capture and interpret cultural experiences (Kirkhart, 1995). Having the CRE review panel provides confidence that cultural differences do not negatively influence the success of the evaluation or impinge on evaluation results.

CRE Products

A **culturally responsive evaluation product** is defined as the item or method used to convey evaluation results. Products can be in a traditional format, such as a written report, but they can also be in the form of a presentation, a videotape, or a collage. Information is presented in a way that is culturally appropriate, and in a format that is understood by all stakeholder groups. The selection of the method used to convey results is made in consultation with the CRE review panel.

Evaluation Impact

During this step of the evaluation, the evaluator ensures that the evaluation products (such as the written reports or videotapes) are distributed to all stakeholder groups. The product or products should be widely distributed, and the results should be explained to all stakeholder groups. It is also important to ensure that the results are useful for all stakeholders and that the results are *perceived* as useful for all stakeholders.

Influence and Impact on the Cultural Group

This step in the evaluation process requires one to focus on the big picture and address the question, How will the program's impact ultimately make a difference in, contribute to, or enhance both cultural and societal factors for African Americans in the larger community? This segment of the evaluation, which is ultimately the responsibility of the program stakeholders to implement, includes suggestions from the CRE evaluators to the program stakeholders. The ultimate goal of the evaluation is for the results to be used to make positive changes or to continue effective programs that could lead to positive cultural or sociopolitical outcomes for the target group.

REFLECTION QUESTION

1. How does the ACESAS incorporate and build on evaluation practices and other select social science theories?

Summary

Culturally responsive evaluation (CRE) is an emerging field of study in evaluation that supports the standards issued by the American Evaluation Association, the American Psychological Association, and the National Association of School Psychologists in relation to culture, assessment, and evaluation. Making culture and issues of social justice relevant to communities and people of color adds to the validity of the evaluation methods as well as the results.

African Americans are a subculture of the U.S. population in which issues of diversity, poverty, racism, and discrimination have created a unique cultural identity and worldview. CRE serves as a course of action to take all relevant factors for this population into consideration when conducting evaluations with this group. The African American Culturally Responsive Evaluation System for Academic Settings (ACESAS) is a logic model designed to provide a visual overview of the steps performed when conducing culturally responsive evaluations in predominantly African American settings. It is our hope that the ACESAS, upon continued use and discussion, will further come to visually represent those key factors that distinguish it from other evaluation models, in order to serve as a guide and frame of reference for culturally responsive evaluators and stakeholder groups.

Key Terms

acculturation, 350
action steps, 368
activities, 360
African American Culturally Responsive Evaluation System for Academic Settings (ACESAS), 360
Afrocentricity, 358
civic capacity, 368
code-switch, 350
collective memory, 354
collectivism, 350
construct, 349
contextual analysis, 365
cultural context, 355
cultural egoism, 354
culturally competent, 363
culturally responsive evaluation (CRE), 348
culturally responsive evaluation product, 369
culturally responsive evaluation review panel, 369
culture, 349
double consciousness, 350
impact, 360
individualism, 350
logic model, 348
moderator, 363
multicultural validity, 369
outcomes, 348
outputs, 360
race, 352
resources or inputs, 360
sankofa bird, 361
social capital, 366
worldview, 354

Further Readings and Resources

Suggested Culturally Responsive Evaluation Study

Zulli, R., & Frierson, H. (2004). A focus on cultural variables in evaluating an Upward Bound program. *New Directions for Evaluation, 102,* 81–93.
This journal article provides an example of a culturally responsive evaluation.

Other Suggested Readings

Hood, S., Hopson, R., & Frierson, H. (2005). *The role of culture and cultural context: A mandate for inclusion, the discovery of truth, and understanding in evaluative practice.* Greenwich, CT: Information Age.
This text provides an overview of current topics addressing culture and cultural context in evaluation.

Taylor-Powell, E., & Henert, E. (2008). *Developing a logic model: Teaching and training guide.* www.uwex.edu/ces/pdande/evaluation/pdf/lmguidecomplete.pdf.
The University of Wisconsin has developed a thorough training manual on logic models.

Organizations and Web Sites

American Evaluation Association Graduate Education Diversity Internship Program (www.eval.org/gedip.htm)
This program offers internships to predoctoral students from groups traditionally underrepresented in evaluation in an effort to cultivate culturally responsive evaluators.

Multiethnic Issues in Evaluation Topical Interest Group of the American Evaluation Association (AEA) (http://comm.eval.org/EVAL/MultiethnicIssuesinEvaluation/Home/Default.aspx)
This is a special interest group within AEA with an emphasis on multicultural issues in evaluation.

Robert Wood Johnson Foundation Evaluation Fellowship Program (http://rwjf-evaluationfellows.org/)
This program is designed for individuals from underrepresented groups in the evaluation field and in organizations. It seeks to diversify the evaluation field for both early-career and nonprofit professionals who seek to build understanding and knowledge of program evaluation.

University of Wisconsin-Extension: Program Development and Evaluation Unit (www.uwex.edu/ces/pdande/evaluation/evallogicmodel.html)
This link to the University of Wisconsin-Extension program contains a resource for training and teaching logic models, templates for logic model development, as well as an online self-study course.

W. K. Kellogg Foundation Logic Model Development Guide (www.wkkf.org/knowledge-center/resources/2006/02/WK-Kellogg-Foundation-Logic-Model-Development-Guide.aspx)
This link provides a comprehensive overview of logic models for use in program evaluation.

CHAPTER 15

WHAT MAKES CRITICAL ETHNOGRAPHY "CRITICAL"?

Angelina E. Castagno

Key Ideas

- Critical ethnography highlights *both* the ways societal structures and institutions shape experience *and* the ability of people to respond and thus shape experience.

- Critical ethnography's goals are to *illustrate* power and oppression and *suggest* paths toward greater equity and justice.

- Critical ethnographers *explicitly* describe our own biases, assumptions, and theoretical backgrounds in order to make our research more transparent.

The biggest struggle for me in this research has been finding the right voice with which to talk about what I observed in the Zion School District. There are many things about which to be critical, but having formed relationships with the participants and generally believing that they are "nice people" make being critical somewhat more difficult. I worry that my analysis will be read as saying they are "bad people." This is not my intention, and, in fact, most of the educators in my study were caring and wanted all of their students to learn and be successful. Much of what I observed, however, reflects racism within the larger society, and in most instances my critiques should be read as being critical of that system and those structures rather than of the individual teachers. In other words, my goal is to illustrate how systems of power and structures of privilege and oppression are played out at the local level. However, there is certainly some measure of critique of individual teachers because we all need to recognize the role we play in creating and sustaining oppressive systems. Unfortunately, the line between these two places is quite thin, and I have struggled to both locate that line and keep my analysis within reach of it. Using ethnography to examine and illustrate structures and systems, however, presents a tension because ethnography, by definition, attempts to get at local practices and understandings. I have, therefore, struggled to shift attention away from individuals as problematic to structures as problematic—but I am not always successful in this endeavor because, I think, the nature of ethnographic research keeps pulling me back to the individual.

Taken from my reflective writing during a yearlong critical ethnographic study of multicultural education in an urban school district (Castagno, 2006, 2008, 2009), this vignette highlights some of the tensions and issues that are central to qualitative researchers conducting critical ethnography. I struggled with balancing a structural account and an individual-cultural account, determining how to best represent the research participants and patterns I observed, negotiating what it means to be critical, and finding my own authorial voice. These struggles, in many ways, define critical ethnography.

In this chapter I provide a broad overview of critical ethnography as a particular methodology within the qualitative research tradition. I begin by discussing the historical and theoretical foundations of critical ethnography. Next I outline some of the defining elements of critical ethnography and then some of the issues that arise in the actual *doing* of critical ethnography. I close by describing some of the most common critiques of critical ethnography, as well as how critical ethnographers have responded to these critiques. Throughout the chapter I draw on both my own and other published critical ethnographic work to illustrate the various points being made.

Beginning to Understand Critical Ethnography

A few words introducing the concept of critical ethnography will help situate the reader, but rest assured I will unpack this information later in the chapter. **Critical ethnography** is a form of research that attempts to account for and highlight the complex relationship between structural constraints on human action and autonomous, active agency by individuals and groups. By **structure** critical ethnographers mean the economic, political, social, historical, and cultural institutions and norms that operate in all contexts. By **agency** critical ethnographers mean the ability of individuals to make choices and shape their experiences so that they are not completely determined by structures. Critical ethnography has grown in response to accounts of structure in which human actors are absent *and* accounts of culture in which structural constraints are absent (Anderson, 1989).

Critical ethnography has both similarities with and differences from traditional ethnography (see Chapter Seven), which is primarily concerned with describing patterns of social life and discussing the meanings of patterns from participants' points of view. Critical ethnography certainly strives for rich, thick description and accurate interpretation of social phenomena, but it has additional goals related to illuminating power differences, injustice, agency, resistance, and larger analyses of structures. Traditional ethnographers employ a more detached, objective, and value-neutral approach to data collection than critical ethnographers believe is possible or desirable. Although all ethnography studies culture, critical ethnography explicitly assumes that various cultures and groups of people are positioned unequally within society and have varied access to power and resources. Critical ethnographers are also clear that representations of culture are never neutral, but are instead shaped by competing interests of funders, researchers, participants, and other community members.

Theoretical and Historical Foundations of Critical Ethnography

Critical ethnography originated in the 1970s with studies of schooling. It developed out of a sort of marriage between previously competing ideas, concepts, and theories. **Classical Marxism** provided one key foundational leg for critical ethnography. Marxism posits that the economic structures in a society determine that society's cultural, familial, legal, political, and other structures. Capitalism requires workers and owners, and it is the relationship between these two groups, and between these groups and what is produced, that shapes everything else in society. Marx viewed capitalism as fundamentally an **exploitative system** (that is, it privileges the owners and oppresses the workers), but this exploitation is hidden in order to ensure its perpetuation. Marxism has been critiqued, however, for being overly **mechanistic** because it models society as a well-oiled machine. Marxism has also been critiqued for being overly **deterministic** because it fails to account for human action. Good critical ethnography is neither mechanistic nor deterministic, but it does take seriously the role of structures within all contexts.

Another foundational leg for critical ethnography is **structuralism.** Drawing on the ideas of Claude Levi-Strauss and Louis Althusser, structuralists assert that all phenomena have a basic structure that determines their elements and characteristics. These structures are real and exist, but they may not be obvious or immediately apparent. Meaning within a community is produced and reproduced through structures—such as the way gender norms are connected to, and carried out through, the institutions of family, work, and education.

And yet another foundational leg can be found in the ideas of **culturalists,** who center the role of human action and culture in explaining social phenomena. Rather than focusing on the role of structures and institutions, culturalists suggest that people and culture have primary roles in shaping meaning and experience. Whereas a structuralist might learn about gender norms by examining employment policies and practices, a culturalist might learn about gender norms by examining the personal interactions among people in a particular setting.

The debates among these competing camps gave birth to critical ethnography. Because Marxists and structuralists advocated the primacy of structures and culturalists advocated the primacy of human agency, the stage was set for a theoretical perspective and methodological approach that merged these two fundamental ideas about structure and agency.

Samuel Bowles and Herbert Gintis's *Schooling in Capitalist America* (1976) offered empirical support for the Marxist and structuralist perspectives by arguing that schools teach differently to students from different social class backgrounds. Specifically, **social reproduction** occurs because working-class children receive an education that prepares them for working-class jobs, middle-class children receive an education that prepares them for middle-class jobs, and class hierarchies are thus passed on from one generation to the next. Bowles and Gintis argued that this reproduction occurs because capitalism requires it. But like Marxism, Bowles and Gintis were critiqued for being overly deterministic and mechanistic.

One year later Paul Willis published *Learning to Labor* (1977), and with it critical ethnography was born. Willis challenged purely structural accounts of schools as institutions of social reproduction by illustrating how British working-class boys produced a culture of opposition to schooling that simultaneously resisted the oppressive education system and contributed to their own social class reproduction. In other words, Willis's analysis accounted for the role of structures while also highlighting the way human agency influences social phenomena. His theory of cultural reproduction offered a merging of the previously competing social theories, and this merging is still what many critical ethnographers attempt in present-day research.

Thus critical ethnography developed in the 1970s as British and American researchers sought ways to resolve the tension between cultural and structural accounts of social and educational processes (Anderson, 1989). In addition to Willis (1977), Jean Anyon (1980), Lois Weis (1985), and Jay MacLeod (987) also produced some of the early work that attempted to marry structural analyses with cultural production explanations in order to highlight human agency in the face of structural constraints. Critical ethnographers initially focused on class issues and, especially, on working-class students' varied responses to schooling (Fine, 1991; Willis, 1997). A common theme in these studies is students as active agents in their education and, oftentimes, as resisting the schooling offered to them. More recent critical ethnographers, such as Michelle Fine, Stacey Lee, and Pauline Lipman, have investigated the intersections of various forms of oppression and continue to provide evidence of the ways class, gender, race, sexuality, language, immigrant status, and other categories are intertwined.

REFLECTION QUESTIONS

1. How and why did critical ethnography emerge as a research methodology?
2. How would you define structure and agency? Why are these concepts important to critical ethnography?

Defining Elements of Critical Ethnography

As with any methodology, critical ethnography is employed differently by different researchers, but there are some common characteristics that can be found in the vast majority of critical ethnographic work. I provided an explanation of critical ethnography at the beginning of this chapter, but I'd like to expand on that explanation here by discussing some of the defining elements of critical ethnography. These elements, in fact, are what make critical ethnography *critical*.

Illuminating Both Structure and Agency

Critical approaches to ethnography (Anderson, 1989; Carspecken, 1996; Carspecken & Walford, 2001; Foley, 1990; Levinson, Foley, & Holland, 1996; Roman & Apple, 1990; Willis, 1977) attend to both the larger social structures and the agency of individual people and groups of people. Both structure and agency are, therefore, illuminated through data and analysis in critical ethnography. Illuminating structure, on the one hand, means showing how economic, political, social, historical, and cultural institutions and norms operate in any given context and confine the options available to individuals. Illuminating agency, on the other hand, means highlighting how people are not completely constrained and how our actions are not always determined by structures. Instead, individuals make choices within a particular context and often resist oppressive and constraining structural forces. Thus highlighting **resistance**—that is, opposition to the marginalization and oppression experienced either by an individual or by a group of which an individual is a member—is an important goal in critical ethnography. In other words, critical ethnographers argue that although people have agency and often resist their oppression, structures bear down on them and confine their arena of possibilities for action.

As I noted earlier, Paul Willis's *Learning to Labor* (1977) offers a classic example of the relationship between structure and agency, but countless critical ethnographic studies since then have done this as well. The vignette with which I opened this chapter reflects this tension in my own research, and, for me, it was difficult to determine the appropriate emphasis between structure and agency. Overemphasizing the structural dynamics of racism within schools implies that individual people play no role and are thus exempt from responsibility for racist practices and outcomes. But overemphasizing the role of individuals in regard to racism within schools implies that the institution of schooling is equitable and that racism is merely the fault of a few irresponsible people and, therefore, is easily fixed. Neither of these explanations fully articulates the reality within schools.

Highlighting Both Micro and Macro Phenomena

Critical ethnography attempts to highlight both local practices and patterns and more general or global practices and patterns. For example, Stacey Lee's ethnography (2005) describes the ways American identity is synonymous with being White within a particular Midwestern high school. She provides thick description of her research context and the Hmong youth with whom she worked, but she uses the data as a sort of window through which to better understand patterns of race, racism, and identity within the U.S. education system. It is this rub between the micro, or local, and the macro, or global, that critical ethnography attempts to articulate. In other words, critical ethnographers know that racism, sexism, classism, and other types of oppression exist, and we attempt to illustrate how this oppression plays out at the local level. But it is also through this illustration of micro patterns and practices that we shed light on macro structures and institutions. As I noted earlier, I struggle (as do others) to articulate this balance in fair and accurate ways.

Drawing On *and* Building Theory

Critical ethnographers are interested in social theory and analyses of social systems, and we attempt to use our research to improve on and build social theory. We share an interest in theoretical concepts like structure, agency, culture, reproduction, and oppression. Further, critical ethnographers attempt to weave theory and rich description. In Angela Valenzuela's *Subtractive Schooling*

(1999), for example, she provides rich description of the schooling experiences of Latina/o youth while also adding much to our understanding of theories of both assimilation and caring. There is much to be learned from Valenzuela's description of schooling so that we can better understand the struggles, successes, and strategies of Latina/o youth in U.S. schools. There is also much to be learned from the variations on caring theory that Valenzuela articulates. Good critical ethnography adds to our understanding of existing theories (such as caring theory in Valenzuela's work) or develops new theoretical insights.

Theory plays an important role in critical ethnography because we rely on theory to provide an interpretive or conceptual framework for both designing the research and analyzing the data. Critical ethnographers may draw on feminist theory, critical theory, queer theory, or critical race theory, for example, to guide our research topic and questions, methods, analysis, and interpretation. This is not to say that critical ethnographers already know what we are going to find or are just looking for what we already know; instead critical ethnographers are explicit about the foundational principles and assumptions from which we are starting. For example, if I approach my research from a critical race theory perspective (Bell, 1992; Crenshaw, Gotanda, Peller, & Thomas, 1995; Delgado & Stefancic, 2001; Dixson & Rousseau, 2006; Ladson-Billings & Tate, 1995), I already assume that racism exists and that race matters in everyday experiences. What I do not know, however, is what racism will look like at a particular site or how race will have an impact on certain people and experiences—these might be some of the things I am hoping to uncover in my research. After collecting data, I also then come back to critical race theory to assist me in making sense of and better understanding my data.

Focusing on Various and Intertwining Power-Related Identities and Oppressions

Critical ethnographers study a range of topics, but our research topics are always related to issues of power. By **power,** I mean access to key resources and knowledge, and the means to exert control over those resources and knowledge within society. Power is differently distributed among and between racial, social class, gender, linguistic, and other groups, resulting in patterns of oppression and privilege. Although critical ethnography is often associated with critical theory and its exclusive focus on social class issues, many critical ethnographers are concerned with *all* forms of social injustice and address issues of race, class, gender, sexuality, and language in our work. It is important to note that many contemporary critical ethnographers examine the intersections of multiple identities and power-related categories. Michelle Fine and Lois Weis's *The Unknown*

City (1998), on the one hand, provides an example of a critical ethnography that is primarily about social class but also devotes considerable attention to race and gender. Stacey Lee's *Up Against Whiteness* (2005), on the other hand, centers an analysis of race and ethnicity while also attending to issues of social class, gender, and language. The primary topic of analysis (for example, race or class) is not what distinguishes critical ethnography. Rather, it is the focus on some aspect of power, privilege, and oppression that is one defining characteristic of critical ethnography.

Reflecting on Issues of Representation and Positionality

Critical ethnographers devote considerable attention to issues of representation and positionality. Although these terms have been used to refer to a variety of issues, I use **representation** here to mean issues related to how we as researchers describe our participants and data, and **positionality** to mean the identities of the researchers in relation to our participants and data.

Two of the most common issues related to representation that critical ethnographers must resolve are how to represent our participants and how to represent certain types of data. Research that focuses on issues of power necessarily involves people who are affected by inequitable resource and power distribution, and questions arise as to whether individuals negatively affected by power hierarchies ought to be described in research as victims, villains, or heroes. These choices are, of course, overly simplistic and fail to account for the actual complexity involved, but the point remains that critical ethnographers sometimes make difficult decisions about how to best represent our research participants.

In a related vein, critical ethnographers sometimes make difficult decisions about how to handle **"hot" data** that has the potential to cause harm or misrepresent an issue. As Michelle Fine and Lois Weis (1998) eloquently note, "We continue to struggle with how to best represent treacherous data; data that may do more damage than good, depending on who consumes/exploits them" (p. 272). Stacey Lee's work (2005) provides another example when she describes the struggle to decide how to talk about "early marriage" practices among the Hmong American families in her research. A topic like "early marriage" could serve to reinforce stereotypes and vilify the Hmong American community, but it could also serve to illuminate both the experiences within families and the dominant structures within schools that judge immigrant youth and communities.

Considering the authorial voice of researchers, Michelle Fine (1994a) outlines three positions qualitative researchers might adopt. First, the

ventriloquist stance assumes the researcher directly transmits information from the research participants. There is no political stance explicit in the research, and the researcher is detached from the participants and attempts to be as invisible in the representation as possible. This position denies that any choice between various perspectives exists and, as a result, conveys descriptions of research that are static and disconnected from the larger context. Second, the **voices stance** positions the research participants at the center and highlights their ideas and experiences that are in opposition to the dominant discourse. The researcher is present, but her positionality is not addressed explicitly. And third, in the **activism stance** the researcher takes an explicit stand against injustice and advocates for greater equity on behalf of those most marginalized.

The third option outlined by Fine is most consistent with critical ethnography because the researcher has a clear agenda and is positioned as an activist. However, in addition to assuming the activism stance, many critical ethnographers also explicitly incorporate **reflexivity** concerning our own positionality. This reflexivity entails deep and critical reflection by the researcher about her own identities and her role in, and impact on, the research. "Positionality is vital because it forces us to acknowledge our own power, privilege, and biases just as we are denouncing the power structures that surround our subjects" (Madison, 2005, p. 7).

Subjectivity is an oft-cited concept within research circles, and although subjectivity and positionality are related, they are not exactly the same. Whereas subjectivity refers to one's own, individual self, positionality refers to the self in relation to others (Madison, 2005). Positionality assumes that we coconstruct reality, and it is the space of overlap or intersection that critical ethnographers must examine and make explicit in our research. There must be a balance, however, so that the research does not become solely about the researcher—taking it out of the realm of critical ethnography and into the sphere of autobiography or autoethnography (see Chapter Eight). Because critical ethnographers are primarily concerned with highlighting and changing inequities, our work must center the people and topic of analysis rather than centering ourselves as researchers.

As in all studies, my positionality and identities certainly played a role in how I was perceived, how people interacted with me, what they said to me, and what they did not say or do in my presence (Emerson, Fretz, & Shaw, 1995; Weis & Fine, 2000). As a White person conducting research with predominantly White teachers, my racial identity was often taken for granted and not questioned. In this sense my whiteness was an asset because White teachers and administrators seemed to assume a sort of compatibility with me and believed that I would share similar ideas about race. I am sure that a number of teachers felt comfortable saying certain things to me because of our shared White identity. Being acutely aware of how I was probably being perceived by most of the White teachers with whom I worked caused me some discomfort, however. I often wondered if I was being dishonest or unethical by not making my beliefs about race and racism explicit to them. It is likely that doing this would have caused tension in a number of the relationships I formed with teachers, and, in the end, I opted to not offer my perspectives about race but also to be honest if I was asked. It is perhaps unsurprising that I was rarely asked about my thoughts on issues of race and racism.

Taking a Stand Against Inequity

In addition to focusing on issues of representation and positionality, critical ethnographers center an agenda of highlighting and changing inequities because we value **equity,** which refers to that which is fair and just. Critical ethnography is concerned with both what is and what could be, or what ought to be (Carspecken, 1996; Madison, 2005; Noblit, Flores, & Murillo, 2004; Thomas, 1993). In other words, critical ethnographers attempt to both describe the current lived realities and advocate more equitable alternatives. Critical ethnographers thus share a value orientation in that we are all concerned about inequity and attempt to use our research toward positive social change (Carspecken, 1996; Carspecken & Apple, 1992). As Phil Carspecken (1996) notes,

> Criticalists find contemporary society to be unfair, unequal, and both subtly and overtly oppressive for many people. We do not like it, and we want to change it. Moreover, we have found that much of what has passed for "neutral objective science" is in fact not neutral at all, but subtly biased in favor of privileged groups. (p. 7)

Through both our research topics and our approaches we strive for a world in which equity prevails—in other words, one in which fairness and justice are prevalent.

Critical ethnography is defined, in part, by its social usefulness—that is, by its ability to highlight and offer alternatives to the many social injustices and inequities in our world. Indeed, "critical ethnography begins with an ethical responsibility to address processes of unfairness or injustice within a particular lived domain" (Madison, 2005, p. 5). Critical ethnographers are explicit about our politics and believe that researchers must be engaged in working for social change, although we sometimes differ on exactly what that means. As an example,

Douglas Foley and Angela Valenzuela (2005) differentiate between critical ethnographers who do cultural critiques, those who write applied policy studies, and those who are involved directly in political movements. Whereas Foley (1990, 1995) describes his work as primarily cultural critique, Valenzuela has been involved in numerous political movements and has served as an expert witness on educational issues in Texas. Both scholars do important critical ethnographic work because, like other critical ethnographers, they attempt to illustrate and disrupt inequity.

REFLECTION QUESTIONS

1. What are the defining characteristics of critical ethnography?
2. What research questions might you pursue that fit with this particular methodology?
3. How might your proposed research make the greatest contribution to increased equity?
4. What do you think about research that has an activism stance?

Doing Critical Ethnography

Critical ethnography shares many methods and goals with more traditional approaches to ethnography. Both attempt to explain social phenomena from the participants' point of view; both privilege local knowledge and experience; and both use participant observation, interviews, focus groups, and general immersion into a local context to generate these insights. The process of doing critical ethnography bears much resemblance to doing ethnography that is interpretive in nature (Schensul, Schensul, & LeCompte, 1999). Immersion is a key part of both ethnographic and critical ethnographic research:

> The ethnographer seeks a deeper immersion in others' worlds in order to grasp what they experience as meaningful and important. With immersion, the field researcher sees from the inside how people lead their lives, how they carry out their daily rounds of activities, what they find meaningful, and how they do so. (Emerson et al., 1995, p. 2)

Both ethnographers and critical ethnographers formulate research questions; consult and are in conversation with the existing research literature; collect data through various means (for example, observation, interviews, document review); and code our data by searching for patterns and outlying cases. Because there is a chapter in this volume on ethnography (Chapter Seven), I will not repeat that information here. Instead I will discuss some of the issues and considerations that critical ethnographers generally face during various phases of the research process.

Background Assumptions

Critical ethnographers ascribe to a set of assumptions that guide our work. As previously explained, these assumptions include (1) that power shapes people's experiences, relationships, and everyday occurrences; (2) that marginalization and oppression exist; (3) that surface-level appearances are not always accurate; and (4) that social change is possible. Critical ethnographers do not spend time attempting to illustrate or prove these basic assumptions because they are already grounded in existing research. We move forward from these previously established points.

Topic Selection

Critical ethnographers can choose from the same range and variation of topics as any other researcher, but the topics are always approached from a particular angle. Our choice of topic and context is often guided by an interest in examining power and oppression, but because we believe power and oppression are always present, we can direct our examination just about anywhere. Indeed, topic selection "begins with a passion to investigate an injustice (for example, racism); social control (language, norms, or cultural rules); power; stratification; or allocation of cultural rewards and resources to illustrate how cultural meanings constrain existence" (Thomas, 1993, p. 36). It can sometimes be difficult to narrow in on a particular area of study because the focus of critical ethnography is often on contexts and situations that are meant to hide the ways power and oppression operate.

Study Design and Method

Decisions about how to design a research project and the methods to employ for data collection are central to all research and greatly influence the degree to which a project is critically oriented. Critical ethnographers identify data sources that are most likely to provide "insider" perspectives of the given topic. We do not assume that all data are equally useful, and we are alert to data sources that may be reinforcing patterns of privilege and oppression and those that may be resisting the status quo. A critical ethnographer may, for example, decide to pay special attention to the voices of gay and lesbian people within a community struggling with homophobia and heterosexism. If the knowledge shared by these individuals contradicts the knowledge offered by straight men and women in the community, the researcher would need to figure out the meanings behind the differences and may decide that the perspectives of the gay and lesbian individuals need to be heard more.

Data Analysis and Interpretation

Although data analysis in critical ethnography follows similar techniques as in other qualitative research (for example, coding, asking questions, making comparisons, looking for patterns and negative cases), critical ethnographers are especially interested in the nonliteral meanings of language and other forms of communication. We might, for example, examine how certain phrases (such as "at risk" or "welfare mothers") carry particular meanings within a community or how silence (that is, the absence of talk) communicates particular messages. Because we assume the presence of unbalanced power relations and structures that are meant to obscure these, we pay close attention to the various, and sometimes competing, meanings embedded in our data.

Writing It Up

Critical ethnographers think about the intended and unintended audiences and consequences of our work. Our goal is to speak truth to power, and yet we also must protect the anonymity of our participants. In other words, although our research must be specific enough to spark changes in policies and practices and among those in positions of power, we have to be careful that the way we write up our research is not compromising the trust and identities of those with whom we conducted the research. We are also alert to instances that merely exoticize or romanticize particular people or circumstances. Because critical ethnography is aimed at social change, we consider which venues will be most effective for sharing our findings.

REFLECTION QUESTIONS

1. What are some key issues critical ethnographers have to think about in the design and implementation of a research project?
2. To what extent can you see yourself doing critical ethnography?

Critiques of Critical Ethnography

Critical ethnography is most commonly subject to at least two broad critiques. The first relates to the political orientation of critical ethnography, and the second relates to issues of representation within critical ethnography.

"It's Politics, Not Research"

One of the most common critiques of critical ethnography relates to **validity** issues, and this critique has come from both within and outside the ethnographic tradition. Both traditional ethnographers and traditional positivist-oriented researchers charge critical ethnography with lacking validity because it is ideological, political, value based, and overly biased. For many qualitative researchers, validity is understood to be the soundness of an argument, which is always mediated by a particular cultural group within a particular context. In other words, for critical ethnographers, research is valid when community members agree that it is an accurate representation of their reality. Although it is true that validity thus depends on what is known about a particular topic at a particular point in time, critical researchers do not ascribe to relativism because we believe a common reality exists and can be known. In order to advocate against oppression, for example, one must believe that oppression exists.

Rather than focusing on validity, some critical ethnographers prefer to think about, and strive for, **trustworthiness**—which has the same idea as validity but does not carry the same connection to positivist traditions. We engage in many of the standard practices to enhance trustworthiness, including member checking, triangulating data sources, and using multiple methods (see Chapter Ten; see also Lincoln & Guba, 1985). But researcher reflexivity is also crucial to enhancing the trustworthiness of critical ethnography. Reflexivity involves reflection around a number of issues, including the relationship between theory and data, the researcher's impact on the data collected, the researcher's biases and assumptions, and the relationship between structure and agency (Anderson, 1989). Undertaking reflective writing like that with which I opened this chapter and holding similar conversations with colleagues are valuable strategies for increasing researcher reflexivity.

Critical ethnographers also respond to questions about validity by pointing out that *all research* is ideological, political, value laden, and biased. The key for critical ethnographers is that whereas most researchers attempt to control or deny these qualities, critical ethnographers are explicit about them and prefer to make our research as transparent as possible. Maintaining particular value orientations certainly shapes a critical ethnographer's research, but it does not determine what the findings will be or what conclusions will be drawn because we engage in standard data analysis techniques (such as coding, making comparisons, searching for patterns and exceptions, and so forth) and draw conclusions that are supported by the data (rather than conclusions that merely confirm our hunches about the data). One's value orientations do shape the research topic chosen, the research questions, and decisions about what to publish and how. Again, however, critical researchers claim that this is true of all researchers—that is, regardless of the methodology used, a researcher always has particular value orientations and epistemologies and those will always have an impact on the research in some way. Thus critical ethnographers would say that our work (like all research) is always *positioned*, but it is not *biased* because our findings and conclusions are data driven rather than value driven.

"It's Either Too Gloomy or Too Romanticized"

Critical ethnography is also sometimes critiqued for the types of representation conveyed in the reporting of research. Critics charge that critical ethnographers are overly pessimistic and offer little hope for practitioners within schools and other social institutions. Indeed, critical ethnographers must find a balance between highlighting oppressive conditions and illuminating spaces of agency, resistance, and opportunities for change. This is a tall order, but critical ethnographers take seriously our responsibility to disrupt inequity and work toward greater justice.

There exists some debate over whether scholars ought to represent historically oppressed groups as victims or as resilient agents who resist and occasionally overcome their systematic marginalization, but critical ethnographers struggle to work around, between, and in spite of this common dichotomy. Lois Weis and Michelle Fine (2000) explain their strategy for maintaining socially just representations:

> We stretch toward writing that spirals around social injustice and resilience; that recognizes the endurance of structures of injustice and the powerful acts of agency; that appreciates the courage and the limits of individual acts of resistance, but refuses to perpetuate the fantasy that "victims" are simply powerless. That these women and men are strong *is not evidence that they have suffered no oppression.* (p. 61)

They provide a useful set of recommendations for conducting and writing research in the interest of social justice; their recommendations include the following (Weis & Fine, 2000):

- Researchers should "dare to speak hard truths with theoretical rigor and political savvy" (p. 62) in an effort to explain accurately why and how the difficult elements of life are intimately tied to historical, structural, and economic relations.

- Researchers should use multiple methods and engage in member checks to increase the validity of our findings.

- Researchers should always consider how our work might be used for "progressive, conservative, and repressive social policies" (p. 65).

These strategies enhance trustworthiness and therefore help guard against research that is inaccurately "gloomy" or "romanticized." It is important to note, however, that critical ethnographers do not avoid certain research topics, data, or conclusions merely because they may make readers uncomfortable. In order to pursue equity, we sometimes have to raise awareness about ugly truths.

REFLECTION QUESTIONS

1. What are the primary critiques of critical ethnography? What do you think about these critiques and the way critical ethnographers respond to them?
2. How willing would you be to conduct research that you might have to defend against critiques like those leveled at critical ethnography?

Summary

In response to these critiques and others, critical ethnography has evolved since its beginnings in the 1970s. In addition to opening up space for analyses of oppressions other than those that are class based, critical ethnography has also opened up space for varied (and sometimes competing) theoretical orientations. Researchers have merged ideas from postmodern theories, queer theories, feminist theories, and countless others. If critical ethnographers are sincere about our goal of highlighting oppression and advocating social change, we must continue to ensure that new and different spaces can continue to be opened within critical ethnography's boundaries.

Critical ethnography is a methodology pursued by researchers with a commitment to equity and the skill to analyze structure and agency, and to highlight the relationships between local and global patterns. Critical ethnographic research focuses on issues of power and oppression and attempts to bring about changes in policies and practices that are more fair and just. Because critical ethnographers are explicit about our value orientations, we are often charged with being overly biased and told that our research lacks validity. Despite these critiques, critical ethnography remains as a useful, trustworthy, and important approach to qualitative research.

Key Terms

activism stance, 381
agency, 374
classical Marxism, 375
critical ethnography, 374
culturalists, 375
deterministic, 375
equity, 382
exploitative system, 375

"hot" data, 380
mechanistic, 375
positionality, 380
power, 379
reflexivity, 381
representation, 380
resistance, 377
social reproduction, 376

structuralism, 375
structure, 374
subjectivity, 381
trustworthiness, 386
validity, 386
ventriloquist stance, 380
voices stance, 381

Further Readings and Resources

Suggested Critical Ethnography Studies

Valenzuela, A. (1999). *Subtractive schooling: U.S.-Mexican youth and the politics of caring.* Albany: State University of New York Press.
This is a well-respected critical ethnography of Mexican American youth.

Willis, P. (1977). *Learning to labor: How working class kids get working class jobs.* New York: Columbia University Press.
This is a now-classic critical ethnography conducted in England among working-class boys.

Other Suggested Readings

Anderson, G. (1989). Critical ethnography in education: Origins, current status, and new directions. *Review of Educational Research, 59,* 249–270.
This article is a review of critical ethnographic theory and research in the field of education.

Carspecken, P. (1996). *Critical ethnography in educational research: A theoretical and practical guide.* New York: Routledge.

This book offers a comprehensive discussion of critical ethnography as a research methodology.

Organizations and Web Sites

American Educational Research Association—Critical Educators for Social Justice (SIG #144) (www.aeracesjsig.org/)
This special interest group of researchers advocates for environmental justice, human rights, and economic democracy.

American Educational Research Association—Critical Examinations of Race, Ethnicity, Class, and Gender in Education (SIG #27) (www.aera.net/default.aspx?menu_id=160&id=931)
This is a special interest group of researchers committed to critical analyses of the intersections of race, ethnicity, social class, and gender.

Council on Anthropology and Education (CAE) (www.aaanet.org/sections/cae/cae-home.html)
This section of the American Anthropological Association comprises researchers who apply anthropological perspectives to the study of education. Many members of CAE conduct critically oriented research.

CHAPTER 16

FEMINIST RESEARCH

Lucy E. Bailey

Key Ideas

- Feminist research seeks to create new knowledge, challenge beliefs and practices that limit human potential, explore the lives of women and other marginalized groups, and facilitate social critique and action to reduce inequities.

- Feminist approaches to research emerged during the 1960s as part of a vibrant period of women's activism and critical questioning in academia.

- Feminist methodologists have offered critiques of traditional approaches to research and have developed innovative approaches to investigate, analyze, and represent the complexity of the social world.

- Feminist researchers argue that all research approaches reflect and strengthen certain agendas and knowledge claims over others and are therefore political by nature.

- There is no one "feminist" methodology; how researchers use methods, conduct research, and embrace certain goals determine whether research is feminist.

- Feminist approaches can be qualitative, quantitative, or mixed-methods; can use varied theories and strategies; and can address diverse topics. Qualitative inquiry is a common approach feminists use to study the lived experiences of marginalized groups and the forces that limit human potential.

- Feminist research follows general "guiding principles" (Fonow & Cook, 1991, 2005).

Feminist approaches to qualitative research encompass a wide range of theories, practices, and methods used to generate knowledge about the social and physical world; to challenge oppressive forces and beliefs (for example, racism, homophobia, sexism, ethnocentrism); and to spur social change that improves the lives of women and other disadvantaged groups—and, by extension, all human lives. In contrast to traditional research approaches that seek to create knowledge about a given phenomenon, feminist research is concerned with knowledge, critique, *and* action. Some feminist researchers consider critique a form of action; for others, action might refer to policy changes, program reform, or group empowerment. Feminist research is potentially emancipatory in nature, providing a vehicle to critique common theories and assumptions and to offer voice and visibility to marginalized groups.

The general principles that guide feminist research include a spirit of critique; a challenge to claims of objectivity in research; consciousness of gender as a force that organizes social life and thought; ethical and equitable research practices; and an action orientation focused on personal, institutional, theoretical, and social transformation (Fonow & Cook, 1991, 2005). The questions that drive feminist projects often emerge from women's lived experiences, such as childbearing or sexual harassment, from revisiting common assumptions and practices through the lens of gender, and from considering the perspectives of diverse groups rendered invisible in history and research. Just as **feminism,** the quest for gender equity, involves diverse groups, beliefs, and practices, feminist research involves diverse researchers, beliefs, and practices. This chapter will describe the historical roots of feminist research, introduce key components of this rich field of inquiry, and provide examples of researchers' use of qualitative methods from a feminist perspective.

Historical Roots of Feminist Research

The roots of feminism and feminist approaches to research stretch back over a century to the origins of the American women's movement, a social movement to advance women's rights that activists launched in Seneca Falls, New York, in 1848. Hundreds of men and women gathered to protest the limited legal, educational, and social rights women held in a democracy founded on the principle that "all men are created equal." Activists recognized that sex and gender were central to organizing law, religion, economics, and social life. From laws that stripped married women of their earnings, property, and children, to limited educational access, to strictures on public speaking, women in diverse circumstances faced profound limitations to their human potential. These reformers boldly proposed a series of resolutions to challenge exclusionary laws and to expand women's opportunities, launching what became the first wave of the women's movement.

The spirit of critique and hope that fueled these early visionaries to protest inequities and act on behalf of the disenfranchised also prompted activists and scholars during the 1960s and 1970s (the second wave of the women's movement) to question conventional approaches to research, critique the knowledge such methodologies generated, and develop a range of feminist practices for studying the social world. Contemporary feminist research approaches emerged during this vibrant period of social critique and activism. Unlike many other approaches to research, feminist methodologies are overtly political and emancipatory in aim.

One significant force shaping the development of feminist inquiry and the development of qualitative research methods is the critique of positivism (see Chapters One and Four). Since the nineteenth century, scientific research has primarily proceeded from a research **paradigm** (a theory of knowledge; how we come to know what we know) called positivism. Paradigms reflect and delineate a set of beliefs about how to investigate phenomena. They shape how researchers conduct inquiry, what researchers and audiences recognize as knowledge, and who is considered a legitimate knower. Although positivist research is rarely identified as such, the majority of research conducted today falls under this paradigm, and it wields significant power in shaping the production of knowledge and legitimizing what counts as good science.

Positivism holds that one true reality exists that trained, objective researchers can discover through the use of appropriate procedures. It relies on **empiricism,** or sensory experience—what one can taste, feel, see, and hear—as the basis for building knowledge claims. One might trek in the field to collect leaves, observe children in a playground, or measure changes in blood chemistry to pursue a given research question. Research guided by this paradigm is generally oriented to discover facts, predict patterns, refine knowledge, and provide information for use in controlling aspects of the social and physical world.

Feminist researchers' gendered critiques of positivist assumptions and approaches prompted the development of a range of creative and emancipatory approaches aligned with feminist aims. During the 1960s and 1970s those agitating for reproductive rights, educational equity, equal pay, and other social issues recognized that gender not only shaped social life but also shaped how scholars conducted research and created knowledge. As with the democratic laws and practices that Seneca Falls activists challenged as patriarchal and exclusionary, scholars noted contradictions between positivist claims of objectivity and **universality** (findings applicable to all) and certain **androcentric** (male-centered) assumptions that guided research practice. For example, philosophical and religious beliefs in women's inferiority permeated Western science for centuries (Hubbard, 1990; Schiebinger, 1993; Tuana, 1993), from Aristotle's claim in the fourth century B.C. that women were "misbegotten men" to physician Edward H. Clarke's research (1873) that "found" that women's pursuit of higher education endangered their reproductive health. Such findings reflected particular beliefs about women and men, mind and body, emotion and rationality, weakness and strength—all produced by male researchers of European ancestry in positions of social power that inevitably shaped their perceptions of the world.

Further, researchers often excluded women and disadvantaged groups (groups who have historically held little social power) as collaborators and participants or deemed their concerns too insignificant to study. Scholars studying "work" ignored women's domestic labor. Biographers narrated the "successful" lives of politicians and military leaders while women who had been restricted from visible public roles evaporated into the historical ether. Historians detailed soldiers' triumphs and military leaders' conquests and overlooked women's efforts to nurse soldiers, provide war supplies, and sustain the home front in the wake of men's absence. Psychologists studying moral development evaluated female participants as less moral than males without considering how gendered assumptions shaped their use of the concept or how different experiences based on race, gender, and class might forge diverse conceptions of morality.

Feminist scholars noted that such research practices did not reflect universal knowledge because they excluded women and people of color as researchers, participants, or subjects and applied concepts that appeared neutral (such as work, morality, or success) in gendered ways that rendered women's lives and experiences invisible. On a more fundamental level, these research approaches proceeded from particular assumptions about the social world, the topics deemed valuable to study, and the questions researchers should ask—all of which shaped the knowledge they generated. Research practices were often based on men's experiences, presented in the guise of *objectivity* and used to generate *universal* truths (Bailey, 2007).

REFLECTION QUESTIONS

1. What are the components of positivism?
2. How is the history of research gendered?
3. How are all research practices political and acts of power?
4. If, historically, women's experiences had been the foundation of research, how might this difference shape our knowledge about the social and physical world?

Guiding Principles of Feminist Research

Critiques of positivism prompted feminist scholars to develop alternative paradigms or ways of knowing, different conceptual frameworks to explain phenomena (**theories**), different rationales and approaches to direct how research should proceed (**methodologies**), new techniques for gathering data (**methods**), and innovative forms to disseminate knowledge (**representation**). Feminist researchers pose varied questions about the social world and mobilize diverse philosophies, theories, methodologies, and methods to gather information and create knowledge.

Across these diverse approaches, feminist researchers generally share a philosophical stance that differs fundamentally from that of positivists: feminists hold that the conduct of research and the knowledge it generates are not—and cannot be—neutral or objective; indeed, such research goals are illusory and counterproductive. All researchers (including those who employ feminist approaches) inevitably absorb the theories, beliefs, and discourses within their social and historical contexts. Researchers' historical context, social location, training, and life experiences shape how they think about the world. Thus, in ways that both complicate and enrich the research process, researchers are inevitably linked to, not outside of and objective toward, the phenomena they study. For many, qualitative research seemed an ideal feminist response to centuries of exploitative and marginalizing research practices. The inclusive in-depth, face-to-face methods provide opportunities to sensitively explore diverse experiences, honor the experience and knowledge of both researcher and participants, and facilitate collaborative relationships.

Despite the affinities between qualitative research and feminist goals, no given framework or technique is inherently feminist. In any research endeavor—whether traditional or critical, quantitative or qualitative—research purpose drives design and methodology. How researchers conceptualize their research and use methods determines whether research is feminist. For example, a research approach used to objectify rather than empower contradicts the principles of feminist methodology. Researchers can conduct survey research, experimental studies, historical research (see Chapter Six), ethnography (see Chapter Seven), or other forms of research from a feminist perspective. Similarly, feminists also use various methods to elicit information. They might conduct interviews, analyze documents, observe interactions, examine photographs, moderate focus groups, distribute surveys, or burrow in archives for traces of women's historical presence.

What distinguishes feminist from conventional research approaches are a general series of **guiding principles** (Fonow & Cook, 1991, 2005) that overlap and vary in practice and continue to evolve as methodology grows increasingly complex. These principles relate to researchers' purpose, theoretical allegiances, and approach to the conduct of inquiry.

Nonobjectivity of Research Practices

First, various scholars, including feminists, scholars of color, and advocates of indigenous approaches to research, argue that research practice is laden with cultural values and subjective beliefs. All researchers occupy particular social roles that shape their experiences, values, and practices. All research practices reflect the cultural beliefs and systems of thought in which they are produced. This inevitability can both enhance and distort research practice. For example, complex systems of racism, colonialism, and sexism have shaped Western thought and research practice historically (see also Chapters Seven, Fourteen, Fifteen, and Seventeen). As a result, the history of science is riddled with researchers' ethnocentric assumptions about the superiority of Western science and racist and sexist assumptions about the presumed inferiority of women and people of color. Researchers in advantaged social positions measured skulls, tracked menstrual cycles, and scrutinized the bodies of women and people of color in search of the physical locus of their presumed inferiority. They then used scientific findings to justify restrictions on their social roles.

These examples underscore the pressing need to cast critical light on *all* research practices: whether findings are laudatory or limiting, they have concrete effects on human lives. Accepting beliefs about particular groups' inferiority as fact, using research to justify their exclusion from higher education where they might contribute to the creation of knowledge, and generalizing research findings from one group to another are not objective practices. They are value-laden acts of power based on particular beliefs about, in this case, race and sex and gender that influence the research undertaken and the knowledge generated.

Some feminists suggest that formulating questions and pursuing research from specific social locations can also enhance research pursuits. For example, feminist **standpoint** theory (Collins, 1990; Harding, 1991, 2004; Hartsock, 1998, 2003) posits that research grounded in the perspectives of those who have been marginalized (women and men of color, gays and lesbians, the impoverished) has potential to offer certain insights and advantages that research grounded in dominant perspectives cannot. Such perspectives, or standpoints, born of particular experiences in socially marginalized locations, can provide a fuller, richer portrait of human experience than researchers working within dominant paradigms have provided historically.

Gender

Second, feminist researchers view gender and its intersections with race, sexuality, (dis)ability, ethnicity, and nationality as factors structuring social life in often unequal ways that merit research scrutiny. From this perspective, such descriptors do not simply refer to whether one is, for example, a male or female, a citizen of a certain nation, or a member of a particular racial group. Rather, the terms refer to socially constructed notions of people and groups that structure research, occupations, families, law, and the intricacies of people's daily lives in a given culture. For example, the category of "intersex" reflects the limits of previously taken-for-granted categories of "male" and "female" to capture the diversity of human biology. Further, whether a shirt buttons on the left or on the right, or where men and women keep their wallets, are not biologically determined; they are gendered social practices that structure men's and women's movement and experience in minute and almost imperceptible ways. Similarly, what is considered a (dis)ability varies in history and context.

On a broader level, the profession of nursing is gendered as *feminine* not simply because women constitute the majority of nurses today but because many consider the caring and compassionate characteristics of the profession feminine whether men or women display them. As one male nurse phrased it in a feminist qualitative study, nursing has "never really been considered a manly thing to do" (Sayman, 2009, p. 150). Gender thus structures men's and women's occupational choices, the experiences of male nurses, messages about nursing in media and textbooks, and the value society accords the profession. Feminist research enacts a critical stance that casts gendered analytic light on significant processes that influence human lives.

Researcher Reflexivity

Feminist methodology is also characterized by varied expressions of researcher **reflexivity.** This concept, which is shared with some other qualitative traditions (see, for example, Chapters Seven, Nine, and Fifteen), refers to researchers' intentional reflections on their research practices. The goal of reflexivity is not to reduce bias; such a goal presumes an objective view is attainable. Rather, in a paradigm that holds that the knower is connected to what is known, reflexivity is a tool for researchers to consider how their assumptions, investments, and decisions shape—often in nourishing and productive ways—the research process. Accordingly, researchers analyze their role in creating knowledge as a standard aspect of inquiry. Reflexivity might include researchers' reflection on their epistemologies and methods; how their identities, standpoint, or training shapes inquiry; or potential audience responses to the research.

Consider this reflection from Mendoza-Denton (2008), a cultural anthropologist who has used sociolinguistics, ethnography, and feminist theory to study cultural practice among Latina gangs. She writes,

> It is a responsibility of anthropologists to explain ourselves, who we are and where we come from . . . given the history of anthropology: deep ethnocentrism; involvement in colonial administration; **anthropometry** (the practice of measuring the human body, historically applied to the sorting of gangsters and criminals, that fueled the foundation of scientific racism); and participation in the practice of display of human beings. . . . We have indeed a sordid story behind us. For these reasons it is essential to clearly set out as much as possible anthropologists' backgrounds, our assumptions, [and] our overt and hidden agendas . . . in order not to repeat some of our past mistakes. (p. 43)

In this reflection, which is relevant to a variety of critical and feminist projects, Mendoza-Denton notes that damaging racist, sexist, and ethnocentric practices have been commonplace in Western research traditions historically. Such traditions obligate researchers to reflect on and render visible how their standpoints, assumptions, and practices shape their research (see, for example, Chapters Fourteen and Fifteen).

Ethical and Equitable Practices

A fourth aspect of feminist research is vigilance to **ethical and equitable research** conduct, which can range in practice from ensuring researchers follow federally mandated **informed consent** protocol (making sure participants understand the procedures to which they are consenting; see also Chapter Two) to involving participants in shaping research design. Feminists work against the legacy of exploiting research subjects and strive to conduct research *with* people (humanizing stance) rather than *on* people (objectifying stance). A detached stance runs counter to feminist principles of **collaboration** and connection, muffles the emotional elements of lived experience, and obscures the human and social dynamics of research.

Like other qualitative approaches, feminist methodologies include such ethical practices as protecting the identities of participants and ensuring research poses no risks or harm beyond that participants might face in their everyday lives. Like other emancipatory approaches (see Chapters Fourteen, Fifteen, and Seventeen), feminist research attends to power inequities in society and in the research process. For example, researchers typically control the direction and outcome of research and often occupy higher social status or possess greater resources than participants. Thus, to minimize power imbalances, feminists might collaborate with participants in research design or data analysis (see Chapter Eighteen). To honor participants' time and energy, researchers might offer gift certificates or assistance with child care. To interrupt researcher authority, they might invite participants to critique their findings.

Like other critical approaches, inquiry conducted from a feminist perspective is also concerned with the **politics of representation.** This phrase highlights the ethical weight of portraying research subjects and findings that have implications for human lives. Research is used to understand human behavior, to develop theories, and to create policy. Accordingly, researchers must consider how they speak for and with their subjects, how they present their work, and how others might interpret or use their findings. For example, researchers examining the experiences of undocumented workers or women activists who live in regions suffused with ethnic and religious conflict must take extreme care in how they collect, preserve, and represent data from women whose safety could be threatened if identified (Gluck, 1991).

Other implications relate to the power of knowledge claims. For example, early feminist research focused narrowly on gender at the expense of other aspects of lived experience (for example, race, class, sexuality, nationality, ethnicity, and the intersections among these entities). Its findings captured white, Western, middle-class women's experiences and ignored significant differences *among* women. Researchers' failure to theorize their own social locations and critique their race-, class-, or heterosexual-based assumptions perpetuated partial and limited knowledge claims and research injustices at odds with researchers' feminist mission. Indeed, scholars of color and postcolonial critics have emphasized that various aspects of women's intersecting identities and social locations (language, class, race, religion, citizenship status) can hold greater significance than sex or gender for shaping women's lives.

Action Orientation

A final guiding principle is an **action orientation.** Like other critical research approaches, feminist inquiry proceeds from the assumption that research is a political and potentially emancipatory enterprise. The mission is not simply to explore, explain, or predict. Although one might *explore* a young woman's experience with eating problems or *explain* the effectiveness of a rape prevention program, the ultimate goal of feminist research is to produce findings that heighten consciousness about injustice, that empower disadvantaged groups, and that transform social institutions, practices, and theories to create a more equitable world. In this view, fundamental social inequities demand the attention of researchers.

Action can take many forms, including critiquing common assumptions, posing alternative views, or developing policies that advance rights. Thus some view critique and theorizing as forms of action. Some research is explicitly **action research** (the purpose of which is to contribute to change in a particular setting; see also Chapter Twelve), whereas some research provides information that others can use to better human lives.

To reflect these principles, feminist researchers have developed innovative forms to portray their research findings. For example, some have found academic conventions inadequate for capturing nuances in lived experience and the complexity of the social world. Standardized reports that require clinical language and tidy formatting can constrain what researchers convey. Some suggest they can also dehumanize participants. Researchers have used poetry (Richardson, 1997) and drama (Visweswaran, 1994) as alternatives to capture emotion simmering in qualitative data and to challenge positivist norms; combined participant voices to convey the collaborative nature of meaning-making; and created messy **multivocal texts** (texts with multiple writers, images, and styles) to challenge easy readings. These forms, which Lather (1991) calls "empowering research designs," challenge traditional ideas of what science can look like.

REFLECTION QUESTIONS

1. What are feminist scholars' primary critiques of the positivist paradigm?
2. What are the guiding principles of feminist inquiry?
3. How does feminist inquiry differ from other approaches?
4. What are the advantages and disadvantages of using innovative forms to share research findings?

RESEARCH SNAPSHOT 1

WOMEN LIVING WITH HIV/AIDS–HIGHLIGHTING THE CHARACTERISTICS OF FEMINIST RESEARCH

The following snapshot of a qualitative study demonstrates the guiding principles of feminist inquiry in action. For *Troubling the Angels: Women Living with HIV/AIDS*, Lather and Smithies (1997) conducted a multiyear study using qualitative methods to explore women's experiences living with HIV/AIDS. The stigma and pain of living with the virus made a humanizing, dialogic, and collaborative approach imperative. As Linda B., who is HIV positive, expressed, "Statistics are human beings with the tears wiped off" (p. xxvi).

Short History

Initially the medical community identified HIV/AIDS as a male disease. Experts were slow to recognize women's vulnerability to the virus and its differing warning signs and consequences for men and women. As a result, women were nearly invisible in the social and research landscape. Few resources were available to women negotiating the practical issues and stigma that accompanied the disease, and most reports were fatalistic.

Chris Smithies, a psychologist, and Patti Lather, a feminist methodologist, identified a pressing need for research that took gender into account. Smithies, who conducted support groups for women living with HIV/AIDS, recognized that women's struggles to find meaning in a devastating disease offered a significant form of knowledge that could help others better understand this invisible population.

Purpose

The purpose of the Lather and Smithies study was multilayered. It included exploring women's experiences *living* with (rather than dying from) a highly stigmatized disease, facilitating the empowerment of those who participated in the study, providing a text that would serve as a resource to others, and increasing awareness of and compassion for those living with the virus. As the researchers expressed, the topic of AIDS "is not so much a story about 'some others' as it is a story of how AIDS shapes our everyday lives, whether we be 'positives' or 'negatives' in terms of HIV status" (p. xiv). The researchers challenged categories of us and them, researcher and participant, and HIV-positive status and HIV-negative status to emphasize that HIV/AIDS affects all of us.

Participants

The twenty-five participants ranged in age from twenty-three to forty-nine. Sixteen of the women were white, and nine were women of color. Reflecting the diversity of women living with HIV/AIDS, many women were mothers or grandmothers; they had varied education levels; one had lost a child to the disease; the majority worked outside the home; and some were "out" to their families, whereas others kept the virus secret. Women attended the support groups as their health

(Continued)

RESEARCH SNAPSHOT 1
WOMEN LIVING WITH HIV/AIDS–HIGHLIGHTING THE CHARACTERISTICS OF FEMINIST RESEARCH (Continued)

and circumstances dictated. Between initial data collection and the final printing of the book, four of the women died.

Methodology

The researchers intended to interview the women to capture their perspectives in depth. As the study unfolded they realized that the support group format facilitated a level of community, dialogue, and energy among the women that individual interviews could not have produced. Support group meetings became their primary data source. (This change in intended research methodology reflects emergent flexible design, a characteristic of qualitative inquiry in which the researcher maintains an open and flexible approach throughout the conduct of research as circumstances and the study demand, as discussed in Chapters Seven and Ten, for example.) They also used observations, interviews, participant-produced documents (e-mails, poetry, and letters), statistics, and activist art. They drew excerpts from their field logs in which they reflected on the research process.

The study was in part naturalistic in the sense that researchers collected data in settings in which women "naturally" experienced living with HIV/AIDS: support groups, retreats, birthday parties, funerals, camping trips. Yet they also shaped the direction of support group conversations through prompts: "What keeps you going?" (p. 8), "What is a really bad day?" (p. 13), "What does that hope look like?" (p. 10), "How do you make sense of this?" (p. 131).

The researchers engaged in collaborative and participatory, rather than objectifying, research practices. They laughed, cried, and disagreed with the women. They celebrated birthdays and mourned deaths. They requested feedback on their findings. They responded to participants' need for visibility and voice. For example, Linda B. asked the researchers, "When are you guys going to publish? Some of us are on deadline, you know" (epigraph). Aware that time takes on different meaning in a study of women with uncertain futures, the researchers published a desktop version of their text to make it available as soon as possible. Rather than adopting the traditional role of research experts, they described their role as "witnesses . . . bearing the responsibility" of telling the women's stories (p. xvi). They also donated a percentage of the book royalties to HIV/AIDS organizations.

In the book, Lather and Smithies reflect on the limits of any researcher's capacity to connect with and understand participant experiences through the concept of **insider/outsider status** (how we are part of or different from the groups we study). Consider this interaction about hiding HIV status:

Chris Smithies (researcher): What's it like to live with such a secret? (p. 5)
Linda B. (participant): It's a double life, it's an absolute double life. You cannot imagine ever in your whole life what it's like. Somebody has cancer, you go and tell them you have cancer, it's oh you poor thing. You say you have AIDS . . . and they can't jump backwards fast enough or far enough. (p. 6)

This excerpt suggests that those who do not negotiate the emotional labor of hiding HIV-positive status on a daily basis cannot fully comprehend the experiences of those who do. Lather and Smithies may have shared a compassionate stance, gender, and often race with participants, yet their HIV-negative status limited their understanding. In fact, participants often felt compelled to teach the researchers their embodied knowledge, reversing the traditional research dynamic of researchers as experts and participants as passive subjects. For example, one participant told Lather as the research progressed, "You've grown so much and gotten a lot smarter than when I first met you" (epigraph).

Analysis

In contrast to traditional approaches in which the researcher's voice is dominant, for this study pages of support group transcripts were included to highlight women's voices. The researchers organized women's narratives into five general themes: life after diagnosis, relationships, making meaning, living/dying with AIDS, and support groups. Their narratives reflect the complexity of women's experiences.

Joanna: It's OK to be a positive woman. (epigraph)
Rosemary: I'm gonna die from stress, not HIV. (p. 11)
Amber: And I didn't even pay my income taxes. (p. 39)
Rita: I'd probably be dead if it wasn't for HIV. (p. 135)
Lisa: I don't have fifty years to be a mother. (p. 79)

The vibrancy of women's *lived* experiences crystallizes against a backdrop of social stigma, and reveals a fuller portrait of the complex phenomenon of HIV/AIDS.

Form

Lather and Smithies shared their findings in an innovative form: a messy, multilayered text intended to reflect the complexity of meaning-making and of living with HIV/AIDS. The text is brimming with information, fact boxes, activist art, poetry, data, and song lyrics. Its split-text format displays transcripts along the top of the page and running commentary from the researchers' field logs along

(Continued)

RESEARCH SNAPSHOT 1
WOMEN LIVING WITH HIV/AIDS–HIGHLIGHTING THE CHARACTERISTICS OF FEMINIST RESEARCH (Continued)

the bottom. It forces the reader's eye up and down, back and forth, choosing what to read. This challenging and confusing form is consistent with the researchers' goals. As Lather expressed, not only is AIDS an unsettling issue but "we *should* be uncomfortable with . . . telling other people's stories" (p. 9).

Summary

This study reflects the broad principles guiding feminist research. It highlights how researchers' perceptions about the social world shape the questions they ask and the research they conduct. It demonstrates the concrete effects of research for human lives. It reveals how gender and gender inequities (as well as class, sexuality, and race) organize social life, including experiences with a deadly virus that might seem, at first glance, a gender-neutral physiological phenomenon.

It also demonstrates research as a potential avenue for self-determination for marginalized groups—an outlet for women to define their experiences in their terms, to teach others, and to agitate for humane responses to a crisis that affects us all. In contrast to traditional qualitative and quantitative approaches in which the researcher adopts a detached stance, Lather and Smithies developed close relationships with the women. They intended to facilitate women's empowerment, to highlight the gendered structure of HIV/AIDS, and to provide readers with resources that better women's lives. These methodological choices are explicitly feminist.

REFLECTION QUESTIONS

1. How is this research design "feminist"? How does it differ from other emancipatory approaches?
2. In what ways was the topic of HIV/AIDS appropriate to study using feminist qualitative methodology?
3. How might a researcher using autoethnography, case study research, or another qualitative design approach this topic? What would be different?

Feminist Approaches

There is no single research model guiding feminist research. Feminist practices are diverse, **interdisciplinary** (drawing from different academic traditions), and driven by research purpose. For example, some researchers focus on law, policy, and curriculum as vehicles to advance women's status; others study how economic forces produce gender, race, and class inequities; and others consider the role of language and systems of thought in creating, and recreating, categories people inhabit, such as "woman" and "sexuality." Each focus reflects different theoretical approaches to formulating and conducting research.

This section will first describe several approaches to developing research questions and then provide examples of two qualitative approaches to feminist inquiry: oral history and ethnography. Oral history seeks to capture individual experiences within their social and cultural contexts; ethnography focuses on cultural practices (see Chapters Six and Seven).

Developing Research Questions

Research begins from any number of philosophical and practical questions about the social world. Questions might arise from the lived experiences of marginalized groups, a concrete problem in a program or community, particular gaps in knowledge about underrepresented groups, or critiques of sexist, heterosexist, or racist assumptions that have shaped knowledge.

Lived Experience
Research questions can emerge from the perspectives and standpoints of disadvantaged groups. Proceeding from the belief that everyone occupies a particular standpoint based on his or her social position, researchers inhabiting social roles with greater advantages might try to step outside the frameworks they assume are universal and consider the issue from the perspective of a disadvantaged person or group. A question to nourish this shift in perspective might be, What would a food program developed from the perspective of our most vulnerable citizens look like? Schmitt and Martin's case study (1999) of activist methods in a rape crisis center reflects this spirit when activists assert, "All we do comes from victims" (p. 364).

Researchers' assumptions shape the questions they formulate, the data they collect to answer their questions, and the knowledge they generate—which in turn shapes human lives and thought. Thus beginning from the standpoint of vulnerable people invites different kinds of questions for examining phenomena.

Concrete Issues

Research might also arise from a concrete issue that merits scrutiny. Perhaps a researcher has noted that a battered women's shelter is underused or a female administrator has advanced more rapidly than her peers. To understand why the women's shelter is underused or how the administrator has advanced, researchers might design an *instrumental* case study to explore each case in depth and *theorize* how they might use findings to improve services or advance other women administrators (see also Chapter Ten).

In the case of the shelter researchers might consider: Who is the center designed to serve? What are the characteristics of the community? How close or collaborative are relations between shelter employees and community residents?

Data collection to answer these questions might include long-term immersion in the setting through doing volunteer work and conducting participant observations. It might include informal interviews with stakeholders, employees, and community members. It might include reviewing shelter documents and police reports to determine how the shelter is used.

Analyzing the data for themes and patterns might reveal gaps between shelter services and community needs. For example, researchers might discover that many community members speak a different language than police officers and shelter employees, that the shelter restricts services to women with very young children, or that some lesbians and women of color feel hesitant to report abuse because it might cast further stigma on their communities (Crenshaw, 1991). Identifying key issues allows researchers to strategize about how to better meet diverse women's needs.

Knowledge Gaps

Researchers might also focus on gaps in knowledge that linger from researchers' disproportionate attention to privileged groups historically. Researchers have worked to sculpt more textured understandings of human lives and social processes on an array of topics: domestic work, sex education, welfare-to-work programs, teaching, letter writing, postpartum depression, midwifery, quilting, reading practices, sex work, cocktail waitressing, and homelessness, to name a few. Such knowledge is not relevant only to women; it benefits us all.

For example, Fonow (2003) examined women's roles in the steel industry and male-dominated labor movement using statistics, historical records, observations, and interviews with women in the United Steelworkers Union. Her study revealed that women's activism helps to forge a collective identity ("Women of Steel"), decrease marginalization in unions, and challenge global changes in manufacturing—powerful forces that affect all workers.

Critique and Revision

Researchers might also question common, taken-for-granted assumptions that shape perspectives and policy. For example, Pillow (2004) challenged the assumption that teen pregnancy is a "crisis" in the United States. She used statistics, media images, and fieldwork in schools to trace sources of negative attitudes toward pregnant and mothering teens, to highlight the racial undercurrents animating the issue, and to explore young women's experiences. In particular, her research revealed schools' failures to meet the mandates of federal policy (Title IX) that since 1972 has explicitly protected the rights of pregnant and mothering students to receive an education equal to that of their peers.

Similarly, researchers have critiqued the trivialization of women's roles and sought to take their labor, activities, and roles seriously. For example, Adams and Bettis (2003) used a feminist lens to analyze cheerleading—a highly feminized activity many dismiss as unimportant. Yet this activity garners significant revenue and endures in popularity; as a giddy twelve-year-old joining a squad phrased it, "I've been waiting for this all of my life" (p. 24). The researchers interviewed cheerleaders in a range of contexts, observed in schools, and analyzed popular films, newspaper reports, and policies. Their data revealed that an activity that the public (and many feminists) see as trivial is suffused with complex racial politics, economic issues, sexual dynamics, and gender messages. Moreover, some girls experienced cheerleading as empowering.

Revisiting common assumptions and topics from a feminist perspective offers new and potentially transformative insights. Audiences can use findings from such studies to reconsider the past, better understand complex social issues, heighten consciousness about discriminatory practices, and develop strategies to combat them.

REFLECTION QUESTIONS

1. What types of questions might lend themselves to a feminist perspective?
2. Why is developing questions an important part of the research process?
3. What makes feminist questions different from other qualitative questions?

Feminist Applications of Qualitative Approaches

Research purpose determines which approaches and methods are appropriate for a given topic, and varied research approaches lend themselves to feminist purposes. Researchers can conduct surveys to capture a broad portrait of social phenomena, study history (Chapter Six), conduct ethnography in which they study particular cultural groups in depth (Chapter Seven), or pursue many other forms of research from a feminist perspective.

Those interested in questions about power or activism in school curricula, in films, on the Internet, in video games, or in newspapers can use content analysis to trace patterns in ideas over time or contradictions in cultural meanings. Others interested in the implications of particular policies for marginalized groups can use feminist policy analysis (Campbell, 2000; Pillow, 2004) to examine how dominant ideas about gender, race, and sexuality shape the policymaking process or how policies might fuel inequities. Those seeking to explore women's lives that do not map onto traditional ideas of success can use oral history. Those interested in gender and cultural processes can use ethnography. Examples of conducting oral history and ethnography from a feminist perspective follow.

Feminist Oral History

Oral history is both a qualitative approach researchers can use to preserve firsthand accounts of people's lives and the final story that is preserved. There are many different ways to conduct oral history and different theories that govern these approaches. Whereas oral history was traditionally used to record the memories of elite leaders or citizens in unique positions in their communities, oral histories conducted from a feminist perspective have often sought to understand the everyday lives of women and other community members. Since the 1970s feminist researchers have used oral history to preserve women's accounts of their lives in their own words and, significantly, to link experiences that feel deeply personal with their broader social and historical context (see Research Snapshot 2). Oral history honors storytelling in everyday language, oral traditions as a method of preserving and transmitting cultural knowledge, and in-depth exploration of important events and individual experiences.

From this perspective, oral histories are potentially emancipatory. All members of societies do not have equal opportunities for expression, for literacy (to read and write), or for occupying social roles with sufficient status to enable voice. Literacy itself is historically, culturally, and geographically specific. Thus oral history can provide voice and visibility to varied groups and convey how marginalized people make meaning of their experiences within dominant discourses. In this view, stories are versions—rather than mirrors—of lives; broader context, norms, and audiences always mediate the stories people sculpt.

Methodology

A narrator's (that is, the person telling his or her own oral history) use of language and her rapport with the researcher are key methodological aspects of oral histories. The primary method researchers use to collect data are in-depth interviews. Researchers traditionally use audiotapes to record interviews, although some may also use video or photography. Rather than using a traditional, structured interview protocol, a researcher might collect an oral history with only a few themes and biographical notes. For example, Middleton (1993) interviewed New Zealand teachers using a three-part, open-ended question. She asked, "I would like you to tell me how and why you became an educator, how and why you came to identify yourself as a feminist, and how your feminism influences your work and activities in education" (p. 70). With prompts from the researcher, participants talked for as long as three hours in the first interview.

Although traditional approaches to oral history often position the researcher as a vehicle for capturing and conveying an individual's story, feminist approaches more often consider oral histories as coconstructed between narrator and researcher. A researcher's questions, prompts, and body language can subtly shape the narrator's account. To attempt to dominate an interview, to impose the researcher's agenda too heavily on a narrator, runs counter to feminist goals of collaborative inquiry. Oral historians must thus balance their research agendas with active listening (Anderson & Jack, 1991). Active listening involves being receptive to varied aspects of communication, including body language, speaking style, silences, and emotion. For example, a narrator's shedding tears when discussing childhood or changing the subject when discussing race may indicate painful or taboo topics. In turn, these communicative forms can shed light on cultural norms and dynamics that shape the narrator's experiences.

Analysis

Conducting oral history from a feminist perspective includes contemplating how such forces as gender, race, and sexuality both shape life experience and structure communication. For example, a woman's devaluing of her domestic labor may reflect her absorption of cultural dismissals of its value. Cultural norms and power dynamics can also shape how narrators tell their stories and what they share. Indigenous women who believe questioning their elders is disrespectful might hesitate to interrupt or clarify responses. Some men might downplay feelings of sadness because social norms link masculinity with rationality and control. Some female narrators might avoid taking charge of an interview, even when encouraged to do this, so as not to appear aggressive or self-aggrandizing.

The theory and purpose of the specific inquiry project shape how researchers analyze oral history data. Some may emphasize memories of key events. Some may link experiences to broader contextual forces, such as a natural disaster, social activism, or community identity. Others may pay particular attention to the intersections among gender, sexuality, race, class, and ethnicity shaping women's lives. Other oral historians may consider *how* a story is told and what it means to the narrator to be as important as the events detailed. What stories does the narrator share, and what meaning do they hold for her or him? What role does the narrator play in the story? (Is she or he a heroine, a victim, a figure hovering on the margins?) When is she or he silent? What might such silences reveal about the narrator's experiences as well as the social norms governing speech? These questions can help guide the researcher's analysis and interpretation.

Form

Oral historians must also consider the politics of representation in the final story they present. A traditional method of preserving oral histories is to preserve the audiotape, or a transcription of the history typed word for word. Others arrange the accounts in themes or time periods significant to the narrator, organization, or community. These choices require subtle interpretive decisions. Perhaps the narrator uses slang or a dialect that readers might judge harshly. How will the researcher represent the style and speech of the respondent authentically and respectfully? Perhaps the narrator shares private information. What should the researcher include in the final account? Perhaps the oral historian and narrator interpret the story differently (Borland, 1991). Who owns the story? There are no straightforward answers to these questions; considering them carefully is foundational to feminist research.

RESEARCH SNAPSHOT 2
FEMINIST ORAL HISTORY—GRANDMOTHER GOES TO THE RACETRACK

The following excerpt from Borland's interview (1991) with her grandmother Beatrice captures the flavor of first-person accounts in which narrators reflect on significant events. It also provides an example of the distinction between traditional and feminist approaches to oral history. In the excerpt Beatrice recounts a day she accompanied her father to the racetrack and placed a bet on a horse against his wishes.

> If I could find a *horse* that right pleased me, and a driver that pleased me . . . *there* would be my choice, you see? So, this particular afternoon . . . I *found* that. Now that didn't happen all the time, by any means, but I found . . . perfection, as far as I was concerned, and I was absolutely *convinced* that *that* horse was going to win. [Her father disapproved of Beatrice's choice, and she responded.] "I am *betting on my horse* and I am betting *ten bucks* on that horse. It's gonna win!"
>
> Father had a fit. *He* had a fit. And he tells everybody three miles around in the grandstand what a fool I am too. . . . [And then the horse won.] I threw my pocketbook in one direction, and I threw my gloves in another direction, and my score book went in another direction and I jumped up and I hollered, to everyone, "you see what know-it-all said! *That's* my father!" (pp. 65, 67).

One distinction between traditional and feminist oral histories becomes evident in Borland's analysis of her grandmother's narrative. To Borland, this story is not simply a textured moment in an individual life. Even the facts of the story—which horse was involved, how much money Beatrice placed on the horse, how her father reacted—are not necessarily important.

The significance lies instead in how Beatrice recounts the tale, the meaning it holds for her, and the glimpses it provides into systems of power shaping her experience as a woman in a particular place and time. Beatrice is the central character in the story. Her recipe for choosing a horse, her resistance to her father's criticism, and her celebration of the horse's win take center stage in the story as a triumphant expression of female autonomy in a male-dominated context. This feminist oral history preserves the account.

REFLECTION QUESTIONS

1. How might feminists use oral histories differently than other researchers?
2. What might an "action orientation" look like in feminist oral history?
3. How would you go about conducting an oral history from a feminist perspective?

Feminist Ethnography

There is no definitive approach to feminist ethnography; it is a flexible methodology researchers use to study culture in detail and depth. The need for feminist ethnographic practices emerged from anthropologists' recognition in the 1970s that the primary focus of ethnography—culture—often dealt solely with male roles. As a result, women often seemed bereft of culture rather than active agents in its creation. Debates continue as to whether ethnography can shake the vestiges of its inequitable origins to embrace truly feminist and emancipatory practices (Abu-Lughod, 1993; Stacey, 1991; Visweswaran, 1994). Indeed, Stacey characterizes the relationship between feminism and ethnography as "unavoidably ambiguous" (p.117).

Ethnography (*writing* culture) is both a research *approach* used to explore the practices and worldviews in a given culture and a *product* of research (the presentation of findings from conducting ethnography). As discussed in Chapter Seven, ethnography relies as much as possible on researchers' direct observations of daily life and practices in the culture of interest. Researchers both participate in and observe the intricacies of cultural practice through long-term immersion in the field. In contemporary ethnography, various groups and settings can constitute cultures: a beauty salon, a mining community, a gang, or a homeschooling organization.

In contrast to traditional ethnography, feminist ethnography generally includes attention to the gendered aspects of culture, the cultural forces that limit women's opportunities, women's roles in their cultural context, and women's agency as cultural actors. For example, ethnographers have studied women's economic activities in Thailand (Wilson, 2004); the work of Latina maids in California (Hondagneu-Sotelo, 2001); African American and white women's experiences with the culture of romance in college (Holland & Eisenhart, 1992); sex education in a New York high school (Fine, 1988); and the moral issues pregnant women face during fetal testing for genetic anomalies and their decisions about whether to continue or terminate their pregnancies (Rapp, 2000).

Methodology

The experiential and dynamic aspects of ethnography lend themselves to feminist inquiry; they offer opportunities to consider the intricacies of daily lives in context, to explore the intersections between gender and culture, and to examine systems of power that constrain women's opportunities. For example, Riemer's research (2001) in workplaces employing former welfare recipients offers insights into the beliefs and organizational practices that shaped the women's ability to thrive in new employment.

Immersion in local culture allows researchers both to hear what people say and to observe what they do in their natural settings—multiple data sources that in concert offer richer, more potentially contradictory, and more substantive information than single data sources can provide. Clifford (1997) has termed this day-to-day immersion in the local as "deep hanging out" (p. 90). The ethnographer's gaze focuses on understanding the worldviews and practices of cultural insiders. Methods must be context-, topic-, and often gender-specific; for example, women may use letter and journal writing more frequently than men; some women may prefer interactive conversation to formal methods; and participants in some cultures, such as in Thailand, may view formal interviews as hierarchical. Thus researchers need to consider gender- and culture-appropriate methods to elicit data. In addition to **jottings** (brief notations of events or terms) and developed field notes (see Chapter Seven) about women's activities, researchers might view social networking Web pages, collect photographs, and examine cultural artifacts to understand cultural processes.

Access and Entry

Researchers must consider how their identities and assumptions can shape ethnographic practice, from developing study questions to accessing a research site, to navigating the field, to writing up accounts. Feminist ethnography, like critical ethnography (see Chapter Fifteen), is concerned with systems of power that shape culture and research. For example, accessing a site can require significant time and resources. As an American anthropologist writes of her fieldwork in Thailand, "There is the bare fact that the United States' great financial and political power underwrites U.S. citizens' ability to conduct research in less wealthy nations such as Thailand. Relatedly, my white identity situated me in a privileged position" (Wilson, 2004, p.27). Researching female refugees, prisoners, graffiti artists, white supremacists, or schoolgirls involves different systems of power, research sites, and preparation.

Conducting ethnography in some settings also requires a degree of freedom to leave family and other work behind for extended periods, a condition that is impossible to meet for some working-class researchers or parents of young children. It requires financial support, specialized training, and sometimes mastery of an additional language, an educational nexus available to few. It may require a researcher to consider safety issues, which face all ethnographers but which may have particular implications for women, sexual minorities (lesbian, gay, bisexual, and transgender individuals), and people with mobility impairments. These factors shape who conducts research and in what ways.

Navigating the Setting

Like traditional ethnographers, feminist researchers must navigate insider/outsider status and power relations within the culture of interest. For some feminist topics, shared experience with key insiders may facilitate rapport and connection—indeed, researchers may be members of the community under study. For example, Rapp (2000) found that having experienced amniocentesis facilitated rapport with women she interviewed in the same situation. Participants considered her an insider. For Bhavnani and Davis (2000), who studied women prisoner's experiences, the researchers' status as nonprisoners and their racial and national identities (which made them outsiders) seemed to evoke less interest than their roles as prison activists and scholars. Navigating different subcultures within the same setting may require careful strategizing, particularly if groups do not get along. Researchers' interactions with one group may jeopardize their access to another group. Such tensions and hierarchies can shape researchers' access to information and the knowledge generated.

Mendoza-Denton (2008) describes her gradual immersion among Latina youth that facilitated her understanding of group culture. Like the participants who educated Lather and Smithies (1997) in the HIV/AIDS study, Latina youth taught Mendoza-Denton specific lessons, such as how to dress, apply makeup, and style hair in line with their cultural codes. As her study unfolded, she reflected,

> The way I dressed changed gradually . . . little side-long glances were flashed in my direction, tactful suggestions were made about relaxing and wearing jeans . . . shopping expeditions were organized . . . sometimes, if we were driving somewhere, the girls would make me pull over on the side of the road and apply makeup so that I could be "presentable." And so gradually people began to treat me differently, and some senior scholars, much to my surprise, complained from just a little eyeliner that I was "going native." (p. 54–55)

Practices of participant observation can be age-, race-, and gender-specific as ethnographers adjust to different cultural norms. Navigating insider/outsider status and nuanced dynamics in a given setting can require strategizing and skill.

Narrative Practices

All ethnographers strive to produce lush descriptions in which details and interactions in the setting under study spring to life. Using empirical data—the sights, sounds, scents, and texture of a setting—the researcher works to capture an insider glimpse of culture. However, the narrative basis of ethnography lends itself to feminist researchers' use of innovative writing forms (drama, autobiographical reflections, multivocal texts) to challenge positivist conventions for research reporting (formal, crisp, authoritative).

Some ethnographers' narrative choices diverge strikingly from traditional ethnographic forms. First, some accounts provide a foreground to the researcher's, rather than the participant's, experience in the field. For example, St. Pierre (2000) has often chosen to narrate methodological reflections of her research among older women rather than represent the women and their words directly. Her choices are theoretically driven and, among other purposes, shift attention to the process rather than the product of inquiry. Some first-person accounts weave the researcher's experiences with accounts of the culture under study to demonstrate the coconstruction of knowledge.

Other texts blend fictional, poetic, and empirical elements. Hurston, a folklorist and novelist, produced a variety of novels that drew from her observations of Southern African American culture (for example, her 1935 collection of folklore, *Mules and Men*). She also incorporated autobiographical narrative into her ethnographic accounts. Richardson (1997) has explored her work through poems, and Visweswaran (1994) has used drama to question dominant conventions and explore ethnographic practice.

Although some dismiss such forms as unscientific, feminist researchers view these methods as important vehicles for exploring experiential knowledge and alternatives to dominant positivist conventions (Visweswaran, 1994). Such techniques are contested; some researchers are concerned that blending autobiographical, novelistic, and dramatic elements with fieldwork may undermine the professional and scientific boundaries of ethnography because these practices blur empirical science and fiction.

RESEARCH SNAPSHOT 3
FEMINIST ETHNOGRAPHY–A RELUCTANT AVON LADY

The following snapshot illustrates elements of a feminist approach to ethnography. It is drawn from Wilson's study (2004) of commercial spaces in Bangkok, Thailand.

(Continued)

RESEARCH SNAPSHOT 3
FEMINIST ETHNOGRAPHY—A RELUCTANT AVON LADY (Continued)

Purpose

Wilson's research explored how globalization shapes identities, relationships, and economic practices in new and complex ways. Her study emerged from interests in women's labor in developing nations and the often unrecognized connections between economic systems and private life.

Setting

For several years, Wilson conducted what is referred to as a multi-sited ethnography. She examined social relationships and economic practices in department stores, go-go bars, shopping complexes, a cable TV marketing office, and direct sales, such as for Avon and Amway.

Methodology

Wilson immersed herself as a participant observer in multiple settings, gathering background information, using such textual sources as popular culture and material artifacts, working part-time in a marketing office, translating English documents, participating in activism on behalf of local women's rights, and conducting informal interviews in both Thai and English. She developed relationships with diverse Thai people.

In this excerpt, Wilson describes a "reluctant Avon lady" (p. 168) who began to sell Avon products. Avon established sales in Thailand in the 1960s. It is a commercial enterprise that attracts diverse Thai vendors, many of them women. Through catalogues, Avon markets a white and American form of femininity internationally. Wilson writes,

> A more unlikely Avon lady than Sila would be hard to find. She had a degree from a leading university with a progressive reputation and was a long term organizer and activist. . . . Sila was called (and sometimes called herself) a tom [representing a Thai gender practice in which females dress and behave in masculine ways, similar to what Americans call "tomboy"]. . . . At Sila's first "training," the agent . . . explained their products and procedures, instructing Sila from catalogues, and offered guidance for selling: "speak nice . . . proper, sweet and polite." Though this advice could hardly have appealed to her temperament, Sila

signed on, paying the equivalent of U.S. $14 to enroll and some more dollars for the start up kit of an Avon bag, catalog and product samples. Sila did not use the Avon bag: "It was ugly. Yellow, pink, brown-tan, colors I don't like . . ." she said, waving her cigarette at the pastel-colored wallpaper that covered my flat . . . [but] she enjoyed the catalogues and used them to sell. "The big one had color," she remembered. (p. 169)

Wilson points out that catalogues were a "critical component of sales" (p. 170) because they showed images of women wearing Avon products. Although Sila initially sold well among women in her social network, she could not identify with the catalogue images and did not know how to market cosmetics to customers. "'It's funny,' she said, 'they'd ask me, is this pretty? How do you use this? and I'd give them a catalogue saying, here look. I couldn't tell them'" (p. 169–171). Her discomfort increased from selling products that the company marketed for profit, that did not live up to their claims, and that she did not use. In fact, she could not learn about them in detail because the labels were in English. She eventually stopped selling Avon products.

Analysis

This snapshot highlights characteristics of feminist ethnography. As with traditional ethnography, Wilson immerses herself in the setting and describes it with depth and detail. Yet she focuses on the gendered aspects of global economic practices—in this example, one Thai worker's experiences within an international company that is marketing beauty products based on white femininity and profiting from direct sales to Thai women. She attends closely to women's working experiences in local contexts and diverse cultural expressions of gender (*tom*). She asks critical questions about the significance of global changes for gender, culture, and identity: "What does it mean for [Sila] . . . to learn corporate rhetoric forged in the United States?" (p. 188).

Form

Although Wilson chose a traditional academic form to represent her work, a key textual practice reflects her feminist attentiveness to the politics of representation. She chose to embed the research she conducted with women in the sex trade within the array of other economic entities she studied—Amway, Avon, department stores. This choice ensured she did not contribute to the Western sensationalism that too often characterizes accounts of exotic, illicit, or sexual practices in non-Western regions. She considered the sex trade along with Avon as part of exploring varied, complex, context-specific practices influenced by globalization.

> **REFLECTION QUESTIONS**
>
> 1. What are the characteristics of feminist ethnography?
> 2. How do traditional ethnography and feminist ethnography differ?

Trusting Feminist Reports

The explicitly emancipatory aim of feminist research, its divergence from traditional research approaches, and others' investments in the claim that science is an objective practice have led some to question the credibility of feminist research. Many feminist researchers continue to follow a checklist of traditional criteria to demonstrate the quality of their work. Researchers use systematic procedures and immerse themselves in the field and in data analysis to ensure they have considered the phenomenon of interest in depth. In writing up their reports, they support their findings with substantive data from interviews, observations, and documents to allow readers to understand and evaluate their interpretive processes. In addition, they might use **triangulation** (taking into account multiple data sources, methods, theories, or researchers); **audit trails** (records of data gathering and analytic procedures); and **peer debriefing** (processing findings with peers). Recording and transcribing interviews can facilitate researchers' immersion in the rhythm of and emotion in participants' speech.

Some common qualitative validity criteria lend themselves to the mission of feminist inquiry. For example, Lather and Smithies (1997) used **member checking** (asking participants to review data or findings for accuracy) to ensure participants could provide feedback on how their lives were represented. Depending on its purpose, a valid feminist study must reflect the guiding principles of feminist inquiry. Readers might begin with the following questions to consider the validity of a feminist study.

1. Do the researchers scrutinize and shed light on gendered structures of social life and research practice?

2. Do the researchers capture the voices of marginalized groups or social processes that contribute to their marginalization?

3. Do the researchers provide detailed data to substantiate their findings and interpretations that offer insights into the phenomenon of interest?

4. Do the researchers employ reflexivity and equitable and ethical research practices that are attentive to power inequities? Do the researchers consider the implications of their findings for the groups under study?

5. Does the research contribute to social critique and facilitate action against oppressive beliefs or systems?

Others use traditional criteria as critical vehicles to reflect rigorously on their data and findings. For example, one measure of validity is seeking **discrepant cases** (examples that contradict findings) in the data set. Cases that do not fit common patterns do not necessarily indicate problems with the initial analysis; rather, they invite researchers to revisit their data, tease out meaningful tensions, and ponder alternative explanations. In this sense, using traditional measures to reflect on a study serves less as an endpoint and more as a springboard to delve deeper into the phenomena of interest.

However, many critical researchers are uncomfortable with such validity checklists as that just listed because they were developed within a positivist paradigm that views the enactment of systematic procedures as an assurance that research findings are true and certain. Although some techniques can be adopted for critical purposes, numerous critical researchers argue that a "one size fits all" approach to validity is reductive because research purposes and practices are not homogenous. For example, a feminist's assertions of validity using traditional criteria—for example, use of systematic procedures, triangulation, and audit trails—will have little meaning if the researcher dehumanizes participants or fails to engage in reflexive practices.

The diversity of contemporary qualitative research has inspired a proliferation of validity categories that transgress traditional forms. For example, some researchers use **catalytic validity,** a form of validity associated with critical research projects intended to provide catalysts for social change. Its premise is straightforward, but its actualization is more complex: if the research purpose is to improve curriculum and empower students in a given classroom, the researcher must demonstrate that curriculum was improved and students were empowered to meet catalytic validity criteria. In this view, following a rote procedural checklist cannot ensure that critical research will accomplish its purpose: to facilitate critique and change. Validity practices, like other aspects of contemporary qualitative inquiry, continue to evolve.

REFLECTION QUESTIONS

1. Why are traditional validity criteria not always a fit for feminist inquiry projects?
2. How would you recognize a "good" feminist study if you encountered it?

Summary

Feminist approaches to research emerged during a period of activism and critical questioning in the 1960s and 1970s. They hold that the creation of knowledge is an inherently political and power-laden enterprise and challenge traditional inquiry approaches that proceed from the assumption that a neutral and objective stance is possible. To feminist and other critical researchers, cultural practices and systems of power always influence research practices. Feminist research is explicitly political and emancipatory in aim.

Feminist approaches have blossomed into a rich and diverse body of practices for investigating phenomena in a range of contexts. These methodologies continue to evolve as new issues emerge and scholars engage in productive debates about practices and approaches. No tool or technique is explicitly feminist; a general set of guiding principles shapes feminist methodologies, which vary widely in practice based on the specific purpose of the study and the researcher's theoretical allegiances. What remain consistent across these efforts are a spirit of critique and the conviction that research should challenge oppressive forces and contribute to tangible changes in people's lives.

Key Terms

action orientation, 399
action research, 400
androcentric, 393
anthropometry, 398
audit trails, 418
catalytic validity, 419
collaboration, 398
discrepant cases, 419
empiricism, 393
ethical and equitable research, 398
feminism, 392
guiding principles, 395
informed consent, 398
insider/outsider status, 402
interdisciplinary, 405
jottings, 413
member checking, 418
methodologies, 395
methods, 395
multivocal texts, 400
paradigm, 393
peer debriefing, 418
politics of representation, 399
positivism, 393
reflexivity, 397
representation, 395
standpoint, 396
theories, 395
triangulation, 418
universality, 393

Further Readings and Resources

Suggested Feminist Studies

Holland, D. C., & Eisenhart, M. A. (1992). *Educated in romance: Women, achievement, and college culture*. Chicago: University of Chicago Press.

This classic feminist ethnography examines African American and white college women's experiences with college culture and its norms of "romance and attractiveness" that influence their achievement.

Luttrell, W. (1997). *School-smart and mother-wise: Working-class women's identity and schooling*. New York: Routledge.

This study focuses on life stories of working-class women and their experiences with schooling as children and adults.

Lather, P., & Smithies, C. (1997). *Troubling the angels: Women living with HIV/AIDS*. Boulder, CO: Westview Press.

This book-length study provides an innovative example of feminist inquiry and discusses many of the dilemmas in conducting feminist research.

Romero, M. (2002). *Maid in the USA*. New York: Routledge.

This classic study of Latina domestic workers sheds critical light on the structural forces and intersections of race, class, and gender that shape women's domestic labor.

Other Suggested Readings

Jaggar, A. (Ed.). (2007). *Just methods: An interdisciplinary feminist reader*. Boulder, CO: Paradigm.

This edited collection of over forty essays introduces different areas of feminist methodologies and the conceptual linkages feminist researchers draw between social power and the creation of knowledge.

Reinharz, S. (with Davidman, L.). (1992). *Feminist methods in social research*. New York: Oxford University Press.

This text provides an early introduction to different feminist research approaches, including chapters on feminist interviewing, ethnography, and discourse analysis.

St. Pierre, E., & Pillow, W. S. (2000). *Working the ruins: Feminist poststructural methods in education*. New York: Routledge.

This edited collection offers a variety of essays on feminist methodology in education that are written from a theoretical perspective termed poststructuralism.

Tong, R. (2008). *Feminist thought: A more comprehensive introduction* (3rd ed.). Boulder, CO: Westview Press.

This text provides a broad introduction to feminist theories, with chapters on such topics as liberal, radical, and postmodern feminisms, which inform the practice of feminist research.

Visweswaran, K. (1994). *Fictions of feminist ethnography.* Minneapolis: University of Minnesota Press.

This text offers a series of theoretical essays and reflections that foreground issues of race, nation, and gender, and that challenge contemporary feminist ethnographic practices.

Organizations and Web Sites

American Educational Research Association (AERA)—Special Interest Group on Qualitative Research (SIG #82) (www.aera.net/Default.aspx?menu_jd=208&id=772)

This special interest group is affiliated with the largest educational association in the country (AERA). It supports scholarship on qualitative methodologies from a variety of perspectives and offers yearly presentation opportunities at the annual AERA conference.

Association for Feminist Anthropology (AFA) (www.aaanet.org/sections/afa)

This organization supports the development of feminist scholarship in anthropology and promotes a variety of equity and human rights initiatives through the American Anthropological Association. The Web site has a variety of useful resources and links.

National Women's Studies Association (NWSA) (www.nwsa.org)

This organization supports feminist scholarship and the field of women's studies. In existence since 1977, NWSA hosts a yearly national conference and offers a variety of resources for scholars and activists.

Sociologists for Women in Society (SWS) (www.socwomen.org/)

This is an international organization of social scientists dedicated to improving women's position in society.

CHAPTER 17

RECLAIMING SCHOLARSHIP: CRITICAL INDIGENOUS RESEARCH METHODOLOGIES

Bryan McKinley Jones Brayboy
Heather R. Gough
Beth Leonard
Roy F. Roehl II
Jessica A. Solyom

Key Ideas

- Critical Indigenous Research Methodologies (CIRM), an overarching line of thinking about methods and philosophies, is rooted in indigenous knowledge systems, is anticolonial, and is distinctly focused on the needs of communities.

- CIRM is rooted in relationships, responsibility, respect, reciprocity, and accountability.

- Research must be a process of fostering relationships between researchers, communities, and the topic of inquiry.

- CIRM recognizes the role of particular components that make it viable for communities, but ultimately it is of little use to create frameworks rooted in these principles if these methodologies do not also promote emancipatory agendas that recognize the self-determination and inherent sovereignty of indigenous peoples.

In academic research we recognize that there is, as Maori scholars Linda Tuhiwai Smith (1999, 2000) and Graham Smith (2000), among others, have noted, an overemphasis on a specific type of science and research, often **positivist** in nature and claiming to hold one singular truth (often referred to as Truth with a capital T). Grounded in a particular worldview inextricably linked to the practice of imperialism and colonialism—and with an unyielding insistence in the notion that Western scientific method and practices, which dominate the academy, are the only legitimate forms of knowledge production—academic research has, to put it politely, become estranged from indigenous communities. A **Critical Indigenous Research Methodologies (CIRM)** perspective, which fundamentally begins as an emancipatory project that forefronts the self-determination and inherent sovereignty of indigenous peoples is rooted in relationships and is driven explicitly by community interests. Given this orientation, the challenge is for scholars and institutions that prepare researcher-scholars to move away from such limited definitions of what kinds of knowledge systems and research processes can be labeled *scientific* and to consider the ways in which indigenous peoples and methodologies inform and frame scientific scholarly inquiry. This chapter responds to a growing call in the academy for rethinking positivist models; for exploring the boundaries outlining indigenous research; and for envisioning anew, or perhaps re-visioning, a research paradigm grounded in indigenous knowledges, beliefs, and practices.

We respond to this call here by offering an overview of CIRM as we interpret this process. In this chapter we present a view of CIRM that is unapologetically rooted in indigenous knowledge systems, is anticolonial, and is distinctly focused on the needs of communities (Battiste, 2000; L. Smith, 1999; St. Denis, 1992; Wilson, 2001b, 2008). In our discussion we attempt to engage in a relationship with those indigenous scholars who have gone before us as we address research concerns, advising current scholars and those who will come after our time of the fundamental need for upholding the basic tenets of CIRM while further refining or adapting analytical frameworks and models that have been developed for specific communities (for example, the Kaupapa Maori approach).

Colonization and the Call for (Re)Claiming an Indigenous Intellectual Life and Thought-World

Writing about CIRM induced a sense of shared anxiety for us. We began the process with a great deal of introspection. We asked ourselves: What is this thing called "Critical Indigenous Research Methodologies"? Who are *we* to write about it? How can we talk about it in terms that capture the commonalities of research methodologies for many indigenous peoples, while at the same time recognizing the nuances in attempting to do this? We must always be mindful of these questions, as we are not alone in this conversation and in fact are able to draw on ongoing discussions that perhaps most notably gained momentum with the publication of Linda Tuhiwai Smith's *Decolonizing Methodologies* (1999), but that had arisen, however briefly, in earlier parts of the twentieth century.

Thus we begin by noting that scholarly arguments presenting a need for indigenous communities to (re)claim research and knowledge-making practices that are driven by indigenous peoples; rooted in recognitions of the impacts of Eurocentric culture on the history, beliefs, and practices of indigenous peoples and communities; and guided by the intention of promoting the anticolonial or emancipatory interests of indigenous communities are not new (see also Chapters Fourteen, Fifteen, and Sixteen). In fact, one of the earliest calls for this kind of research and knowledge-making surfaced in the scholarly literature in the early 1900s when Seneca scholar Arthur C. Parker (1916) published his article "The Social Elements of the Indian Problem" in the *American Journal of Sociology*. Almost fifty years later the late Lakota scholar Vine Deloria Jr. presented a similar call when he published *Custer Died for Your Sins: An Indian Manifesto* (1969). These scholarly works presented several important considerations for the creation of indigenous research methodologies. For example, although Parker did not provide a framework for establishing an indigenous research methodology per se, he did offer a sophisticated argument for why an intellectual framework, guided by indigenous epistemological, ontological, and axiological beliefs, is needed. (We use **epistemologies** to mean ways of knowing or how peoples come to know the things they know. **Ontologies** refer to how we engage the world [how people "be"]. **Axiologies** refer to how people value what is right—in other words, axiologies refer to particular types of value systems.)

In the process of laying down "seven charges, out of perhaps many more, that the Indian makes at the bar of American justice" (p. 254), Parker (1916) recognized the detrimental effects of colonization on the intellectual lives of indigenous peoples and reasoned that

> human beings have a primary right to an intellectual life, but civilization has swept down upon groups of Indians and, by destroying their relationships to nature, blighted or banished their intellectual life, and left a group of people mentally confused. . . . The Indians must have a thought-world given back. Their intellectual world must have direct relation to their world of responsible acts and spontaneous experiences. (p. 258)

The phrase "The Indians must have a thought-world given back" raises some concern for us as it seems to beg the question: *Given back by whom?* We agree that systematic attempts were and continue to be made to ensure that the intellectual life of Indians was blighted or banished (or, more literally, silenced and ignored). However, indigenous epistemological, ontological, and axiological beliefs have remained and *survived*. This chapter is a testament to this as it is largely driven by the work of indigenous scholars. (Brayboy [Lumbee], Leonard [Deg Hit'an Athabascan], and Roehl [Aleut] are indigenous people, and Solyom and Gough are allies [of Puerto Rican/Hungarian and Semitic/Anglo descent, respectively]). For us, this suggests that an intellectual life or an intellectual thought-world is not being given back by anyone. Rather, it is resurfacing through the growing contributions of indigenous scholar–community members around the world. Ultimately we believe that while Parker presents us with a thoughtful argument for asserting an indigenous intellectual life and thought-world, Deloria (1969), in his classic text *Custer Died for Your Sins*, makes a more direct contribution concerning the role of research and intellectualism among indigenous peoples by naming what the research and thought processes are actually about. That is, the tasks are *not* for indigenous communities to be *given back* a thought-world. Rather, the task is for indigenous peoples to *reclaim* our intellectual lives by developing practices that are based in practices guided by indigenous beliefs, actions, and experiences.

In terms of research, we believe *the right to an intellectual life* described by Parker (1916) and others necessitates an engagement in the research process and the philosophy behind that process. In many ways Parker was a visionary who served to foreground the arguments that would arise decades later. His work frames the need for indigenous research methodologies as rooted in the recognition of basic *human, community, and civil rights* and recognizes that indigenous peoples think and behave in ways unique to their worldviews and experiences. Later, Cree scholar Shawn Wilson (2008) similarly argued,

> There is a need to examine how an Indigenous research paradigm can lead to a better understanding of and provision for the needs of Indigenous people. Appreciating the differences Indigenous people have in terms of their ontology, epistemology, methodology, and axiology can lead to research methods that are more fully integrated with an indigenous worldview. (pp. 20–21)

Drawing from the works of such scholars as Parker, Deloria, L. Smith, Wilson, and many others, this chapter is our attempt to add our voices to the conversations, and although it is neither exhaustive nor as deeply involved as we would hope, it is an effort to engage the work of those who have come before us and to offer something to those who have yet to engage in academic research. And, with great humility, we seek to honor and amplify indigenous voices and to reflect back what we already know to be true: that indigenous communities have for centuries engaged in empirical research, developed and refined as an integral process of living through engaged observation, both for survival and for continued growth.

REFLECTION QUESTIONS

1. What kinds of connections can you envision among epistemologies (ways of knowing), ontologies (ways of being), axiologies (value systems), and the research process?
2. What are the implications of arguing that indigenous thought-worlds have survived and need to resurface within research rather than be given back?

Note on Methods Versus Methodologies

Before delving any further into the discussion on methodologies, it is important to acknowledge the distinction between **methods** (the tools used to collect data) and **methodologies** (the theoretical and philosophical considerations of how to engage in the process of doing research). Whereas the former represents a toolbox or how-to guide, the latter informs our theoretical understandings about the process. As the theory behind how and why we do research, research methodology drives the assumptions we make and our choice of topic and methods and situates us in a particular geopolitics of time and space. Methodology determines whether we are looking for the Truth, a point of view, a structural cause or an individual failing, an answer, or a question. It determines whether we will believe we own what we find or whether we believe we enter into a relationship with those ideas to learn from them, to care for them, and to pass them on to the next generation. Methodologies, driven by beliefs about the nature of truth and data, encourage us to consider not only how to engage in the process of research but also *why* and *to what end* we engage in it in the first place. We will expand more on the historical and traditional forms of methodologies that have guided Western academic research as well as their epistemological, ontological, and axiological implications later in the chapter. We now turn, however, to a more general discussion of the concept of research as it relates to indigenous communities.

What Makes *Research* Such a Dirty Word?

In order to fully engage in our goal of offering an overview of CIRM, it is necessary for us to consider the lasting impression the notion of research has left on indigenous communities. Scholars have noted that knowledge and research, their (re)production and value, have historically been embedded within a framework driven by colonialist and imperialist interests (for a more detailed argument see Duran & Duran, 2000; Henderson, 2000; L. Smith, 1999; Wilson, 2008).

Maori scholar Linda Tuhiwai Smith (1999) explains the specific nature of one connotation of the term *research* and its practice when she states, "From the vantage point of the colonized . . . the word 'research' . . . is probably one of the dirtiest words in the indigenous world's vocabulary" (p. 1). *Research* for Indigenous communities invokes past, and notably present, incidents of abuse; exploitative research practices; looting of cultural knowledge, artifacts, and even bodies and genetic material; anthropological recastings of histories, cultural practices, and understandings of self, community, and sovereignty through outsiders' eyes; and a placing of study and knowledge outside the community such that community members become objects to be studied and the knowledge produced fails to reflect indigenous values (Battiste & Henderson, 2002; Deloria, 1969; Hart, 2010; L. Smith, 1999). Moreover, the history of relegating indigenous thought-worlds to the periphery (if they are acknowledged at all) by many of those engaged in research created a research paradigm used to discredit and sometimes eradicate indigenous knowledges and thought-worlds (Parker, 1916) by placing indigenous worldviews in direct opposition to Western ones. Mi'kMaq scholar Marie Battiste (2002) observes,

> For as long as Europeans have sought to colonize Indigenous peoples, Indigenous Knowledge has been understood as being in binary opposition to "scientific," "western," "Eurocentric," or "modern" knowledge. Eurocentric thinkers dismissed Indigenous Knowledge in the same way they dismissed any socio-political cultural life they did not understand: they found it to be unsystematic and incapable of meeting the productivity needs of the modern world. (p. 5)

In many ways the principles behind, and the processes of, colonization advance, develop, and promote research philosophies and practices that continue to transform the (re)production of knowledge; knowledge that controls and dismisses indigenous or "other" knowledges, beliefs, and practices as inferior. (Western) scientific method has historically been presented as neutral, objective, and representative of the Truth. Research grounded in these methods has functionally served to vivisect the world, cutting across interconnections, lives, cultural knowledge, and bodies, often with good intentions and occasionally espousing a critical approach even as it reproduces the status quo. Such dissections leave the *objects* of research scarred, producing and reproducing knowledge that defines the borders of exclusion and projects denigrated caricatures of the *other* to be internalized as grotesque truths about one's own being and community. This kind of research produces real consequences in the lives of the indigenous peoples researched, consequences reflecting the severed and dismembered processes from which they were generated. Understood in this light, research is *dirty* in large part because it has been used to systematically oppress, colonize, brutalize, and suppress indigenous peoples for generations (for additional arguments engaging this theme see Battiste & Henderson, 2002; Blaut, 1993; Kawagley, 1995, 2006).

Unfortunately, the recognition and identification of research engagement as a practice promoting and (pre)serving colonialist interests have created a significant divide between indigenous academics and indigenous communities. In fact, Deloria (1969) argues that research has in many ways been of no use to indigenous peoples. He suggests that the reason research and academic knowledge are considered to be useless stems from the differences between the epistemologies, ontologies, and axiologies driving Western theories and those guiding the lives of indigenous peoples. Deloria reminds us of the importance of **praxis**—the place where theory and practice come together in noticeable and important ways—when engaging in research involving indigenous communities by pointing out that "abstract theories create abstract action. Lumping together the variety of tribal problems and seeking the demonic principle at work is intellectually satisfying. But it does not *change* the real situation" (p. 86, italics added). Later he argues, "Academia, and its by-products, continues to become more irrelevant to the needs of the people" (p. 93). Linda Tuhiwai Smith (1999) made similar observations about the disconnect between the objectives and goals of (Western) research(ers) and those of indigenous communities: "Research was talked about [in indigenous communities] both in terms of its absolute worthlessness to us, the indigenous world, and its absolute usefulness to those who wielded it as an instrument" (p. 3).

However, Graham Smith (2000), although recognizing the reasons indigenous communities may remain distrustful of researchers, even those who are indigenous, cautions indigenous communities from being too quick to dismiss indigenous research(ers) by pointing out,

> There is good reason to be concerned that some Indigenous academics become "ivory tower intellectuals," disconnected from Indigenous communities and concerns, mere functionaries for the colonization of

our peoples.... Rather than dismissing all intellectual contributions as being unworthy and problematic, we should be seeking out those whose work is supportive and useful and ensuring that they are able to contribute to the struggle with appropriate support and guidance from the community. (pp. 213–214)

This statement presents a series of implications for considerations pertaining to the *methods* driving a CIRM approach as well as considerations pertaining to the question of *why* we engage in the research process. For G. Smith, the main point is that there is need for indigenous academics working for the people. He goes on to suggest that both support and guidance must come *from* communities and bluntly points out, "If Indigenous academics, despite the burden, are not accountable to both community and academy, then they ought to be!" (p. 213).

Writing to this point, Linda Tuhiwai Smith (1999, 2000) and Graham Smith (2000) add that indigenous scholars must consider, and engage in, the transformation of scholarly inquiry. This transformation either includes (re)moving inquiry from a process centered on promoting the interests of non-indigenous individuals or portraying indigenous or non-majority communities as defeated and broken. Instead they argue that the process of scholarly inquiry should seek to understand the complexity, resilience, contradiction, and self-determination of these communities, and should be driven by a desire to serve community interests (as defined by the communities themselves). Aleut scholar Eve Tuck (2009) addresses this directly when she suggests that research should be aimed at a fundamental transformation of how stories are reported, taken up, and used in marginalized communities and to what end they are used. Indeed, she challenges scholars to consider if they are engaging in damage-centered research and suggests a move to desire-based scholarship. Tuck explains,

In damage-centered research, one of the major activities is to document pain or loss in an individual, community, or tribe. Though connected to deficit models—frameworks that emphasize what a particular student, family, or community is lacking to explain underachievement or failure—damage-centered research is distinct in being more socially and historically situated. It looks to historical exploitation, domination, and colonization to explain contemporary brokenness, such as poverty, poor health, and low literacy. Common sense tells us this is a good thing, but the danger in damage-centered research is that it is a pathologizing approach in which the oppression singularly defines a community.... In a damage-centered framework, pain and loss are documented in order to obtain particular political or material gains. (p. 413)

Ultimately, the reframing of research agendas through transformational visions and responsiveness to the colonial underpinnings of research methodologies is the essence of critical indigenous research. Tuck notes that desire-based research is

> an antidote [that] stops and counteracts the effects of a poison, and the poison I am referring to here is not the supposed damage of Native communities, urban communities, or other disenfranchised communities but the frameworks that position these communities as damaged. (p. 416)

Although we recognize that the contentious history of research in indigenous communities has led the very mention of the word to be received with apprehension and suspicion, and understandably so, we believe there lies a possibility for framing research as rooted in a strength-based manner that is about doing exactly what L. Smith (1999, 2000), Tuck (2009), and others call for. That is, we remain hopeful that research methodologies centered on promoting cooperative, collaborative efforts between formally trained researchers and indigenous communities—essentially redefining relationships between and among researchers and the researched to establish truly collaborative relationships in which power is viewed as a shared resource—can serve an important role in (re)defining the nature, scope, and function of research such that the needs of communities can be addressed in meaningful, productive, and respectful ways.

REFLECTION QUESTIONS

1. What makes the genealogy of research in indigenous communities important?
2. Why are scholars calling for a (re)claiming of research by indigenous peoples?

Epistemological, Ontological, and Axiological Considerations in Research

In the last decade indigenous scholars have been engaged in a series of conversations about the need for indigenous peoples to become more assertive about conducting, participating in, and driving relevant research on indigenous issues and within indigenous communities (Cook-Lynn, 2000; Harris, 2002; Hart, 2010; Henderson, 2000; G. Smith, 2000; L. Smith, 1999, 2000; Tuck, 2009;

Weber-Pillwax, 2001; Wilson, 2001a, 2001b, 2008). As a result of these conversations there has emerged a more explicit call for defining the boundaries of indigenous research and for laying out a vision of a research paradigm grounded in indigenous knowledges, beliefs, and practices. Before we outline a framework for CIRM, let us first offer an overview of the epistemological, ontological, and axiological assumptions promoted by traditional, generally Eurocentric forms of research.

Many traditional forms of positivist research seek an ultimate Truth that assumes the world can be defined through the development of finite, disconnected **taxonomies** (scientific classifications); these specific ways of conducting research claim to be rooted in objective, neutral hypotheses that will reveal "the" singular Truth. Traditional research perspectives often individualize the pursuit of knowledge such that the acquisition of knowledge is driven by individual interests and by the pursuit of knowledge for knowledge's sake. Oftentimes researchers embedded in a positivist framework seek to isolate variables in living organisms and create research initiatives that will derive enough information to allow researchers to predict and control natural occurrences—including human behavior. For example, Western methodologies often assume the power to define taxonomically what is human or nonhuman, animate or inanimate, organic or inorganic, living or lifeless, natural or unnatural, rational or irrational. In addition to promoting rigid definitions and labels, Western scientific methodologies may seek to exclude other epistemologies and methodologies that focus on the processes and qualities of relationships between and among humans and the worlds they inhabit (Deloria, 1969; Kawagley, 2006; L. Smith, 1999). This philosophical orientation to knowledge, its pursuit and uses, conflicts with indigenous perspectives that value seeking knowledge for the purpose of serving others.

Inherent in this vision of research is the supremacy of Western understandings of science as a framing mechanism for research. Western conceptions of science, referred to simply as *science*, become the golden and guiding rule. Linda Tuhiwai Smith (1999) explains,

> Research "through imperial eyes" describes an approach which assumes that Western ideas about the most fundamental things are the only ideas possible to hold, certainly the only rational ideas, and the only ideas which can make sense of the world, of reality, of social life and of human beings.... It is research which is imbued with an "attitude" and a "spirit" which assumes a certain ownership of the world.... There are people out there who in the name of science and progress still consider indigenous peoples as specimens, not as humans. (p. 56)

As suggested by L. Smith, colonized research, taught in the Western academy as *good* research, is problematic in several respects. First and foremost, this singular approach, which assumes its own superiority, functions to silence, erase, appropriate, dominate, own, and oppress that which it encounters in the world—be it people, knowledge systems, or alternate visions of how the world could be. We want to be clear that research can, and should, serve multiple purposes in terms of its contributions. The primary motivation within a CIRM framework, however, is for the research and researcher(s) to serve indigenous communities, acting as a tool of the community to meet the community's needs and to advance emancipatory goals of self-determination and sovereignty. Perhaps Wilson (2001b) explains this best when he writes,

> One major difference between the dominant paradigms and an Indigenous paradigm is that the dominant paradigms build on the fundamental belief that knowledge is an individual entity: the researcher is an individual in search of knowledge, knowledge is something that is gained, and therefore knowledge may be owned by an individual. An Indigenous paradigm comes from the fundamental belief that knowledge is relational. Knowledge is shared with all of creation. (p. 176)

There is an immediate connection made evident here between research and knowledge. It raises the question of how **relationality**—the ways in which relationships are enacted and connected—functions within the context of research and presents implications for the ownership, utility, and sharing of knowledge. Wilson encourages us to consider who owns the knowledge generated from research and in what ways knowledge might not only be wholly relational, but sacred to specific communities and not meant to be shared in broader contexts. We would argue that in a CIRM framework knowledge is not a commodity; instead, it is information gained or accumulated in order to serve the needs of those with whom we are in relation. In other words, the knowledge acquired and generated through indigenous research is intended to serve others. Moreover, whereas many critical methodological theories operate within a social justice framework based in relationality, CIRM reflects indigenous peoples' extension of the term *social* beyond the human realm, to include areas such as environmental, plant, animal, and spiritual realms.

Thus far our discussion of indigenous methodologies, building on the work of others, promotes an axiological, or value-based, claim that is specifically rooted in an anticolonial agenda and that places emphasis on serving the needs of indigenous peoples. Weber-Pillwax (2001) explains this when she writes, "I could also make a value statement and say that 'whatever I do as an Indigenous researcher must be hooked to the community' or 'the Indigenous research has to benefit the community'" (p. 168). This axiological commitment means that research must be driven by purposes that (re)position the motives of the researcher away from motives of control and individual gain—motives associated with preserving, promoting, upholding, and enforcing a colonialist agenda—to a position in which communities are primarily served. In essence we are suggesting that CIRM moves away from "ivory tower intellectuals" (G. Smith, 2003, p. 213) to community-serving, community-rooted intellectuals.

What Is a Critical Indigenous Research Methodologies Framework?

To our knowledge, there are no direct definitions of what specifically constitutes a Critical Indigenous Research Methodology; however, we do have a sense of how and in what ways indigenous scholars have begun to critically address the call for indigenous-based research and practices. Denzin and Lincoln (2008) suggest that one way to begin to conceptualize CIRM is by considering the following position: "Critical indigenous inquiry begins with the concerns of Indigenous people" (p. 2), and the concerns of indigenous peoples are not necessarily confined to a dichotomous opposition of human concern versus environmental concern. Moreover, for Evans, Hole, Berg, Hutchinson, and Sookraj (2009), discussions of indigenous methodologies need to include a consideration of *who* are engaging in the research and *how* they do so. For them, an indigenous methodology "can be defined as research by and for Indigenous peoples, using techniques and methods drawn from the traditions and knowledges of those peoples" (quoted in Denzin, Lincoln, & Smith, 2008, p. x). This definition recognizes a direct connection between ensuring that indigenous research methodologies include beliefs that are based on indigenous principles of relating *and* of sharing knowledge. This definition also raises another important consideration: that is, separating indigenous methodologies from indigenous knowledges not only is faulty—it also removes any sense of indigeneity from the methodology. **Indigeneity** is broadly defined as the enactment and engagement of being an indigenous person. In other words, methodologies inherently carry with them the ways in which those who are guided by them view the world. This worldview is inherently a part of one's knowledge system.

Research as Service

Still other scholars have presented a specific purpose that an indigenous research methodology should fulfill. According to Hart (2010), "An Indigenous Methodology includes the assumption that knowledge gained will be utilized practically" (p. 9). Hart's observation suggests there is a significant need for putting knowledge or research to practical use and echoes the work of other scholars who suggest research must address particular challenges or specific issues if it is going to be useful for indigenous peoples (Deloria, 1969; G. Smith, 2000; L. Smith, 1999, 2000; Weber-Pillwax, 2001; Wilson, 2001a, 2008). This serves as a further reminder that a CIRM approach is driven by service and is tied to well-being, rather than an approach that views knowledge accumulation as the end goal. Thus there is a clear sense in CIRM of the need to conduct research rooted in transformative processes that assist communities in ways that meet their needs.

The literature is also clear on the idea that a community's needs are best assessed by the community itself. Members of a community understand the local context, challenges, and resources; it is up to them to identify needs. Explaining how researchers engage communities on this level, Lumbee scholar Robert Williams (1997) draws on his experience as director of an indigenous legal clinic at the University of Arizona, writing that the clinicians in the practice go out into communities, listen to people there, and become "story hearing fools" (p. 764). This process of becoming "story hearing fools" largely ensures that communities drive the practices and research in which practitioners and researchers engage.

The community-driven nature of CIRM should not be taken as an argument that this kind of research is in any way anti-intellectual or nonempirical; rather, it helps to justify CIRM as a process that serves the needs of the people—*as defined by the people*—as well as to advance intellectual inquiries further in ways consistent with indigenous understandings of empiricism, multisensory learning, service, and responsibility. This focus on engaging in research endeavors that directly address the needs and concerns facing indigenous communities, it has been argued, serves as one example of what may differentiate a CIRM framework or paradigm from a traditionally Western one. Consider Perry Gilmore and the late David Smith's writings (2005) wherein they argue, "The notion that one should seek knowledge for knowledge's sake is revered in Western traditions of scholarship. Indigenous research seeks to contribute both to academic and local communities" (p. 82). Although we would note that there is often overlap and intermingling between academic and local knowledge, nevertheless this theme of connection between research by and research for indigenous peoples is echoed in multiple places and carries significant implications for what the role of the researcher is and how it is perceived (see also Chapter Eighteen concerning community participation).

The Four R's of CIRM: Relationality, Responsibility, Respect, and Reciprocity

In response to the call by the indigenous researchers to (re)claim an indigenous intellectual life and thought-world, we suggest a framework built on relationality, responsibility, respect, and reciprocity. This CIRM perspective shares similarities with other critical perspectives—notably its commitment to research that is driven by the community, that serves the needs of the community, and that ultimately works to recognize basic human, community, and civil rights. However, other facets of CIRM make it distinct from other critical approaches, as will be elaborated in the next sections.

Relationality

For us, the genesis of Critical Indigenous Research Methodologies is rooted in relationships. CIRM posits that knowledge is relational and thus not owned by the individual, presenting serious considerations for how we understand the purposes of data and their analyses as well as the purposes of knowledge production and acquisition for indigenous communities. This implication will be further explored in the following section. For now, we want to note our belief that knowledge is both relational and **subjective,** not based on objective truths that are often thought to define research; that is, objectivity in indigenous research *is not* a goal researchers should necessarily strive for. As Harris (2002) points out, "For many Indigenous people the notion of objectivity is preposterous because every aspect of Creation is continually interacting; the observer is interacting with the observed, and, therefore logically cannot be divorced from it" (p. 188). Many other critical research paradigms embrace the concepts of subjectivity and relationality; in contrast to CIRM, however, these other paradigms are still operating under very different assumptions about the world than are those paradigms grounded in indigenous worldviews (for example, worldviews that are human-centered or in which subjectivity may also include the metaphysical or spiritual realms).

Metís scholar Cora Weber-Pillwax (2001) also recognizes the role of subjectivity when she states, "Indigenous Research Methodologies are those that enable and permit Indigenous researchers to be who they are while engaged actively as participants in the research processes that create new knowledge and transform who they are and where they are" (p. 174). Linda Tuhiwai Smith (1999) extends Weber-Pillwax's point when she argues, "Indigenous research approaches problematize the insider model in different ways because there are multiple ways of both being an insider and an outsider in indigenous contexts" (p. 137).

As we argue that CIRM, as a research stance, is rooted in relationships, we understand that this may not be as evident to readers as it is to us. In part, we want to make two important points concerning our argument for the importance of relationships in CIRM.

The first point is that research must be a *process* of fostering relationships between researchers, communities, and the topic of inquiry. Embedded in this process is a need to engage from a position of trust; researchers must be trustworthy and held accountable, as Graham Smith (2000) so clearly articulates. Linked to this, the second point is that CIRM acknowledges that there are multiple ways to be in relationship. This starts with a real sense of protocol for conducting research: communities must be approached, permission must be granted, and research must be engaged in with benevolent intent, taking into account generations past, present, and future. The research itself is also conducted with a particular sense of humility; every legitimate relationship necessitates the discarding of egos and requires the researcher to recognize the responsibilities that emerge from the relationship.

Other critical methodologies also make similar points concerning research. We acknowledge that some of the defining traits of CIRM are shared with other critical methodologies. We do not want to argue that all of CIRM is unique; rather, we want to point out that the totality of CIRM, driven by notions of sovereignty and self-determination, makes it unique and important. The connections to other critical methodologies point to the fact that CIRM stands in solidarity with these methodologies.

Along these lines, Nicholls (2009) argues for an understanding of relationality as methodology when, quoting Linda Tuhiwai Smith (1999), she states, "Indigenous Methodologies tend to approach cultural protocols, values and behaviours as an integral part of methodology" (p. 120). Nicholls further suggests that "relationality, in this context, is ontology, epistemology, and axiology" (p. 120). The behavioral aspects (ontology) of CIRM are driven by the beliefs (epistemology), which are framed by a value system (axiology). Within this value set, Maori scholar Russell Bishop (2005) notes that "researchers are expected to develop prevailing relationships with participants" (p. 117) on the terms outlined by the community. This expectation presents one of the responsibilities linked to the relationships.

Responsibility

The link between relationships and responsibilities is critical. From a CIRM perspective, research is situated within complex relationships that necessitate multiple responsibilities on the part of the researcher. Indeed, Wilson (2001b) speaks directly to this point when he notes,

> What is an Indigenous Methodology? . . . To me an Indigenous Methodology means talking about relational accountability. As a researcher you are answering to *all your relations* when you are doing research. You are not answering questions of validity or reliability or making judgments of better or worse. Instead you should be fulfilling your relationships with the world around you. So your methodology has to ask different questions: rather than asking about validity or reliability, you are asking how am I fulfilling my role in this relationship? What are my obligations in this relationship? (p. 177)

Embedded in Wilson's words is an outline for thinking about CIRM that suggests indigenous-based research methodologies go beyond an individual-oriented way of engaging the world. Recognizing the importance of relationships, as we have previously noted, requires the researcher to think about how research affects others beyond himself or herself. Relationships exist between people, animals, places, and ideas. In a sense, this relatedness to other living objects/beings in the world situates peoples as just one part of a larger cosmos, not the center of it. To this end, if we have relationships with other peoples, things, animals, and places, we are necessarily responsible to them. As people we learn from, rely on, and survive and thrive because of that which surrounds us. Ideas, as part of the research process, implicate these same sets of relational protocols and responsibilities. Our ideas matter: how and if we pursue them and what becomes of those ideas after research ends—these things have long-lasting repercussions for those with whom we are in relationship. CIRM necessitates careful thought, consultation, and collaboration to care for both the ideas, or knowledge, it generates and the living beings those ideas influence.

Respect

Naturally emerging from relationships and responsibilities is the importance of respect. **Respect** is a key component of CIRM and is demonstrated in Linda Tuhiwai Smith's earlier mention of protocols (1999) and Bishop's reference (2005) to expectations of building relationships. Respect is one of those things that emerge from the process of building and engaging in relationships. Relationships must be built on mutual and ongoing respect, or the research cannot be conducted ethically. Linda Tuhiwai Smith (1999) continues by writing,

> The term "respect" is consistently used by indigenous peoples to underscore the significance of our relationships and humanity. Through respect, the place of everyone and everything in the universe is kept in balance and harmony. Respect is a reciprocal, shared, constantly interchanging principle which is expressed through all aspects of social conduct. (p. 120)

Valid relationships are vital to research and are enacted through processes of respect, as she notes.

Reciprocity

From the three R's (relationality, responsibility, and respect) that are central to CIRM there emerges a fourth element: reciprocity. **Reciprocity** here moves beyond a "quid pro quo" line of thinking in research and relationships to one that reflects more of a "pay it forward" notion. That is, we take so that we can give to and provide for others—in order to survive and to thrive. In so doing we are bounded, through these relationships, to care for those things around us. This notion flows through the CIRM research process, which is, at its core, relational.

Yupiaq scholar Oscar Kawagley (1995, 2006) notes that indigenous worldviews contain a sense of responsibility and reciprocity. Cree scholar Michael Anthony Hart (2010), drawing on the work of Rice (2005), states, "Another dominant aspect is reciprocity, or the belief that as we receive from others, we must also offer to others" (p. 7). Within reciprocity is a clear sense of relatedness and that whatever is received makes its way back around to others. There is another aspect of reciprocity that contains, as Linda Tuhiwai Smith (2000) explains,

> [a] level of accountability in regard to developing transformative outcomes for the indigenous communities [researchers] purport to be serving. If a person is genuinely working on behalf of the community, then the community will also be part of the whole process, not simply be passive recipients of a grand "plan" developed outside themselves. (p. 213)

In other words, reciprocity happens through ongoing processes and relationships with others. Relationality, respect, responsibility, reciprocity, *and* accountability thus animate CIRM and guide all aspects of the research process.

Living Research: Indigenous Empiricism, Multisensory Listening, and Indigenous Epistemologies

For us, another important point in considering CIRM is to acknowledge that indigenous peoples have always engaged in research. We are empirical peoples, as Kawagley (1995, 2006) notes, and research for Native peoples is certainly not a new concept. Indigenous peoples used, and continue to use, our knowledge of the world, gained through generations of empirical observation and sensuous engagement of the world, toward hunting, farming, fishing, and meeting the day-to-day challenges of being in the world. Indeed, traditionally for indigenous peoples research has been engaged toward a high-stakes goal—survival.

A critical aspect to surviving has been the ability of indigenous peoples to research through listening, or more specifically through **multisensory listening**. For indigenous peoples, this means we listen with more than just our ears: we engage in listening through sight, touch, and smell. We listen to our gut; we listen to our memories; and we listen to what the old mountains and the wily coyotes care to share with us. In the past—and for many of us still, in the present—this was (is) true. Listening, or gathering data by observation and by engaging with the world through the seasons, means understanding how fish or caribou migrate; or when to plant corn, beans, and other foodstuffs; or when or where to build protective living structures. Research in this context, through long periods of observation, notes how the wind blows before a big storm comes and how this is different from how it normally blows. In the following quote, Iñupiat scholar Paul Ongtooguk (2000) clearly articulates the empirical knowledge necessary to survive in the Arctic:

> It was not mere hope and persistence that allowed Iñupiat society to develop in the North. Traditional Iñupiat society was, and is, about knowing the right time to be in the right place, with the right tools to take advantage of a temporary abundance of resources. Such a cycle of life was, and is, based on a foundation of knowledge about and insight into the natural world. Such a cycle of life was, and is, dependent upon a people's careful observations of the environment and their dynamic response to changes and circumstances. Developing this

cycle of life was critical to the continuance of traditional Iñupiat society. (para. 5)

Native Hawaiian (Kanaka Maoli) scholar Manulani Aluli Meyer (2001) eloquently adds that these ways of knowing reflect a kind of listening or experiencing through "senses . . . developed by culture" (p. 144). Noting that "knowledge has a genesis, a place of origin" (p. 148), Meyer reminds us that listening itself is relational, invoking genealogies of place and of family come and gone. Although detailing the depths of indigenous knowledge systems is well beyond the scope of this work, indigenous epistemologies are in many ways at the heart of the embodied research (that is, it is taken up through the senses, in part), of which listening is just one part.

Our fundamental understanding, then, is that indigenous peoples have used research processes informed by particular epistemological, ontological, and axiological understandings of the world for millennia, and that the physical senses, the intellect, and intuition are all integral parts of these processes. CIRM calls for this type of multisensory listening and culturally embedded ways of knowing within research. In making such a call, CIRM recognizes the validity of indigenous research as a set of time-tested, empirical methods of knowledge production, subject as they have been across generations to revision and updating based on observed changes in the environment. Moreover, CIRM calls on the researcher to *really listen*.

Within the CIRM context, respect for multisensory listening, embodied intellect, and traditional worldviews that understand cause and effect as living, integrated systems reaching through time and space are all elements that intersect with the four R's: relationality, responsibility, respect, and reciprocity (and accountability). These elements are embedded within the larger CIRM context of service, sovereignty, and self-determination. Both conceptually and in being, this rich combination, imbued with local worldviews, knowledges, and practices, guides not only research protocols but larger epistemological, ontological, and axiological questions about the research process: how it came to be; to what end it will be put; how the relationships embedded within it will progress long after grant dollars are spent; or how each generation will teach the next the research that, through lived experience and thoughtful action, has become encoded in place names, language, stories, planting, fishing, hunting, literature, and family ways of doing. CIRM is evolving and in many ways (re)hearing its own voice as well as the voices of community members past and present. In the process of this evolution there has emerged a particular call for a critical perspective on methodologies. It is to addressing the *critical* nature of these methodologies that we now turn.

> **REFLECTION QUESTIONS**
>
> 1. How are the four R's that the authors explain connected?
> 2. Why does listening need to be multisensory?

What Makes the "Critical" Critical?

Quechua scholar Sandy Grande (2008) writes, "By virtue of living in the Whitestream world, indigenous scholars have no choice but to negotiate the forces of colonialism, to learn, understand, and converse in the grammar of empire as well as develop the skills to contest it" (p. 234). Given the history of colonialism and its lasting effects on indigenous communities, indigenous research(ers) are faced with a number of struggles in the attempt to establish a research paradigm that is consistent with indigenous worldviews and practices. Engaging in these efforts means resisting the manner in which research has been traditionally conceptualized and practiced in the academy. Resisting research paradigms that have shaped the academy for so long by (re)defining indigenous paradigms means that, by its very nature, research based in indigenous frameworks almost always becomes politicized. This is especially the case when non-indigenous researchers choose to acknowledge and engage work based on an indigenous knowledges and methodologies framework.

By now it should be clear that research rooted in an **indigenous methodologies paradigm**, a theoretical and philosophical approach that places high priority on building relationships and serving the needs and interests of indigenous communities, carries with it a set of commitments to dialogue, community, self-determination, and cultural autonomy (Denzin et al., 2008). In fact, Linda Tuhiwai Smith (2000) directly proposes a guiding principle for a CIRM when, echoing the work of Graham Smith (2000), she argues that "in terms of Kaupapa Maori, the most important question is related to issues of social justice" (p. 231). For her, social justice as a guiding principle includes (but is not limited to) addressing issues that will assist Maori peoples in reclaiming items stolen by colonizers, including land claims, "histories," and "resources" (p. 232). These claims are rooted in treaty rights.

Herein lies the key component for us in considering what makes indigenous research methodologies *critical*. The **critical component** is that the methodologies recognize particular (group-based)—legal and inherent—rights of indigenous peoples and work toward a vision of justice determined by communities and in relation to things like land, histories, and resources. Thus engaging in research from an indigenous methodologies paradigm entails an understanding not only of the history and practices of indigenous communities but also of how research may be used to advance the *political* and *social justice* goals of indigenous communities. Linda Tuhiwai Smith (1999) further notes,

> The research agenda is conceptualized here as constituting a programme and set of approaches that are situated within the decolonization politics of the indigenous peoples' movement. The agenda is focused strategically on the goal of self-determination of indigenous peoples. Self-determination in a research agenda becomes something more than a political goal. It becomes a goal of social justice which is expressed through and across a wide range of psychological, social, cultural and economic terrains. It necessarily involves the processes of transformation, of decolonization, of healing and of mobilization as peoples. (pp. 116–117)

When it comes to a *Critical* Indigenous Research Methodologies framework, we believe that—although it is important to have indigenous research methodologies that are rooted in indigenous practices of relationality, respect, reciprocity, and responsibility—it is of little use to create frameworks rooted in these principles if these methodologies do not also promote emancipatory agendas that recognize the self-determination and inherent sovereignty of indigenous peoples. CIRM thus requires researchers not only to be community-serving, community-rooted intellectuals but also to root their endeavors in the land and all of the politics that implies (see also Chapters Fourteen, Fifteen, and Sixteen).

Where Do We Go from Here? Moving Forward and the Reclamation of Voice

Indigenous scholars within the academy continue to voice a concern that has been expressed within communities for decades: that indigenous knowledge should be protected and respected (Battiste, 2000, 2002; Battiste & Henderson, 2002; G. Smith, 2000; L. Smith, 2000). It is only through the development of research frameworks and practices that are centered on serving indigenous communities and indigenous practices that we can actively work toward answering the call that Parker (1916) and Deloria (1969) put forth decades ago. If indigenous peoples are to reclaim our research and our intellectual voices, indigenous research(ers) must (re)claim and (re)define how research is understood and taken up. Graham Smith (2000) echoes the concerns of Parker and Deloria to assert the need for indigenous peoples to pursue self-determination and reclaim an intellectual life that honors and respects indigenous knowledges as he explains,

> My message . . . is that we have the option to set our own courses with respect to realizing our dreams and aspirations, and therefore we ought to be considering developing resistance initiatives around that kind of philosophy, initiatives that are positive and proactive. We must *reclaim* our own lives in order to put our destinies in our own hands. (p. 211, italics added)

Resistance to CIRM

It is not surprising that this process of reclaiming an indigenous research methodology and thought-world has been met with resistance from non-indigenous colleagues. Echoing some of Parker's concerns (1916) just after the close of the nineteenth century, Cook-Lynn (2000) explains,

> At the close of the [twentieth] century, the efforts that indigenous peoples have made to speak for themselves and their peoples, either through their own works or through the interpretative works of translators, are being subjected to abuse and scholarly/political attacks that goes far beyond the normal critical analysis of academic work. (p. 80)

Thus indigenous scholarship, when it is engaged, suffers from the same practices and treatment that relegated indigenous worldviews to the periphery in the first place. Not engaging indigenous research is a **hegemonic method** by which the "Whitestream world" (Grande, 2008, p. 234) can discredit, ignore, or deny an intellectual life for indigenous peoples (see, for example, Battiste, 2002). **Hegemony** is a term first coined by Italian philosopher Antonio Gramsci (Gramsci, Hoare, & Nowell-Smith, 1971) to indicate how a society comes to believe that the manner in which things, like Western research, are engaged in has always been that way; it erases the fact that these beliefs have been influenced by imperial and colonial practices that have silenced and subverted the voices and thoughts of indigenous people for centuries. In this way, the power to name or determine the beliefs and practices of the community has come to rest on the shoulders of those responsible for colonizing these spaces rather than on those who have always inhabited the space(s). Viewed in this light, we can see that there is little that is "commonsense" or "natural" about the ways in which research has historically been taken up in indigenous communities.

Cook-Lynn (2000) goes on to note, "It can be argued that pretending the work does not exist or pretending ignorance of it is one of the methods of discrediting the work" (p. 89). Ignoring, silencing, and hiding critical indigenous scholarship and its concomitant methods and methodologies are hegemonic practices. These practices of discrediting end up denying, once again, the basic human rights of indigenous peoples to develop their own intellectual lives and thought-worlds, defined not in the Cartesian sense but on indigenous terms. CIRM, then, must be **counterhegemonic**, calling attention to actions that seek to disrupt the "commonsense" nature of research and thinking that accompany mainstream ideas and research, as well as anticolonial.

Similarly, Graham Smith (2000) points to another trend that has surfaced in an attempt to discredit the work of indigenous scholars. That is, attacking the credibility of the work serves to place into question the accountability the research(er) has to the academic community *and* to the indigenous community that is being served by the research.

> Within the postmodern analysis, there is often an emphasis on the critique—that is, on what has gone wrong—at the expense of providing transformative strategies and outcomes. Many academics have their research shaped by the institution in which they work—for example, in order to fulfill the institution's academic expectations that research be positivistic and so on. A lot less emphasis is put on the critique that's developed out of the organic community context (it's not seen as real academic work). To put this another way, many Maori academics complain that we have to perform to two levels of accountability. Our academic credibility does not just depend on the institution we work for and the number of papers or books we produce. Our academic credibility is also set in very powerful ways by the communities in which we are located. (G. Smith, 2000, p. 213)

Echoing some of G. Smith's concerns, Cook-Lynn (2000) points out that scarier still are the methodologies that are rising in *response to* indigenous efforts to engage in indigenous-centered research and practices:

> [Questioning the] veracity and authority of representational stories, questioning liberation theology, politics, and mediation—these have emerged as the disciplinary methodologies used to interpret and analyze the singular native voice. In the process much of what is written and

published as the American Indian literary voice of the twentieth century is subject to analysis as either inauthentic or too transgressive and counterhegemonic, and often is discredited in literature as not even aesthetically pleasing. (p. 81)

This strategic response by those opposed to CIRM in discrediting the long-silenced voices of indigenous peoples is unsurprising given the history of Western research practices concerning indigenous communities.

Indigenous researchers embracing CIRM may also find their efforts are trivialized as a certain fawning for a former utopia that cannot be achieved and as such may be dismissed as irrelevant, obsolete, or nonpracticable by current researchers. Such views dismiss thousands of years of indigenous research because lifestyles engaged in by indigenous peoples in the past are viewed as nonviable in today's modern societies; these views represent a failure to understand that those traditions and forms of engaging in research do not remain in the past but continue to influence the present. That is, as indigenous researchers we are linked to the past through traditions, some of which are embedded in research done by our ancestors, but this does not mean indigenous researchers are *stuck* in the past. The past matters for the present in that we are all constructed by traditions that morph through their use and engagement.

That said, indigenous researchers may find themselves on sandy ground and at a distinct researching disadvantage in an academy dominated by an almost unwavering belief in a singular epistemological approach grounded in Western understandings of science and in which academicians mistakenly assume the goal of CIRM is to time-travel back to a precontact era. To be clear, CIRM does not pretend that the goal is to flash back to precontact times (although wouldn't that be something?!?). Rather, CIRM is grounded in a belief that by centering indigenous worldviews, values, beliefs, and traditions (old and new), it is possible to rehabilitate academic research into a responsible community member—into research that sustains, supports, and provides sustenance to those who dare to envision healthy, thriving futures grounded in indigenous worldviews and considerations of self-determination and sovereignty.

Response to Critiques

Moreover, it is imperative that indigenous scholars respond directly to the critiques while simultaneously not becoming distracted by them. In order to do this, we argue that indigenous scholarship should stay focused on the relational aspects of the research and the justice-oriented nature of the work. Indeed,

Cook-Lynn (2000) notes that to not engage in critical research is a denial of a "*basic human right*" (p. 86, italics added). She goes on to argue that the denial of indigenous peoples' right, "to *express* [themselves] collectively and historically in terms of continued self-determination, is a kind of genocide that is perhaps even more immoral than the physical genocide of war and torture" (p. 86). Cook-Lynn's sentiment might be best addressed by Linda Tuhiwai Smith (1999), who writes,

> The denial by the West of humanity to indigenous peoples, the denial of citizenship and human rights, the denial of the right to self-determination—all these demonstrate palpably the enormous lack of respect which has marked the relations of indigenous and non-indigenous peoples. (p. 120)

Notably, Cook-Lynn's and Smith's commentaries bear striking resemblance to Parker's work (1916) in their analysis of the importance of self-determination and the right to an intellectual life.

CIRM responds to the critique surrounding indigenous scholarship by moving the focus of the arguments away from an emphasis on dismissals to a focus aimed squarely at addressing particular issues of (in)justice. CIRM calls for attention to the needs of peoples and communities. Linda Tuhiwai Smith (1999) is again insightful when she notes, "Reclaiming a voice in this context has also been about reclaiming, reconnecting and reordering those ways of knowing which were submerged, hidden or driven underground" (p. 69). Ultimately the reclamation project of CIRM is a vital component of this work. We envision, in the foreseeable future, methodologies that do not succumb to the bitter politics of *being right* but ones that focus on *doing right*—that is, working toward fulfilling the needs of communities, asserting a right to intellectual and scholarly freedoms and creativity, and engaging the research process with integrity.

Summary

According to Maori scholar Linda Tuhiwai Smith (1999), "From the vantage point of the colonized . . . the word 'research' . . . is probably one of the dirtiest words in the indigenous world's vocabulary" (p. 1). This is because research invokes, for indigenous communities, past and present incidents of abusive, exploitative research practices. Yet many indigenous scholars, although recognizing the reasons for why indigenous communities remain distrustful of researchers, argue that research can serve beneficial purposes when it is driven by community interests and undertaken with attention paid to the complexity, resilience, contradiction, and self-determination of these communities. For this reason indigenous scholars have been calling for indigenous communities to (re)claim research and knowledge-making practices that are (1) driven by indigenous peoples, knowledges, beliefs, and practices; (2) rooted in recognition of the impact of Eurocentric culture on the history, beliefs, and practices of indigenous peoples and communities; and (3) guided by the intention of promoting the anticolonial or emancipatory interests of indigenous communities. CIRM is a response to this call.

A CIRM perspective fundamentally begins as an emancipatory project rooted in relationships and is driven explicitly by community interests. Admittedly, CIRM shares similarities with other critical perspectives, most notably in its commitment that research should be driven by the community; that it should serve the needs of the community; and that the research endeavor should work to ultimately recognize basic human, community, and civil rights. However, other facets of CIRM make it distinct from other critical approaches. Specifically, CIRM is rooted in indigenous knowledge systems and recognizes the role of indigenous beliefs and practices in the construction and acquisition of knowledge—this recognition serves to influence the techniques (methods) and expectations guiding the research process. CIRM recognizes that indigenous peoples think and behave in ways unique to their worldviews and experiences and thus places a heavy emphasis on the role relationships, responsibility, respect, reciprocity, and accountability play in our interactions with the human, physical, and spiritual world around us.

In addition, CIRM is driven by a belief that information and knowledge are sometimes esoteric; that the knowledge uncovered through scientific inquiry does not solely belong to the researcher; and that the acquisition of knowledge requires one to enter into a relationship with those ideas—to learn from them, to care for them, and to pass them on to the next generation. From a CIRM perspective, knowledge is sacred and to be entrusted with it carries great responsibility, thus adding a seriousness to subsequent decisions researchers make in terms of how and when to ask for information and how and when to share the knowledge with which they have been entrusted. Finally, CIRM specifically recognizes the political positioning of indigenous peoples in contemporary societies and reasons that it is of little use to create frameworks rooted in these principles of relationships, reciprocity, and responsibility if these methodologies do not also promote emancipatory agendas that recognize the self-determination and inherent sovereignty of indigenous peoples.

Key Terms

axiologies, 425
counterhegemonic, 445
critical component, 442
Critical Indigenous Research Methodologies (CIRM), 424
epistemologies, 425
hegemonic method, 444
hegemony, 444
indigeneity, 434
indigenous methodologies paradigm, 442
methodologies, 426
methods, 426
multisensory listening, 440
ontologies, 425
positivist, 424
praxis, 429
reciprocity, 439
relationality, 433
respect, 438
subjective, 436
taxonomies, 432

Further Readings and Resources

Suggested Readings

Kawagley, A. O. (2006). *A Yupiaq worldview: A pathway to ecology and spirit* (2nd ed.). Prospect Heights, IL: Waveland.

In this study Kawagley explores both memories of his Yupiaq grandmother, who raised him with the stories of the Bear Woman and respectful knowledge of the reciprocity of nature, and his own education in science as it is taught in Western schools.

Smith, L. T. (1999). *Decolonizing methodologies: Research and indigenous peoples*. London: Zed Books.

The book is divided into two parts. In the first, Smith critically examines the historical and philosophical base of Western research; in the second, she sets an agenda for planning and implementing indigenous research, as part of the wider project of reclaiming control over indigenous ways of knowing and being.

Smith, L.T.T.R. (2000). Kaupapa Maori research. In M. Battiste (Ed.), *Reclaiming indigenous voice and vision* (pp. 225–247). Vancouver: University of British Columbia Press.

In this chapter, Smith points to the ways that Maori peoples are working to reclaim their sense of research. By turning to Kaupapa Maori theory, scholars can engage in critique and resistance in a way that also points to a need to exert control and exercise notions of sovereignty. All of this, she argues, is a move toward helping Maori peoples address the significant issues they face.

Wilson, S. (2008). *Research is ceremony: Indigenous research methods*. Halifax, Nova Scotia: Fernwood.

Wilson describes a research paradigm shared by indigenous scholars in Canada and Australia. By portraying indigenous researchers as knowledge seekers, he demonstrates how this paradigm can be put into practice.

Organizations and Web Sites

AlterNative: An International Journal of Indigenous Peoples (www.alternative.ac.nz/)
This peer-reviewed, interdisciplinary journal is dedicated to the analysis and dissemination of indigenous knowledge that uniquely belongs to cultural, traditional, tribal, and aboriginal peoples as well as first-nations from around the world.

American Education Research Association—Special Interest Groups on Indigenous Peoples of the Americas (SIG #48) and Indigenous Peoples of the Pacific (SIG #146) (www.aera.net/Default.aspx?menu_id=396&id=5480)
These SIGs promote a better understanding of theoretical-, policy-, and practice-related research pertaining to educational issues for indigenous peoples of North America, the Pacific, and the Pacific Rim, including indigenous ways of knowing and indigenous practices.

Center for Indian Education at Arizona State University (http://coe.asu.edu/cie/)
This interdisciplinary research and service organization promotes studies in American Indian/Alaska Native policy and administration that contribute to the quality of scholarship and effective practices in education, professional training, and tribal capacity building. It sponsors conferences and colloquia and publishes the *Journal of American Indian Education*.

Hoʻokulāiwi: ʻAha Hoʻonaʻauao ʻŌiwi (Center for Native Hawaiian and Indigenous Education) (http://hookulaiwi.com/)
The center is an educational partnership to prepare teachers and educational leaders for working with Hawaiian communities. It also offers original insights into Native Hawaiian knowledge and practices and how these can be used in classrooms.

Journal of American Indian Education (http://jaie.asu.edu/)
This professional journal publishes papers directly related to the education of American Indian/Alaska Natives; it also invites scholarship on educational issues pertaining to native peoples of the world, such as First Nations (Aboriginal People of Canada), Native Hawaiians, Maori, Indigenous Peoples of Latin America, and others.

CHAPTER 18

DEMOCRATIZING QUALITATIVE RESEARCH

Ernest R. House

Key Ideas

- Researchers often encounter situations in which there are strong conflicting perspectives, values, and interests.

- One way to handle such differences is to democratize the research by including diverse perspectives in the study.

- Deliberative democratic research involves key stakeholders in the study, promotes dialogue with and among stakeholders, and enhances deliberation about research findings.

- There are many ways to involve stakeholders, depending on experience, available resources, and the ingenuity of the researcher.

- Not all research situations are suited to engaging in democratic research.

It is tough to do research studies in settings in which there are strong conflicting perspectives, values, and interests. Perhaps nowhere are these problems more acute than where there are class, cultural, and ethnic differences. One way of dealing with these differences is to incorporate them into the research itself. I will discuss a study in which such differences were pronounced and how I handled them. My democratizing approach to planning and conducting studies can work with any of the research approaches presented in this book.

The Denver Study

In 1999 I received a phone call from a lawyer in Boston representing the Congress of Hispanic Educators. Years before, this group had sued the Denver Public Schools for segregating minority students. The original desegregation lawsuit involved bussing students, but the case had evolved over time into one about language and culture. The federal court now required the Denver Public Schools to provide native language instruction to students who did not understand English. The U.S. Justice Department joined the suit as coplaintiff. Each group—the school district, the Hispanic educators, and the Justice Department—was represented by lawyers.

The court agreement specified in detail educational services the district should provide, such as teacher qualifications, criteria for enlisting and exiting students, and the size of classes. Federal court judge Richard Matsch (who presided over the Oklahoma City bombing trial of Timothy McVey) needed someone to monitor whether the school district was fulfilling its obligations. After consulting various parties, the judge appointed me court monitor based partly on previous work I had done in New York and Chicago. I envisioned a study to monitor the implementation of the educational program and report these findings to the court, the plaintiffs, and the school district. I expected considerable differences of opinion and political conflict from various **stakeholder** groups, that is, those groups that had the most to gain or lose in the program.

Language, Class, and Cultural Politics

Denver had a school population of seventy thousand students; fifteen thousand of these students could not speak English very well. They were overwhelmingly Spanish speakers, mostly recent immigrants from Mexico and Latin America. A few were Russian or Vietnamese speakers. Many students were illegal immigrants whose parents had come to Denver during the boom economy of the 1990s, when the Colorado population increased by 30 percent. The parents of the students built houses, cooked food, washed cars, and performed basic manual labor for the city and state. It is the policy of most American schools to accept students who appear at the school door and not question their citizenship. Denver schools followed this policy.

The city itself was dominated by an Anglo business establishment, and Anglos displayed ambivalent attitudes toward these recent immigrants. The Denver program was titled the English Language Acquisition (ELA) program to signal that its purpose was to teach English, not maintain Spanish. Bilingual instruction was a hot political issue, as it is in most of the United States. The old Latino part of town had become so crowded with the new immigrants that Latinos were moving to other parts of the city. African Americans—long-established residents—were being pushed out of their neighborhoods. Tensions between blacks and Latinos were high. Some blacks saw the Latinos as taking the available affordable housing and undercutting them for jobs. Political power was shifting as tens of thousands of Latinos moved in. When the study began, the governing school board was dominated by Anglos, but two Latinas had just been elected. As the study progressed, more Latino members joined the board.

Furthermore, many teachers and administrators in the Denver schools were Latinos who had come from southern Colorado and northern New Mexico, descendants of the old Santa Fe culture. Santa Fe, founded in 1610, is the oldest capital city in the United States. These people have a distinct cultural identity predating Anglo settlement by centuries, and they consider themselves Spanish Americans, not Mexican. Other teachers and administrators were Chicanos, United States–born descendants of Mexicans whose ancestors had come from Mexico generations before, usually as migrants to pick crops.

These two Latino groups spoke both English and Spanish and staffed many educational positions in the Denver schools. Although they identified with the new Latino immigrants, they also saw them as different. The immigrants came from poor rural villages, mostly in Mexico, and were sparsely educated in any language. Ethnic, cultural, and class differences among the Latino groups themselves generated misunderstandings. For example, some immigrants took their children out of school for weeks to return to their home villages in Mexico for fiestas, which infuriated some professional educators. The teachers and administrators saw the loss of a month of school time as a serious setback for the students.

Some immigrant parents wanted their children to go directly into English classes so they could learn enough English to quit school, find jobs, and help the family. Again, this was not what the professional educators thought best for the students. Most new immigrants wanted their children in Spanish classes first, then in English classes after three years. That was the way the program was structured, accommodating a gradual transition to English classes. According to the court agreement, parents had the choice as to what classes their children should take, but the school district had a strong preference that students be placed according to their limited English ability.

Over the years of the lawsuit (this is a famous legal case called the Keyes case), some school officials and some plaintiffs had deepened their distrust of each other. Each side considered the other suspect. Some school personnel suspected the plaintiffs wanted to build a Latino political base in Denver; some plaintiffs thought the schools did not really want to provide good educational services for these students. In my early encounters with both sides, these hostile attitudes came through forcefully. I was told that the other side was untrustworthy. Personalities rubbed each other the wrong way: such-and-such was "unprofessional"; so-and-so was "a snake in the grass." Much stronger language was expressed. When the monitoring began, passions were inflamed in some quarters, and the bilingual program was controversial.

Research Plan

My plan was to reduce distrust among these parties by involving the major stakeholders in the research study and by making my own actions transparent. I did not want any group to see me as siding with the other groups or as being duplicitous. Circumstances were ripe for misunderstanding. When I first announced that I was trying to make the monitoring study transparent, one administrator told me that was a big mistake. Why didn't I just act with the authority of the court? The other side had no choice but to accept my research findings. In any case, the opposition was not going to change.

To foster mutual understanding, I brought the representatives of the contending parties together face-to-face twice a year to discuss the research findings and to allow the parties significant input into the process. Because many participants were lawyers, adversarial by occupation (and some would say nasty by disposition), the meetings had some contentious encounters. Although I set the agenda for the meetings and chaired them, I could not anticipate what would occur when the parties met. I structured interaction around information and issues we, the court monitors, and they thought significant. In general, the sessions were cordial, whatever people said about each other privately.

REFLECTION QUESTIONS

1. Who would you identify as the important audiences for this proposed study?
2. What research questions do you think this study will try to answer?

At the beginning I intended to use data from the district's new management information system to identify schools that appeared deficient in implementing the program. However, the implementation of the data system fell far behind schedule. I had to do something else. People expected me to provide findings that would indicate whether the program was being implemented successfully. I constructed a checklist based on key elements of the program. By visiting schools, I could judge whether each school was in compliance. I submitted the checklist to all parties to ensure the items on the checklist were the most significant program features. People made useful suggestions, and I revised the checklist. I visited a few schools to see what collecting the data would be like. With more than one hundred schools involved, there was no way I could collect the data myself. Sampling schools—choosing some to represent the entire district—did not seem viable either because determining whether each school was in compliance was important.

I hired two retired school principals from Denver to visit and rate the schools using the checklist. It would have been easier to use graduate students, but graduate students would have had little credibility with administrators and teachers, and it would be too easy for principals to fool them. By contrast, the former principals knew how the Denver schools worked. When they were fed a suspect explanation they could sense it; they had been in similar positions, and they knew the program, the personnel, and the students. Because they were former principals from the school district, the central office trusted them. Because they were Latinas, spoke fluent Spanish, and had supported the ELA program and the Hispanic educator lawsuit from the beginning, the plaintiffs also trusted them. Without the trust from both sides, there was no sense in collecting the data.

The former principals did lack research experience, and sometimes they reverted to their former roles as helpers by acting as consultants. I had to prevent this, because this behavior would bias the findings. I held regular meetings with them to discuss their findings school by school and to remind them they were researchers now. It is surprising how well people can assume a role once the role expectations are clear. To help separate their opinions from the monitoring, I added a section to the checklist where they could provide their professional observations, with the understanding that these comments did not have to be based on the elements of the legal agreement. That helped them (and me) sort out their ratings of schools from other (often invaluable) insights. They felt better because their professional insights did not go unrecognized.

Discussing what was going on with the former principal–data collectors helped me construct an image of how the program was functioning overall and in depth. From them I had insights into what was happening and why that I could never have learned otherwise. For example, we might discover that a school principal was undercounting the number of eligible students deliberately. Why would the principal do that? I would have no idea. My colleagues might suggest that the principal was concerned about losing her expert veteran teachers who had been with her for a long time. The legal agreement stipulated that when numbers of eligible students reached a certain level, Spanish language teachers must be introduced to provide instruction. That could mean that regular teachers would have to transfer to other schools. The principal was therefore protecting her veteran teachers. Although we could not solve the problem, we could alert the school district staff to seek solutions. Alerting the district and the court to problems in particular schools was part of our job. In some research this reporting might be a breach of confidentiality, but in this study reporting problems of implementation was our basic task.

Enlisting these two former principals as coresearchers was one of the best things I did in the study. They not only could communicate with immigrant parents, teachers, and administrators but also were able to detect when things were awry when I had no idea. I could not have obtained this inside knowledge using a more traditional research approach, for example by using data collectors who had no special knowledge of the program. As a check on our site visits, I encouraged the ELA program staff to challenge our findings about particular schools when they disagreed. They were forthcoming when they thought we were wrong, and we hashed out disagreements face-to-face. Eventually the ELA staff members developed their own similar checklist so they could anticipate which schools had problems and fix them.

REFLECTION QUESTIONS

1. In what ways might clarifying role expectations have helped the former principals?
2. What biases might have influenced these former principals as they collected data?

As the management information system improved, I also developed quantitative indicators of progress in program implementation based on district data. One indicator was the percentage of eligible students enrolled in the program. The other indicator was whether students with the least English ability were placed in appropriate classes. Again, I discussed these indicators with all parties until everyone accepted them as measures that showed the progress of the program. Higher percentages of students in appropriate places meant the program was being successfully implemented. The development of the information system was slow and tortuous, reflecting how difficult it is to obtain accurate information in such organizations. Data had to be collected at the school level, entered into the data system, and aggregated. Errors plagued the process every step of the way. It cost the district a huge effort to obtain reliable data, but school district personnel managed it over two or three years.

When the data were reasonably accurate, our quantitative indicators showed gradual improvement year by year. Improvement was slower than anticipated, as is often the case in new programs. The indicators also showed which particular schools were in trouble. By combining our on-site checklists with the school-by-school indicators, we had a cross-check on where things stood. When schools looked bad, we revisited them to look again, and the district sent staff members to these schools to tackle problems. Finally, we could combine the checklist findings and school indicators to provide a summary of where the implementation of the ELA program stood at any given time. Good profiles of individual schools obtained by our data collectors were expected to be matched with increases in the percentages of students in the program and in the appropriate classes within the program.

Constant Change

Constant change in the school district was a complicating disturbance. School principals were retiring, resigning, and being replaced or promoted constantly. New principals meant a new situation, and we revisited schools that had new principals. Students dropped out, moved mid-term, went back to Mexico, or disappeared from the school rolls altogether. Some schools had more than 100 percent student turnover. Of course, student turnover was not unexpected.

More surprising was the turnover in school superintendents. In the six years of the monitoring study there were five different superintendents in charge of the Denver school district. Principals were accustomed to running their buildings without much interference, and each new superintendent disrupted long-standing patterns of behavior. Each superintendent had different goals for the district, and each reorganized the district administration. I had to establish a professional relationship with each new superintendent, and I had to give superintendents time to understand my role and figure out how their plans would affect the monitoring. The ELA program directors also changed. There were four during the study. I admired these people and the difficult challenges they faced. They were responsible for implementing the court agreement, yet had no line authority within the school district. They could persuade others or refer problems up the chain of command, but they could not order principals or teachers to do anything. Yet when things went wrong they were held personally accountable. Some lasted a long time; some not. Establishing a working relationship with them was critical for me and my two colleagues.

Power Shifts

Meanwhile, I met with interested groups in the community, including the militants, both those opposed to the program and those wanting Spanish in all schools. I listened, responded to their concerns, and included some of their ideas in my investigations. I followed up on information these groups provided. I turned down no one wanting to offer views, though I did not accept their information at face value. For example, the most militant Latino group wanted Spanish language classes to be maintained in all schools along with English classes. I met with the leader in a café that served as political headquarters and listened to her concerns. There was little I could do about continued Spanish classes for all students because the court agreement precluded it. That was beyond the purview of the study. However, I did investigate certain practices reinforcing her view that the district was insincere in providing services to students in the program.

My periodic, written summary reports went to the court. As court documents, the reports were public information the media seized on. I asked the school district and plaintiffs how they thought I should handle the media. Bilingual education was such a hot topic I knew the reporters would be after comments. All parties preferred that I not talk to the media. In their view, it would inflame the situation and make implementation of the program more difficult. I took their advice, referred inquiries to the parties themselves, and made no comments outside my written reports. The media accepted this stance reluctantly and quoted my reports in the newspapers.

After six years of monitoring, the program was almost fully implemented. The conflict seemed defused, at least for the time being. The opposing parties could meet in a room without casting insults at each other. I am not saying the groups loved each other, but they could manage their business together rationally. The strife and distrust was much less than when we started. The school district had established its own monitoring system. Even so, the plaintiffs were reluctant to let the district out of the court ruling.

District politics had shifted, with more Latinos having been elected to the school board. In fact, the daughter of the man who had sponsored the original lawsuit became chair of the school governing board, and the last superintendent, a lawyer who had been the mayor's chief of staff, adopted a strong pro-Latino attitude. (He was appointed a U.S. senator in 2009.) Under these circumstances, one plaintiff lawyer and the district lawyer thought the monitoring was no longer necessary. The plaintiff lawyer had long disagreed with us about whether the district was forcing students into mainstream classes inappropriately. We could find no evidence for that, but he thought we did not look in the right places. It seemed advisable to end the study because one side had gained the upper hand politically, and we had already been evaluating for three years longer than originally planned.

I had a mixed reaction to ending the study. I wanted to resolve the lawsuit in court, but that wasn't my assignment, and at the time the district had no motivation to take the case back to court. On a more positive note, however, the district and plaintiffs had reached a new level of understanding and cooperation. They could work things out without a third party. Time to quit.

Deliberative Democratic Research

The approach employed in Denver is called **deliberative democratic research** and evaluation. It has three guiding principles: (1) inclusion of all major stakeholder views, values, and interests; (2) dialogue among researchers and stakeholders so they understand one another; and (3) deliberation with and by all parties (House & Howe, 1999). This approach encourages the participation of major stakeholders in the study, with stakeholder views tested against other views and the available evidence. The legitimacy of the approach rests on fair, inclusive, and open procedures for deliberation, in which those taking part in discussion are not intimidated or manipulated.

The first principle is **inclusion** of all relevant major interests. It would not be right for researchers to provide research only to the most powerful stakeholders or the highest bidders. That would bias the research toward special interests. Nor would it be right in democracies to let sponsors revise findings and delete any conclusions they do not like in order to maximize their own interests. Inclusion of all major stakeholder interests is mandatory. Otherwise we would have stakeholder bias in the research, which usually means bias in favor of the most powerful. The inclusion principle does not mean researchers must take all stakeholder views at face value or believe everything stakeholders say. No doubt some views are better grounded than others. Research should contribute to public consideration on the basis of merit, not power.

The second democratic principle is **dialogue**. Researchers should not presume to know what others think without engaging them in dialogue. Too often researchers take the perspectives of sponsors as definitive or presume they know how things stand when they do not. One safeguard against such error is to engage in dialogue with all stakeholders. This admonition comes from minority and feminist spokespeople in particular, who have said repeatedly, "You only *think* you know what we think. You don't!" Again, researchers need not take all views at face value. But they should hear and understand all views in order to assess them.

A second task of dialogue is to discover "real" interests. Researchers should neither make assumptions about what the interests of the parties are nor take those interests as set in stone. Stakeholders may change their mind about where their interests lie after they examine other views. There is a serious concern that engaging in extensive dialogue will cause researchers to be biased toward some stakeholders, or perhaps to be too sympathetic to program developers or sponsors. Certainly that is a significant danger, but being ignorant of stakeholder views or misunderstanding their views are also dangers.

The third principle is **deliberation**. Deliberation is a cognitive process grounded in reasons, evidence, and valid arguments, including the methodological canons of research. The special expertise of researchers plays a critical role. Value claims (beliefs)—as with any difficult and contested issues—are subject to argument, discussion, and explanation. People's ideas are not assumed to be set in stone, fixed, or unquestionable. It is assumed that all parties will listen to other people's arguments politely, even if not everyone agrees. For example, in discussions involving school district personnel and the lawyers, we presented data we had collected and conducted discussions about what the data meant. All parties continued deliberating until we could reach agreement. If we could not agree, we might collect more data. Of course, we could never reach agreement on everything in these deliberations. The model here resembles deliberation in which the jury members are considering evidence that has been presented in court.

If inclusion and dialogue are achieved but deliberation is not, we might have authentic interests represented, but have the issues not well considered. If inclusion and deliberation are achieved but dialogue is inadequate, we might misrepresent participant interests and views, resulting in conclusions based on false interests. Finally, if dialogue and deliberation are achieved but not all stakeholders are included, the research may be biased toward special interests—stakeholder bias. The democratic aspiration is to arrive at unbiased conclusions by processing all relevant information from all parties.

No doubt such an approach extends the research role beyond the traditional one. The rationale is that because many views, values, and interests are considered, the conclusions will be more accurate, fair, and acceptable. The approach employs traditional data collection techniques, plus procedures for involving stakeholders. These procedures may be as familiar as convening focus groups or as unusual as involving stakeholders in helping construct conclusions. No particular techniques are required. What works in one place to facilitate involvement, dialogue, and deliberation might not work elsewhere.

The deliberative democratic approach is derived from past experiences with politicized studies, from research and evaluation theory, and from philosophy and political science (see, for example, Gutmann & Thompson, 1996). Compatible ideas have been advanced in England by MacDonald (MacDonald & Kushner, 2004; see also Kushner, 2000; Norris, 1990; Simons 1987) and by Karlsson and his colleagues in Sweden Hanberger, 2006; Karlsson, 1996; Karlsson Vestman & Segerholm, 2009). The Scandinavians have carried democratic concepts further than anyone else in their governing institutions. The ideas in this chapter reflect the American approach (House & Howe, 1999; Ryan & DeStefano, 2000).

REFLECTION QUESTIONS

1. At this stage, how would you define the terms *inclusion, dialogue,* and *deliberation*?
2. In what ways does the deliberative democratic approach differ from other forms of research?

Research Methods and Democratic Procedures

I distinguish between the traditional research methods employed in Denver and the procedures that made the approach more democratic, although there is overlap. The traditional research methods included the qualitative checklist completed by coresearchers and the quantitative indicators based on data from the management information system. The checklist was drawn from the court agreement that specified program details, including how students were selected, what language tests were administered to them, how students were exited to mainstream classes, and how teachers were trained and qualified. We paired this qualitative information with the information on indicators.

Certain procedures democratized the study by increasing inclusion, dialogue, and deliberation. For example, when I constructed the checklist I took the draft to key stakeholders and made changes based on their feedback. I did the same with the indicators. In this way I involved stakeholders in the research without compromising the accuracy of the findings. What I did not do was have the stakeholders themselves collect the data or analyze them. In my view, that would have risked bias. I controlled the data collection and analysis while involving stakeholders. I did have stakeholders discuss findings and draw their conclusions. No doubt there are other ways of including stakeholders without compromising the data, such as using the Internet or separating the evaluation into smaller tasks that stakeholders could handle on their own.

At the beginning of the study I identified the major stakeholders, which included the judge, district administrators and lawyers, program staff, principals, teachers, and staff in schools, plus the district governing board. Plaintiff stakeholders included the lawyers for the Congress of Hispanic Educators and the U.S. Justice Department. As a practical matter, I could not communicate with all stakeholders, which meant I had to choose groups to focus on. Given the legal imperatives, I focused on the administrators, lawyers, and program staff. To a considerable degree, the lawsuit defined the issues.

Which stakeholders to include is a matter of researcher judgment. There are no hard and fast rules, although major stakeholders will be evident in most studies. The question will be which to exclude as a practical matter. Procedures for encouraging dialogue consisted of one-on-one meetings, group meetings, document exchanges, school visits, and interviews with staff, faculty, parents, and students. Procedures encouraging deliberation included discussions of findings, face-to-face meetings, reports to the judge and media, and discussions with the governing board. The Internet presents intriguing possibilities that we did not pursue in this study. One might present data, collect data, and conduct discussions and deliberations online without meeting face-to-face. There is no reason to be limited to the procedures we employed.

For example, Karlsson (1996) evaluated a five-year program that provided care and leisure services for children ages nine through twelve in Eskilstuna, Sweden. The program aimed for more efficient organization of such services and new pedagogical content, which were to be achieved through new school-age care centers. Politicians wanted to know how the services could be organized, what the pedagogical content would be, what the centers would cost, and what the children and parents wanted the centers to be.

A first stage of the study was to identify stakeholder groups and choose representatives from them, including politicians, managers, professionals, parents, and children. Once having done that Karlsson surveyed parents and interviewed other stakeholders on these issues, asking each group the following questions:

Politicians—What is the aim of the program?

Parents—What do parents want the program to be?

Management—What is required to manage such a program?

Staff union—What do the staff unions require?

Cooperating professionals—What expectations are there from those who work in this field?

Children—What expectations do the children have?

This information was summarized and communicated to the stakeholder groups in the form of four different metaphors of ideal types of school-age care centers. The metaphors for the centers were the workshop, the classroom, the coffee bar, and the living room.

The second stage of the study focused on implementing the centers, twenty-five altogether, serving five hundred students. In this stage Karlsson employed a "bottom-up" approach—as opposed to the "top-down" approach of the first stage—by first asking children how they experienced the centers. Next, parents and cooperating professionals, then managers and politicians, were interviewed. Karlsson achieved dialogue by presenting to later groups what the prior groups had said and asking for their reaction. In the first two stages the format of the dialogue allowed a certain amount of distance and space among participants.

In the third stage the goal was face-to-face dialogue and establishing a more mutual and reciprocal relationship. The aim was to develop genuine and critical dialogue that could stimulate new thoughts among stakeholders and bring conflicts into open discussion. Karlsson arranged four meetings with representatives from the stakeholder groups. To ensure everyone could have a say, four professional actors played out short scenes illustrating critical questions and conflicts. The actors involved the audiences in dialogue through scenarios showing the problems (identified from the data) and enlisted the audience members to help the actors solve the problems. For example, the actors might demonstrate the difficulty students had in expressing their ideas to the professionals running the social program and enlist the audience's help in resolving that issue.

About 250 representatives participated in four performances, which were documented by video and each edited to twenty minutes. These videos were used later in meetings with other parents, politicians, and staff. The aim was to develop understanding of program limitations and possibilities, especially for disadvantaged groups, which would enable the powerless to have some influence. Karlsson's study was a particularly ambitious one that had access to considerable resources and took place over a three-year period. Longer timelines provide opportunities to do more unusual things.

REFLECTION QUESTIONS

1. How would you summarize the procedures used in Karlsson's study (1996)?
2. What about this study makes it a deliberative democratic approach?

Ten Caveats in Using a Democratic Approach

Any approach to conducting research has its limitations and difficulties. That is particularly true of new approaches like democratic studies. On the one hand, the approaches are exciting because they offer new possibilities for research. On the other hand, the studies may be more difficult to conduct because they are new. Here are several caveats—things to be aware of and look out for—for those attempting to democratize their research studies.

Cultural Acceptability

There is no sense trying to do such research in settings that are not democratic. It is difficult enough to democratize research without having the culture work against you. Democratic research requires the underpinning of democratic culture, and democratic culture varies even within and between democratic societies. One cannot take ideas from one society and employ them in another without adjustments. Sometimes transplanting ideas is not possible at all.

The deliberative democratic conception that Howe and I developed was strongly influenced by MacDonald's and Karlsson's ideas, but formulated for American circumstances (House & Howe, 1999). Politics and policies in the United States are driven increasingly by wealthy elites. Much of this elite influence is exercised through advertising, publicity, and control of government agendas without adequate consideration by the public. Policies and programs often favor special interests rather than the public interest. Some scholars have addressed this problem by stressing deliberative democratic processes as a way of testing ideas (Gutmann & Thompson, 1996).

When one steps outside democratic societies, cultures are too different for democratic approaches to be useful. For example, when Karlsson (Karlsson Vestman & Segerholm, 2009) tried to employ deliberative democratic procedures in Russia, he discovered that in Russian organizations information not coming from the top down lacks legitimacy. Research processes are culturally bound and must be adapted to the cultures in which they are practiced.

Cultural Diversity

Cultures are not internally uniform or unified. For example, the Latino community in Denver consisted of three separate groups: the recent immigrants, those of Chicano descent, and the descendants of the early inhabitants of the region. The descendants of the Santa Fe culture and Chicanos held professional positions and had ambitions to send their children to universities. Most recent immigrants were trying to survive economically. Many immigrants wanted their children to learn English quickly so the children could quit school and get jobs to help the family, an ambition antithetical to those of professional educators. Latinos shared some views and values (in regard to family, language, and religion), but also held some different values (in regard to education, career, and citizenship).

Faithful Representation

Of course, such differences raise questions about who is representing whose views. In Denver, Latino interests were advanced by lawyers, but many lawyers came from other social classes and different ethnic groups. The lawyers had interests and views different from those of the groups they represented. As a practical matter researchers cannot involve all stakeholders directly. Faithful representation of stakeholder interests is a tough problem to sort out in democratic research. Indeed, it is a tough problem in democracies generally. Whom do the politicians in Washington really represent?

Authentic Processes

There is a tendency for governments to pretend to want democratic involvement when they do not. Too often officials have determined what their policies or programs should be and merely want to legitimate them. They hold public hearings adorned with the rhetoric of public involvement, but the processes are for show and have little influence on what the government has already decided. Such ruses usually fool few, partly because these attempts are common, unfortunately.

Structured Interaction

Deliberative democratic research is directed at reaching sound conclusions. To accomplish this researchers need structure. Discussions cannot be so unstructured as to let anyone express opinions at any time or proceed in an undisciplined fashion. In trying to be fair, there is a temptation to abandon rules and structures, letting people vent their feelings and frustrations. Research is not therapy or counseling. Unhampered emoting and rambling discursions result in withdrawal by other participants who sense the process is going nowhere. For these reasons open public hearings are not usually productive.

Focusing on Issues
Keeping everyone focused on specific issues and on bringing evidence, discussion, and deliberation to bear is a productive way of keeping things moving. It is not necessary that everyone like each other or agree on all matters. In fact, that is unlikely. What is useful is for participants to agree to resolve specific issues. The process includes jointly determining what new evidence might shed light on contested issues. Focusing on issues, not on feelings, is a better way to go.

Rules and Principles
Researchers need rules and principles for dealing with culturally different people. The rules should not be rigid or inflexible; ideally, they can be adjusted to people and circumstances. One should not, however, abandon all rules because different cultures are involved. Guiding principles are necessary. After all, deliberative democratic research is democratic, not anarchic. Researchers are operating within a democratic framework, not without a framework.

For example, in Denver I decided early on that I would meet with any group that had a legitimate claim, including militant groups, such as those who did not want Spanish language instruction at all and also those who wanted bilingual schools. My listening to these groups was not popular with the plaintiffs or school officials. But I followed through with the principle of being informed about other views not represented in our discussions. Meeting with these groups also provided a chance to inform them about what we were doing, sometimes reducing suspicions.

Collaboration
The researcher's role in deliberative research is one of collaboration, not capitulation. In Denver I had certain methods for processing data. Even though I wanted to involve stakeholders, I could not cede some methods to the contending parties without ruining the honesty and accuracy of the research, in my view. At one point we reached a critical juncture when the plaintiffs wanted us researchers, my two colleagues and I, *not* to make summary judgments but to give the plaintiffs the data and let them decide. I could see why they wanted to do this; they themselves could decide whether schools were in compliance. But if I had ceded this point, the monitoring would have failed. The contending parties would be unlikely to agree on something in the future that they could not agree on now. I insisted we take the issue back to the judge and let him decide. I was ready to let the study go at that point. I thought the judge would

recognize the necessity of impartial court monitors' making these judgments, and I suspect the plaintiffs realized the judge would see it that way too. They desisted.

Balance of Power

Power imbalances are a big threat to democratic dialogues. They disrupt and distort discussion. The powerful may dominate discussions as others are intimidated, silenced, or disengaged. There should be a rough balance of power among participants for reasoned discussions to occur. If one party has overwhelming power, members of that party can enforce their will and often do so. In Denver the power balance changed during the project. The district increasingly became controlled by those more favorable to Latino interests. This shift resulted from changes in the governing board, district administration, and city politics, ultimately leading to termination of the study.

Constraints on Self-interest

Democratic processes work only if people do not act excessively in their own self-interest. Corruption can undermine democracies when people in power grab what they can for themselves and manipulate democratic processes. The public interest is then lost. Frankly, I do not know how to prevent such usurpation other than by promoting an esprit that we are all in this together for our mutual advantage. If others do not see it that way and act selfishly, their behavior distorts democratic processes. That is true in democratic governments and in democratic research.

Democratic research is an approach that has merit under certain conditions, particularly when strong differences among groups are operating. Involving stakeholders requires time and resources, and there is no reason to conduct democratic studies unless the circumstances are appropriate. If the differences among stakeholders are not strong, if the resources for conducting democratic studies are not available, or if some conditions mentioned as caveats pertain, it may not be advisable to attempt democratic studies. Democratic research is no panacea for all problems, but then neither is democracy.

Some Guidelines for Conducting Deliberative Democratic Research

The purpose of the following checklist is to guide research from a deliberative democratic perspective. Such research incorporates democratic processes within a study to secure better conclusions. The aspiration is to construct valid conclusions where there are conflicting views. The approach extends impartiality by including relevant interests, values, and views so that conclusions can be unbiased in value as well as in fact. Relevant value positions are included, but they are subject to criticism the way other findings are. Not all value claims are equally defensible. The researcher is still responsible for unbiased data collection, analysis, and sound conclusions. The three **guiding principles of democratic research** are inclusion, dialogue, and deliberation, which work in tandem with the professional canons of research validity.

Principle 1: Inclusion
The research study should consider the interests, values, and views of major stakeholders involved in the program or policy under review. This does not mean that every interest, value, or view need be given equal weight, only that all relevant ones should be considered in the design and conduct of the research. For example, we attended to many views in the Denver study that we did not weigh equally with those of the key stakeholders.

Principle 2: Dialogue
The study should encourage extensive dialogue with stakeholder groups and sometimes dialogue among stakeholders. The aspiration is to prevent misunderstanding of interests, values, and views. However, the researcher is under no obligation to accept views at face value. Nor does understanding entail agreement. The researcher is responsible for structuring the dialogue.

Principle 3: Deliberation
One might consider the model for deliberation to be jury deliberation, as when a jury weighs evidence presented in court in order to reach a verdict. Jury members discuss the evidence, give some evidence heavier weight, argue with each other, ask for more evidence and clarification by the judge, and so on. Deliberation is not a neat process or a straightforward one, but it is necessary to arrive at balanced, well-considered conclusions. Democratic studies should provide for extensive deliberation. Stakeholders participate in deliberation to discover their true interests. The researcher is responsible for structuring the deliberation and for the validity of the conclusions.

The three guiding principles might be implemented by addressing specific questions (see Exhibit 18.1). The questions overlap each other, as might dialogue and deliberation processes. For example, some procedures that encourage dialogue might also promote deliberation. Ultimately, there is no one way to democratize studies. It depends on the resourcefulness, ingenuity, and interest of the researcher.

EXHIBIT 18.1
CONSIDERATIONS FOR IMPLEMENTING GUIDING PRINCIPLES

1. **Inclusion**
   a. Whose interests are represented in the research?
      - Specify the interests involved in the program and research.
      - Identify relevant interests from the history of the program.
      - Consider important interests that emerge from the cultural context.
   b. Are all major stakeholders represented?
      - Identify those interests not represented.
      - Seek ways of representing missing views.
      - Look for hidden commitments, such as political or personal relationships that might bias the study.
   c. Should some stakeholders be excluded?
      - Review the reasons for excluding some stakeholders.
      - Consider if representatives represent their respective groups authentically.
      - Clarify the evaluator's role in structuring the research.

2. **Dialogue**
   a. Do power imbalances distort or impede dialogue and deliberation?
      - Examine the situation from the participants' points of view.
      - Consider whether participants will be forthcoming under the circumstances.
      - Consider whether some will exercise too much influence.
   b. Are there procedures to control power imbalances?
      - Do not take sides with factions.
      - Partition vociferous factions, if necessary.
      - Balance excessive self-interests.
   c. In what ways do stakeholders participate?
      - Secure commitments to rules and procedures in advance.
      - Structure the exchanges carefully around specific issues.
      - Structure forums suited to participant characteristics.
   d. How authentic is the participation?
      - Do not organize merely symbolic interactions.
      - Address the concerns put forth.
      - Secure the views of all stakeholders.

(Continued)

> **EXHIBIT 18.1**
>
> **CONSIDERATIONS FOR IMPLEMENTING GUIDING PRINCIPLES (Continued)**
>
>   e. How involved is the interaction?
> - Balance depth with breadth in participation.
> - Encourage receptivity to other views.
> - Insist on civil discourse.
>
> 3. **Deliberation**
>   a. Is there reflective deliberation?
>   - Organize resources for deliberation.
>   - Clarify the roles of participants.
>   - Have experts play critical roles where relevant.
>   b. How extensive is the deliberation?
>   - Review the main criteria.
>   - Account for all the information.
>   - Introduce important issues neglected by stakeholders.
>   c. How well considered is the deliberation?
>   - Fit all the data together coherently.
>   - Consider likely possibilities and reduce these to the best.
>   - Draw the best conclusions for this context.

> **REFLECTION QUESTION**
>
> 1. How might the ideas of inclusion, dialogue, and deliberation be applied when using another research approach outlined in this text?

Summary

Researchers often encounter situations in which there are strong conflicting values, interests, and perspectives among the major stakeholders in a study. Sometimes these conflicting views can disrupt the research. One way to handle such situations is to democratize the research. This is done by including key stakeholder views, encouraging extensive dialogue with and among stakeholders to reduce misunderstandings, and enhancing opportunities for deliberating about the findings. One model for such extended deliberation is deliberation by jury in a legal trial, whereby the evidence and its implications are assessed, debated, and examined in depth. Not all situations are suitable to democratic research. The approach must be culturally acceptable and sufficiently resourced. One hopes that studies that are more democratic will make the findings more accurate, more just, and more usable.

Key Terms

authentic processes, 465
balance of power, 467
collaboration, 466
constraints on self-interest, 467
cultural acceptability, 464
cultural diversity, 465

deliberation, 460
deliberative democratic research, 459
dialogue, 459
faithful representation, 465
focusing on issues, 466

guiding principles of democratic research, 468
inclusion, 459
rules and principles, 466
stakeholder, 452
structured interaction, 465

Further Readings and Resources

Suggested Deliberative Democratic Research Study

Karlsson, O. (1996). A critical dialogue in evaluation: How can interaction between evaluation and politics be tackled? *Evaluation, 2*, 405–416.
Karlsson applies the approach as outlined in this chapter.

Other Suggested Readings

Gutmann, A., & Thompson, D. (1996). *Why deliberative democracy?* Princeton, NJ: Princeton University Press.
Two political scientists present the case for deliberative democracy in general.

Hanberger, A. (2006). Evaluation of and for democracy. *Evaluation, 12*(1), 17–37.
This article presents a Swedish analysis of how democratic research fits into the larger framework of governmental decision making.

House, E. R. (2004). Deliberative democratic evaluation. In S. Mathison (Ed.), *Encyclopedia of evaluation* (pp. 104–108). Thousand Oaks, CA: Sage.
This is a brief account of the deliberative democratic approach.

House, E. R., & Howe, K. R. (1999). *Values in evaluation and social research.* Thousand Oaks, CA: Sage.
This book provides the most complete account of deliberative democratic research and evaluation and its philosophical rationale in the American setting.

Howe, K. R., & MacGillivary, H. (2009). Social research attuned to deliberative democracy. In D. H. Mertens & P. E. Ginsberg (Eds.), *The handbook of social research ethics* (pp. 565–579). Thousand Oaks, CA: Sage.
This chapter contains an analysis of how deliberative democratic research fits into contemporary political theory as well as a discussion of a few democratic research studies.

Karlsson, O. (1996). A critical dialogue in evaluation: How can interaction between evaluation and politics be tackled? *Evaluation, 2,* 405–416.
The Swedish approach to democratic evaluation is presented in this article by its leading proponent.

Karlsson Vestman, O., & Segerholm, C. (2009). Dialogue, deliberation, and democracy in educational evaluation: Theoretical arguments and a case narrative. In K. E. Ryan & J. B. Cousins (Eds.), *The Sage international handbook of educational evaluation* (pp. 465–482). Thousand Oaks, CA: Sage.
This chapter examines the challenges of implementing evaluation methods in a cultural and political context other than the one in which these were developed (in this case, implementing the idea and practice of a dialogic, democratic evaluation approach developed in Sweden for use in Russia).

Kushner, S. (2000). *Personalizing evaluation.* London: Sage.
Kushner's book offers an interpretation of the British approach to democratic research.

MacDonald, B., & Kushner, S. (2004). Democratic evaluation. In S. Mathison (Ed.), *Encyclopedia of evaluation* (pp. 109–113). Thousand Oaks, CA: Sage.
The British tradition of democratic evaluation is presented by its originator.

Norris, N. (1990). *Understanding educational evaluation.* London: Kogan Page.
Norris's is perhaps the most scholarly account of the British approach to democratic research.

Ryan, K. A., & DeStefano, L. (Eds.). (2000). *Evaluation as a democratic process: Promoting inclusion, dialogue, and deliberation* (New Directions for Evaluation, no. 85). San Francisco: Jossey-Bass.
Proponents, critics, and those who practice deliberative democratic evaluation discuss its features.

Simons, H. (1987). *Getting to know schools in a democracy.* London: Falmer.
This book offers a lucid exposition of the British tradition of democratic research as it is applied to schools.

REFERENCES

Abu-Lughod, L. (1993). *Writing women's worlds: Bedouin stories.* Berkeley: University of California Press.

Abu-Lughod, L. (2000). *Veiled sentiments: Honor and poetry in a Bedouin society.* Berkeley: University of California Press.

Adams, N., & Bettis, P. J. (2003). *Cheerleader! An American icon.* New York: Palgrave.

Adams, T. E. (2005). Speaking for others: Finding the "whos" of discourse. *Soundings, 88,* 331–345.

Adams, T. E. (2006). Seeking father: Relationally reframing a troubled love story. *Qualitative Inquiry, 12,* 704–723.

Adams, T. E. (2008). A review of narrative ethics. *Qualitative Inquiry, 14,* 175–194.

Adams, T. E. (2011). *Narrating the closet: An autoethnography of same-sex attraction.* Walnut Creek, CA: Left Coast Press.

Akbar, N. (1975, October). Address presented at the Black Child Development Institute Annual Meeting, San Francisco, CA.

Allen, C. J., & Garner, N. (1996). *Condor qatay: Anthropology in performance.* Long Grove, IL: Waveland.

Allport, G. W. (1937). *Personality: A psychological interpretation.* New York: Holt, Rinehart and Winston.

American Anthropological Association (AAA). (2004). *Statement on ethnography and institutional review boards.* www.aaanet.org/stmts/irb.htm.

American Evaluation Association (AEA). (2004). *Guiding principles for evaluators.* www.eval.org/Publications/aea06.GPBrochure.pdf.

American Indian Higher Education Consortium. (2009). *Indigenous evaluation framework: Telling our story in our place and time.* Unpublished manuscript, Alexandria, VA.

American Psychological Association. (2003). *Guidelines on multicultural education, training, research, practice, and organizational change for psychologists.* Washington DC: Author.

Analytic Technologies. (2010). *Anthropac Version 4.98.* Lexington, KY: Analytic Technologies. www.analytictech.com/anthropac/apacdesc.htm.

Anderson, G. (1989). Critical ethnography in education: Origins, current status, and new directions. *Review of Educational Research, 59,* 249–270.

Anderson, K., & Jack, D. C. (1991). Learning to listen: Interview techniques and analyses. In S. B. Gluck & D. Patai (Eds.), *Women's words: The feminist practice of oral history* (pp. 11–26). New York: Routledge.

Anfara, V. R., Brown, K. M., & Mangione, T. L. (2002). Qualitative analysis on stage: Making the research process more public. *Educational Researcher, 31*(7), 28–38.

Anyon, J. (1980). Social class and the hidden curriculum of work. *Journal of Education Policy, 161*, 67–72.

Asad, T. (1995). *Anthropology and the colonial encounter.* Amherst, NY: Prometheus Books.

Asante, M. F. (1998). *The Afrocentric idea.* Philadelphia: Temple University Press.

Atkin, J. M. (1991, April). *Teaching as research.* Paper presented at the American Educational Research Association Annual Convention, Chicago.

Atkinson, P. (1997). Narrative turn or blind alley? *Qualitative Health Research, 7*, 325–344.

Atkinson, P., & Delamont, S. (2006). Rescuing narrative from qualitative research. *Narrative Inquiry, 16*, 164–172.

Atkinson, R. (1998). *The life story interview.* Thousand Oaks, CA: Sage.

Atkinson, R. (2007). The life story interview as a bridge in narrative inquiry. In D. J. Clandinin (Ed.), *Handbook of narrative inquiry* (pp. 224–245). Thousand Oaks, CA: Sage.

Australasian Evaluation Society. (2006). *AES Ethics Committee.* www.aes.asn.au/about.

Bailey, L. (2007). Feminist critiques of educational research and practices. In B. J. Bank (Ed.), *Gender and education: An encyclopedia* (pp. 107–115). Westport, CT: Praeger.

Bakhtin, M. (1981). *The dialogic imagination: Four essays* (C. Emerson & M. Holquist, Trans.). Austin, TX: University of Texas Press.

Bamberg, M. (2004). Narrative discourse and identities. In J. C. Meister, T. Kindt, W. Schernus, & M. Stein (Eds.), *Narratology beyond literary criticism* (pp. 213–237). New York: Walter de Gruyter.

Barone, T. (1983). Things of use and things of beauty: The story of the Swain County High School arts program. *Daedalus, 112*(3), 1–28.

Barone, T. (1992). Beyond theory and method: A case of critical storytelling. *Theory into Practice, 31*, 142–146.

Barone, T. (1995). Persuasive writings, vigilant readings, reconstructed characters: The paradox of trust in educational storysharing. *International Journal of Qualitative Studies in Education, 8*, 63–74.

Barone, T. (2001). *Touching eternity: The enduring outcomes of teaching.* New York: Teachers College Press.

Barone, T., & Eisner, E. (2006). Arts-based educational research. In J. Green, G. Camilli, & P. Elmore (Eds.), *Handbook of complementary methods in education research* (pp. 93–107). New York: Lawrence Erlbaum.

Barone, T., & Eisner, E. (2011). *Arts based research.* Thousand Oaks, CA: Sage.

Barresi, J., & Jukes, T. J. (1997). Personology and the narrative interpretation of lives. *Journal of Personality, 65*, 693–719.

Barthes, R. (1977). *Image, music, text* (S. Heath, Trans.). New York: Hill and Wang. (Original work published 1968)

Barton, D., & Hamilton, M. (2000). Literacy practices. In D. Barton, M. Hamilton, & R. Ivanic (Eds.), *Situated literacies: Reading and writing in context* (pp. 7–15). New York: Routledge.

Battiste, M. (Ed.). (2000). *Reclaiming indigenous voice and vision*. Vancouver: University of British Columbia Press.

Battiste, M. (2002). *Indigenous knowledge and pedagogy in First Nations education: A literature review with recommendations*. Paper prepared for the National Group on Education and the Minister of Indian Affairs Canada (INAC). Ottawa, Ontario: Indian and Northern Affairs.

Battiste, M., & Henderson, J. Y. (2002). *Protecting indigenous knowledge and heritage: A global challenge*. Saskatoon, Saskatchewan: Purich.

Beattie, C. (1989). Action research: A practice in need of a theory. In G. Milburn, I. F. Goodson, & R. J. Clark (Eds.), *Re-interpreting curriculum research: Images and arguments* (pp. 110–120). London: Falmer.

Becker, H. S., Geer, B., Hughes, E. C., & Strauss, A. L. (1961). *Boys in white: Student culture in medical school*. New Brunswick, NJ: Transaction.

Behar, R. (1993). *Translated woman*. Boston: Beacon.

Bell, D. (1992). *Faces at the bottom of the well: The permanence of racism*. New York: Basic Books.

Benard, H. R. (1988). *Research methods in cultural anthropology*. Thousand Oaks, CA: Sage.

Benstock, S. (1991). *Textualizing the feminine: On the limits of genre*. Norman: University of Oklahoma Press.

Berg, M. J., Kremelberg, D., Dwivedi, P., Verma, S., Schensul, J. J., Gupta, K., et al. (2010). The effects of husband's alcohol consumption on married women in three low-income areas of greater Mumbai. *Aids and Behavior, 14*, 126–135.

Berg, M. J., & Schensul, J. J. (Eds.). (2004). Participatory action research with youth (Special issue). *Practicing Anthropology, 26*(2).

Berliner, D. C. (2009). Research, policy, and practice: The great disconnect. In S. D. Lapan & M. T. Quartaroli (Eds.), *Research essentials: An introduction to designs and practices* (pp. 295–313). San Francisco: Jossey-Bass.

Bernard, H. R. (2000). *Social research methods: Qualitative and quantitative approaches*. Thousand Oaks, CA: Sage.

Bernard, H. R. (2005). *Research methods in anthropology: Qualitative and quantitative approaches* (4th ed.). Walnut Creek, CA: AltaMira.

Berry, K. (2005). To the "speechies" themselves: An ethnographic and phenomenological account of emergent identity formation. *International Journal of Communication, 15*, 21–50.

Bhabha, H. (1993). *Location of culture*. New York: Routledge.

Bhavnani, K., & Davis, A. (2000). Women in prison: Researching race in three national contexts. In F. W. Twine & J. W. Warren (Eds.), *Racing research, researching race: Methodological dilemmas in critical race studies* (pp. 227–246). New York: New York University Press.

Bird, R. B. (2007). Fishing and the sexual division of labor among the Meriam. *American Anthropologist, 109,* 442–451.

Birren, J. E., & Deutchman, D. E. (1991). *Guiding autobiography groups for older adults: Exploring the fabric of life.* Baltimore: Johns Hopkins University Press.

Bishop, R. (1996). Addressing issues in self-determination and legitimation in Kaupapa Maori research. In B. Webber (Ed.), *He paipai korero* (pp. 143–160). Wellington: New Zealand Council for Educational Research.

Bishop, R. (2005). Freeing ourselves from neocolonial domination in research. In N. K. Denzin & Y. S. Lincoln (Eds.), *The Sage handbook of qualitative research* (3rd ed., pp. 109–138). Thousand Oaks, CA: Sage.

Blagov, P. S., & Singer, J. A. (2004). Four dimensions of self-defining memories (specificity, meaning, content, and affect) and their relationship to self-restraint, distress, and repressive defensiveness. *Journal of Personality, 72,* 481–511.

Blaut, J. M. (1993). *The colonizer's model of the world: Geographical diffusionism and Eurocentric history.* New York: Guilford Press.

Bledsoe, K. L. (2005). Using theory-driven evaluation with underserved communities: Promoting program development and program sustainability. In S. Hood, R. Hopson, & H. Frierson (Eds.), *The role of culture and cultural context: A mandate for inclusion, the discovery of truth, and understanding in evaluative theory and practice* (pp. 179–199). Greenwich, CT: Information Age.

Blumenfeld-Jones, D. (2006, April). *The shattered mirror: Curriculum, art and critical politics.* Vice-presidential address presented at the annual meeting of the American Educational Research Association Division B (Curriculum Studies), San Francisco.

Blumer, H. (1969). *Symbolic interactionism: Perspective and method.* Berkeley: University of California Press.

Bochner, A. P. (1984). The functions of human communication in interpersonal bonding. In C. C. Arnold & J. W. Bowers (Eds.), *Handbook of rhetorical and communication theory* (pp. 544–621). Boston: Allyn & Bacon.

Bochner, A. P. (1994). Perspectives on inquiry II: Theories and stories. In M. L. Knapp & G. R. Miller (Eds.), *Handbook of interpersonal communication* (pp. 21–41). Thousand Oaks, CA: Sage.

Bochner, A. P. (2000). Criteria against ourselves. *Qualitative Inquiry, 6,* 266–272.

Bochner, A. P. (2001). Narrative's virtues. *Qualitative Inquiry, 7,* 131–157.

Bochner, A. P. (2002). Perspectives on inquiry III: The moral of stories. In M. L. Knapp & J. A. Daly (Eds.), *Handbook of interpersonal communication* (3rd ed., pp. 73–101). Thousand Oaks, CA: Sage.

Bochner, A. P., & Ellis, C. (1995). Telling and living: Narrative co-construction and the practices of interpersonal relationships. In W. Leeds-Hurwitz (Ed.), *Social approaches to communication* (pp. 201–213). New York: Guilford Press.

Bochner, A. P., & Ellis, C. (2006). Communication as autoethnography. In G. J. Shepherd, J. St. John, & T. Striphas (Eds.), *Communication as . . .: Perspectives on theory* (pp. 110–122). Thousand Oaks, CA: Sage.

Borchard, K. (1998). Between a hard rock and postmodernism: Opening the Hard Rock Hotel and Casino. *Journal of Contemporary Ethnography, 27*, 242–269.

Borland, K. (1991). "That's not what I said": Interpretive conflict in oral narrative research. In S. B. Gluck & D. Patai (Eds.), *Women's words: The feminist practice of oral history* (pp. 63–75). New York: Routledge.

Bourdieu, P. (1990). *In other words: Essays towards a reflexive sociology* (M. Adamson, Trans.). Stanford, CA: Stanford University Press.

Bourgois, P. (1995). *In search of respect: Selling crack in El Barrio*. New York: Cambridge University Press.

Bowles, S., & Gintis, H. (1976). *Schooling in capitalist America*. New York: Basic Books.

Boykin, A. W. (1986). The triple quandary and the schooling of Afro-American children. In U. Neisser (Ed.), *The school achievement of minority children* (pp. 51–92). Mahwah, NJ: Lawrence Erlbaum.

Boylorn, R. M. (2006). E pluribus unum (Out of many, one). *Qualitative Inquiry, 12*, 651–680.

Boylorn, R. M. (2008). As seen on TV: An autoethnographic reflection on race and reality television. *Critical Studies in Media Communication, 25*, 413–433.

Brabeck, M. M., & Brabeck, K. M. (2009). Feminist perspectives on research ethics. In D. M. Mertens & P. E. Ginsberg (Eds.), *The handbook of social research ethics* (pp. 39–53). Thousand Oaks, CA: Sage.

Brayboy, B. K., & Deyhle, D. (2000). Insider outsider: Research in American Indian communities. *Theory into Practice, 39*, 163–169.

Britzman, D. (2000). "The question of belief": Writing poststructural ethnography. In E. A. St. Pierre & W. S. Pillow (Eds.), *Working the ruins: Feminist poststructural theory and methods in education* (pp. 27–40). New York: Routledge.

Brouwer, D. C. (2004). Corps/corpse: The U.S. military and homosexuality. *Western Journal of Communication, 68*, 411–430.

Brown-Smith, N. (1998). Family secrets. *Journal of Family Issues, 19*, 20–42.

Brown v. *Board of Education*, 347 U.S. 483 (1954).

Brugge, D., & Missaghian, M. (2003). *Protecting the Navajo people through tribal regulation of research*. Research Ethics and Environmental Health. www.researchethics.org/articles.asp?viewrec=27.

Bruner, J. S. (1986). *Actual minds, possible worlds*. Cambridge, MA: Harvard University Press.

Bruner, J. S. (1990). *Acts of meaning*. Cambridge, MA: Harvard University Press.

Brunswik, E. (1956). *Perception and the representative design of psychological experiments*. Berkeley: University of California Press.

Bryant, A. (2002). Re-grounding grounded theory. *Journal of Information Technology Theory and Application, 4*, 25–42.

Bryant, A., & Charmaz, K. (Eds.). (2007). *The Sage handbook of grounded theory*. Thousand Oaks, CA: Sage.

REFERENCES

Burford, T. I. (2005). *Race narratives, personality traits, and race self complexity: Towards an understanding of the psychological meaning of race*. Unpublished manuscript, Howard University, Washington DC.

Burford, T. I., & Winston, C. E. (2005). *The Guided Race Autobiography*. Washington DC: Howard University Identity and Success Research Laboratory.

Burton, R. (2007). *The anatomy of melancholy* (Vol. 1). Teddington: Echo Library. (Original work published 1638)

Cahnmann, M. (2006). Reading, living, and writing bilingual poetry as scholARTistry in the language arts classroom. *Language Arts, 83*, 342–352.

Campbell, D. T., & Stanley, J. C. (1963). *Experimental and quasi-experimental designs for research*. Chicago: Rand McNally College.

Campbell, N. (2000). *Using women: Gender, drug policy, and social justice*. New York: Routledge.

Carlyle, T. (1841). *Heroes, hero worship and the heroics in history*. Toronto: Archibald MacMechan.

Carspecken, P. (1996). *Critical ethnography in educational research: A theoretical and practical guide*. New York: Routledge.

Carspecken, P., & Apple, M. (1992). Critical qualitative research: Theory, methodology, and practice. In M. LeCompte, W. Millroy, & J. Preissle (Eds.), *The handbook of qualitative research in education* (pp. 507–553). San Diego, CA: Academic Press.

Carspecken, P., & Walford, G. (Eds.). (2001). *Critical ethnography and education*. New York: Routledge.

Cashmore, E. (2003). *Encyclopedia of race and ethnic studies*. New York: Routledge.

Castagno, A. (2006). *Uncertain but always unthreatening: Multicultural education in two urban middle schools*. Unpublished dissertation, University of Wisconsin, Madison.

Castagno, A. (2008). "I don't want to hear that!": Legitimating whiteness through silence in schools. *Anthropology & Education Quarterly, 39*, 314–333.

Castagno, A. (2009). Commonsense understandings of equality and social change: A critical race theory analysis of liberalism at Spruce Middle School. *International Journal of Qualitative Studies in Education, 22*, 755–768.

Caulley, D. N. (2008). Making qualitative research reports less boring: The techniques of writing creative nonfiction. *Qualitative Inquiry, 14*, 424–449.

Chappell, S. (2009). *Evidence of utopianizing toward social justice in young people's community-based art works*. Unpublished dissertation, Arizona State University, Tempe.

Charmaz, K. (1991). *Good days, bad days: The self in chronic illness and time*. New Brunswick, NJ: Rutgers University Press.

Charmaz, K. (1999). Stories of suffering: Subjects' tales and research narratives. *Qualitative Health Research, 9*, 369–382.

Charmaz, K. (2000). Grounded theory: Objectivist and constructivist methods. In N. K. Denzin & Y. S. Lincoln (Eds.), *Handbook of qualitative research* (2nd ed., pp. 509–535). Thousand Oaks, CA: Sage.

Charmaz, K. (2003). Grounded theory. In J. A. Smith (Ed.), *Qualitative psychology: A practical guide to research methods* (pp. 81–110). London: Sage.

Charmaz, K. (2006). *Constructing grounded theory: A practical guide through qualitative analysis.* London: Sage.

Charmaz, K. (2008). Grounded theory as an emergent method. In S. N. Hesse-Biber & P. Leavy (Eds.), *Handbook of emergent methods* (pp. 155–170). New York: Guilford Press.

Charmaz, K. (2009). Shifting the grounds: Constructivist grounded theory methods for the twenty-first century. In J. Morse, P. Stern, J. Corbin, B. Bowers, K. Charmaz, & A. Clarke (Eds.), *Developing grounded theory: The second generation* (pp. 127–154). Walnut Creek, CA: Left Coast.

Charmaz, K., & Bryant, A. (2010). Grounded theory. In B. McGaw, P. Peterson, & E. Baker (Eds.), *The international encyclopedia of education* (3rd ed., pp. 401–406). Oxford, England: Elsevier.

Chen, H.-T. (1990). *Theory-driven evaluations.* Thousand Oaks, CA: Sage.

Chilisa, B. (2005). Educational research within postcolonial Africa: A critique of HIV/AIDS research in *Botswana. International Journal of Qualitative Studies in Education, 18,* 659–684.

Christians, C. (2005). Ethics and politics in qualitative research. In N. K. Denzin & Y. S. Lincoln (Eds.), *The Sage handbook of qualitative research* (3rd ed., pp. 139–164). Thousand Oaks, CA: Sage.

Clandinin, D. J., & Connelly, F. M. (1995). *Teachers' professional knowledge landscapes.* New York: Teachers College Press.

Clandinin, D. J., & Connelly, F. M. (2000). *Narrative inquiry: Experience and story in qualitative research.* San Francisco: Jossey-Bass.

Clandinin, D. J., & Rosiek, J. (2007). Mapping a landscape of narrative inquiry: Borderland spaces and tensions. In D. J. Clandinin (Ed.), *Handbook of narrative inquiry: Mapping a methodology* (pp. 35–76). Thousand Oaks, CA: Sage.

Clark, E. H. (1873). *Sex in education, or, a fair chance for the girls.* Boston: James R. Osgood.

Clarke, A. E. (2005). *Situational analysis: Grounded theory after the postmodern turn.* Thousand Oaks, CA: Sage.

Clifford, J. (1983). On ethnographic authority. *Representations, 1*(2), 118–146.

Clifford, J. (1986). Introduction: Partial truths. In J. Clifford & G. E. Marcus (Eds.), *Writing culture* (pp. 1–26). Berkeley: University of California Press.

Clifford, J. (1988). *The predicament of culture: Twentieth-century ethnography, literature, and art.* Cambridge, MA: Harvard University Press

Clifford, J. (1997). *Routes: Travel and translation in the late 20th century.* Cambridge, MA: Harvard University Press.

Clifford, J., & Marcus, G. (1986). *Writing culture: The poetics and politics of ethnography.* Berkeley: University of California Press.

Cobb, M. (2006). *God hates fags: The rhetorics of religious violence.* New York: New York University Press.

Coles, R. (1989). *The call of stories: Teaching and the moral imagination.* Boston: Houghton Mifflin.

Collins, P. H. (1990). *Black feminist thought.* Boston: Unwin Hyman.

Connelly, F. M., & Clandinin, D. J. (1990). Stories of experience and narrative inquiry. *Educational Researcher, 19*(5), 2–14.

Conway, M. A., & Pleydell-Pearce, C. W. (2000). The construction of autobiographical memories in the self-memory system. *Psychological Review, 107,* 261–288.

Cook-Lynn, E. (2000). How scholarship defames the Native voice . . . and why. *Wicazo Sa Review, 15*(2), 79–92.

Corbin, J., & Strauss, A. (2008). *Basics of qualitative research: Techniques and procedures for developing grounded theory* (3rd ed.). Thousand Oaks, CA: Sage.

Coulter, C. (2003). *Growing up immigrant in an American high school. Unpublished dissertation,* Arizona State University, Tempe.

Council of National Psychological Associations for the Advancement of Ethnic Minority Interests. (2000). *Guidelines for research in ethnic minority communities.* Washington, DC: American Psychological Association.

Couser, G. T. (1997). *Recovering bodies: Illness, disability, and life writing.* Madison: University of Wisconsin Press.

Cram, F. (2009). Maintaining indigenous voices. In D. M. Mertens & P. E. Ginsberg (Eds.), *The handbook of social research ethics* (pp. 308–322). Thousand Oaks, CA: Sage.

Cram, F., Ormond, A., & Carter, L. (2004, October 28–30). Researching our relations: Reflections on ethics and marginalization. Paper presented at the Kamehameha Schools 2004 Research Conference on Hawaiian well-being. Kea'au, Hawaii. www.ksbe.edu/pase/pdf/KSResearchConference/2004presentations/.

Crapanzano, V. (1985). *Tuhami: Portrait of a Moroccan.* Chicago: University of Chicago Press.

Crawley, S. L. (2002). "They still don't understand why I hate wearing dresses!" An autoethnographic rant on dresses, boats, and butchness. *Cultural Studies <=> Critical Methodologies, 2,* 69–92.

Crenshaw, K. W. (1991). Mapping the margins: Intersectionality, identity politics, and violence against women of color. *Stanford Law Review, 43,* 1241–1299.

Crenshaw, K., Gotanda, N., Peller, G., & Thomas, K. (Eds.). (1995). *Critical race theory: The key writings that formed the movement.* New York: New Press.

Cressey, D. R. (1953). *Other people's money: A study in the social psychology of embezzlement.* Glencoe, IL: Free Press.

Creswell, J. W. (2005). *Planning, conducting and evaluating quantitative and qualitative research* (2nd ed.). Upper Saddle River, NJ: Pearson Education.

Creswell, J. W. (2007). *Qualitative inquiry and research design: Choosing among five approaches* (2nd ed.). Thousand Oaks, CA: Sage.

Creswell, J. W. (2009). *Research design: Qualitative, quantitative, and mixed methods approaches* (3rd ed.). Thousand Oaks, CA: Sage.

Cross, W. E. J. (1991). *Shades of black: Diversity in African-American identity.* Philadelphia: Temple University Press.

Daly, K., & Dienhart, A. (1998). Navigating the family domain: Qualitative field dilemmas. In S. Grills (Ed.), *Doing ethnographic research: Fieldwork settings* (pp. 97–120). Thousand Oaks, CA: Sage.

Darts, D. (2004). *Visual culture jam: Art, pedagogy and creative resistance.* Unpublished dissertation, University of British Columbia, Vancouver.

Delamont, S. (2009). The only honest thing: Autoethnography, reflexivity and small crises in fieldwork. *Ethnography and Education, 4,* 51–63.

Delgado, R., & Stefancic, J. (2001). *Critical race theory: An introduction.* New York: New York University Press.

Deloria, V., Jr. (1969). *Custer died for your sins: An Indian manifesto.* New York: Avon.

Delpit, L., & Dowdy, J. (2002). *The skin that we speak: Thoughts on language and culture in the classroom.* New York: New Press.

Denzin, N. K. (1989a). *Interpretive biography.* Thousand Oaks, CA: Sage.

Denzin, N. K. (1989b). *The research act: A theoretical introduction to sociological methods* (3rd ed.). Englewood Cliffs, NJ: Prentice Hall.

Denzin, N. K. (2000). The art of interpretation, evaluation, and presentation. In N. K. Denzin & Y. S. Lincoln (Eds.), *Handbook of qualitative research* (2nd ed., pp. 479–485). Thousand Oaks, CA: Sage.

Denzin, N. K., & Lincoln, Y. S. (1998). Introduction. In N. K. Denzin & Y. S. Lincoln (Eds.), *The landscape of qualitative research: Theories and issues* (Vol. 1, pp. 1–44). Thousand Oaks, CA: Sage.

Denzin, N. K., & Lincoln, Y. S. (Eds.). (2005). *The Sage handbook of qualitative research* (3rd ed.). Thousand Oaks, CA: Sage.

Denzin, N. K., & Lincoln, Y. S. (2008). Introduction: Critical methodologies and indigenous inquiry. In N. K. Denzin, Y. S. Lincoln, & L. T. Smith (Eds.), *Handbook of critical and indigenous methodologies* (pp. 2–20). Thousand Oaks, CA: Sage.

Denzin, N. K., Lincoln, Y. S., & Smith, L. T. (Eds.). (2008). *Handbook of critical and indigenous methodologies.* Thousand Oaks, CA: Sage.

Derrida, J. (1980). *Writing and difference* (A. Bass, Trans.). Chicago: University of Chicago Press. (Original work published 1967)

de Saussure, F. (1983). *Course in general linguistics* (R. Harris, Trans.). London: Duckworth. (Original work published 1916)

Dewey, J. (1960). *Quest for certainty.* New York: Putnam.

Dey, I. (1993). *Qualitative data analysis.* London: Routledge.

Diamond, N. (1970). Fieldwork in a complex society: Taiwan. In G. D. Spindler (Ed.), *Being an anthropologist* (pp. 113–141). New York: Holt, Rinehart and Winston.

Dibble, N. & Rosiek, J. (2002). White out: A case study introducing a new citational format for teacher practical knowledge research. *International Journal of Education & the Arts, 3*(5). www.ijea.org/v3n5/index.html.

Dickson-Gomez, J., Convey, M., Hilario, H., Corbett, M., & Weeks, M. (2007). Unofficial policy: Access to housing, housing information and social services among homeless drug users in Hartford, Connecticut. *Substance Abuse Treatment, Prevention, and Policy, 2*(8), 1–14.

Diefenbach, G. J., Disch, W. B., Robison, J. T., Baez, E., & Coman, E. (2009). Anxious depression among Puerto Rican and African-American older adults. *Aging & Mental Health, 13,* 118–126.

REFERENCES

Dilthey, W. (1989). *Introduction to the human sciences: An attempt to lay a foundation for the study of society and history*. Princeton, NJ: Princeton University Press.

Disch, W. B., Schensul, J. J., Radda, K. E., & Robison, J. T. (2007). Perceived environmental stress, depression, and quality of life in older, low income, minority urban adults. In H. Mollenkopf & A. Walker (Eds.), *Quality of life in old age* (pp. 151–165). The Netherlands: Springer.

Dixson, A., & Rousseau, C. (Eds.). (2006). *Critical race theory and education: All God's children got a song*. New York: Routledge.

Dodd, S. J. (2009). LGBTQ: Protecting vulnerable subjects in all studies. In D. M. Mertens & P. E. Ginsberg (Eds.), *The handbook of social research ethics* (pp. 474–488). Thousand Oaks, CA: Sage.

Downs, A. (2005). *The velvet rage: Overcoming the pain of growing up gay in a straight man's world*. Cambridge, MA: Perseus.

Du Bois, W. E. B. (2005). *The souls of black folk*. New York: Penguin. (Original work published 1903)

Dukes, W. F. (1965). N = 1. *Psychological Bulletin*, *64*, 74–79.

Dunlop, R. (1999). *Boundary Bay: A novel*. Unpublished dissertation, University of British Columbia, Vancouver.

Duque, R. L. (2009). Review: Catherine Kohler Riessman (2008). Narrative methods for the human sciences. *Forum Qualitative Sozialforschung/Forum: Qualitative Social Research*, *11*(1), Art. 19. www.qualitative-research.net/index.php/fqs/article/view/1418/2906.

Duran, B., & Duran, E. (2000). Applied postcolonial clinical and research strategies. In M. Battiste (Ed.), *Reclaiming indigenous voice and vision* (pp. 209–224). Vancouver: University of British Columbia Press.

Dykins Callahan, S. B. (2008). Academic outings. *Symbolic Interaction*, *31*, 351–375.

Ecker, D. (1966). The artistic process as qualitative problem solving. In E. Eisner & D. Ecker (Eds.), *Readings in art education* (pp. 57–68). Waltham, MA: Blaisdell.

Eisner, E. (1991). *The enlightened eye: Qualitative inquiry and the enhancement of educational practice*. New York: Macmillan.

Eisner, E. (2002). *The arts and the creation of mind*. New Haven, CT: Yale University Press.

Elliott, J. (1988, April). *Teachers as researchers: Implications for supervision and teacher education*. Paper presented at the American Educational Research Association Annual Convention, New Orleans, LA.

Ellis, C. (1986). *Fisher folk: Two communities on Chesapeake Bay*. Lexington: University Press of Kentucky.

Ellis, C. (1991). Sociological introspection and emotional experience. *Symbolic Interaction*, *14*, 23–50.

Ellis, C. (1993). "There are survivors": Telling a story of a sudden death. *Sociological Quarterly*, *34*, 711–730.

Ellis, C. (1995a). Emotional and ethical quagmires in returning to the field. *Journal of Contemporary Ethnography*, *24*, 68–98.

Ellis, C. (1995b). *Final negotiations: A story of love, loss, and chronic illness*. Philadelphia: Temple University Press.

Ellis, C. (1995c). The other side of the fence: Seeing black and white in a small, southern town. *Qualitative Inquiry, 1*, 147–167.

Ellis, C. (2002). Shattered lives: Making sense of September 11th and its aftermath. *Journal of Contemporary Ethnography, 31*, 375–410.

Ellis, C. (2004). *The ethnographic I: A methodological novel about autoethnography*. Walnut Creek, CA: AltaMira.

Ellis, C. (2007). Telling secrets, revealing lives: Relational ethics in research with intimate others. *Qualitative Inquiry, 13*, 3–29.

Ellis, C. (2009a). *Revision: Autoethnographic reflections on life and work*. Walnut Creek, CA: Left Coast.

Ellis, C. (2009b). Telling tales on neighbors: Ethics in two voices. *International Review of Qualitative Research, 2*, 3–28.

Ellis, C., & Bochner, A. P. (2000). Autoethnography, personal narrative, reflexivity: Researcher as subject. In N. K. Denzin & Y. S. Lincoln (Eds.), *Handbook of qualitative research* (2nd ed., pp. 733–768). Thousand Oaks, CA: Sage.

Ellis, C., & Ellingson, L. (2000). Qualitative methods. In E. Borgatta & R. Montgomery (Eds.), *Encyclopedia of sociology* (pp. 2287–2296). New York: Macmillan.

Ellis, C., Kiesinger, C. E., & Tillmann-Healy, L. M. (1997). Interactive interviewing: Talking about emotional experience. In R. Hertz (Ed.), *Reflexivity and voice* (pp. 119–149). Thousand Oaks, CA: Sage.

Ellison, C. M. (2004). Talent Development professional development evaluation model: A paradigm shift. *New Directions for Evaluation, 101*, 63–78.

Elms, A., & Heller, B. (2007). Twelve ways to say "lonesome": Assessing error and control in the music of Elvis Presley. *Handbook of psychobiography* (pp. 142–157). New York: Oxford University Press.

Elze, D. (2003). Gay, lesbian, and bisexual youths: Perceptions of their high school environments and comfort in schools. *Children & Schools, 25*, 225–239.

Emerson, R., Fretz, R., & Shaw, L. (1995). *Writing ethnographic fieldnotes*. Chicago: University of Chicago Press.

Erikson, E. H. (1958). *Young man Luther: A study in psychoanalysis and history*. New York: Norton.

Erikson, E. H. (1968). *Identity, youth, and crisis*. New York: Norton.

Erikson, E. H. (1969). *Gandhi's truth: On the origins of militant nonviolence*. New York: Norton.

Evans, M., Hole, R., Berg, L. D., Hutchinson, P., & Sookraj, D. (2009). Common insights, differing methodologies: Toward a fusion of indigenous methodologies, participatory action research, and white studies in an urban Aboriginal research agenda. *Qualitative Inquiry, 15*, 893–910.

Evans-Pritchard, E. E. (1940). *The Nuer: A description of the modes of livelihood and political institutions of a Nilotic people*. Oxford, England: Clarendon Press.

Fetterman, D. M. (1989). *Ethnography: Step by step*. Thousand Oaks, CA: Sage.

Fine, G. A. (1993). Ten lies of ethnography. *Journal of Contemporary Ethnography, 22,* 267–294.

Fine, G. A. (2003). Towards a people ethnography: Developing a theory from group life. *Ethnography, 4*(1), 41–60.

Fine, M. (1988). Sexuality, schooling, and adolescent females: The m*issing discourse of desire. Harvard Educational Review, 58,* 29–53.

Fine, M. (1991). *Framing dropouts: Notes on the politics of an urban high school.* Albany: State University of New York Press.

Fine, M. (1994a). Dis-stance and other stances: Negotiations of power inside feminist research. In A. Gitlin (Ed.), *Power and methods* (pp. 13–55). New York: Routledge.

Fine, M. (1994b). Working the hyphens: Reinventing self and other in qualitative research. In N. K. Denzin & Y. S. Lincoln (Eds.), *The Sage handbook of qualitative research* (pp. 70–82). Thousand Oaks, CA: Sage.

Fine, M., & Macpherson, P. (1992). Over dinner: Feminism and adolescent bodies. In M. Fine (Ed.), *Disruptive voices: The possibilities of feminist research* (pp. 175–202). Ann Arbor: University of Michigan Press.

Fine, M., Torre, M. E., Boudin, K., Bowen, I., Clark, J., Hylton, D., et al. (2003). Participatory action research: From within and behind prison bars. In P. M. Camic, J. E. Rhodes, & L. Yardley (Eds.), *Qualitative research in psychology: Expanding perspectives in methodology and design* (pp. 173–198). Washington, DC: American Psychological Association.

Fine, M., & Weis, L. (1998). *The unknown city: The lives of poor and working-class young adults.* Boston: Beacon.

Firth, R. (1936). *We the Tikopia: A sociological study of kinship in primitive Polynesia.* London: Allen and Unwin.

Fischer, M. M., & Abedi, M. (2002). *Debating Muslims: Cultural dialogues in postmodernity and tradition.* Madison: University of Wisconsin Press.

Fitzpatrick, J. L., Sanders, J. R., & Worthen, B. R. (2003). *Program evaluation: Alternative approaches and practical guidelines* (3rd ed.). New York: Longman.

Flanders, N. (1973). Basic teaching skills derived from a model of speaking and listening. *Journal of Teacher Education, 24,* 24–37.

Foley, D. (1990). *Learning capitalist culture: Deep in the heart of Tejas.* Philadelphia: University of Pennsylvania Press.

Foley, D. (1995). *The heartland chronicles.* Philadelphia: University of Pennsylvania Press.

Foley, D., & Valenzuela, A. (2005). Critical ethnography: The politics of collaboration. In N. Denzin & Y. L. Lincoln (Eds.), *The Sage handbook of qualitative research* (3rd ed., pp. 217–242). Thousand Oaks, CA: Sage.

Fonow, M. (2003). *Union women: Forging feminism in the United Steelworkers of America.* Minneapolis: University of Minnesota Press.

Fonow, M., & Cook, J. (Eds.). (1991). *Beyond methodology: Feminist scholarship as lived research.* Bloomington: Indiana University Press.

Fonow, M., & Cook, J. (2005). Feminist methodology: New applications in the academy and public policy. *Signs, 30,* 2211–2236.

Foster, E. (2008). Commitment, communication, and contending with heteronormativity: An invitation to greater reflexivity in interpersonal research. *Southern Communication Journal, 73,* 84–101.

Fraser, S., & Gerstle, G. (Eds.). (1989). *The rise and fall of the New Deal order, 1930–1980.* Princeton, NJ: Princeton University Press.

Freire, P. (1973). *Education for critical consciousness.* New York: Seabury.

Freeman, M. (2009). *Hindsight: The promise and peril of looking back.* New York: Oxford University Press.

Freud, S. (1949). *An outline of psychoanalysis* (J. Strachey, Trans.). New York: Norton. (Original work published 1940)

Freud, S. (1955). *Leonardo da Vinci and a memory of his childhood/A study in psychosexuality* (A. A. Brill, Trans.). New York: Vintage Books. (Original work published 1910)

Frierson, H., Hood, S., & Hughes, G. (2002). A guide to conducting culturally responsive evaluations. In J. Frechtling, H. Frierson, S. Hood, & G. Hughes, *The 2002 user-friendly handbook for project evaluation* (pp. 63–73). Washington, DC: National Science Foundation.

Gall, M. D., Gall, J. P., & Borg, W. R. (2003). *Educational research: An introduction* (7th ed.). Boston: Allyn & Bacon.

Geertz, C. (1973). *The interpretation of cultures.* New York: Basic Books.

Gilmore, P., & Smith, D. M. (2005). Seizing academic power: Indigenous subaltern voices and counternarratives in higher education. In T. L. McCarty (Ed.), *Language, literacy, and power and schooling* (pp. 67–88). Mahwah, NJ: Lawrence Erlbaum.

Gingrich-Philbrook, C. (2005). Autoethnography's family values: Easy access to compulsory experiences. *Text and Performance Quarterly, 25,* 297–314.

Ginsberg, P. E., & Mertens, D. M. (2009). Frontiers in social research ethics: Fertile ground for evolution. In D. M. Mertens & P. E. Ginsberg (Eds.), *The handbook of social research ethics* (pp. 580–612). Thousand Oaks, CA: Sage.

Giroux, H. (2004). Cultural studies and the politics of public pedagogy: Making the political more pedagogical. *Parallax, 10*(2), 73–89.

Glaser, B. G. (1978). *Theoretical sensitivity.* Mill Valley, CA: Sociology Press.

Glaser, B. G. (1998). *Doing grounded theory: Issues and discussions.* Mill Valley, CA: Sociology Press.

Glaser, B. G. (2001). *The grounded theory perspective I: Conceptualization contrasted with description.* Mill Valley, CA: Sociology Press.

Glaser, B. G. (2005). *The grounded theory perspective III: Theoretical coding.* Mill Valley, CA: Sociology Press.

Glaser, B. G., & Strauss, A. L. (1965). *Time for dying.* Chicago: Aldine.

Glaser, B. G., & Strauss, A. L. (1967). *The discovery of grounded theory.* New York: Aldine.

Gluck, S. B. (1991). Advocacy oral history: Palestinian women in resistance. In S. B. Gluck & D. Patai (Eds.), *Women's words: The feminist practice of oral history* (pp. 205–220). New York: Routledge.

Golafshani, N. (2003). Understanding reliability and validity in qualitative research. *Qualitative Report, 8,* 597–607.

Goodall, H. L. (2001). *Writing the new ethnography.* Walnut Creek, CA: AltaMira.

Goodall, H. L. (2006). *A need to know: The clandestine history of a CIA family.* Walnut Creek, CA: Left Coast.

Goodenough, W. H. (1970). *Description and comparison in cultural anthropology.* Chicago: Aldine.

Gramsci, A., Hoare, Q., & Nowell-Smith, G. (1971). *Selections from the Prison Notebooks of Antonio Gramsci.* New York: International.

Grande, S. (2008). Red pedagogy: The unmethodology. In N. K. Denzin, Y. S. Lincoln, & L. T. Smith (Eds.), *Handbook of critical and indigenous methodologies* (pp. 233–254). Thousand Oaks, CA: Sage.

Graves, J. L. (2001). *The emperor's new clothes: Biological theories of race at the millennium.* New Brunswick, NJ: Rutgers University Press.

Gredler, M .E. (1996). *Program evaluation.* Englewood Cliffs, NJ: Prentice Hall.

Greene, D. M., & Walker, F. R. (2004). Recommendations to public speaking instructors for the negotiation of code-switching practices among black English-speaking African American students. *Journal of Negro Education, 74,* 435–442.

Greenspan, H. (1998). *On listening to Holocaust survivors: Recounting and life history.* Westport, CT: Praeger.

Grills, S. (1998). On being nonpartisan in partisan settings: Field research among the politically committed. In S. Grills (Ed.), *Doing ethnographic research: Fieldwork settings* (pp. 76–94). Thousand Oaks, CA: Sage.

Gruber, J. (1970). Ethnographic salvage and the shaping of anthropology. *American Anthropologist, 72,* 1289–1299.

Grumet, M. (1988). *Bitter milk: Woman and teaching.* Amherst: University of Massachusetts Press.

Guba, E. G., & Lincoln, Y. S. (1989). *Fourth generation evaluation.* Thousand Oaks, CA: Sage.

Gust, S. W., & Warren, J. T. (2008). Naming our sexual and sexualized bodies in the classroom: And the important stuff that comes after the colon. *Qualitative Inquiry, 14,* 114–134.

Gutmann, A., & Thompson, D. (1996). *Why deliberative democracy?* Princeton, NJ: Princeton University Press.

Halbwachs, M. (1992). *On collective memory* (L. A. Coser, Ed. & Trans.). Chicago: University of Chicago Press. (Original work published 1941)

Halpern, D. F. (2009). *Undergraduate education in psychology: A blueprint for the future of the discipline* (3rd ed.). Washington DC: American Psychological Association.

Hamilton, D. (1977). Making sense of curriculum evaluation: Continuities and discontinuities in an educational idea. *Review of Research in Education, 5,* 318–347.

Hammersley, M., & Atkinson, P. (1983). *Ethnography: Principles in practice.* London: Tavistock.

Hanberger, A. (2006). Evaluation of and for democracy. *Evaluation, 12*(1), 17–37.

Harding, S. (1991). *Whose science? Whose knowledge?* Ithaca, NY: Cornell University Press.

Harding, S. (Ed.). (2004). *Feminist standpoint theory reader: Intellectual and political controversies.* New York: Routledge.

Harrell, C. J. P. (1999). *Manichean psychology: Racism and the minds of people of African descent*. Washington DC: Howard University Press.

Harris, H. (2002). Coyote goes to school: The paradox of indigenous higher education. *Canadian Journal of Native Education, 26*(2), 187–196.

Harris, R. (2011). A case study of extended discourse in an ASL/English bilingual classroom. Unpublished doctoral dissertation, Gallaudet University, Washington DC.

Harris, R., Holmes, H., & Mertens, D. M. (2009). Research ethics in sign language communities. *Sign Language Studies, 9*, 104–131.

Harrison, D., & Trabasso, T. (Eds.). (1976). *Black English: A seminar*. Hillsdale, NJ: Lawrence Erlbaum.

Hart, M. A. (2010). Indigenous worldviews, knowledge, and research: The development of an indigenous research paradigm. *Journal of Indigenous Voices in Social Work, 1*(1), 1–16.

Hartsock, N. (1998). *The feminist standpoint revisited and other essays*. Boulder, CO: Westview Press.

Hartsock, N. (2003). The feminist standpoint: Developing the ground for a specifically feminist historical materialism. In S. Harding & M. Hintikka (Eds.), *Discovering reality: Feminist perspectives on epistemology, metaphysics, methodology and philosophy of science* (2nd ed., pp. 283–310). Dordrecht: Kluwer Academic.

Haverkamp, B. E. (2005). Ethical perspectives on qualitative research in applied psychology. *Journal of Counseling Psychology, 52*, 146–155.

Heckathorn, D. D. (1997). Respondent-driven sampling: A new approach to the study of hidden populations. *Social Problems, 44*, 174–199.

Heine, S. J. (2008). *Cultural psychology*. New York: Norton.

Henderson, J. Y. (2000). Ayukpachi: Empowering Aboriginal thought. In M. Battiste (Ed.), *Reclaiming indigenous voice and vision* (pp. 209–224). Vancouver: University of British Columbia Press.

Hermans, H. J. M. (1988). On the integration of nomothetic and idiographic research methods in the study of personal meaning. *Journal of Personality, 56*, 785–812.

Hermans, H. J. M., Kempen, H. J. G., & van Loon, R. J. P. (1992). The dialogical self: Beyond individualism and rationalism. *American Psychologist, 47*, 22–33.

Hertz, R. (Ed.). (1997). *Reflexivity and voice*. Thousand Oaks, CA: Sage.

Hilliard, A. (1991). Why we must pluralize the curriculum. *Educational Leadership, 49*(4), 12–16.

Hinchman, L. P., & Hinchman, S. (1997). *Memory, identity, community: The idea of narrative in the human sciences*. Albany: State University of New York Press.

Holland, D. C., & Eisenhart, M. A. (1992). *Educated in romance: Women, achievement, and college culture*. Chicago: University of Chicago Press.

Holman Jones, S. (2005). Autoethnography: Making the personal political. In N. K. Denzin & Y. S. Lincoln (Eds.), *The Sage handbook of qualitative research* (3rd ed., pp. 763–791). Thousand Oaks, CA: Sage.

Holton, J. A. (2007). The coding process and its challenges. In A. Bryant & K. Charmaz (Eds.), *The Sage handbook of grounded theory* (pp. 265–289). Thousand Oaks, CA: Sage.

REFERENCES

Hondagneu-Sotelo, P. (2001). *Domestica: Immigrant workers cleaning and caring in the shadows of affluence*. Berkeley: University of California Press.

Hood, S. (2009). Evaluations for and by Navajos. In K. E. Ryan & J. B. Cousins (Eds.), *The Sage international handbook of educational evaluation* (pp. 447–464). Thousand Oaks, CA: Sage.

hooks, b. (1994). *Teaching to transgress: Education as the practice of freedom*. New York: Routledge.

Hoonaard, V. D. H. (2002). *Walking the tightrope: Ethical issues for qualitative researchers*. Toronto: University of Toronto Press.

Hoonaard, V. D. H. (2011). *The seduction of ethics: The transformation of the social sciences*. Toronto: University of Toronto Press.

Hopson, R. K. (2003). *Overview of multicultural and culturally competent program evaluation: Issues, challenges, and opportunities*. Woodland Hills, CA: The California Endowment.

Hopson, R. K. (2009). Reclaiming knowledge at the margins: Culturally responsive evaluation in the current evaluation movement. In K. E. Ryan & J. B. Cousins (Eds.), *The Sage international handbook of educational evaluation* (pp. 429–446). Thousand Oaks, CA: Sage.

Hopson, R. K., & Kirkhart, K. E. (2011). Strengthening evaluation through cultural relevance and competence. Session at the American Evaluation/Centers for Disease Control and Prevention Summer Institute, Atlanta, GA.

House, E. R. (1980). *Evaluating with validity*. Beverly Hills, CA: Sage.

House, E. R. (1993). *Professional evaluation: Social impact and political consequences*. Thousand Oaks, CA: Sage.

House, E. R. (1996). A framework for appraising educational reforms. *Educational Researcher, 25*(7), 6–14.

House, E. R. (2001). Responsive evaluation (and its influence on democratic deliberative evaluation). *New Directions for Evaluation, 92*, 23–30.

House, E. R. (2011). Conflict of interest and Campbellian validity. In H. T. Chen, S. I. Donaldson, & M. M. Mark (Eds.), *Advancing validity in outcome evaluation: Theory and practice* (New Directions for Evaluation, no. 130, pp. 69–80). San Francisco: Jossey-Bass.

House, E. R., & Howe, K. R. (1999). *Values in evaluation and social research*. Thousand Oaks, CA: Sage.

House, E. R., & Howe, K. R. (2000). Deliberative democratic evaluation. *New Directions for Evaluation, 85*, 3–12.

House, E. R., & Lapan, S. D. (1988). The driver of the classroom: The teacher and school improvement. In R. Haskins & D. MacRae (Eds.), *Policies for America's public schools: Teachers, equity, and indicators* (pp. 70–86). Norwood, NJ: Ablex.

Hubbard, R. (1990). *The politics of women's biology*. New Brunswick, NJ: Rutgers University Press.

Hurston, Z. N. (1935). *Mules and men*. New York: Harper & Row.

Husserl, E. (1982). *Ideas pertaining to a pure phenomenology and to a phenomenological philosophy—First Book: General introduction to a pure phenomenology*. The Hague: Nijhoff. (Original work published 1913)

Iser, W. (1974). *The implied reader.* Baltimore: Johns Hopkins University Press.

Isherwood, C., & Macaulay, A. (2010, March 31). One loves it. One loathes it. "That's life." *New York Times.* www.nytimes.com/2010/04/01/theater/01tharp.html?th&emc=th.

Jefferson, G. (2004). Glossary of transcript symbols with an introduction. In G. H. Lerner (Ed.), *Conversation analysis: Studies from the first generation* (pp. 13–31). Philadelphia: John Benjamins.

Johnson, A. P. (2008). *A short guide to action research* (3rd ed.). Boston: Allyn & Bacon.

Johnson, B. M. (1995). Why conduct action research? *Teaching and Change, 3*(1), 90–104.

Johnson, E. (2005). The use of contextually relevant evaluation practices with programs designed to increase participation of minorities in science, technology, engineering and mathematics (STEM) education. In S. Hood, R. Hopson, & H. Frierson (Eds.), *The role of culture and cultural context: A mandate for inclusion, the discovery of truth, and understanding in evaluative theory and practice* (pp. 217–235). Greenwich, CT: Information Age.

Johnson, R. B., Onwuegbuzie, A. J., & Turner, L. A. (2007). Toward a definition of mixed methods research. *Journal of Mixed Methods Research, 1,* 112–134.

Jones, A., Sterling, H., Pollack, D., Doshier, S., Yeknik, C., Falls, D., et al. (1999, September). *Action research and educational practice.* Paper presented at the 12th annual conference of the Arizona Educational Research Organization, Flagstaff.

Jones, J. (2003). TRIOS: A psychological theory of the African legacy in American culture. *Journal of Social Issues, 59,* 217–241.

Jordan, B., & Henderson, A. (1995). Interaction analysis: Foundations and practice. *Journal of the Learning Sciences, 4,* 39–103.

Josselson, R., & Lieblich, A. (Eds.). (1993). *The narrative study lives.* Thousand Oaks, CA: Sage.

Jung, C. G. (1961). *Memories, dreams, reflections* (R. Winston & C. Winston, Trans.). New York: Vintage.

Kaestle, C. F., & Vinovskis, M. (1980). *Education and social change in nineteenth-century Massachusetts.* Cambridge, MA: Cambridge University Press.

Kaplan, I. M. (1991). Gone fishing, be back later: Ending and resuming research among fishermen. In W. B. Shaffir & R. A. Stebbins (Eds.), *Experiencing fieldwork: An inside view of qualitative research* (pp. 232–237). Thousand Oaks, CA: Sage.

Karlsson, O. (1996). A critical dialogue in evaluation: How can interaction between evaluation and politics be tackled? *Evaluation, 2,* 405–416.

Karlsson Vestman, O., & Segerholm, C. (2009). Dialogue, deliberation, and democracy in educational evaluation: Theoretical arguments and a case narrative. In K. E. Ryan & J. B. Cousins (Eds.), *The Sage international handbook of educational evaluation* (pp. 465–482).

Katz, M. B. (1968). *The irony of early school reform: Educational innovation in mid-nineteenth century Massachusetts.* Cambridge, MA: Harvard University Press.

Kawagley, A. O. (1995). *A Yupiaq worldview: A pathway to ecology and spirit.* Prospect Heights, IL: Waveland.

Kawagley, A. O. (2006). *A Yupiaq worldview: A pathway to ecology and spirit* (2nd ed.). Prospect Heights, IL: Waveland.

Keene, J. D. (2001). *Doughboys, the Great War, and the remaking of America*. Baltimore: Johns Hopkins University Press.

Kemmis, S. (1993). Action research and social movement: A challenge for policy research. *Education Policy Analysis Archives, 1*(1), 1–6.

Kemmis, S. (2009). Action research as a practice-based practice. *Educational Action Research, 17*, 463–474.

Kemmis, S., & McTaggart, R. (Eds.). (1982). *The action research planner*. Geelong, Victoria, Australia: Deakin University Press.

Kemmis, S., & McTaggart, R. (Eds.). (1988). *The action research planner* (3rd ed.). Geelong, Victoria, Australia: Deakin University Press.

Kemmis, S., & McTaggart, R. (2003). Participatory action research. In N. K. Denzin & Y. S. Lincoln (Eds.), *Strategies of qualitative inquiry* (2nd ed., pp. 134–164). Thousand Oaks, CA: Sage.

Kidd, S. A., & Kral, M. J. (2005). Practicing participatory action research. *Journal of Counseling Psychology, 52*, 187–195.

Kiesinger, C. E. (2002). My father's shoes: The therapeutic value of narrative reframing. In A. P. Bochner & C. Ellis (Eds.), *Ethnographically speaking: Autoethnography, literature, and aesthetics* (pp. 95–114). Walnut Creek, CA: AltaMira.

Kirkhart, K. E. (1995). Seeking multicultural validity: A postcard from the road. *Evaluation Practice, 16*, 1–12.

Kitchener, K. S., & Kitchener, R. F. (2009). Social science research ethics: Historical and philosophical issues. In D. M. Mertens & P. E. Ginsberg (Eds.), *The handbook of social research ethics* (pp. 5–22). Thousand Oaks, CA: Sage.

Kondo, D. (1990). *Crafting selves: Power, gender, and discourses of identity in a Japanese workplace*. Chicago: University of Chicago Press.

Kostick, K. M., Schensul, S. L., Jadhav, K., Singh, R., Bavadekar, A., & Saggurti, N. (2010). Treatment seeking, vaginal discharge and psychosocial distress among women in urban Mumbai. *Culture, Medicine and Psychiatry, 34*, 529–547.

Kuhn, T. S. (1962). *The structure of scientific revolutions*. Chicago: University of Chicago Press.

Kuhn, T. S. (1970). *The structure of scientific revolutions* (2nd ed.). Chicago: University of Chicago Press.

Kuper, A. (1973). *Anthropologists and anthropology: The British School (1922–1972)*. New York: Pica.

Kushner, S. (2000). *Personalizing evaluation*. London: Sage.

Kusserow, A. D. (2002). *Hunting down the monk*. Rochester, NY: BOA Editions.

Labov, W. (1972). The transformation of experience in narrative syntax. In W. Labov (Ed.), *Language in the inner city: Studies in black English vernacular* (pp. 354–396). Philadelphia: University of Philadelphia Press.

Ladson-Billings, G. (1994). *The dreamkeepers: Successful teachers of African American children*. San Francisco: Jossey-Bass.

Ladson-Billings, G. (1995a). But that's just good teaching! The case for culturally relevant pedagogy. *Theory into Practice, 43,* 159–165.

Ladson-Billings, G. (1995b). Toward a theory of culturally relevant pedagogy. *American Educational Research Journal, 32,* 465–492.

Ladson-Billings, G. (1998). Teaching in dangerous times: Culturally relevant approaches to teacher assessment. *Journal of Negro Education, 67,* 255–266.

Ladson-Billings, G. (2005). *Beyond the big house: African American educators on teacher education.* New York: Teachers College Press.

Ladson-Billings, G., & Tate, W. (1995). Toward a critical race theory of education. *Teachers College Record, 97,* 47–64.

LaFrance, J., & Crazy Bull, C. (2009). Researching ourselves back to life: Taking control of the research agenda in Indian Country. In D. M. Mertens & P. E. Ginsberg (Eds.), *The handbook of social research ethics* (pp. 135–149). Thousand Oaks, CA: Sage.

Landrine, H., & Klonoff, E. A. (1996). *African-American acculturation: Deconstructing race and reviving culture.* Thousand Oaks, CA: Sage.

Lapan, S. D. (1986). *Teacher thinking: Can it be translated into valid teacher evaluation?* Paper presented at the Center for Excellence in Education, Northern Arizona University, Flagstaff.

Lapan, S. D. (2004). Evaluation studies. In K. deMarrais & S. D. Lapan (Eds.), *Foundations for research: Methods of inquiry in education and the social sciences* (pp. 235–248). Mahwah, NJ: Lawrence Erlbaum.

Lapan, S. D., & Armfield, S. W. J. (2009). Case study research. In S. D. Lapan & M. T. Quartaroli (Eds.), *Research essentials: An introduction to designs and practices* (pp. 165–180). San Francisco: Jossey-Bass.

Lapan, S. D., & Haden, C. M. (2009). Program evaluation. In S. D. Lapan & M. T. Quartaroli (Eds.), *Research essentials: An introduction to designs and practices* (pp. 181–201). San Francisco: Jossey-Bass.

Lapan, S. D., & Quartaroli, M. T. (Eds.). (2009). *Research essentials: An introduction to designs and practices.* San Francisco: Jossey-Bass.

Lareau, A. (2000). *Home advantage: Social class and parental intervention in elementary education.* Lanham, MD: Rowman & Littlefield.

Lather, P. (1991). *Getting smart: Feminist research and pedagogy with/in the postmodern.* New York: Routledge.

Lather, P., & Smithies, C. (1997). *Troubling the angels: Women living with HIV/AIDS.* Boulder, CO: Westview Press.

LeCompte, M. D., & Goetz, J. P. (1982). Problems of reliability and validity in ethnographic research. *Review of Educational Research, 52,* 31–60.

LeCompte, M. D., & Schensul, J. J. (1999). *Analyzing and interpreting ethnographic data.* Walnut Creek, CA: AltaMira.

LeCompte, M. D., & Schensul, J. J. (Eds.). (2010). *Designing and conducting ethnographic research* (Vol. 1). Lanham, MD: AltaMira.

Lee, S. (2005). *Up against whiteness: Race, school, and immigrant youth.* New York: Teachers College Press.

Lemley, C. (2006). *Recovering language, reclaiming voice: Menominee language revitalization programs.* Unpublished dissertation, University of Wisconsin-Madison, Madison.

Lempert, L. B. (2007). Asking questions of the data: Memo writing in the grounded theory tradition. In A. Bryant & K. Charmaz (Eds.), *The Sage handbook of grounded theory* (pp. 244–264). Thousand Oaks, CA: Sage.

Levinson, B., Foley, D., & Holland, D. (Eds.). (1996). *The cultural production of the educated person: Critical ethnographies of schooling and local practice.* Albany: State University of New York Press.

Lewin, K. (1946). Action research and minority problems. *Journal of Social Issues, 2*, 34–46.

Lewin, K. (1948). *Resolving social conflicts: Selected papers on group dynamics.* New York: Harper & Row.

Lewis, A. E. (2004). What a group? Studying whites and whiteness in the era of color blindness. *Sociological Theory, 22*, 623–646.

Lieblich, A., Tuval-Mashiach, R., & Zilber, T. (1998). *Narrative research: Reading, analysis, and interpretation* (Vol. 47). Thousand Oaks, CA: Sage.

Limón, J. E. (1994). *Dancing with the devil: Society and cultural poetics in Mexican-American South.* Madison: University of Wisconsin Press.

Lincoln, Y. S. (1997). Self, subject, audience, and text: Living at the edge, writing in the margin. In W. G. Tierney & Y. S. Lincoln (Eds.), *Representation and the text: Reframing the narrative voice* (pp. 37–56). Albany: State University of New York Press.

Lincoln, Y. S. (2009). Ethical practices in qualitative research. In D. M. Mertens & P. E. Ginsberg (Eds.), *The handbook of social research ethics* (pp. 150–169). Thousand Oaks, CA: Sage.

Lincoln, Y. S., & Guba, E. G. (1985). *Naturalistic inquiry.* Beverly Hills, CA: Sage.

Lincoln, Y. S., & Guba, E. G. (2000). Paradigmatic controversies, contradictions, and emerging confluences. In N. Denzin & Y. S. Lincoln (Eds.), *Handbook of qualitative research* (2nd ed., pp. 163–188). Thousand Oaks, CA: Sage.

Lipsitz, G. (2006). *The possessive investment in whiteness: How white people profit from identity politics.* Philadelphia: Temple University Press.

Logan, R. W., & Winston, M. R. (1982). Dictionary of American Negro biography. New York: Norton.

Lowenstein, T. (2005). *Ancestors and species. New and selected ethnographic poetry.* Exeter, England: Shearsman Books.

Lyotard, J.-F. (1984). *The postmodern condition: A report on knowledge* (G. Bennington & B. Massumi, Trans.). Minneapolis: University of Minnesota Press.

MacDonald, B., & Kushner, S. (2004). Democratic evaluation. In S. Mathison (Ed.), *Encyclopedia of evaluation* (pp. 109–113). Thousand Oaks, CA: Sage.

Mack, K. M., Rankins, C. M., & Winston, C. E. (in press). Black women faculty at historically black colleges and universities: Perspectives for a national imperative. In H. T. Frierson & W. F. Tate (Eds.), *Beyond stock stories and folk tales: African Americans' paths to STEM fields.* Bingley, England: Emerald Group.

MacLeod, J. (1987). *Ain't no makin' it: Leveled aspirations in a low-income neighborhood.* Boulder, CO: Westview Press.

Madison, D. S. (2005). *Critical ethnography: Method, ethics, and performance.* Thousand Oaks, CA: Sage.

Madison, D. S. (2006). The dialogic performative in critical ethnography. *Text and Performance Quarterly, 26,* 320–324.

Mahmood, S. (2005). *Politics of piety: The Islamic revival and the feminist subject.* Princeton, NJ: Princeton University Press.

Mahoney, M. J. (2004). What is constructivism and why is it growing? *PsycCRITIQUES, 49,* 360–363.

Makagon, D. (2004). *Where the ball drops: Days and nights in Times Square.* Minneapolis: University of Minnesota Press.

Malinowski, B. (1922). *Argonauts of the western Pacific.* Long Grove, IL: Waveland.

Mangum, A. M. (2006). *Emotion and race narratives: Are emotions represented in the narrative reconstruction of the earliest autobiographical memory of race?* Unpublished manuscript, Howard University, Washington DC.

Manswell-Butty, J. L., Daniel Reid, M. & LaPoint, V. (2004). A culturally responsive evaluation approach applied to the Talent Development school-to-career intervention program. *New Directions for Evaluation, 101,* 37–47.

Marcus, G. E. (1998). *Ethnography through thick and thin.* Princeton, NJ: Princeton University Press.

Marcus, G. E. (2007). Ethnography two decades after writing culture: From the experimental to the baroque. *Anthropology Quarterly, 80,* 1127–1145.

Marcus, G. E., & Cushman, D. (1982). Ethnographies as texts. *Annual Review of Anthropology, 11,* 25–69.

Marcus, G. E., & Fisher, M. M. J. (1986). *Anthropology as cultural critique: An experimental moment in the human sciences.* Chicago: University of Chicago Press.

Mark, M. M., & Gamble, C. (2009). Experiments, quasi-experiments, and ethics. In D. M. Mertens & P. E. Ginsberg (Eds.), *The handbook of social research ethics* (pp. 198–213). Thousand Oaks, CA: Sage.

Mark, M. M., Henry, G. T., & Julnes, G. (2000). *Evaluation: An integrated framework for understanding, guiding, and improving public and nonprofit policies and programs.* San Francisco: Jossey-Bass.

Martin, J., & Meezan, W. (Eds.). (2003). *Research methods with gay, lesbian, bisexual, and transgender populations.* Binghamton, NY: Haworth.

Martin, W. E., & Bridgmon, K. D. (2009). Essential elements of experimental and quasi-experimental research. In S. D. Lapan & M. T. Quartaroli (Eds.), *Research essentials: An introduction to designs and practices* (pp. 35–58). San Francisco: Jossey-Bass.

Marvasti, A. (2006). Being Middle Eastern American: Identity negotiation in the context of the war on terror. *Symbolic Interaction, 28,* 525–547.

Masco, J. (2006). *The nuclear borderlands: The Manhattan Project in post–Cold War New Mexico.* Princeton, NJ: Princeton University Press.

Maso, I. (2001). Phenomenology and ethnography. In P. Atkinson, A. Coffey, S. Delamont, J. Lofland, & L. Lofland (Eds.), *Handbook of ethnography* (pp. 136–144). Thousand Oaks, CA: Sage.

Maurer, B. (2005). *Mutual life limited: Islamic banking, alternative currencies, lateral reasoning.* Princeton, NJ: Princeton University Press.

McAdams, D. P. (1985). *Power, intimacy, and the life story: Personological inquiries into identity.* New York: Guilford Press.

McAdams, D. P. (1997). The guided autobiography [Data collection instrument]. Evanston, IL: Foley Center for the Study of Lives, School of Education and Social Policy, Northwestern University. www.sesp.northwestern.edu/foley/instruments/guided/.

McAdams, D. P. (2001). The psychology of life stories. *Review of General Psychology, 5,* 100–122.

McAdams, D. P. (2008). The Life Story Interview [Data collection instrument]. Evanston, IL: Foley Center for the Study of Lives, School of Education and Social Policy, Northwestern University. www.sesp.northwestern.edu/foley/instruments/interview. (Original work published 1995)

McAdams, D. P. (2009). *The person: An introduction to the science of personality psychology* (5th ed.). Hoboken, NJ: Wiley.

McAdams, D. P., Bauer, J. J., Sakaeda, A. R., Anyidoho, N. A., Machado, M. A., Magrino-Failla, K., et al. (2006). Continuity and change in the life story: A longitudinal study of autobiographical memories in emerging adulthood. *Journal of Personality, 74,* 1371–1400.

McAdams, D. P., & Logan, R. L. (2004). What is generativity? In E. de St. Aubin, D. P. McAdams, & T. Kim (Eds.), *The generative society: Caring for future generations* (pp. 15–31). Washington, DC: American Psychological Association.

McAdams, D. P., & Pals, J. L. (2006). A new big five: Fundamental principles for an integrative science of personality. *American Psychologist, 61,* 204–217.

McAdams, D. P., Reynolds, J., Lewis, M., Patten, A., & Bowman, P. J. (2001). When bad things turn good and good things turn bad: Sequences of redemption and contamination in life narrative, and their relation to psychosocial adaptation in midlife adults and in students. *Personality and Social Psychology Bulletin, 27,* 208–230.

McCrae, R. R., & Costa, P. T., Jr. (1987). Validation of the five-factor model of personality across instruments and observers. *Journal of Personality and Social Psychology, 52,* 385–405.

McCrae, R. R., & Costa, P. T., Jr. (1999). A five-factor theory of personality. In L. A. Pervin & O. P. John (Eds.), *Handbook of personality: Theory and research* (2nd ed., pp. 139–153). New York: Guilford Press.

McNiff, J. (2007). My story is my living educational theory. In D. J. Clandinin (Ed.), *Handbook of narrative inquiry: Mapping a methodology* (pp. 308–329). Thousand Oaks, CA: Sage.

Mead, M. (1928). *Coming of age in Samoa: A psychological study of primitive youth for Western civilization.* New York: William Morrow.

Mendoza-Denton, N. (2008). *Homegirls: Language and cultural practice among Latina youth gangs*. Malden, MA: Blackwell.

Merriam, S. B. (1998). *Qualitative research and case study applications in education: Revised and expanded from case study research in education* (2nd ed.). San Francisco: Jossey-Bass.

Merriam, S. B. (2009). *Qualitative research: A guide to design and implementation*. San Francisco: Jossey-Bass.

Mertens, D. M. (2009). *Transformative research and evaluation*. New York: Guilford Press.

Mertens, D. M. (2010). *Research and evaluation in education and psychology: Integrating diversity with quantitative, qualitative, and mixed methods* (3rd ed.). Thousand Oaks, CA: Sage.

Mertens, D. M., Fraser, J., & Heimlich, J. E. (2008). M or F?: Gender, identity and the transformative research paradigm. *Museums and Social Issues, 3*(1), 81–92.

Mertens, D. M., & Ginsberg, P. (2008). Deep in ethical waters: Transformative perspectives for qualitative social work research. *Qualitative Social Work, 7*, 484–503.

Mertens, D. M., Holmes, H. M., & Harris, R. L. (2009). Transformative research and ethics. In D. M. Mertens & P. E. Ginsberg (Eds.), *The handbook of social research ethics* (pp. 85–102). Thousand Oaks, CA: Sage

Meyer, M. A. (2001). Our own liberation: Reflections on Hawaiian epistemology. *Contemporary Pacific, 13*(1), 124–148.

Middleton, S. (1993). *Educating feminists: Life histories and pedagogy*. New York: Teachers College Press.

Mi'kmaq College Institute. (2006). *Research principles and protocols: Mi'kmaw ethics watch*. http://mrc.uccb.ns.ca/prinpro.html.

Miles, M. B., & Huberman, A. M. (1994). *Qualitative data analysis: An expanded sourcebook* (2nd ed.). Thousand Oaks, CA: Sage.

Miller, J. (1992). Exploring power and authority issues in a collaborative research project. *Theory into Practice, 31*, 165–172.

Miller, J. (1998). Autobiography and the necessary incompleteness of teachers' stories. In W. Ayers & J. Millers (Eds.), *A light in dark times: Maxine Greene and the unfinished conversation* (pp. 145–154). New York: Teachers College Press.

Miller, J. (2005). *Sounds of silence breaking: Women, autobiography, curriculum*. New York: Peter Lang.

Mills, G. E. (2003). *Action research: A guide for the teacher researcher* (2nd ed.). Upper Saddle River, NJ: Prentice Hall.

Minkler, M., & Wallerstein, N. (Eds.). (2003). *Community-based participatory research for health*. San Francisco: Jossey-Bass.

Mishler, E. (1990). Validation in inquiry-guided research: The role of exemplars in narrative studies. *Harvard Educational Review, 60*, 415–442.

Mishler, E. (2004). Historians of the self: Restorying lives, revising identities. *Research in Human Development, 1*, 101–121.

Mitchell, R. (2008). Interpretive transgressions. In L. Mazzei & A. Jackson (Eds.), *Voice in qualitative inquiry: Challenging conventional, interpretive, and critical conceptions in qualitative research* (pp. 77–96). New York: Routledge.

REFERENCES

Moewaka Barnes, H., McCreanor, T., Edwards, S., & Borell, B. (2009). Epistemological domination: Social science research ethics in Aotearoa. In D. M. Mertens & P. E. Ginsberg (Eds.), *The handbook of social research ethics* (pp. 442–457). Thousand Oaks, CA: Sage.

Monaghan, E. J. (1989). Literacy instruction and gender in colonial New England. In C. Davidson (Ed.), *Reading in America: Literature and social history* (pp. 53–80). Baltimore: Johns Hopkins University Press.

Moonzwe, L., Schensul, J. J., & Kostick, K. (in press). The role of MDMA (Ecstasy) in coping with negative life situations among urban young adults. *Journal of Psychoactive Drugs, 42*(3).

Moore, T. S. (2009). *The student tutor experience in a problem-based learning course: A case study*. Unpublished doctoral dissertation, Northern Arizona University, Flagstaff.

Moro, P. (2006). It takes a darn good writer: A review of *The Ethnographic I*. *Symbolic Interaction, 29*, 265–269.

Morse, J. M., Stern, P. N., Corbin, J., Bowers, B., Charmaz, K., & Clarke, A. E. (2009). *Developing grounded theory: A second generation*. Walnut Creek, CA: Left Coast Press.

Mosher, H. (in press). Creating participatory ethnographic videos. In J. J. Schensul & M. D. LeCompte (Eds.), *Specialized ethnographic methods: Book 4. Ethnographer's toolkit* (2nd ed.). Lanham, NJ: AltaMira.

Munro, P. (1993). Continuing dilemmas of life history research: A reflexive account of feminist qualitative inquiry. In D. Flinders & G. Mills (Eds.), *Theory and concepts in qualitative research: Perspectives from the field* (pp. 163–177). New York: Teachers College Press.

Munro-Hendry, P. (2007). The future of narrative. *Qualitative Inquiry, 13*, 487–497.

Murdock, G. P. (1971). *Outline of cultural materials* (4th rev. ed., 5th printing, with modifications). New Haven, CT: Human Relations Area Files.

Murray, H. A. (1938). *Explorations in personality*. New York: Oxford University Press.

Murray, H. A. (1943). *The Thematic Apperception Test: Manual*. Cambridge, MA: Harvard University Press.

Narayan, K. (1993). How native is a "native" anthropologist? *American Anthropologist, 95*, 671–685.

Nasby, W., & Read, N. W. (1997). The life voyage of a solo circumnavigator: Integrating theoretical and methodological perspectives. *Journal of Personality, 65*, 785–1068.

Nathan, R. (2006). *My freshman year: What a professor learned by becoming a student*. New York: Penguin.

National Commission for the Protection of Human Subjects of Biomedical and Behavioral Research. (1979). *The Belmont report: Ethical principles and guidelines for the protection of human subjects of research* (DHEW Publication No. OS 78–0012). Washington DC: Government Printing Office.

Nicholls, R. (2009). Research and indigenous participation: Critical reflexive methods. *International Journal of Social Research Methodology, 12*, 117–126.

Noblit, G., Flores, S., & Murillo, Ed. (Eds.). (2004). *Postcritical ethnography: An introduction*. Cresskill, NJ: Hampton.

Noguera, P. A. (2008). *The trouble with black boys . . . and other reflections on race, equity, and the future of public education*. San Francisco: Jossey-Bass.

Norris, N. (1990). *Understanding educational evaluation*. London: Kogan Page.

Ntseane, P. G. (2009). The ethics of the researcher-subject relationship: Experiences from the field. In D. M. Mertens & P. E. Ginsberg (Eds.), *The handbook of social research ethics* (pp. 295–307). Thousand Oaks, CA: Sage.

Office of Strategic Services Assessment Staff. (1948). *Assessment of men: Selection of personnel for the Office of Strategic Services*. New York: Rinehart.

Oliva, M. (2000). Shifting landscapes/shifting langue: Qualitative research from the in-between. *Qualitative Inquiry, 6*, 33–58.

Ongtooguk, P. (2000). Aspects of traditional Iñupiat education. *Sharing Our Pathways, 5*(4), 8–12. www.ankn.uaf.edu/sop/sopv5i4.html#ongtoogook.

Osborne, R., & McPhee, R. (2000, December). *Indigenous terms of reference (ITR)*. Paper presented at the 6th UNESCO-ACEID International Conference on Education, Bangkok.

Parker, A. C. (1916). The social elements of the Indian problem. *American Journal of Sociology, 22*, 252–267.

Pascoe, C. J. (2007). *Dude, you're a fag: Masculinity and sexuality in high school*. Berkeley: University of California Press.

Patton, M. Q. (1987). *How to use qualitative methods in evaluation*. Thousand Oaks, CA: Sage.

Patton, M. Q. (1997). *Utilization-focused evaluation: The new century text* (3rd ed.). Thousand Oaks, CA: Sage.

Patton, M. Q. (2002). *Qualitative research and evaluation methods* (3rd ed.). Thousand Oaks, CA: Sage.

Paulson, S., & Willig, C. (2008). Older women and everyday talk about the ageing body. *Journal of Health Psychology, 13*, 106–120.

Pelias, R. J. (2000). The critical life. *Communication Education, 49*, 220–228.

Pelias, R. J. (2007). Jarheads, girly men, and the pleasures of violence. *Qualitative Inquiry, 13*, 945–959.

Penn Towns, D., & Serpell, Z. (2004). Successes and challenges in triangulating methodologies in evaluations of exemplary urban schools. *New Directions for Evaluation, 101*, 49–62.

Perkins, L. (1987). *Fanny Jackson Coppin and the Institute for Colored Youth, 1837–1902*. New York: Garland.

Perlmann, J. (1988). *Ethnic differences: Schooling and social structure among the Irish, Italians, Jews and blacks in an American city, 1880–1935*. Cambridge, MA: Cambridge University Press.

Petryn, A. (2002). *Life exposed: Biological citizens after Chernobyl*. Princeton, NJ: Princeton University Press.

Phellas, C. N. (2005). Cypriot gay men's accounts of negotiating cultural and sexual identity: A qualitative study. *Qualitative Sociology Review, 1*(2), 65–83.

Pillow, W. (2004). *Unfit subjects: Educational policy and the teen mother*. New York: Routledge.

Pinnegar, S., & Dayne, J. G. (2007). Locating narrative inquiry historically: Thematics in the turn to narrative. In D. J. Clandinin (Ed.), *Handbook of narrative inquiry: Mapping a methodology* (pp. 3–34). Thousand Oaks, CA: Sage.

REFERENCES

Plummer, K. (2001). The call of life stories in ethnographic research. In P. Atkinson, A. Coffey, S. Delamont, J. Lofland, & L. Lofland (Eds.), *Handbook of ethnography* (pp. 395–406). Thousand Oaks, CA: Sage.

Polkinghorne, D. (1988). *Narrative knowing and the human sciences.* Albany: State University of New York Press.

Press, A. L., & Cole, E. R. (1999). *Speaking of abortion: Television and authority in the lives of women.* Chicago: University of Chicago Press.

QSR International. (2010). *NVivo 9.* Doncaster, Victoria, Australia: Author. www.qsrinternational.com/products_nvivo.aspx.

Radcliffe-Brown, A. R. (1952). Letters to the editor. *American Anthropologist, 54,* 275–277.

Radda, K. E., Schensul, J. J., Disch, W. B., Levy, J. A., & Reyes, C. Y. (2003). Assessing human immunodeficiency virus (HIV) risk among older urban adults: A model for community-based research partnership. *Family & Community Health, 26,* 203–213.

Radway, J. A. (1984). *Reading the romance: Women, patriarchy, and popular literature.* Chapel Hill: University of North Carolina Press.

Ramirez-Valles, J., Heckathorn, D., Vázquez, R., Diaz, R., & Campbell, R. (2005). From networks to populations: The development and application of respondent-driven sampling among IDUs and Latino gay men. *AIDS and Behavior, 9,* 387–402.

Rapp, R. (2000). *Testing women, testing the fetus: The social impact of amniocentesis in America.* New York: Routledge.

Ravitch, D., & Vinovskis, M. A. (Eds.). (1995). *Learning from the past: What history teaches us about school reform.* Baltimore: Johns Hopkins University Press.

Reinharz, S. (1997). Who am I? The need for a variety of selves in the field. In R. Hertz (Ed.), *Reflexivity and voice* (pp. 3–20). Thousand Oaks, CA: Sage.

Rice, B. (2005). *Seeing the world with Aboriginal eyes: A four dimensional perspective on human and non-human values, cultures and relationships on Turtle Island.* Winnipeg, Manitoba, Canada: Aboriginal Issues Press.

Richardson, L. (1997). *Fields of play: Constructing an academic life.* New Brunswick, NJ: Rutgers University Press.

Richardson, L., & Lockridge, E. (1991). The sea monster: An ethnographic drama. *Symbolic Interaction, 14,* 335–340.

Richardson, M. (1975). Anthropologist—the myth teller. *American Ethnologist, 2,* 517–533.

Riemer, F. J. (2001). *Working at the margins: Moving off welfare in America.* Albany: State University of New York Press.

Riemer, F. J. (2008). Becoming literate, being human: Adult literacy and moral reconstruction in Botswana. *Anthropology & Education Quarterly, 39,* 444–464.

Riemer, F. J. (2009). Ethnography research. In S. D. Lapan & M. T. Quartaroli (Eds.), *Research essentials: An introduction to designs and practices* (pp. 203–222). San Francisco: Jossey-Bass.

Riessman, C. K. (1993). *Narrative analysis* (Qualitative Research Methods Series 30). Thousand Oaks, CA: Sage.

Riessman, C. K. (2008). *Narrative methods for the human sciences.* Thousand Oaks, CA: Sage.

Riessman, C. K., & Speedy, J. (2007). Narrative inquiry in the psychotherapy professions. In D. J. Clandinin (Ed.), *Handbook of narrative inquiry* (pp. 426–456). London: Sage.

Robison, J., Schensul, J. J., Coman, E., Diefenbach, G. J., Radda, K. E., Gaztambide, S., et al. (2009). Mental health in senior housing: Racial/ethnic patterns and correlates of major depressive disorder. *Aging & Mental Health, 13,* 659–673.

Rogers, K. L. (2004). Lynching stories: Family and community memory in the Mississippi Delta. In K. L. Rogers, S. Leydesdorff, & G. Dawson (Eds.), *Trauma: Life stories of survivors* (pp. 113–130). New Brunswick, NJ: Transaction.

Rogge, W. M. (1967). The teacher is his own best change agent. *Accent on Talent, 1*(4), 1, 4.

Rogoff, B. (1990). *Apprenticeship in thinking: Cognitive development in social context.* New York: Oxford University Press.

Roman, L., & Apple, M. (1990). Is naturalism a move away from positivism? Materialist feminist approaches to subjectivity in ethnographic research. In E. Eisner & A. Peshkin (Eds.), *Qualitative inquiry in education: The continuing debate* (pp. 38–74). New York: Teachers College Press.

Rorty, R. (1982). *Consequences of pragmatism (essays 1972–1980).* Minneapolis: University of Minnesota Press.

Rorty, R. (1989). *Contingency, irony, and solidarity.* Cambridge, England: Cambridge University Press.

Rosaldo, R. (1989). *Culture and truth: The remaking of social analysis.* Boston: Beacon.

Rosiek, J., & Atkinson, B. (2007). The inevitability and importance of genres in narrative research on teaching practice. *Qualitative Inquiry, 13,* 499–521.

Rouse, J. (1978). *The completed gesture: Myth, character, and education.* New York: Skyline.

Rumsey, A. (2000). Orality. *Journal of Linguistic Anthropology, 9,* 170–172.

Ryan, K. A., & DeStefano, L. (Eds.). (2000). *Evaluation as a democratic process: Promoting inclusion, dialogue, and deliberation* (New Directions for Evaluation, no. 85). San Francisco: Jossey-Bass.

Saberwal, S. (1969). Rapport and resistance among the Embu of central Kenya (1963–1964). In F. Henry & S. Saberwal (Eds.), *Stress and response in fieldwork* (pp. 47–62). New York: Holt, Rinehart and Winston.

Said, E. W. (1979). *Orientalism.* New York: Vintage.

Saldaña, J. (2008). Second chair: An autoethnodrama. *Research Studies in Music Education, 30,* 177–191.

Salemink, O. (2000). *Colonial subjects: Essays on the practical history of anthropology.* Ann Arbor: University of Michigan Press.

Salganik, M. J., & Heckathorn, D. D. (2004). Sampling and estimation in hidden populations using respondent-driven sampling. *Sociological Methodology, 34,* 193–240.

Sanjek, R. (1990). On ethnographic validity. In R. Sanjek (Ed.), *Fieldnotes: The making of anthropology* (pp. 385–418). Ithaca, NY: Cornell University Press.

Sarbin, T. R. (1986). The narrative as a root metaphor for psychology. In T. R. Sarbin (Ed.), *Narrative psychology: The storied nature of human conduct* (pp. 2–21). New York: Praeger.

Sarsby, J. (1984). The fieldwork experience. In R. F. Ellen (Ed.), *Ethnographic research: A guide to general conduct* (pp. 87–132). San Diego, CA: Academic Press.

Sayman, D. (2009). *Man enough to care: A qualitative study of male nurses.* Unpublished doctoral dissertation, Oklahoma State University, Stillwater.

Schafer, R. (1981). Narration in the psychoanalytic dialogue. In W. J. Mitchell (Ed.), *On narrative* (pp. 25–29). Chicago: University of Chicago Press.

Schensul, J. J. (2008). Method. In L. M. Givens (Ed.), *The Sage encyclopedia of qualitative research methods* (p. 522). Thousand Oaks, CA: Sage.

Schensul, J. J., Chandran, D., Singh, S. K., Berg, M., Singh, S., & Gupta, K. (2010). The use of qualitative comparative analysis for critical event research in alcohol and HIV in Mumbai, India. *Aids and Behavior, 14*, 113–125.

Schensul, J. J., Diamond, S., Disch, W., Bermudez, R., & Eiserman, J. (2005). The diffusion of Ecstasy through urban youth networks. *Journal of Ethnicity in Substance Abuse, 4*(2), 39–73.

Schensul J. J., & LeCompte, M. D. (1999). *The ethnographers' toolkit (Vols. 1–7).* Lanham, MD: Rowman & Littlefield.

Schensul, J. J., Levy, J. A., & Disch, W. B. (2003). Individual, contextual, and social network factors affecting exposure to HIV/AIDS risk among older residents living in low-income senior housing complexes. *JAIDS Journal of Acquired Immune Deficiency Syndromes, 33*(Suppl. 2), S138–S152.

Schensul, S. L., Oodit, G., Schensul, J. J., Ragobur, S., & Bhowon, U. (1994). *Young women, work, and AIDS-related risk behavior in Mauritius* (Phase I Research Report Series, no. 2). Washington DC: International Center for Research on Women.

Schensul, J. J., Robison, J., Reyes, C. Y., Radda, K., Gaztambide, S., & Disch, W. B. (2006). Building interdisciplinary/intersectoral research partnerships for community-based mental health research with older minority adults. *American Journal of Community Psychology, 38*, 79–93.

Schensul, S. L., Schensul, J. J., & LeCompte, M. D. (1999). *Essential ethnographic methods: Observations, interviews, and questionnaires.* Walnut Creek, CA: AltaMira.

Scheper-Hughes, N. (2001). *The global traffic in human organs: A report presented to the House Subcommittee on International Operations and Human Rights, United States Congress on June 27, 2001.* www.publicanthropology.org/TimesPast/Scheper-Hughes.htm.

Schiebinger, L. (1993). *Nature's body: Gender in the making of modern science.* Boston: Beacon.

Schmitt, F. E., & Martin, P. Y. (1999). Unobtrusive mobilization by an institutionalized rape crisis center: "All we do comes from victims." *Gender & Society, 13*, 364–384.

Schön, D. C. (1983). *The reflective practitioner: How professionals think in action.* New York: Basic Books.

Schultz, W. T. (2007). *Handbook of psychobiography.* New York: Oxford University Press.

Schwandt, T. (1989). Solutions to the paradigm conflict. *Journal of Contemporary Ethnography*, *17*, 379–407.

Scientific Software. (2010). *ATLAS.ti 6.0*. Berlin, Germany: ATLAS.ti Scientific Software Development GmbH. www.atlasti.com/fileadmin/atlasti/downloads/atlas.ti6_brochure_2009_en.pdf.

Scriven, M. S. (1991). *Evaluation thesaurus* (4th ed.). Thousand Oaks, CA: Sage.

Seidman, I. (1998). *Interviewing as qualitative research: A guide for researchers in education and the social sciences* (2nd ed.). New York: Teachers College Press.

Seidman, I. (2006). *Interviewing as qualitative research: A guide for researchers in education and the social sciences* (3rd ed.). New York: Teachers College Press.

Shadish, W. R. (1995). The logic of generalization: Five principles common to experiments and ethnographies. *American Journal of Community Psychology*, *23*, 419–428.

Shadish, W. R., Cook, T. D., & Campbell, D. T. (2002). *Experimental and quasi-experimental designs for generalized causal inference*. Boston: Houghton Mifflin.

Shaffir, W., & Stebbins, R. (1991). *Experiencing fieldwork*. Thousand Oaks, CA: Sage.

Shaffir, W., Stebbins, R., & Turowetz, A. (1980). *Fieldwork experience*. New York: St. Martin's Press.

Shavelson, R. J., & Stern, P. (1981). Research on teachers' pedagogical thoughts, judgments, decisions, and behavior. *Review of Educational Research*, *51*, 455–498.

Silverman, D. (2001). *Interpreting qualitative data: Methods for analyzing talk, text and interaction* (2nd ed.). London: Sage.

Simons, H. (1987). *Getting to know schools in a democracy*. London: Falmer.

Simons, H. (1977). Case-studies of innovation. In D. Hamilton, B. MacDonald, C. King, D. Jenkins, & M. Parlett (Eds.), *Beyond the numbers game: A reader in educational evaluation* (pp. 178–180). Berkeley, CA: McCutchan.

Sinclair, M. (2007). A guide to understanding theoretical and conceptual frameworks. *Evidence-Based Midwifery*, *5*, 39.

Singer, E. O., & Schensul, J. J. (in press). Negotiating Ecstasy risk, reward and control: A qualitative analysis of drug management patterns among Ecstasy-using inner city youth. *Drug Use and Misuse*, *47*.

Singer, J. A. (2004). Narrative identity and meaning-making across the adult lifespan: An introduction. *Journal of Personality*, *72*, 437–459.

Singer, J. A. (2005). *Personality and psychotherapy: Treating the whole person*. New York: Guilford Press.

Singer, J. A., & Moffitt, K. H. (1991). An experimental investigation of specificity and generality in memory narratives. *Imagination, Cognition, and Personality*, *11*, 233–257.

Singer, J. A., & Salovey, P. (1993). *The remembered self: Emotion and memory in personality*. New York: Free Press.

Smith, B. H. (1981). Narrative versions, narrative theories. In I. Konigsberg (Ed.), *American criticism in the poststructuralist age* (pp. 62–186). Ann Arbor: University of Michigan Press.

Smith, C. P. (1992). *Motivation and personality: Handbook of thematic content analysis*. New York: Cambridge University Press.

REFERENCES

Smith, G. H. (2000). Protecting and respecting indigenous knowledge. In M. Battiste (Ed.), *Reclaiming indigenous voice and vision* (pp. 209–224). Vancouver: University of British Columbia Press.

Smith, L. T. (1999). *Decolonizing methodologies: Research and indigenous peoples.* London: Zed Books.

Smith, L. T. T. R. (2000). Kaupapa Maori research. In M. Battiste (Ed.), *Reclaiming indigenous voice and vision* (pp. 225–247). Vancouver: University of British Columbia Press.

Smith, M. M. (1998). *Debating slavery: Economy and society in the antebellum American South.* Cambridge, MA: Cambridge University Press.

Snow, C. P. (1993). *The two cultures.* Cambridge, England: Cambridge University Press. (Original work published 1959)

Spence, D. P. (1982). *Narrative truth and historical truth: Meaning and interpretation in psychoanalysis.* New York: Norton.

Spivak, G. (1987). *In other worlds: Essays in cultural politics.* New York: Routledge.

Spradley, J. (1979). *The ethnographic interview.* New York: Holt, Rinehart and Winston.

Springgay, S. (2008). *Body knowledge and curriculum: Pedagogies of touch in youth and visual culture.* New York: Peter Lang.

Stacey, J. (1991). Can there be a feminist ethnography? In S. B. Gluck & D. Patai (Eds.), *Women's words: The feminist practice of oral history* (pp. 111–119). New York: Routledge.

Stake, R. E. (1967). The countenance of educational evaluation. *Teachers College Record, 68,* 523–540.

Stake, R. E. (1983). Program evaluation, particularly responsive evaluation. In G. F. Madaus, M. S. Scriven, & D. L. Stufflebeam (Eds.), *Evaluation models: Viewpoints on educational and human services evaluation* (pp. 287–310). Boston: Kluwer-Nijhoff. (Reprinted from keynote address presented at conference on New Trends in Evaluation, Göteborg, Sweden, October 1973)

Stake, R. E. (1995). *The art of case study research.* Thousand Oaks, CA: Sage.

Stake, R. E. (2005). Qualitative case studies. In N. K. Denzin & Y. S. Lincoln (Eds.), *The Sage handbook of qualitative research* (3rd ed., pp. 443–466). Thousand Oaks, CA: Sage.

Stake, R. E. (2006). *Multiple case study analysis.* New York: Guilford Press.

St. Denis, V. (1992). Community-based participatory research: Aspects of the concept relevant for practice. *Native Studies Review, 8*(2), 51–74.

Stern, P. N. (2007). On solid ground: Essential properties for growing grounded theory. In A. Bryant & K. Charmaz (Eds.), *The Sage handbook of grounded theory* (pp. 114–126). Thousand Oaks, CA: Sage.

Stewart, A. J. (1994). Toward a feminist strategy for studying women's lives. In C. Franz & A. J. Stewart (Eds.), *Women creating lives: Identities, resilience and resistance* (pp. 11–35). Boulder, CO: Westview Press.

Stewart, A. J., Franz, C., & Layton, L. (1988). The changing self: Using personal documents to study lives. *Journal of Personality, 56,* 41–74.

Stewart, K. (1996). *A space on the side of the road.* Princeton, NJ: Princeton University Press.

Stone, C. N., Henig, J. R., Jones, B. D., & Pierannunzi, C. (2001). *Building civic capacity: The politics of reforming urban schools*. Lawrence: University Press of Kansas.

St. Pierre, E. A. (2000). Nomadic inquiry in the smooth spaces of the field: A preface. In E. A. St. Pierre & W. S. Pillow (Eds.), *Working the ruins: Feminist poststructural theory and methods in education* (pp. 258–283). New York: Routledge.

St. Pierre, E., & Pillow, W. S. (2000). *Working the ruins: Feminist poststructural methods in education*. New York: Routledge.

Strathern, M. (2005). *Kinship, law and the unexpected: Relatives are always a surprise*. New York: Cambridge University Press.

Strauss, A. L. (1987). *Qualitative analysis for social scientists*. Cambridge, England: Cambridge University Press.

Strauss, A., & Corbin, J. (1990). *Basics of qualitative research: Grounded Theory Procedures and Techniques*. Thousand Oaks, CA: Sage.

Strauss, A., & Corbin, J. (1998). *Basics of qualitative research: Techniques and procedures for developing grounded theory* (2nd ed.). Thousand Oaks, CA: Sage

Stufflebeam, D. L. (2001). Evaluation models. *New Directions for Evaluation, 89*, 7–98.

Stufflebeam, D. L. (2003). The CIPP Model for evaluation. In D. L. Stufflebeam & T. Kellaghan (Eds.), *The international handbook of educational evaluation* (pp. 31–62). Boston: Kluwer Academic.

Stufflebeam, D. L., Gullickson, A., & Wingate, L. (2002). *The spirit of Consuelo: An evaluation of Ke Aka Ho'ona*. Kalamazoo: Evaluation Center of Western Michigan University. http://rszarf.ips.uw.edu.pl/ewalps/teksty/consuelo_eval.pdf.

Stufflebeam, D. L., & Shinkfield, A. J. (2007). *Evaluation theory, models and applications*. San Francisco: Jossey-Bass.

Sullivan, M. (2009). Philosophy, ethics and the disability community. In D. M. Mertens & P. E. Ginsberg (Eds.), *The handbook of social research ethics* (pp. 69–84). Thousand Oaks, CA: Sage.

Symonette, H. (2004). Walking pathways toward becoming a culturally competent evaluator: Boundaries, borderlands, and border crossings. In M. Thompson-Robinson, R. Hopson, & S. SenGupta (Eds.), *In search of cultural competence in evaluation: Toward principles and practices* (New Directions for Evaluation, no. 102, pp. 95–110). San Francisco: Jossey-Bass.

Symonette, H. (2009). Cultivating the self as responsive instrument: Working the boundaries and borderlands for ethical border-crossings. In D. M. Mertens & P. E. Ginsberg (Eds.), *The handbook of social research ethics* (pp. 279–294). Thousand Oaks, CA: Sage.

Szala-Meneok, K. (2009). Ethical research with older adults. In D. M. Mertens & P. E. Ginsberg (Eds.), *The handbook of social research ethics* (pp. 507–518). Thousand Oaks, CA: Sage.

Taussig, M. (1991). *Shamanism, colonialism, and the wild man: A study in terror and healing*. Chicago: University of Chicago Press.

Taussig, M. (1997). *Magic of the state*. New York: Routledge.

Taussig, M. (2005). *Law in a lawless land: Diary of a Limpieza in Colombia*. Chicago: University of Chicago Press.

REFERENCES

Taylor-Powell, E., & Henert, E. (2008). *Developing a logic model: Teaching and training guide*. www.uwex.edu/ces/pdande/evaluation/pdf/lmguidecomplete.pdf.

Tedla, E. (1996). *Sankofa: African thought and education*. New York: Peter Lang.

Tedlock, B. (1991). From participant observation to the observation of participation: The emergence of narrative ethnography. *Journal of Anthropological Research, 47*, 69–94.

Terry, R. L. (2008). *Race self complexity within multiracial college students: Negotiating the suppression of multiracial integration*. Unpublished manuscript, Howard University, Washington DC.

Thomas, J. (1993). *Doing critical ethnography*. Thousand Oaks, CA: Sage.

Thomas, V. G. (2004). Building a contextually responsive evaluation framework: Lessons from working with urban school interventions. *New Directions for Evaluation, 101*, 3–23.

Thompson, E. P. (1977). *William Morris: Romantic to revolutionary*. London: Merlin.

Thornberg, R. (2007). Inconsistencies in everyday patterns of school rules. *Ethnography & Education, 2*, 401–416.

Thornberg, R. (2008a). A categorisation of school rules. *Educational Studies, 34*, 25–33.

Thornberg, R. (2008b). School children's reasoning about school rules. *Research Papers in Education, 23*, 37–52.

Thornberg, R. (2009). The moral construction of the good pupil embedded in school rules. *Education, Citizenship and Social Justice, 4*, 245–261.

Thornberg, R. (2010a). Schoolchildren's social representations on bullying causes. *Psychology in the Schools, 47*, 331–327.

Thornberg, R. (2010b). A student in distress: Moral frames and bystander behavior in school. *Elementary School Journal, 110*, 585–608.

Thornberg, R. (2011). *Consultation barriers between teachers and non-school consultants*. Unpublished manuscript, Department of Behavioural Sciences and Learning, Linköping University, Linköping, Sweden.

Thornberg, R. (in press). Informed grounded theory. *Scandinavian Journal of Educational Research*.

Thornberg, R., Halldin, K., Petersson, A., & Bolmsjö, N. (2011). Victimizing of school bullying: A grounded theory. Unpublished manuscript, Department of Behavioural Sciences and Learning, Linköping University, Linköping, Sweden.

Tickle, N. (2003). *You can read a face like a book: How reading faces helps you succeed in business and relationships*. Mountain View, CA: Daniels.

Tillmann, L. M. (2008). Father's blessing: Ethnographic drama, poetry, and prose. *Symbolic Interaction, 31*, 376–399.

Tillmann, L. M. (2009). Body and bulimia revisited: Reflections on "A Secret Life." *Journal of Applied Communication Research, 37*, 98–112.

Tillmann-Healy, L. M. (2003). Friendship as method. *Qualitative Inquiry, 9*, 729–749.

Tololyan, K. (1987). Cultural narrative and the motivation of the terrorist. *Journal of Strategic Studies, 10*, 217–233.

Tomkins, S. S. (1979). Script theory. In H. E. Howe Jr. & R. A. Dienstbier (Eds.), *Nebraska symposium on motivation* (Vol. 26, pp. 201–236). Lincoln: University of Nebraska Press.

Toyosaki, S., Pensoneau-Conway, S. L., Wendt, N. A., & Leathers, K. (2009). Community autoethnography: Compiling the personal and resituating whiteness. *Cultural Studies <=> Critical Methodologies, 9*, 56–83.

Traustadottir, R. (2001). Research with others: Reflections on representation, difference, and othering. *Scandinavian Journal of Disability Research, 3*, 9–28.

Trimble, J., & Fisher, C. (Eds.). (2006). *The handbook of ethical research with ethnocultural populations and communities*. Thousand Oaks, CA: Sage.

Tripathi, B., Sharma, H., Pelto, P., & Tripathi, S. (2010). Ethnographic mapping of alcohol use and risk behaviors in Delhi. *AIDS and Behavior, 14*, 94–103.

Tsing, A. L. (2004). *Friction: An ethnography of global connection*. Princeton, NJ: Princeton University Press.

Tuana, N. (1993). *The less noble sex: Scientific, religious, and philosophical conceptions of woman's nature*. Bloomington: Indiana University Press.

Tuck, E. (2009). Suspending damage: A letter to communities. *Harvard Educational Review, 79*, 409–427.

Tyack, D., & Cuban, L. (1995). *Tinkering toward utopia: A century of public school reform*. Cambridge, MA: Harvard University Press.

U.S. Department of Health and Human Services. (2003). *Privacy protection for research subjects: "Certificates of Confidentiality."* Washington DC: Author. www.hhs.gov/ohrp/humansubjects/guidance/certconpriv.htm.

U.S. Department of Health & Human Services, National Institutes of Health. (2011). *Certificates of confidentiality*. Washington DC: Author. www.grants.nih.gov/grants/policy/coc.

Valenzuela, A. (1999). *Subtractive schooling: U.S.-Mexican youth and the politics of caring*. Albany: State University of New York Press.

Van Maanen, J. (1988). *Tales of the field: On writing ethnography*. Chicago: University of Chicago Press.

Vargas, L. A., & Montoya, M. E. (2009). Involving youth in research within complex cultural settings: Ethics and law. In D. M. Mertens & P. E. Ginsberg (Eds.), *The handbook of social research ethics* (pp. 489–506). Thousand Oaks, CA: Sage.

Vidich, A., & Bensman, J. (1958). *Small town in mass society*. Princeton, NJ: Princeton University Press.

Visweswaran, K. (1994). *Fictions of feminist ethnography*. Minneapolis: University of Minnesota Press.

Weber-Pillwax, C. (2001). What is indigenous research? *Canadian Journal of Native Education, 25*(2), 166–174.

Webster, C. (2006). Change the nation. On *Change the nation* [CD]. Oakland, CA: Youth Movement Records.

Webster, L., & Mertova, P. (2007). *Using narrative inquiry as a research method: An introduction to using critical event narrative analysis in research on learning and teaching*. London: Routledge.

REFERENCES

Weis, L. (1985). *Between two worlds: Black students in an urban community college.* Boston: Routledge & Kegan Paul.

Weis, L., & Fine, M. (2000). *Speed bumps: A student-friendly guide to qualitative research.* New York: Teachers College Press.

White, R. W. (1938). The case of Earnst. In H. A. Murray (Ed.), *Explorations in personality* (pp. 615–627). New York: Oxford University Press.

Wholey, J. S., Hatry, H. P., & Newcomer, K. E. (Eds.). (1994). *Handbook of practical program evaluation.* San Francisco: Jossey-Bass.

Whyte, W. F. (1943). *Street corner society.* Chicago: University of Chicago Press.

Williams, R. (1997). Vampires anonymous and critical race analysis. *University of Michigan Law Review, 95,* 741–765.

Willis, P. (1997). *Learning to labor: How working class kids get working class jobs.* New York: Columbia University Press.

Wilson, A. (2004). *The intimate economies of Bangkok: Tomboys, tycoons, and Avon ladies in the global city.* Berkeley: University of California Press.

Wilson, A. (2005). The effectiveness of international development assistance from American organizations to deaf communities in Jamaica. *American Annals of the Deaf, 150,* 292–304.

Wilson, S. (2001a). Self-as-relationship in indigenous research. *Canadian Journal of Native Education, 25*(2), 91–92.

Wilson, S. (2001b). What is an indigenous research methodology? *Canadian Journal of Native Education, 25*(2), 175–179.

Wilson, S. (2008). *Research is ceremony: Indigenous research methods.* Halifax, Nova Scotia: Fernwood.

Wilson, W. J. (1987). *The truly disadvantaged: The inner city, the underclass, and public policy.* Chicago: University of Chicago Press.

Wilson, W. J., & Chaddha, A. (2009). The role of theory in ethnographic research. *Ethnography, 10,* 549–564.

Winfield, A. G. (2007). *Eugenics and education in America: Institutionalized racism and the implications of history, ideology, and memory.* New York: Peter Lang.

Winston, C. E., Philip, C. L., & Lloyd, D. L. (2007). The Identity and Success Life Story Method: A new paradigm for digital inclusion. *Journal of Negro Education, 76,* 31–42.

Winston, C. E., & Winston, M. R. (in press). Cultural psychology and racial ideology: An analytic approach to understanding racialized societies and their psychological effects on lives. In J. Valsiner (Ed.), *Oxford handbook of culture and psychology.* New York: Oxford University Press.

Winter, D. G. (1973). *The power motive.* New York: Free Press.

Winter, D. G. (1987). Leader appeal, leader performance, and the motive profiles of leaders and followers: A study of American presidents and elections. *Journal of Personality and Social Psychology, 52,* 196–202.

Winter, D. G. (1996). *Personality: Analysis and interpretation of lives.* New York: McGraw-Hill.

REFERENCES

Wisler, C. (1991). *Designing evaluations.* Washington DC: U. S. General Accounting Office, Program Evaluation and Methodology Division. http://archive.gao.gov/t2pbat7/144040.pdf.

W. K. Kellogg Foundation. (2004). *Logic model development guide.* Battle Creek, MI: Author. www.wkkf.org/knowledge-center/resources/2010/Logic-Model-Development-Guide.aspx.

Wolcott, H. F. (1990). *Writing up qualitative research.* London: Sage.

Wolcott, H. F. (1999). *Ethnography: A way of seeing.* Walnut Creek, CA: AltaMira.

Worthen, B. R., Sanders, J. R., & Fitzpatrick, J. L. (1997). *Program evaluation: Alternative approaches and practical guidelines* (2nd ed.). New York: Longman.

Wyatt Knowlton, L., & Phillips, C. C. (2009). *The logic model guidebook: Better strategies for great results.* Thousand Oaks, CA: Sage.

Yin, R. K. (2003). *Case study research: Design and methods* (3rd ed.). Thousand Oaks, CA: Sage.

Yin, R. K. (2004). *The case study anthology.* Thousand Oaks, CA: Sage.

Yoshino, K. (2006). *Covering: The hidden assault on our civil rights.* New York: Random House.

Znaniecki, F. (1934). *The method of sociology.* New York: Farrar & Rinehart.

INDEX

Page references followed by *fig* indicate an illustrated figure; followed by *t* indicate a table; followed by *e* indicate an exhibit.

A
ACCESS (software), 99
Acculturation, 350
ACESAS (African American Culturally Responsive Evaluation System for Academic Settings): acronym of the, 348–349; description of, 347–348, 360–362; framework for, 362–363; logic model components, 364–370; purpose of the, 363–364; sankofa bird model of, 361*fig*–362
ACESAS logic models: contextual analysis component, 365–366; CRE action steps component, 368–369; CRE products component, 369; CRE team component, 366–367; CRE team resources component, 367–368; cultural and sociopolitical influences component, 364–365; evaluation impact component, 369; influence and impact on cultural group component, 370
Acting (practitioner research), 299, 300–301

Action orientation, 399–400
Action research, 292, 400. *See also* Practitioner action research
Action steps (CRE), 368–369
Active listening, 409
Activism stance, 381
Activities (logic model), 360
Aesthetic qualities of arts-based research, 286
African American communities: CRE (culturally responsive evaluation) implemented in, 357–358; culture of, 350–352; worldview of, 354
African American culture: characteristics of, 350–352; individualism to collectivism continuum of, 350
African Americans: acculturation of, 350; *Brown v. Board of Education* decision on education desegregation of, 350; double consciousness of, 350; implications of racial group classification for, 353–354; narrative inquiry into experiences of, 220–221; Tuskegee experiments (1933–1972) on, 21–22
African Ancestry, 122

The Afrocentric Idea (Asante), 358
Afrocentricity, 358
Agency: biography and life story, 112; critical ethnography, 374, 377–378; historical, 148–149; relationship of structure and, 378
Alternative representations, 267
American Anthropological Association (AAA), 34, 98, 169
American Educational Research Association (AERA), 31, 273, 294
American Evaluation Association (AEA), 31, 326, 329, 357, 358
American Indian Higher Education Consortium, 360
American Journal of Sociology, 425
American Psychological Association (APA), 31, 357–358
American Sign Language, 23
American sociological Association (ASA), 31
Analytic induction, 179
Analytic summaries, 99
Androcentric (male-centered) assumptions, 393–394

Anthropology as Critique: An Experimental Moment in the Human Sciences (Marcus and Fisher), 181
Anthropometry, 398
APA's Council of National Psychological Association for the Advancement of Ethnic Minority Interests, 31
APA's Joint Task Force of Division, 17, 31
Archival documents, 151–152
Archival research, 90
Argonauts of the Western Pacific (Malinowski), 180
Aristotle, 5, 394
Artifacts: ethnographic data collection using, 175–176; as primary sources, 152
Arts-based research: background of, 272–274; *Boundary Bay: A Novel* (Dunlop) example of, 280–282; description of, 271–272; *Evidence of Utopianizing Toward Social Justice in Young People's Community-Based Art Works* (Chappell) example of, 282–284; genre blurring technique used in, 273; learning from, 284–285; planning and conducting, 277–279; purposes of, 274–276; trusting, 285–286
Assent, 35. *See also* Informed consent
Atlas-ti (software), 99
Audiences: cast study research outcomes for, 244; program evaluation, 322
Audiovisual documentation, 90, 95*t*, 312*t*
Audit trails, 418
Authenticity: catalytic, 30; as deliberate democratic research caveat, 465; description of, 29; educative, 30; ontological, 30; tactical, 30
Autobiography, 225, 227–228
"Autobiography and the Necessary Incompleteness of Teachers' Stories" (Miller), 238
Autoethnography: benefits of, 204–206; Carolyn's introduction to, 193–195; community, 203; crisis of confidence concerns about, 196; critical responses to, 206–209; epiphanies recorded by, 198–200; ethnography aspect of, 199; forms of, 202–204; generalizability of, 207; helping insiders and outsiders to understand the culture, 199; identity politics of, 196; methods used for, 198–200; narrative inquiry through, 238; origins and development of, 196–198; outcomes for Tony and Carolyn, 209–210; participant observers in, 199; reliability and validity of, 207; Tony's introduction to, 190–193; writing, 200–201. *See also* Ethnography; LGBTQ youth
Autonomy: feminist oral history on female, 410–411; researcher, 303, 314*e*
Axiological belief systems, 22–23
Axiologies: as consideration in research, 431–434; definition of, 425

B

Balance (or fairness), 30
Belmont Report: on norms for research, 19–20; three ethical principles identified in, 19, 22, 23–28; on voluntary informed consent, 32–33
Beneficence: definition of, 22; transformative perspective of, 23–24
Biases: CRE (culturally responsive evaluation) approach to, 356; minimizing, 255*e*; program evaluator, 339; researcher, 255; triangulating analyst to minimize, 340
Biography: definition of, 142; as narrative inquiry genre, 225, 226
Biography and life story research: contemporary design of, 112–116; data analytic methods used for, 125–131; data collection methods and tools used for, 116–123; data processing used in, 124–125; description of, 107–108; dissemination of findings, 133; historical roots in psychology, 109–110; key theoretical underpinnings of, 110–112; reliability and validity issues of, 131–133. *See also* Historical research; Life story research study
"Black English," 351
Body Knowledge and Curriculum: Pedagogies of Touch in Youth and Visual Culture (Springgay), 276
Body maps, 96*t*
Bottom-up view of history, 146–147
Boundary Bay: A Novel (Dunlop) [arts-based research], 280–282
Bounded system, 91
Bracketed interview, 255
Brown v. Board of Education, 350

INDEX

C

Canonical stories, 204–205
Case histories (or case records), 244
Case method, 244
Case studies: characteristics of, 245–247; description of, 244; instrumental, 246–247; intrinsic, 246; purposes of, 246–247; types of, 247
Case study reports: alternative representations of, 267; descriptive and interpretive, 266–267e; naturalistic generalization of, 267; thick description of, 267
Case study research: case study reports component of, 266–268; description of, 243–244; implementing, 261–265; planning, 247–261. *See also* Dental hygiene student tutor study
Case study research implementation: coding, 263–264e; data analysis, 263–264e; data collection, 261–262t; member checking, 265–266e; two-column journaling template for, 262t; validity issues, 265
Case study research planning: bounding or limiting the case, 248–249; data collection, 251–255; dental hygiene student tutor study, 248e; writing study questions, 249 250e
Cases: bounding of the, 245–246, 248–249; description of, 243; seeking discrepant, 419
casework, 244
Catalytic authenticity, 30
Catalytic validity, 419
Categories: core, 48; defining gaps among, 60; ethnographic typologies and taxonomies from, 178; focused coding, 46, 48–51; generating and refining grounded theory, 50; historical categories of analysis, 157–158; initial (or open) coding, 44–46, 47t; tentative conceptual, 49–50; theoretical coding, 51–54; theoretical saturation of, 61–62, 178–179, 253; theoretical sensitivity to relationships between, 62–63
Categories of analysis, 157–158
Causal chains, 80–81
Census, 74
Centers for Disease Control and Prevention, 360
Certainty: epistemological predisposition toward, 272–273; John Dewey on quest for, 272
Certificate of confidentiality, 35
Change the Nation (Youth Movement Records album), 283–284
Chicago School, 6
Child informed consent, 35
CIPP Evaluation Model, 325, 333, 362
CIRM (critical indigenous research methodologies): colonization and call for (re)claiming, 424–427; critical component of, 442–443; description of, 424, 434; empiricism and multisensory listening approach of, 440–441; epistemological, ontological, and axiological research considerations, 431–434; future directions of, 443–444; impact of traditional research on indigenous communities, 428–431; indigenous methodologies paradigm of, 442; reciprocity of, 439–440; relationality of, 436–437; research as a service approach of, 435–436; resistance and critique of, 444–446; respect of, 438–439; response to critiques of, 446–447; responsibility of, 438. *See also* Indigenous/native communities
Civic capacity, 368
Class issues: classical Marxism approach to, 375; as The Denver Study issue, 452–454
Classical Marxism, 375
Co-constructed narratives, 204
Code of Ethics of the American Sociological Association (ASA), 169
Code-switch, 350–351
Coding: Atlas-ti or NVivo software used for, 98–99; case study research, 263–264e; description of, 44, 98–99; ethnographic data analysis, 177–178; focused, 46, 48–51, 57e–58e; initial (or open coding), 44–46, 47t; thematic content analysis, 129–131; theoretical, 51–54. *See also* Data; Data analysis
Collaborative (or participatory) approach: deliberate democratic research, 466–467; description of, 78
Collective memory, 354
Collectivism culture, 350
Colonization: of indigenous/native communities, 424–427; reclaiming indigenous identity/knowledge from, 431–434
Communication: active listening, 409; CIRM's practice of multisensory

listening, 440–441; deliberative democratic principle of dialogue, 459–460, 468, 469e–470e
Community autoethnographies, 203
Community mapping, 90
Comparative case studies, 247
Competency: cultural, 31–32; researcher, 31–32
Conceptual models: case study research, 249–250e; data analysis approach for, 99; domains identified using, 80–81; formulating, 79–81; HIV/AIDS study, 81, 86–87fig; strategies used to create, 86. *See also* Theoretical (or conceptual) frameworks
Confidentiality: certificate of, 35; IRB requirements for, 37; research issue of, 36–37
Confirmability, 29
Conflict of interest validity, 7
Congress of Hispanic Educators, 462
Consequence (narrative), 221
Constant comparative method, 46, 178
Construct: of culture, 349; of race, 349, 353
Constructivist paradigm: biography and life story research, 113; data collection in grounded theory, 44; description of, 22–23; grounded theory research using, 43
Contemporary Ethnography Across the Disciplines (CEAD) conference [2010], 184
Context: case study research observation, 257; CRE logic model component on, 365–366; cultural, 355;

definition of historical, 143–144; historical research, 143–145
Contextual analysis (CRE model), 365–366
Convenience sampling, 60
Core category, 48
Council for World Mission/London Missionary Society, 176
Counterevidence, 150
Counterhegemonic, 445
CRE (culturally responsive evaluation): ACESAS logic model components used for, 364–370; benefits of, 358–359; description of, 348, 349, 355; implementing in African American community settings, 357–358; origin of, 355. *See also* Culture/cultures
CRE evaluators: characteristics of, 355–357; cultural competencies of, 356–357
Credibility: description of, 29; program evaluation, 338. *See also* Trustworthiness; Validity
Crisis of confidence, 196
Criterion sampling, 84
Critical component of CIRM, 442–443
Critical ethnography: comparing traditional ethnography and, 374–375; critiques of, 386–388; elements of, 377–383; introduction to, 374–375; practices of doing, 383–385; theoretical and historical foundations of, 375–377; validity and trustworthiness of, 386–387. *See also* Ethnography
Critical ethnography elements: drawing on and building

theory, 378–379; focus on power-related identities and oppressions, 379–380; micro and macro phenomena, 378; reflecting on representation and positionality, 380–382, 387; structure and agency, 374, 377–378; taking a stand against inequity, 382–383
Critical events: description of, 219; narrative inquiry using, 219–221
Critical life episode, 117
Critical (or interpretive) traditions, 296
Critical perspective, 8–9
Critical persuasion, 274
Critical researchers, 77–78
Critical social action, 296
Cultural acceptability, 464
Cultural competencies: ACESAS approach to, 363–364; CRE evaluators, 356–357; description of, 31–32
Cultural consensus modeling, 89
Cultural context, 355
Cultural diversity, 465
Cultural egoism, 354
Cultural history, 142
Cultural interpretation, 165
Culturalists, 375–376
Culturally responsive evaluation product, 369
Culturally responsive evaluation review, 369
Culture/cultures: characteristics of African American, 350–352; code-switching between two different, 350–351; construct of, 349; definition of, 349; deliberate democratic research caveats related to, 464–465; difference between

INDEX

race and, 352–353; helping insiders and outsider to understand the, 199; individualism and collectivism, 350; informants on their, 165–166; as issues in The Denver Study, 452–454; meaning in context of, 126; respectful research in relationship of language and, 26. *See also* CRE (culturally responsive evaluation); Society

Custer Died for Your Sins: An Indian Manifesto (Deloria), 425, 426

Cyclical philosophy of history, 156

D

Data: critical ethnographic approach to "hot," 380; ethnographic, 176–180; process of biography and life story, 124–125; quantitative historical, 153–154; transcription of audio or video, 125. *See also* Coding; Information; Triangulation

Data analysis: analytic summaries used during, 99; Atlas-ti or NVivo software used for, 98–99; biography and life story approaches to, 125–131; case study research, 263–264*e*; critical ethnography, 385; description of, 98; discourse analytic question asked during, 127; ethnographic, 176–180; general analytic mind-set adopted during, 126–127; interpretation, 125–126; Ke Aka Ho`ona project evaluation, 334, 336; thematic content analysis approach to, 129–131; triangulating for, 99–100. *See also* Coding

Data collection: audit trails of, 418; case study research, 251–255, 261–262*t*; constructivist grounded theory on, 44; cultural level of, 89–90; example of depression study, 74–75; individual level of, 90–91; issues to consider for, 43–44; Ke Aka Ho`ona project evaluation, 334, 335*t*; main classes of individual and community levels of, 88*t*; participation element of qualitative, 70–71; practitioner action research, 308–312*t*; researcher position in, 88–91

Data collection instruments: case study research, 255–261; designing valid, 256; Developmental Success Matrix (DSM), 122; Flanders Interaction Analysis, 257, 259; guided autobiography, 118–119, 121, 126; Guided Race Autobiography (GRA), 121–123; Identity and Success Life Story Method (ISLSM), 120–121*fig*, 133; law of the instrument tendency to reuse, 311–312; Life Story Interview, 117–119, 127; Life Story Telling (LST), 121; NEO Personality Inventory, 122; program evaluation use of, 334; Self-Defining Memory Task, 119–120, 126

Data collection methods: archival research, 90; audiovisual documentation, 90, 95*t*, 312*t*; Biography and life story research design, 112–116; bounded system and semibounded system, 91; case study research, 255–261; community mapping, 90; cultural consensus modeling, 89; data recording, 123; ethnographic research, 171–176; focus groups, 173; individual-level network data, 91; journaling, 262*t*, 312*t*; logs, 312*t*; network research, 89–90; non-participant participant observer, 172; selecting, 92–97; surveys, 91, 173–174, 256–257. *See also* Interviews; Methods; Observation

Data recording: biography and life story research use of, 123; case study research use of, 260*e*

Decolonizing Methodologies (Smith), 425

Deductive analysis, 177

Deficit orientation, 305

Deliberate democratic research: The Denver Study example of, 452–459; description and principles of, 459–461; guidelines for conducting, 467–470*e*; research methods and democratic procedures of, 461–464; ten caveats for using, 464–467

Deliberate democratic research caveates: authentic processes, 465; balance of power, 467; collaboration, 466–467; constraints on self-interest, 467; cultural acceptability, 464; cultural diversity, 464; faithful representation, 465; focusing on issues, 466; rules and principles, 466; structured interaction, 465–466

INDEX

Deliberate democratic research guidelines: deliberation, 468, 470*e*; dialogue, 468, 469*e*–470*e*; inclusion, 468, 469*e*; overview of, 467–468
Deliberate democratic research principles: deliberation, 460; dialogue as, 459–460; inclusion as, 459
Deliberation guideline, 468, 470*e*
Dental hygiene student tutor study: case, limits, and purpose, 248*e*; case study research questions used in, 250*e*; coding during the, 264*e*; contrary findings of, 265*e*; data recording during, 260*e*; descriptive statement of patterns and findings, 267*e*; example of questions linked to data sources/types, 252*e*; excerpt of tutor interview protocol, 258*e*–259*e*; member checking during, 266*e*; minimizing bias, 255*e*; pilot and field testing interview protocol of, 27*e*; researcher skill development in, 254*e*; theoretical or conceptual framework, 2250*e*. *See also* Case study research
The Denver Study: background information on, 452; bilingual language debate during, 452–453; constant change impact school district during, 457; district's English Language Acquisition (ELA) program, 452, 455–456, 457; language, class, and cultural politics impacting, 452–454; research plan used for, 457; school district power shifts during, 458–459; stakeholder groups in the, 452

Dependability, 29
Depression study in older population, 72–75*t*
Descriptive case study reports, 266, 267*e*
Design. *See* Methodology
Designing Evaluations (GAO manual), 337–338
Deterministic (Marxism), 375
Developmental Success Matrix (DSM), 122
Dewey, John, 272
Dialogue principle, 459–460, 468, 469*e*–470*e*
Dilthey, Wilhem, 6
Diplomatic (or political) history, 142
Disciplined inquiry, 4–5
Discourse analytic question, 127
Discrepant cases, 419
Dissemination: biography and life story research, 133; critical ethnography findings, 385; culturally responsive evaluation product for, 369; program evaluation, 336–337
Documentation: archival, 151–152; audiovisual, 90, 94*t*, 312*t*; cameras and digital recorders for, 97; "ethnographic broadside" desire for, 167; ethnographic use of written records and, 175–176; network research, 89–90; photography, 95*t*
Domains: description of, 80; portrayed as causal chains, 80–81; predictor and outcomes, 80
Dora case study (Freud), 128
Double consciousness, 350
Doughboys, the Great War, and the Remaking of America (Keene), 141
Duration, 82

E

Ecological validity, 7
Educative authenticity, 30
Emic perspective (insider-participant), 12, 87, 165
Empiricism/empirical information: description of, 4–5; feminist research, 393; indigenous, 440–441
Epiphanies, 198–200
Epistemological research, 7
Epistemologies: as consideration in research, 431–434; definition of, 425
Equity: critical ethnographic stand against, 382–383; definition of, 382; women's movement for, 392–393
Erickson, Erik, 110
Ethical and equitable research, 398
Ethical issues: axiology study of, 22; Code of Ethics of the American Sociological Association (ASA), 169; confidentiality, 36–37; constructivist paradigm framing of, 22–23; ethical norms for research, 28–37; ethical principles of research, 21–28; feminist research practices, 398–399; guidance for ethical conduct of research, 20–21; informed consent, 32–36; IRB (institutional review board) role in, 21, 33, 34, 97–98; program evaluators and, 327*t*–328*t*; relational ethics, 204, 205–206; research dilemmas related to, 20; researcher as instrument, 21; transformative paradigm framing of, 22, 23–28. *See also* Research
Ethical norms: of feminist research, 398–399; validity,

INDEX

rigor, and qualitative research, 28–30
Ethical principles: *Belmont Report's* identification of three, 19, 22; beneficence, 22, 23–24; justice, 22, 27–28; respect, 22, 25–26
Ethnic Differences: Schooling and Social Structure Among the Irish, Italians, Jews and Blacks in an American City, 1880–1935 (Perlmann), 154
Ethnographers: cultural interpretation of, 165; emic perspective of, 12, 87, 165; ethnographic realism style of writing by, 180–181; etic perspective of, 12, 165; fieldwork of, 169–170; how they begin their research, 167–169; participant-observer role of, 172, 175
Ethnographic data: iterative nature of, 176; organizing, 176–177
Ethnographic data analysis: analytic induction approach to, 179; coding used for, 177–178; constant comparative method of, 178; deductive and inductive, 177; theoretical saturation outcome of, 178–179; typologies or taxonomies developed during, 178
Ethnographic data collection: focus groups, 173; interviews, 172–173; key informants used for, 175; non-participant participant observer, 172; participant observation, 171–172; projective techniques used in, 174; surveys, 173–174; written records and artifacts used during, 175–176

Ethnographic interviews, 172–173
Ethnographic mapping, 85
Ethnographic realism, 180–181
Ethnographic research: current state of, 183–184; data collection methods used in, 171–176; data and data analysis in, 176–180; emic perspective (insider-participant) of, 12, 87, 165; how to begin, 167–169; introduction to, 163–164; overview of, 165–167; thick description characterization of, 165, 201; validity of, 182–183
Ethnographic surveys, 173–174
Ethnographic writing: polyphonic or heteroglossic styles of, 181; realism of, 180–181; reflexivity strategy used in, 181; representation used in, 181; trope (or common theme) of, 180; vignettes of, 180
Ethnographies: indigenous/native, 202; narrative, 202; reflexive, 203
Ethnography: comparing critical and traditional, 374–375; definition of, 165; feminist research use of, 412; informed consent requirements of, 169; institutional review boards (IRBs) role in, 169; as iterative, 176; multi-sited, 166–167; naturalistic, 166; salvage, 167. *See also* Autoethnography; Critical ethnography
Etic perspective (outsider-researcher), 12, 165
Evaluation: autoethnography, 206–209; culturally responsive evaluation (CRE),

348, 349; description of, 322. *See also* Program evaluation
Evaluation Center of Western Michigan University, 325, 330–331
Event-specific life experience, 116
Evidence of Utopianizing Toward Social Justice in Young People's Community-Based Art Works (Chappell) [arts-based research], 282–284
Executive summary, 336
Experience: biographical and life story research use of, 116–117; critical life episode from, 117; event-specific life, 116; feminist research questions drawn from lived, 405; lifetime period, 116; narrative specificity on, 116; transactional, 222–223; understood through stories, 218–219. *See also* Narrative inquiry; Stories
Exploitative system, 375
External evaluations, 339
External reliability, 182–183
External validity: representativeness and, 132; transferability parallels to, 29
Extreme (or midpoint) sampling, 84–85

F

Fairness (or balance), 30
Feminism: definition of, 392; research evolution of, 27–28
Feminist ethnography: description of, 412; methodology used for, 412–413; narrative practices used in, 414–415; navigating thee setting, 414; Reluctant Avon Lady study, 415–417; researcher access and entry in, 413–414

Feminist oral history: emancipatory potential of, 408; Grandmother goes to the Racetrack (Borland interview), 410–411; revelations possible from, 409–410

Feminist research: design and questions used for, 405–411; ethnographic approach used in, 412, 415–417; gender studies of, 397; guiding principles of, 395–400; historical roots of, 392–394; methodology used for, 395, 409, 412–413; nonobjectivity of, 396; overview of, 392; qualitative approaches used in, 407–408; trusting validity of, 418–419; *Women Living with HIV/AIDS*, 400–404. *See also* Women

Feminist researchers: access and entry by, 413–414; narrative practices used by, 414–415; navigating the setting, 414

Feminist standpoint theory, 396

Field tests: case study research, 256; tutor study example of, 257*e*

Fieldwork: ethnographic, 169–170; four stages of, 171; full cycle of activities required for, 170–171

Findings. *See* Dissemination

Flanders Interaction Analysis, 257, 259

Focus groups, 173

Focused coding: description and overview of, 46, 48–51; example of memo taken during, 57*e*–58*e*; examples of, 49*t*; following comparisons which may help during, 50

Focused in-depth interviews, 94*t*

Focusing (practitioner research), 298, 300

Formative evaluation questions, 332

Formative model of research, 73*fig*

Freud, Sigmund, 109–110, 128

Full cycle of activities, 170–171

"The Future of Narrative" (Munro-Hendry), 236

G

Gandhi's Truth (Erikson), 110

Gaps among categories, 60

Gatekeepers, 168

Gayness experience. *See* Authoethnography

Gender issues: evolution of research on, 27–28; feminist oral history revelations on, 409; feminist research focus on, 397

General analytic mind-set, 126–127

Generalizability: arts-based research naturalistic, 285; autoethnography, 207; case study research naturalistic, 267; narrative inquiry, 231, 232; psychological, 285; sampling, 84

Generativity, 286

Genre blurring, 273

GIS mapping software, 99

"Grand tour question," 116

Grounded theory: analytic induction similarities to, 179; description of, 12, 41–42; inductive logic of, 41, 42; iterative method of, 41–42

Grounded theory research: coding data in, 44–54; constructivist perspective of, 43; data gathering in, 43–44; issues to consider for, 42–43; memos and memo writing during, 54–59; theoretical sampling and saturation during, 60–62; theoretical sensitivity and using the literature during, 62–63

Guided autobiography instrument, 118–119, 121, 126

Guided Race Autobiography (GRA), 121–123

Guiding principles: *Belmont Report's* three ethical, 19, 22, 23–28; feminist research, 395–396; program evaluation, 326–328*t*

Guiding Principles for Evaluators (APA), 357–358

Gulf Coast oil spill disaster (2010), 244

H

Haiti earthquake (2010), 234, 235

Hegemonic method, 444–445

Hegemony, 444–445

Heteroglossic text, 181

Heuristic purpose, 274

Historical actors, 147–149

Historical agency, 148–149

Historical imagination, 144

Historical research: context of, 143–145; finding a topic, 139–141; sources used to find evidence, 149–155; specialized topic areas of, 142–143; topic categories, 142–143. *See also* Biography and life story research

Historical truth, 132

Historiography, 155, 157

History: case histories (or case records), 244; the how of historical research evidence, 149–155; investigative drama of, 138–139; oral, 225, 229–230, 408, 409–410;

INDEX

philosophies of, 156; types of, 142–143; the what of, 139–143; the when and historical context of, 143–145; the where and foci of, 145–147; the who of historical actors, 147–149; the why of historical interpretation and analysis, 155–158

HIV/AIDS studies: conceptual model designed for, 81, 86; initial conceptual model of older adults and exposure to, 87*fig*; *Women Living with HIV/AIDS*, 400–404

"Hot" data, 380

Housing/injection drug users study, 77–78

Human individuality, 111

Human Relations Area Files (HRAF), 177

Husserl, Edmund, 6

Hypothesis, description of, 5

I

Identity: critical ethnographic focus on power-related, 379–380; Menominee, 223–224; policies of, 196

Identity and Success Life Story Method (ISLSM), 120–121*fig*, 133

Identity and Success Research Lab (ISRL), 130–131

Idiographic approach to personality, 109

Illumination, 286

Immigration law case study, 244

Impact (logic models), 360

In-depth ethnographic interviews, 173

In-depth interviews: cameras and digital recorders to record, 97; description of, 90; focused, 94*t*; open-ended, 94*t*; sampling plan for depression study, 75*t*; semistructured, 94*t*; structured, 94*t*

Incident-by-incident coding, 45–46

Incisive arts-based research, 286

Inclusion principle, 459, 468, 469*e*

Indigeneity, 434

Indigenous empiricism, 440–441

Indigenous methodologies paradigm, 442

Indigenous/native communities: CIRM for reclamation of voice by, 443–444; CIRM serving research needs as defined by, 435–436; colonization of, 424–427; ethnographies of, 202; hegemony used as denial of, 444–445; negative connotation of research to, 428–431; political and social justice goals of, 443. *See also* CIRM (critical indigenous research methodologies)

Individual-level network data, 91

Individualism culture, 350

Inductive analysis, 177

Inductive process: description of, 12; of grounded theory, 41, 42

Informants: case research study, 252–253; ethnography, 166–167, 175; program evaluation, 334. *See also* Participants

Information: empirical, 4–5; quantitative historical, 153–154; ventriloquist stance by researchers on, 381; *Vestehen* approach to gathering, 6. *See also* Data; Knowledge

Informed consent: *Belmont Report* on voluntary, 32–33; children and, 35; ethnographic research and, 169; feminist research, 398; obtaining signatures for, 33–34; older adults and, 35–36; qualitative research designs and, 34–35; role of IRBs in, 33, 34. *See also* Assent; Qualitative research

Initial (or open) coding: analytical questions to aid in, 45; constant comparative method used for, 46; description of, 44–45; examples of, 47*t*; incident-by-incident, 45–46; line-by-line, 45–46

Injection drug users/housing study, 77–78

Inputs (or resources): ACESAS logic model on, 367–368; logic model component of, 360

Insider/outsider status, 402

Institute for Community Research, 81

Institutional review boards (IRBs): confidentiality requirements of, 37; data collection review and approval by, 97–98; description of, 21; ethnographic research permissions from, 169; voluntary informed consent role of, 33, 34

Instrumental case studies, 246–247

Instrumental (or technical) transfer, 295

Instruments. *See* Data collection instruments

Intellectual history, 142

INDEX

Interactive interviews, 203
Interdisciplinary research, 405
Internal evaluations, 339–340
Internal reliability, 183
Internal validity, 132
Interpretation: critical ethnography, 385; data analysis, 125–126; ethnographic cultural, 165; historical analysis and, 155–158
Interpretive case study reports, 266–267
Interpretive (or critical) traditions, 296
Interpretivist perspective: defining the research questions using, 79; description of, 8–9; methodological decisions guided by, 76–77
Interrogatory purpose, 274
Intersubjective modes of knowledge production, 237
Interview instruments: Developmental Success Matrix (DSM), 122; Guided Race Autobiography (GRA), 121–123; Identity and Success Life Story Method (ISLSM), 120–121*fig*; Life Story Interview, 117–119; Life Story Telling (LST), 121; Self-Defining Memory Task, 119–120; stimulated recall (S-R), 308–312. *See also* Data collection methods
Interview protocol: case study research, 257; tutor study excerpt of, 258*e*–259*e*
Interviews: bracketed, 255; cameras and digital recorders to record, 97; case study research, 256–257*e*; ethnographic, 172–173; guided autobiography method of, 118–119;

incident-by-incident coding of, 45–46; interactive, 203; line-by-line coding of, 45–46; member checks for accuracy of, 183; oral, 152–153; practitioner action research, 312*t*; reflexive, dyadic, 203; sampling plan for depression study in-depth, 75*t*; selecting methods for in-depth, 94*t*; semistructured, 90, 117; stimulated recall (S-R) approach to, 308–312; unstructured, 116–117
Intrinsic case studies, 246
Introspection (or reflexivity): critical ethnographic, 381–382; ethnographic, 181; feminist research, 397–398
Intuitionist/pluralist evaluation perspective, 323–324
Items for classifications, 96*t*
Iterative (ethnography), 176
Iterative method, 41–42

J

Jeffersonian method, 125
Jottings, 413
Journals: case study template for keeping, 262*t*; practitioner action research, 312*t*
Jung, Carl, 128
Justice: definition of, 22, 27; indigenous/native goals for social, 443; transformative perspective on, 27–28

K

K&M (Kemmis and McTaggart) design models, 305*t*
Ke Aka Ho`ona project evaluation: background information on, 330–331; criteria used for, 332*e*; data analysis during, 334, 336;

data collection during, 334, 335*t*; evaluation questions used during, 333*t*; feedback workshops held during, 337; selecting standards for, 333–334. *See also* Program evaluation
Kellogg Foundation, 330, 331, 360
Key informants: case research study, 252–253; ethnographic, 165–166, 175; program evaluation, 334
Knowledge: indigenous empirical, 440–441; intersubjecctive modes of producing, 237; narrative inquiry outcome of reflexive, 225–226; personal practical, 224–225; program evaluation used to generate, 341; research-based, 4. *See also* Information
Knowledge gaps of research, 406
Krackplot (software), 99
Ku Klux Klan, 351

L

Language: "Black English" and "Standard English," 351; as The Denver Study issue, 452–454; respectful research in relationship of culture and, 26
Law of the instrument, 311–312
Learning from the Past: What History Teaches Us About School Reform (Ravitch and Vinovskis), 141
Learning to Labor (Willis), 376, 378
Leonardo da Vinci and a Memory of his Childhood (Freud), 109–110
Lewin, Kurt, 293–294, 305*t*

INDEX

LGBTQ youth: certificate of confidentiality provided to, 35; narrative inquiry research on, 237. *See also* Autoethnography
Life course perspective, 112
Life Story Interview, 117–119, 127
Life story research study, 225, 228–229. *See also* Biography and life story research
Life Story Telling (LST), 121
Life-story model of identity, 115
Lifetime period experience, 116
Line-by-line coding, 45–46
Listening: active, 409; CIRM's practice of multisensory, 440–441
Listings and pilesorts, 96*t*
Logic models: ACESAS, 364–370; description of, 359–360; diagram illustration of simple, 331*fig*; evaluation stages represented by, 348; program evaluation, 329–330
Logs (practitioner action research), 312*t*
Longitudinal case studies, 247
Low-inference descriptors, 183

M

Macro phenomena, 378
Mapping: maps not to scale, 95*t*; maps to scale, 95*t*; social maps, 96*t*
Margaret Mead, 167–168
Marxism, 375
Masking, 124
Master, universal narratives, 197
Mauritius Family Planning Association, 81
MDMA (Ecstasy) research, 77
Meaning, 126

Mechanistic (Marxism), 375
Member checking: case study research, 265–266*e*; ethnographic, 183; feminist research, 418; practitioner action research, 316; program evaluation, 340
Memo writing: description of, 54–55; early example, 55*e*–56*e*
Memory sorting, 59
Memory/memories: critical life episode, 117; event-specific life, 116; guided autobiography of, 118–119; Life Story Telling (LST), 121; lifetime period, 116; narrative specificity on, 116; self-defining, 115
Memos: description of, 54; example taken during focused coding, 57*e*–58*e*
Menominee identity, 223–224
Metaphorical purpose, 279
Method selection: guide to qualitative research tool and, 93*t*–96*t*; in-depth interview, 94*t*; issues to consider for, 92, 97; mapping, 95*t*–96*t*; observation tools and, 93*t*; other elicitation techniques, 96*t*; visual documentation, 95*t*
Methodological decisions: defining the research questions, 79; formulating a conceptual model, 79–81; issues to consider when making, 75–76; paradigms guiding, 7–9, 22–28, 43, 44, 76–78; sampling in qualitative research, 84–85; on where, when, and with whom study is conducted, 81–84
Methodology: ACESAS, 347–349, 362–370;

biography and life story research design, 112–116; CIPP Evaluation Model, 325, 333, 362; CIRM (critical indigenous research methodologies), 423–448; CRE (culturally responsive evaluation), 348, 349, 355, 357–359; critical ethnography, 384–385; description of, 10, 70, 71–72; distinguishing methods from, 11, 427; feminist research, 395, 409, 412–413; making decisions related to, 75–85; mixed-method design, 10, 113–114; narrative inquiry use of qualitative, 221–225; practitioner action research, 303–305*t*; program evaluation, 329–337; sampling plan for in-depth interviews, 75*t*; study population used in, 72–74
Methods: deliberate democratic research, 461–463; description of, 10, 70, 85–86; distinguishing methodology from, 11, 427; feminist research, 395; hegemonic, 444–445. *See also* Data collection methods
Micro phenomena, 378
Microsoft ACCESS, 99
Midpoint (or extreme) sampling, 84–85
Minority report, 336
Mixed-methods design: biography and life story research, 113–114; description of, 10
Mixed-paradigm research, 77
Moderator (ACESAS), 363
Move-testing, 294
Mules and Men (Hurston), 415
Multi-sited ethnographies, 166–167

Multicultural validity, 369
Multiple case studies, 247
Multiple site case studies, 247
Multisensory listening, 440–441
Multivocal texts, 400
Mumbai health study, 79, 83, 84–85
Muslim cultural center near WTC site study, 89

N
Narrative ethnographies, 202
Narrative inquiry: authentic representation and reproduction in, 234–235; Christine Lemley's position on, 216–217; critical events approach to, 219–221; description of, 215, 216; generalizability in, 231, 232; genres of, 225–230; how to begin, 236–238; objectivity in, 231–232; positivist approach to, 236; qualitative research methodology used for, 221–225; reflexive knowledge outcome of, 225–226; reliability in, 231; research questions to ask for, 233; responses to critique of, 230–235; Roland Mitchell's position on, 217–218; therapeutic benefits of storytelling in, 234; understanding experiences through stories and, 218–219; validity in, 231, 232–234. *See also* Experience; Stories
Narrative inquiry genres: autobiography as, 225, 227–228; biography as, 225, 226; life story research as, 225, 228–229; oral history as, 225, 229–230, 408; overview of, 225–226

Narrative mode of thought, 111
Narrative specificity, 116
Narrative theories of personality, 114–115
Narrative truth, 132
Narratives: authentic representation and reproduction of, 234–235; co-constructed, 204; feminist researcher use of, 414–415; master, universal, 197; personal, 202; qualitative research use of, 221; raw, 219; specificity of, 116; truth of, 132. *See also* Stories
National Commission (1979), 28
National Institutes of Health, 35
National Science Foundation (NSF), 355
Native Americans. *See* Indigenous/native communities
Naturalistic ethnography, 166
Naturalization generalizability: arts-based research, 285; case study research, 267
Nazi medical experiments, 21
NEO Personality Inventory, 122
Network research, 89–90
Nomothetic approach to personality, 109
Non-participant participant observer, 172
The Nuer: A Description of the Modes of Livelihood and Political Institutions of a Nilotic People (Evans-Pritchard), 166
NVivo (software), 99

O
Objectivity: confirmability parallels, 29; narrative inquiry, 231–232

Observation: autoethnographic, 199; cameras and digital recorders used in, 97; case study research use of, 257, 259–260; emic perspective (insider-participant) of, 12, 87, 165; etic perspective (outsider-researcher) of, 12, 165; guide to selecting tools for, 93t; network research, 89–90; non-participant participant observer, 172; obtrusive, 88; open-ended nonparticipatory, 93t; participant, 171–172; participatory, 93t; practitioner action research, 299, 301, 312t; structured, 93t. *See also* Data collection methods
Observation plan, 257
Observe in real time, 260
Observing (practitioner action), 299, 301
Obtrusive observations, 88
Office of Strategic Services (OSS), 110
Ontological authenticity, 30
Ontological research, 7
Ontologies: as consideration in research, 431–434; definition of, 425
Open coding. *See* Initial (or open) coding
Open-ended in-depth ethnographic interviews, 173
Open-ended in-depth interview, 94t
Open-ended nonparticipatory observation, 93t
Oppression: classical Marxism on, 375; critical ethnographic focus on, 379–380; resistance to, 377–378. *See also* Power/power dynamics

Oral histories: description of, 225; example of, 229–230; feminist, 408, 409–411. *See also* Stories
Oral interviews, 152–153
Outcome domains, 80
Outcomes (program), 348
Outputs (logic models), 360
Outsider/insider status, 402

P
Pajek (software), 99
Paradigmatic mode of thought, 111
Paradigmatic science, 275
Paradigmatic text, 281–282
Paradigms: constructivist, 22–23, 43, 44, 113; description of, 7, 76; feminist, 393; guiding methodological decisions, 76–78; indigenous methodologies, 442; interpretivists, 8–9, 76–77, 79; mixed-paradigm, 77; positivists, 7, 76, 236, 393, 432; quantitative and qualitative, 11; transformative, 22, 23–28
Participant observers/observation: autoethnographic, 199; ethnographic, 171–172
Participants: informed consent of, 2–36; masking, 124; positionality of, 71; pseudonyms used for, 124; voices stance taken by, 381. *See also* Informants; Sampling; Study population
Participation, 70–71
Participatory action research: description of, 292; respect demonstrated during, 26. *See also* Practitioner action research
Participatory observation, 93*t*

Participatory (or collaborative) approach: deliberative democratic research and, 466–467; description of, 78
Peer debriefings, 418
Person-centered psychology, 109
Personal narratives, 202
Personal practical knowledge, 224–225
Personality: idiographic approach to, 109; narrative theories of, 114–115; NEO Personality Inventory, 122; nomothetic approach to, 109
Personaology, 109
Phenomenologically truthful, 285–286
Philosophy: definition of, 156; philosophies of history, 156
Photographic documentation, 95*t*
Pilesorts and listings, 96*t*
Pilot tests: case study research, 256; tutor study example of, 257*e*
Planning (practitioner research), 298, 300
Pluralist/intuitionist evaluation perspective, 323–324
Political (or diplomatic) history, 142
Politics of representation, 399
Polyphonic text, 181
Population validity, 7
Positionality: critical ethnography, 380–382; description of, 12
Positivists/positivism: assumptions regarding truth of taxonomies, 432; description of, 7, 76; feminist research, 393; narrative inquiry using, 236
Postmodernism, 156

Power/power dynamics: critical ethnographic focus on, 379–380; critical ethnographic stand against inequity of, 382–383; deliberative democratic research and issues of, 467; The Denver Study on school district shifts in, 458–459; feminist oral history revelations on, 409. *See also* Oppression
Practical reasoning, 207
Practices (people's), 170
Practitioner action research: characteristics of, 302–303; choosing the study questions, 306–307*t*; data collection for, 308–312*t*; designs of, 303–305*t*; guidelines and suggestions for, 314*e*–315*e*; historical perspective of, 293–294; Mr. Crane, Sixth-Grade Teacher scenario of, 298–299, 301–302; Ms. Drake, Courtroom Lawyer scenario of, 299–302; overview of, 292–293; professional practice of, 294–298; spiral (or spiraled) cycle of, 301–302, 303; structure for, 312–313; traditions shaping, 296–297; validity and member checking of, 315–316. *See also* Action research; Participatory action research
Practitioner research, 298
Practitioner self-reflection, 298, 302
Praxis, 429
The Predicament of Culture: Twentieth-Century Ethnography, Literature, and Art (Clifford), 181
Predictor domains, 80
Presentism, 144

INDEX

Primary sources: archival documents as, 151–152; artifacts as, 152; description of, 150, 151; oral interviews as, 152–153; public records as, 151; quantitative information as, 153–154
Problem focus, 167
Problem solving: practitioner action research conceived bas, 294; qualitative, 277–279
Program antecedents, 324
Program evaluation: audience and stakeholder interest in, 322; CIPP Evaluation Model, 325, 333, 362; culturally responsive evaluation (CRE), 348, 349; description of, 322–332; design of, 329–337; Historical foundations of, 324–326; member checking during, 340; perspectives of, 323–324; reporting results of, 336–337; stages represented by logic model, 348; uses of, 341; validity of findings, 337–340. *See also* Ke Aka Ho'ona project evaluation; Research
Program Evaluation and Methodology Division (U.S. GAO), 337
Program evaluators: bias of, 339; competence of, 327*t*; CRE (culturally responsive evaluation), 355–357; external, 339; guiding principles for, 326–328*t*; integrity and honesty of, 327*t*; internal, 339–340; respect for people, 328*t*; responsibilities of, 328*t*; systematic inquiry by, 327*t*. *See also* Researchers
Program outcomes, 324

Program transactions, 324
Programs: countenance model of, 324; description of, 322; evaluation used to improve, 341; outcomes of, 348
Progressive philosophy of history, 156
Providential philosophy of history, 156
Pseudonyms, 124
Psychobiography, 110
Psychodynamic approach to questions, 127
Psychological generalizability, 285
Psychology: biography and life story research historical roots in, 109–110; biography and life story research theoretical basis from, 110–112; person-centered, 109
Psychosocial construction, 115
Public records, 151
Purposeful (or purposive) sampling, 334
Purposeful sampling, 253

Q
Qualitative control, 279
Qualitative problem solving: phase one: random qualities, 277–278; phase two: tentative relationships between qualities, 278; phase three: an emerging theme, 278–279; phase four: a developing theme, 279; phase five: work that is judged complete, 279; definition of, 277
Qualitative research: axiological belief systems and, 22–23; democratizing, 451–471; emic perspective (insider-participant) used in, 12, 87, 165; Etic perspective (outsider-researcher) used in,

12; feminist applications of, 407–408; historical roots of, 6–9; informed consent issue of, 34–35; interpretivist or critical perspectives of, 8–9; introduction to, 3–4; methodology and methods used in, 10, 11, 70–101; narrative inquiry use of methodological, 221–225; truth as contextual and time-specific in, 8; validity, rigor, and ethics in, 28–30. *See also* Informed consent; Research
Qualitatively based surveys, 92
Quantitative research: description of, 4; true experiments as characterizing, 5
Questionnaires, 312*t*. *See also* Research questions

R
Race: collective memory of, 354; construct of, 349, 352, 353; difference between culture and, 352–353
Racial group classification, 353–354
Random sampling, 253, 334
Raw narratives, 219
Reasoning (practical), 207
Recall time, 82–83
Reciprocity: as CIRM component, 439–440; definition of, 439
Recovering Language, Reclaiming Voice: Menominee Language Revitalization Programs (Lemley), 223
Reflexive, dyadic interviews, 203
Reflexive ethnographies, 203
Reflexive knowledge, 225–226
Reflexivity (or introspection): critical ethnographic, 381;

INDEX

ethnographic, 181; feminist research, 397–398
Refocusing (practitioner action), 299, 301
Relational ethics, 204, 205–206
Relationality of CIRM, 436–437
Relevance of Culture in Evaluation Institute (RCEI), 367
Reliability: autoethnography, 207; biography and life story research, 131–133; dependability parallel to, 29; external, 182–183; internal, 183; narrative inquiry, 231
Reluctant Avon Lady research (feminist ethnography), 415–417
Representation: case study research alternative, 267; critical ethnography, 380–382, 387; deliberate democratic research caveat of faithful, 465; ethnographic, 181; external validity relationship to, 132; feminist research, 395; narrative inquiry, 234–235; politics of, 399
Research: androcentric (male-centered) assumptions driving, 393–394; archival, 90; arts-based, 271–286; autoethnography, 189–210; biography and life story, 107–134; case study, 243–268; CIRM approach to, 424–448; critical ethnography, 373–389; deliberative democratic, 452–471; ethical norms for, 28–37; ethnographic, 163–188; feminist, 391–420; grounded theory, 43–54; historical, 138–158;

interdisciplinary, 405; methods and methodology of, 10–11; mixed-paradigm, 77; narrative inquiry, 215–239; negative connotation to indigenous peoples, 428–431; network, 89–90; paradigm frameworks used in, 7, 11, 22, 23–28, 43, 44, 76–77; participatory action, 26; practitioner action, 291–317; quantitative, 3–9, 12. *See also* Ethical issues; Program evaluation; Qualitative research
Research methodology. *See* Methodology
Research methods. *See* Methods
Research questions: defining the qualitative, 79; discourse analytic, 127; feminist approach to, 405–407; formative, 332; narrative inquiry, 233; practitioner action, 306–307*t*; program evaluation, 331–333*t*; psychodynamic approach to, 127; summative, 331–332; writing case study, 249–250*e*. *See also* Questionnaires
Research questions "grand tour," 116
Research-based knowledge, 4
Researcher biases: case study research, 255; CRE (culturally responsive evaluation) approach to, 356; program evaluation, 339; triangulating analyst to minimize, 340; tutor study approach to minimizing, 255*e*
Researcher competencies: case study research, 254*e*; cultural, 31–32, 356–357,

363–364; description of, 31–32; program evaluators, 327*t*
Researcher as instrument, 21
Researcher position, 255
Researchers: activism stance by, 381; autonomy of, 303, 314*e*; biases of, 255*e*, 339, 340, 356; critical, 77–78; data collection position of, 88–91; ethnographers, 12, 87, 163–185; instrument role of, 21; knowledge gaps from disproportionate attention of, 406; memos/memo writing by grounded theory, 54–59; participatory or collaborative approach by, 78; reflexivity of, 181, 381, 397–398; traditional, 293; ventriloquist stance taken by, 381. *See also* Program evaluators
Resistance, 377–378
Resources (or inputs): ACESAS logic model on, 367–368; logic model component of, 360
Respect: as CIRM component, 438–439; definition of, 22; transformative perspective on, 25–26
Respondent-driven sampling, 85
Responsibility of CIRM, 438
Revision (practitioner action), 299, 301
Revisionist histories, 157
Rigor norms, 28–30
The Rise and Fall of the New Deal Order (Fraser and Gerstle), 141

S

Safed pani (white discharge) compliant (Mumbai women), 79

The Sage Handbook of Qualitative Research (Denzin and Lincoln), 22
Salvage ethnography, 167
Sampling: convenience, 60; criterion, 84; extreme or midpoint, 84–85; for in-depth interviews in depression study, 75*t*; initial, 60; purposeful, 253; purposeful (or purposive), 334; qualitative research approach to, 84–85; random, 253, 334; respondent-driven, 85; targeted, 85; theoretical, 60–62, 84; thought, 129. *See also* Participants
Sankofa bird (ACESAS model), 361*fig*–362
Saturation: case study research, 253; ethnographic research, 178–179; grounded theory research, 60–62
Schooling in Capitalist America (Bowles and Gintis), 376
Scientific method: description of, 5; origins of, 5
"Second Chair: An Autoethnodrama" (Saldaña), 285
Secondary sources: description of, 150, 154–155; historiography of, 155
Selective coding, 48
Self-defining memories, 115
Self-Defining Memory Task, 119–120, 126
Self-interest constraints, 467, 467
Self-reflection, 298, 302
Semibounded system, 91
Semistructured in-depth interview, 94*t*
Semistructured interviews, 90, 117

Sensitizing concepts, 53
Sequence (narrative), 221
"The Shattered Mirror: Curriculum, Art and Critical Politics" (Blumenfeld-Jones), 275
Showing writing technique, 200–201
Simmel, Georg, 6
Single case studies, 247
Site mapping, 85
Social capital, 366
"The Social Elements of the Indian Problem" (Parker), 425
Social history, 142
Social maps, 96*t*
Social reproduction, 376
Socially significant arts-based research, 286
Society: critical ethnographic support of equity in, 382–383; gatekeepers of, 168; key informants of, 165–166, 175; people's practices in, 170. *See also* Culture/cultures
The Souls of Black Folk (Du Bois), 350
Specialized topic areas, 142–143
Spiral (or spiraled) cycle, 301–302, 303
SPSS (software), 99
Stakeholders: cast study research outcomes for, 244; CRE consideration of civic capacity of, 368; The Denver Study, 452; intrinsic case studies communicated to, 246; program evaluation, 322
Standpoint theory, 396
Stimulated recall (S-R), 308–311
Storied thought, 112

Stories: autoethnography, 189–210; biography and life story research, 107–134; canonical, 204–205; historical truth of, 132; master, universal narratives, 197; narrative truth of, 132; showing and telling techniques, 200–201; therapeutic benefits of, 234; understanding experiences through, 218–219; witnessing through, 205. *See also* Experience; Narrative inquiry; Narratives; Oral histories
Street Corner Society (Whyte), 175
Structuralism, 375
Structure: critical ethnography focus on, 374, 377–378; deliberative democratic research, 465–466; relationship of agency and, 378
Structure in-depth interviews, 94*t*
Structured interaction, 465–466
Structured observation, 93*t*
Study population: case examples of depression research, 72–74; description of, 72, 83; methodological decisions related to, 83–84; selecting the, 73*fig*–75. *See also* Participants
Study validity, 315. *See also* Validity
Subjectivity: CIRM and role of, 436–437; critical ethnographic, 381
Subtractive Schooling (Valenzuela), 37–379
Summative evaluation questions, 331–332

INDEX

Surveys: case study research, 256–257; ethnographic, 173–174; qualitatively based, 91

T

Tactical authenticity, 30
Targeted sampling, 85
Taxonomies: ethnographic, 178; narrative inquiry to form, 221; positivist research assumptions about, 432
Technical (or instrumental) transfer, 295
Telling writing technique, 200–201
Temporal order, 112
Thematic content analysis, 129–131
Theoretical coding: description and overview of, 51–54; examples of Glaser's coding families, 52t–53; sensitizing concepts related to, 53
Theoretical generalizations, 132
Theoretical (or conceptual) frameworks, 249–250e. *See also* Conceptual models
Theoretical sampling, 60–62, 84
Theoretical saturation: case study research, 253; ethnographic research, 178–179; grounded theory research, 60–62
Theoretical sensitivity, 62–63
Theories: biography and life story research, 114–116; classical Marxism, 375; critical ethnography, 375–377; critical ethnography's drawing on and building, 378–379; culturalists, 375–376; feminist research, 395;
feminist standpoint, 396; instrumental case studies used to build cases for new, 246–247; life-story model of identity, 115; narrative theories of personality, 114–115; praxis intersection of practice and, 429; psychosocial construction, 115; structuralism, 375
Thick description: autoethnography, 201; case study reports, 267; ethnography, 165
"Things of Use and Things of Beauty" (arts-based research), 277
Thought: narrative mode of, 111; paradigmatic mode of, 111; storied, 112
Thought sampling, 129
Timing: determining study, 82; practitioner action research, 303; recall time consideration, 82–83
Tinkering Toward Utopia: A Century of Public School Reform (Tyack and Cuban), 141
Title IX, 407
Top-down view of history, 146–147
Traditional researchers, 293
Transactional experience, 222–223
Transactive space, 283
Transcription of data, 125
Transferability, 29
Transformative paradigm, 22
Triangulating analyst, 340
Triangulation: case study research data, 251–252; description of, 99–100; ethnographic data, 182–183; feminist research data, 418; practitioner action research data, 316; program
evaluation data, 338–339. *See also* Data
Trope (common theme), 180
Troubling the Angels: Women Living with HIV/AIDS (Lather and Smithies), 400–404
True experiments, 5
Trustworthiness: critical ethnography, 386–388; feminist reports, 418–419. *See also* Credibility; Validity
Truth: deliberate democratic research faithful representation of, 465; historical, 132; narrative, 132; phenomenologically truthful, 285–286
Tuskegee experiments (1933–1972), 21–22
Tutor study. *See* Dental hygiene student tutor study
The 2002 User-Friendly Handbook for Project Evaluation (NSF), 355
Typologies (ethnography), 178

U

UCINET (software), 99
Unit of analysis, 81
United Way, 360
Universality, 393
University of Connecticut Health Center, 81
University of Mauritius, 81
University of Waikato (New Zealand), 184
The Unknown City (Fine and Weis), 379–380
Unstructured interview, 116–117
Up Against Whiteness (Lee), 380
U.S. Department of Health and Human Services, 35
U.S. General Accounting Office (GAO), 337

U.S. Gulf Coast oil spill disaster (2010), 244
U.S. Justice Department, 462
Utilitarian evaluation perspective, 323

V

Valid instrument design, 256
Validity: autoethnography, 207; biography and life story research, 131–133; case study research, 265–266*e*; catalytic, 419; conflict of interest, 7; critical ethnography, 386–387; ecological, 7; ethical norms of qualitative research, 28–30; ethnographic, 182–183; external, 29; feminist research, 418–419; internal, 132; member checking for, 183, 265–266*e*, 316, 340, 418; multicultural, 369; narrative inquiry, 231, 232–234; population, 7; practitioner action research, 315–316; program evaluation, 337–340; sampling, 84; seeking discrepant cases to establish, 419. *See also* Credibility; Study validity; Trustworthiness
Validity checks, 86–87
Value negation, 276
Ventriloquist stance, 381
Vestehen research, 6
Video documentation, 90, 95*t*
Vignettes, 180
Visual Culture Jam: Art, Pedagogy and Creative Resistance (Darts), 276
Voice in Qualitative Inquiry: Challenges Conventional, Interpretive, and Critical Conceptions in Qualitative Research (2008), 220
Voices stance, 381
Voluntary informed consent: *Belmont Report* on, 32–33; children and, 35; ethnographic research and, 169; feminist research, 398; obtaining signatures for, 33–34; older adults and, 35–36; qualitative research designs and, 34–35; role of IRBs in, 33, 34

W

W. K. Kellogg Foundation, 330, 331, 360
Weber, Max, 6
Western Michigan University Evaluation Center, 325, 330–331
Whig histories, 157
White, Robert, 110
Witnessing, 205
Women: feminism argument on historic exclusion of, 393–394; Title IX mandate on equality of, 407; *Women Living with HIV/AIDS* study on, 400–404; women's movement for equal rights of, 392–393. *See also* Feminist research
Women's movement, 392–393
World Trade Center (WTC) attacks [2001], 89
Worldview: African American communities, 354; biography and life story research and, 113; historical analysis and interpretation research and, 155–158; postmodernism philosophy on, 156
Writing Culture: The Poetics and Politics of Ethnography (Clifford and Marcus), 181
Writing reports. *See* Dissemination

Y

Young Man Luther (Erikson), 110
Youth Movement Records (Oakland), 283